W9-CKI-222

Ready-To-Wear
Apparel Analysis

Ready-To-Wear Apparel Analysis

Patty Brown

JOHNSON COUNTY COMMUNITY COLLEGE

MACMILLAN PUBLISHING COMPANY
NEW YORK

MAXWELL MACMILLAN CANADA, INC.
TORONTO

MAXWELL MACMILLAN INTERNATIONAL
NEW YORK   OXFORD   SINGAPORE   SYDNEY

Editor: David Chodoff
Production Supervisor: Marcia Craig
Production Manager: Valerie Sawyer
Cover Designer: Robert Freese
Cover photographs: Background: Ted Horowitz/The Stock Market;
top inset: Gabe Palmer/The Stock Market; middle and
bottom insets: George DiSario/The Stock Market
Illustrations: Hadel Studio and Caroline Plaisted

This book was set in Century Schoolbook by Ruttle, Shaw & Wetherill, Inc.,
printed and bound by The Book Press, Inc.
The cover was printed by The Lehigh Press, Inc.

Brown, Patty (Patricia Kay)
    Ready-to-wear apparel analysis / Patty Brown.
        p.   cm.
    Includes bibliographical references and index.
    ISBN 0-02-315611-2
    1. Clothing trade.   2. Clothing factories—Quality control.
3. Quality of products.   I. Title.
TT497.B74   1992
687′ .068′5—dc20   90-28148
                                         CIP

Macmillan Publishing Company
866 Third Avenue, New York, New York 10022

Macmillan Publishing Company is part of
the Maxwell Communication Group of Companies

Maxwell Macmillan Canada, Inc.
1200 Eglinton Avenue East
Suite 200
Don Mills, Ontario M3C   3N1

    LIBRARY OF CONGRESS CATALOGING-IN-PUBLICATION DATA

Brown, Patty (Patricia Kay)
    Ready-to-wear apparel analysis / Patty Brown.
        p.   cm.
    Includes bibliographical references and index.
    ISBN 0-02-315611-2
    1. Clothing trade.   2. Clothing factories—Quality control.
3. Quality of products.   I. Title.
TT497.B74   1992
687′ .068′5—dc20   90-28148
                                         CIP

Printing: 1 2 3 4 5 6 7   Year: 2 3 4 5 6 7 8

To my parents

Quality is never an accident. . . .
It is the will to produce a superior thing.

Attributed to John Ruskin,
nineteenth-century social critic

Preface

The purpose of this book is to provide students of textiles and apparel with a method for evaluating the quality of ready-to-wear apparel. The book takes an industry approach, integrating the study of traditional clothing construction with that of apparel production. The resulting body of knowledge and related vocabulary are important tools for anyone pursuing a career in the apparel industry. To make informed business decisions, you must understand how clothing is manufactured and appreciate the features that affect cost and quality.

A familiarity with what constitutes apparel quality and how it is achieved enhances effectiveness on every level:

- Designers, manufacturers, and retail product developers establish standards that maximize quality but balance with cost limitations.
- Suppliers of machinery, materials, and services meet the industry's needs.
- Manufacturers communicate quality expectations to contractors.
- Wholesale representatives educate retail buyers about quality features.
- Retail buyers choose garments that perform well and deliver value to the consumer.
- Advertisers and marketers promote quality features to the target market.
- Retail salespeople communicate quality features to consumers.
- Consumers make better purchase decisions.

In short, anyone can benefit from a knowledge of apparel quality.

Chapter 1 defines apparel quality and establishes a framework for examining how consumers evaluate quality and value. It also examines the quality control efforts of the apparel industry. Chapter 2 overviews the apparel industry and outlines the mass-production process, including the use of new technology. Costing and pricing are also discussed. Chapter 3 summarizes information gained from apparel labels, both required and voluntary. Sizing is discussed in depth.

Chapter 4 reviews the effect of fabric on the performance of the garment. The influence of fibers, yarns, fabric structure, and finishes is presented; readers will benefit from a previous exposure to basic textiles. Chapter 5 introduces the stitch classes and types contained in *U.S. Fed. Std. No. 751a: Stitches, Seams, and Stitchings*. The advantages and disadvantages of each stitch class are examined. Chapter 6 discusses the seam classes and types contained in *U.S. Fed. Std. No. 751a*. It also identifies seam defects and features that ensure seam integrity. Chapter 7 presents edge treatments used to finish raw edges, with emphasis on hems, facings, bindings, bands, and plackets.

Chapter 8 explains how garments are shaped by darts and dart substitutes. It also contains a discussion of underlying fabrics and other devices that lend shape and support to the garment. Chapter 9 examines style variations, with emphasis on waistbands, collars, sleeves, cuffs, and pockets. Chapter 10 presents functional and decorative details, including trims, ornamental stitchings, and pattern matching. Chapter 11 discusses methods of garment closure, including buttons and buttonholes, zippers, and miscellaneous fasteners.

Chapter 12 concentrates on the evaluation of fit and on garment alteration at the point of sale. This chapter also discusses fitting special markets.

Although the evaluation of quality as discussed in this book relies on a visual analysis of garments, Appendix A presents a list of ASTM and AATCC standards for laboratory test methods that may be used in objectively quantifying the evaluation of certain performance features. Appendix B contains schematic diagrams of all the seam and stitching types in *U.S. Fed. Std. No. 751a.* Appendix C outlines the apparel production operations for which each seam and stitching type is used and lists the appropriate stitch types to use.

Throughout the book, the focus is on the aesthetic and functional performance of garments. Each chapter concentrates on identifying the physical features that produce desirable aesthetic and functional performance. At the end of each chapter, a quality checklist, a list of new terms, review questions, and related activities allow you to practice and apply the content of that chapter. The concepts come to life when you apply them to real garments where you work, where you shop, and in your own wardrobe. Related resources are provided at the end of the text to aid in pursuing topics further. While exploring the following pages, I hope you develop a better understanding of apparel production and an increased appreciation of apparel quality that serve you well.

Acknowledgments

Thank you to Margaret McWhorter and Kitty Dickerson, who encouraged me to write this text. And thank you to Jim Reid of Quick-Rotan for his assistance along the way. Those who read early drafts of the manuscript offered helpful suggestions; they include Margaret McWhorter, Lark Caldwell, Barbara Cunningham, Jane Wilsdorf, and Jerry Navlyt, along with reviewers John Donnellan, University of Massachusetts; Helen Douty, Auburn University; Sharron Lennon, Indiana University; Karen Leonas, University of Georgia; Phyllis Miller, University of Tennessee; Anita Racine, Cornell University; Theresa Robinson, Middle Tennessee State University; Margaret Tierney, Ohio State University; and Jane Workman, Southern Illinois University. Carl Locke did an outstanding job on the photography. Samples for photography were kindly lent by Texas Christian University, Johnson County Community College, and The Fashion Group of Kansas City. Texas Christian University also deserves recognition for providing the grant that funded the research leading to this text. Many companies and organizations in the apparel industry have generously shared their expertise and resources: Amalgamated Clothing and Textile Workers Union, American Textile Manufacturers Institute, Angelica Uniforms, Bobbin International, Cotton Incorporated, Crafted With Pride in U.S.A. Council, Everest and Jennings Avenues, Hal Hardin Apparel, International Fabricare Institute, International Ladies Garment Workers Union, International Linen Promotion Commission, Jack Henry, Kurt Salmon Associates, Lands' End, Lee Apparel Company, Microdynamics, Monsanto Chemical Company, Union Special Corporation, Winning Ways, and the Wool Bureau. Thanks also to the many colleagues, friends, and family who have lent moral support. And thank you to my husband, Paul, who was patient and supportive through it all.

Contents

8

Shape and Support: Creating a Three-Dimensional Garment

9

Style Variations: Focus on Design Features

10

Details: Aesthetic and Functional Extras

11

Closures: Securing Garment Openings   235

12

Fit and Alteration: Point of Sale Concerns   260

Related Resources   284

APPENDIX A

APPENDIX B

APPENDIX C

1

Apparel Quality: The Concern of Consumers and Industry

CHAPTER OBJECTIVES

1. Define apparel quality.
2. Examine how consumers evaluate quality.
3. Explore the relationship between price and quality.
4. Understand the function of a quality department.

Quality is a key factor in the production, marketing, buying, and selling of ready-to-wear apparel. To pursue a career in the fashion industry, you need a clear understanding of apparel quality. Your success in this industry will depend upon your ability both to recognize degrees of quality and to know how quality standards can be met. Everyone involved in the apparel industry is influenced by the need to achieve an ap-

propriate balance between quality and price. The goal is to provide apparel products that best meet your customers' expectations.

Ready-to-Wear apparel (RTW) is clothing that is mass-produced. Also called *ready-made* or *off the rack,* in its broadest sense this clothing includes any garment that is not custom-made for the wearer. Both RTW buyers and sellers are conscious of **apparel quality,** its degree of excellence and conformance to requirements, or the extent to which a garment meets expectations.

A quality-conscious apparel company meets the wants and needs of consumers, and its business grows as satisfied customers make repeat purchases. Therefore, everyone benefits from an emphasis on quality. Apparel companies include both **manufacturers,** who produce apparel and sell it to retailers; and **retailers,** who buy apparel from manufacturers and sell it to the consumers who wear it. Apparel quality knowledge equips you to deliver products that meet the wants and needs of your company's *target market,* the group of consumers it aims to serve. Paying attention to quality helps you turn **consumers,** the general buying public, into **customers,** consumers who buy from your company.

No one is *against* quality, though some place it on a priority level below other business concerns. These people argue that paying attention to quality increases the costs of doing business. However, the combination of returns, complaints, ill will, and lost sales caused by lack of quality really cost more in the long run.

Successful businesses offer consumers at least one of three things: *something different, something better,* or *something cheaper.* To generate sales, many manufacturers and retailers provide ready-to-wear that reflects the latest fashion trends (something different) or the lowest price (something cheaper), with little concern for other aspects of apparel quality and value. Although color, style, price, and fit initially "sell" a garment by attracting attention, other features determine the consumer's ultimate satisfaction. This phenomenon calls for a focus on the overall quality and value of the garment (something better).

Quality Features

Apparel quality has two dimensions: (1) physical features, or what the garment *is;* and (2) performance features, or what the garment *does* (Solinger 1980). *The physical features of a garment determine its performance* (Figure 1-1). Therefore, consumers purchase garments with specific physical features that they believe will fulfill their performance expectations. For example, a consumer chooses a blouse made of silk (a physical feature) because silk typically produces desirable performance (e.g., lustrous beauty and comfort).

PHYSICAL FEATURES

A garment's **physical features** provide its tangible form and composition. Physical features include the garment's design, materials, and construction. **Design** provides the plan for the garment's style. For example, is the skirt slim or full? **Materials** include the fabrics and other components used to produce the garment. For instance, are the overalls made of denim or corduroy? **Construction** refers to the methods used to assemble the garment. For example, what types of stitches are used?

A garment's physical features are *intrinsic attributes;* they cannot be altered without changing the garment itself. This text concentrates on intrinsic cues that can be used to evaluate quality.

PERFORMANCE FEATURES

A garment's **performance features** determine the standards it meets and how it benefits the consumer. Performance features include the garment's aesthetic performance and functional performance.

Aesthetic performance refers to *attractiveness.* Do the design, materials, and construction of the garment fulfill appearance expectations? Do the design elements (color, line, shape, form, and texture) of the garment reflect good design principles (balance, proportion, emphasis, rhythm, and unity)? Does the garment possess classic or current fashion trends desired by consumers? And does the garment meet the consumer's personal preferences regarding appearance? These questions are important to ask when evaluating ready-to-wear because design impacts the visual appeal of clothing and therefore consumer acceptance of it. However, a thorough discussion on evaluating design aesthetics is outside the focus of this text (see Related Resources: Design and Style).

Functional performance includes performance features other than appearance, namely the garment's utility and durability. *Utility* refers to usefulness. For example, does the garment fit? Is it comfortable? Is it easy to care for? Does it function appropriately for the intended use? *Durability* or *serviceability* refers to how well the garment retains its structure and ap-

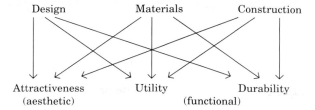

PHYSICAL
FEATURES   Design   Materials   Construction

PERFORMANCE
FEATURES   Attractiveness   Utility   Durability
            (aesthetic)   (functional)

Figure 1-1 *The physical features of a garment determine its performance.*

pearance after wear and care. Does it resist shrinking? Do the seams remain intact? Does the zipper continue to zip?

Aesthetic and functional performance occasionally overlap. For example, fit may be an aesthetic feature (attractive fit versus unattractive fit) or a functional feature (comfortable fit versus uncomfortable fit).

SELLING POINTS AND BUYING BENEFITS

Emphasizing a garment's quality by enumerating its benefits to the consumer is a valuable sales and marketing technique. Today's increasingly well-educated shoppers appreciate information about the quality of the apparel products they buy, preferring to make purchase decisions based on facts.

Selling points are the physical features of a garment that make it desirable. However, effectively promoting a garment involves more than merely citing a list of selling points. Ideally, you interpret those selling points to the consumer in terms of buying benefits. **Buying benefits** are the performance advantages that result from the garment's physical features. They explain how each feature fulfills the consumer's wants and needs. For example, the statement, "This shirt is 100% cotton," is a selling point, but not nearly as meaningful to consumers as the statement of an associated buying benefit, for example, "Because this shirt is 100% cotton, it is cool and comfortable." The more technical the selling point, the more important to translate it into buying benefits for the consumer.

Knowing the selling points of the merchandise and understanding the buying benefits the consumer is seeking enhance business success on every level, from personal selling to marketing and manufacturing. Lands' End catalogs use this technique effectively. Note the use of selling points and the associated buying benefits to promote the quality of a man's tie in Figure 1-2. And be alert to selling points and buying benefits as you read this text.

Variations in Quality Perceptions

Consumers use a variety of criteria to evaluate quality (see Related Resources: Variations in Consumer Quality Perceptions). The unique combination of performance factors used by a particular consumer depends on a number of conditions: (1) the intended use of the garment,

At Lands' End, the back of a tie is every bit as important as the front.

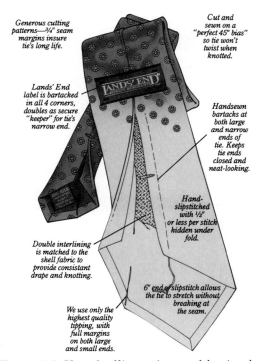

Generous cutting patterns—¾″ seam margins insure tie's long life.

Cut and sewn on a "perfect 45″ bias" so tie won't twist when knotted.

Lands' End label is bartacked in all 4 corners, doubles as secure "keeper" for tie's narrow end.

Handsewn bartacks at both large and narrow ends of tie. Keeps tie ends closed and neat-looking.

Hand-slipstitched with ½″ or less per stitch hidden under fold.

Double interlining is matched to the shell fabric to provide consistant drape and knotting.

6″ end of slipstitch allows the tie to stretch without breaking at the seam.

We use only the highest quality tipping, with full margins on both large and small ends.

Figure 1-2 *Use of selling points and buying benefits to promote the quality of a man's tie. (Reprinted courtesy of Lands' End Catalog. © Lands' End, Inc.)*

(2) cultural influences on the consumer, (3) demographics and psychographics, and (4) individual standards. These conditions determine a particular consumer's requirements and expectations for a particular garment. They also determine the selling points and buying benefits that are important to the consumer.

END USE

The **end use,** or intended use, of a garment affects how the consumer assesses quality. For example, a high-quality wedding gown possesses aesthetic characteristics—it is beautiful and flattering to the wearer. A functional characteristic, such as ease of care, has little or no importance to a bride who wears the dress only one time. On the other hand, ease of care is a major quality indicator for children's play clothing and is important to most parents. In another example, young teenage consumers typically want the latest fashion (an aesthetic characteristic). Durability (a functional characteristic) is relatively unimportant to them because fashion will probably make their wardrobe obsolete before it physically wears out. In contrast, adults tend to be interested in *investment dressing,* the purchase of classic apparel such as coats and suits that can be worn several seasons; thus, utility and durability are important to them.

CULTURAL DIFFERENCES

The features used to define apparel quality change over time. Hand-stitched seams and boned bodices, important in a high-quality garment a hundred years ago, are not relevant to modern definitions of ready-to-wear quality. And the stone washed, abraded, and torn jeans popular in the 1990s would have been abhorrent to quality-conscious consumers in the 1950s.

Cultural differences make it possible for a garment considered of high quality in one culture to be considered of low quality in another because of varying standards and expectations. An example is garments made of madras-plaid cotton fabric when it was originally imported to the United States from India. At first, U.S. consumers perceived the garments to be low quality because the natural dyes faded and ran when the garments were laundered. When U.S. consumers adopted the Indian notion that the fading of madras is a desirable part of its natural beauty and character, madras-plaid garments were perceived to be of high quality.

DEMOGRAPHICS AND PSYCHOGRAPHICS

The demographics and psychographics of a target market help determine the wants and needs of the consumers in it. *Demographics* are statistics that describe a population, including age, income, education, occupation, and other factors that affect a consumer's product preferences. For example, statistics on the aging of the U.S. population led Levi's to develop their popular Dockers brand pants for men. The loose fit of Dockers is more comfortable and more flattering to the expanding waistline of a person approaching middle age than are tight pants. Another demographic influence on the apparel industry is the increase in families having few children but earning high incomes. This creates a demand for luxury children's clothing, such as leather jackets instead of cloth coats for toddlers.

Demographics are most useful when considered along with psychographics. *Psychographics* characterize people according to their lifestyle values—interests, attitudes, and opinions. Understanding these things about consumers helps predict what they expect and desire of a garment because their values influence their clothing behavior. For example, a consumer interested in aesthetics considers features such as color and design as most important in judging quality. Another consumer assessing the same garment, but with the attitude that clothing should be comfortable, makes a quality judgment based on features such as the roominess or weight of the garment.

INDIVIDUAL STANDARDS

Individual standards affect the perception of quality. Consumers with high standards are dissatisfied when a garment does not meet their expectations; others with lower expectations might be relatively pleased and satisfied with the performance of the same garment. For example, if one consumer expects to wear a pair of shorts four years, but they last three, the consumer is dissatisfied. But if another consumer expects to wear the shorts only two years, and they last three, the consumer is satisfied.

Many consumers lack the ability to objectively evaluate quality. Although everyone has experience in wearing clothing, the average consumer is not trained to evaluate it. However, consumers do not necessarily base their quality judgment on the *inherent* quality of a garment, but instead upon their *perception* of its quality. Thus, *in the consumer's mind,* the perceived quality *is* the real quality of the garment.

Perceived Quality Model

A consumer's main question when making a purchase decision is, "How will the garment perform for me when I wear it?" Before shopping for clothing, consumers establish the aesthetic and functional performance standards they think the garment should meet. While shopping, they compare possible purchases to these standards. However, because these processes usually happen informally and subconsciously, many consumers are unaware of *how* they decide what to buy.

Figure 1-3 features the **perceived quality model,** which illustrates the process consumers use to evaluate the overall quality of a garment. The perceived quality model quantifies a consumer's evaluation of the *desirability,* or overall quality, of a garment. Although the actual process is not formal and conscious, the model shows how consumers form perceptions about apparel quality.

The model demonstrates that no two purchase decisions are made in exactly the same way. It contrasts how different consumers evaluate the same garment, and how the same consumer evaluates two different garments or types of garments. You may find the model useful in examining your own purchase motivations and those of others.

APPLICATION OF THE MODEL

Table 1-1 illustrates how two hypothetical consumers, A and B, evaluate the same T-shirt using the perceived quality model. To evaluate a garment using the model, follow these steps:

1. *Select* the features that affect the quality of the garment you are evaluating. Consumers consider different things to assess quality, so the features vary from person to person and depend on the type of garment being evaluated. Any number and combination of factors may be used. Note in Table 1-1 that Consumer A considers more features than does Consumer B when evaluating a T-shirt.*

2. *Weight* each performance feature to reflect its *importance* in determining quality. The weights represent the percentage of the feature's influence on your quality evaluation. Adding the weights should total 100 percent, illustrating that, together, the features account for the overall quality evaluation of the garment. Different consumers value some things more than others, so the weights vary from person to person and with the type of garment. Note the different weights assigned to various performance features by Consumer A and Consumer B.

3. *Rate* how well the garment meets expectations for each performance feature on a scale of 0 to 100, with 100 as the highest rating. The ratings depend entirely on your attitudes about

---

* Because most consumers use price as a cue to quality, it may be included as a feature in the model. However, doing so changes the model from one that measures perceived quality to one that measures perceived value (see discussion concerning Figure 1-5).

$$Q = \sum_{f=1}^{n} w_f r_f$$

Overall quality score =
Sum of (weight of each feature × rating of each feature)

Q = overall quality score; a number ranging from 0 to 100 representing a consumer's evaluation of a garment's quality, with 100 as maximum quality and 0 as absence of quality

Σ = sum

n = number of features used in the evaluation; varies depending on consumer and garment

f = feature used in evaluating a garment's quality; the features used depend on the consumer and the garment

w = weight; a percentage ranging from 0 to 100 representing the contribution or importance of the feature to the overall quality evaluation, with the weights of all features totaling 100%

r = rating; a number ranging from 0 to 100 representing how well the garment performs on that feature, with 100 as maximum performance and 0 as absence of performance

Figure 1-3 Perceived quality model. (Adapted from models in Ajzen, I., and J. Fishbein, 1980, Understanding Attitudes and Predicting Social Behavior En-glewood Cliffs, NJ: Prentice-Hall; and Maynes, E.S. (1976), Decision-Making for Consumers: An Introduction to Consumer Economics, New York: Macmillan.

TABLE 1-1

Comparison of two consumers' evaluations of a T-shirt using the perceived quality model

Consumer A's Perceived Quality Evaluation:

Feature	Weight (Importance)		Rating		Contribution to Quality
Brand name	10%	×	70	=	7
Color	10%	×	60	=	6
Comfort	5%	×	20	=	1
Country of origin	5%	×	70	=	3.5
Durability	2.5%	×	10	=	.25
Ease of care	2.5%	×	10	=	.25
Fabric	5%	×	40	=	2
Fit	10%	×	60	=	6
General appearance	30%	×	60	=	18
Shrinkage	5%	×	60	=	3
Style/fashion	15%	×	80	=	12
TOTAL	100%				59
					OVERALL QUALITY SCORE

Consumer B's Perceived Quality Evaluation:

Feature	Weight (Importance)		Rating		Contribution to Quality
Color	50%	×	70	=	35
Fit	10%	×	90	=	9
General appearance	15%	×	60	=	9
Style/fashion	25%	×	80	=	20
TOTAL	100%				73
					OVERALL QUALITY SCORE

the garment's performance. Thus, ratings vary from person to person. Note the different ratings assigned to the T-shirt by Consumer A and Consumer B.

4. *Multiply* the weight, or importance, of each feature by its rating to determine the contribution of the feature to the quality evaluation.

5. *Add* the contribution of all the features to calculate the *overall quality score* for the garment. There is no "minimum" quality score, above which all consumers think a garment is high quality and below which all consumers agree that a garment is low quality. The overall quality score that constitutes an acceptable level depends upon the individual consumer. However, if we establish an overall quality score of 70 as average, Consumer A finds the T-shirt unacceptable (overall quality score 59) and Consumer B finds it acceptable (overall quality score 73). A consumer who likes the T-shirt very much would have an even higher quality score for it.

DETERMINANT ATTRIBUTES

A consumer's overall satisfaction with the quality of a garment may be measured: (1) at the point of sale, (2) later, when the garment is in use, or (3) when the garment is discarded. The features that have the greatest effect on the consumer's satisfaction at any of these times are called *determinant attributes*. At the point of sale, the aesthetic features of the garment are typically determinant. However, if functional features are unsatisfactory when the garment is worn, they eventually replace aesthetics as determinants of the consumer's satisfaction (or more accurately, at that point, dissatisfaction). The following sections illustrate the differences in quality perception at the point of sale and when the garment is in use. The examples of the perceived quality model, for the sake of brevity, include only the broad categories of "aesthetic performance" and "functional performance." These features represent the multiple aesthetic and functional features that a real consumer would evaluate separately.

Point of Sale. Consumers easily judge a garment's aesthetic performance at the point of sale just by looking at it. The attractiveness of a garment affects consumers emotionally and psychologically; a consumer is unlikely to purchase a garment that does not meet his or her aesthetic standards. Aesthetic features of a garment, such as color, style, and fit, initially attract or repel consumers. *In fact, color, style, and fit, all aesthetic features, are three of the four* most common determinants of consumers' clothing purchase decision* (Galbraith 1981). Yet evaluation of these dimensions is subjective; beauty cannot be quantified. Aesthetic judgments are largely influenced by personal tastes and current fashions. Also, the wearer's height, weight, figure type, and coloring interact with the appearance of the garment, making it more eye-pleasing or less so.

Consumers cannot accurately evaluate a garment's functional performance at the point of sale. They may estimate some aspects of functional performance, such as comfort or freedom of movement, by trying on the garment. Or they may try to predict functional performance, based on the design, materials, or construction of the garment. However, most aspects of functional performance are *latent,* or hidden until the consumer wears and cares for the garment. Galbraith (1981) determined that most consumer dissatisfaction with apparel results from problems involving size/fit, seams that pucker and burst, buttons that fall off, improper choice and application of interfacings, uncomfortable

* Price is the other determinant factor in purchase decision making (see pages 9–12).

and inaccurate care labels, fabric shrinkage, color change, pilling, snagging, edge wear, holes in pockets, and stain/soil retention. Consumers can see and accurately predict few, if any, of these functional defects at the point of sale. They buy a garment *assuming* that it will function adequately in use, without really knowing whether it will or not. Therefore, because functional performance is largely unknown at the point of sale, it does not greatly influence most consumers' purchase decisions.

In the example in Table 1-2, the hypothetical consumer bases most of his decision about suit quality on aesthetics, assigning it a weight of 70%. He bases the remaining 30 percent of the quality judgment on functional performance. The consumer rates aesthetics low (10) for a hypothetical gray suit and high (90) for a hypothetical blue suit. Because aesthetics is visually determined at the point of sale, he rates the suits so differently because of differences in their appearances. However, the consumer cannot visually determine the functional performance of the two suits at the point of sale, so he assumes both will function adequately and gives each suit a rating of 70.

When the ratings are totaled, the blue suit achieves a higher overall quality score at the point of sale than does the gray suit. If we establish a score of 70 as average, or acceptable, we conclude that the consumer views the gray suit as being of "low quality" and the blue suit as being of "high quality." As in most cases, *aesthetic features determine the apparel purchase decision.* In some cases, functional performance rather than aesthetics is determinant at the point of sale. For instance, a serious runner is more concerned about comfortable exercise clothes than attractive ones. However, in most cases, aesthetics is usually predominate.

TABLE 1-2

Point-of-sale quality of two suits, as evaluated by a hypothetical consumer

Feature	Weight	Gray Suit Point-of-Sale Rating	Blue Suit Point-of-Sale Rating
Aesthetics	70%	× 10 = 7	× 90 = 63
Function	30%	× 70 = 21	× 70 = 21
	100%	28	84
		OVERALL POINT-OF-SALE QUALITY SCORE	OVERALL POINT-OF-SALE QUALITY SCORE

In Use. Although not accurately predicted at the point of sale, the functional performance of the garment becomes obvious in use. For example, how warm a garment is, how much it fades, and how easily it tears are easily determined, but only after the garment is used. At that time, the consumer re-evaluates the garment, comparing actual performance to point-of-sale expectations about performance. Because aesthetic performance is accurately predicted at the point of sale, its influence on the in-use quality evaluation remains the same. However, because functional performance is unpredictable at the point of sale, its influence on the in-use quality evaluation may change. Therefore, functional performance becomes critical to later consumer satisfaction.

Reconsider the consumer, who was discussed previously, evaluating the gray and blue suits. Table 1-3 shows how the quality judgment of the consumer may change after the suits are put into use. After wearing and caring for the suits, the consumer gathers data on their functional performance, which affects the in-use quality evaluation.

In use, the consumer rates the function of the gray suit high (90) and the function of the blue suit low (10). Note the impact of these ratings on the overall quality scores of each suit. Poor function in the presence of excellent aesthetics creates dissatisfaction with the blue suit (in-use quality score = 66). However, excellent function in the absence of excellent aesthetics does not create satisfaction with the gray suit (in-use quality score = 34). This leads us to the realization of an important fact: *Adequate aesthetic performance is required to create satisfaction, and adequate functional performance is required to prevent dissatisfaction* (Swan and Combs 1976).

Another phenomenon causes the in-use quality score of a garment to differ dramatically from the point-of-sale quality score. The importance, or weight, assigned to each performance feature *may change* when the garment is worn. This occurs because some features, depending upon their in-use performance, increase or decrease in importance. For example, durability might be weighted low at the point of sale. If the garment quickly wears out, however, durability becomes a very important feature in evaluating the in-use quality of the garment, and the weight assigned to durability is raised accordingly, increasing its influence on the overall quality score.

Achieving in-use consumer satisfaction should be as important to an apparel manufacturer and/or retailer as delivering satisfaction at the point of sale. Granted, satisfaction at the point of sale determines whether or not the consumer buys the garment. But in-use satisfaction affects the consumer's feelings of good will or ill will toward the brand and/or retailer, and determines whether or not the consumer makes repeat purchases. Therefore, companies that ignore functional performance, and rely exclusively on the aesthetic appeal of their products, ignore their own futures.

Consumers assess their *ultimate* satisfaction with a garment at the time they discard it. When consumers get rid of items they no longer wear, they objectively evaluate how well the garment performed compared to their original expectations for it. A garment that ultimately fulfills the consumer's expectations of quality leads to satisfaction that translates into an increased loyalty to the brand and/or retailer. A garment that ultimately fails to meet the consumer's expectations leaves the consumer dissatisfied, eroding loyalty to the brand and/or

TABLE 1-3

In-use quality of two suits, as evaluated by a hypothetical consumer

Feature	Weight	Gray Suit In-Use Rating	Blue Suit In-Use Rating
Aesthetics	70%	× 10 = 7	× 90 = 63
Function	30%	× 90 = 27	× 10 = 3
	100%	34	66
		OVERALL IN-USE QUALITY SCORE	OVERALL IN-USE QUALITY SCORE

retailer. Therefore, providing garments that meet or exceed consumers' quality expectations contributes to long-term business success.

Relating Price and Quality

In addition to intrinsic features, apparel has *extrinsic attributes,* those that can be altered without changing the garment. Like intrinsic cues, extrinsic cues influence quality evaluations. Extrinsic cues include (1) the price of the garment, (2) its manufacturer, (3) brand name, (4) country of origin, (5) image and reputation of retailer, and (6) hanger, hang tags, and packaging. All these cues are visible at the point of sale. They carry connotations of quality and influence the consumer's perception of the garment's quality, either positively or negatively.

Of the extrinsic cues, consumers pay the most attention to *price.* Price is a major determinant of consumers' apparel purchase decisions for several reasons. First, consumers rely heavily on price as a quality cue. Second, they compare a garment's price and perceived quality to determine value. Third, whether or not a consumer can afford to purchase a particular garment depends upon price.

PRICE LINES

Ready-to-wear is categorized according to price lines (Figure 1-4). **Price lines** are clusters of merchandise at various price levels, from most expensive to least expensive. Price lines categorize retailers, departments within retail stores, and manufacturers as "high end," "low end," or somewhere in between. *Off-pricing* or *discounting* can occur within any price line. Off-price retailers sell goods at lower prices than the manufacturer's suggested retail price. They

profit by selling large quantities of merchandise and/or by keeping operating costs low.

Exclusive Price Lines. Couture and haute couture are the highest price lines of ready-to-wear. In its purest sense, **couture** (koo tur′) refers to high-quality clothing *custom made,* or made to measure, for a specific individual. It originated in Paris, where designers made couture clothing (literally "fine sewing" in French) for their private customers. **Haute couture** (ōt koo tur′) is a term reserved for the most fashionable and exclusive couture apparel. True couture and haute couture are associated with exceptionally fine fabrics, careful and detailed construction, excellent fit and astronomical prices, often $10,000 or more for a dress. **Bespoke** is a comparable term for high-quality, custom-made men's suits, usually from London.

Some designers, mainly in Europe, still have couture houses where they make true couture clothing for a few wealthy clients. But these same designers also produce ready-to-wear lines, from which they make far greater profits due to larger sales volumes and mass-manufacturing techniques. Thus, *couture* has become a diluted term, often used to describe high-price, designer-name ready-to-wear rather than custom-made clothing. For example, "American couture" usually refers to ready-to-wear. Although expensive, these garments cost much less than true couture.

In its highest sense, **designer clothing** is synonymous with couture or haute couture. As a price line, however, it includes work by popular designers who make only ready-to-wear; although they may make high-quality garments, they are not considered among the ranks of the couture designers. In fact, the term *designer* has been so overused that it sometimes refers to any merchandise that bears the name of a designer, not necessarily a famous one. Designer names have experienced such popularity that some so-called designer apparel carries the name of a nonexistent person and is equivalent to an ordinary brand name. Thus, the price for designer merchandise varies widely.

Mass Merchandise Price Lines. Other important ready-to-wear price lines are budget, moderate, and better, often equated with the retailer's lingo of "*good, better,* and *best.*" The apparel industry encourages consumers to associate quality and price by using references to quality and price synonymously in this manner.

High End/Most Expensive	Haute Couture
	Couture
	Designer
	Bridge
	Better
	Moderate
Low End/Least Expensive	Budget

Figure 1-4 Ready-to-wear price lines.

The majority of apparel falls into one of these price lines. Budget, moderate, and better constitute the *mass merchandise* or *volume market,* where large quantities of goods are sold. These price lines are dominated by brand names as opposed to designer names. The French term for ready-to-wear, **prêt à porter** (prĕt′ ah por tay′) or **prêt** for short, refers to goods in the mass merchandise price lines. It means, literally, "ready to carry."

Better represents the highest of the mass merchandise price lines. Notice how quality is associated with the idea of paying more, a popular marketing tactic. Better lines frequently feature well-known brands and relatively low-price designer names. In some stores, a price line called **bridge** falls between better and designer merchandise, "bridging" the gap between the two; bridge may also refer to goods between better and moderate. **Moderate** price lines serve as the middle ground, moderate-price goods associated with moderate quality standards, for the average consumer. **Budget** is the lowest of the mass merchandise price lines. Consumers usually assume that budget goods meet lower quality standards than other price lines. Therefore, for marketing purposes budget goods are often given a more appealing name such as *popularly priced, value priced,* or *bargain.*

Remember that price lines are relative. For example, "moderate sportswear" in an exclusive department store may be "better sportswear" to a mass merchandiser. For example, brands such as Liz Claiborne and Pendleton may be considered as moderate merchandise in one store, better merchandise in another, and bridge merchandise in a third. Thus, the same price lines, in different stores, do not necessarily encompass the same **price points** (specific dollar price amounts).

PRICE AS A CUE TO QUALITY

Price influences the consumer's perception of apparel quality. Most consumers believe that there is a positive relationship between price and quality; they assume that a garment with a high price meets high quality standards. Sayings such as, "You get what you pay for," perpetuate this idea. A high price often lends an aura of quality to a garment; if a price seems too low, the quality of the garment is suspect.

While not necessarily related to quality, extrinsic cues such as price, brand, and retailer's reputation are nevertheless used by consumers in assessing quality. Consumers are especially likely to use price as a cue to quality because, unlike the performance of a garment, price is visible and known. And price is a number that can be easily compared to the prices of other garments, unlike the difficulty of comparing elusive characteristics such as durability.

This is not to say that price and other extrinsic cues are more important than the intrinsic aspects of the product. However, especially in the absence of other information, price is important to the consumer's quality evaluation. When the consumer cannot readily see other differences in two similar garments, price is the main piece of information available for use in evaluating quality. It appears that consumers rely on price as a quality indicator because they are trying to make an informed decision. However, the more other quality cues available, the less likely it is that price influences quality judgments.

One would think that the higher the price of the garment, the better the quality of its design, materials, and construction. However, cost of production does not by itself determine price (see Chapter 2), and price does not necessarily reflect quality. High-quality goods can be found at low prices, and a high price does not guarantee high quality. Several research studies show that reliance on price to evaluate apparel quality yields inaccurate results (see Related Resources: Price as a Cue to Quality).

Consumers rely on price as a quality indicator because *sometimes* price aids them in making a successful quality evaluation. For some garments a high price reflects superior design, materials, and/or construction. Sproles (1977) found support for this general idea when he investigated the relationship between the price of various products and the inherent quality as determined through objective tests and established standards. Sproles' findings indicate a positive relationship between price and quality for about 50 percent of the products studied. For those products, when the price is higher, the quality is higher, and when the price is lower, the quality is lower. However, the other half of the products studied does not demonstrate such a relationship. In fact, over 10 percent actually appear to display negative relationships between price and quality; when price went up, quality went down! For the products Sproles studied, if consumers base their quality evaluations entirely on price, they would make many poor decisions.

VALUE

The relationship between quality and price is expressed in terms of **value.** An item of apparel is a *fair value* if it delivers quality comparable to the price paid. An *overpriced* garment furnishes little quality for the price, and a *bargain* offers high quality compared to the price paid.

Perceived value is a determinant factor in a consumer's decision whether or not to purchase a garment. If the garment seems a fair value or a bargain, the consumer's perception of value motivates buying. Perceived value is also assessed when the garment is removed from use, as the wearer appraises his or her ultimate satisfaction with the garment compared to the price paid.

Perceived Value Graph. The **perceived value graph** in Figure 1-5 represents how consumers make decisions based on the *price* of a garment and *perceived quality*. Notice the position of the various points on the graph. The points representing garments with high perceived quality/low price fall into the bargain sector. The points representing garments with high price/low perceived quality fall into the overpriced sector. The points representing equal price and perceived quality are on the fair value line. Luxury goods are at the upper end, where both price and perceived quality are high. So-called "sleazy" or cheap merchandise is found at the lower end, where both price and perceived quality are low. The value graph illustrates that the consumer must perceive the quality of a garment as equal to or greater than the price before making a purchase.

Cost Per Wear. In purely economic terms, the value of a garment depends on how much it costs to wear it. The purchase price divided by the number of times the garment is worn determines the **cost per wear.** An expensive garment is a better cost-per-wear value than an inexpensive one *if* the expensive item is worn more frequently or over a longer period of time. For example, if a $200 coat is worn 50 times before being discarded, it is a better value than a $100 coat worn only 20 times. The $200 coat costs $4 per wear; the $100 coat costs $5 per wear (Figure 1-6). However, an inexpensive garment is a better cost-per-wear value than an expensive garment if neither is worn much.

Consumers commonly apply the cost-per-wear formula when durability is important. However, it can also be used when other factors, such as comfort or styling, affect the relationship between the purchase price of a garment and the number of times a garment is worn. For example, evening dresses are usually worn only a limited number of times because the wearer is unwilling to be seen in the same evening dress more than a few times, or because the dress goes out of fashion before it physically wears out. A $400 evening dress worn 2 times costs $200 per wear, whereas a $200 evening dress worn the same number of times costs only $100 per wear. If a garment requires dry cleaning, the cost of care influences the cost per wear; for example, a washable sweater has a lower cost per wear than a *Dry Clean Only* sweater of the same price.

Paying a high price to obtain a high-quality product is a poor use of economic resources if it does not lower the cost per wear. However, a

Figure 1-5 Perceived value graph illustrates the relationship of price and perceived quality.

$\dfrac{\text{Number of times a garment is worn}}{\text{Purchase price}}$	$=$ Cost per wear
$\dfrac{\text{Coat worn 50 times}}{\$200 \text{ purchase price}}$	$=$ $4 per wear
$\dfrac{\text{Coat worn 20 times}}{\$100 \text{ purchase price}}$	$=$ $5 per wear
$\dfrac{\text{Dress worn 2 times}}{\$400 \text{ purchase price}}$	$=$ $200 per wear
$\dfrac{\text{Dress worn 2 times}}{\$200 \text{ purchase price}}$	$=$ $100 per wear

Figure 1-6 Formula for calculating cost per wear, and examples.

high price that translates into a low cost per wear is a good economic choice. Of course, the decision to purchase a garment is often based on factors other than the best use of economic resources. For instance, if a child looks charming in a fancy party dress, the emotional appeal of the dress to a grandparent makes "cost per wear" irrelevant, even if the child wears the dress to only one event before outgrowing it.

Apparel Life Expectancy. The **International Fabricare Institute (IFI),** association of professional dry cleaners and launderers, promotes the *Fair Claims Guide for Consumer Textile Products.** It defines the value of clothing of various ages. The Fair Claims Guide suggests that certain apparel categories imply certain life expectancy rates if the garment is cared for as recommended (Table 1-4). It estimates how long a garment reasonably may be expected to last, considering normal wear, care, and fashion change. The Fair Claims Guide is widely used in the arbitration of apparel serviceability disputes; for example, replacement value is calculated based on the degree to which the garment's life expectancy has been used up and the condition of the garment. In addition, the Fair Claims Guide is useful as a yardstick to which all garments may be compared. Individuals responsible for manufacturing and selling ready-to-wear apparel should be aware of these guidelines and be sure that products meet them.

Assuming that the Fair Claims Guide is viewed as reasonable by consumers, garments that meet the guidelines should satisfy most consumers' expectations of serviceability. Consumers probably have justifiable reason to complain about a garment's poor performance when it does not meet the criteria of the Fair Claims Guide.

Industry Efforts to Control Quality

The apparel industry consciously pursues quality in an effort to produce clothing that meets consumer expectations. Determining the wants and needs of consumers helps manufacturers

* For more information, contact International Fabricare Institute, 12251 Tech Road, Silver Spring, MD 20904.

and retailers establish appropriate quality standards for the merchandise they produce and sell. Companies that offer garments most closely meeting the expectations of the target market have the greatest chance for success in selling to and satisfying those consumers.

Consumers' aesthetic expectations are easier to discern than their functional expectations. Shoppers cast their votes in the form of dollars at the cash register for the colors and styles they prefer; sales figures send a clear message to the industry regarding which aesthetic characteristics they like and dislike. However, the apparel industry does not get such a clear message regarding functional performance preferences. Consumers are neither satisfied nor dissatisfied with the utility or durability of a garment at the point of sale; they cannot identify garments that meet or fail to meet functional performance standards until after wear and care. Companies that pursue and acquire an understanding of functional performance expectations have a clear advantage in ensuring that they provide the level of in-use performance that consumers want. For example, merchandisers at The Lee Company wear jeans to work every day so they get to know their product better. This company policy enables them to clearly see the consumer's perspective of their product, and to pinpoint and correct in-use performance problems rather than concentrating only on point-of-sale aesthetics.

QUALITY DEPARTMENTS

Many large manufacturers and some retailers have **quality departments** that establish quality standards and search for ways to consistently achieve the desired level of quality. These are sometimes called **quality assurance (QA)** or **quality control (QC)** departments. Quality-minded companies monitor the conformance of garments to quality standards through a program of inspection, laboratory and wear testing, and the analysis of returned merchandise.**

Quality departments promote the principle that quality cannot be ignored all through the manufacturing process and "inspected in" to the garment at the end. Moving beyond merely inspecting finished goods for defects, modern qual-

* The professional organization for people interested in apparel quality is the **American Society for Quality Control (ASQC),** Textile and Needle Trades Division, 230 West Wells Street, Milwaukee, WI 53203.

TABLE 1-4
Average life expectancy of textile items in years
(Reprinted courtesy of International Fabricare Institute.)

Apparel		Household Furnishings
Bathing Suits 2	Fabric, lined & unlined . . . 3	Bedspreads 6
Bathrobes	Rubber and plastic 3	Blankets
Lightweight 2	Shirts	Heavy wool and
Heavy or quilted 3	Dress 3	synthetic fibers 10
Wool 3	Sports 2	Lightweight 5
Blazers	Wool or silk 2	Electric 5
Cotton and blends 3	Ski Jackets	Comforters 5
Imitation suede* 3	(including down) 2	Down 5
Wool 4	Skirts 2	Curtains
Coats and Jackets (Outerwear)	Slacks	Sheer 3
Children's 2	Lounging and active sport . 2	Glass fiber 3
Cotton and blends 3	Dress 3	Draperies
Down 3	Socks 1	Lined 5
Fur 10	Sport Coats	Unlined 4
Imitation fur or suede* . . . 3	Cotton and synthetic	Sheer 3
Leather and suede 5	blends 3	Glass fiber 4
Plastic 2	Imitation suede* 3	Sheets & Pillow Cases 2
Wool 4	Wool and wool blends 4	Slipcovers 3
Blouses 3	Suits	Table Linen
Choir Robes 6	Cotton and synthetic 2	Fancy 5
Dresses	Summer-weight wool 3	Other 2
Casual 2	Imitation suede* 3	Towels 3
Office 3	Silk 3	Upholstery Fabrics 5
Silk 2	Washable 2	
Evening	Winter-weight wool 4	
High fashion 3	Sweaters 3	
Basic 5	Ties 1	
Formal Wear 5	Underwear	
Gloves	Foundation garments 1	
Fabric 1	Panties 1	
Leather 2	Slips 2	
Rainwear & Windbreakers	Uniforms 1	
Film & plastic coated . . . 2	Vests 2	

* Nonwoven only. Life expectancy for coated or flocked articles is two years.

Author's note: The life expectancies in this table may be conservative and do not take into account factors such as style, fabrication, quality of construction, or frequency of use.

ity departments attempt to identify the causes of defects and propose solutions. The responsibilities of a comprehensive quality department include planning for quality at all stages by overseeing the design, materials, and construction of garments. Planning for quality and building it into the garment at every step are the only ways to ensure quality (see Related Resources: Industry Efforts to Control Quality).

Instilling a commitment to quality in employees throughout the company, from management to production workers, is essential. If workers get the idea that management talks about quality but rewards high production, they concentrate on production. But if workers believe that management genuinely cares about quality and rewards those who make it possible, they care about quality too.

Retailers with quality departments recognize the importance of maintaining a consistently positive image by selling quality apparel to their customers. Rather than relying solely on manufacturers to deliver high-quality apparel to them, they monitor the items they buy and sell to ensure that all goods meet the standards of their organization. The most common function of retail quality departments is measuring samples of incoming garments to check their conformance to fit specifications. However, some of these departments have requirements as comprehensive as those of the most sophisticated manufacturer. They may establish all types of performance specifications and perform physical tests to ensure conformance to those standards. As an example, a retail quality department may require little boys' jeans to be made of denim with a specified level of abrasion resistance. Then they test incoming jeans to see that the product meets the specification.

SPECIFICATIONS

The establishment of specifications is one of the most important responsibilities of a quality department. **Specifications** or **specs** are exact standards for the production of a garment. Think of specifications as the recipe for producing a garment. They serve as a tool for communicating the desired quality standards regarding the design, materials, and construction of a garment. Specifications represent a conscious effort to build desired levels of performance into a garment. They are developed with the consumer's requirements in mind, as well as cost limitations. Specifications serve to inform people about and to involve them in the pursuit of quality standards at all phases of the manufacturing process. These standards are useful in-house as well as when assigning work to others and when procuring goods from materials sources, such as fabric mills and trim houses.

Retailers find specifications useful as well. Retail buyers may purchase according to the company's preset requirements. This helps them to concentrate on the precise wants and needs of their customers and to communicate these wants and needs to the manufacturer.

If accurately written, specifications allow garments to be conceptualized on one side of the globe and produced on the other side of the world exactly as designed. As more companies do business internationally, language and cultural barriers increase the chance for misunderstood intentions unless written specifications are used to clearly communicate standards. Great distances and high shipping costs make it difficult or impractical to return goods that do not meet expected standards, so specs are vital in getting things right the first time.

Quality specifications must be continually enforced to protect the image of a quality-oriented business. And manufacturers or retailers who grow "too fast" are often plagued by quality problems. These companies must meet the challenge of maintaining the quality standards that originally made them popular, but for a vastly increased volume of goods. Firms that do not establish and enforce strict methods to control quality tarnish their reputations by offering low-quality garments to the public, eventually damaging their business.

Establishing Specifications. Before establishing specifications, the important performance features and the desired level of performance for each feature must be identified. These criteria may be specified without stating *how* they should be achieved. For example, a manufacturer may simply require seams of a certain strength. More commonly, however, the physical features of the product—its design, materials, and construction—are specified. For example, the manufacturer might specify the seam type, stitch type, thread type, and number of stitches per inch for the seams of a garment in an effort to achieve the desired seam strength. Of course, specifying the design, materials, and construction is effective only if it results in the desired performance.

Specifications should balance required levels of performance with the cost limitations of the price line. This is vital for the final product to be not only of high quality but also a good value. To keep costs low, most manufacturers and retailers write specifications that state the lowest level of performance they find acceptable.

Many informal, oral specifications are used in the apparel industry. A manufacturer may, for example, call a contractor and mention that a certain seam type is to be used on the blouses the contractor is making. However, the trend is toward more formal, written specs. The explicit directions contained in written specifications are more clearly understood, more apt to be followed, and more readily enforceable than oral specifications.

The U.S. government recognizes the importance of specifications in communicating quality requirements. The government has established extensive specifications for the production of apparel for the armed services. This ensures that all manufacturers bidding on a contract submit a bid based on the production of exactly the same design, using the same quality and quantity of materials and construction. Government specs allow for clear-cut rejection of any garments that do not meet minimum standards.

Consequently, military garments are of fairly consistent quality, regardless of the manufacturer, which highlights the benefits of written specifications.

The more detailed the specifications, the less room for misunderstanding. Of course, a balance should be struck between specifications that are complete enough to cover all the pertinent points and specs that are unnecessarily tedious. Specifications sheets sent to contractors are generally quite comprehensive, covering every detail of production. But specs for in-house use or between companies that deal with one another frequently may include minimum specifications that are less detailed, as in Figure 1-7. In lieu of specifications, some companies provide *caution sheets*, which highlight the most important information that production workers should know to achieve quality results.

Tolerances. Reasonable specifications include plus-or-minus tolerances. A **tolerance** is the difference between the allowable minimum and maximum of a specification (Figure 12-1). For example, specifying that seams be stitched using exactly 12 stitches per inch is an unrealistic standard, considering the wide range of sewing machines and operators used to construct a single garment. A realistic specification is 12 stitches per inch, plus-or-minus 1 stitch per inch. This provides a more reasonable range of 11–13 stitches per inch, achievable on different machines and by different operators.

Unreasonable specifications have little chance of being met, making them unenforceable and useless. For instance, a too-rigid standard is that the side seam and sleeve seam must meet *exactly* where they intersect under the arm, a specification nearly impossible to achieve. This specification sets an impractical goal that is more frustrating than constructive. However, if a tolerance of plus-or-minus ¼″ is set, so that the seams must meet within ¼″ of one another, the goal is achievable. Making the tolerance stricter, plus-or-minus ⅛″, tightens quality standards. Or making it more lenient, plus-or-minus ½″, loosens quality standards. For in-house use and for contractors with whom they work regularly, manufacturers may establish standard tolerances for various operations so they do not need to restate the tolerance each time they write a specification.

Tolerances provide a realistic way to control quality when mass-manufacturing. However, state tolerances only when slight differences are acceptable. If, for example, a manufacturer specifies seven buttons on a shirt front, no tolerance need be stated.

INSPECTION

Most quality programs include a visual **inspection** or **audit** of garments for monitoring and regulating quality. Inspectors examine fabrics and other raw materials for flaws and check their conformance to specifications upon receipt. However, most inspection efforts concentrate on the assembly process. Quality inspectors examine garments for construction faults and other defects that occur during production. For example, a pocket accidentally sewn shut is clearly an unacceptable defect. In other situations, causing a garment to pass or fail inspection depends on the tolerances allowed in the specifications and the judgment of the inspector. For instance, a crooked line of stitches may be acceptable or unacceptable, depending on whether or not the inspector decides the stitches deviate too much from the standard.

Using traditional inspection methods, production workers or their supervisors visually inspect the goods produced for conformance to quality standards. The evaluation consists of a visual examination of the construction of the garment. A conflict of interest exists in this method because the same people responsible for achieving high production are also responsible for achieving high quality. If they must choose, they tend to favor high production over quality. Separate quality departments that complement a visual examination with test data and that are not responsible for meeting production quotas eliminate this conflict of interest. Nevertheless, quality does not belong to the quality department; everyone should share in the responsibility for quality.

Sewing machine operators are generally paid according to the number of pieces they complete rather than by the hour. Thus, they have more incentive to work rapidly than to work accurately. Operators should be informed by management about the quality standards to be achieved and the allowable tolerances for those standards, and be held accountable for work performed. To encourage them to work accurately, companies usually dock (do not pay) operators for completed garments that do not meet standards.

The aim of any manufacturer's inspection system is more than to detect defective gar-

Style #	1430			Sketch/Swatches

Season	Fall	Year	1990
Sizes	10-20	Label	H H

Description
Appliquēd jacket/skirt + bodice joined at waist. Red/Black combo (one color only)

Self Color: 3997 Black
(skirt + appliqué)

Trim 1 Color: 1111 F I Red
(jacket)

Trim 2 Color: 8 Red
(bodice)

Body Part	Vendor/Number	Content	Width	Price per yd.	Yd. per garment
Self	Charter Indio Solids 5403	50 poly/50 rayon	58/60	2.95	1 yd. 19"
Trim 1	Charter Indio Solids 5403	50 poly/50 rayon	58/60	2.95	1 yd. 28"
Trim 2	Thompson peach silk 426	100 poly	44/45	2.95	1 yd. 12"
Interfacing	2205			7.95	1 yd. 14"
Headers	net			4.35	24"

Notions	Vendor/Number	Length	Width
Thread	to match		
Belt keepers	RI 00352		
Belt	Cobra 2845w/ gold harness buckle		2
Skirt hem tape	to match	53	
Zipper	to match	14	
Jacket shoulder pad	(curved) C4731196 c wht		
Elastic		27 1/4	1/4
Embroidery	National Appliqué		
Labels	Machine Wash Warm Delicate Cycle Tumble Dry Low Cool Iron		

Figure 1-7 *Specifications sheet. (Courtesy of Hal Hardin Apparel.)*

ments and prevent their shipment. When defective garments are found, inspectors identify the source of problems in the production process. Records of inspection results can pinpoint and eliminate such problems. Inspection thus helps improve the quality of future production as it monitors the current production run.

Retailers may also have inspection programs. Retailers that inspect incoming merchandise are able to maintain a consistent image for quality by removing the defective merchandise before sending it to the sales floor. They ensure that garments are consistently sized to meet fit specifications. Retailers that monitor the quality of the goods they sell are able to identify vendors that send them low-quality merchandise and to eliminate sources that are unable to meet quality standards.

Most producers perform a **final inspection** at the end of the assembly process, in addition to or substituting for in-process inspection. This visual inspection resembles the type of thorough examination that quality-conscious consumers give garments at the point of sale. Inspectors designate garments that fully meet quality specifications as *firsts* to be sold at full price. They send garments with minor defects to be reworked. Or they designate them as *seconds* or *irregulars* to be sold, sometimes without a brand label, below full price in factory outlets or by

Marking and Cutting Instructions

Spread F/F ✓   Fu/1w   Fu/2w   Other

Patterned Fabrics: Spike _____   Pattern Repeat _____   Match _____

Description	Skirt	Jacket	Bodice	# pcs.
Self	8			8
Trim 1		8		8
Trim 2			9	9
Interfacing		3	3	6
Headers		2		2
Total Number of Pieces				33

Out of House Work?

Yes ✓   No _____

(jacket front for appliqué)

Specifications	Size 10	12	14	16	18	20
Cut waist elastic	26½	27½	29	30½	32	33½

Seam Allowance Specifications

Operation	Seam Allow	Edge Finish	Operation	Seam Allow	Edge Finish
Bodice center back	5/8	serge	Waistline join	3/4	elastic casing
Bodice sides	1/2	pink	Skirt bottom hem	2"	with tape
Bodice sleeves	1/2	pink	Jacket sides	3/8	serge
Bodice shoulders	1/2	pink	Jacket sleeves	3/8	serge
Bodice armholes	1/2	pink	Jacket armholes	3/8	serge
Bodice sleeve hems	1"	serge	Jacket sleeve hems	1"	serge
Skirt center back	1/2	into pleat	Jacket bottom hem	1½"	serge

Misc. Pattern or Construction notes:

Press interfacing to bodice front + back neck facing + to jacket front and back neck facing. Sew front skirt pocket with ½" seam + flat stitch; sew rest of pocket with side seams. ④ Laid-in pleats in sleeve crown -- center pleat makes box.

Figure 1-7 (continued).

retailers dealing in such merchandise. Garments that are unsalable are discarded as *scraps*.

Producers of complex garments tend to perform **in-process inspections,** inspections done during assembly. In-process inspection requires more time spent on inspection, but results in a higher proportion of first-quality garments. It builds quality into the product by catching defects early. Workers at each phase of production get immediate feedback about their work and rework their own mistakes, which makes them feel responsible for quality. The industry trend is toward in-process inspection.

Some quality departments perform **100% inspections;** they require inspectors to examine each garment. The inspector rejects defective garments and accepts the rest. A 100% inspection is thorough but costly in terms of labor, and fatigued inspectors, under pressure to inspect every garment, frequently fail to detect a defective garment and it gets shipped. Small companies tend to perform 100% inspection.

Some quality departments use **random sampling** or **statistical sampling** to inspect for quality. The inspector examines a representative sample of the garments produced rather than all of them. This eliminates the labor spent in inspecting every garment but still detects the majority of defectives. The company establishes an **acceptable quality level (AQL)** for each *lot* or group of garments. If the inspector finds fewer than the limit of defective garments in a random sample of garments taken from the lot, the entire lot is accepted. If the inspector finds more than the limit, the entire lot is rejected. Statistically, this method detects the majority of defects and is cost efficient because it requires less labor than 100% inspection. Users of this system believe that the small percentage of defective garments that slip through is acceptable considering the cost savings. Many large companies use statistical sampling inspection methods.

LABORATORY AND WEAR TESTING

Some manufacturers and a few large retailers perform physical testing to objectively determine the functional quality of apparel. Unlike aesthetic performance, functional performance can be measured with wear tests and laboratory tests. Testing monitors garments for conformance to established standards.

Wear testing, or wearing and caring for the garment under normal circumstances, helps determine how the interaction between the design, the materials, and the construction of the garment affects overall performance. Companies that wear test garments get the truest sense of how the garment performs in use.

Some manufacturers and few retailers perform extensive **laboratory testing** on the garments they produce to ensure quality. However, only very large manufacturers and retailers can justify the expense of operating their own quality laboratory; sometimes smaller companies hire independent quality laboratories to perform testing for them. Laboratory quality testing may be very simple or extremely complex. Equipment ranges from a home washing machine and dryer to sophisticated, computer integrated instrumentation. The *American Society for Testing and Materials (ASTM)* and the *American Association of Textile Chemists and Colorists (AATCC)* publish standards for textile testing to provide industry-wide consistency (see Chapter 4 and Appendix A).

Unfortunately, many manufacturers do not test the garments they produce and most retailers do not test the garments they sell. And, if they do perform tests, they do not usually inform consumers about the results. Consequently, consumers are deprived of data about the garment's performance that could help them make more enlightened purchase decisions; they remain reliant on the few clues obtained from visually inspecting the garment.

ANALYSIS OF RETURNS

It is a consumer's right and responsibility to communicate with the industry by returning unsatisfactory merchandise. However, consumers **return** only about 10 percent of defective garments to the retailer (Latture 1981), even though they report dissatisfaction with over 20 percent of their clothing purchases (Best and Andreasen 1976). Because most people do not return garments with which they are dissatisfied, a return by a single customer may represent the dissatisfaction of many others, so each return should be taken seriously. Consumers fail to return defective garments for a number of reasons:

1. If the price of a garment is low, consumers may have low expectations for the garment and thus do not return it when it fails. If consumers pay a lot for a garment, they expect more from it and are more apt to return it when it fails.

2. If the price of a garment is low, the consumer may not consider it worth the time and trouble to make the return. Consumers are more apt to return high-price than low-price garments because their time and trouble are better rewarded.

3. Because most people own many garments, when one garment fails, a consumer is not forced to return the failed garment for lack of anything else to wear.

4. Consumers often accept the blame for choosing a defective garment even though the defect may have been latent at the time of purchase. They feel that somehow they "should have known better." As a result, consumers fail to return garments with performance problems that are the manufacturer's responsibility, not the consumer's.

5. Retailers' return policies (and sometimes retail employees' reception of returns) discourage returns. For example, if the consumer loses the receipt for a garment that turns out to be defective, he or she is not permitted or does not feel entitled to return it.

Returns benefit both consumers and the apparel industry. Consumers gain the benefit of having a defective garment replaced or their money refunded. Businesses benefit from the opportunity to win back the consumer's good will, and they can gain a better understanding of consumer expectations through an analysis of returns.

An analysis of merchandise returned by consumers helps retailers trace which vendors' goods are most frequently returned. They can reward vendors with good quality records by buying from them again and can eliminate sources of consumer dissatisfaction. Retailers should always **return to vendor (RTV)** any defective goods they receive. If they discard them to avoid the trouble of returning them, they deny the manufacturer feedback from consumers about the in-use performance of their products.

If a manufacturer carefully analyzes returned goods, quality problems can be pinpointed and corrected in future production. Although the apparel industry is never thrilled to see goods returned by dissatisfied consumers, an analysis of returned goods is an excellent way to find out about garment failures that occurred after the sale, and thus to improve future products.

Summary

Quality is important to building a successful apparel business. Quality is defined as the degree to which a garment meets expectations. Consumers perceive quality differently, depending on the end use of the garment; and on cultural influences, demographics and psychographics, and individual standards. Quality apparel results when the intrinsic physical features of a garment—its design, materials, and construction—produce the aesthetic (attractiveness) and functional (utility and durability) performance desired by the consumer. Enumerating the buying benefits related to each of the garment's selling points helps consumers understand how the garment fulfills their wants and needs.

Quality evaluation is quantified by the perceived quality model, in which the consumer weights the importance of and rates each of the features of the garment being judged to find out the contribution of each characteristic to the overall quality evaluation. The sum of the contributions of all the features yields an overall quality score for a garment that is useful in comparing two different garments or types of garments evaluated by the same consumer, or in examining how different consumers evaluate the same garment.

Aesthetic features generally determine the consumer's evaluation of the garment's quality, or desirability, at the point of sale. But functional features become more important when the garment is put into use. The apparel industry maximizes consumer satisfaction by providing garments with quality aesthetic performance and minimizes consumer dissatisfaction by providing garments with quality functional performance. Ultimate consumer satisfaction, rather than merely satisfying consumers at the point of sale, is the goal of forward-looking companies.

Extrinsic aspects, such as price, brand, and retail store reputation also influence the consumer's perception of quality. Price lines include the exclusive lines: haute couture, couture/ bespoke, designer; and the mass merchandise price lines: better, moderate, and budget. Bridge lines occur between price lines. Price lines often cause consumers to associate price and quality. However, price is an inadequate predictor of apparel quality.

The perceived value of a garment expresses the relationship between its price and its perceived quality. Garments with equal price and perceived quality are fair values; overpriced garments have a higher price than perceived quality; and bargains have higher perceived quality than price. Economical values are calculated in terms of cost per wear, the price of the garment divided by the number of times it is worn.

A comprehensive industry approach builds quality into apparel products by establishing specifications, with reasonable tolerances, according to customers' expectations. Manufacturers inspect 100% of production or a random sample to check conformance to standards. In-process inspections detect defects early, but some manufacturers perform only final inspections. In addition to inspection, wear and laboratory tests ensure conformance to specifications. An analysis of returns provides feedback about customer dissatisfaction with the garment. Through such efforts, the apparel industry strives to provide apparel that not only attracts consumers but satisfies them.

New Terms

If you can define each of these terms and differentiate between related terms, you have gained a good working vocabulary for discussing the topics in this chapter. The terms are listed in the order in which they appear in the chapter.

ready-to-wear apparel (RTW)
apparel quality
manufacturer
retailer
consumer
customer
physical feature
design
materials
construction
performance feature
aesthetic performance
functional performance
selling point
buying benefit
end use
perceived quality model
price line
couture
haute couture
bespoke
designer clothing
prêt à porter/prêt
better
bridge
moderate
budget
price point
value
perceived value graph
cost per wear
International Fabricare Institute (IFI)
quality department
quality assurance (QA)
quality control (QC)
American Society for Quality Control (ASQC)
specifications/specs
tolerance
inspection/audit
final inspection
in-process inspection
100% inspection
random/statistical sampling
acceptable quality level (AQL)
wear testing
laboratory testing
return
return to vendor (RTV)

Review Questions

1. Define apparel quality.

2. How do the physical features of a garment and the performance of a garment differ?

3. List the three main physical dimensions and the two main performance dimensions of apparel.

4. Why are buying benefits more important to the customer than selling points?

5. Which performance dimension is more important at the point of sale? Which performance dimension becomes more important when the garment is in use?

6. Why do consumers differ in their individual perceptions of quality?

7. What is the difference between the intrinsic and extrinsic features of a garment?

8. List, in order from most expensive to least expensive, the various price lines defined in this chapter. Discuss the meaning of each.

9. How is a price line different from a price point?

10. Discuss the relationship of quality, price, and value.

11. Explain the concept of cost per wear.

12. What is the role of a modern quality department?

13. How are specifications useful in the pursuit of quality?

14. Compare and contrast 100% inspection and random sample inspection. What are the advantages and disadvantages of each method?

15. How are customer returns helpful to retailers and manufacturers?

Activities

1. Study the perceived quality model presented in this chapter. Do you think the model explains the way consumers actually make apparel purchase decisions? Why or why not?

2. Buy two similar garments for comparison (e.g., two T-shirts or two pairs of jeans).

a. Evaluate the garments at the point of sale, using the perceived quality model.

b. Wear and care for the garments over the course of the current term.

c. Evaluate the garment in use, using the perceived quality model.

d. What differences did you find in your point-of-sale and in-use evaluations? Explain.

3. Establish performance criteria for different types of garments. For example, what are the typical attractiveness, utility, and durability expectations for the following classifications of merchandise:

a. wedding gowns
b. baseball uniforms
c. tailored suits
d. infant sleepers
e. swimsuits

4. Establish performance criteria for different target markets for the same type of garment. For example, what are the typical attractiveness, utility, and durability expectations of customers who buy the following classifications of merchandise:

a. jogging shorts
b. men's casual shorts
c. women's casual shorts
d. toddlers' shorts
e. biking shorts

5. Using a catalog, list the selling points and buying benefits the retailer uses to promote three different products. Could the use of selling points and buying benefits be more effective? If so, how?

6. Visit a major department store. Identify the locations of their budget, moderate, and better goods. What terms does the store use to differentiate between these departments?

7. Survey five friends. Which do they use more in evaluating apparel quality, price or their own knowledge about quality? How much does the price of a garment tell them about the quality of the apparel they buy? Based on your findings, to what extent does price influence consumers' perception of apparel quality?

8. For two similar garments in your wardrobe, estimate the cost per wear of each. Determine which is the better value from a cost-per-wear standpoint. Compare your results with those of your classmates.

9. Visit the quality department of a manufacturer or major retailer.

a. What details do their specifications cover?
b. How do they set specifications?
c. Do their specifications include tolerances?
d. What inspection methods do they use?
e. What testing methods do they employ?
f. How do they analyze returned merchandise?

2

Overview of the Industry: The Big Picture

CHAPTER OBJECTIVES

1. Outline the organization and structure of the apparel industry.

2. Describe the steps in mass producing ready-to-wear.

3. Discuss the costing process, and the relationship of cost and price.

4. Explore current trends affecting the industry.

To gain insight into the evaluation of ready-to-wear quality, you need to understand the past, present, and continuing evolution of the apparel industry. The industry has grown during the past century into a complex manufacturing and distribution system to meet the demands of today's market. Trends that impact its further development center around the expansion of world markets and the advancement of computer applications and rapid communications networks.

History of the Apparel Industry

The apparel industry is a fairly new one, with most of its growth in the nineteenth and twentieth centuries. Clothing in the United States was hand produced before 1850. Virtually all of it was custom made for a specific individual. Sailors, soldiers, miners, and slaves wore low-quality ready-to-wear, but it was not considered proper attire for others. Ready-to-wear was known as *slops*, and was worn only by the lower class.

Two main factors in the late 1800s contributed to the eventual acceptance of ready-to-wear by the general public (Kidwell 1975). First, there was a demand for it. The middle class increased, as a result of the same industrialization that made the sewing machine and mass production possible. These people wanted clothing to show their middle class status, but not at the cost of custom made. Second, custom tailors responded to supply the demand by producing off-the-rack garments in their spare time. The Civil War created the need for military uniforms, which further spurred the development of ready-to-wear. Soldiers were measured and the results compiled to develop a sizing system so that uniforms could be mass-produced rather than custom made. Traditional tailoring methods were simplified to produce reasonably priced ready-to-wear uniforms. The establishment of size standards and relatively simple production methods paved the way for the mass-manufacturing of clothing for the general public.

The technology, labor supply and distribution systems of the late nineteenth and early twentieth centuries were ripe for the growth of the mass-produced, ready-to-wear apparel industry in the United States. The Industrial Revolution was a major factor, with the advent of the sewing machine around 1850. Improved machines for cutting and pressing were developed at about the same time. Parallel advances in textile technology and the growth of a domestic textile industry made fabrics available in great variety and at reasonable prices. An influx of immigrants with sewing skills provided the labor force that made the mass production of apparel feasible. And as important as any other factor, the rapid expansion of department stores, specialty stores, and mail-order houses made possible the mass distribution of ready-to-wear apparel.

By 1860, the men's ready-to-wear industry produced everything from work clothes to formalwear. The women's ready-to-wear industry made slower inroads in the market, at first concentrating mainly on undergarments and cloaks. Women's dresses and other fashion garments of the era were complicated to construct and fit, and underwent frequent style changes

that made them unprofitable to mass-produce. However, when the simple skirt and shirtwaist became popular for women in the 1890s, ready-to-wear gained a firm foothold in the women's market. The trend toward simpler dressing continued into the twentieth century. By 1910, all items of women's clothing could be purchased ready-made.

Today's Apparel Industry

U.S. consumers purchase over $100 billion of apparel annually. The modern apparel industry is a global structure of firms, all intent on providing ready-to-wear to these and other consumers around the world. Textiles and apparel are often referred to as a single industry, but in fact are two separate though closely related industries: (1) the textile industry, composed of fiber, yarn, fabric, and some findings producers; converters that dye, print, and finish cloth; and wholesale representatives who sell fabrics and findings to apparel producers; and (2) the apparel industry, made up of apparel manufacturers and contractors; apparel wholesale representatives who sell garments to retailers; and apparel retailers, including department and specialty stores, chain stores, mass merchandisers, discount stores, mail-order retailers, and direct sellers. Retailers sell the finished goods to the consumer (Figure 2-1). Together, the textile and apparel manufacturing complex is annually about a $50 billion industry in the United States. The complex includes about 5,000 textile mills and about 20,000 apparel plants.

Apparel is produced by a manufacturer, a contractor, or a combination of both. Technically, the manufacturer is the firm completely responsible for the design, production, and sale of finished garments to the retailer. The company *profits* from the difference between the cost of producing and distributing the garment and the price at which it is sold to the retailer.

When manufacturers operate their own factories, they are called **inside shops.** Manufacturers with in-house production have several advantages over those that depend on contractors, including

1. Fewer communication problems.
2. Tighter control of quality.

Textile Production	Fabric and Findings Manufacturers/Converters
Fabrics and Findings Wholesale	Sales Representatives
Apparel Production	Apparel Manufacturers/Contractors
Apparel Wholesale	Sales Representatives
Retail	Retail Stores/Mail-Order Companies/Direct Sellers
Consumer	Customers

Figure 2-1 *Textile and apparel industry flow chart.*

3. No need to physically move garments back and forth to contractors, saving time and money.

4. More control over timing, making it easier to meet delivery dates.

Manufacturers may hire out part or all of the work to independent **contractors,** sometimes called **jobbers.** A contractor that does all the work to produce a manufacturer's design is called a *cut, make, and trim (CMT)* contractor. *Subcontractors* perform highly specialized functions (e.g., permanent pleating) for other contractors. Contractors and subcontractors make money from their labor input.

Manufacturers that use contractors, or **outside shops,** have more flexibility, including

1. No investment in plants and equipment, which enables them to present their designs to the public with little initial investment.

2. No need to train employees or deal with personnel problems and demands.

3. No need to build factories during peak times or if business grows; merely to hire additional contractors.

4. No need to maintain idle plants and workers between seasons or if business slows; simply to hire fewer contractors.

Subcontractors perform specialty work more quickly and economically than inside shops because they can afford the specialized equipment to do jobs such as pleating, quilting, and embroidery. They spread the cost of the equipment over many jobs, whereas an individual manufacturer cannot justify buying equipment that is only used a few times.

Large companies and inside shops dominate the men's apparel industry. The fairly basic nature of menswear allows these manufacturers to steadily produce relatively unchanged products over a long period of time. On the other hand, the women's apparel industry, characterized by frequent style changes, consists of many small and often new companies that are constantly adjusting to the latest fashion trends. The flexibility contractors offer is critical to these manufacturers.

Wholesale representatives or **sales reps** are agents of the manufacturer; they sell the finished garments to retailers. Manufacturers hire their own sales reps or contract independent agents. Wholesale representatives sell to retail buyers in showrooms at market centers and visit buyers to show them new lines. Wholesalers make money from the commission they earn on the goods they sell to retailers. Retailers profit from the difference between the cost of buying the garment from the manufacturer and the price at which it is sold to the final consumer.

The Mass-Production Process

Most apparel is mass-manufactured in a series of steps which vary slightly from firm to firm. Each part of the process impacts the quality of the finished garment. The usual production sequence is as follows: (1) design, (2) quick costing, (3) sample pattern, (4) sample garment, (5) production costing, (6) production pattern, (7) grading, (8) marker making, (9) cutting, (10) assembly, and (11) finishing.

The industry recognizes its need for improved use of technology if it is to remain internationally competitive. Computers and computer-linked technologies are revolutionizing the way the apparel industry operates. The ideal of many companies is **computer integrated manufacturing (CIM),** in which all computerized facets of the business are electronically linked for efficient management. The computer improves the speed and accuracy of many production processes, such as design, pattern making, grading, marking, cutting, sewing and pressing. And it enhances management's ability to analyze situations, make cost-effective decisions and communicate with others.

Every September in Atlanta, Georgia, apparel manufacturers gather for the *Bobbin Show* and **American Apparel Manufacturers Association (AAMA)** convention, showcasing new equipment and facilitating the exchange of ideas.* The **Textile/Clothing Technology Corporation,** better known as **(TC)2** (tee see squared), pursues technological advances year round.** They research the practicality, productivity, and profitability of new equipment and manufacturing systems. (TC)2 represents a coalition of industry, education, government, and labor. (TC)2 concentrates on research and development into cutting edge manufacturing techniques and training to advance apparel manufacturing technology and enhance the competitiveness of the U.S. industry.

* For more information, contact the American Apparel Manufacturers Association at 2500 Wilson Boulevard, Suite 301, Arlington, VA 22201.

** For more information, contact (TC)2, 706 Hillsborough Street, Raleigh, NC 27603.

DESIGN

In general, **designers** originate ideas for the creation of new styles by *draping* fabric on a form, by *sketching* new styles, or by suggesting changes in existing styles. The designer may *knock off* or copy, with or without modification, successful designs shown by other firms. A series of related designs make up a comprehensive package called a **line,** or a **collection,** which suggests higher prices. *Fashion-forward* lines, such as junior sportswear lines, consist of the newest design concepts. *Classic* lines, such as men's suits, merely update standard designs. Firms producing *staple* or *basic* lines, such as underwear, may show little or no change from one season to the next. Small firms or those producing classic or basic garments may not have a designer; minor changes in design and fabrication are made in proven *bodies* or styles from season to season and are decided by the production manager, who oversees production. Some large firms have replaced designers with **merchandisers,** who formulate and build the line to satisfy the company's target market. A few large retailers also hire merchandisers to develop merchandise suited to the target customer.

Manufacturers use **computer-aided design/ computer-aided manufacturing (CAD/CAM)** systems to aid the design process (see Related Resources: CAD/CAM). CAD maximizes designer creativity and speeds design and marketing in numerous ways. Relatively few manufacturers use CAD systems for design because of the high cost of the equipment; many small companies cannot afford it. However, as the technology continues to become more affordable, and as more designers are trained to use it, CAD for apparel design is certain to become commonplace. CAD systems offer tremendous possibilities, although few companies that own CAD systems take advantage of all its technological potential. For example, CAD can

1. Eliminate time-consuming sketching by allowing the designer to draw an original design on-screen and make changes in it without redrawing it each time.

2. Allow the designer to recombine or change elements of garments in memory, from past seasons, to create new designs.

3. Scan actual garments or pictures of garments into memory, where the designer modifies

Figure 2-2 CAD system. (Courtesy of Microdynamics, Inc.)

them as desired (Figure 2-2). Companies use this feature to adapt to their own use historical garments, competitors' styles, or samples bought in another country.

4. Scan existing fabric swatches into memory, enabling the designer to duplicate print motifs that formerly took hours to draw by hand.

5. Apply colors and prints to garment designs on-screen. The computer mixes literally millions of colors as directed by the designer and instantly applies them to the design. Colors can be lightened, darkened, or changed in hue at the touch of a button, eliminating time-consuming hand coloring of sketches.

6. Provide predrawn garments from memory for the designer to alter.

7. Allow the designer to experiment endlessly with the size, shape, orientation, and color of designs at a touch, and to store favorites for later access.

8. Communicate designs to contractors via *electronic graphic interchange (EGI)* and *electronic data interchange (EDI)*. Fax (short for *facsimile*) communicates data from computer to computer over the phone line. The graphic output arrives, along with the written specifications, at the contractor's production facilities across town or around the world in a matter of seconds.

9. Show lines to retail buyers on-screen. Only a few manufacturers and retailers have compatible CAD systems at this time, but soon buyers may be able to preview manufacturers' lines from around the world without leaving their offices. The main disadvantage of viewing a line on the computer is that the garment may look different when made up in fabric than it does as a concept on the computer screen. For example, the color may not be accurate.

10. Show potential designs to merchandisers for approval via fax or in person. CAD allows easy editing of the design, enabling the designer to refine and tailor it to meet the merchandiser's requirements.

11. Provide camera-ready copy of designs for advertisements and catalogs before the actual garments are produced. This feature is helpful to mail-order retailers, who must plan their catalogs many months in advance.

12. Require sample garments to be produced only of the designs chosen for production. Traditionally, manufacturers make samples of many garments each season, some of which are not chosen for the line and others of which are not chosen for production. Samples ordinarily cost between $10 and $300 each to make, depending on the garment, due to fabric and labor costs, and some samples are made several times before the design is approved. Because buyers can approve designs and see lines on-screen, samples are not needed until the design is tested in fabric for production. The need for fewer samples reduces costs. Also, eliminating early sample making allows the line to be designed much closer to the selling season—eight to ten weeks closer—so the designer can make more accurate decisions about what will sell well.

SAMPLE PATTERNS

Sample-pattern makers convert designs into **sample patterns** that, when the pieces are sewn together, create sample garments. The pattern maker develops a pattern piece for each part of a garment, making the necessary changes in the company's basic pattern, the **sloper** or **basic block** (Figure 8-1). A company derives its basic block through a process called *drafting,* in which a pattern is drawn using the body measurements of the typical target customer. A computerized **pattern design system (PDS)** speeds pattern making and can improve its accuracy. The block is entered into the computer using a *digitizer;* the pattern maker then directs the computer to make the changes in the pattern on-screen (Figure 2-3). Pattern design systems are an example of CAD/CAM.

SAMPLE GARMENTS

A *sample hand* or *sample maker* constructs each garment according to the sample pattern from a sample cut of fabric to produce a **sample** of the garment. If the designer is not satisfied with the sample, it is reworked or remade; for example, a different sleeve style might improve the garment. The production manager and the design or merchandising staff then review the salability and profitability of each sample, suggest minor changes, and choose the best designs to include in the line. Finally, **duplicates** of each sample chosen for the line are produced to show to retail buyers.

Retail buyers view the line and place orders for the styles or **numbers** that they think will sell best in their stores. After manufacturers determine the styles ordered in sufficient quantity to justify production, they order the fabric and findings necessary to make those styles; the remaining styles are dropped from the line.

PRODUCTION PATTERNS

The styles chosen for production go to the *production pattern maker* or *pattern engineer,* who analyzes how the garments are made. The pattern maker develops the **production patterns** or **hard patterns,** for optimum fabric utilization and ease of assembly, and determines how each garment can be most economically mass-manufactured while retaining the look of the original design. Any unnecessary curves, fullness, seams, or details are eliminated from the sample pattern to produce an efficient production pattern. A knowledgeable and skillful production pattern maker reduces wastefulness and streamlines designs without destroying their essence. As when making the sample pattern, a computerized pattern design system speeds the process of making a production pattern and can improve accuracy.

GRADING

Grading the pattern involves increasing and decreasing its dimensions to reflect the various

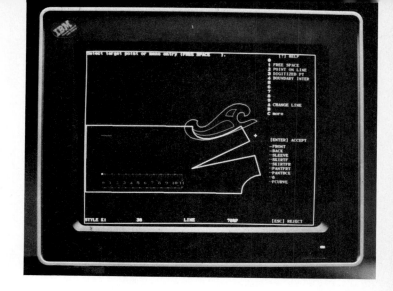

Figure 2-3 *"Microdesign" brand pattern design system, an example of CAD/CAM. (Courtesy of Microdynamics, Inc.)*

sizes to be produced. Grade rules may reflect even amounts of change between sizes, or different amounts. For example, a standard grade for misses sizes is a 1″ difference (at bust, waist, and hips) between sizes 6, 8, and 10; a 1½″ difference between sizes 10, 12, 14, and 16; and a 2″ difference between sizes 16, 18, 20, and 22. The graded *nest* consists of all the sizes of graded patterns, superimposed on one another. Computer grading using a CAM system quickly and accurately grades the pattern to all the desired sizes automatically, eliminating the painstaking task of manual grading. For example, Figure 2-4 illustrates the computer graded pattern pieces for a leotard with numerous insets of different colors. This points out convincingly how valuable CAD/CAM is. Manually distributing the grade throughout all these pieces would be extremely time consuming. CAD/CAM does it automatically with the touch of a button. The computer changes the original pattern according to grade rules entered by the pattern grader for how much and where each incremental increase and decrease in size and shape is to be made. Thus, the accuracy of the original or base pattern (usually made in a size from the middle of the size range) affects the accuracy of all the other sizes. Many companies have CAD/CAM systems for computerized pattern grading or contract out their pattern grading to firms that do. However, some firms still manually grade their patterns, which requires a skilled pattern grader for good results.

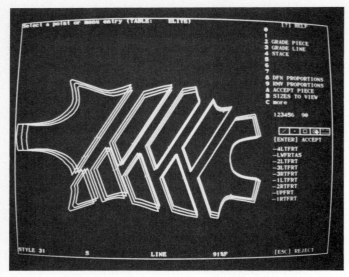

Figure 2-4 Computerized pattern grading system, an example of CAD/CAM. (Courtesy of Microdynamics, Inc.)

MARKER MAKING

The **marker** indicates how all the pattern pieces of the garment are arranged on the fabric to achieve the most efficient layout. Sometimes even in ideal circumstances, 10 to 15 percent of the fabric is *fallout,* or wasted areas between the pattern pieces. Saving an inch of fabric here or an inch there over thousands of yards ultimately has a pronounced effect on company profits, so marker planning receives close attention. The goal is a *tight marker,* which uses the fabric efficiently with minimal waste. Large pieces are generally placed first, and small pieces are fitted in where possible. The marker maker continues to move the pieces around until a tight marker is achieved. To achieve better **material utilization (MU),** the marker maker may allow some pattern piece edges to overlap. If the overlapping is slight, it does not affect the final dimensions of the garment. However, it may affect seam strength, so manufacturers of higher quality garments avoid overlapping pattern pieces. Another tactic for increasing material utilization involves tilting pattern pieces slightly rather than placing them perfectly straight on the fabric. Again, manufacturers of better garments avoid this practice because it causes the finished garment to hang crooked (see Chapter 4 and Chapter 12).

Making a marker manually involves the unwieldy task of shifting the pattern pieces around until they are squeezed together as closely as possible. Then the marker maker traces the pattern pieces onto the paper marker, which is the same width as the fabric, to provide guidelines for the cutter.

Many marker makers use CAD/CAM systems, which allow them to move small-scale pattern pieces around on the computer screen until the most efficient layout is achieved (Figure 2-5). Some of the features of computerized marker making are that it

1. Allows marker makers to see the entire marker at the same time, allowing them to visualize a greater variety of possible arrangements of the pattern pieces.

2. Keeps track of the percent of material utilization at all times so the marker maker can readily assess various arrangements of the pieces.

3. Positions pieces as closely together as possible where the marker maker indicates placement.

4. Automatically overlaps pieces a programmable amount if overlapping improves material utilization.

5. Automatically tilts pieces a programmable amount if tilting improves material utilization.

6. Arranges pieces so that patterns such as stripes and plaids match in the finished garment (see Chapter 10). This is important, because if matching is neglected at this stage, the patterns cannot be matched later in the assembly process.

7. Color codes pattern pieces on the screen according to size so the marker maker readily identifies smaller and larger pieces that otherwise appear identical.

8. Automatically superimposes the straight edges of side-by-side pieces; the shared cutting line saves fabric and speeds cutting.

9. Enlarges hard-to-see areas of the marker.

10. Plans ideal points for splicing the ends of fabric pieces.

11. Identifies locations where fabric defects can be placed without affecting the garment.

12. Stores markers for later use in nonbulky form compared to traditional paper markers.

13. Makes duplicate markers quickly and at low cost. This is important for producers of basic garments, who use the same marker over and over.

14. Transmits markers via phone lines to remote factory locations.

The computer generally helps the marker maker achieve 1 to 4 percent higher fabric efficiency in companies producing fashion goods, where under ordinary circumstances 20 percent fallout is not uncommon. Most companies producing basic goods have developed efficient markers over the years (often over 95 percent material utilization), so they realize a lower percentage of improvement when they use computerized marker making. However, even small improvements in material utilization add up fast!

The computer *plotter* generates the full-scale paper marker at the touch of a button. Or the computer stores the marker in its memory and uses it to guide automatic computerized cutting, eliminating the need for a person to guide the cutting.

The use of CAD/CAM systems for marker making is growing rapidly because of their accuracy, speed, and ultimate cost savings for apparel producers; computerized marker making systems can pay for themselves in improved material utilization alone. Many companies that do not have computerized marker making contract out their markers to companies that do; others continue to rely on manual methods.

CUTTING

Cutting affects the quality of the finished garment before assembly ever begins. Cutters are relatively well paid among apparel factory workers because of the skill and accuracy their job demands. If they cut a garment inaccurately, it cannot be sewn accurately; poor cutting plagues the entire assembly process. Cutting is the only production step that is performed on many garments simultaneously; in all other cases each garment is handled separately. Thus, any cutting error affects not one but many garments.

The cutter layers the fabric back and forth on a long table, with the assistance of a device called a *spreader,* in preparation for cutting. To save time and reduce costs, most firms cut many *plies,* or layers, of fabric at one time. Most *lay-ups,* or stacks, are only a few inches high. However, some are as high as 14 inches and contain nearly 500 plies. Such lay-ups generally lead to inaccurate cutting on traditional cutting tables. However, state-of-the-art cutting rooms contain *vacuum tables,* which use suction to compress

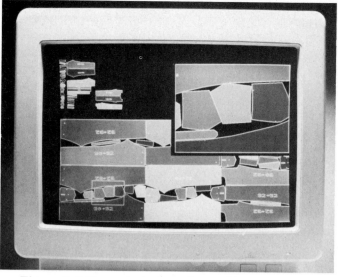

Figure 2-5 *Computerized marker making system, an example of CAD/CAM. (Courtesy of Microdynamics, Inc.)*

and stabilize multiple plies of fabric, holding them in place. Vacuum tables allow the economical and accurate cutting of tall lay-ups, even on difficult-to-handle, slippery, and bulky fabrics.

Cutters in most factories use a *straight knife* with a straight, vertically vibrating blade. *Round knives* have a rotating, circular blade instead. These electric knives automatically stop to sharpen themselves during cutting to remain razor-sharp. A human or a computer guides the cutting process around the outline of each pattern piece on the marker. Alternatively, a *band knife* is mounted in the cutting table and the cutter moves the fabric past it.

A human cutter follows the lines of the marker, but a computerized cutter guides the cut according to the marker stored in its memory. Faster than humans, computers cut accurately at speeds up to 800 inches per minute, and the computer plans the route the knife is to take for maximum efficiency. Although computerized cutting has replaced the human cutter in many large factories, its high initial cost prohibits other companies from installing it.

A few factories have the capability to cut with computer-guided laser beams or high-pressure water jets. However, lasers can cut only one ply or a few plies at a time, and water jets can cut lay-ups no higher than about an inch. Companies specializing in small production runs may find them useful, but these technologies are not practical for large runs.

Small, complex pattern pieces are sometimes

cut out using a **die,** similar to a cooky cutter. For example, a cutter for a glove factory would have difficulty using a knife to cut accurately around the finger shapes of a glove piece. Instead, a heavy weight presses the sharp edges of the die, in the shape of the glove pattern piece, into the layers of fabric, cutting consistently every time. Dies cut out collars, cuffs, belt loops, and other small pieces for basic garments, such as men's shirts and slacks. For fashion-oriented companies with new styles each season, however, the cost and lead time involved in casting new dies for each new style make die cutting impractical.

After cutting, the cut pieces are marked, if necessary. Marks on the fabric enable **operators** (people who sew the garment together) to align seams and other pieces properly and construct the garment accurately. For example, marks indicate pocket placement and dart tip locations. Notches at edges, hot or cold drill holes, needles carrying marking fluid or wax, or occasionally, thread marks *(tailor's tacks)* are used to mark the cut pieces for sewing. Marks should be accurate, visible until the operation requiring them is complete, and not visible in the finished garment.

ASSEMBLY

Most factories produce garments on an **assembly line.** The cut pieces are tied together into **bundles.** Identification tickets attached to the bundles tell the style number, the operation to be performed on the bundle, and the pay rate for performing it. Each operator completes the same task on a bundle of garments before passing it on to the next operator. As operators complete a bundle, they save the bundle ticket, which helps calculate the **piecework** pay of each worker, based on how many bundles he or she completes.

Each garment passes through many different hands as it is assembled one step at a time. For example, a man's tailored jacket, generally considered the most complex garment to construct, requires at least 115 separate operations. On the other hand, a simple T-shirt requires as few as 8 operations (Union Special 1983).

Some progressive manufacturers use modular manufacturing or unit production systems which replace the traditional assembly line and its bundles (see Related Resources: Sewing Room Technology). **Unit production systems (UPS)** send garments to each operator's station

via computer-controlled, overhead transporters. Computers help track the progress of individual garments through the factory and direct them to operators who need work. Unit production systems improve the flow of garments through the factory and eliminate the time spent in handling bundles. Operators *cross-train* for several jobs so they can work where they are needed most. The unit production system optimizes operator productivity and reduces the time a garment spends in the sewing room from several weeks to less than a day! For example, in the traditional bundle system, if the collar setters finish more garments than the sleeve setters, bundles of collared garments wait for sleeves. If the sleeve setters finish garments faster than the collar setters, the sleeve setters sit idle at their machines waiting for collared garments to work on. The unit production system sends each garment directly from a collar setter to a sleeve setter who needs work; if the sleeve setters get behind, a worker who was setting collars starts setting sleeves.

Modular manufacturing groups operators into teams, or modules. The team produces one garment at a time. The operators stand at their work stations and rotate to different machines as they work, becoming familiar with all the steps in producing the garment. And they inspect their team's own work, catching and correcting mistakes as soon as they happen. Early experiments with modular manufacturing show that, besides inspiring teamwork, it also enhances quality and increases production. To make a garment using modular manufacturing or the unit production system takes as little time as shown in these examples:

T-shirt	3 minutes
Pull-on pant	6 minutes
Zip-front pant	17 minutes
Unconstructed jacket	25 minutes
Lined blazer	40 minutes
Tailored coat	120 minutes

(Glock and Kunz 1990; King 1988).

A wide variety of technologically advanced sewing machines, some computerized, help operators speedily and accurately execute the various steps in assembling a garment. Some sewing machines automatically or semiautomatically complete complex construction processes such as shirt collars and tailored jacket pockets. Sewing machine technology continues to de-skill many apparel manufacturing processes. But even automated sewing machines still require human operators, causing the apparel industry to remain very labor intensive. And although some operators use automated and semiautomated equipment, many use manual sewing machines that require considerable skill to operate.

To reduce the apparel industry's heavy reliance on human labor, *robotics*—the use of robots—is growing in importance. More than other industries, apparel production has defied full automation because of the soft, flexible nature of fabric, which prevents the production of uniform-quality goods by robots. But researchers are seeking and finding ways to overcome the problems inherent in handling cloth. Already, robots handle small parts and perform complex and repetitive sewing operations in a few factories. Vision systems and tactile sensing systems help robots locate fabric pieces and detect their orientation, enabling the robot to align and sew the pieces together correctly. For example, a newly developed robot sews a sleeve seam and vent in 17 seconds versus 2 minutes for the manual process (Brockett 1989). Although perfecting robotics for the apparel industry will require a huge investment in technology, you can expect to see an increase in the use of robots for garment production.

PRESSING AND FINISHING

After assembly, some garments (e.g., underwear and swimwear) require no pressing, but most require minimal pressing (e.g., T-shirts, slips, and nightgowns) or extensive pressing (e.g., tailored pants and jackets). Garments are commonly pressed using a combination of heat, steam, and pressure. Pressers usually use an industrial steam iron similar to a home iron or a heavy *buck press* like the ones you see at the dry cleaners. There is also specialty pressing equipment shaped like the parts of the garment; for example, the shoulder area of the jacket or the leg of a pair of pants. Some pressing equipment sponges the fabric with water or blows puffs of steam to improve pressing. Vacuum-suction pressing tables extract steam from pressed fabrics to minimize garment distortion after pressing. A limited amount of pressing is computer guided for consistent results. Manufacturers may pass some types of garments through a steam tunnel to remove wrinkles.

Well-pressed garments make a good impression on consumers and command a higher price than unpressed or poorly pressed garments. A beautiful press job sometimes disguises poor construction to an extent. On the other hand, poor pressing makes even a well-constructed garment look like a low-quality piece. Evidence of poor pressing includes the impressions of seams and other details pressed through so that they are visible on the outside of the garment. Scorching, melting, water marks, and shine also indicate poor pressing technique. *Shine* is a change in the fabric's surface appearance resulting from too much pressing. If a finished garment is thoroughly pressed or **off-pressed** it not only smooths the garment and enhances its construction; it also helps the garment fit smoothly. High-quality garments are also **underpressed,** or pressed during construction, in addition to the final pressing. Because pressing requires extra labor, it is sometimes neglected to reduce costs. But the importance of pressing is evidenced by the extensive use of hand-held steamers by retailers to steam out shipping wrinkles in garments.

Quality inspectors check for defects, remove spots of dirt or oil that got on the fabric during production, and clip loose and dangling threads. Hang tags are attached. Then the garment is hung and bagged or folded and packaged. Although packaging does not affect the function of the garment, it affects appearance at the point of sale and, consequently, the consumer's perception of the quality of the garment. For example, if two garments are otherwise equal, but one is hung on an expensive wooden hanger and the other is hung on an inexpensive plastic hanger, the one on the wooden hanger will more likely be judged as high quality. For this reason, department and specialty stores regularly remove garments from shipping hangers and place them on special store hangers to make the garment look worthy of a higher selling price. After packaging, shipping clerks *pick* or fill orders by selecting the requested styles, sizes, and colors from inventory; finally, the finished goods are boxed and shipped to the retailer.

Costing

Costing is the process of estimating the total cost of producing a garment, including the cost of materials and labor as well as the general expenses of operating the business. Early in the design process, manufacturers determine a **pre-cost** or **quick cost** for each garment based on a rough sketch and list of required materials. They base this preliminary estimate, or "best guess" of what it will cost to produce the garment, on their judgment and past experience. The quick cost is usually accurate within 10 to 15 percent of the actual cost of production and gives the manufacturer some idea of whether the style can be produced and sold at a profit. The quick cost helps the manufacturer decide whether to reject the style, accept it as part of the line, or send it back to the designer or merchandising staff for changes to reduce its cost.

PRODUCTION COSTING

After it is accepted as part of the line, a garment must be accurately costed. This detailed cost estimating is known as **production costing.** Manufacturers base production costing on a sample or detailed sketch of the garment, accompanied by written specifications.

Production costing used to be a simple, straightforward process. Manufacturers calculated costs with great accuracy because they produced similar styles from year to year. Fashion, competition and production methods changed relatively slowly. Today, frequent style changes, stiff international competition and rapidly advancing technology make costing much more complex and accuracy more crucial than ever. Some large companies calculate each element of cost to the nearest $.0001 *per each* (per garment) to ensure accurate prediction of total costs. Other manufacturers merely calculate their costs to the nearest $.01 *per dozen*.

Most manufacturers cost garments manually; some use computers to assist them. To perform computerized costing, first the manufacturer stores the time and costs required to execute various sewing operations into the computer's memory. When they cost a garment, they enter the operations required to construct it, and the cost and amount of materials it requires. The computer then calculates the estimated cost of producing the garment.

A *costing sheet* is used for production costing (Figure 2-6), which is more detailed than quick costing. The costing sheet contains a sketch of the garment and a style number to identify it. The sheet also may record the size range, colors, selling season, and other pertinent information.

The cost sheet includes the four main elements included in costing a garment: (1) fabric, (2) findings, (3) labor, and (4) overhead (see Related Resources: Costing).

Fabric Costs. Fabric is generally the most significant factor in costing a garment. Fabric accounts for 40 to 50 percent of the total cost of most garments. In many cases, evaluating the quality and the amount of fabric used in a garment indicates better than any other factor the overall cost of producing it. The generous use of fabric; heavy or dense fabric (such as wool coatings); fabric with rare fibers, complex fabrication, or expensive finishes; fabric with patterns that require matching; and fabric currently in high demand and low supply can all add significantly to the cost of a garment.

To determine fabric costs, the manufacturer estimates the amount of fabric required to produce a style, including a waste factor. The total cost of the fabric equals the number of yards needed multiplied by the price per yard, plus delivery charges and inspection costs.

Findings Costs. **Findings, notions,** or **sundries** include all materials other than fabric required to produce a garment. For example, most cost sheets incorporate as findings such items as thread, trimmings (ribbon and lace), closures (buttons and zippers), miscellaneous materials (elastic and shoulder pads), wet processing chemicals (bleaches and softeners), and packaging materials (hangers and plastic bags).

The cost of findings significantly affects the cost of a garment and requires accurate estimation. For example, the yards of thread used for sewing may cost only a few cents per garment. However, a manufacturer that produces thousands of garments must account for thread costs to accurately predict total costs.

Labor Costs. *Labor costs* include the cutting, sewing, pressing, and finishing operations required to produce a garment. They may also cover the cost of designing, sample making, pattern making, grading, and marker making. Labor accounts for a large portion, sometimes as much as half, of the total cost of garments produced in developed countries such as the United States. In low-wage countries, labor requirements have less impact on the total cost of the garment.

Each individual operation in the production of a garment contributes to its labor costs. To

ESTIMATE SHEET

SEQ. NO.	ITEM CODE		Description	Qty / Unit	@	Amount
			60" Body	22.50 Yd. @	2.38	63.68
				Yd. @		
			60" Trim	2.25 Yd. @	2.90	6.53
				Yd. @		
			60" Lining	1.25 Yd. @	1.615	2.02
						72.23
	BI 000	BIAS	MAT. REQ. 7/8" UE (Trim) 21	Yd. @	48.12	1.01
		BIAS	MAT. REQ.	Yd. @	MY	
		BIAS	MAT. REQ.	Yd. @		
		DECT		Yd. @		
		ELAS		Yd. @		
	BN 7	BTN	24/1/4 ball Navy 24	Ea. @	1.16	.19
		BTN		Ea. @	gr.	
		FSTN		Ea. @		
		FSTN		Ea. @		
		CUFF		Ea. @		
		TAPE		Yd. @		
		TAPE		Yd. @		
		VEL		Yd. @		
		VEL		Yd. @		
	TH6XX	THD	70/3 Spun Poly 2000	Yd. @		.86
	TR0XX	THD	40/3 80	Yd. @		.05
		THD		Yd. @		
	ZP999	ZIP	24" CB Coil 12	Ea. @	.24 ea	2.88
	L5599	LABEL	Size Label #55 12	Ea. @		.15
		LABEL		Ea. @		
		EMB		Ea. @		
		MISC.				
		MISC.				
	PF016	PKG	Poly bag 12	Ea. @		.18
	CN004	CTN	#4 .33	QTY.		.16
		OC				
			SUB. TOTAL			5.48

DATE 8 | 17 | 90   **STYLE** Dress

INQ. NO. 12560   **PROD. NO.** | **GG** | **SUB** | **INV**

FOR   **SAMPLE** 1501

QTY. 150 **DOZ.** 0 **EA**   **SIZES** 4-22

SIZE DEPENDENT   DESCRIPTION

Make like sample made for the customer.

To be assembled using type 512 serge stitch seam.

To have 2" blindstitch bottom hem.

To have front and back princess line gore seams.

To have L/R inserted pocket bags cut from body material.

TOTAL MATERIAL COST 77.71

FACTORY

SEW LABOR 20.55

CUTTING LABOR	2.25
TOTAL LABOR	22.80
VARIABLE OVERHEAD %	31.92
TOTAL MFG. COST	132.43
OVERHEAD	20.00
TOTAL COST PER DOZ.	152.43

Figure 2-6 *Costing sheet. (Courtesy of Angelica Uniforms.)*

aid in costing, time and motion engineers measure and record the time required to perform each operation. Automation reduces labor costs compared to manual production (although increased equipment costs may offset the reduction). Large production runs justify automation more than do small quantities; thus, basic goods can be produced with lower labor costs than can fashion goods. Even without automation, operators familiar with sewing basic styles work faster—translating into lower labor costs—than those learning to sew a new style every few weeks. To reinforce these ideas, examine a $30 men's basic dress shirt and a $30 women's fashion blouse. The dress shirt usually contains considerably more labor-intensive detail for the same price.

Overhead Costs. **Overhead costs** are the expenses of operating the business beyond the direct costs of producing garments. They include the factory, equipment, taxes, and utilities; the salaries of supervisors, managers, and their staffs; and employee benefits such as insurance and pensions. In addition, overhead includes selling costs, such as advertising, marketing, and the sales commissions (typically 7 to 10 percent of wholesale price) paid to the sales reps who sell the line to retail buyers. Distribution costs, covering items such as shipping and warehousing, are also considered a part of overhead.

RELATIONSHIP OF COST TO PRICE

It is important to remember that the terms *cost* and *price* mean different things, depending on your perspective. In general, *cost* refers to the dollar amounts *you pay to others. Price* refers to the dollar amounts *others pay to you.*

Accurate costing helps manufacturers establish the **wholesale price** of garments, the price they charge retailers. Although the estimated cost of a garment does not automatically determine its wholesale price, manufacturers use cost figures as a guideline, and rely on accurate costing to help them set profitable wholesale prices. For the manufacturer to make a profit, the wholesale price must be higher than the actual cost of producing the garment. But a too-high wholesale price discourages buyers. So how does the manufacturer decide on a wholesale price?

When pricing apparel, producers are apt to price the garment according to "how much it looks like it's worth" more than any other factor. Thus, a familiarity with supply and demand in the marketplace is more important than cost in determining the correct price of a garment. A wise manufacturer determines the **market potential price** of a garment, the highest price that can be charged without dampening sales too much. For example, a company that produces a "hot" style that is in demand can sell the style for a high price, especially if the product has little competition. On the other hand, if a manufacturer produces a style that is plentiful, with many other manufacturers offering similar goods, the price of the item must be low enough to compete.

Generally, manufacturers aim for an average profit margin, but the profit margin on particular garments may vary widely. For example, a manufacturer's target profit may be 6 percent of the wholesale price, but the company makes more profit on some garments, and less on

others, and hopes to average out to 6 percent overall. In fact, sometimes firms sell a few garments at a loss, to attract buyers to the line; such items are referred to as **loss leaders.**

When pricing garments, manufacturers also consider their price line reputation. Most companies position their products in the same general price range from season to season so buyers know what to expect from them; consistency is important. Companies that produce one price line this season and another price line the next lose business because buyers want to count on the same resources for specific price lines from season to season. The wholesale price must allow an adequate retail markup and still result in a suitable retail price.

Like manufacturers, retailers also consider market forces when they establish the **retail price,** the price they charge the consumer. However, as a general rule to cover operating expenses and still make a profit, retailers approximately double the wholesale cost to obtain the retail price of a garment, a practice called *keystoning.*

METHODS FOR CUTTING COSTS

Good management practices reduce overhead costs, but other cost reductions occur by making changes in the garment, which affects the cost of producing it. Producing a garment at or below a certain cost enables it to fit into a designated price line. *Trade-offs* or *compromises* in design, materials, and/or construction are sometimes necessary to produce a garment at the desired cost. Discerning manufacturers compromise features that impact the overall performance of the garment least, or those which customers do not care about. Unfortunately, some manufacturers forfeit features that are not noticeable to customers at the point of sale, but which contribute to quality. For example, low-quality shoulder pads look as good as high-quality shoulder pads at the point of sale but shrink, curl and twist after wear and care. The reward of profits for sacrificing such features tempts some manufacturers to make changes that result in low-quality goods.

In an ideal situation, desired performance balances with cost limitations, enabling the manufacturer to sell the garment at a reasonable price, make a profit, *and* satisfy customers (Figure 2-7). A garment that fulfills the consum-

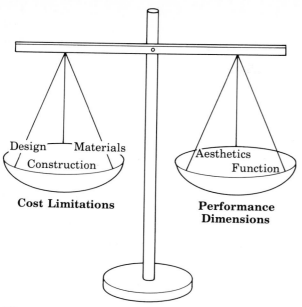

Figure 2-7 *Manufacturers must balance aesthetic and functional performance with cost limitations.*

er's expectations at a price he or she is willing to pay, without unnecessary features that inflate cost, represents this balance. But a perfect balance is difficult to achieve.

Reducing Materials Costs. When attempting to reduce costs, manufacturers scrutinize fabric costs first because of their significant contribution to total costs. For example, if a large company spends $50 million per year for fabric, a mere one percent savings translates into a half million dollars! Tactics for reducing fabric costs range from using a less expensive fabric or utilizing production methods that reduce waste, to modifying the style, fit, or construction of the garment to require less fabric. Manufacturers also employ techniques such as narrow seams and hems, shallow pleats, sparse gathers, and less-than-generous sizing to achieve lower fabric costs. These fabric-saving changes in a garment's style, fit, and construction may affect quality adversely. For example, *skimpy* (less than generously cut) swimsuits for women hike up in back, unlike those cut long enough and full enough to provide better coverage. And wrap-around robes, skirts, and dresses that barely overlap expose the body more than those cut generously enough to fully overlap. In another case, knit sport shirts often have too-short tails that come untucked easily. But shirts with *tennis tails* (cut longer in back than in front)

stay tucked in when the wearer moves and reaches.

Skilled pattern makers reduce fabric usage without sacrificing quality. They may, for example, add an extra seam where it does not affect appearance, comfort, or durability. The resulting two smaller pattern pieces require less fabric than the one larger piece. The fabric savings more than offsets the labor cost of sewing the two pieces together. Changing style elements to reduce fabric requirements may or may not compromise quality. For instance, some customers do not notice or care if the manufacturer eliminates the belt loops and back pockets on a pair of casual pants. But other customers, who want to wear a belt or put their wallet in the back pocket, view these cost-cutting measures as detracting from quality.

The cost of findings dramatically influences the cost of a garment. Manufacturers use fewer and less costly details and closures to reduce findings costs. For example, a slightly less expensive button or a six- rather than seven-button shirt front reduces the manufacturer's costs significantly when producing thousands of garments. Consumers may or may not notice such changes. Be sure to consider findings when comparing the quality of one garment to another seemingly identical garment, to detect differences that affect cost.

Reducing Labor Costs. Labor costs, especially in complex garments, significantly impact total costs. Naturally, garments requiring many construction steps have high labor costs. And operations requiring skilled operators cost more than those performed by less-skilled operators. Eliminating some steps and simplifying complicated, labor-intensive construction details, such as unusually shaped seams, pockets, and linings, reduce labor costs. For example, a row of stitches simulating a seam costs less to produce than an actual seam. Changing the type of stitches or seams affects production costs, because some stitch and seam types cost less to make than others (Figure 6-5). Sewing the garment faster also lowers labor costs. Some techniques for reducing labor costs affect the performance of the garment very little. In other cases, efforts to save on labor cause manufacturers to "cut corners," reducing the aesthetic or functional performance of the garment. Automation of procedures lowers labor costs (but raises equipment costs).

Current Trends Affecting the Industry

A number of current trends are shaping the way the apparel industry operates. For example, changes in retail buying practices and the growth of private label merchandise and specification buying blur the distinction between retailers and manufacturers. Increased apparel imports and efforts to expand apparel exports are causing domestic apparel manufacturers to become increasingly competitive. Advances in computer applications modify industry practices as technology becomes ever more sophisticated.

PRIVATE LABELS

As stores struggle for unique images, improved profits, and expanding market shares, many retailers rely increasingly on private label merchandise. **Private label** apparel is developed by or for a specific retailer, as opposed to **national brands,** which are developed by a manufacturer and sold to many retailers. In the traditional **per sample buying** used to acquire national brands, buyers select merchandise from manufacturers' lines. In contrast, private-label merchandise gives retailers more control over what they offer to consumers because private labels are acquired through specification buying. Retailers employ **specification buying** whenever they request goods made to meet their requirements and standards rather than choosing from manufacturers' lines.

Private labels are nothing new. Large department stores and specialty store chains have carried them for years. The proliferation and popularity of national brands in the mid- to late 1900s caused many retailers to move away from private-label merchandise, but now many of these stores are increasing their reliance on private labels again. Even small retailers may carry private labels; noncompeting retailers (for example, from different cities) band together to form buying groups large enough to share the costs of developing private labels.

About 10 percent of all apparel is private-label merchandise, although many retailers carry greater amounts, especially in classifications that lend themselves to the strategy. For example, 85 percent of men's and boys' underwear remains nationally branded. However, 40 percent of sweaters in better department and specialty stores are sold under private labels (Private Label 1988). A few stores carry nothing but private labels (see Related Resources: Brand Name).

The simplest form of private label development occurs when a retailer hires a manufacturer to put a store label on merchandise the manufacturer already produces. At the other extreme, a retailer personally oversees the whole manufacturing process from design through production, to create products unique to its store. In these cases, technically, *retailers* become *manufacturers* that hire contractors to execute the design and production processes. Likewise, manufacturers are increasingly becoming retailers; for example, Esprit, a sportswear maker with retail stores. Both trends represent an increasing vertical integration within the apparel industry. **Vertical integration** occurs when the same firm is responsible for multiple steps in the production or marketing of an apparel product. Examples of vertical integration include making the fiber and the fabric, making the fabric and the garment, making the garment and selling it to the ultimate consumer, or any combination of these steps.

Advantages of Private Labels. Retailers usually profit more from successful private labels than from national brands. National brands do little to build the reputation of a store; many competing retailers sell the same merchandise. Customer loyalty belongs to the national brand and usually follows it to the store with the lowest price; offering a low price on national-brand merchandise builds store traffic, yet hurts profits. Conversely, because private labels are exclusive, a popular one translates into loyalty to the retailer who sells it. Consumers cannot buy the same brand from a competing retailer, so they cannot directly compare it or its price at other stores. Without direct price competition, retailers carrying successful private brands sell them at attractive profits. The Limited, a specialty shop, is an example of a company that increased market share and profits by building brand recognition and customer loyalty to its products, first with their Forenza brand and then with a number of other successful private labels. Retailers that understand their target market are well equipped to develop private labels.

Disadvantages of Private Labels. The downside of private labels for retailers is that initially the retailer must promote the private label to establish its popularity. Until demand grows, private labels are not very profitable. And private labels that never catch on with consumers pose great financial risks for retailers. On the other hand, highly advertised national brands with established reputations create in-store traffic immediately, as consumers seek out their favorite brands. And well-known, national-brand merchandise commands higher prices than comparable merchandise with less-well-known, private labels.

Another disadvantage is that building and running a successful private-label program requires a knowledge not only of customer wants and needs, but of garment production and quality standards. Traditional buyers are not always equipped for the job. Some retailers hire independent product development consultants to formulate the right apparel products for their target customers. Others employ product development managers to assist buyers or substitute for buyers. Product developers establish quality specifications for design, materials, methods of construction, and sizing. And they help make decisions about product features to upgrade or downgrade and how best to balance performance and cost limitations.

INTERNATIONAL TRADE

The United States *imports* or buys from other countries more textile and apparel products than it *exports* or sells to other countries, leading to a *trade deficit*. The U.S. textile and apparel trade deficit has been growing for many years (Figure 2-8).

Manufacturers in the United States have traditionally paid most of their attention to the domestic market instead of thinking in terms of the world market. Demand for U.S.-made clothing is considerable in many other countries, and increased exports would narrow the trade deficit. Nevertheless, fewer than 10 percent of U.S. apparel companies export their products (Vigdor 1989). However, the main cause of the textile and apparel trade deficit is the amount of apparel the United States imports from other countries. The world supply of apparel production capacity will continue to exceed world demand for the forseeable future; only the most competitive firms will survive.

Imports. Perhaps about half of all apparel sold in the United States today is imported (see Related Resources: Imports). The chief advantage of imported apparel is low cost. The cost of apparel imports into the United States is low because of the labor costs in many other countries. Although U.S. apparel workers (paid an average of about $6.00 per hour) are not highly paid by American standards, they earn more than apparel workers in most other parts of the world; in some poor, developing countries apparel workers earn as little as $.20 per hour. A very labor-intensive industry, apparel manufacturing is an ideal industry for countries with little capital to invest but with plenty of unskilled

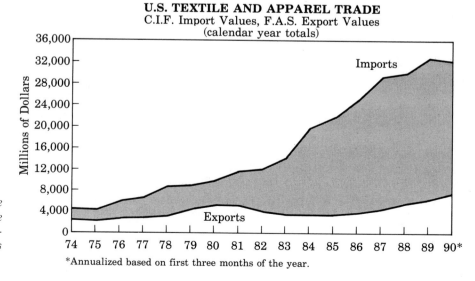

Figure 2-8 *Growth in the U.S. textile and apparel trade deficit. (Courtesy of American Textile Manufacturers Institute, Inc.)*

workers willing to accept wages far below the U.S. minimum wage. And what seem like low wages to most Americans are very desirable to impoverished people in these countries, who welcome any opportunity to raise their standard of living. U.S. manufacturers find it difficult to compete with foreign manufacturers that have the advantage of low labor costs.

The competitive force of imports has kept apparel prices relatively low for U.S. consumers. Since the early 1970s, wholesale apparel prices have risen only about half as fast as the prices of other products. However, although imported apparel is purchased by the retailer at a lower cost than domestic goods, it is not always sold at a lower price to consumers. Many retailers mark up low-cost imports more than domestic goods, selling them at the same or nearly the same price but making higher profits. Domestic apparel manufacturers argue that this practice makes imports no bargain for U.S. consumers.

Offshore Production. Despite the complaints of U.S. apparel manufacturers about the dent imports make in the domestic apparel industry, some of them also benefit from the advantages of importing. They practice **offshore production**—contracting with foreign producers to make goods. Because of lower labor costs, a number of well-known U.S. brands are mostly or entirely produced offshore according to their U.S. manufacturer's specifications. U.S. apparel workers' unions do not like this practice and refer to it as "job exporting." About one-third of all apparel imports result from this international **sourcing** (finding a contractor) by manufacturers. Another one-third is accounted for by the international sourcing of retailers acquiring private label merchandise (the majority of private label merchandise is made offshore). Thus, only the remaining one-third of apparel imports is marketed here directly by foreign companies (Glock and Kunz 1990).

Domestic apparel manufacturers may cut garments and then send the cut pieces to a low-wage country to be sewn, often in Central or South America because of their proximity. When the garment is shipped back to the United States, the manufacturer pays a tariff only on the *value added* to the garment; in other words, only on the labor costs of producing the garment. This provision is allowed under **Chapter 98** in the internationally developed Harmonized Commodity Description and Coding System, called

the **Harmony System (HS)** for short.* It formerly was allowed under **Item 807** in the U.S. Tariff Schedule. Thus, you may hear someone say, "We 807ed those jackets," referring to sending the cut pieces offshore to be made. Both Chapter 98/Item 807 and offshore production make it financially attractive for many U.S. manufacturers to import goods into the United States.

Regulation of International Trade. An international agreement called the **General Agreement on Tariffs and Trade (GATT)** promotes free trade. Under GATT is the **Multi-Fiber Arrangement (MFA),** which seeks an orderly growth in the openness of world trade, allowing countries to encourage industrial growth in developing nations and at the same time minimize disruption of their domestic apparel industries. The MFA allows for treaties between two nations, called *bilateral agreements*. These agreements include provisions for *tariffs*, otherwise known as *duties* or taxes, placed on imported apparel. The agreements also set up *quotas*, which limit the number of items that may be imported. The United States applies strict quotas mainly to developed nations whose goods are considered a threat to the domestic apparel industry, such as apparel from Taiwan, South Korea, the Republic of China, and Hong Kong, who together account for over half of the apparel imported into the United States. More lenient standards are applied to poor, developing countries given *most favored nation (MFN)* trading status.

Tariffs and quotas enforced by the U.S. Customs Service are not entirely effective in controlling imports. Even after paying the tariff, the cost of imported apparel is often still lower than goods produced domestically. Also, the regulations provide loopholes that allow imports to enter the United States at a higher rate than planned. For example, although it is illegal, countries sometimes transship goods to a country with a more favorable tariff or quota position than their own; from there they are shipped to the United States. And some foreign governments, to establish an industrial economy in their countries, financially *subsidize* the production of apparel. This allows manufacturers in

* For more information, contact U.S. Customs Service, P.O. Box 7407, Washington, DC 20044.

those countries to sell goods at a price lower than their cost of production, giving them an unfair advantage over producers in other countries; *dumping* occurs when manufacturers sell goods for a lower price abroad than in their own country.

There is much political controversy over whether or not the United States should legislate greater control of textile and apparel imports. Those with one view, **free trade,** favor unrestricted imports in the interest of the free flow of goods between nations. Free traders believe that if goods can be made better or at a lower cost in some other country, they should be. They argue that the world is best served by a free market, global economy. This group includes most retailers.* Those with the opposing view, called **protectionism** or **fair trade** by its proponents, favor regulating imports to protect the domestic industry. They use the term *fair trade* because they believe the United States should be no more open to accepting imports from other countries than these countries are to accepting U.S. exports. Fair traders include most U.S. manufacturers and labor unions representing U.S. textile and apparel workers. They have had some success in lobbying for legislation to protect the industry against imports, but not enough to prevent the closing of factories and the displacement of many workers in recent decades.

The U.S. textile and apparel industry employs over two million workers. Along with workers in related industries, they account for about 10 percent of the national industrial work force. The majority of workers in the apparel industry are women and minorities. They tend to have little education and few other employment options. Because the textile and apparel industry provides so many jobs, advocates of fair trade believe the industry and its workers warrant protection.

QUICK RESPONSE

In an effort to compete with imports, U.S. apparel manufacturers developed the notion of **Quick Response (QR).** Quick Response is a strategy for responding more quickly to the retailer's needs than foreign manufacturers can.

* For more information, contact the **National Retail Merchants Association (NRMA),** 100 W. 31st Street, New York, NY 10001.

66 WEEKS

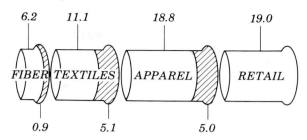

Figure 2-9 *Traditional textile and apparel pipeline (dark sections) versus Quick Response textile and apparel pipeline (light sections). (Courtesy of American Textile Manufacturers Institute, Inc.)*

It attempts to make domestically produced goods more profitable for U.S. retailers than imported goods, offsetting foreign manufacturers' advantage of low labor costs (see Related Resources: Quick Response).

Quick Response concentrates on compressing the textile and apparel pipeline. The **textile and apparel pipeline** is the channel of distribution through which a garment passes, from the fiber producer all the way to the ultimate consumer. The pipeline consists of three main sections: (1) fiber/fabric producers, (2) apparel manufacturers, and (3) retailers. Quick Response speeds the flow of goods through the pipeline by implementing advanced technology and good management practices. Figure 2-9 illustrates a typical textile and apparel pipeline of 66 weeks when traditional methods are used (the dark sections of the pipeline). However, the garment is **in-process,** or having work done on it, only 11 of those weeks. The remaining 55 weeks—or 83 percent of the time—the garment is in **inventory,** the time goods are in the factory waiting to be processed or in a warehouse waiting to be sold. Quick Response commonly cuts the cycle from over 60 weeks to fewer than 40 weeks. Incorporating Quick Response at *all* phases of the pipeline reduces the total length of a typical 66-week pipeline even more dramatically (the light sections of the pipeline).

The Quick Response management philosophy accomplishes these dramatic results by streamlining production, and reducing both in-process

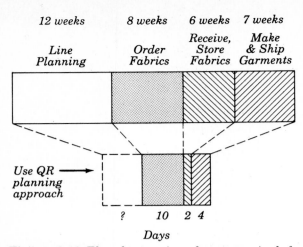

12 weeks	8 weeks	6 weeks	7 weeks
Line Planning	*Order Fabrics*	*Receive, Store Fabrics*	*Make & Ship Garments*

Use QR planning approach →

? 10 2 4

Days

Figure 2-10 *The shorter time frame required for planning and producing apparel using Quick Response. (Courtesy of American Textile Manufacturers Institute, Inc.)*

time and inventory time. For example, without Quick Response, a T-shirt that requires under three minutes in-process time takes two to eight days to flow through the production cycle; pants that involve twenty minutes in-process time often require ten days in production; a tailored coat requiring two hours in-process time takes up to six weeks to move through the factory (Brockett 1989). Quick Response incorporates the use of improved technology (e.g., CAD/CAM, UPS) to speed both planning and production and manage them more efficiently. It also incorporates the **just in time (JIT)** notion, signifying that there is no wasted time between each step of production. Suppliers provide the right quantity and quality of materials "just in time" for the next process, reducing inventory and inspection costs.* Figure 2-10 illustrates the shorter time frame for planning and manufacturing under the Quick Response system compared to traditional methods.

The concept of Quick Response is in its infancy; it is by no means an accomplished fact throughout the apparel industry. The pipeline contains numerous bottlenecks because some suppliers, manufacturers, and retailers have been reluctant to adopt the Quick Response philosophy and the technology required to execute it. However, many recognize the benefits of

Quick Response and consider it a goal worth pursuing.

Quick Response benefits retailers because buyers can buy goods closer to the selling season, making it easier to buy the "right" styles in the "right" numbers to meet customer demands. Shortening the *lead time,* the time from order placement to receipt of the goods, reduces the retailers' risks of making the wrong buying decision or missing out on a major trend. In contrast, retailers must select apparel purchased abroad far in advance of the selling season to allow time for shipping and clearing U.S. customs. Prompt delivery of Quick Response merchandise translates into promptly filled reorders, reducing warehousing and inventory costs and *stockouts,* when a store runs out of an item. In fact, with a two-week faster delivery time retailers can increase their sales 15 percent while simultaneously decreasing their inventories (Weintraub 1986). Thus, they are willing to pay a premium price for goods with fast delivery.

Many retailers are happy to buy domestic goods because they do not require expensive foreign buying trips, and they eliminate worries about fluctuating currency exchange rates, Third World instabilities, and filled quotas that cause goods to be held up by U.S. Customs. Domestic manufacturers extend credit terms, whereas foreign manufacturers require advance payment, tying up the retailer's money. And domestic goods involve lower shipping and insurance costs, no brokers' fees, and none of the other "hidden" costs of importing. Quick Response allows time to reorder fast-selling items while they are still popular, an impossibility with most imports. In addition, domestic manufacturers accept returns of and can send timely replacements for goods that do not meet specifications. Most foreign manufacturers do not accept returns and do not have time to send replacements before the selling season ends. All the benefits of domestically produced goods translate into retail sales and profit increases.

Quick Response gives U.S. manufacturers little advantage over sophisticated manufacturers in developed countries. However, QR does not suit most foreign manufacturers as much as it benefits U.S. manufacturers for two reasons. First, U.S. manufacturers' geographical proximity to U.S. retailers gives domestic producers an advantage in faster shipping times, providing a truly quicker response. Second, QR depends upon an investment in expensive modern technology and not upon a low-cost labor supply.

---

* The *Textile and Apparel Linkage Council (TALC),* the *Sundries and Apparel Findings Linkage Council (SAFLINC),* and the *Fabric Suppliers Linkage Council (FASLINC)* help manufacturers and their suppliers work together more closely, an important aspect of Quick Response.

Thus, QR is not feasible in developing countries whose main advantage over the United States is low-cost labor.

COMPUTER COMMUNICATIONS

The implementation of Quick Response requires immediate and constant communication between various segments of the apparel pipeline. This is made possible by electronic data interchange through computer-to-computer hookups. Electronic data interchange provides a vital link within companies and between companies by allowing the tracking of raw materials and finished garments at all phases of production, distribution, and sale. It creates greater coordination and cooperation between segments of the apparel pipeline. The majority of major retailers and manufacturers currently use some form of electronic data interchange in their day-to-day operations; those who do not will soon be left behind.

Bar codes are an essential element of the language of computer communications within the apparel industry. The price tags on most garments contain a **Universal Product Code (UPC),** a bar code like the ones used on groceries (Figure 2-11).* A bar code is a "fingerprint" for a product. A laser beam reads the width of the black lines and the spaces between the lines of the bar code. It translates that information into the 12-digit UPC number printed below the bar code. The first digit is a systems character; all apparel products start with a 0, 4, or 7. Digits two through six identify the *vendor* (manufacturer), and digits seven through eleven identify a particular product of that vendor. The last number is a check digit (see Related Resources: Bar Codes).

Most major retailers, manufacturers, and trade groups have endorsed the Universal Product Code for use on apparel. Its use is also endorsed by **Voluntary Interindustry Communications Standards (VICS),** a group with representatives from all facets of the apparel industry who determine the standards for electronic data interchange for the industry. However, a few retailers, during their transition to UPC, continue to use the older *Optical Character Recognition (OCR)* system, a series of com-

* The *UPC Data Communications Guidelines for General Merchandise and Apparel* can be obtained for about $30 from the *Universal Code Council,* P.O. Box 1244, Dayton, OH 45401.

① A number system character that identifies the product category. There are currently seven categories.

② A five digit number that identifies the manufacturer . . . assigned by the Uniform Code Council, Inc.

③ A five digit product code number that is assigned and controlled by the manufacturing company. This number is unique for each of the manufacturer's products including each size, flavor, color, etc.

④ A check digit.

Figure 2-11 *Universal Product Code (bar code).*

puter-read numbers without a bar code. When both OCR and UPC are included on the same ticket, it is referred to as *Dual Technology Vendor Marking (DTVM).*

Only a few retailers and manufacturers are equipped to take full advantage of all that bar codes offer. But you can expect the use of bar codes to grow steadily because of their many possibilities for improving business efficiency, which include

1. Encoding of product features such as vendor, color, size, style, and price so that the information serves as a substitute for a verbal description of the item. This is extremely helpful to retailers; for example, a department store may have as many as two million different UPCs in stock, compared with only about twenty-five thousand for a large grocery store (Thall 1988).

2. Speeding up checkout time for retail customers. The retailer programs the computer so that the *point of sale (POS) terminal* (the computerized cash register) associates the garment's bar code with its current retail price, even if the garment is on sale or has been marked down.

3. Substituting for each company's own numbering system of **stock keeping units (SKUs),** creating uniformity throughout the industry.

4. Providing all the necessary information for keeping track of inventory, subtracting sales and markdowns, adding new shipments and customer returns, and reordering items if and when necessary.

5. Making possible a fast and accurate **physical inventory** or count of every piece of merchandise by scanning each item's UPC.

6. Enabling manufacturers to mark goods at the factory (referred to as **vendor marking**). Manufacturers send vendor-marked merchandise directly to the retail store with UPC tickets attached. The garments do not need to pass through a retail distribution center for marking; instead, the retailer puts them directly on the selling floor.

7. Communication between retailers and manufacturers regarding inventory levels (i.e., which items are selling well and which are not). For example, the retailer scans the bar code at the point of sale, and the electronic data from the bar code is transmitted via phone from the retailer's computer to the manufacturer's computer. This computer-to-computer communication provides immediate feedback to the manufacturer when a sale is made.

8. Generation of automatic reorders for basic goods based on information about what sells. This reduces retail stockouts and replaces fast-selling items quickly.

9. Tracking sales of basic goods and helping to chart trends for the sale of fashion goods.

and finishing. The computer is increasingly used in mass production, but the apparel industry remains very labor intensive.

The main factor affecting the cost of a garment is the quality and quantity of the fabric. Also considered when costing a garment are the quality and quantity of the findings and labor, plus the overhead costs associated with conducting business. The price of the garment must be set higher than its cost to allow for a profit. Manufacturers often try to reduce the costs of producing a garment. Sometimes this can be done without sacrificing quality, but often cutting costs affects quality.

Current trends affecting the industry include the move toward private labels and specification buying and away from national brands. Another trend is the increase in apparel imported by U.S. retailers. Many U.S. manufacturers also take advantage of lower labor costs in foreign countries through offshore production and Chapter 98/Item 807 programs. The rising number of imports has prompted U.S. manufacturers to adopt a philosophy of Quick Response to compete with foreign manufacturers. Quick Response depends heavily on proximity to retailers and new technology. Examples of technology that is increasing efficiency for manufacturers who can afford the capital investment include the following: computer aided design and computer aided manufacturing; sewing room innovations (for example, unit production systems, modular manufacturing, and robotics); and increased electronic data interchange between retailers and manufacturers who rely on Universal Product Codes/bar codes.

Summary

The ready-to-wear apparel industry involves fiber, fabric, and other materials producers; apparel manufacturers, contractors, subcontractors, wholesalers, and retailers. Apparel manufacturers design, cut, and assemble garments, and sell them to retailers; retailers sell the finished garments to consumers. Contractors are hired to perform portions of the manufacturing process. Wholesalers sell the manufacturer's products to retailers for a commission.

Steps in the mass-production process include the design of the garments, making sample patterns and samples, making production patterns, grading, marker making, cutting, assembling,

New Terms

If you can define each of these terms and differentiate between related terms, you have gained a good working vocabulary for discussing the topics in this chapter. The terms are listed in the order in which they appear in the chapter.

inside shop
contractor/jobber
outside shop
wholesale representative/sales rep
computer integrated manufacturing (CIM)

American Apparel Manufacturers Association
  (AAMA)
Textile/Clothing Technology Corporation/(TC)2
designer
line/collection
merchandisers
computer-aided design/computer-aided
  manufacturing (CAD/CAM)
sample pattern
sloper/basic block
pattern design system (PDS)
sample
duplicate
number
production pattern/hard pattern
grading
marker
material utilization (MU)
die
operator
assembly line
bundle
piecework
unit production system (UPS)
modular manufacturing
off-pressed
underpressed
costing
precost/quick cost
production costing
findings/notions/sundries
overhead costs
wholesale price
market potential price
loss leader
retail price
private label
national brand
per sample buying
specification buying
vertical integration
offshore production
sourcing
Chapter 98 of Harmony System/Item 807
General Agreement on Tariffs and Trade
  (GATT)
Multi-Fiber Arrangement (MFA)
free trade
protectionism/fair trade
National Retail Merchants Association
  (NRMA)
Quick Response (QR)
textile and apparel pipeline
in-process
inventory

just in time (JIT)
bar code
Universal Product Code (UPC)
Voluntary Interindustry Communications
  Standards (VICS)
stock keeping unit (SKU)
physical inventory
vendor marking

Review Questions

1. What factors were responsible for the growth and acceptance of the U.S. ready-to-wear industry in the 1800s?

2. Compare the advantages and disadvantages of inside and outside shops.

3. How does a manufacturer differ from a contractor?

4. List the steps of the mass production process, beginning with the original concept for a garment.

5. How are computers used to assist in the production of ready-to-wear?

6. List the four main elements that must be considered when costing a garment. Which is generally the most significant?

7. List ten examples of how a manufacturer might cut costs.

8. What part does the cost of producing a garment play in establishing its wholesale price?

9. Discuss the advantages and disadvantages of private label merchandise for retailers.

10. Why has the amount of apparel imported into the United States increased in recent decades?

11. Discuss the advantages and disadvantages of unrestricted imports of apparel into the United States from the following points of view:
  U.S. manufacturer
  U.S. retailer
  U.S. consumer
  U.S. government
  foreign government of a developed country
  citizen of an undeveloped country

12. Explain the concept of Quick Response. How does it benefit U.S. manufacturers and retailers?

13. How does the use of UPC bar codes benefit apparel manufacturers and retailers?

Activities

1. Visit apparel manufacturers in your area. Compare and contrast their production processes from design through shipping the product. Or view videotapes on apparel manufacturing.

2. Examine blank copies of costing sheets from area apparel manufacturers. What elements do they have in common? How could they be improved?

3. Research a major apparel manufacturer. Write for an annual report and related information and read articles about the company. Interview someone who works for the company, if possible. Answer the following questions:
   a. Who owns the company?
   b. Who is the target customer?
   c. What classifications of merchandise does the company produce?
   d. What price line or lines are produced?
   e. Is production done in-house or by contractors?
   f. Where, geographically, is the production done?
   g. What is the annual sales volume?
   h. What retailers carry the company's lines?

4. Visit an historic costume collection to compare early ready-to-wear to modern ready-to-wear. Or, in a costume history book, compare fashions from the early and mid 1800s to fashions of the late 1800s and early 1900s. What are the most obvious differences? Which era's fashions lent themselves better to mass production?

5. Examine a garment and choose three features that you, as a manufacturer or retailer, would be willing to sacrifice to cut costs. Choose three features that you, as a consumer, would be willing to sacrifice to cut costs. Are the features you chose as a manufacturer or retailer the same as those you chose as a consumer? Why or why not?

6. Examine two similar garments sold for different prices. What influenced the difference in the prices—fabric costs, findings costs, labor costs, or some other factors?

7. In a store where you work or shop, find out which items are private labels and which are national brands. Approximately what percentage of each are present?

8. Where do you think the garment you are wearing right now was made? Check to see if you are correct. Compare results with other students.

9. Examine the labels of all the clothes in your closet. What percentage of your wardrobe is imported? Made in the U.S.A.?

10. Hold a class debate on free trade versus fair trade. What are the main points of each position?

11. Does the store where you work or shop record prices using bar codes? How do they use the information they gather? Are there other advantages?

3

Labels: Informing Consumers

CHAPTER OBJECTIVES

1. Discuss the requirements of federal laws for apparel labeling.
2. Recognize standard care terms and symbols.
3. Define the generally accepted size classifications and sizes used for childrenswear, womenswear, and menswear.
4. Discuss problems associated with sizing.
5. Understand the impact of voluntary labels on consumer perceptions of quality

Ready-to-wear garments contain a variety of labels and tags that convey information to those evaluating apparel quality. Clearly and accurately written labels provide a means for you to learn about the garment; they enable you to aid your customer in making informed decisions about selecting and caring for their clothing. A familiarity with labeling laws helps you determine whether or not the labels on a garment meet federal requirements. Of course, manufacturers may voluntarily furnish additional label information not required by law.

Apparel **labels** must be permanent and must remain legible throughout the useful life of the garment. Information may be woven in or printed on the label, but some printed labels tend to become illegible over time (Figure 5-8). Woven labels are generally comfortable to wear and give consumers an impression of quality. Nonwoven labels cost less but tend to be harsh and scratchy, and are apt to curl up. Manufacturers should provide comfortable labels so that consumers do not cut them out, which defeats the purpose of labeling. Sometimes consumers also cut out unsightly labels that show through the garment.

Labels require secure attachment. Manufacturers glue or sew labels into garments. Glued labels generally indicate lower-price garments than do sewn-in labels. Labels sewn in as a loop are less apt to roll but cost more to apply than those sewn in flat. Including a label in a seam costs less than tacking it into the garment as a separate process. As an alternative, sometimes label information is stamped directly on the garment; for example, inside the neckband of men's dress shirts.

Producers typically locate permanent labels inside the center back of a garment, at the neck or waist. Otherwise, they position the label in a conspicuous location elsewhere inside the garment. For packaged garments, both the garment and packaging must be labeled unless the garment's label is visible through the package.

Mandatory Labels

U.S. law mandates that all apparel sold in the United States contain permanent labels that fulfill the requirements of the *Textile Fiber Products Identification Act* and the *Care Labeling Rule*. Garments must also display labels that meet the requirements of the *Wool Products Labeling Act* and the *Fur Products Labeling Act,* if applicable. These laws are administered by the Federal Trade Commission (FTC).*

Other nations have different laws regulating apparel labeling. Companies involved in international trade need to familiarize themselves with the labeling requirements of those nations. Otherwise, the goods may not be accepted. For example, U.S. Customs requires imported apparel that does not conform to U.S. labeling laws to be properly labeled before it enters the country.

TEXTILE FIBER PRODUCTS IDENTIFICATION ACT

The **Textile Fiber Products Identification Act (TFPIA)** became effective in 1960. The TFPIA requires labels to disclose three things to consumers: (1) fiber content, (2) manufacturer, and (3) country of origin. TFPIA labeling

* To obtain copies of the Acts or to report violations, contact the Federal Trade Commission, Washington, DC 20580.

must be permanently affixed to all garments sold in the United States (see Related Resources: Fiber Content Labeling).

Fiber Content. A garment's fiber content affects its appearance, ease of care, comfort, durability, and cost (see Chapter 4). Labels meeting TFPIA requirements disclose the percentage of each fiber in the garment's fabric, in order of predominance by weight (Figure 3-1). The percentages should be accurate to within 3 percent. The label lists any fiber constituting less than 5 percent of the total weight as *other fiber* unless the fiber makes a significant contribution to the performance of the garment. For example, spandex affects elasticity even if present as only a small portion of the total fiber used. Garments of unknown fiber content must be so labeled; for example, *of undetermined fiber content.* The fibers used in garment trimmings, such as lace or ribbon, need not be identified if they cover less than 15 percent of the garment's surface area, but the fiber content label should include the term *exclusive of decoration.* If fiber ornamentation, such as embroidery, constitutes less than 5 percent of the total weight, it need not be identified but the label should read *exclusive of ornamentation.* The fiber content of elastic need not be identified if it covers less than 20 percent of the surface area of the garment, but the label should read *exclusive of elastic.* The label should identify the fiber content of linings or interlinings added for warmth separately from that of the garment.

The TFPIA requires that labels refer to fibers by generic names, in English. A **generic name,** as established by the Federal Trade Commission, denotes a family of fibers with a similar chemical composition. The law permits a trademark to accompany the generic name. A **trademark** is a registered brand name for the generic fiber made by a particular producer (Table 4-2). For example, *polyester* is a generic name; *Dacron* is a trademark for polyester fibers produced by DuPont. The trademark and generic name must appear in lettering of the same size and importance and on the same side of the label. The law forbids terms implying the presence of fibers which are not a part of the garment and terms which are promotional in nature. For example, *silky luster* may not be used to describe the properties of rayon fibers.

Occasionally, a manufacturer intentionally mislabels the fiber content of a garment so that consumers will think it contains more costly or desirable fibers than it actually does. For example, a garment labeled *cashmere* may contain sheep's wool instead of fibers from the Kashmir goat; a garment labeled *down* may contain feathers instead of the fine, fluffy down fibers that grow under the feathers of waterfowl. Another form of mislabeling uses the correct fiber names but inflates the percentage of the more desirable fiber. Of course, sometimes fiber content mislabeling is unintentional. In any case, mislabeling often goes undetected. Some trade organizations, such as the Wool Bureau, perform laboratory analyses of random garment samples to police the accuracy of fiber content labels. A few manufacturers and retailers also randomly analyze for fiber content labeling accuracy. However, most manufacturers merely accept the fiber content information provided by their suppliers and most consumers do not question the fiber content on the labels of the garments they buy.

Manufacturer. All garments must contain labels identifying their manufacturer. The manufacturer's name, trademark, or identification number as registered with the Federal Trade Commission must appear on the label. The reputation of the manufacturer who produced the garment influences the consumer's perception of the quality of the garment, because consumers expect garments made by a specific manufacturer to be of consistent quality.

A producer's **registered identification number** is the number you see following the letters **RN** (registered number) on garment labels. Some older manufacturers have a WPL, or Wool Products Labeling, number instead of an RN number. The RN or WPL pinpoints the maker of the garment. Table 3-1 contains a list of a few prominent manufacturers and their RN/WPL

Figure 3-1 *Examples of apparel labels.*

numbers.* RNs and WPLs enable consumers or federal regulators to determine the producer of a garment, should the need arise. When off-price retailers cut out brand name labels, they must leave the RN label intact to identify the garment's manufacturer.

Country of Origin. Labels on apparel sold in the United States must identify **country of origin,** or where the garment was produced. Because of perceptions about the quality of imported apparel and due to the effect of apparel imports on the U.S. economy, country of origin is a noteworthy part of apparel labeling for customers who want to "buy American." In fact, clothing is the type of merchandise that consum-

* *The RN & WPL Encyclopedia* can be obtained for about $175 from The Salesmans Guide, National Register Publishing Co./Division of Macmillan, 1140 Broadway, Suite 1203, New York, NY 10117-0130.

TABLE 3-1
Examples of RN and WPL numbers

FOUR-IN-HAND SHOP TIES UNL	RN39323
FOUR-O-EIGHT FASHION INC	RN22921
FOURRES SPORT WALT STIELF LTD	RN44959
FOURSOME FASHION INC	RN49874
FOURTEEN CARROT INC	RN 75117
FOURTH AVENUE CONTEMPORARY SPORTSWEAR	RN 70435
THE FOURTH LITTLE PIG	RN 69904
FOUSHEE MFG CO	RN59188
FOWLES & COMPANY	WPL09511
FOWNES BROS & CO INC	WPL09522

ers are most likely to scrutinize for country of origin (East vs. West 1988).

Luxury imported apparel constitutes a limited portion of total imports. Unlike low-price imports, consumers perceive these goods to be of high quality because of the mystique of the label; for example, "Made in France" or "Made in Italy." Many luxury imports indeed do possess high quality, especially those made of natural resources that are the specialties of certain nations. For instance, wools from Britain, silks from China, linens from Ireland, leathers from Italy, and cottons from Egypt are among the finest available. In other cases, luxury goods represent uncommon quality in labor, made possible by generations of experience in a particular craft and an emphasis on factors other than lowering costs and increasing production volume. For example, London is known for its exquisite menswear tailoring and Paris for its couture fashions.

Low-price imports constitute the majority of apparel imports and represent direct competition for the U.S. industry (see Chapter 2). Customers often associate these low-price imports with low quality and low fashion appeal. However, *country of origin is not a valid clue to quality;* no consistent evidence exists to show that one country of origin indicates higher or lower quality than another. The sophistication, fashion appeal, fit, and durability of low-price imported apparel, which admittedly was inferior years ago, has improved dramatically so that stereotypes about low-price imported apparel are no longer valid. By the same token, although many U.S. manufacturers have excellent quality records, others have low quality standards. High quality and low quality result from conformity or nonconformity to quality standards, not from country of origin. By setting high standards and following established specifications, manufacturers anywhere in the world can produce quality apparel.

To alert consumers to country of origin, since 1984, garments made in the United States must bear a label reading *Made in U.S.A.* And garments made in the United States of non-U.S. materials are labeled *Made in U.S.A. of imported fabric.* To determine country of origin, the manufacturer is required to go back one step and name the country where the garment was last substantially transformed. For example, if part of the garment is assembled in another country, the label must read *Made in (name of other country), finished in the U.S.A.* Clothing made in other countries must be labeled *Made in (name of country).* Chapter 98/Item 807 goods of U.S. fabric that are cut and sent offshore to be sewn are labeled *Made in (name of country where assembled) of U.S. materials.* Descriptions in mail-order catalogs also must disclose whether garments are made in the United States or imported and whether the fabric is domestic or imported.

WOOL PRODUCTS LABELING ACT

Since 1939, the **Wool Products Labeling Act (WPLA)** has regulated the labeling of garments containing hair fibers. The terms *wool* and *pure wool* refer to wool fibers that previously have not been made into a fabric; *new wool* and *virgin wool* refer to fibers that previously have not been processed in any way. *Recycled wool* refers to wool previously fabricated, possibly used, and then reclaimed into fiber form. Recycled wool, also called *shoddy,* represents lower aesthetic quality than new fibers; otherwise, it performs well and is as warm to wear as new wool. Recycled wool is confined to interlinings and, occasionally, outer fabrics for low-price coats.

FUR PRODUCTS LABELING ACT

The **Fur Products Labeling Act (FPLA)** regulates the labeling of garments made of fur still attached to the animal skin. The act, in place since 1952, requires fur products to carry a label bearing the English name of the animal and only that name. It also requires the label to indicate the country of origin of the fur. The label must disclose if the fur is waste fur or has been used, damaged, dyed, bleached, or otherwise treated to artificially change the color.

CARE LABELING RULE

The **Care Labeling Rule,** in effect since 1972, requires that apparel carry a permanently affixed care label providing full instructions for the regular care of the garment (see Related Resources: Care). A care label is an implied warranty by the manufacturer that if the customer follows the care instructions, the garment will retain its appearance. The rule requires the manufacturer to recommend only one care method, although other methods may work as well. The care label must clearly and thoroughly tell the customer how to care for the garment. It must specify washing, bleaching, drying, ironing, and/or dry cleaning procedures and warn against procedures that harm the garment. The rule does not allow care labels that are promotional in nature; for example, *Never Needs Ironing* is unacceptable. Ironically, the law does not require that a care label suggest a care method that cleans the item effectively, merely that the recommended care method not harm the garment.

All ready-to-wear apparel sold to the public must be permanently care labeled, with the exception of garments that withstand any care method, and items such as hosiery on which a label would detract from appearance or usefulness. However, such garments must provide care information to the customer on the product package or on a temporary care label. Garments consisting of more than one piece require only one care label, although a label in each piece is preferable. If the manufacturer locates care information on the back of a label, the front must state *Over For Care, Care Information on Reverse Side,* or a similar instruction.

Care plays an important role in maintaining the existing quality of a garment. Ideally, the care label recommends a care method that minimizes shrinkage, color loss, and deterioration of the garment. Manufacturers that impart an understanding of appropriate care procedures to consumers through care labeling avoid returns of garments that did not perform well because of improper care.

Some consumers use care labels in evaluating ready-to-wear. For example, one consumer avoids garments that require ironing or dry cleaning, while another expects such care requirements. In either case, the care label affects the consumer's perception of the quality of the garment. Care labels allow the consumer to estimate the maintenance costs for the garment, which influence the garment's ultimate cost and value.

Standard Care Terms. The Federal Trade Commission supplies a *Glossary of Standard Terms,* a list of the terms required for care labeling and definitions for the terms (Table 3-2). The glossary enables manufacturers to write care labels consistent with those of other manufacturers; this simplifies care labels for consumers. Manufacturers use the terms in the glossary in various combinations to describe the care procedures they recommend for the garments they produce. The definitions provided in the glossary further explain the brief instruc-

tions given on care labels to describe exactly how to care for the garment. Unfortunately, most consumers are unfamiliar with these definitions and use only the general terms on the care label to guide their care decisions.

The Care Labeling Rule requires that all washing instructions suggest a particular method of washing—machine wash or hand wash. Drying instructions also must suggest a method—tumble dry, line dry, or dry flat. If the label does not mention ironing, the garment should not require ironing.

The label must be specific about the variation of the method to use if other variations harm the garment. For example, if a label says *Machine Wash,* the consumer can assume that any water temperature and cycle is safe. Otherwise, the label must state, for instance, *Machine Wash, Cold, Delicate Cycle.* If the label does not prohibit bleach in conjunction with washing instructions, the consumer can assume that any form of bleach is safe. If the garment could harm other garments being washed with it, the label must so warn; for example, *Wash Separately* or *Wash with Like Colors.* If the label states *Dry Clean,* the consumer can assume that any dry cleaning procedure is safe; the label must qualify the type of solvent or other aspect of the process if not all procedures are safe. If trim on the garment requires special care, the label must warn *Remove Trim.* Warnings need be given only for variations of the care procedure recommended on the label, not for all possible procedures. In other words, if the label states *Dry Flat,* it does not have to warn *Do Not Tumble Dry.*

Reasonable Basis for Care Labels. The Care Labeling Rule requires apparel manufacturers to have a **reasonable basis** for the care instructions they recommend. A reasonable basis includes evidence such as tests, current technical literature, past experience, or industry experience. For example, the manufacturer should have proof that washing will harm a garment that is labeled *Dry Clean Only.*

Only the apparel manufacturer possesses complete information about the garment and all its components. Therefore, it makes sense that the apparel manufacturer, not the consumer, is responsible for determining a safe care method for the garment. Manufacturers should test the ability of the garment to withstand the recommended care procedure, even though testing increases costs, because garments with inaccurate

TABLE 3-2

Glossary of Standard Care Terms according to the Federal Trade Commission's Care Labeling Rule

1. Washing, Machine Methods

   a. *Machine wash*—a process by which soil may be removed from products or specimens through the use of water, detergent or soap, agitation and a machine designed for this purpose. When no temperature is given, e.g., "warm" or "cold," hot water up to 150°F (66°C) can be regularly used.
   b. *Warm*—initial water temperature setting 90° to 110°F (32° to 43°C) (hand comfortable).
   c. *Cold*—initial water temperature setting same as cold water tap up to 85°F (29°C).
   d. *Do not have commercially laundered*—do not employ a laundry which uses special formulations, sour rinses, extremely large loads or extremely high temperatures or which otherwise is employed for commercial, industrial or institutional use. Employ laundering methods designed for residential use or use in a self-service establishment.
   e. *Small load*—smaller than normal washing load.
   f. *Delicate cycle* or *Gentle cycle*—slow agitation and reduced time.
   g. *Durable press cycle* or *Permanent press cycle*—cool down rinse or cold rinse before reduced spinning.
   h. *Separately*—alone.
   i. *With like colors*—with colors of similar hue and intensity.
   j. *Wash inside out*—turn product inside out to protect face of fabric.
   k. *Warm rinse*—initial water temperature setting 90° to 110°F (32° to 43°C).
   l. *Cold rinse*—initial water temperature setting same as cold water tap up to 85°F (29°C).
   m. *Rinse thoroughly*—rinse several times to remove detergent, soap, and bleach.
   n. *No spin* or *Do not spin*—remove material start of final spin cycle.
   o. *No wring* or *Do not wring*—do not use roller wringer, nor wring by hand.

2. Washing, Hand Methods

   a. *Hand wash*—a process by which soil may be manually removed from products or specimens through the use of water, detergent or soap, and gentle squeezing action. When no temperature is given, e.g., *warm* or *cold,* hot water up to 150°F (66°C) can be regularly used.
   b. *Warm*—initial water temperature 90° to 110°F (32° to 43°C) (hand comfortable).
   c. *Cold*—initial water temperature same as cold water tap up to 85°F (29°C).
   d. *Separately*—alone.
   e. *With like colors*—with colors of similar hue and intensity.
   f. *No wring or twist*—handle to avoid wrinkles and distortion.
   g. *Rinse thoroughly*—rinse several times to remove detergent, soap, and bleach.
   h. *Damp wipe only*—surface clean with damp cloth or sponge.

3. Drying, All Methods

   a. *Tumble dry*—use machine dryer. When no temperature setting is given, machine drying at a hot setting may be regularly used.
   b. *Medium*—set dryer at medium heat.
   c. *Low*—set dryer at low heat.
   d. *Durable press* or *Permanent press*—set dryer at permanent press setting.
   e. *No heat*—set drying to operate without heat.
   f. *Remove promptly*—when items are dry, remove immediately to prevent wrinkling.
   g. *Drip dry*—hang dripping wet with or without hand shaping and smoothing.
   h. *Line dry*—hang damp from line or bar in or out of doors.
   i. *Line dry in shade*—dry away from sun.
   j. *Line dry away from heat*—dry away from heat.
   k. *Dry flat*—lay out horizontally for drying.
   l. *Block to dry*—reshape to original dimensions while drying.
   m. *Smooth by hand*—by hand, while wet, remove wrinkles, straighten seams and facings.

TABLE 3-2 *(continued)*

4. Ironing and Pressing

a. *Iron*—Ironing is needed. When no temperature is given iron at the highest temperature setting may be regularly used.

b. *Warm iron*—medium temperature setting.

c. *Cool iron*—lowest temperature setting.

d. *Do not iron*—item not to be smoothed or finished with an iron.

e. *Iron wrong side only*—article turned inside out for ironing or pressing.

f. *No steam* or *Do not steam*—steam in any form not to be used.

g. *Steam only*—steaming without contact pressure.

h. *Steam press* or *Steam iron*—use iron at steam setting.

i. *Iron damp*—articles to be ironed should feel moist.

j. *Use press cloth*—use a dry or a damp cloth between iron and fabric.

5. Bleaching

a. *Bleach when needed*—all bleaches may be used when necessary.

b. *No bleach* or *Do not bleach*—no bleaches may be used.

c. *Only nonchlorine bleach, when needed*—only the bleach specified may be used when necessary. Chlorine bleach may not be used.

6. Washing or Dry Cleaning

a. *Wash or dry-clean, any normal method*—can be machine washed in hot water, can be machine dried at a high setting, can be ironed at a hot setting, can be bleached with all commercially available bleaches and can be dry-cleaned with all commercially available solvents.

7. Dry Cleaning, All Procedures

a. *Dry clean*—a process by which soil may be removed from products or specimens in a machine which uses any common organic solvent (for example, petroleum, perchlorethylene, fluorocarbon) located in any commercial establishment. The process may include moisture addition to solvent up to 75% relative humidity, hot tumble drying up to 160°F (71°C) and restoration by steam press or steam-air finishing.

b. *Professionally dry clean*—use the dry-cleaning process but modified to ensure optimum results either by a dry-cleaning attendant or through the use of a dry-cleaning machine which permits such modifications or both. Such modifications or special warnings must be included in the care instruction.

c. *Petroleum, Fluorocarbon,* or *Perchlorethylene*—employ solvent(s) specified to dry-clean the item.

d. *Short cycle*—reduced or minimum cleaning time, depending upon solvent used.

e. *Minimum extraction*—least possible extraction time.

f. *Reduced moisture* or *Low moisture*—decreased relative humidity.

g. *No tumble* or *Do not tumble*—do not tumble dry.

h. *Tumble warm*—tumble dry up to 120°F (49°C).

i. *Tumble cool*—tumble dry at room temperature.

j. *Cabinet dry warm*—cabinet dry up to 120°F (49°C).

k. *Cabinet dry cool*—cabinet dry at room temperature.

l. *Steam only*—employ no contact pressure when steaming.

m. *No steam* or *Do not steam*—do not use steam in pressing, finishing, steam cabinets or wands.

8. Leather and Suede Cleaning

a. *Leather clean*—have cleaned only by a professional cleaner who uses special leather or suede care methods.

labels that suggest ruinous care methods lead to dissatisfied customers; accurate care labeling pays for itself in the form of fewer returns and more satisfied customers.

Unfortunately, not all manufacturers take their care labeling responsibility seriously. For example, it is a common practice for apparel manufacturers to use care labels provided by the fabric producer rather than making their own determination about a care procedure for the garment. This ignores the interaction of the fabric with other garment components and with the construction of the garment. For instance, do the interfacing and shoulder pads withstand the same care as the fabric? Will the trim and closures accept the same care as the fabric? Manufacturers who overlook such questions often produce erroneous care labeling, resulting in garment failure when the customer follows the suggested care procedures. For example, the thread used to sew together the sweater shown in Figure 3-2 shrank when washed, distorting the armhole seams. Although the care method suggested on the label did not harm the sweater fabric, it made the sweater unwearable because

the manufacturer did not test the effect of the care method on the thread.

Many customers do not trust care labels. They may have had experience in which following the care label led to garment failure. Or they may have successfully used a care method other than the one suggested on the label. Because manufacturers are required by law to list only one care method, not to list all possible care methods, other safe care methods sometimes exist besides the one on the label. Also, some manufacturers practice low labeling with respect to care. **Low labeling** involves recommending a more conservative care method than the garment requires. For example, the label may recommend *Dry Clean* rather than other methods that are equally safe and effective, as well as simpler and less expensive. Manufacturers low label because it allows them to recommend a safe care method without performing costly testing, and because it releases them from liability if the garment fails because the consumer decides to ignore the label and use a harsher care method.

Following Care Labels. When consumers notice that garments appear to be low labeled, or when following care labels leads to garment failure, consumers begin to believe they can do a better job than the manufacturer of determining care methods. Although consumer "guessing" about the appropriate care for garments may meet with occasional success, it may also lead to ruining garments through inappropriate care. For example, consumers use information such as the fiber content of the garment to decide how to care for a garment. But variations in fibers, yarns, fabrications, and finishes that the consumer cannot see may cause the garment to require a different care method than the fiber content might suggest. For instance, although it is true that most cotton fabrics are washable, the dye in some cotton fabrics bleeds when washed and the fabric requires dry cleaning. Another example is that most children's sleepwear has a flame retardant finish and certain care procedures damage the finish, rendering it ineffective. Care labels on children's sleepwear must warn against laundering with soap and nonphosphate detergents, although the fiber content might suggest to consumers that these care processes are safe. Or, a garment that might otherwise be washable may contain buttons, trim, or other components that are not washable. Consumers cannot tell these things

Figure 3-2 Sleeve distorted by thread that shrank when garment was laundered according to the care method recommended on the label.

from the fiber content label or by looking at or feeling a garment. Thus, consumers who ignore care labels take a risk which, when their methods meet with failure, is their fault and not that of the manufacturer. Rather than taking care decisions into their own hands, consumers should communicate with manufacturers about dissatisfaction with suggested care methods to encourage accurate and useful care labeling.

Care Symbols. A few countries have developed care symbols, sometimes called **sure care symbols,** to indicate to consumers the recommended care for a garment. For example, Britain, Canada, Japan, and Ginetex (a group of European countries including Germany and France) each has developed their own system of care labeling using symbols. A single, consistent set of care symbols recognized internationally does not exist. However, the **International Standards Organization (ISO)** in Geneva, with representatives from many nations, currently is developing a standard set of international care symbols to provide universally understood care labeling.* Until ISO completes the work, the International Fabricare Institute (IFI) suggests that U.S. manufacturers use the set of symbols illustrated in Figure 3-3. These symbols consolidate the common elements from the systems of several different countries. The system uses five basic symbols—a tub shape representing washing, a square representing drying, a triangle representing bleaching, an iron representing ironing, and a circle representing dry cleaning. If the symbols are printed in one of three colors—red, amber or green—like a traffic light, red means *stop,* amber means *caution,* and green means *go ahead* with regard to the action represented by the symbol. The color of the symbols is not significant if they are blue or black. An "X" over the symbol means *do not use it* or *do not do it.* If dots are added to the symbols, the number of dots indicates the recommended temperature of the procedure, with more dots representing a higher temperature.

Care symbols overcome language barriers in providing care instructions for garments that are imported or exported, which is important as international trade in apparel continues to grow. In the United States, the Care Labeling Rule permits the use of the symbols in addition to, but not as a substitute for, the required written care instructions. These symbols are useful only to the extent that consumers understand them, which at the present time in the United States is not the case.

FLAMMABLE FABRICS ACT

Most apparel burns readily, but the **Flammable Fabrics Act,** established in 1953, prohibits the sale of highly flammable apparel. The Flammable Fabrics Act is administered by the Consumer Product Safety Commission (CPSC).* The strictest federal flammability regulations govern children's sleepwear (see Chapter 4). The law does not require labels on children's sleepwear to inform the consumer that the garment complies with federal regulations, but many manufacturers indicate compliance as a service to the consumer and to promote the garment. The law does require that each garment be permanently labeled with a *Garment Production Unit number (GPU)* and a *Fabric Production Unit number (FPU)* to identify its producers in case of a fire-related incident. Manufacturers are required to retain records on each piece of children's sleepwear produced to verify compliance with the law.

Voluntary Apparel Labels

Much of the information included on apparel labels is voluntary; manufacturers use size, brand name, certification, union, and "Crafted With Pride" labels to market products. Because such information is not required by law, the manufacturer may choose to provide it on permanent labels or hang tags, or not at all. Informative labels help consumers form accurate expectations about the garment. For example, size labeling is clearly necessary in helping consumers make purchase decisions. Labels that express not only the selling points but the buying benefits of the garment serve as "silent salespeople," to convince the consumer concerning the quality of the garment.

* For more information, contact the U.S. member organization of ISO, the **American National Standards Institute (ANSI),** 1430 Broadway, New York, NY 10018.

* To obtain copies of the Act or to report violations, contact the Consumer Product Safety Commission, Washington, DC 20207.

INTERNATIONAL CARE SYMBOLS

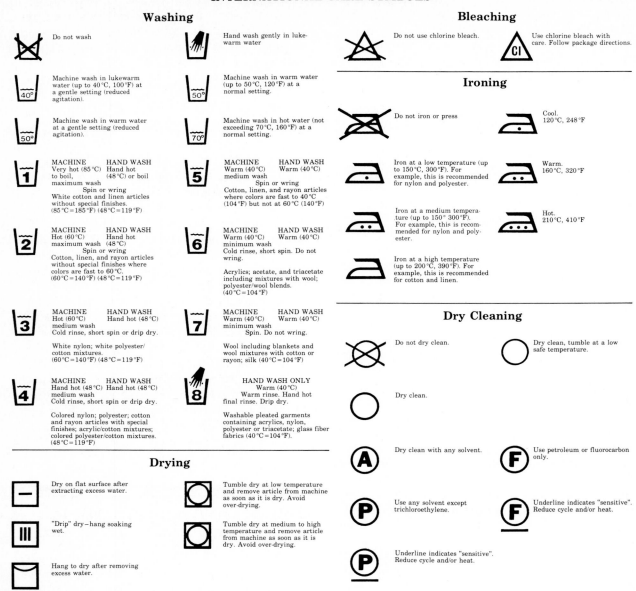

Figure 3-3 *International care symbols. (Courtesy of International Fabricare Institute.)*

SIZE

Size labeling suggests to consumers the suitability of a garment for their body dimensions. The labeled size of a garment is intended to help determine whether or not that particular garment will fit a particular individual.* However, lack of conformity to a consistent apparel size labeling system in the United States makes size helpful only in narrowing down the choices of

what to try on first and in comparing two otherwise identical garments of different sizes. Sizes are grouped together into **size classifications,** according to the sex, age, and/or body type of consumers (see Related Resources: Size).

Consumers use sizes and size classifications in trying to locate a garment that fits; manufacturers and retailers use them as an assortment planning device and as a marketing tool. The industry offers a variety of sizes and size classifications to fit and appeal to the full range of consumers.

* See Chapter 12 for a discussion of the elements of good fit.

Voluntary Standards. As anyone trying on clothing quickly recognizes, there is no such thing as a "perfect size 10." Because every manufacturer cuts garments from an individually developed block, the fit of garments produced by different manufacturers varies considerably. A size 4 dress made by one company and a size 8 dress made by another may fit the same woman. Variations in sizes from company to company are partly the result of each firm's effort to develop a distinctive fit that differentiates their goods in the marketplace and fits their target consumer better than garments produced by the competition. Although the lack of size standardization often irritates consumers, it has some benefits. A variety of cuts and fits produced by different manufacturers translates into a variety of cuts and fits available to consumers. If all clothing conformed to the same strict size standards, anyone with an other-than-average figure could not find clothing that fits. Of course, variations in fit between two garments with the same size label and made by the same manufacturer reflect poor quality control.

Voluntary standards for U.S. sizing were published by the National Bureau of Standards in 1945. The standards were revised in 1970 to reflect the changes in Americans' bodies, and withdrawn in 1983 because of the need to revise them again. Since that time, there has been no recognized standard for apparel sizing in the United States. The American Society for Testing and Materials (ASTM) is currently developing new standard tables of body measurements on which sizes can be based, but will not complete the work for several years.*

In the meantime, the withdrawn voluntary size standards are available from the U.S. Department of Commerce's National Institute of Standards and Technology (NIST), formerly the National Bureau of Standards.** Portions of the voluntary standards are presented in this chapter because they are the only size standards available. Review them to get a general idea about sizes and size classifications, but do not be surprised to see other sizes and classifications in stores and catalogs. Although most manufacturers loosely follow the withdrawn voluntary standards as a guideline for establishing sizes and size classifications, each interprets the numbers and categories differently. For the time being, "anything goes" in sizing, as manufacturers and retailers (especially mail-order firms) search for the best way to size garments and classify sizes.

In general, expensive lines tend to *run large*—larger than most other garments of the same labeled size; they are cut to fit generously because the high price allows for liberal use of fabric. Expensive lines that run large are sometimes referred to as **vanity sized,** because they appeal to the vanity of consumers who want to think of themselves as wearing a small labeled size. Conversely, some high-price lines run small, because they aim at a target market that is small-framed. An example is Adolfo, a favorite designer for former First Lady, Nancy Reagan. Generally, however, low-price garments tend to *run small*—smaller than most other garments of the same labeled size—in an effort to conserve fabric. When someone suggests that a garment runs *true to size,* it fits about the same as most other garments of the same labeled size.

The voluntary standard sizes encompass the majority of people. However, many manufacturers do not make and most retailers do not carry all the sizes in a classification because few consumers require the extremely small and the extremely large sizes. Catalog retailers and some specialty stores are most apt to carry the full range of sizes. Yet some individuals require sizes even smaller or larger than those included in the voluntary size standards. Manufacturers producing apparel for these people develop sizes using the extreme ends of the standards as a starting point.

Expressed as Body Measurements. The main problem with apparel sizing is not the lack of standardization, but that size labeling has no real meaning to consumers. Sizing frustrates consumers instead of providing them with guidance in locating garments that fit. The solution lies in labeling clothing with the body measurements the garment fits. Size labeling expressed in terms of body measurements gives useful information to consumers. It is used by mail-order retailers and some other retailers and manufacturers concerned with maintaining a quality reputation for providing good fit. Informative size labeling that relates directly to *body measurements* helps companies satisfy consumers.

Currently, most sizes are not expressed as body measurements (the exception is men's apparel). Early sizing systems evolved with the

---

* ASTM D 4910-89 Standard Tables of Body Measurements for Infants, Ages 0 to 18 Months has been released for use.
** For more information, contact National Institute of Standards and Technology, Gaithersburg, MD 20899.

idea that women did not want to reveal their body measurements when shopping, causing the development of numbers which represent body measurements but obscure them at the same time. Thus, most sizes are expressed as arbitrarily chosen numbers or letters that correlate with sets of unrevealed body measurements (exceptions are the height/weight charts on panty hose packages and childrenswear labels). Unfortunately, when body measurements are not revealed to the consumer, the size designations are almost meaningless. Thus, most sizes are relative rather than absolute, useful only for the assumption that a garment labeled with a larger size is bigger than a garment labeled with a smaller size.

Lettered Sizing. Lettered sizing has grown increasingly popular in recent years. The stretch provided by knit fabrics and the popularity of loose fits have encouraged this trend. **Lettered sizing** uses the size designations of *S* = small, *M* = medium, and *L* = large. It usually includes the extension *XL* = extra large, and sometimes *XXL* and *XXXL* for yet larger sizes and *XS* = extra small. Collapsing size categories into lettered sizes reduces the number of size divisions from seven or eight to just three or four. However, consumers cannot find an accurate fit within S, M, L, and XL as easily as they can within numbered sizes, which provide finer differences between sizes.

Lettered sizing is prevalent in low-price lines because it eliminates the need for precise sizing, and because it is more economical to produce fewer sizes. Foreign manufacturers who have difficulty in achieving accurate sizing for the U.S. market turn to lettered sizing because of its simplicity. Many retailers like lettered sizing because, by eliminating the need to carry so many sizes, it allows them to carry a greater number of styles and colors. Consumers easily identify with lettered sizing, although it often gives them little real assistance in finding a garment that fits; S, M, L, and XL have little standardization from manufacturer to manufacturer and no consistent correlation to body measurements. In fact, S, M, L, and XL are used without any differentiation for unisex garments, menswear, womenswear, and childrenswear.

Sometimes garment length is also designated with lettered sizing. When they do not provide length in inches, manufacturers commonly use *P* = Petite or *S* = Short, *A* = Average or *R* = Regular, and *L* = Long or *T* = Tall.

One-size-fits-all sizing is an attempt by manufacturers and retailers to further collapse sizing by providing garments that have the ability to stretch to fit many figure types and sizes. But one-size-fits-all apparel cannot be expected to accurately fit figure types at either size extreme. Perhaps the more accurate label for these garments is "one size fits most."

Childrenswear. Although the voluntary size standard for **childrenswear** bases sizes on age, you should *never base size selection on the age of the child.* For example, not all children are born the same size, so "newborn size" is a misnomer because some children are born too large to ever wear a "newborn size" garment. Children also grow at widely varying rates, requiring the use of *height* and *weight* rather than age to achieve proper fit. Most manufacturers of childrenswear provide charts on the label or on the package indicating the height and weight ranges that the garment fits. Always purchase clothing for children according to these guidelines rather than the garment's numerical or lettered size.

Childrenswear size classifications overlap somewhat. For example, a 24-month infants' size and a toddlers' size 2 fit approximately the same body dimensions, as do a toddlers' size 4 and a children's size 4. However, the garments differ in the amount of ease and length allowed for the differences in the locomotion of an infant, a toddler, and a child; also, infants' and toddlers' clothing bottoms are cut larger than children's to accommodate the thickness of diapers.

Like adult apparel, childrenswear is increasingly letter sized S, M, L, XL. This is common for garments such as sweaters, knit shirts, sleepwear, and underwear, and for all types of garments in low-price lines.

Infants. Childrenswear begins with **infants'** or **babies' sizes,** for infants from birth to approximately 18 months or when the child is old enough to walk. The voluntary standard size designations range from 3 months to 36 months and correlate with *height* and *weight*. Many retailers carry infants' sizes only up to 24 months (Table 3-3); some carry size 0 for newborns. But remember that age is not a good indicator of size; purchase garments according to the infant's height and weight. Infants' sizes are cut full to accommodate diapers. Lettered sizing for infantwear usually consists of XS, S, M, L, and XL; sometimes *NB* (for newborn) substitutes for XS. Some manufacturers use the lettered size

TABLE 3-3
Infants' sizes

Infants' size	3 mo.	6 mo.	12 mo.	18 mo.	24 mo.
Height	24	26½	29	31½	34
Weight	13	18	22	26	29

designations NB (newborn) and *1B* (1 babies') through *4B* (4 babies').

Toddlers and Children. **Toddlers' sizes** are for the child from 18 months to approximately 3 years of age, the early walking stage. Toddlers are characterized by a short, round figure with an undefined waistline. The voluntary standard sizes range from 1T to 4T, although many retailers carry only sizes 2T to 4T. The sizes correlate with *height* and *weight* (Table 3-4). S, M, L, XL may be used instead of numbered size designations.

TABLE 3-4
Toddlers' sizes

Toddlers' size	2T	3T	4T
Height	34	37	40
Weight	29	34	38

Children's sizes, also known as *preschool, juvenile,* or *little boys'/little girls'* sizes, typically fit children approximately three to six years old. Children are taller and slimmer than toddlers but still have an undefined waistline. The voluntary standard sizes range from 2 to 6, plus 6X. Many childrenswear retailers carry only sizes 4 to 6 plus 6X for girls, and 4 to 7 for boys (borrowing size 7 from boys' sizes). Children's sizes, like infants' and toddlers', correlate with *height* and *weight* (Table 3-5). S, M, L, XL also may be used.

Girls. **Girls' sizes** fit girls approximately 7 to 11 years old. The bustline is undefined and the waistline slightly delineated. The voluntary standard sizes range from 7 to 18, although many retailers carry only 7 to 14. Girls' sizes correlate with *height, chest, waist, and hip* measurements in the voluntary size standard (Table 3-6). It also suggests the body build categories of *slim, regular,* and *chubby.* Manufacturers and retailers usually choose more appealing terms for chubbies; for example, *pretty plus* and *size up.*

Some retailers carry an additional size classification, not included in the voluntary standard. They call this classification *preteen, teen, junior high, subteen,* or *young juniors.* It is designed for girls with a more defined waistline who are not yet ready for junior sizes. These sizes typically run from 6 to 14.

Boys. **Boys' sizes** fit boys approximately 7 to 17 years old. The boys' figure is characterized by developing shoulders and a delineated waistline. Voluntary standard sizes range from 2 to 24, although many retailers carry only the even-numbered sizes 8 to 20. The voluntary size standard correlates boys' sizes to *height, weight, chest, and waist* measurements (Table 3-7). It also suggests the body build categories, *slim, regular,* and *husky.*

Some retailers offer boys' sizes 8 to 14 and an additional size classification for sizes 16 to 20. Not included in the voluntary size standard, they call this size classification *prep, student, teen,* or *cadet* to appeal to bigger boys not yet ready for young men's sizes.

TABLE 3-5
Children's sizes

Children's size	2	3	4	5	6	6X
Height	34	37	40	43	46	48
Weight	29	34	38	44	49	54

TABLE 3-6
Girls' sizes

Girls' size	7	8	10	12	14
Height	51	53	55	57½	60
Weight	60	66	74	84	96
Bust/Chest	26	27	28½	30	31½
Waist	22½	23	24	25	26
Hip	27½	28½	30	32	34

Womenswear. **Womenswear** is clothing for adult females. Womenswear uses a complex sizing system. In theory, womenswear sizes are labeled with numbers that correlate with height, bust, waist, hip, and other measurements. In practice, womenswear sizes vary widely among manufacturers and often bear little correlation to any standard. Perhaps rapid style changes in womenswear from season to season have made attention to sizing a low priority for manufacturers. However, women's former willingness to try on multiple garments to find one that fits may be ending, forcing manufacturers to improve sizing methods.

Outerwear. **Outerwear** refers to clothing seen by others when it is worn; for example, dresses, blouses, pants, skirts, jackets, coats, and sweaters. Outerwear sizes for womenswear fall into four basic categories: (1) *junior,* (2) *misses,* (3) *women's* and (4) *half size.* These size classifications refer to general figure types (Figure 3-4). Ironically, the average "woman" does not wear "women's sizes" but "misses sizes." How-

ever, some manufacturers refer to clothes sized for the average, misses figure as "women's sizes" to differentiate them from "men's sizes." This inconsistent usage further confuses the sizing issue, pointing to the need to rename womenswear size classifications for greater clarity.

Within the four womenswear size classifications, there are sizes used for outerwear, often referred to as **dress sizes.** When someone asks a woman, "What size do you wear?," usually the reference is to her dress size. Most dresses and other outerwear are labeled with these sizes. According to the voluntary size standard, dress sizes correlate with the *bust, waist,* and *hip* measurements in Table 3-8. However, as discussed in the following sections, the industry adheres to the voluntary size standard for womenswear only loosely or not at all.

Outerwear is occasionally sized according to body measurements. *Bottoms* (e.g., pants and skirts) are sometimes labeled with waist or hip measurement. In addition, other factors such as hip shape (slim, average, full) and leg length (short, regular, tall) may be used. *Tops* (e.g.,

TABLE 3-7
Boys' sizes

Boys' size	8	10	12	
Height	50	54	58	
Weight	59	73	87	
Chest	26½	28	29½	
Waist	23½	24½	25½	
Boys' size	14	16	18	20
Height	61	64	66	68
Weight	100	115	126	138
Chest	31½	33	34½	36
Waist	26½	27½	28½	29½

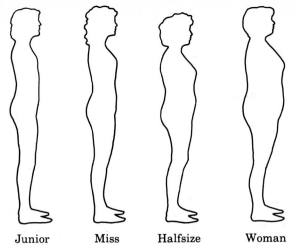

Junior   Miss   Halfsize   Woman

Figure 3-4 *Womenswear figure types and size classifications.*

blouses and sweaters) are sometimes labeled with bust measurement. Some producers use lettered sizing to label outerwear.

MISSES SIZES. **Misses sizes** fit the adult woman of average proportions and average height; they are also commonly referred to as **Missy sizes.** The voluntary standard suggests misses sizes as even numbers from 6 to 22, although many retailers carry only sizes 6 to 14. They often merchandise the larger misses size designations as *large sizes* or *women's sizes* (see next section). Although the smallest standard misses size is 6, it is possible to find sizes 4, 2, and even 0; these may be examples of vanity sizes or efforts to fit women smaller than those included in the standard.

Misses sizes subdivide into **Petites,** for the shorter woman of average proportions. Petites are designated with a *P* after the misses size and typically run from size 2 to 12. **Talls,** for the taller woman of average proportions, are designated with a *T* after the misses size. Clothing for petites and talls should be proportioned and designed to flatter the wearer's height. For example, short jackets and small-scale details flatter the petite figure, whereas long jackets and bold details generally look better on the tall figure.

WOMEN'S SIZES. **Women's sizes** fit the adult woman of average height who has a full, mature figure. Women's sizes feature a longer torso and longer sleeves than misses sizes. The voluntary standard lists women's sizes as even numbers 34 to 52, although these designations are used

to a very limited degree. *Large size* or *women's* departments and specialty stores are increasingly likely to designate women's sizes with what should be misses size designations; for example, even-numbered sizes 16 to 20 or 14 to 24. In such cases, it is unclear whether the garments are designed for a large misses figure type or a true women's figure type—the two do differ slightly. However, you can see how size is a marketing tool as well as a fitting tool. At any rate, large sizes should be designed to flatter the full figure. Some manufacturers produce *tall women's* sizes, and *super women's* sizes (larger than size 52), though these are not divisions of the voluntary size standard.

HALF SIZES. **Half sizes** accommodate the shorter-than-average adult woman who has a full, mature figure. The voluntary standard lists half sizes as even numbers from 12½ to 26½. Half sizes feature a lower, fuller bustline, shorter sleeves, and a higher, larger waistline than misses sizes. They should be designed to flatter the full, short figure. For larger but short women, some manufacturers produce *stout* sizes (for example, sizes 34½ to 52½), though this is not a division of the voluntary size standard.

Few stores promote half sizes or stout sizes because of their somewhat negative connotation. In fact, the use of half sizes is very rare these days. Instead, to appeal to consumers, retailers usually market these sizes as *women's petites* and size them using misses size designations, typically 8 to 16. Women's *petites* generally are merchandised in *large size* or *women's* areas. This use of the word *petite* draws attention to the fact that petite means "short," not "small."

The styling of half size apparel usually reflects the tastes and lifestyles of mature adults, suitable to the majority of wearers. However, there are exceptions, and a younger half-size woman has difficulty finding clothing to reflect her age, in her size.

JUNIOR SIZES. **Junior sizes** fit a short, slender, youthful figure. They feature a higher bustline and a higher waistline than misses sizes. The voluntary standard lists junior sizes as odd numbers from 3 to 17, although many retailers carry only sizes 5 to 13. *Junior Petite* sizes, designated by a *P* after the junior size, are for a woman shorter than the average junior; they are rather rare. A very few manufacturers produce tall junior sizes, designated by a *T* after the junior size.

TABLE 3-8

Womenswear sizes

Misses size	6	8	10	12	14
Bust	31½	32½	33½	35	36½
Waist	22½	23½	24½	26	27½
Hip	33½	34½	35½	37	38½

Misses size	16	18	20	22	
Bust	38	40	42	44	
Waist	29	31	33	35	
Hip	40	42	44	46	

Women's size	34	36	38	40	42
Bust	38	40	42	44	46
Waist	30	32	34	36½	39
Hip	39	41	43	45	47

Women's size	44	46	48	50	52
Bust	48	50	52	54	56
Waist	41½	44	46½	49	51½
Hip	49	51	53	55	57

Half size	12½	14½	16½	18½	
Bust	36	38	40	42	
Waist	28	30	32	34	
Hip	37	39	41	43	

Half size	20½	22½	24½	26½	
Bust	44	46	48	50	
Waist	36½	39	41½	44	
Hip	45	47	49	51	

Junior size	3	5	7	9	
Bust	31	31	32	33	
Waist	20½	21½	22½	23½	
Hip	32	33	34	35	

Junior size	11	13	15	17	
Bust	34½	36	37½	39	
Waist	25	26½	28	29½	
Hip	36½	38	39½	41	

A tall junior size is not a division of the voluntary size standard and, in fact, is a contradiction in terms.

Although it is true that, for example, "Junior is a size, not an age," there is some justifiable stereotyping of size classifications and ages. The majority of junior-size customers are young, so the styling of junior apparel is typically oriented to youthful fashion trends. However, there are exceptions to these generalizations, making it difficult for older junior-size women to find clothing styled appropriately for their age and lifestyle, in their size.

Double ticketing involves labeling clothing with both a junior size and a missy size, for example, 3/4, indicating that it fits either a junior size 3 or a misses size 4. Because there are significant differences in the body types of juniors and misses sizes, it seems unlikely that double-ticketed garments fit both body types equally well unless the garment is one without exacting fit requirements.

Underwear. **Underwear** is clothing worn beneath outerwear. **Lingerie** or **intimate apparel** refers to underwear as well as loungewear and sleepwear. Because it is subject to repeat purchases, and because a smooth, comfortable fit is important, consumers expect consistent fit each time they purchase underwear. And because underwear is a fairly basic item, most manufacturers size it similarly. Low-price line underwear is often labeled with lettered sizing. However, numerical sizing allows an exact fit and is usually used in high-price lines.

Bras are sized by a two-part system. The first part, **bra size,** is a number. It equals the under bust measurement (the rib cage just below the bust) plus 5 or 6 inches, whichever results in an even number (above a 38-inch under bust measurement, add only 3 or 4 inches). The second part, **cup size,** is a letter ranging from *AAA* to *F*. Measure the bust at its fullest point and determine cup size by finding the difference between this measurement and bra size, as shown in Table 3-9. For example, if the bust measurement is 1 inch different from the bra size, the customer requires an A cup; 2 inches, a B cup; 3 inches, a C cup; and so on.

Numbered sizes on panties correlate with hip measurements (Table 3-10). Half slips are sized by waist measurement and length from the waist in inches; full slips by dress size or bra size and length from the waist in inches; and camisoles and sleepwear by dress size or bra

TABLE 3-9

Bra cup sizes

If bust measurement is	Cup size is
same or less than bra size	AAA
up to ½ inch larger than bra size	AA
up to 1 inch larger than bra size	A
up to 2 inches larger than bra size	B
up to 3 inches larger than bra size	C
up to 4 inches larger than bra size	D
up to 5 inches larger than bra size	DD/E
up to 5½ inches larger than bra size	F

size. Girdles are sized by waist measurement and hip development (the difference between waist and hip measurement). The customer has straight hips if they are up to 8 inches larger than her waist, average hips if 8 to 10 inches larger, and full hips if 10 inches or more larger.

Menswear. **Menswear** encompasses clothing for adult males. Men's figures have fully developed shoulders, a tapered waist, and slim hips. Menswear includes **men's clothing** (men's suits, jackets, pants, and coats), **sportswear** (casual separates), and **furnishings** (other items, such as shirts, ties, underwear, sleepwear, and accessories). Most menswear sizing is expressed in terms of body measurements, an example worthy of imitation by womenswear producers. The **men's size** classification includes clothing that fits the average adult man. Because men's numerical sizes are expressed as body measurements, there is no voluntary size standard for menswear.

Men's sizes sometimes use a body build category in addition to the numerical size to indicate the type of figure the garment fits. Examples include *short* for the shorter man; *tall* or *long* for the taller man; *slim* for the slender build; *regular* for the average height and aver-

TABLE 3-10

Womenswear panty sizes

Hip measurement (in inches)	Panty size
33–34	4
35–36	5
37–38	6
39–40	7
41–42	8
43–45	9
46–48	10

age build; and *big, portly,* or *stout* for the full build. However, garments in all these categories are sized using the same system as regular men's sizes, unlike the use of multiple size classifications for womenswear. Lettered sizing is widely used within some men's merchandise classifications, especially sportswear, sweaters, sleepwear, and underwear.

Menswear sizing is considerably more consistent from manufacturer to manufacturer than is womenswear sizing. Granted, men's figures are somewhat more standard than women's, which have more curves. And perhaps the more basic nature of menswear has allowed its manufacturers greater opportunity to perfect sizing. Whatever the reason, menswear is more likely than womenswear to fit as indicated by its labeled size.

Young men's sizes are designed for young men with developing builds. Although a division of the voluntary size standards, in practice they are sized with body measurements just like men's sizes. Young men's sizes contain the smaller men's sizes and reflect the youthful styling generally preferred by young men; they parallel the junior category for young women. They are cut proportionately smaller than men's sizes. Adult men with small statures sometimes experience difficulty in finding clothes appropriate for their age and lifestyle in young men's departments, or clothes their size in men's departments.

Jackets. Men's jacket and coat sizes are based on the wearer's *chest* circumference and his overall *height.* A number denotes the chest measurement, typically an even number ranging from 32 to 50. Most men wear sizes 38 to 44; smaller sizes may be found in young men's and larger sizes in big and tall men's. Most retailers carry jackets with increments of 1 inch in the chest measurement between sizes up to size 44, with 2-inch increments thereafter; some carry only even sizes.

A letter accompanying chest measurement denotes height, with *S* for short, *R* for regular, and *L* for long. Thus, a 42R jacket, the most common size, represents a 42-inch chest and average height. Most retailers carry few shorts because it is easier to shorten garments than to lengthen them.

Pants. Men's pants sizes are based on two numbers. The first number correlates with the wear-

er's *waist* circumference, typically ranging from 32 to 40 inches. Waist sizes smaller than 32 inches are found in young men's and waist sizes larger than 40 inches in big and tall men's. Many retailers stock pants in 1-inch increments in waist measurement between sizes up to size 32, with 2-inch increments thereafter; some stock only even waist sizes. Few are willing to carry the large inventories required to stock every waist size.

The second number in a pants size represents the inseam measurement, typically ranging from 29 to 34 inches. The *inseam* is the length of the seam on the inside of the leg, from the crotch to the hem of the slacks. For example, a size 30/32 denotes a 30-inch waist and a 32-inch inseam. Some pants leave the factory unhemmed to fit a wider range of inseams.

Body build categories may be used to indicate the amount of fullness in the hips and thighs. Pants sizes may also include *rise,* which is the measurement from crotch level to waist level (short, regular, or long; see Chapter 12).

Furnishings. Men's sport shirts are usually sized S, M, L, XL. Short-sleeved dress shirt sizes are based on neck circumference. Long-sleeved dress shirt sizes are based on two numbers, one denoting the wearer's *neck circumference* and the other denoting his *sleeve length.* For example, a 15/34 shirt size indicates a 15-inch neck circumference and a 34-inch sleeve length. Neck sizes typically range from $14\frac{1}{2}$ to 17 inches, with $\frac{1}{2}$-inch increments between sizes. Smaller neck sizes are found in young men's and larger neck sizes in big and tall men's. Sleeve length is measured from the center back of the neck, across the shoulder, along the arm behind the elbow, and to the wrist bone (Figure 3-5). High-quality shirts meet exact standards of sleeve length with 1-inch increments between sleeve lengths, which typically range from 30 to 34 inches (with shorter lengths found in young men's and longer lengths in big and tall men's). So many different neck size/sleeve length combinations require the manufacturer to produce and the retailer to stock many different stock keeping units (SKUs). In low-price lines, shirtmakers often lump sleeve lengths together. For example, a sleeve length of 32/33 denotes that the shirt sleeve fits a man with a sleeve length of either 32 to 33 inches. The manufacturer puts two buttons on the cuff; buttoning the cuff tighter "fits" the shorter sleeve length; buttoning the cuff looser "fits" the longer length (Figure 7-20). This

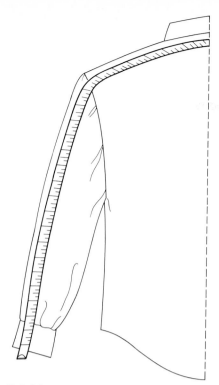

Figure 3-5 *Measuring men's shirt sleeve length.*

TABLE 3-11

Comparison of different sizing systems

Misses Sizes		
U.S. size	*G.B.* size	*Continental* size
6		34
8		36
10	32	38
12	33	40
16	35	42
18	38	44
20	39	48

international trade; they are a practical solution to the size labeling of garments for import and export. They provide meaningful information about size because they are based on body measurements. Some mail-order retailers use pictograms to communicate size or measuring information to consumers in catalogs.

BRAND

A brand name, trademark, or logo on a garment often influences how the consumer perceives the quality of the garment. In some cases, little-known brands provide equal or better quality than well-known brands, but the consumer hesitates to purchase the little-known brand. If a producer builds a deserved reputation for qual-

reduces the number of sizes the manufacturer must produce but provides less exact fit.

Manufacturers size undershirts, sweaters, and pajamas by chest measurement or S, M, L, XL. Undershorts (boxers and briefs) are sized by waist measurement or S, M, L, XL.

International Sizing. Complicating the size issue further, with an increase in the international trade of apparel comes the difficulty of communicating the size of imported and exported garments. Not only does language and the method of sizing vary in different countries, but the U.S. consumer measures the human body in inches and pounds rather than centimeters and kilograms. The three major sizing systems in the world are *U.S. sizes, British sizes,* and *European* or *Continental sizes* (Table 3-11). Most countries size using some variation of these three systems.

Some countries convey size information without words, through **pictograms** (Figure 3-6). The body measurements critical to the fit of the particular garment are indicated on a sketch of the human body. Pictograms overcome language barriers, and they are easy for consumers to understand. At a glance, they give the shopper an idea of whether or not a garment will fit. Expect an increase in the use of pictograms for

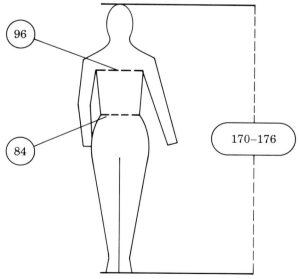

Figure 3-6 *Pictogram size labeling for man's suit. Metric measurements convert to chest girth = 38", waist girth = 33", and height = 5′ 7″ to 5′ 9″.*

ity apparel, a brand name serves as a cue to quality; in other cases, consumers may incorrectly associate a well-known brand name with a certain level of quality, just because it is currently fashionable. Become familiar with brand names and the quality level with which they are generally associated, but evaluate their actual quality objectively (see Related Resources: Brand Name).

National Brands. Manufacturers develop **national brands,** also called **name brands** or **manufacturer's brands,** and make them available to any retailer who wants to buy them for resale to consumers. National brands became dominant in the ready-to-wear industry during the mid- to late-twentieth century. Examples of national (actually international) brand names include Levi's, Esprit, and Liz Claiborne (Table 3-12).

Licensing. Items that bear a famous name are not necessarily designed or manufactured by that individual. Designers and other individuals or companies may **license** their names, trademarks, or logos for use on merchandise produced by others. In a licensing agreement, the individual or company (*licensor*) is paid a fee by a manufacturer (*licensee*) for the privilege of affixing the licensor's name, trademark, or logo to the licensee's products. Licensors may or may not have input into the actual design of such products. However, they are usually concerned about the quality of the merchandise because it is a direct reflection on their name in the eyes of the public. Accessories, fragrances, and home furnishings are examples of products frequently bearing the licensed name of famous apparel designers. In fact, some high-fashion designers make more money from their licensing agreements than from the apparel segment of their business. The names of sports figures, movie and music stars, cartoon characters, and products such as the Coco-Cola and Crayola brands are commonly licensed for use on apparel.

Private Labels. Retailers develop and sell merchandise exclusive to their stores under **private labels** (see Chapter 2). A private label, also called a **private brand** or **store brand,** represents the retailer rather than a manufacturer. In many cases, customers are unaware that a particular private label belongs to the retailer because the names of most private labels sound just like national brands. Examples of private labels include J.C. Penney's Worthington brand of womenswear, The Gap's Gapsport brand of sportswear, and Hartmarx's Hickey-Freeman brand of men's suits. Private labels featuring celebrity endorsements, such as Jaclyn Smith for K-Mart, are referred to as **signature labels** or **signature brands.**

Retailers have a great stake in ensuring the quality of private label merchandise, because consumers associate the quality level of the merchandise with the retailer, not the manufacturer. Retailers retain or lose customers depending on the strength or weakness of their private labels.

Counterfeit Goods. **Counterfeit goods** are fakes or copies of currently popular branded apparel, accompanied by the *illegal* use of the rightful producer's brand name or trademark. Counterfeit goods steal the profits of the legitimate manufacturer, diluting the reputation for quality and reducing the value of the brand name or trademark. If officials detect counterfeit goods, they confiscate the merchandise and prosecute those responsible.

Hang Ten's two feet, Izod's alligator, and Oshkosh B'Gosh, Inc.'s triangle on the back of their

TABLE 3-12

Examples of brand names for various merchandise classifications

Levi's (jeans)
Lee (jeans)
Bali (bras)
Gunne Sax (dresses)
Chaus (women's sportswear)
Leslie Fay (dresses)
Jessica McClintock (bridal)
Campus Casuals (women's sportswear)
Izod (sportswear)
Ocean Pacific (sportswear)
Jockey (underwear)
Hanes (T-shirts)
Pendleton (wools)
Health-tex (children's)
London Fog (raincoats)
Esprit (juniors sportswear)
Vassarette (women's intimate apparel)
Guess (jeans)
Danskin (leotards)
Olga (women's intimate apparel)
Catalina (women's swimwear)
Van Heusen (men's shirts)
Carter's (children's)
Liz Claiborne (sportswear)

overalls are all trademarks, registered with the U.S. Patent and Trademark Office; they cannot be copied legally. Some companies, such as Levi's (known for the trademarked arched stitching on the back pockets of their jeans), Nike (known for the trademarked Swoosh design on the sides of their athletic shoes), and Ocean Pacific (with the registered OP trademark), have resorted to "fingerprinting" their labels. They print them with information that is invisible to the eye but readable by laser, enabling them to easily confirm suspected counterfeit goods bearing look-alike labels (Bender 1984). If you walk the streets of New York City, you will see counterfeit Rolex brand watches, Gucci brand purses, and other counterfeit merchandise sold by street vendors. Many of these goods are produced overseas and sold through nontraditional outlets. However, occasionally a reputable retailer is duped into buying counterfeit merchandise. This happened, for example, during the peak popularity of Calvin Klein brand jeans, when retailers were desperate for the product and some did not investigate their sources.

Knock-Offs. Knock-offs are entirely different from counterfeit goods. A **knock-off** is the copy or near-copy of a design under a different brand name. No law prohibits knocking off a designer's ideas, a common practice in low- and moderate-price lines. Apparel designs are rarely patented or copyrighted; thus, knock-offs are perfectly legal and acceptable. For example, designer Victor Costa readily acknowledges knocking off the evening wear styles of couture designers. He produces his interpretations of the couture originals at a fraction of the cost, making dresses affordable to many. Thus, knock-offs enable consumers at other price levels to enjoy new fashion trends. Firms that specialize in knock-offs often use less costly materials and streamline the design for fabric and labor efficiency, to produce designs resembling the original but at a much lower cost.

CERTIFICATION LABELS

Occasionally, an apparel label contains a **certification,** or seal of approval. This indicates that the garment has met the certifying agency's standards for quality. Usually, no information about the standards is included on the label, only the fact that the certifying agency approved

the garment. Therefore, a certification is only as good as the standards and the reputation of the agency issuing it. Some certifying agencies are independent; others exist to promote a specific fiber. Figure 3-7 contains examples of some well-known certification labels.

The *Woolmark* and the *Woolblend Mark* registered trademarks certify that the wool fibers contained in a garment meet the *Wool Bureau's* standards of quality for fiber content, colorfastness, abrasion resistance, tensile strength, dimensional stability, and other factors. The Wool Bureau also awards its *Superwash* trademark label to washable wool apparel that meets quality standards.

The *Cotton Seal*, a registered trademark of *Cotton Incorporated*, identifies products made in the United States of 100% U.S.-grown cotton.

Woolmark and Woolblend Symbols   Cotton Seal

 Pure Western European Linen. The L Symbol is the registered trademark of the Confederation Internationale du Lin et du Chanvre (CILC).

Figure 3-7 Certification labeling. (Woolmark and Woolblend Mark courtesy of the Wool Bureau. Cotton Seal symbol and NATURAL BLEND symbol courtesy of Cotton Incorporated. The L symbol submitted by the International Linen Promotion Commission. Wear-Dated logo courtesy of Monsanto Chemical Company. Crafted With Pride registered certification mark courtesy of Crafted With Pride in U.S.A. Council.)

The *NATURAL BLEND* trademark identifies products containing a minimum of 60% U.S. cotton. The symbols certify a garment's naturalness and comfort. The Cotton Seal is used only on products sold in the United States.

The *L* trademark symbol of the *Confederation Internationale du Lin et du Chanvre (CILC)* certifies garments made from pure Western European linen and assures customers that the product has passed rigid quality controls. The International Silk Association is currently developing a certification label for silk products.

Wear-Dated, a registered trademark of *Monsanto,* is a seal of approval that indicates the garment, which contains fibers made by Monsanto, has passed a series of laboratory tests. "Wear-Dated Apparel" meets standards for seam strength, colorfastness, shrinkage, and abrasion resistance. Monsanto fully guarantees the garment, not just the fabric, for one year.

The U.S. apparel industry promotes domestically made apparel by drawing attention to country of origin and relating it to quality. The impetus for promotional "Made in the U.S.A." labeling resulted from surveys that suggested a majority of consumers perceive U.S.-made apparel to be of higher quality than foreign-made apparel (see Related Resources: Crafted With Pride). Several of these studies also suggested that many U.S. consumers did not notice country of origin labels when shopping. This prompted the implementation of advertising to focus consumer attention on country of origin in order to capitalize on some consumers' expressed preferences for domestically produced goods and to enhance the image of U.S.-made goods in the eyes of others. The **Crafted With Pride in the U.S.A.** registered certification mark campaign is the work of the *Crafted With Pride in U.S.A. Council.* It appeals to the patriotism of consumers as well as to their desire for value (Figure 3-7). The Crafted With Pride in U.S.A. Council also coordinates the advertisement of Miss America's and other celebrities' endorsements of U.S.-made apparel, featuring the theme, *Made in the U.S.A.—It Matters to Me* and *What a Feeling—Made in the U.S.A.* Evidence suggests that since the Crafted With Pride campaign began, the amount of attention consumers pay to country of origin labeling has increased, and so have sales.*

* For more information, contact the Crafted With Pride in U.S.A. Council, 1045 Avenue of the Americas, New York, NY 10018.

UNION LABELS

Union labels are sewn into garments produced in **union shops,** or factories where the workers are union members. Union labels indicate that a garment was produced under fair labor practices as defined by the union. They offer assurance that the workers who made the garment were not mistreated or misused, as sometimes happens in apparel factories around the world where employees have few rights. And union labels represent the union members' pride in their work. According to consumers' attitudes toward labor unions, union labels affect their perceptions of a garment's quality.

Unions arose out of the factory system in the United States during the early part of the twentieth century. The factories that sprang up to meet the rising demand for ready-to-wear apparel in the late 1800s and early 1900s often operated as **sweatshops.** The factory owner reaped profits from the sweat of the workers, many of whom were newly arrived immigrants, both children and adults. Many owners took advantage of workers, who had few other employment options. People were overworked and underpaid in crowded, poorly lit, unsafe, and unsanitary conditions.

Labor unions were formed in the 1800s to organize apparel workers, but invariably were small, isolated, and weak local entities that did not succeed in winning rights for workers. The first national union, the **International Ladies Garment Workers Union,** or **ILGWU,** was founded in 1900, uniting the many small unions into one powerful organization that today fights for and wins rights for apparel factory workers. In 1914, a union formed to represent workers in the men's ready-to-wear industry. This union later merged with unions in the textile and shoe industries to become the **Amalgamated Cloth-**

Figure 3-8 *Union labels. (Courtesy of International Ladies Garment Workers Union and Amalgamated Clothing and Textile Workers Union.)*

ing and Textile Workers Union of America, or **ACTWU.** Figure 3-8 shows the labels of the ILGWU and the ACTWU.

Summary

The information on apparel labels provides an important tool for evaluating apparel quality. Responsible manufacturers and retailers provide accurate and informative labels; good consumers express their concern about labels that are inaccurate or inadequate.

Federal laws require certain label information on all apparel products. Labels fulfilling the Textile Fiber Products Identification Act disclose the garment's fiber content, manufacturer, and country of origin. Labels list the fiber content by percentage in order of predominance by weight. The manufacturer's name, registered trademark, or RN (registered number)/WPL (Wool Products Labeling) number. The country where the garment was last substantially transformed is listed as the country of origin, and the origin of the fabric, if different, also must be disclosed. The Care Labeling Rule requires the manufacturer to suggest a suitable care method for the garment. Only one method need be suggested, but the manufacturer should have a reasonable basis for it. Consumers should follow the care label, not make a judgment about how to care for the garment based on fiber content. Standard terms for care labeling aid in writing consistent instructions. Optional care symbols help overcome language barriers in communicating suggested care methods. The Wool Products Labeling Act and Fur Products Labeling Act provide for accurate labeling of those products.

Some label information on garments is voluntary. Voluntary labels include size, brand, certification, and union labels. These labels help consumers gain additional information about the garment and help retailers sell the garment.

Size labeling is very important to most consumers, but there is no legislation controlling it. Most manufacturers loosely base their current size labeling on the U.S. voluntary size standards that were withdrawn in 1983. Childrenswear sizes are divided into infants', toddlers', children's, girls', and boys' categories. Use height and weight charts and body measure-ments when buying childrenswear. Womenswear sizes are divided into four basic categories, misses, women's, half sizes, and junior. The numerical sizes within these categories correlate to body measurements. Men's sizes are usually expressed as body measurements, making them more consistent and meaningful to consumers than are women's sizes. For example, jacket sizes are based on chest measurement and height, shirt sizes on neck circumference and sleeve length, and pants sizes on waist measurement and inseam.

Lettered sizing (S, M, L, XL) is used in many apparel categories. It is more suitable to knit garments and those not requiring an exact fit than for woven and tailored garments, where it is found only in low-price lines. Lettered sizing eliminates fine differences in sizing but is economical because it requires the production of fewer sizes.

There is widespread inconsistency in apparel sizing from manufacturer to manufacturer, especially in womenswear. However, the answer to sizing problems lies not in standardization but in expressing sizes in terms of the body measurements the garment fits. Pictograms help explain this relationship visually. Manufacturers and retailers who develop consistent and meaningful size labeling satisfy consumer expectations in the search for garments that fit.

Label Quality Checklist

If you can answer yes to the following questions regarding garments you evaluate, they meet mandatory labeling requirements.

- Are fibers identified by their generic name, in order of predominance by weight?
- If the trademark name of the fiber is used, does it appear on the same side of the label and in the same size type as the generic name?
- Is the manufacturer of the garment identified by name, registered trademark, and/or registered number (RN or WPL)?
- Is the country of origin identified on the label?
- If the garment is made of wool, is the type of wool identified according to the Wool Products Labeling Act?

- If the garment is made of fur, is the type of fur identified according to the Fur Products Labeling Act?
- Does the label clearly specify the washing, bleaching, drying, ironing, and/or dry cleaning method that should be followed to care for the garment?
- Does the suggested care method have a reasonable basis?
- In infants' or childrens' sleepwear, sizes 0–6X or 7–14, does the label warn against care procedures that damage the flame resistant finish on the garment? Does the label contain a GPU and FPU number?

If you can answer yes to the following questions regarding the garment you are evaluating, the labels contain voluntary information.

- Does the care label have sure care symbols?
- Does the garment feature a national brand or private brand label?
- Does the garment have a certification or seal of approval label?
- Does the garment have a union label?
- Does the garment have a size label, preferably one that relates to the body measurements it fits?
- Are pictograms used to explain the garment's dimensions as they relate to body measurements?
- For high quality, is the label woven cloth, not printed paper?
- For high quality, is the label stitched in, not glued on?

New Terms

If you can define each of these terms and differentiate between related terms, you have gained a good working vocabulary for discussing the topics in this chapter. The terms are listed in the order in which they appear in the chapter.

label
Textile Fiber Products Identification Act (TFPIA)
generic name
trademark
registered identification number (RN)
country of origin
Wool Products Labeling Act (WPLA)
Fur Products Labeling Act (FPLA)
Care Labeling Rule
reasonable basis
low labeling
sure care symbols
International Standards Organization (ISO)
American National Standards Institute (ANSI)
Flammable Fabrics Act
size
size classification
vanity sized
lettered sizing
one-size-fits-all sizing
childrenswear
infants'/babies' sizes
toddlers' sizes
children's sizes
girls' sizes
boys' sizes
womenswear
outerwear
dress size
misses/missy sizes
petites
talls
women's sizes
half sizes
junior sizes
double ticketing
underwear
lingerie/intimate apparel
bra size
cup size
menswear
men's clothing
sportswear
furnishings
men's sizes
young men's sizes
pictograms
national/name/manufacturer's brand
license
private label/private or store brand
signature label/brand
counterfeit goods
knock-off
certification
Crafted With Pride in the U.S.A.
union shop

sweatshop
International Ladies' Garment Workers Union
  (ILGWU)
Amalgamated Clothing and Textile Workers
  Union of America (ACTWU)

Review Questions

1. What perceptions about a garment's quality do consumers form, based on labels?

2. What label information is required on all garments sold in the United States? What information is voluntary?

3. Explain the specifics of the Textile Fiber Products Identification Act for disclosing the fiber content of a garment.

4. Discuss the purpose and requirements of country of origin labeling.

5. What are the specific requirements of the Care Labeling Rule?

6. Who enforces federally mandated apparel labeling?

7. Why should consumers follow care labels rather than choosing a care method of their own?

8. What information does a certification label or seal of approval provide?

9. Name the two major unions representing apparel factory workers.

10. What is the main problem with apparel sizing? What is the solution?

11. Discuss the advantages and disadvantages of lettered sizing (S, M, L, XL) versus numerical sizing.

12. List and describe the four size classifications of women's outerwear.

13. List the body part/parts that are measured to size the following women's garments: dresses, coats, blouses, skirts, pants, bras, panties, girdles, full slips, half slips, and sleepwear.

14. List the body part/parts that are measured to size the following men's garments: jackets, slacks, shirts, sweaters, undershirts, and undershorts.

15. What are the major size classifications of childrenswear?

Activities

1. Examine the labels of ten different garments in your closet or in a retail store for conformance to the TFPIA and the Care Labeling Rule. Do you find any violations? If so, explain.

2. Write a letter to a manufacturer telling of your dissatisfaction with the care label directions on a garment they produced that you purchased. Support your argument with facts from the Care Labeling Rule.

3. Survey five friends. Which do they think is of higher quality, apparel made in the United States or in other countries? Have them name three countries that come to mind when you mention high-quality apparel and three countries that come to mind when you mention low-quality apparel. What are the perceptions of your friends regarding the relationship between quality and country of origin?

4. Survey five friends. Do they always, sometimes, or never read care labels before purchasing apparel? Does the care label influence their likelihood of purchasing the garment? Do they always read the care label before caring for a garment? Do they always follow the suggested care procedure on the label? In your opinion, how could they improve their use of care labels?

5. Examine children's sleepwear in a store or catalog. What information about flammability is provided?

6. Visit an apparel manufacturer. Ask:
   a. what testing is done to ensure accurate labeling
   b. what kind of labels are used (woven/printed/paper/cloth)
   c. how labels are attached
   d. what labeling concerns the manufacturer has
Or write to the Federal Trade Commission and obtain a copy of the publication "Writing a Care Label."

7. Measure three garments of the same numbered or lettered size and the same general style, but different brands. Take measurements in each area of the garment that is important for good fit. Compare the measurements of the three garments and explain any differences you find.

8. Visit a department store. Compare the number of national brands versus the amount of private label merchandise. Does the ratio vary from department to department?

9. Visit a department store or look at a mass merchandiser's catalog. How are size classifications used as a marketing tool? How did they influence store or catalog layout?

10. Using a child you know, compare the size indicated by their age to the size indicated by their height and weight. Why should height and weight be used rather than age to decide on a child's size?

4

Fabric: The Essential Quality Indicator

CHAPTER OBJECTIVES

1. Explain how fabric quality is evaluated.

2. Define the fabric performance features that affect garment performance.

3. Review the physical features of fabrics: fibers, yarns, fabrication, dyes, prints, and finishes.

4. Discuss the impact of a fabric's physical features on fabric performance.

Of all the components used to produce ready-to-wear, fabric makes the greatest single contribution to the cost and quality of a garment (Cole 1983). There is a direct correlation between fabric quality and apparel quality (Mehta 1985). Although high-quality fabric does not guarantee a high-quality garment, fabric provides a foundation for quality. The fabric interacts with other garment components and with the design and construction of the garment to affect overall quality. Therefore, the evaluation of fabric is integral to assessing apparel quality.

Although this chapter is no substitute for a basic textiles course, it serves as a review of the physical features and associated performance features of fabrics. And it relates fabric features to garment performance (see Related Resources: Fabric).

Fabric Performance

Fabric is the textile material from which manufacturers produce ready-to-wear. The performance of the fabric does not necessarily predict the performance of the finished garment, but the two are strongly related. The right fabric is required for the garment to meet aesthetic and functional performance expectations. Manufacturers establish the required aesthetic and functional performance standards for a fabric based on the design of the garment, the intended end use of the garment, and on fashion trends, consumer preferences, and cost limitations. For example, a loose, flowing design calls for a fluid fabric. A garment that receives heavy wear requires a durable fabric. Consumers may favor either knits or wovens, depending on current trends.

ESTABLISHING FABRIC SPECIFICATIONS

The apparel manufacturer purchases fabrics from the textile mill according to required specifications. Specifying performance standards for the fabric or the desired physical features of the fabric communicates expectations to the textile mill. In the absence of clearly defined specifications, the apparel manufacturer is likely to receive fabrics that do not meet desired standards. Many manufacturers establish and enforce fabric specifications according to the *Worth Street Textile Market Rules*.* The Worth Street Rules establish the procedures for buying and selling textiles by defining specifications and tolerances for standard types of fabric.

ASTM and AATCC Standards. The American Society for Testing and Materials (ASTM) and the American Association of Textile Chemists and Colorists (AATCC) publish standard test methods for quantifying the functional performance of textile fibers, yarns, fabrics, and finishes (see Appendix A). Some manufacturers use these tests to check samples of the piece goods they receive for conformance to specifications. For example, is the fabric as strong as

specified? Some retailers perform tests on the finished garment to ensure that it meets their specifications. The specification of ASTM and AATCC standards enables textile mills and manufacturers to clearly communicate in the same "language" about performance requirements for fabrics and some other garment components such as thread and zippers.**

ASTM's Committee D-13 on Textiles has established performance expectations for fabrics used in some types of garments (Table 4-1). Manufacturers and fabric suppliers use these guidelines to establish specifications for and to evaluate the quality of fabrics intended for certain end uses.

KES and Fast. Apparel manufacturers are interested in a fabric's *ease of production*. Producers avoid many construction difficulties that detract from the garment's quality through an informed choice of fabrics and an advanced awareness of fabric properties. The ease or difficulty with which the manufacturer cuts, sews, presses, dyes, finishes, and packages a garment influences both quality and costs. For example, it is difficult to produce a garment from a fabric with a slick surface. Such a fabric causes production difficulties and requires extra time, skilled operators, and/or special equipment to achieve good results. Weak fabrics and fabrics that ravel pose additional production problems. Because of the effect on manufacturing costs and quality, a fabric's ease of production ultimately affects the consumer in the form of the retail price paid and value received.

In an effort to quantify the statement of difficult-to-measure fabric performance specifications, Sueo Kawabata of Japan developed the **Kawabata Evaluation System for Fabrics (KES)** (Fortess 1985). The KES can be used to objectively rate fabric properties, both aesthetic and functional. These ratings describe aesthetic dimensions that were formerly described only subjectively. Kawabata developed KES by correlating the physical measurements of various fabric attributes to the subjective perceptions of human judges. The KES ratings predict the suitability of a fabric for mass manufacturing, in-

---

* *Worth Street Textile Market Rules* is available for about $6 from the **American Textile Manufacturers Institute (ATMI)**, 1101 Connecticut Avenue, N.W., Washington, DC 20036.

** *Annual Book of ASTM Standards* on Textiles is available for about $142 from American Society for Testing and Materials (ASTM), 1916 Race Street, Philadelphia, PA 19103-1187. *AATCC Technical Manual* is available for about $69 from American Association of Textile Chemists and Colorists (AATCC), P.O. Box 12215, Research Triangle Park, NC 27709.

TABLE 4-1

Fabric performance specifications available from American Society for Testing and Materials (ASTM)

Specifications for	End Use
D 4110-82	Bathrobe, Dressing Gown, and Pajama Fabrics, Knitted, Men's and Boys'
D 3784-81	Bathrobe and Dressing Gown Fabrics, Woven, Men's and Boys'
D 4154-83	Beachwear and Sport Shirt Fabrics, Knitted and Woven, Men's and Boys'
D 4235-83	Blouse and Dress Fabrics, Knitted, Women's and Girls'
D 4233-83	Brassiere Fabrics, Knitted and Woven, Women's and Girls'
D 4232-83	Career Apparel Fabrics, Dress and Vocational, Men's and Women's
D 3995-81	Career Apparel Fabrics, Knitted, Dress, and Vocational, Men's and Women's
D 3781-79	Coat Fabrics, Knitted Rainwear and All-Purpose, Water-Repellent, Men's and Boys'
D 3779-81	Coat Fabrics, Woven Rainwear and All-Purpose, Water-Repellent, Women's and Girls'
D 4116-82	Corset-Girdle Combination Fabrics, Knitted and Woven, Women's and Girls'
D 4109-82	Coverall, Dungaree, Overall, and Shop Coat Fabrics, Woven, Men's and Boys'
D 4118-82	Coverall, Dungaree, Overall, and Shop Coat Fabrics, Woven, Women's
D 4038-88	Dress and Blouse Fabrics, Woven, Women's and Girls'
D 3778-88	Dress Coat Fabrics, Dry-cleanable Woven, Women's and Girls'
D 4115-82	Dress Glove Fabrics, Knitted and Woven, Women's and Girls'
D 3477-84	Dress Shirt Fabrics, Woven, Men's and Boys'
D 4119-82	Dress Shirt Fabrics, Knitted, Men's and Boys'
D 3782-79	Dress Suit Fabrics and Sportswear Jacket, Slack, and Trouser Fabrics, Knitted, Men's and Boys'
D 3780-88	Dress Suit Fabrics and Sportswear Jacket, Slack, and Trouser Fabrics, Woven, Men's and Boys'
D 3562-83	Dress Topcoat and Dress Overcoat Fabrics, Woven, Men's and Boys'
D 4522-86	Feather-Filled and Down-Filled Products
D 3783-88	Flat Lining Fabrics, Woven, for Men's and Boys' Apparel
D 4114-82	Flat Lining Fabrics, Woven, Women's and Girls' Apparel
D 4153-82	Handkerchief Fabrics, Woven, Men's, Women's, and Children's
D 4035-81	Necktie and Scarf Fabrics, Knitted
D 3785-81	Necktie and Scarf Fabrics, Woven
D 3655-81	Overcoat and Jacket Fabrics, Sliver Knitted, Men's and Women's
D 3819-88	Pajama Fabrics, Woven, Men's and Boys'
D 4234-83	Robe, Negligee, Nightgown, Pajama, Slip, and Lingerie Fabrics, Knitted, Women's and Girls'
D 4117-82	Robe, Negligee, Nightgown, Pajama, Slip, and Lingerie Fabrics, Woven, Women's and Girls'
D 4156-83	Sportswear Fabrics, Knitted, Women's and Girls'
D 4155-83	Sportswear, Shorts, Slacks, and Suiting Fabrics, Woven, Women's and Girls'
D 3782-79	Sportswear Jacket, Slack, and Trouser Fabrics, Dress Suit Fabrics, Knitted, Men's and Boys'
D 3996-81	Swimwear Fabrics, Knit, Men's, Women's, and Children's
D 3994-88	Swimwear Fabrics, Woven
D 3820-88	Underwear Fabrics, Woven, Men's and Boys'

cluding its ease of construction and the finished appearance of garments made from it. However, KES is a complex system of tests requiring considerable time, equipment, and training.

An Australian system called **Fabric Assessment by Simple Testing (FAST)** has been drawing a lot of attention as a less costly alternative to KES. FAST measures only four main fabric characteristics critical to garment appearance and performance. The fabric is tested for these four factors: compression, bending, extension, and dimensional stability (these terms are defined later in the chapter). The tests require a minimum of time, equipment, and training. FAST can be used to estimate a fabric's hand and tailorability based on a computer's interpretation of the test results; thus, it is an economical approach. FAST helps manufacturers identify potential problems with fabrics and avoid costly fabric pitfalls such as seam pucker by testing a sample of the fabric before purchasing it. Preliminary data show FAST to be a satisfactory method, although not as sophisticated and detailed as the KES (Rees 1990).

KES and FAST are crucial to the advancement of automated apparel production, which depends on the ability to identify unique fabric characteristics and then to engineer robots to handle them. Both KES and FAST are experimental, and only a few manufacturers have adopted them. But as the systems become more widely used by manufacturers, subjectivity in fabric selection will be replaced by objective instrumental testing. In the meantime, the specification of many fabric characteristics remains relatively imprecise.

Defects. Most apparel manufacturers inspect incoming fabrics or **piece goods** for defects. Defects detract from the aesthetic appearance of a garment and sometimes from its functional performance. Common fabric flaws include broken, knotted, or thick yarns; *barré* (streaks), foreign material, spots, soil, and holes. Other defects include bowing and skewing; shading; and prints that are smudged, off-grain, or out of registration (these terms are defined later in the chapter). The *put-up,* or amount of fabric on a roll, also is verified.

Some manufacturers make no attempt to cut around flaws. Instead, they inspect the finished garments and reject those with serious defects. Other manufacturers *flag* or mark defects and cut around them. The monotony of manual fabric inspection often fatigues the inspector, who may then overlook defects. Some firms use computerized fabric inspection systems for smooth-surface, solid-color fabrics. Computerized scanning equipment detects fabric defects and marks them with metallic flags. Electronic spreading equipment detects the metallic flags so the fabric flaws can be placed in between pattern pieces or where they will not be noticeable in the finished garment.

Manufacturers of high-price apparel may consider any fabric defect unacceptable in the finished garment. Manufacturers of low-and moderate-price garments may accept minor flaws and flaws located in low-visibility areas. For example, a flaw in the shirttail is less objectionable than one on the collar or chest.

Low-visibility areas include seam and hem allowances, facings and linings, and near the crotch of pants and the underarm of sleeves.

A number of fabric grading systems are used in the industry, including the *Ten Point System,* the *Graniteville System,* and the *Four Point System,* all of which serve as methods to quantify the number and severity of fabric defects found during an inspection. The **Four Point System** is the most popular fabric rating system used in the apparel industry; it is endorsed by the American Society for Quality Control and the U.S. Government. The system is used to assign penalty points to a fabric based on the number and size of defects. A fabric that receives four or fewer points per linear yard (or 40 points per 100 yards) is typically considered first quality. A fabric receives more points if it has more and/or more serious defects compared with a fabric that receives fewer points. Manufacturers producing high-price apparel usually specify fabrics with fewer points per 100 yards than do manufacturers of low-price apparel. If manufacturers detect more points per 100 yards than were specified, they may return the substandard fabric to the textile mill and try to acquire replacement goods in time to keep up with the production schedule. Or the manufacturer may use the low-quality fabric "as is" because of a lack of time to acquire replacement goods. The latter results in inferior-quality finished garments. If these garments are sold as first-quality, they risk damaging the manufacturer's reputation.

Some apparel manufacturers accept fabric ratings from trusted suppliers; the textile mill rates the fabric and communicates the fabric's rating to the apparel manufacturer. This enables the manufacturer to send piece goods of known quality straight to the cutting table upon receipt, eliminating the costs of inspecting the fabric a second time.

AESTHETIC PERFORMANCE OF FABRIC

The aesthetic performance or attractiveness of a fabric refers to the appearance of the fabric as it complements the appearance of the garment. Fabric plays an important part in the aesthetic performance of the garment. However, fabric must be considered in concert with the design and construction of the garment because design, materials, and construction interact to produce the total aesthetic effect of the garment.

Fabric aesthetics include color, pattern, color

consistency, luster, opacity, and hand. All these elements of the aesthetic performance of a fabric are difficult to describe because of their subjective nature; they do not lend themselves to objective measurement. For example, it is more difficult to accurately specify the luster of a fabric than the strength of a fabric.

Color and Pattern. Color is perhaps the single most important feature in initially attracting consumers to garments. Manufacturers request fabric samples to consider various colored and patterned fabrics. **Lab dips** are fabric samples that illustrate the possible colorations from which the manufacturer can choose. However, the "beauty" or "goodness" of a color or pattern is subjective; there are no laboratory tests for evaluating the "quality" of colors or choosing the "best" design for a patterned fabric. The aesthetic evaluation of color and pattern depends on fashion trends, personal preferences, and an awareness of design elements and principles.

Color Consistency. Achieving *color consistency* within the same garment or ensemble is important. However, manufacturers find it understandably difficult to buy or dye fabrics, trims, buttons, zippers, belts, and other components—all of different raw materials—to match. For example, dyeing an acrylic knit dress and a leather belt to match requires the formulation of different dyes to produce the same color in each item.

Color consistency of fabric within the same garment or outfit is also important. Fabric producers can dye only a limited number of yards of fabric in each batch or **dye lot.** Although they make every effort to exactly duplicate the dye "recipe" each time, there are slight shade differences from dye lot to dye lot. Producers number each dye lot to differentiate it from other dye lots. After dyeing, the producer usually inspects the fabric under strong light, and fabrics of the same shade are grouped together into matching **shade lots.** This is done manually by human experts or automatically by computerized optical scanners. Preferably, apparel manufacturers cut all the parts of a garment or coordinated outfit from the same dye lot, but at the very least cut them from the same shade lot.

Shading refers to the absence of color consistency, when parts of garments or outfits differ slightly in color from one another. Shading results when the manufacturer cuts various parts

of the same garment or outfit from rolls of fabric dyed in different dye lots. Lines built on the modular dressing concept (for example, the Units and Multiples brands) present special challenges to maintaining color consistency. Coordinating garments purchased months apart or in different stores are expected to match, even though they come from different dye lots. Manufacturers of these lines must pay special attention to shading from batch to batch. However, even within the same dye lot or same piece of fabric there may be differences in shade caused by uneven dyeing.

Shading can be subtle or noticeable, depending upon its severity. If the sleeve of a garment is from a different dye lot than the body of the garment, or if the pants of a suit are cut from a different dye lot than the jacket, even a slight difference in fabric shade is noticeable in the finished garment or outfit. Shading detracts from the appearance of a garment, especially if it appears at a focal point like a front band, yoke, collar, or sleeve (Figure 4-1).

Garment pieces from the same dye lot or shade lot must be stamped, stickered, or otherwise marked after cutting so that operators sew only pieces of the same shade together. You occasionally see stickers for this purpose inside garments at the point of sale if the manufacturer does not remove them. Some makers of better goods attach hang tags with dye lot numbers to finished garments so consumers can select coordinated separates of the same shade.

Dichroism occurs when light strikes the fab-

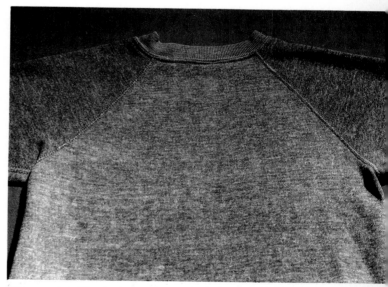

Figure 4-1 *Shading evident in body and sleeves of sweatshirt.*

ric differently from one end to the other, causing a difference in shade. Corduroy, velvet, and other napped fabrics display *end-to-end shading* of this type (Figure 4-12).

Metamerism refers to the apparent change in a color due to a change in lighting. For example, colors appear different in daylight than they do under incandescent or fluorescent light; components that appear to match under one light may clash under different lighting. This makes it difficult to control color consistency because consumers wear their clothing in many different types of lights. Manufacturers can minimize the effects of metamerism through careful dye selection. To be on the safe side, however, they recommend that consumers match colors under the type of light in which the clothes will be worn.

Most fabrics have a definite *face* (front or *right side*) and *back* (*wrong side*). However, some fabrics must be examined closely to differentiate the two. If this difference is not observed when the fabric is spread, cut, and sewn, some or all of the garment pieces may be sewn together with the wrong side of the fabric on the outside of the garment. This can cause shading in the finished garment.

Luster. *Luster* is the amount of light the fabric reflects. Terms such as *dull, matte,* and *diffused* refer to fabrics with little or no luster; *shiny* and *lustrous* refer to those with high luster. Fabrics with smooth, flat surfaces tend to have great luster because a flat surface reflects more light than a surface with contours.

Opacity. The *opacity* of a fabric refers to the amount of light that passes through it; opacity affects the appearance of the finished garment. Fabrics that have high light permeability and can be seen through are *sheer.* Fabrics that have low light permeability and cannot be seen through are *opaque.* Fabrics that have medium light permeability but cannot be clearly seen through are *translucent.* Fabrics with inadequate opacity for the end use of the garment require a lining or should not be used.

Hand. **Hand** is a broad term for the *kinesthetic* or movement aspects of a fabric. Hand refers not to the comfort but to the emotional sensations resulting from touching, moving, or squeezing the fabric with the human hand. Because of the difficulty in quantifying emotions, Kawabata concentrated on quantifying hand when he de-

veloped his evaluation system. The KES makes an invaluable contribution in this area because the hand of a fabric is critical to ease of garment production and to the aesthetic and functional performance of the finished garment. Apparel producers require the ability to equate various fabric hands with ease of production and to objectively specify fabric hand. Hand encompasses the following aspects of the fabric.

1. *Drapability/flexibility* or ease of bending, from *pliable/limp/fluid* (high) to *firm/stiff/crisp* (low). Drapability is the aspect perhaps most nearly synonymous with the concept of hand. It refers to how easily the fabric bends, and consequently how it hangs, falls, clings, flows, sags, pleats, or gathers. Drapability is one of the most important characteristics of a fabric in achieving the desired design effect in the finished garment. The amount of drapability desirable in a fabric depends upon the garment design. For instance, tailored suits demand firm, crisp fabrics. Other designs, such as cowl necklines or harem pants, depend upon soft, drapable fabrics for the desired effect.

2. *Compressibility* or ease of squeezing, from *soft* (high) to *hard* (low).

3. *Extensibility* or ease of stretching, from *stretchy* (high) to *nonstretchy* (low).

4. *Resilience* or ability to recover from deformation, from *springy/alive* (high) to *limp* (low).

5. *Density* or weight per volume, from *compact* (high) to *loose/open* (low).

6. *Surface contour/texture* or variation in the surface, from *rough/coarse* (high) to *smooth* (low).

7. *Surface friction/texture* or surface resistance to slipping, from *harsh* (high) to *slippery* (low).

8. *Thermal character* or apparent temperature, from *cool* (high) to *warm* (low) (Annual Book of ASTM Standards 1989).

FUNCTIONAL PERFORMANCE OF FABRIC

The functional performance of a fabric refers to its utility and durability as a component of the garment. Utility includes the influence of the fabric on these garment characteristics: (1) shape retention, (2) appearance retention, (3) comfort, (4) ease of care, and (5) safety. Durability refers to the serviceability of the fabric regarding these characteristics of the garment:

(1) strength, (2) abrasion resistance, and (3) degradation by chemicals and other elements of the environment.

As for aesthetic performance, the functional performance of a garment is not determined fully by the fabric. The design, materials, and construction of a garment interact to determine utility and durability. For example, although fabric provides warmth, so can the design (a high collar to keep wind off the neck). And although fabric influences serviceability, so can construction (strong stitches and seams).

Dimensional Stability. One of the most important performance characteristics of a garment is **dimensional stability,** the ability to maintain original shape and size. Dimensional stability affects the function of the garment in terms of appearance retention and fit; for close-fitting garments it also affects comfort. Producing dimensionally stable garments, especially knitwear, is one of the big challenges for the textile and apparel industry; many garments shrink or stretch in use.

Elongation and Elasticity. If a fabric is extensible, it *elongates* or *stretches* in use. Permanent stretch occurs if the fabric does not return to its original dimensions. *Elasticity* or *memory,* the fabric's ability to return to its original size after being stretched, helps maintain the garment's appearance. Elasticity is associated with quality, especially in knit fabrics. Without elasticity, garments stretch out of shape and remain stretched. Some garments stretch during wear and do not recover; for example, jackets with sagging elbows and pants with sagging knees exhibit a lack of elasticity. Other garments stretch when laundered; to avoid stretching they may require dry cleaning, or hand washing and *blocking* (arranging garment to original shape and size and allowing it to dry flat).

Shrinkage. Shrinkage occurs when a garment becomes smaller, usually when it is laundered. Shrinkage is a major cause of consumer dissatisfaction because it not only affects the appearance of the garment but makes it uncomfortable and sometimes unwearable. Consumers have come to expect certain garments, for example 100% cotton blue jeans, sweatshirts, and T-shirts, to shrink when laundered (Figure 4-2). Many consumers attempt to compensate for shrinkage by purchasing an overly large garment so it will fit after laundering. But how

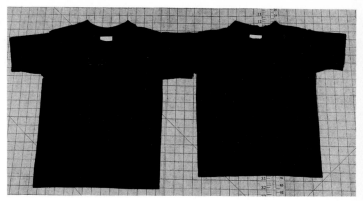

Figure 4-2 T-shirts before and after multiple launderings. Laundered T-shirt exhibits shrinkage and loss of color.

much will the garment shrink? The consumer can only guess. Some manufacturers provide consumers with the results of shrinkage testing on the label, for example, "Guaranteed not to shrink more than 2%." People in the apparel industry recognize that a 2 to 3 percent change in a garment of woven fabric, or a 3 to 5 percent change in a garment of knit fabric, represents a change of one full size. However, the percentage of shrinkage is not useful to the average consumer. A more meaningful guideline in obtaining the desired fit is, for example, "Guaranteed not to shrink more than one-half inch in length." The law does not require apparel labels to disclose shrinkage, but if they state that the garment is preshrunk, they are required to provide the maximum percentage of *residual shrinkage* (the remaining potential shrinkage).

Shrinkage results from either relaxation shrinkage or felting shrinkage. The majority of shrinkage in apparel is *relaxation shrinkage.* Fabrics are gradually stretched as they are produced or as the garment is produced. As the fabric gradually relaxes to its original dimensions when the garment is washed and dried, relaxation shrinkage occurs. Relaxation shrinkage is the main reason why cotton fabrics tend to shrink; for example, the T-shirts in Figure 4-2. The cotton fiber is easily elongated during processing. When a garment is made from a cotton fabric that has been stretched and has not been treated to prevent shrinkage, relaxation shrinkage occurs. Because they are more easily stretched in production, knit fabrics are subject to two to three times more relaxation shrinkage when laundered than are wovens (Hudson 1988).

The problem with relaxation shrinkage is that it does not occur until after the garment is worn and laundered. Therefore, consumers cannot predict it at the point of sale. Although it is difficult to prevent relaxation shrinkage entirely, quality-conscious apparel manufacturers avoid stretching fabrics during production. For example, after spreading a knit fabric, some manufacturers allow it to relax overnight before cutting. Unscrupulous manufacturers or contractors may purposely stretch a fabric before cutting it to yield more garments, resulting in severe relaxation shrinkage. Unfortunately, the problem does not become evident until the garments are worn and laundered.

Felting shrinkage occurs when fibers mat together because of moisture, heat, and/or agitation. This form of shrinkage is common in wool fabrics. Felting may cause a garment to shrink to half its original size, and the process is largely irreversible. Felting can be prevented by certain finishing processes.

Most shrinkage is *progressive*; although the first laundering causes the majority of shrinkage, additional shrinkage continues to occur in subsequent launderings. It is difficult for the manufacturer to control progressive shrinkage. However, fabrics or garments may be preshrunk so that the garment does not shrink much when the consumer wears and cares for it.

Some manufacturers predict shrinkage and oversize garments, allowing enough excess ease so that the garment shrinks to its labeled size after laundering, a practice called *shrink grading*. For example, Levi's effectively marketed "shrink-to-fit" jeans and thus capitalized on the otherwise undesirable fact that their jeans progressively shrink. However, shrink-graded garments present problems. At the point of sale, consumers cannot determine with certainty the in-use fit of the garment. For example, if the consumer buys a shrink-graded garment that fits desirably at the point of sale, it will be too small after laundering. Thus, the manufacturer must educate consumers about shrink-graded garments and must accurately predict shrinkage to ensure that garments fit properly after laundering. Because of the problems with shrink grading, many manufacturers are preshrinking garments instead of shrink grading.

Appearance Retention. The fabric must maintain its original appearance for the garment to remain useful. The ability of a fabric to stay the same color; retain creases; resist wrinkling, snagging, and pilling; and withstand the heat of care processes determines whether the garment maintains its original appearance.

Colorfastness. **Colorfastness** is the ability of the fabric to retain its original color (Figure 4-2). Colorfastness refers to color retention in reaction to laundering (bleach, water, detergent, heat), light, dry cleaning solvents, perspiration, and other chemicals. Colorfast is a relative term; no garment is completely colorfast. Expect some loss of color because of the limitations of technology. However, some fabrics are much more colorfast than others.

A loss or change in the garment's original color is a major source of consumer dissatisfaction. Consumers may accept faded jeans, but most other items with colors that streak or fade are discarded as unwearable, even if structurally sound. Sometimes color loss or change is so slight that the consumer does not notice unless it is compared to the original color. For example, sometimes one part of a coordinated outfit is worn and laundered more than the other, causing it to fade. When the consumer wants to wear the pieces together again, they no longer match in color.

Lack of colorfastness may be expressed in a variety of ways:

1. *Fading* refers to the lightening of a color because of the loss or breakdown of the dye. Clothes sometimes fade in the retail store under the bright lights in display windows or on the selling floor. Most fading at the consumer level is due to repeated laundering or to sunlight exposure for garments worn outdoors.

2. *Frosting* occurs when color leaves the surface of the fabric due to abrasion. Notice it on the hems and pocket edges of denim jeans, especially those that have been stone washed.

3. *Crocking* is the transfer of a fabric's color to another surface through rubbing; it occurs under dry or wet conditions. For example, the dye from your new blue jeans might crock onto your skin.

4. *Bleeding* is the migration of color from a wet fabric into water and sometimes, from there, onto another fabric. For instance, a red trim might bleed onto a white garment when laundered.

5. *Yellowing* or *graying* is the noticeable color change in white or light-colored garments. Many dress shirts end up in thrift shops because of yellowing or graying.

The law does not require labeling regarding the colorfastness of garments. Some garment labels include the word *colorfast,* but this has no objective definition and is merely a marketing tool used to appeal to consumers' desire for colorfast garments.

Wrinkle Resistance. Creases appear in most fabrics when pressure, heat, and/or moisture are applied to the folded or compressed fabric. *Wrinkle resistance,* the ability of a fabric to avoid undesirable creases, is generally a desirable feature (except when a wrinkled look is fashionable). The fabric's resilience determines whether or not a garment that becomes wrinkled will remain wrinkled, affecting both appearance and ease of care. In other cases, *crease retention,* the ability of a fabric to retain creases, is desirable. Crease retention keeps the style crease on pant legs and the creases of pressed pleats sharp.

Snag and Pill Resistance. Snagging and pilling detract from a garment's appearance and its usefulness. *Snags* are pulls in the fabric made when the yarns catch on a sharp object. *Pills* are fuzz balls, or balls of tangled fibers that form on the surface and are held there by one or more fibers (Figure 4-3). Pills may form all over a garment, but are most likely where the garment receives abrasion; for example, in the underarm area, inside collars, and on sleeves and cuffs (Chapter 11). Some fabrics have a greater resistance than others to snagging and pilling.

Heat Resistance. Heat resistance is the ability to withstand the heat of high washing, drying, and ironing temperatures without deforming the fabric. For example, some fabrics cannot withstand hot ironing temperatures, leading to *scorching,* the charring of the fabric evidenced by brown or black stains. **Thermoplastic** or heat sensitive fibers melt when exposed to high temperatures—a critical problem when the garment is tossed about in a hot washing machine or dryer or when it is pressed with a hot iron. However, fabrics made from thermoplastic fibers can be **heat set** to retain desirable creases such as pleats and the creases on pant legs. Heat setting also keeps garments made of thermoplastic fibers permanently wrinkle free. And melting can be desirable; for example, when fusible fabrics (made from thermoplastic fibers) are joined using heat instead of stitches.

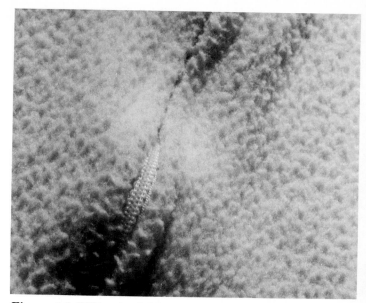

Figure 4-3 *Pilling in children's sleeper. Also note zipper exhibits zipper hump.*

Comfort. Many factors help determine comfort. The fabric's *hand* is an important influence. A stiff or heavy fabric or one with a rough texture, for example, makes the garment uncomfortable to wear. The extensibility of the fabric affects comfort and the ability of the garment to fit a variety of people. *Comfort stretch* is minimal stretch, which provides ease of motion. *Power stretch* or *action stretch* is a high degree of elongation, required in activewear; for example, dance leotards.

Insulation. The ability of the fabric to transmit air, heat, moisture, and electricity also helps determine the comfort. *Air permeability,* the rate at which air passes through a fabric, refers to the fabric's ability to "breathe." Air permeability and *thermal conductivity,* the rate at which heat passes through a fabric, both affect comfort. Fabrics with high air permeability and thermal conductivity are good choices for hot-weather clothing and active sportswear because they help release body heat and cool the wearer. Fabrics with low air permeability and thermal conductivity are desirable for cold-weather clothing because they help retain body heat. Clothing that retains body heat is especially important for infants and the elderly, whose bodies are inefficient at temperature regulation.

Researchers measure the thermal or insulative value of clothing (encompassing not only the fabric but the design, materials, and construction of the garment) according to its clo value. *Clo* is a unit of measurement approximately equal to the insulation required to keep a resting person comfortable at room temperature, or roughly the insulation value of typical indoor clothing. Thus, a garment with a high clo value would keep you warmer than one with a low clo value.

Moisture Transfer. Absorbency is the ability of a fabric to take in moisture. **Wicking ability** is the rate at which a fabric diffuses moisture; and *moisture retention* is the rate at which a fabric dries. All three factors contribute to comfort in both hot-weather and cold-weather clothing. High absorbency allows the fabric to absorb perspiration. It also makes the fabric easy to dye, easy to launder, and resistant to static cling. Low moisture retention allows the fabric to dry quickly. However, the most important factor is wicking ability. Good wicking ability helps the fabric carry moisture along its surface and away from the body. Wicking cools the body in hot conditions by aiding in the evaporation of perspiration and, in cold conditions, carries perspiration away so that the wearer does not get wet and chilled. For example, ski socks need good wicking characteristics so that, as the feet perspire, the fabric carries away the moisture to keep the feet dry and therefore warm. Conversely, rainwear fabrics require low water permeability rather than absorbency for comfort.

Static Cling. Static cling is caused by low electrical conductivity. *Electrical conductivity* is the ability of the fabric to conduct electrical charges. Fabrics with good electrical conductivity avoid the buildup of static electricity. Garments with excess static tend to cling or billow, affecting comfort and also the garment's appearance. Generally, absorbent fibers have little problem with static buildup.

Ease of Care. For many consumers, the *ease of care* of a fabric is an important utility feature because of its effect on the care of the garment. The fabric and other materials used in the garment should have the same launderability or dry cleanability so that the finished garment retains its appearance and function after care.

Ease of care also refers to the garment's tendency to resist soiling and wrinkling. For example, the ability of a fabric to resist perspiration staining is very important for men's white dress shirts. Fabrics are generally easy to care for if they are soil resistant, absorbent, resilient, strong, abrasion resistant, dimensionally stable, colorfast, and resistant to heat and chemicals. Washable garments typically cost less to care for than do dry cleanable garments. Garments that require special treatment, such as hand washing, drying flat, or ironing take extra time to care for properly.

Safety. One of the main issues in clothing *safety* for the general public is flame resistance. *Flame resistance* does not imply that a garment is fireproof. It means that the fabric resists catching fire, burns more slowly than ordinary fabrics and self-extinguishes or easily extinguishes after the flame is removed. However, flame-resistant fabrics *do* burn.

The Flammable Fabrics Act establishes the most stringent requirements for infants' and children's sleepwear; it must meet minimum standards for flame resistance. Infants' and children's sleepwear includes clothing sizes 0–6X and 7–14 worn primarily for sleeping and related activities. Included are nightgowns, pajamas, robes, and other sleep-related accessories, excluding diapers and underwear. The Flammable Fabrics Act also sets forth standards for rating fabrics as follows:

- *Class 1:* normal flammability (suitable for clothing)
- *Class 2:* intermediate flammability
- *Class 3:* rapid and intense burning (unsuitable for clothing)

The purpose of these standards is to discourage the use of any dangerously flammable fabrics to make apparel. However, more stringent rulings for general wearing apparel are under consideration.

Another safety consideration for fabric is its ability to reflect light. Special, highly *light-reflective* fabrics are useful for biking and jogging clothing and for some occupational clothing.

Strength and Abrasion Resistance. The strength of a fabric is a measure of how well it resists deformation by external forces. **Tensile strength** or **tenacity** refers to the ability of the fabric to resist a pulling force. Strength may also be measured in *tear strength* (ability to resist tearing) or *bursting strength* (ability to withstand pressure without rupturing). Obviously, all three are closely related to garment durability.

Abrasion resistance refers to the amount of rubbing action a fabric can withstand without being destroyed. *Edge abrasion* at hems and other folded edges particularly prone to abrasion often results if a fabric has low abrasion resistance. Some parts of garments are subjected to more abrasion than others; for example, cuffs, elbows, seats, and knees. Abrasion-resistant fabrics are important for durability; they are especially critical in apparel categories such as children's play clothing or occupational clothing that is subjected to intense abrasion.

Yarn slippage is the tendency of the yarns in a fabric to shift under stress. Yarn slippage often occurs near the seams of snug-fitting garments (Figure 6-3). Yarn slippage reduces durability and is unattractive.

Resistance to Degradation. Fabrics must withstand degradation from the environment. For example, a durable garment is made of fabric with the following characteristics:

1. *Chemical resistance,* the ability to withstand degradation by chemicals. For example, active sportswear should withstand perspiration, and swimwear should withstand salt water and chlorine. Fabrics should withstand the cleansing agents required to care for the garment; for example, bleaches, detergents, and/or dry-cleaning solvents.

2. *Launderability,* the ability to withstand the mechanical, thermal, and chemical actions of laundering.

3. *Dry cleanability,* the ability to withstand the dry-cleaning process.

4. *Insect resistance,* the ability to repel moths, silverfish, and other insects which destroy the fabric by eating it.

5. *Mildew resistance,* the degree to which the fabric can resist the growth of fungi, which may stain or weaken the fabric.

6. *Sunlight resistance,* the ability of a fabric to absorb sunlight without being damaged or destroyed. Fading is a common problem in retail stores, where garments are degraded by sunlight in display windows facing the outdoors. Clothing worn by people who spend a lot of time outdoors also requires sunlight resistance.

Storage conditions play as important a part as the fabric itself in the last three factors. Clothing should be cleaned and stored in a well-ventilated, dark place with relatively low temperature and humidity to avoid degradation by insects, mildew, and sunlight.

Physical Features of Fabric

The physical features of a fabric determine its performance. No single physical feature is solely responsible for the performance of the fabric. Instead, the interplay between all the physical dimensions of the fabric determine its performance. Understanding how the physical properties of a fabric influence its aesthetics, utility, durability, and cost is important for evaluating fabric and garment quality. The physical features of a fabric include its fibers and yarns, the structure of the fabric, and how it is dyed, printed, and finished.

The quality of the fabric is not the sole determinant of a garment's quality, but it is a critical ingredient. As you study the following pages, note the relationship between the physical features of a fabric and the resulting performance features, discussed earlier in the chapter.

FIBERS

Fibers are the raw materials from which fabrics are made; they are the basic building blocks of a fabric. An individual fiber is a fine, hairlike structure. Knowing the fiber content of a fabric helps predict the aesthetic and functional performance of the fabric and the garment. The type of fiber or fibers from which a fabric is produced strongly influences the fabric's characteristics. Fiber content affects the aesthetics, comfort, durability, shape and appearance retention, ease of care, and other performance characteristics as well as the cost of the fabric. For example, fibers affect the hand of the fabric, including its texture and drape, because some fibers are inherently soft and others are stiff. Fiber content also affects the dimensional stability of the fabric. For example, wool fibers have a tendency to stretch and to shrink under adverse conditions. Other fibers, such as nylon, have the ability to return to their original length after being stretched, which improves the dimensional stability of nylon fabrics. A fiber with high abrasion resistance contributes to the durability of the fabric. Comfort factors such as the absorbency, moisture transmission and retention, water repellency, air and thermal conductivity, and electrical conductivity of a fabric are greatly affected by the properties of the fibers used to make the fabric. The luster of the fiber influences the luster of the fabric. Some fibers are fuzzy, making them likely to hide soil and to retain trapped soil, affecting the appearance and ease of care of the fabric. In addition to influencing fabric performance, fiber content is listed on the label of the garment and therefore affects the consumer's perception of quality.

Natural Fibers. Fibers fall into two broad categories, **natural fibers,** which occur naturally in the environment, and manufactured fibers. The natural fibers used in apparel include

1. *Protein fibers*—silk, wool, and other fibers from animal sources;
2. *Cellulosic fibers*—cotton, linen, and its close relative, ramie, and other fibers from plant sources; and
3. *Miscellaneous natural fibers*—rubber and metal.

In general, natural fibers are most costly and considered to be more luxurious than manufactured fibers. Consumers typically associate natural fibers with beauty, comfort, durability, and cellulosics with the tendency to wrinkle.

Manufactured Fibers. **Manufactured fibers** or **man-made fibers** are formed through human effort. The manufactured fibers used in apparel include

1. *Regenerated cellulosics* made from plant fibers—rayon, acetate and triacetate; and
2. *Synthetics* made from petroleum products—nylon, polyester, acrylic, modacrylic, olefin, and spandex.

In addition to their generic names, manufactured fibers have registered trade names, or brand names that identify the fiber producer. For example, *Lycra* is a brand of spandex made by DuPont (Table 4-2).

The characteristics of manufactured fibers vary widely. Synthetics, such as nylon and polyester, are associated with low to moderate absorbency, making them uncomfortable in hot,

humid weather. But regenerated cellulosic fibers, especially rayon, are typically more absorbent and more comfortable than synthetics. The strength and resilience of manufactured fibers ranges from very low to very high, depending on the type of fiber and particular variation. Synthetic fibers tend to be stronger and more durable than regenerated cellulosics. The strength of synthetic fibers makes fabrics likely to pill because the strong fibers cling to fuzz balls that form on the fabric surface and do not let them fall off. Synthetic fibers are generally more resilient than regenerated cellulosics and natural fibers, so they are less apt to wrinkle and to require ironing. Unlike some regenerated cellulosics and natural fibers, synthetics can usually be heat set. This gives synthetic fabrics the ability to resist or retain creases as desired. Synthetics are generally more resistant to mildew, insects, fire and chemicals than regenerated cellulosics and natural fibers.

Fiber Performance. People often make assumptions about the performance of a fabric based on fiber content. However, the particular fabric in which a fiber is found may perform quite differently than one might guess from knowing the fiber content. For example, nylon is a very strong fiber. But nylon hosiery runs easily if the yarns are very fine and the structure of the fabric is very delicate.

The relationship of the fabric and other components of the garment also affects performance. For example, a consumer might assume that a garment made of polyester is durable because polyester fibers are generally durable. But if the stitches securing the seams are weak, the garment is not very durable.

Fibers that look and feel alike may perform quite differently in use. High-quality and low-quality fibers exist within each fiber type. Manufactured fibers have limitless variations; they can be engineered to possess any number of characteristics. Therefore, it is impossible to accurately generalize about their performance. For example, different rayons vary widely in their durability. If a label reads *100% Rayon* the consumer may assume a level of durability higher or lower than that particular variation of rayon possesses. However, the fiber properties of the fabric in a garment cannot be determined visually but must be described on the label.

Blends of more than one fiber type increase or decrease the characteristics contributed by

Text continued on page 86.

TABLE 4-2

Generalizations about common apparel fibers

Generic Fiber: *cotton,* the most widely used apparel fiber in the United States
—from seed pod of cotton plant
—*Pima* and *Egyptian* varieties are high quality
chief uses: warm weather apparel, underwear, sleepwear
cost: moderate, slightly more expensive than man-made fibers
performance: appears dull; wrinkles easily unless specially finished; absorbent; draws heat from body; feels cool in hot, humid weather; moderate strength; colorfastness often a problem; deteriorated by mildew and sunlight; drapes well; easy to cut and sew; dyes readily; most rigorous care, machine wash and dry; exhibits relaxation shrinkage when laundered, especially in knitted fabrications, unless preshrunk; iron at high temperature

Generic Fiber: *linen*
—from stem of flax plant
—*Belgian* and *Irish* linen are finest
chief uses: warm weather apparel
cost: expensive luxury fiber, constitutes less than 1% of apparel fibers used
performance: crisp, lustrous, wrinkles easily; absorbent; draws heat from body; cool in hot, humid weather; strong; tends to crack at creases or folds; does not shed lint; easy to cut and sew; most rigorous care, dry clean; if machine washed and dried, may wrinkle, lose crispness, and exhibit relaxation shrinkage; iron at high temperature

Generic Fiber: *ramie*
—from stem of ramie plant
—frequently used in imported garments after cotton quotas are filled
chief uses: warm weather apparel, especially sweaters; blends with polyester, cotton, linen, and acrylic are common
cost: less expensive than linen
performance: aesthetics similar to linen; highly lustrous; wrinkles easily; somewhat stiffer than linen; absorbent; draws heat from body; cool in hot, humid weather; stronger than linen; colorfast; brittle and difficult to twist into yarns and to weave; easy to cut and sew; dyes readily; most rigorous care, same as linen

Generic Fiber: *silk*
—from silkworm cocoons
—*raw silk* has not been de-gummed; *tussah silk* is coarse, uneven staple fibers from wild silkworms
chief uses: elegant suits, dresses, blouses, neckties, scarves
cost: expensive luxury fiber, constitutes less than 1% of apparel fibers
performance: dry hand; lustrous; wrinkles easily; luxurious hand; absorbent; lightweight; retains body heat; cool in summer, warm in winter; strong but not especially durable; deteriorated by sun and perspiration; does not stretch or shrink; dyes may bleed; drapes well; in filament form is slippery to cut and sew and may show needle holes; in spun form is easy to cut and sew; dyes readily; most rigorous care, dry clean or hand wash, cool, gentle, soap, line dry; no harsh detergents; no chlorine bleach; iron at low temperature

Generic Fiber: *wool*
—from the fleece of sheep
—some of the highest quality comes from *Merino* and *Rambouillet* breeds
—*lambswool* is soft first shearing from lambs
chief uses: cool weather apparel, especially sweaters; tailored suits and coats
cost: relatively expensive; finer wool is more expensive than coarser wool
performance: varies from dull/fuzzy to smoother/somewhat lustrous; resists wrinkling; wrinkles fall out; absorbent; some wool is scratchy; retains body heat; stretches but can recover; shrinks; rela-

cont'd

TABLE 4-2 (continued)

tively weak fiber, but fabric can be fairly durable, depending on structure; finer wool is less durable; moths can destroy unless mothproof finish is added; malleable so tailors well; does not ravel easily; dyes readily; colorfast; most rigorous care dry clean or hand wash, cool, gentle, soap, dry flat; shrinks when machine washed and dried unless specially finished; no harsh detergents; no chlorine bleach; iron at low temperature

Generic Fiber: *specialty hair fibers*
        —from the fleece of animals other than sheep, for example, *mohair, cashmere, alpaca, angora, camel, vicuña*

chief uses: same as wool

cost: vicuña is as expensive as a good fur coat; cashmere and camel are also expensive luxury fibers; others are generally more expensive than wool

performance: aesthetics similar to wool; slightly more lustrous; retain body heat; most are softer, fluffier, smoother, and less scratchy than wool; most are slightly less durable than wool; ease of production similar to wool; most have somewhat less body than wool; most rigorous care, same as wool

Generic Fiber: *rayon*
        —regenerated cellulose
        —most rayon is *viscose* or *high wet modulus (HWM)/high performance (HP)*; HWM rayon is much more durable than viscose rayon

trade name examples: Avisco, Avril (HWM), Coloray, Fortisan, Zantrel (HWM)

chief uses: imitates natural fibers in light- and medium-weight apparel

cost: varies widely, low to moderate

performance: dull to lustrous; wrinkles easily unless HWM; absorbent; low strength unless HWM; tends to stretch and not recover well unless HWM; exhibits some relaxation shrinkage; deteriorated by mildew; drapes well; in filament form, difficult to cut and sew; prone to seam slippage; dyes readily; most rigorous care, dry clean; iron at low temperature; HWM rayons may suggest machine wash and dry and iron at slightly higher temperature

Generic Fiber: *acetate* and *triacetate* (a refinement of acetate)
        —regenerated cellulosics

trade name examples of acetate: Avron, Celaperm, Celara, Chromspun, Estron

trade name examples of triacetate: Acele, Arnel

chief uses of acetate: light- and medium-weight apparel, especially linings, silklike bridal and formal wear and lingerie

chief uses of triacetate: apparel that needs to be heat set

cost: relatively low

performance: lustrous; acetate wrinkles easily, triacetate does not wrinkle easily; acetate moderately absorbent, more absorbent than triacetate; retains body heat; relatively weak; acetate prone to shrinking and stretching unless treated, triacetate resists shrinking and stretching; acetate may fade or change color from exposure to atmosphere; drapes well; ravels; stitching holes show; seams often pucker; slippery to cut and sew; can be difficult to dye; no chlorine bleach; most rigorous care for acetate, dry clean, iron at low temperature; most rigorous care for triacetate, hand or machine wash and dry, iron at low temperature

Generic Fiber: *nylon*
        —petroleum derivative

trade name examples: Anso, Antron, Blue C, Cantrece, Caprolan, Crepeset, Enkaloft, Enkalure, Zeflon

chief uses: hosiery, lingerie, blended with other fibers to add strength, wind-resistant garments

cost: varies widely, low to medium

performance: dull to lustrous; does not wrinkle easily; moderately absorbent; lightweight; does not carry heat from body; may build up static; very strong and durable; tends to pill; resists abrasion; excellent elasticity; in filament form, difficult to cut and sew; may be difficult to dye; prone to oily stains; most rigorous care, machine wash and dry, iron at low temperature; light colors may pick up other colors when laundered

TABLE 4-2 *(continued)*

Generic Fiber: *polyester,* second most widely used apparel fiber in the United States
       —petroleum derivative

trade name examples: Avlin, Dacron, Encron, Fortrel, Kodel, Quintess, Trevira

chief uses: used to imitate other fibers or blended to improve characteristics of other fibers, cotton/ polyester blends are common

cost: varies widely, from low to moderate, but lower than most natural fibers; often added to blends to reduce cost and/or improve some dimensions of performance

performance: can imitate most other fibers; dull to lustrous; does not wrinkle easily; low absorbency, but wicks moisture well; retains body heat; tends to pill; strong and durable; dimensionally stable; in filament form, difficult to cut and sew; details may be heat set; dyes readily; prone to oily stains; known for easy care; most rigorous care, usually machine wash and dry, iron at low temperature; usually can be dry cleaned

Generic Fiber: *acrylic* and *modacrylic*
       —petroleum derivatives

trade name examples of acrylic: Acrilan, Bi-Loft, Creslan, Orlon, Zefran

trade name examples of modacrylic: SEF, Verel

chief uses of acrylic: sweaters, to imitate wool

chief uses of modacrylic: fake fur, pile fabrics, flame-resistant sleepwear

cost: varies widely, low to moderate

performance: aesthetics similar to wool, does not wrinkle easily; low absorbency; fairly comfortable; some acrylics prone to stretching and shrinking, especially knits; details can be heat set; acrylic fair to good strength, modacrylic weaker; modacrylic inherently flame retardant; easy to cut and sew; resists dyeing; prone to oily stains; most rigorous care, machine wash and dry; acrylic iron at medium temperature, modacrylic iron at very low temperature; dry clean deep pile/fur fabrics

Generic Fiber: *olefin*
       —petroleum derivative

trade name examples: Accord, Marvess, Tyvek

chief uses: thermal socks and underwear

cost: fairly low

performance: waxy; nonabsorbent but wicks moisture away from the body; extremely lightweight; strong; fairly easy to cut and sew; very difficult to dye; very heat sensitive; most rigorous care, machine wash and line dry, iron at cool temperatures

Generic Fiber: *spandex*
       —petroleum derivative

trade name examples: Byrene, Cleerspan, Glospan, Lycra, Spandelle

chief uses: blended with other fibers to add stretch to foundation garments, swimwear and active sportswear, support hose

cost: high, but only a small percentage is needed to achieve stretch—as low as 3 percent of total fiber weight

performance: shiny; stretches more than 500 percent; recovery from stretch almost as good as rubber; such a small percentage is used in a blend that it usually does not affect garment comfort except for adding stretch; weak, but twice as strong as rubber; resistant to sun and chemicals such as perspiration, suntan oil, chlorine, and sea water; slippery to cut and sew; details can be heat set; dyes readily; most rigorous care, machine wash and dry, no chlorine bleach, iron at low temperature

Generic Fiber: *rubber*
       —natural or manufactured (petroleum derivative)

chief uses: elastic thread, to introduce stretch into garments

cost: lower than spandex

performance: rubber yarns are covered with other fibers that determine aesthetics; stretches more than 700 percent; excellent elasticity; becomes brittle over time; needles can pierce and damage

cont'd

TABLE 4-2 (*continued*)

rubber yarns; very low strength compared to spandex; deteriorates with age and exposure to heat, sun, and chemicals such as perspiration, suntan oil, and salt water; most rigorous care, machine wash; heat destroys rubber; chlorine bleaches and dry-cleaning solvents degrade and harden rubber

Generic Fiber: *metal*
          —natural fiber derived from minerals
trade name example: Lurex
chief uses: decorative threads or to reduce static buildup
cost: varies from inexpensive to expensive
performance: shiny if visible; excellent conductor of electricity; little or no drapability and resiliency; heavy; cannot be dyed, must be coated for color; durable

each fiber to the fabric. In a good blend, the qualities of all fibers in the blend are evident. The characteristics of the fiber present in the highest percentage generally dominate. Usually the fabric must have at least 15 percent of a fiber for that fiber to have an important impact on performance; exceptions are spandex and other elastomers. Care for blends must take into consideration the most delicate component of the blend.

Although generalizations about the properties of fibers may lead to erroneous conclusions about garment performance, fiber content is strongly related to fabric performance and provides a valuable clue to predict garment performance. The aesthetic and functional performance generally associated with each generic fiber is summarized in Table 4-2. Cost, chief uses, and the most rigorous care suggested for the raw fiber are included. It is not certain that a garment with a particular fiber content will withstand the care methods discussed in Table 4-2. The manufacturer determines the proper care for a garment by testing the finished garment, not based on fiber content. Therefore, the care methods listed in Table 4-2 do not directly relate to the care labels in most garments. In addition to the raw fiber, garment care labels also take into account the yarn and fabric structure, dyes and finishes used; and other components of the garment, such as the trim, which may require more delicate care than the raw fiber. Therefore, the care methods listed are merely examples of the most rigorous care the fiber can withstand in its raw state, before being restricted by additional yarn, fabrication, dye, print, finish, and other garment component and construction considerations.

Plastic. The most common plastic used in apparel applications is *vinyl*. Like many other synthetic materials, vinyl is a petroleum derivative. The most common vinyl material is *polyvinyl chloride (PVC)*. Vinyl is widely used in raincoats and to imitate leather in jackets and other apparel, as well as in belts, shoes, and other accessories. It costs considerably less than leather, and garments are cut from large sheets of vinyl more efficiently than from irregularly shaped leather hides. Vinyl is generally considered to be of lower quality than leather because it tends to stiffen and crack with age. Also, vinyl melts if exposed to high temperatures. Vinyl is uncomfortable to wear next to the skin because it is not absorbent and does not breathe. The hand of vinyl depends on how much plasticizer the producer adds; more plasticizer results in a more flexible product. The producer adds air bubbles during the manufacturing process to create *foamed vinyls* or *expanded vinyls*; the air bubbles make these vinyls good insulators for cold-weather clothing. They closely imitate leather. Most vinyls may be wiped clean with a damp cloth or machine washed, but not machine dried. Another synthetic, leather-like fabric more costly than vinyl is Ultrasuede R, a blend of polyester fibers and polyurethane plastic.

Leather. *Leather* is the *tanned* or preserved skin or hide from an animal. Manufacturers use leather to make jackets, coats, and other apparel as well as shoes, belts, and accessories. Consumers prize leather for its beauty and durability. They find it comfortable to wear because of its ability to breathe.

Top grain or **genuine leather** is the top layer of the hide. It represents the highest quality leather and the most expensive. Other layers of the hide are referred to as **splits.** Manufacturers sometimes give splits an artificial grain that looks like top grain, but splits are slightly rougher, do not wear as well, and cost less than top grain. *Suede* results when a manufacturer naps the leather, giving it a fuzzy surface.

Fashion greatly affects the demand for various types of leathers from different animals. Unblemished hides yield the most attractive and costly leathers. The thickness of the split, the rarity of the animal from which it is taken, and the tanning and finishing processes chosen also affect the cost and quality of leather. Hides go through an extensive tanning process to become leather, which partly explains their expense. Placement of pattern pieces on small, individual, irregular hides is not as efficient as on wide, even-width stacks of manufactured fabrics, another factor contributing to the cost of leather garments.

Leather and imitation leathers require special construction techniques; regular methods may damage them. Stitches weaken these fabrics, so long stitches should be used. Seams and hems may be glued or fused instead of stitched. Fasteners other than buttons and buttonholes may be used. Because these fabrics retain needle puncture marks, alteration of garments made from these fabrics is limited. Seams and stitched hems cannot be let out without exposing the needle holes. Large leather garments require seams to piece several hides together because of the limited size of the animal. For example, most leather pants for adults have a seam across the leg because the hide is not long enough to cover the length of the leg.

Fur. *Fur* is an animal skin or hide with the hair still attached; it is used to make luxurious coats and jackets, and for trims and accessories. Consumers value fur for its warmth and beauty.

Fashion greatly affects the demand for various types of fur from different animals. The Fur Products Labeling Act regulates the labeling of fur garments. Most fur today is taken from ranch-raised animals rather than from animals trapped in the wild. Responsible furriers use fur only from species that are not endangered. Nevertheless, animal rights activists oppose the wearing of fur because it requires killing the animal for its coat.

The cost of a fur depends on the rarity of the animal from which it came and upon its quality. Fur quality relates to the softness, fluffiness, and density of the fur, and its color and luster. Fur from female animals tends to be softer and more desirable than fur from males. Plus, female pelts are smaller, making garments produced from them more costly. Animals raised in cold climates and fed nutritious diets tend to have dense, lustrous fur. How well the furs within a garment match one another also affects quality. Furs go through an expensive dressing process, which helps explain their cost.

Fur garments require special construction techniques. The methods chosen help determine cost. **Fully-let-out** fur garments are by far the most expensive. Letting out involves cutting the pelts into narrow diagonal strips. These strips are sewn back together so that each pelt becomes a long, narrow panel that covers the length of the wearer's body. Fully-let-out furs lend a slimming appearance to the wearer. Letting out requires hours of hand labor and must be done by a highly skilled furrier. **Skin-on-skin** garments contain whole pelts sewn together. They are much less costly to produce than fully-let-out furs.

YARNS

A group of fibers is twisted or *spun* into a continuous strand called a **yarn.** Yarns are the "threads" used to make fabrics. A fabric's yarns affect functional and aesthetic performance—for example, hand, including drapability and texture; luster; durability, including strength and abrasion resistance; and comfort. The two main types of yarns are (1) spun and (2) filament. Several individual or *single* yarns of either type may be twisted together to create larger, stronger, *ply* yarns.

Spun Yarns. **Spun yarns** are composed of short fibers called *staple fibers.* All natural fibers, except for silk, are staples. Manufactured fibers occur as filaments but may be cut into staples, if desired. When staple fibers are spun into yarns, the many fiber ends sticking out from spun yarns give them a dull appearance and a slightly rough texture. Fabrics made from spun yarns are comfortable because they do not lie flush against the body. They ravel and shift less, press flatter, pucker less, and show wrinkles and construction errors less than do filament yarns.

Carded or Combed. As one of the steps in creating a yarn, the yarn producer *cards* the staple fibers to semi-orient them in a parallel manner. The producer may also *comb* the yarn if it contains long staple fibers. Combing removes short fibers and further orients the remaining fibers in a parallel manner. Carded yarns are fuzzy and soft. Combed yarns are smoother and more lustrous than carded yarns, partly because of the longer fibers and partly because they are more tightly twisted. Combed yarns retain their appearance longer and are less likely to pill than carded yarns. Combed yarns cost more than carded yarns and are a sign of quality. Carded and combed are terms usually applied to cotton yarns.

Woolen or Worsted. Woolen refers to carded wool yarns; *worsted* indicates combed wool yarns. Worsted yarns cost more than woolen yarns and are a sign of quality. Worsted yarns are used in menswear and hard-finish suitings. Worsted fabrics wear well but have a tendency to become shiny in areas of hard wear; for example, the elbows of a jacket. Woolen fabrics are generally loosely woven and bulky. They tend to lose their shape more easily than worsteds. Woolen yarns are used in sweaters and soft, cold-weather suitings. Woolen yarns are good insulators.

Filament Yarns. **Filament yarns** are composed of long fibers called *filaments.* All manufactured fibers are filaments (unless they are cut to staple length). The only natural fiber occurring in filament form is silk.

Because they contain long fibers, filament yarns are very smooth. Fabrics made from filament yarns have a lustrous appearance (unless they are delustered) and resist wrinkling. Filament yarns are usually stronger than staple yarns of comparable size and fiber content. They are also generally less absorbent than staple yarns and less comfortable because they tend to stick to the skin when wet. Filament yarns involve fewer steps so they cost less to make than staple yarns. In apparel production, filament-yarn fabrics ravel and shift during cutting and sewing because they are slippery. Thus, they cost more to cut and sew than comparable fabrics made from spun yarns, and it is more difficult to achieve smooth, attractive results. They tend to pucker and show wrinkles and construction errors. Therefore, a garment of filament-yarn fabric generally costs more than a comparable garment of staple-yarn fabric.

Most filament yarns are *texturized,* which adds crimp and dimension. Although still economical, texturizing filament yarns makes them more comfortable to wear, less apt to wrinkle, and easier to cut and sew. It helps the yarn stretch and recover from stretch. Texturizing makes the yarn somewhat dull. It increases the tendency of the yarn to snag or pill.

Novelty Yarns. *Novelty* yarns or *fancy* yarns are used to achieve special effects in fabrics. For example, *tweed* yarns have bits of contrasting colored fiber added to the plain yarn; *bouclé* yarns have decorative loops; *slub* yarns are thick and thin. Novelty yarns add to the design effect of the fabric and to its cost. Novelty yarns tend to decrease abrasion resistance because the uneven surface of the yarns wears unevenly and is prone to snagging. They require a looser fabric structure than plain yarns, making the fabric prone to snagging and yarn slippage. The uneven surface of novelty yarns also traps and hides soil; it does not show soil readily but is difficult to clean.

Yarn Twist. The amount of *twist,* measured in the number of turns per inch, is an important property of yarn. Tightly twisted yarns are stronger, finer, less apt to snag and pill, and generally retain their appearance longer than loosely twisted yarns. Tightly twisted yarns can be packed closely together, creating durable fabrics, which are generally wrinkle resistant. These yarns are generally associated with increased cost and quality. In some applications, loosely twisted yarns are desirable because they create a soft, lofty, drapable fabric. But the fabric is also subject to pilling, snagging, and abrasion.

High twist generally adds luster to staple fibers, but decreases the luster of filament fibers. Extremely high levels of twist create crinkly looking *crepe* yarns. They add texture to the fabric but are prone to shrinkage.

Yarn Size. *Yarn size* or diameter affects the performance of the fabric. Large, coarse yarns tend to be stronger and more durable than small, fine yarns with the same amount of twist. The large yarns create fabrics with a rougher texture and stiffer hand and which are less drapable; these are thick, warm, opaque fabrics that do not wrinkle easily. Because large yarns cannot be packed as closely together as small yarns, the fabric may be prone to yarn slippage.

Yarn size is designated in various ways, depending on the type of fiber used in the yarn. The size of staple-fiber yarns is designated by **yarn number.** There are different yarn numbering systems for cotton, woolen, and worsted yarns. Yarn numbering is an indirect system;

the larger the number, the smaller the yarn. The numbers are based on pounds and yards, so they are not well suited for international use.

Filament yarn sizes are designated by **denier.** Denier is a direct system; the larger the number, the larger the yarn. Denier is based on the metric system, so it is useful internationally. Denier is also used to refer to the diameter of filament fibers.

For international use, the **Tex** system is suggested, although Tex has not yet been formally adopted in the United States. Tex is the weight (in grams) of 1,000 meters of fiber or yarn. Tex is well suited to international use because it is a direct system, based on the metric system, and designates the diameters of any type of fiber and yarns made of any type of fiber.

FABRIC STRUCTURE

The *structure* of a fabric or how it is fabricated affects its aesthetic and functional performance. Fabric structure affects the hand of the fabric, including its drapability and texture. The structure of the fabric also affects luster, ability to stretch and breathe, and strength and abrasion resistance. Fabrics can be formed in a number of ways. The two most common methods of forming a fabric are weaving and knitting.

Weaving. *Weaving* is the most common method of creating fabrics. *Warp* yarns are interlaced with *filling* or *weft* yarns at right angles to make the fabric. Woven fabrics are firm and strong. They can be easily tucked, pleated, dyed, and printed. They are better at blocking wind than knits. Because of their interlaced structure, woven fabrics have low stretch, ravel at cut edges, and are prone to seam pucker.

Woven fabrics vary from plain to complex weaves. All weaves are some variation of the plain weave, twill weave, or satin weave (Figure 4-4). These weaves refer to different arrangements of the yarns within the fabric.

1. In **plain weave** fabrics, the filling yarns pass alternately over and under the warp yarn. Plain weave fabrics are the simplest and the most common. They can be woven more compactly than other types of weaves and, because of their simplicity, lend themselves to being printed. These fabrics are more prone to wrinkling than other fabric constructions. Examples of plain weaves include calico, challis, muslin, percale, chambray, and gingham.

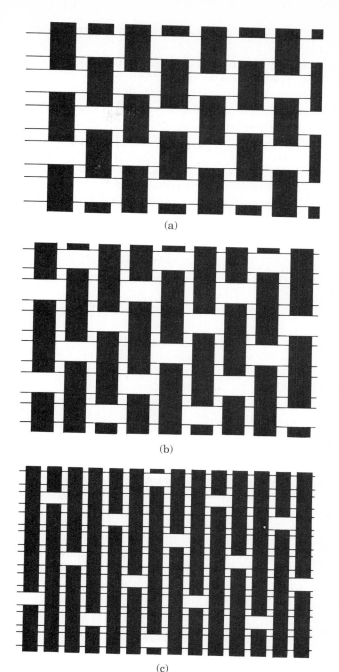

Figure 4-4 *Weaves: (a) plain weave, (b) twill weave, and (c) satin weave.*

2. In **twill weave** fabrics, the filling yarns *float* or pass over or under two or more warp yarns in a staggered progression, producing a characteristic diagonal rib on the surface of the fabric. Twill weave fabrics are very durable. The floats allow the yarns to move, helping them to resist abrasion. If the ribs of a twill weave fabric are flattened, the fabric develops shiny spots. Common twill weaves include denim and gabardine.

3. In **satin weave** fabrics, the filling yarns pass over or under several warp yarns at one time. This produces a long float, which gives satin weave fabrics their characteristic smooth, lustrous surface. More floats and fewer interlacings yield a drapable fabric. The floats are prone to snagging, yarn slippage, and abrasion, making satin weave fabrics the least durable type of woven fabric. Fabrics with long floats, including *jacquard* weaves which have complex designs woven into the fabric, should be handled carefully to avoid marring their surfaces. Most fabrics made with a satin weave are called, simply, satin.

Knitting. *Knitting* is the other major method of creating fabric used in apparel. The yarns in a knit fabric are a series of connected loops. The interlooped structure of knits allows them to stretch more than wovens, making them comfortable to wear. The amount of stretch depends on variations in the knitting technique. Because they stretch, knits are likely to lose their original shape. Knit fabrics pose more challenges for apparel manufacturers than woven fabrics. Manufacturers must take care not to stretch knit fabrics; if the fabric is stretched, it later relaxes to its original size and causes relaxation shrinkage in the finished garment. Often, knit garments demonstrate relaxation shrinkage in their length, causing them to grow shorter and wider.

Knitting is faster and less costly than weaving. Knit fabrics tend to wrinkle less than wovens. They are more subject to pilling and snagging because they do not hold the yarns and fibers in place as rigidly as do wovens. Knits are generally good insulators in still air, but are cool to wear if there is a breeze. They are less opaque than comparable-weight wovens. Many knit fabrics have a tendency to curl at the edges. They rarely have problems with seam pucker, but seam grin is a problem (Figure 6-3). If a loop snags and breaks, the knit structure comes undone; for example, a run in a pair of hose.

Weft Knits. In **weft knits** or **filling knits,** the yarns run horizontally across the fabric (Figure 4-5). Hand knitting is an example of weft knitting. The majority of knits used in apparel are weft knits, including those used to make sweaters and sweatshirts. An example is *jersey,* a plain weft knit used to make T-shirts. You can distinguish jersey by the rows of flat, vertical lines on the front of the fabric and the horizontal ribs on the back of the fabric. The loops that run up and down the face or front of a plain knit fabric are **wales.** The loops that run across the back of an ordinary, plain knit fabric are **courses.** Weft knits tend to run if a loop is severed; a whole row of loops may disconnect, especially if the yarn or fiber type is smooth. If a sewing needle cuts a single yarn of the fabric during construction of the garment, the fabric runs. Therefore, needle cutting is a major concern to manufacturers sewing on knits. The edges of jersey fabrics ravel and curl, so apparel producers need to allow extra seam width to compensate.

Most weft knits are knitted on circular machines that produce a tubular fabric. Producers split the tube of fabric and flatten it so that it can then be cut and sewn. In the case of T-shirts and sweatshirts, producers knit a narrow tube the desired circumference of the finished garment and leave it in tube form, eliminating the

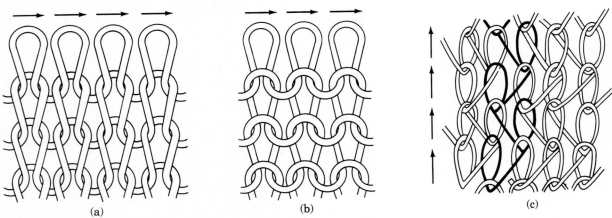

Figure 4-5 *Knits: (a) wales on face of weft knit, (b) courses on back of weft knit, and (c) warp knit.*

need for side seams. Unfortunately, the construction of circular knits gives them a tendency to twist in the finished garment (Figure 4-11).

Weft knits include other single knits such as purl knits, rib knits, and interlocks, as well as double knits. A *purl knit* resembles the back of a jersey fabric on both sides. Purl knits are bulkier than plain knits and are used mainly in heavier garments.

Rib knits alternate wales and courses on their face to create the stretchiest and most elastic knit fabric. Rib knits or *ribbing* is used at the neck, wrist, and hem of sweaters, T-shirts, and sweatshirts to allow the openings to stretch for dressing and undressing. A 2-inch-wide piece of rib knit in a sweater can stretch to 20 inches (Hudson 1988), so rib knits require a large quantity of yarn in their structure to permit such a high degree of stretch. When relaxed, rib knits are loftier than other knits because of the excess yarn.

The front and back of *interlock knits* look like the front of a plain knit. Interlock knits are a variation of the rib knit and look like two layers of rib knit fabricated together. Interlock knits are therefore thicker, heavier, and more dimensionally stable than jersey knits. They are less apt to stretch during production or when worn or cared for. They are also less apt to run and their edges do not ravel or curl like jersey. Interlock knits are used by many manufacturers who produce high-quality knit shirts and dresses.

Most weft knit fabrics are *single knits*, a single layer. *Double knits* are two single knit fabrics interlocked as one. Double knits do not all look like the stereotypical polyester double knits popular in past decades; fabrics that are technically double knits come in a variety of versatile looks. Double knits are heavier and have greater dimensional stability than single knits. They do not have as much stretch as other knits but they retain their shape better. Their edges do not curl or ravel. This makes them the easiest knits to cut and sew. They cost more than single knits.

Warp Knits. In **warp knits,** the yarns run parallel to the length of the fabric. Warp knitting machines interloop many yarns simultaneously across the width of the fabric; the loops interlock diagonally. The wales and courses of warp knits appear similar to those of weft knits, except the courses of warp knits lie somewhat more diagonally than horizontally.

Warp knits are produced as flat goods, never as tubes. They do not run or ravel and they have greater dimensional stability than weft knits. The main types of warp knits used in apparel are tricot and raschel. *Tricot* is a flat single knit, usually made of nylon filament yarn, used to make panties, slips, and other lingerie. It accounts for the majority of warp knits. *Raschel* knits are open, lacy-looking knits. Another type of warp knit, *Simplex,* is common in swimwear.

Other Fabric Structures. A variety of other fabric structures are significant for use in the apparel industry, including the following.

1. *Fiberweb* or *nonwoven* fabrics result from neither weaving nor knitting, but are created directly from fibers by matting the fibers together with various techniques, including heat, adhesives, and tufting. Apparel manufacturers mainly use fiberwebs inside garments to provide shape; fiberwebs are typically less costly than other types of fabric. The durability of fiberwebs varies widely. A fiberweb inside the garment should endure wear and care as well as the fashion fabric and other components of the garment, but low-quality fiberweb fail before the rest of the garment. Felt is an example of a fiberweb.

2. *Bonded* fabrics are two distinct fabrics glued together as one. *Laminated* fabrics are a layer of fabric adhered to a layer of foam. Bonding and laminating are mainly used to add body to low-quality fabrics. The main problems with low-quality bonded and laminated fabrics are uneven shrinking or separation of the two layers.

3. *Film* fabrics are continuous sheets of fabric made directly from a polymer solution; for example, vinyl. Film fabrics are strong, durable, and easy to sew only if they are bonded or laminated.

4. *Lace* is a fabric structure resulting from twisting and knotting the yarns around one another (Figure 10-5). Although lace originated as a handcraft, almost all lace today is machine made. For example, machine-made laces imitate crocheted and tatted laces so well that they are difficult to tell from handmade. The cost of lace is related to its fiber content and the complexity of its production; knitted laces are the least expensive form of lace. Some laces can be made on more than one type of machine.

Count or Gauge. The count or gauge of a fabric identifies how densely it is fabricated.

Thread count or **yarn count** refers to the number of yarns per square inch of woven fabric; **cut** or **gauge** refers to the number of loops per square inch of knit fabric. Fabrics with high thread counts cost more than comparable fabrics with low thread counts because they contain more fiber. In general, the higher the thread count or gauge, the higher the quality of the fabric. An exception to this is a fabric intentionally woven or knitted loosely for design effect; for example, gauze.

Fabrics with low thread count are subject to raveling, fraying, and yarn slippage. The yarns shift if they are not held firmly in place, as are the yarns of tightly woven fabrics. Fabrics with high thread counts are durable, dimensionally stable, abrasion resistant, and resist snagging and pilling. High-thread-count fabrics have body and they press flat, making them suitable for tailored garments. Because so many yarns are packed into each square inch, they allow little air to penetrate, so they tend to be warm to wear. They are generally more opaque than fabrics with low thread counts. Fabrics with high thread counts may be initially water repellant but, once wet, they dry slowly. Because the yarns are packed so tightly together, they resist easing and have a tendency toward seam pucker (Figure 6-2). They are also stiffer and wrinkle more than low-count fabrics. The density of the fabric structure affects ease of garment production; dense fabrics are difficult for knives and needles to penetrate. Fabrics with low thread counts tend to be drapable; however, if the fabric does not have the desired amount of body, its hand is described negatively as *limp* or *sleazy*. The ratio of lengthwise and crosswise yarns in a fabric affects its durability. *Balanced* fabrics, with about the same size and number of lengthwise and crosswise yarns, are stronger and more durable with less yarn slippage than unbalanced fabrics.

Fabric Weight. The *weight* of a fabric should be appropriate for the garment design. Lightweight fabrics are suitable for styles with gathering or delicate details. Tailored styles or bold details require slightly heavier fabrics with more body. The weight of a fabric depends on fiber type, yarn size, and the fabric's count or gauge.

1. *Top weights* include light-weight fabrics suitable for making shirts, blouses, and dresses. They are sometimes referred to as shirt weight,

blouse weight, or dress weight. Top weights generally weigh between 2 and 5 *ounces per square yard* of fabric.

2. *Bottom weights* include somewhat heavier fabrics suitable for making pants, skirts, jackets, and coats. They are sometimes referred to as pant weight, skirt weight, suit weight, or coat weight. Bottom weight fabrics range from 7 to 15 ounces per square yard. Heavy coating fabrics can weigh over 20 ounces per square yard (Hudson 1988).

3. Heavy top weights and light bottom weights are sometimes referred to as *mid weights*.

Fabric weight offers an excellent clue to garment cost and quality when comparing similar garments. Heavy fabrics generally cost more than light fabrics because they contain more yarn and fiber; an expensive fabric often indicates an expensive garment. For instance, jeans made of heavyweight denim probably cost more to produce than those made of lightweight denim. A sweatshirt made of heavyweight fleece probably costs more to produce than one made of lightweight fleece. Mail-order catalogs often call attention to the heavy weight of the fabric in a garment as a sign of quality. There are exceptions to these generalizations. For example, when considering fabrics intended to be very fine and lightweight, a light fabric may cost more than a heavy one. This is true if fine yarns and additional labor are required to create the lightweight fabric than is used, for example, to make a fine silk scarf.

Fabric Thickness. The *thickness* of the fabric greatly affects how comfortable a garment is to wear. The thicker the fabric, the warmer it is, up to about one-quarter inch (Solinger 1980). Thick fabrics allow less air to penetrate and help the wearer retain body heat. The thickness of a fabric depends on yarn size and fabric structure.

For the manufacturer, fabric thickness affects ease of production. Very thin and very thick fabrics are difficult to handle and require special techniques for cutting and sewing. The manufacturer may need to reduce bulk in seams and hems.

Fabric Grain. One of the major considerations in garment quality is the orientation of the fabric's grain. Just as furniture makers observe and use the grain of wood to create a desired effect, garment manufacturers should use the grain in fabric to its best advantage. *Grain* is the orientation of the yarns that make up the fabric. The two sets of yarns that make up a woven fabric should be interlaced at right angles to one another. While, technically, knit fabrics do not have a grain, most of the same general directional rules apply in their use.

The appropriate handling of fabric grain affects the aesthetic and functional quality of the finished garment. Attention to grain is important throughout construction but is most critical during cutting. If cut incorrectly, trueness of grain cannot be restored to the garment.

Lengthwise Grain. The **lengthwise grain** or **warp** runs parallel to the **selvages,** the woven edges of the fabric (Figure 4-6). It consists of the yarns that are held taut by the loom during weaving. Therefore, the mill makes the lengthwise yarns the strongest to withstand the tension of the weaving process. Lengthwise yarns are very stable, not apt to stretch or shrink, and hang straighter than other yarns. For these reasons, lengthwise yards are usually worn lengthwise on the body, perpendicular to the floor. Manufacturers cut most pattern pieces on the lengthwise grain, with the length of the pattern piece parallel to the lengthwise grain.

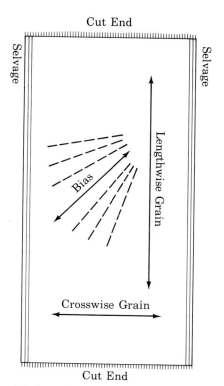

Figure 4-6 *Lengthwise and crosswise grains, bias and true bias.*

Crosswise Grain. The **crosswise grain** or **weft** consists of the yarns woven over and under the lengthwise yarns to create the fabric. The crosswise grain runs at a 90-degree angle to the lengthwise grain and the selvages (Figure 4-6). The crosswise grain is slightly less strong, less stable, and does not hang as straight as the lengthwise grain. Therefore, the crosswise yarns are usually worn going around the body, parallel to the floor; the manufacturer places most pattern pieces with their length running perpendicular to the crosswise grain of the fabric.

If the producer cuts pattern pieces on the crosswise grain, with the length of the pattern piece running in the same direction as the crosswise grain, the effect on the hang of the finished garment may be imperceptible. But crosswise layouts are generally less desirable than cutting the pattern pieces on the lengthwise grain because of the superior qualities of the lengthwise yarns.

In only a few cases it is preferable to cut pieces on the lengthwise grain, but to have this grain run around the body instead of up and down. For example, waistbands require stability around the waist and should be cut so that the lengthwise grain goes around the body. Collars, cuffs, and other minor pattern pieces may be cut this way for the same reason.

Sometimes major pattern pieces are cut on the crosswise grain, to maximize fabric usage or to create special effects. For example, on border print fabrics (with the design along one selvage edge), if a dress design calls for the border print to run around the hem, the skirt is cut on the crosswise grain.

Straight-of-Grain. **Straight-of-grain** includes both the lengthwise and crosswise grains because they follow the straight yarns of the fabric. Unless there are design reasons for doing otherwise, manufacturers should lay out pattern pieces on the straight-of-grain, in the lengthwise direction. Figure 4-7 shows the commonly accepted placement of grainlines on the human body for a basic garment. The lengthwise grain runs straight down the body at the center front and center back. The crosswise grain is perpendicular to the lengthwise grain at bust/chest and hip levels. For sleeves, the lengthwise grain runs straight down the center of the arm from shoulder to elbow. The crosswise grain is perpendicular to the lengthwise grain at bust/chest level.

To create various effects, a designer alters the

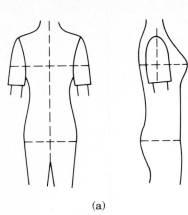 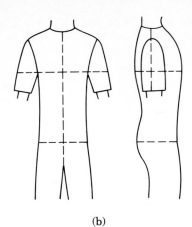

(a)　　　　　　　　　　　　　　　　　　(b)

Figure **4-7** *Correct positions of fabric grain on (a) female and (b) male bodies.*

position of the lengthwise grainline and changes the way the garment hangs. Pattern pieces cut on the lengthwise grain, crosswise, bias, or true bias create various results. Figure 4-8 illustrates how a skirt appears with the lengthwise grain placed at center front, side front, and at the side seam of the skirt.

Most manufacturers use the lengthwise grain to follow the length of the body and the crosswise grain around the body. However, it is often difficult to distinguish between the lengthwise and crosswise grains just by looking at a garment unless you are familiar with the fabric. A close examination of the fabric usually reveals more lengthwise yarns per square inch than crosswise yarns. Also, if a woven fabric is stretched, the lengthwise grain generally stretches less than the crosswise grain.

Bias and True Bias. The bias and true bias of a fabric are not considered grains, but rather directions, of the fabric. Technically, any direction that is not the lengthwise grain or crosswise

grain may be referred to as **bias**. The **true bias** occurs at a 45-degree angle to the lengthwise and crosswise grains of woven fabrics. Usually when a garment is "cut on the bias," that refers to the true bias (Figure 4-6). The true bias of a woven fabric has several interesting features (the bias direction on knit fabrics does not share these characteristics). True bias is the most stretchy part of a woven fabric because its stretch is impeded by few yarn interlacings. Garments or pieces of garments cut on the true bias drape and roll beautifully and hang close to the body, emphasizing contours.

For these reasons, many high fashion designers include bias cuts in their creations, especially for evening wear. Full skirts cut on the true bias are flattering to the wearer and elegant. Bows, neckties, cowl necklines, and jacket and coat under collars utilize the graceful drape and roll of the true bias. The stretch and roll of true bias makes it ideal as binding for curved as well as straight edges. Bias cuts are not used much in low-price lines. A bias layout wastes

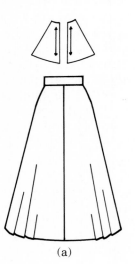 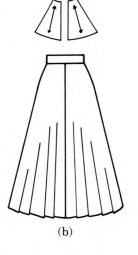 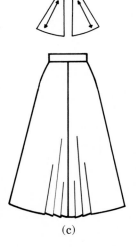

(a)　　　　　　　　　　(b)　　　　　　　　　　(c)

Figure **4-8** *Different drape of skirts cut on various grains: (a) lengthwise grain at center front, (b) lengthwise grain in center of each gore, and (c) lengthwise grain at side seams.*

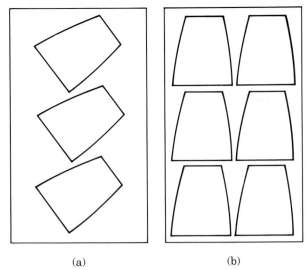

(a)   (b)

Figure 4-9 *(a) bias layout is less fabric-efficient than (b) straight-of-grain layout.*

considerably more fabric than a straight-of-grain layout for the same garment (Figure 4-9), as much as 40 to 60 percent more (Hudson 1988). Also, bias-cut garments are difficult to sew because they tend to stretch out of shape during construction.

A garment cut on the bias is easily identified upon close examination. The fabric's straight-of-grain lies on the diagonal, oriented at a 45-degree angle to the center front of the garment. *Do not confuse* the bias with the appearance of a twill fabric like denim or gabardine. Examine a pair of jeans, which are cut on the straight-of-grain, and notice that the diagonal ridges of the denim fabric result from its twill weave, not from being cut on the bias.

Garments with proper grain alignment hang straight and maintain their shape. Garments cut only slightly off-grain do not hang perfectly but the problem may be very subtle. In such cases, a close examination of the position of the lengthwise and crosswise yarns of the fabric is necessary to reveal the accuracy with which the garment was cut on grain. Garments which are cut extremely off-grain have a noticeably crooked hang. Evidence of the misuse of fabric grain includes twisted pant legs, twisted torsos, twisted sleeves, uneven hems, undesirable sagging and wrinkling in fitted garments, and pleats that fall open. When making the marker, some manufacturers tilt the pattern pieces slightly off-grain (usually not more than 3 percent) to increase material utilization. How far off-grain the manufacturer allows the pieces to

be cut depends on the tolerances established. For low-quality garments, several inches off-grain may be allowed.

Some manufacturers tilt the pieces of tight-fitting pants, cutting them slightly off-grain so they can stretch (because of the introduction of bias) to fit a wider range of people. And the bias helps the pants cling to the body. However, too much tilt causes the pants legs to twist because they are not cut on straight-of-grain.

Off-Grain Fabrics. When the fabric grain becomes distorted during processing, the fabric is referred to as **off-grain;** the lengthwise and crosswise yarns do not lie at perfect right angles to one another as they should. Using off-grain fabrics results in finished garments that do not hang straight. The two main forms of fabric grain distortion are bowing and skewing (Figure 4-10). Sometimes during the processing of a fabric, the selvage edges feed faster than the center of the fabric. The result is a *bowed* fabric, in which the lengthwise yarns are straight but the crosswise yarns *arc* across the fabric. If, during the processing of a fabric, one side feeds faster than the other selvage, a *skewed* fabric results. In this case, the crosswise yarns *slant* from one selvage to the other. In some fabrics, both bowing and skewing are present. Woven fabrics are more subject to skewing, and knit fabrics to bowing.

In many cases, grain defects do not become apparent until after the garment has been laundered and the yarns relax and return to their original positions. A difficult problem for jeans manufacturers is compensating for the natural skew of denim fabrics, even those of high quality, resulting from the twill weaving process.

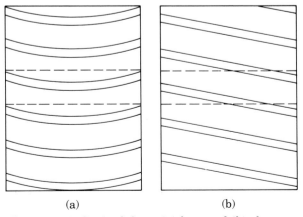

(a)   (b)

Figure 4-10 *Grain defects: (a) bow and (b) skew.*

Tilting the garment pieces on the fabric slightly, in the opposing direction, helps compensate for the tendency of the twill weave to twist the fabric. T-shirts and other garments made from circular knit fabrics frequently twist after laundering. The fabric is skewed as a natural result of the circular knitting process, causing the finished garment to twist (Figure 4-11). The manufacturer must compensate for this skew to avoid twist in the finished garments. Sewing operators contribute to twist if they feed seam plies at uneven rates. Production pattern makers contribute to twist if they develop pattern pieces with nonsymmetrical flare or taper; pattern pieces must have equal amounts of flare or taper on both sides of the grain line for the garment to hang straight.

If an off-grain fabric is permanently heat set, the fabric grain cannot right itself, so the grain defect is not noticeable in the finished garment. An exception is when a pattern (e.g., stripe or plaid) is woven into the fabric. In such a case, the skewing of the pattern draws attention to the fact that the grain is not straight.

Grain distortions and their effect on garment appearance are relative. Thus, garments cut slightly off-grain or from slightly off-grain fabrics may be acceptable if the problem is imperceptible in the final garment. However, manufacturers of high-quality clothing strive to produce "grain perfect" garments.

Directional Fabrics. Some fabrics are *directional*; they have a definite top end and bottom end that must be observed in cutting. Directional fabrics include napped fabrics such as velvet, velveteen, and corduroy, and pile fabrics; for example, fake fur. All the nap or pile must lie in the same direction in the finished garment, usually so that the wearer brushes the nap or pile down the body. This causes the least disturbance of the nap or pile during normal wear. Directional fabrics also include *one-way designs* such as floral prints with all the flower stems pointing down, teddy bear prints with all the heads pointing up, and vertically uneven stripes, checks, and plaids. A patterned fabric should be carefully examined to determine if it has a one-way design versus an *all-over design,* which is not directional.

A directional fabric usually is spread with each ply of the fabric face up, a layout called **nap-one-way (NOW).** The manufacturer orients the tops of all the garment pieces in the same direction on the fabric. This does not allow as fabric-efficient a layout as **nap-either-way (NEW),** the face to face layout for ordinary, nondirectional fabrics.

When the fabric has a direction that must be observed within the same garment but which can vary from garment to garment, the fabric may be spread **nap-up-and-down (NUD).** Pieces from alternating layers are sewn together so that the direction of the fabric is consistent within each garment. For example, in Figure 4-12 the two children's corduroy overalls of the same style appear to vary in color—one appears light and the other dark; they were cut from alternating layers of an NUD layout. This causes them to reflect light differently, and the finished garments appear to have been cut from two different colors of fabric.

DYES

Dyes add color to the undyed, unbleached fabrics, also called **greige goods** (pronounced *gray goods*). Most dyes are water-soluble chemicals that bond with the fibers or build up on or within the fibers. The type of dye used influences the aesthetic and functional performance of the fabric. Dyes affect the fabric's strength, abrasion resistance, luster, absorbency, and dimensional stability. For example, different dyes alter the amount of stretch in a knit fabric. Dyes influence the hand of the fabric, including its drape,

Figure 4-11 *Twist in a knit shirt.*

texture, and ease of production. The type of dye used helps determine how the garment should be laundered or dry cleaned. The color of the dye affects the fabric's opacity; dark colors are typically more opaque, or have more *covering power,* than light colors. Dyeing is a merchandising decision as much as a technical decision because color is critical to consumers when considering which garment to purchase.

Dyestuffs. *Dyestuffs* are the various chemicals used to color fabrics. Some types and colors of dyes are more colorfast than others; some fade more than others in reaction to light, water, detergents, or bleaches. Colorfastness must be balanced with the desire for a particular color because, in some cases, the desired color is not available in the most colorfast dye. These problems are the concerns of dye chemists, who formulate the best dye type for the fiber, type of garment (for example, swimwear should be colorfast to sunlight and chlorine), stage of application, and desired color. However, the cost to buy and then to apply dyestuffs varies considerably, so sometimes the dye chemist makes compromises.

A consumer cannot tell by looking at a fabric or garment the type of dye used and how colorfast it is. Sometimes labels describe the colorfastness of the garment; however, there is no legislated meaning for the term *colorfast* on a label. **Vat dyes** are one of the most colorfast types of dyes. The use of the term *vat dyed* on a label usually indicates excellent colorfastness (depending on the fiber type) and is perhaps the only evidence the consumer has of good colorfastness, beyond assurances from the manufacturer. Some garments are, because of their color and the limitations of technology, less colorfast than others; consumers should be informed about what to expect from such garments so the wearer will not be disappointed when the garment loses color. Manufacturers need to set minimum standards and perform product testing to ensure good colorfastness. Their reputation and the satisfaction of their customers depend upon it.

Dye Application. Fabrics can be dyed in the fiber, yarn, fabric, or garment stage. It is not usually possible to identify the stage in which dye was added by examining a garment, although some processes may be eliminated from consideration. The main methods of dye application include the following:

Figure 4-12 *These two children's corduroy overalls were cut out with the nap running in opposite directions, making them appear different in color.*

1. **Solution dyeing,** or **dope dyeing,** is the dyeing of manufactured fibers before the fibers are formed, while they are still in the liquid stage. Fabrics made from such fibers have the greatest colorfastness because the dye penetrates and is locked inside the fiber. This process, as well as the dyeing of natural fibers in the fiber stage, may be called **fiber dyeing.** Fiber dyeing produces the most even dyeing results in the finished fabric. The main disadvantage of fiber dyeing is that manufacturers have to commit to color decisions far in advance of the selling season, as much as two years before. To reduce the risk of making the wrong color decision, manufacturers fiber dye only basic-colored garments. They make fashion-color decisions closer to the selling season to reduce the risk of making an incorrect prediction about what color will be most popular.

2. **Yarn-dyed** fabrics receive their dyes in the yarn stage. This is the last chance to add color for stripes, plaids, and other designs that are to be woven in, not printed on. Yarn-dyed fabrics tend to be more evenly colored than piece-dyed fabrics. However, if poorly dyed, the dye does not penetrate the center of the yarn, leading to uneven results.

3. **Piece-dyed** fabrics are dyed in the fabric stage. This is the easiest and least expensive stage for adding color and probably the most common. Traditionally, the fabric is dyed and the garment is made from the colored fabric.

This allows color commitments to be made close to the selling season.

4. There is an increasing trend toward **garment dyeing.** The manufacturer produces the garment from greige goods and then dyes the finished garment. The big advantage of garment dyeing is that the manufacturer can make color decisions at the last minute, dyeing garments in the proven best-selling colors and avoiding a large inventory of colors that are not popular. For example, The Gap contracts the production of thousands of basic white T-shirts and then dyes them according to the best-selling colors as needed. Garment dyeing works best on knit fabrics made of cotton or other absorbent fibers, but it is used on a variety of fabrics. It is mainly limited to solid-color fabrics, although, occasionally, patterns are chemically imprinted on the greige goods. The patterns "pop," or appear due to a reaction between the chemical imprinting and the dye formulation, when the garment is dyed.

A disadvantage of garment dyeing is that it requires extra skill and care to achieve even dyeing; streaky, uneven coloring often results. Any dyeing errors are costly because not only is the fabric ruined, but the cost of producing the garment is lost as well. A number of other problems are inherent in garment dyeing. Fasteners may rust or stain the garment when they get wet or are exposed to chemicals in the dyeing process. Sometimes garment shrinkage occurs during the dyeing process, garment parts cut from different rolls of fabric accept the dye differently, or threads are abraded or broken during dyeing. Findings, for example the thread or lining, may not dye to the same color as the fashion fabric and, as a result, may not match the finished garment. Needle holes or chews from poor sewing often accept too much dye, making them very noticeable. Labels undesirably may accept dye, interfering with their appearance or readability. However, the challenges of garment dyeing are being met by manufacturers for whom the benefits of garment dyeing outweigh the disadvantages.

PRINTING

Printing is the application of designs onto the fabric using dyes or pigments in limited areas. Patterns, for example flowers or geometric designs, can be printed on or woven into fabrics. Generally, printed-on patterns are less costly than woven-in designs because of the complexity of weaving a patterned fabric.

A good-quality printed design is clear, focused, and sharp, not smudged. If the producer applies different colors in sequence, each color should be precisely lined up or **in registration.** A print that is *out of registration* has white areas in the design or places where the colors overlap. Patterns containing numerous colors and details are generally costly to produce. Patterned fabrics, whether printed on or woven in, tend to mask wrinkling, puckering, soiling, and construction errors in the garment better than solid fabrics, improving ease of production.

Designs should be printed onto the fabric on the straight-of-grain. When plaids, checks, stripes, or other obviously directional designs are printed onto a fabric in a skewed or bowed manner, they appear crooked on the finished garment. If the design is printed only slightly off-grain, the manufacturer should cut the garment straight with the directional pattern rather than on the straight-of-grain. Although the garment may not hang perfectly straight, it looks straighter than a garment that hangs straight but has a crooked stripe or plaid. If the design is printed drastically off-grain, the fabric should not be used but be returned to the mill.

For durability of a printed design, the dyes or pigments used to create the design must be absorbed by the fabric. A heavy application of color is generally more durable than a light application, but even more important is that the color bond to the fiber or be absorbed by the fiber. Some knit fabrics do not absorb printed-on dyes, but merely hold them on the surface of the wales of the fabric. When the garment is stretched during wear, separation of the wales distorts the printed design.

Manufacturers use several methods to apply prints to fabrics, including the following:

1. *Direct printing* involves applying a pattern by directly rolling it onto the fabric using a series of differently colored cylinders. The cost of preparing the rollers makes direct printing suitable only for large runs.

2. *Jet printing* is a relatively new technique. It utilizes a computer that directs streams of dye from jets toward the fabric in a predetermined pattern.

3. *Screen printing* applies colored ink, using a squeegee, through a screen that has some areas blocked off to create a stencil. A series of screens are used to apply different colors to

achieve multicolored designs. The ink is then heat cured. Screen printers print entire fabrics or apply designs to finished garments like T-shirts and sweatshirts. Screen print ink is best absorbed by fabrics that are made entirely or mostly of cotton. The more ink deposited on the fabric, the more durable the screen-printed design. The formulation of the ink and how it is cured also affect durability. Poorly cured screen prints crack or peel readily in use. High-quality screen prints are in registration; all the colors fall within their intended areas and do not overlap other areas. The manufacturer should dispose of the chemical by-products used in screen printing in an environmentally sound manner. Overall, screen prints cost less per garment than transfer printing if a large quantity of the same graphic is run, but for small runs the cost of designing the screens is prohibitive.

4. *Transfer printing* involves transferring a design from a specially printed paper to the fabric using heat and pressure. Heat transfer prints can be chosen by the consumer and applied by the retailer to the fronts of T-shirts and sweatshirts at the point of sale because the process requires a minimum of equipment. It is also used by manufacturers to apply designs to garments either before or after they are sewn. Transfer prints adhere best to garments that are made entirely or mostly of synthetic fibers. The durability of heat transfer prints depends on the amount of heat, pressure, and time used to transfer the design. For durability, the design must deeply penetrate and bond with the fabric, rather than adhering only to the surface.

If properly executed, heat transfer printing allows greater design clarity, better penetration of the fibers, and therefore a more durable design, and less pollution (except for the paper waste) than screen printing. Transfer printers achieve a variety of three-dimensional, foil, and other special effects, including sometimes combining transfer prints with screen prints. Heat transfer prints tend to crack and peel over time, especially when exposed to high washing and drying temperatures. Transfer prints are more economical than screen prints for small runs. Paper, not garments, is kept in stock, lowering inventory costs for transfer printing versus screen printing.

FINISHES

A myriad of *finishes,* mechanical and chemical fabric treatments, is available for imparting de-sirable performance characteristics to fabrics. Almost any performance aspect of a fabric can be improved through the application of the appropriate finish. For example, finishes affect the strength or absorbency of the fabric. However, some finishes enhance one aspect of performance but detract from another, stiffening the fabric's hand too much, for instance. In such cases, the manufacturer must choose a level of finish that achieves the best overall performance possible with the available technology.

Usually, consumers cannot see fabric finishes. Therefore, manufacturers should inform consumers about the presence and performance features of various fabric finishes. In addition, fabric finishes often affect whether or not garments are washable or dry cleanable; many finishes are damaged by improper care. The manufacturer's recommended procedures should be followed to preserve the finish and ensure that the garment performs as expected. Many finishes gradually diminish over the life of the garment, regardless of care, but appropriate care maintains the finish for as long as possible.

Garment Washing. **Garment washing** or **garment rinsing** is perhaps the most important *wet-process* finish for jeans and other casual clothing in recent years. The completed garment is washed before it is sold to the consumer. Garment washing softens, preshrinks, and sometimes fades the garment before it goes to the consumer. Garment washing minimizes the shrinkage experienced by the consumer; thus it is sometimes called prewashing or preshrinking because it eliminates the majority of relaxation shrinkage in the garment before it reaches the consumer. Consumers can try on garment-washed apparel at the time of purchase, knowing that the fit will not change drastically after home laundering. Many consumers have become accustomed to purchasing garments that are too large and expecting them to shrink after laundering. Garment washing requires the reeducation of consumers to buy garments of the correct size and to expect little shrinkage after laundering. Garment washing adds as much as 10 percent to the cost of the garment. Manufacturers must install giant washing and drying facilities, and the production problems inherent in garment dyeing are also present in garment washing.

Stone washed, acid washed, frosted, and other distressed-look, wet-process finishes for jeans and casual clothing are achieved by garment washing in conjunction with the use of rocks or other abrasives, and bleaches or other chemicals, that alter the surface appearance of the fabric. Clothing that has been physically or chemically abraded by garment washing is not as durable as other apparel. Holes may appear in the folded edges at hems, pockets, or waistbands at the point of sale. Consumers should be aware of the decreased durability of such apparel. They need to understand the trade-off of durability for the distressed look. Manufacturers should try to achieve a reasonable balance between the distressed look and the durability of the garment. Fabrics may be prewashed to preshrink them before they are cut and sewn, but that does not produce the preferred, naturally worn look achieved by wet processing the finished garment.

Mechanical Finishes. *Mechanical finishes* are generally used to alter the appearance and texture of the fabric surface. A few of the most common mechanical finishes are summarized in Table 4-3. Some of these finishes have trademark names registered by their producers.

Chemical Finishes. *Chemical finishes* are added to enhance a variety of performance dimensions. Shrinkage control, garment washing, durable press, and sizing are a few of the main chemical finishes. Other common chemical finishes are summarized in Table 4-4. Many of these finishes have trademark names registered by their producers.

Durable press is a chemical finish that helps garments maintain their shape and their pressed appearance after many washings and wearings. Such finishes are also called **permanent press,** although the finish is not permanent. Fabric producers apply the durable-press chemical finish to the fabric and then bake the fabric in a curing oven to bond the finish to it. Fabrics may be finished with a durable-press finish before the garment is made, or the durable-press finish may be applied after the garment is constructed. If the finish is applied in the garment stage, alterations are difficult because creases from the original seam lines remain after alteration, and new creases cannot be pressed in. If applied in the fabric stage, the finish causes the fabric to resist being shaped into a garment.

Durable-press garments require little or no ironing; wrinkles fall out. However, wearers of garments finished with a durable-press may notice some problems, depending on the particular type of finish used (some durable-press processes

TABLE 4-3
Mechanical finishes for fabrics

compression: compressing the fabric to return it to its original dimensions to control relaxation shrinkage. Sometimes combined with chemical shrinkage control finishes. Examples include the *Sanforized* trademark on cotton and cotton blend fabrics, and its related labels, Sanforized Plus, Sanforized Plus 2, Sanfor Knit and Sanfor Set. All guarantee residual shrinkage of less than 1 percent.

heat set: used to control shrinkage of fabrics made from thermoplastic fibers. The amount of heat that will soften the fiber without melting is applied; then the fabric is cooled. After heat setting, the fabric will not shrink or wrinkle unless the heat set temperature is exceeded. Heat setting is also used to permanently set details, such as creases or pleats, into a garment. Details that have been heat set maintain their shape throughout the life of the garment unless the heat setting temperature is exceeded.

napped: fibers pulled up from the yarns to make the surface soft, thick, and warm.

brushed: nap or pile of the fabric raised by brushing.

embossed: decorative textures pressed into the fabric; *moiré*, a watermark design, is an example.

glazed: polished finish combining resins/wax/starch and heavy pressing; some glazes are more permanent than others.

TABLE 4-4
Chemical finishes for fabrics

shrinkage control: used alone or in addition to compressive shrinkage techniques to maintain dimensional stability of fabrics; for example, allow wool fabrics to be machine washed without shrinking.

sizings: starches or resins added to the fabric to improve the appearance of and add body to fabrics. Sizings add to the aesthetic value of the garment at the time of purchase by making the surface smooth and crisp. They are often used on low-quality fabrics to improve their appearance and hand. Although some sizings are semipermanent, most are temporary. Temporary sizings can mislead consumers into buying garments that they would not otherwise purchase. After laundering, if the sizing washes out, the garment may be limp and lifeless, have little luster, and require ironing, leaving the consumer dissatisfied.

mercerization: strengthens cotton and linen; makes the fabric lustrous and absorbent.

water repellent: helps fabric repel light rain and resist wet spotting and staining; important for raingear and other outerwear; well-known trademarks are Zepel and Scotchgard; not durable to care processes, but can be reapplied by dry cleaner or consumer

waterproof: completely repels rain; most are uncomfortable to wear because the fabric cannot breathe.

moth repellent: repels moths in wool fabrics.

soil release: increases the absorbency of fabrics; increased absorbency also improves the launderability of the fabric, helping it repel and release soil and stains and reduce static buildup; generally improves fabric hand; some reduce durable press characteristics and cause yellowing or dullness.

antistatic: increases fabric's ability to absorb water and therefore conduct electrical charges; important for lingerie and some work uniforms.

softeners: give fabrics a pleasant hand but generally decrease absorbency; consumer use of fabric softeners in the laundry helps maintain softness and antistatic characteristics; restrict use of softeners on diapers, terry cloth robes, and other garments intended to be absorbent

flame retardant: makes fabrics flame resistant. By law, flame-retardant finishes used on children's sleepwear must withstand 50 machine washings. They also must be nontoxic and noncarcinogenic (not cancer causing). Garments with flame-retardant finishes require special care even though they look and feel like other garments; consumers must follow the manufacturer's suggested care instructions.

antibacterial: prevents perspiration odor; found in some socks

---

are better than others). Durable-press garments tend to attract oily stains and sometimes have an offensive odor. The finishes sometimes cause the seam of the garment to pucker and also reduce strength and abrasion resistance of the garment. But many consumers are willing to accept the limitations of the durable-press finish in return for its easy-care advantages. For example, uniforms often have a durable-press finish. These finishes are superior to **wash and wear** finishes, which reduce wrinkling but require some touch-up pressing.

Summary

Quality fabric is a prerequisite for a quality garment. Fabric alone cannot predict garment quality. The fabric interacts with the design, other materials, and construction of the garment to yield its overall performance. However, fabric is an essential indicator because it makes the greatest single contribution to the cost and quality of the garment.

The design of a garment, its end use and price

line, fashion trends, and personal preferences determine the required performance characteristics of the fabric in a garment. Aesthetic performance specifications include standards for color, color consistency (no shading), luster, opacity and hand (drapability, compressibility, extensibility, resilience, density, texture, thermal character). Most aesthetic performance standards are subjective and difficult to accurately measure and specify. Most functional performance standards can be objectively measured and specified. Standards for measuring and rating fabric performance have been established by the ASTM, AATCC, KES, and FAST. Functional performance specifications deal with utility dimensions of the fabric; for example, its number and severity of flaws; ease of production; shape retention (resistance to shrinking or stretching); appearance retention (colorfastness and resistance to wrinkling, snagging, pilling, and heat); comfort (breathability, warmth, absorbency, and electrical conductivity); ease of care; and safety. Functional performance specifications also relate to the durability of the fabric, including its tear and bursting strength, abrasion resistance, resistance to yarn slippage, and ability to withstand degradation by mechanical and chemical means and natural elements.

The performance of the fabric is a result of the interaction of the physical dimensions, including the fibers, yarns, fabric structure, dyes, prints, and finishes. Fibers are the basic building blocks of a fabric and provide important clues to fabric performance. Though fibers have some characteristics in common with others of their same type, either natural or manufactured, individual fibers vary considerably in performance. They are spun into yarns, the threads from which fabrics are made. Staple-yarn fabrics are duller looking and generally more comfortable to wear than filament-yarn fabrics. High-quality yarns usually have high twist. Weaving, the interlacing of yarns, is the most common method for producing fabric. Knitting, the interlooping of yarns, is a more economical fabrication than weaving. Knits tend to be comfortable but dimensionally unstable because they stretch. Fabrics with a high thread count or gauge tend to be stable and of high quality. Heavyweight fabrics generally cost more and are of higher quality than lightweight fabrics. To hang straight, garments should be cut on the straight of the fabric's grain. They may be cut on the bias for special effects. Directional fabrics should be laid out so that the fabric's direction

is consistent in the finished garment. Dyes add color to fabrics. The earlier the dye is added, the more colorfast, but adding the color later gives the producer more flexibility in following fashion trends. Prints should be clear, durable, on-grain, and in registration. Chemical and mechanical finishes are applied to enhance garment performance. For example, they can reduce shrinkage and wrinkling, and increase body and luster.

Fabric Quality Checklist

If you can answer yes to each of these questions regarding the garment you are evaluating, it contains high-quality fabric. The ability of the garment to meet many of these performance standards cannot be evaluated visually, but must be determined through laboratory or wear testing.

- Is the fabric free of flaws? If not, are the flaws inconspicuous?
- Is the appearance of the fabric compatible with the design and end use of the garment?
- Is the color consistent within the garment or ensemble (no shading)?
- Is the hand (including drapability and texture) of the fabric suitable for the design of the garment?
- Does the fabric lend itself to the mass production process?
- Does the fabric retain its original shape and size (resist shrinking and stretching)?
- Is the fabric adequately colorfast?
- Does the fabric retain desirable creases?
- Does the fabric resist undesirable wrinkling?
- Does the fabric resist snagging and pilling?
- Does the fabric resist heat damage?
- Is the fabric comfortable?
- Does the fabric stretch if stretch is necessary for comfort and good fit?
- Does the fabric breathe?
- Is the fabric warm or cool, as called for by the end use of the garment?
- Is the fabric absorbent?
- Does the fabric have good wicking ability?
- Does the fabric resist static cling?

- Is the fabric easy to care for?
- Is the fabric safe (for example, fire resistant)?
- Is the fabric durable?
- Does the fabric resist tearing and bursting?
- Does the fabric withstand abrasion?
- Do the yarns resist shifting?
- Does the fabric resist chemical and mechanical degradation?
- Can the fabric withstand insects, mildew, and sunlight?
- Are the yarns tightly twisted?
- Is the thread count or gauge high?
- Is the garment cut on the straight-of-grain (or on the bias for special effects)?
- Are prints durable, clear, on-grain, and in registration?
- Are finishes permanent or semipermanent?
- Is leather top grain and free of blemishes?
- Are furs soft and lustrous? Are fur garments made using fully-let-out versus skin-on-skin construction?

New Terms

If you can define these terms and differentiate between related terms, you have gained a good working vocabulary for discussing the topics in this chapter. The terms are listed in the order in which they appear in the chapter.

fabric
American Textile Manufacturers Institute (ATMI)
Kawabata Evaluation System for Fabrics (KES)
Fabric Assessment by Simple Testing (FAST)
piece goods
Four Point System
lab dips
dye lot
shade lot
hand
dimensional stability
colorfastness
thermoplastic
heat set
wicking ability
tensile stength/tenacity

yarn slippage
fibers
natural fibers
manufactured/man-made fibers
blend
top grain/genuine leather
split
fully-let-out
skin-on-skin
yarn
spun yarn
filament yarn
yarn number
denier
Tex
plain weave
twill weave
satin weave
weft/filling knit
wales
courses
warp knit
thread/yarn count
cut/gauge
lengthwise grain/warp
selvage
crosswise grain/weft
straight-of-grain
bias
true bias
off-grain
nap-one-way (NOW)
nap-either-way (NEW)
nap-up-and-down (NUD)
greige goods
vat dye
solution/dope/fiber dyeing
yarn dyed
piece dyed
garment dyeing
in registration
garment washing/rinsing
durable/permanent press
wash and wear

Review Questions

1. Explain the relationship of fabric quality to garment quality.

2. What percentage of shrinkage represents one full size in a garment of woven fabric?

3. What steps can manufacturers take to reduce garment shrinkage experienced by consumers?

4. How does fiber content affect fabric performance?

5. Summarize the general characteristics of natural fibers versus manufactured fibers.

6. How does fiber content impact the care of the finished garment?

7. Discuss the effect of yarn type, twist, and size on fabric performance.

8. Compare and contrast the characteristics of woven fabrics and knit fabrics.

9. List and describe the three main types of weaves. Repeat for the two main types of knits.

10. What is the significance of thread count or gauge?

11. Why should a garment be cut on-grain? Which grain is typically placed parallel to the length of the body and why?

12. Describe the characteristics of garments cut on the bias.

13. What are the advantages and disadvantages of garment dyeing?

14. List the criteria for a high-quality printed design.

15. Discuss how finishes can improve fabric and garment performance.

Activities

1. Visit an apparel manufacturer. Ask to see their fabric and garment testing facilities. Find out:
   a. what instrumental and other tests they perform
   b. how they establish performance criteria for the fabrics they use
   c. how they inspect for flaws
   d. the number and type of acceptable flaws
   e. how they deal with flaws through the manufacturing process
   f. how they inspect for color consistency
   g. steps they take to avoid shading in the finished garment

2. Purchase three one-half-yard pieces of fabric. Describe the fabric's physical and performance features, including the hand of the fabric. For each piece of fabric, select a picture of a garment for which the fabric is suitable and another for which it is unsuitable.

3. Purchase a new garment. Measure it before and after laundering. How much did it shrink in length and in width (inches and percentage)? Why did it shrink (or not shrink)? Compare results with your classmates.

4. Purchase two new, identical, colored garments. Wash one five times. Evaluate the garments' colorfastness, crocking, frosting and mark-off by comparing the two after each washing. Compare results with your classmates.

5. Examine a sweater that you have worn several times. Has the fabric pilled? If not, why not? If so, why? Where is the pilling concentrated and why?

6. Examine a leather garment. What special construction techniques were used and why?

7. Examine a fur garment. What special construction techniques were used and why?

8. Using ½″ strips of colored paper, with one color as the warp and one color as the filling, weave a sample of the plain weave, the twill weave, and the satin weave. Find an example of each weave in your wardrobe.

9. Pull and twist a cotton ball into a yarn. Note the impact of increased twist on yarn strength, fineness, and luster.

10. Compare a similarly styled low-price and high-price garment. What differences, if any, do you see in the thread count of the fabric and in its weight and thickness?

11. Examine a low-price and a high-price example of the following garments for use of grain and grain trueness. Do you find any differences based on price? On classification?
   a. men's necktie
   b. jeans
   c. men's shirt
   d. skirt
   e. T-shirt
   f. jacket

12. Squeeze the fabric of a durable press garment in your fist for 15 seconds and release. Repeat on a garment of similar fabric without a durable press finish. What differences do you see?

5

Stitches: Holding the Garment Together

CHAPTER OBJECTIVES

1. Differentiate between stitch types.
2. Evaluate the advantages and disadvantages of various stitch types.
3. Discuss the influence of stitch length and tension, needles and threads, and other features on stitch performance.

Stitches hold a garment together; therefore, stitch quality is a critical gauge of apparel quality. The care a manufacturer uses in establishing stitch specifications often represents the overall quality standards used in producing the garment. The thoughtful selection of stitch types and the appropriate choice of factors such as stitch length, tension, needles, and threads positively influence stitch, and thus garment, performance. The evaluation of the stitches in a garment contributes important information for judging its overall quality.

Stitch Performance

Stitches are the thread interloopings used to make *seams,* the joints between two pieces of fabric that are sewn together (see Chapter 6) and *stitchings,* which perform functions other than joining pieces of fabric together. *Edge finish stitchings (EF)* finish garment edges (see Chapter 7) and *ornamental stitchings (OS)* add decoration (see Chapter 10).

Stitches are by far the most widely used technique for assembling apparel. Consumers accept stitches more readily than they accept stitchless techniques such as adhesives and ultrasonic welding. Gluing is mainly useful in leather and leatherlike garments. Ultrasonic welding melts and fuses together fabrics with at least 65% synthetic (thermoplastic) fibers, and costs about one-tenth as much as stitches (Moreland 1985). However, fusing is well accepted only in raingear, to seal the seams, making them waterproof. For other fabrics and other end uses, these methods, although less costly, tend to be less durable, less comfortable, and less attractive than stitches. Alternative methods of joining fabrics will likely be further developed to improve their performance; meanwhile, stitches are the basis of most garment construction.

Stitches help determine the functional and aesthetic performance of a garment. Their durability, comfort, and attractiveness are important performance considerations determined by the end use and design of the garment, the type of fabric used, and the location and purpose of the stitches. Cost limitations also affect the choice of stitches.

Strong, durable stitches relate directly to seam strength and garment durability. Weak, nondurable stitches lead to premature seam failure. Garments that receive hard wear and heavy laundering require more durable stitches than those worn for special occasions. Locations subject to stress require stronger stitches than low-stress locations. Highly stressed seams also require extensible stitches. For example, one of the most common places for seam rupture is the seam joining the sleeve to the body of the garment. Another common place for seam failure is the seat seam (center back seam) of pants. These highly stressed seams are cut on the bias of the fabric, which provides stretch. However, if the stitches used to sew the seams do not stretch with the fabric, the stitches rupture.

Garments made of knit fabrics, such as swimsuits and sweaters, require more extensible stitches than those made of woven fabrics. The stitches must withstand the amount of stretch to which the fabric is subjected without rupturing. To test for adequate stitch extensibility, stretch a garment seam in a high-stress area. Adequately extensible stitches do not rupture.

Stitches affect the wearer's comfort. For underwear, sleepwear, and active sportswear in which physical activity may cause the stitches to chafe the skin, comfort is particularly impor-

tant. Infants, the very elderly, and bedridden people have a special need for comfortable stitches because their skin is thin and sensitive. Some stitch and thread types are more comfortable than others.

Uniform stitches placed in a straight line (or smoothly curved line on curved seams) contribute to the attractiveness of the garment. Stitches that cause puckers, holes, snags, or runs, or that allow the seams to spread open or fail, detract from the garment's appearance. Some stitches are attractive for decorative stitching; others are appropriate only for use inside the garment.

Physical Features of Stitches

The desired aesthetic and functional performance of stitches is achieved by controlling the following physical features of stitches: stitch type; stitch length and width; needle type, size and condition; thread type and size; tension and other sewing machine adjustments; and operator accuracy. Manufacturers choose the physical features of stitches based on desired stitch performance, balanced with cost. Manipulating the physical features results in various levels of performance and cost.

STITCH TYPE

Stitch type impacts functional and aesthetic performance. Several different stitch types may be used in constructing a single garment (Figure 5-1). Each stitch type has performance advantages and disadvantages and purposes for which it is best suited. Manufacturers consider the fabric of the garment, the location and purpose of the stitches, and the style, fit, and end use of the garment to determine which types of stitches to use. The cost of stitches depends on the amount of labor, thread, and fabric required and the sewing machine used.

Lockstitch and Chainstitch Sewing Machines. Most machine-made stitches are formed by either a **lockstitch** sewing machine or a **chainstitch** sewing machine. Lockstitch machines rely on *interlocking* threads; chainstitch machines rely on *interlooping* threads. Lockstitch and chainstitch machines both feature a *needle thread*. The needle thread enters the fabric from above, carried by the sewing machine needle. The needle thread feeds from a large cone or other type of thread package. The difference in lockstitch and chainstitch machines lies in the delivery of the *underthread,* which enters the fabric from below.

Lockstitch Machines. Lockstitch machines feature an underthread called a *bobbin thread.* The bobbin thread feeds from a small, round *bobbin,* a cylinder of thread located beneath the needle. As the machine sews, a rotary hook, or shuttle hook, revolves around the bobbin. The rotary hook catches the needle thread when the needle brings it down through the fabric. The rotary hook carries the needle thread all the way around the bobbin; then the needle pulls the needle thread back up to the top of the fabric again. The needle thread and bobbin thread become interlocked, forming a lockstitch.

To achieve high sewing speeds, the size of the bobbin around which the rotary hook must revolve is limited. Because of its limited size, a bobbin can hold only about 100 yards of thread. Operators must remove and replace the bobbin frequently during sewing, interrupting productivity and increasing labor costs. A single operator may make over 100 bobbin changes in an eight-hour shift. Each time, the operator must refill the bobbin or insert a prewound bobbin purchased from the thread company.

Chainstitch Machines. Most chainstitch machines feature one or more underthreads, called *looper threads,* instead of a bobbin thread (some chainstitch machines have no underthreads). Each looper thread is carried back and forth by a moving arm, either a *looper* or a *spreader.* The looper or spreader holds the underthreads in position to interloop with the needle thread every time the needle brings it down. This repeated action forms a chain of thread on the underneath side of the fabric, creating the chainstitch.

Looper threads feed from large cones of thread; no bobbin is required. This allows the operator to sew without the interruption of changing the bobbin, making chainstitches less costly in labor than are lockstitches.

U.S. Fed. Std. No. 751a. U.S. Fed. Std. No. **751a: Stitches, Seams, and Stitchings** sche-

matically diagrams the conformation of each stitch type and defines it. The original purpose of the Federal Standard was to achieve greater uniformity in sewn products, such as military uniforms, that the government contracts out for construction. Because of its usefulness, the Federal Standard has been adopted by the apparel industry for general use. It enables designers, manufacturers, contractors, and retailers to differentiate between stitch types and communicate about them more accurately, eliminating misunderstood specifications. The stitch types are illustrated, which makes the Federal Standard well suited to international communication. Some manufacturers remain unfamiliar with the Federal Standard, but could benefit from becoming acquainted with its advantages because the Federal Standard includes most, but not all, stitch types used in ready-to-wear. This chapter discusses the most widely used stitch types within each class. Refer to a copy of *U.S. Fed. Std. 751a* for a complete listing.*

Stitch Classes. *U.S. Fed. Std. No. 751a* established six classes of stitches. The general performance of stitches in the six classes is summarized in Table 5-1. The classes used to categorize stitches are as follows:

Stitch class 100	Simple chainstitches
Stitch class 200	Hand stitches and their machine simulations
Stitch class 300	Lockstitches
Stitch class 400	Multithread chainstitches
Stitch class 500	Overedge stitches
Stitch class 600	Cover stitches

The first digit of a three-digit number identifies each stitch class. The second and third digits of the number identify the stitch type within the class (Figure 6-4). For example, 503 and 521 are stitch types within the 500 class. Stitch types within a class are similar but vary in the number and exact arrangement of threads. The Federal Standard is the best available tool for identifying stitches, and it is used widely in the industry to designate stitch types. Appendix C lists the stitch types used for various garment construction operations. To make multiple rows of the same stitch type, each row

* *U.S. Fed. Std. No. 751a* can be obtained for about $6 from General Services Administration, Specifications Section, Room 6654, 7th and D Streets, Washington, DC 20407.

DRESS SHIRT

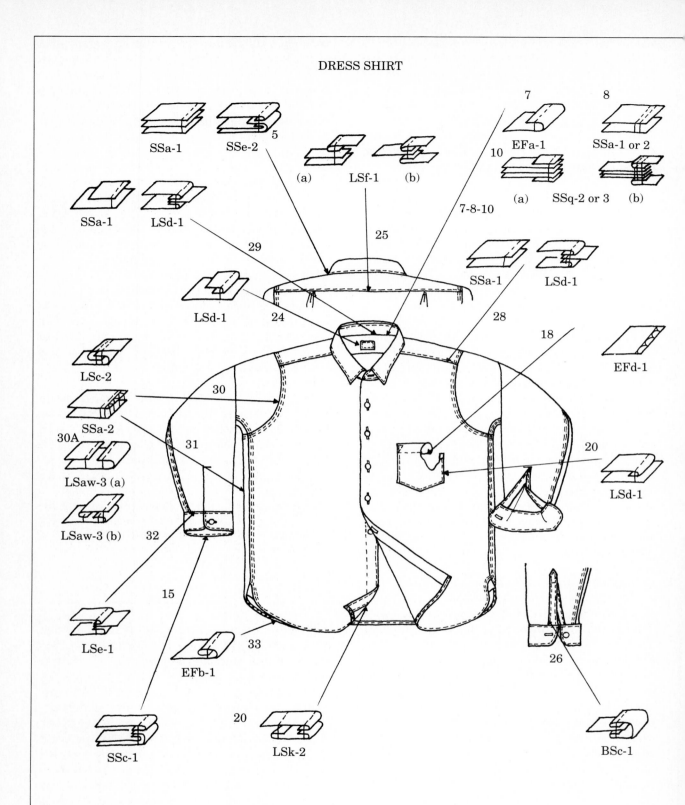

Figure 5-1 *Stitches, seams, and stitchings used to make a man's dress shirt. (Courtesy of Union Special Corporation.)*

OP. DESCRIPTION	SEQUENCE OF OPERATIONS	
	Stitch/Seam	Est. Doz./Hr.
Collars		
1. Fuse collar & band		50
2. Attach plastic stays	301 SSa-1	30
3. Runstitch collar	301 SSa-1	15
4. Trim, turn, & press collar points		
5. Topstitch collar	301 SSe-2(b)	16
6. Trim collar edge		
7. Hem collar band	301 EFa-1	20
8. Attach collar band to collar	301 SSa-1	15
9. Turn & press collar band		
10. Sew-down collar band	301 SSq-2(b)	18
11. Buttonhole collar band		
12. Button sew collar band	101	37
13. Trim & notch collar band	Hand	
Cuffs		
14. Precrease cuffs		
15. Topstitch cuffs	301 SSc-1	7-½
16. Buttonhole cuffs		25
17. Button sew cuffs	101	24
Pockets		
18. Serge pocket tops	504 EFd-1	40
19. Precrease pockets		
Fronts & Backs		
20. Hem button stay (Rt side)	401 EFb-1(inv)	30
21. Buttonhole front (Rt)		10
22. Set center plait	401 LSm-2	25
23. Button sew front	101	10
23a. Set pocket to Lt front	301 LSd-1	18
24. Attach label to yoke	301 LSd-1	16
25. Set back to yoke	401 SSa-1	20
Sleeves		
26. Attach sleeve facing	301 BSc-1	12-½
27. Tack sleeve facing	301	10
Assembly		
28. Join shoulder seam	401 SSa-1	15
29. Attach & sew-down collar	301 LSf-2(b)mod	4
30. Set sleeves	401 LSc-2	8
ALT. (French sleeving)	301 LSaw-3(b)	8
31. Side seam & close sleeves	401 LSc-2	8
32. Set cuffs	301 LSe-1	7-½
33. Hem bottom	301 EFb-1	7-½
34. Trim & inspect	Hand	

may be sewn separately. More commonly, however, independent, parallel rows of stitches are sewn simultaneously using a multineedle machine. Special machines allow multiple needles to negotiate sharp corners so that the rows of stitches stay parallel at collar and lapel points and other corners.

100-Class Stitches. Stitches in the **100 class** are **single-thread chainstitches** (Figure 5-2). These chainstitches are categorized separately from their nearest relatives, 400-class chainstitches, because they usually are made using only a needle thread with no underthread. The needle thread interloops with itself on the back of the fabric to form a simple chain.

ADVANTAGES. The loops of their chainlike structure give 100-class stitches extensibility. The use of only one thread for most 100-class stitches makes them economical. They are useful for **basting,** or temporary stitches, because they are easily unraveled.

DISADVANTAGES. Simple chainstitches represent low-quality standards because they lack durability. The last stitch must be secured or the stitches may *unravel* or come undone (also called *run back*). The 100-class stitches unravel easily because each stitch is secured only by its interlooping with the next stitch. Pulling a loose thread from a broken or unsecured stitch unravels all the stitches. These stitches are prone to seam grin, so called because the stitches of the seam show, or grin, when the seam is stressed (Figure 6-3).

VARIATIONS. Variations of 100-class stitches secure hems, sew on buttons, and make buttonholes and tacks at high speeds. However, 100-class stitches are not the most durable choice in any of these cases.

The most common stitch type of the 100 class is the *101*. It is a continuous row of straight stitches on the face of the fabric and a continuous chain of interlooped stitches on the back side. The 101 stitches are used to close bags of pet food. The *103* is a blindstitch. A **blindstitch** joins layers of fabric without the needle thread fully penetrating the top layer (Figure 7-3), and it should be imperceptible, or nearly so, from the outside of the garment. The depth of the stitches must be adjusted so that each one barely catches a few yarns of the outermost layer of fabric, securing the other layers to it but re-

TABLE 5-1
Summary of stitch class performance

Class 100

description	simple chainstitches, interlooped
cost	very inexpensive
durability	flexible but unravels easily
appearance	plain on face, single chain on back
comfort	less comfortable than 300
limitations	unravels too easily for use in quality apparel
special features	uses only one thread

Class 200

description	hand stitches/machine simulations, one thread up and down through fabric
cost	extremely high if by hand, by machine varies
durability	machine is more durable
appearance	machine is more uniform, hand may be less noticeable
comfort	hand is softer
limitations	decorative and specialty uses, not used for structural seams
special features	most are made on specialty machines

Class 300

description	lockstitches, interlocked
cost	labor costs higher than 400 but requires less thread
durability	strong, not very extensible
appearance	seams do not grin but tend to pucker, reversible
comfort	very comfortable, flat, nonbulky
limitations	bobbin must be changed, slowing production, not very extensible
special features	hard to unravel, 301 is most widely used stitch in industry

Class 400

description	multithread chainstitches, interlooped
cost	labor costs less than 300 but requires more thread
durability	strong, more extensible than 300
appearance	seam grin, less likely to pucker than 300
comfort	slightly less comfortable than 300 unless soft thread is used, bulkier than 300
limitations	can abrade, catch, and unravel easily
special features	main competition of 300s, combines with 500s in most safety stitches, can cover bottom of seam

Class 500

description	overedge stitches, interlooped
cost	labor costs less than 300 but requires more thread
durability	very extensible, strong, safety stitches very durable
appearance	seam grin a problem, not likely to pucker
comfort	less comfortable than 300 unless soft thread is used, somewhat bulky
limitations	can be used only on edges
special features	stitches seam, trims, and finishes edge simultaneously, most widely used in knitwear industry

Class 600

description	cover stitches, interlooped
cost	labor costs less than 300 but requires more thread
durability	very extensible, strong
appearance	several threads show face and back, not likely to pucker
comfort	less comfortable than 300 unless soft thread is used, stitch somewhat bulky but seam often not
limitations	stitches flat seams
special features	joins abutted or overlapped edges, covers top and bottom of seam simultaneously

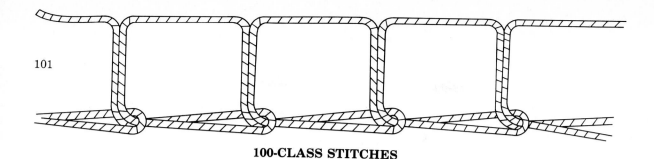

100-CLASS STITCHES

Appearance

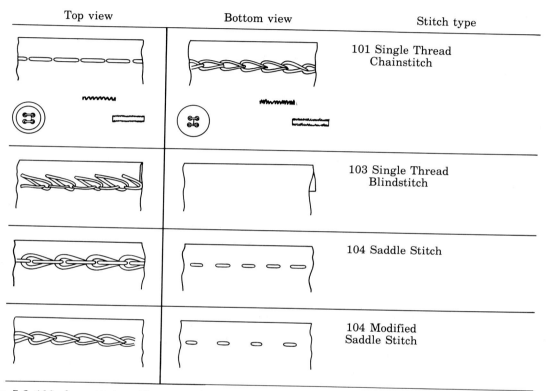

Top view	Bottom view	Stitch type
		101 Single Thread Chainstitch
		103 Single Thread Blindstitch
		104 Saddle Stitch
		104 Modified Saddle Stitch

Figure 5-2 *100-class stitches. (Courtesy of Union Special Corporation.)*

maining as inconspicuous as possible. Although they are used for hemming (see Chapter 7), 100-class blindstitches lack durability but are easily removed for hem alteration. The *104* stitches are decorative saddle stitches.

200-Class Stitches. Stitches in the **200-class** originated as **hand stitches.** Manufacturers use **machine-made versions** of 200-class stitches for decorative and other special purposes. The stitches are created on machines that pass a single thread through one side of the material and then the other. These machine imitations are produced much faster than actual hand-made stitches, which are found only occasionally in ready-to-wear. The 200 class does not include all the hand stitches and machine imitations of hand stitches used in ready-to-wear, only those classified for use in government procurement.

ADVANTAGES. Machine imitations of hand stitches are similar in durability, uniformity, and cost to other types of machine stitches. Though hand stitches are rarely found in ready-to-wear apparel, they are desirable in some cases because they provide shape, control, flexibility, and softness. They are used only where their cost is justified by the price of the garment. For example, high-quality men's neckties are hand slipstitched and tacked by hand for soft drape and attractive knotting. Finely tailored and couture clothing often feature hand stitches,

PHYSICAL FEATURES OF STITCHES **111**

lending the connotation of craftsmanship and quality. Some handwork is used in moderate-price apparel when relatively low production numbers do not justify mechanization of certain processes. Examples include sewing on closures, such as hooks and eyes; or decorative features, such as feathers. This occurs more often in womenswear than menswear because of frequent fashion changes which defy the cost-effective mechanization of some production processes.

DISADVANTAGES. Machine imitations of hand stitches are similar in performance to other types of machine stitches. However, hand stitches are generally less durable and less uniform than machine stitches. Hand stitches drastically lower production speeds and increase costs compared to machine stitches. For these reasons, almost all ready-to-wear apparel is sewn entirely by machine.

VARIATIONS. Figure 5-3 illustrates variations of the 200-class stitch. Stitch type *202* is a **backstitch.** Backstitching is a very secure form of stitching where one small stitch is taken backward (on the outside of the garment) for every

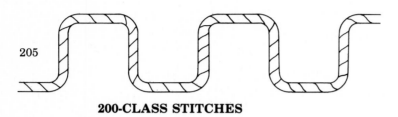

205

200-CLASS STITCHES

Appearance		Stitch Type	
Top View	Bottom View		
		202	Backstitch
			Prickstitch (Form of Backstitch)
		203	Decorative Chainstitch
		204	Catch Stitch/ Herringbone Stitch
		205	Running Stitch
			Saddle Stitch (Form of Running Stitch)

Figure 5-3 200-class stitches.

large stitch taken forward (on the inside of the garment). A variation of the 202 is the **pick-stitch,** or **prickstitch.** Pickstitches are tiny, decorative backstitches used to flatten and define lapel edges on jackets. They are also used to insert zippers by hand in couture clothing. Stitch type *203* is a **decorative chainstitch.** It is identical to the 101 stitch except the chain appears on the face side of the fabric rather than the back side. Stitch type *204* is a **catchstitch.** The catchstitch looks like a series of uneven *X*'s. It is a flexible, extensible stitch as well as a decorative one. Manufacturers use catchstitches to attach labels in high-price clothing and to perform other tacking jobs.

The simplest 200-class stitch is the *205,* the **running stitch.** The running stitch is created by the needle being passed up and down through the fabric, always moving forward, creating a space between each stitch. Manufacturers use long running stitches to *baste* or temporarily join garment pieces. **Saddle stitches** are decorative running stitches, ¼" to ½" long, used to accent the edges of lapels, pockets, and yokes, particularly of men's western wear. The **slip-stitch** is an "invisible" form of the running stitch. Slipstitches join a folded edge to another ply of fabric. The stitches are hidden in the fold. Manufacturers use slipstitches to attach linings at the armholes of high-quality tailored jackets and to close men's neckties.

300-Class Stitches. Stitches in the **300 class** are **lockstitches.** Lockstitches are composed of a needle thread interlocked with a bobbin thread. The threads interlock between the plies of fabric (Figure 5-4).

ADVANTAGES. Because the stitches are interlocked between the fabric plies, lockstitches appear identical on both sides; they are reversible. The stitches are flat and smooth on both sides, making them comfortable and protecting the thread from abrasion. The 300-class stitches are very tight and secure. Each stitch interlocks with the stitch on either side of it, so 300-class stitches resist unraveling of the stitches. They require less thread than other stitch types; they cause little bulk.

DISADVANTAGES. Lockstitches are not very extensible; they rupture easily if stretched or strained. They cause more seam pucker than other stitch types because most of the thread lies between the plies of the seam, crowding the area. The 300-class stitches require the operator to frequently interrupt the sewing process to replace the bobbin, making lockstitches relatively costly in terms of labor. Also, lockstitch machines stitch 3,000 to 5,000 **stitches per minute (SPM),** slower than most other types of industrial sewing machines. Lockstitches are difficult and time consuming to unravel when repairing or altering a garment.

VARIATIONS. The *301* stitch is the most popular stitch in the 300 class and the *most frequently used stitch in the production of apparel.* The 301, also called the **plain stitch** or **straight stitch,** is the same stitch made by conventional, home-sewing machines. The 301 results in a single, straight, continuous row of stitches on both sides of the fabric (Figure 5-5). It is widely used to sew seams in woven-fabric garments and to construct garment details. The 301 is popular for several reasons. It offers a flat, uniform, reversible appearance, plus comfort and durability. And it is the tightest of all stitch formations, minimizing seam grin.

The *304* is a **zigzag stitch.** The needle moves from side to side to produce a symmetrical zigzag pattern. The chief advantage of zigzag stitches is their elasticity; they stretch when the seam is stretched so that the stitches do not rupture. Manufacturers use zigzag stitches to attach lace and elastic and to sew underwear, foundation garments, and swimwear. Closely spaced zigzag stitches create buttonholes and tacks. Lockstitched buttonholes and tacks are more costly but more durable than if chainstitched.

The *308* and *315* are **multiple-stitch zigzag stitches.** The stitches resemble a 304 zigzag and are made in much the same way except that each diagonal portion of the zigzag is made up of more than one stitch. Stitch types *306, 313,* and *314* are **lockstitch blindstitches.** Like blindstitches in the 100 class, they join plies of fabric with stitches that are imperceptible, or nearly so, from the outside of the garment. Lockstitch blindstitches are the most durable type of blindstitch. Manufacturers use them to secure hems in high-quality garments.

400-Class Stitches. Stitches in the **400 class** are **multithread chainstitches** or **double-locked chainstitches** (Figure 5-6). The term "chainstitch" usually refers to the 400-class multithread chainstitch rather than to chainstitches in the 100 class. Multithread chainstitches are

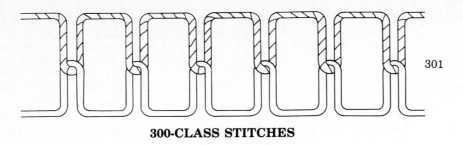

300-CLASS STITCHES

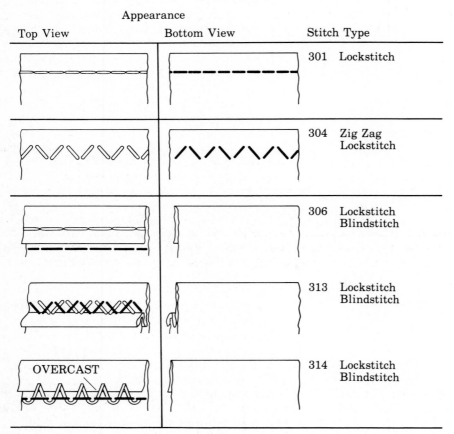

Appearance		Stitch Type
Top View	Bottom View	
		301 Lockstitch
		304 Zig Zag Lockstitch
		306 Lockstitch Blindstitch
		313 Lockstitch Blindstitch
OVERCAST		314 Lockstitch Blindstitch

Figure 5-4 300-class stitches. (*Courtesy of Union Special Corporation.*)

formed by a needle thread passing through the fabric and interlooping with one or more looper threads. The 400-class stitches are widely used in the apparel industry.

ADVANTAGES. The 400-class chainstitches have some advantages over their closest competition, 300-class lockstitches. Because they do not require bobbins, chainstitches help achieve high production speeds. Chainstitch machines can achieve speeds up to 9,000 SPM. Chainstitches are more extensible than lockstitches because of their looped structure, which stretches somewhat when stressed. This prevents the chainstitch from rupturing as easily as the lockstitch. Chainstitches are less likely than lockstitches to cause seam pucker because

most of the thread is outside the fabric plies. They do not require bobbins, making them relatively less costly to produce than lockstitches. Chainstitches are quick and easy to unravel if the garment needs repair or alteration.

DISADVANTAGES. Chainstitches have several disadvantages when compared to lockstitches. Chainstitches create a looser seam than do lockstitches and are more prone to seam grin. They also require more thread and thus create a bulkier seam than do lockstitches. Because chainstitches are formed outside the fabric layers rather than imbedded in between the layers like lockstitches, they may be less comfortable unless a soft thread is used. Because the thread is built up on the fabric, it abrades away more easily than that of lockstitches, which hug the fabric surface. The raised loops of chainstitches are easy to rupture on rings or jewelry, and the chainstitch is less durable than the lockstitch after rupturing. Pulling on a loose looper thread from a broken or unsecured stitch, in the direction of the stitching, unravels all the stitches. The double-locked structure of 400-class chainstitches makes them more immune to unraveling than 100-class chainstitches, but not nearly as resistant as lockstitches.

VARIATIONS. The most common of the 400 stitches is the *401*, the **two-thread chainstitch.** It consists of a needle thread interlooping with a looper thread. Because of their strength and extensibility, 401 chainstitches are more suitable than 301 lockstitches for sewing elastics, knit-fabric garments, or seams in woven-fabric garments subject to stretch and stress; for example, crotch seams, armhole seams, and elastic applications.

The 401 looks like a 301 lockstitch on the face of the fabric, but you can distinguish it by the double loops visible on the back (Figure 5-7). One must examine closely to differentiate the double loops of the desirable two-thread chainstitch from the single loops of the undesirable 101 single-thread chainstitch. 401 stitches are significantly stronger and more durable than 101 stitches.

The *402* is a **cording stitch.** It secures creases, such as those on the fronts of pant legs or the backs of gloves. Two rows of straight stitches appear on the face side with a looper thread on the back. The *404* and *405* are **bobbinless zigzag stitches.** They resemble a plain, lockstitch zigzag on the face side, but interloopings are visible on the back side. They serve the same purposes as lockstitch zigzags but are more elastic.

The *406* and *407* are **bottom cover stitches** or **bottom-covering chainstitches.** They feature two or three parallel rows of straight stitches visible on the face side. The many thread interloopings on the back side of these bottom cover stitches flatten the area and conceal raw edges by covering them with thread (Figure 5-8). Manufacturers use bottom cover stitches to make belt loops, to attach elastics and bindings to underwear, to hem T-shirts, and to flatten seam allowances of seams after they are sewn. For example, T-shirt and sweatshirt neckline seams (sometimes only the back half) are improved with the addition of a bottom cover

Figure 5-5 *Face and back of 301 stitch.*

stitch. Although requiring two runs through the machine, once to sew the seam and once to flatten it with the bottom cover stitch, the finished seam is comfortable and attractive.

500-Class Stitches. The term **overedge** is probably the best descriptive term for the **500-class stitches** (Figure 5-9); these are formed, as the description implies, over the edge of the fabric, encasing the edge in thread interloopings. Overedge stitches, an advanced form of chainstitch, sew a seam and simultaneously finish its raw edges to prevent raveling. **Overlock, serge, overseam, overcast,** and **merrow** also refer to 500-class stitches. Serging and merrowing generally refer to sewing on the edge of a single ply of material rather than to sewing a seam.

Overedge stitches are made on small, unconventional sewing machines called *overedgers.*

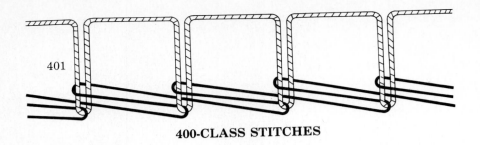

401

400-CLASS STITCHES

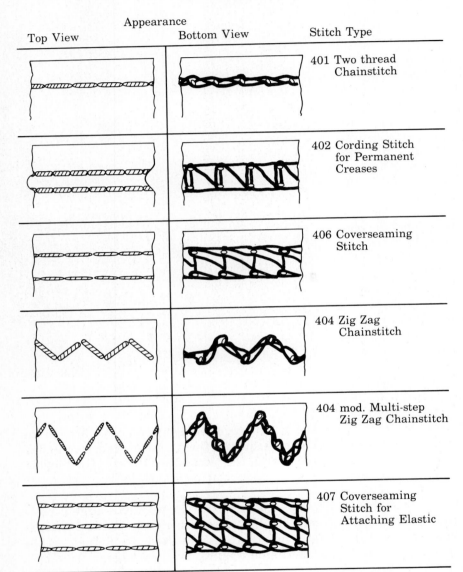

	Appearance		
Top View		Bottom View	Stitch Type

401 Two thread Chainstitch

402 Cording Stitch for Permanent Creases

406 Coverseaming Stitch

404 Zig Zag Chainstitch

404 mod. Multi-step Zig Zag Chainstitch

407 Coverseaming Stitch for Attaching Elastic

Figure 5-6 400-class stitches. *(Courtesy of Union Special Corporation.)*

Overedgers stitch *only* at the edge of a fabric, unlike conventional sewing machines used to make other classes of stitches, which can sew anywhere. Overedgers have a knife attachment that evenly trims the edge of the fabric just before the stitches are made, finishing the raw edge and preventing it from raveling. The stitches are formed over the trimmed edge by looper and/or spreader mechanisms that carry threads to the fabric edge where they interloop. Overedgers are well-suited to stitching and finishing narrow seams at garment edges. They cannot stitch within the body of a garment. They cannot stitch wide seams; their width is limited to about three-eighths inch. They can stitch straight or gently curved seams, but have diffi-

Figure 5-7 *Face and back of 401 stitch.*

Figure 5-8 *Face and back of bottom cover stitch. Also note illegible printed label.*

culty stitching around intricate curves or sharp angles.

ADVANTAGES. Overedge stitches are the most extensible of all the stitch classes because of their many interloopings. The ability to stretch without breaking has made them the workhorse of the knitwear industry. They are also popular in garments made of woven fabrics. Because they cover the raw edge of the material, overedge stitches neaten and prevent fabric edges from raveling better than any other stitch class. Manufacturers sometimes use overedge stitches to finish the raw edges of individual garment pieces before the garment is assembled. Overedge stitches cause little seam pucker because most of the thread bulk is outside the seamline. Seams sewn with overedge stitches require nar-

row seam allowances, conserving fabric. Sometimes the stitches compress the plies of thick fabric to lessen bulk. Overedge stitches require a lot of thread, but they reduce labor when used instead of separate seaming and seam finishing operations because they perform both steps simultaneously. And they sew fast—up to 9,000 SPM. Overall, they are an economical choice.

DISADVANTAGES. Overedge stitches have a fairly loose stitch formation, which makes them prone to seam grin. Most overedged seams cannot be pressed open to reduce bulk because the plies are sewn together at the edges. This is unacceptable for some garments and fabrics. Overedge stitches require more thread than most other stitch types. The presence of all that thread can make overedge stitches uncomfortable, but if the interloopings are flat and a soft thread is used, the stitches are adequately comfortable. Although overedge stitches rarely rupture as a result of stress, they do rupture if one

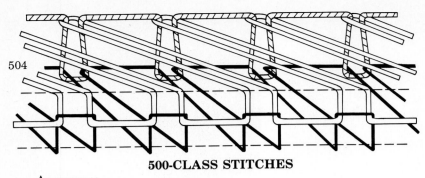

504

500-CLASS STITCHES

Appearance

Top View	Bottom View	Stitch Type	Application
1 Thread	Ndl. Thd.	501	Break-open Seaming (easily unraveled) Note: No purl
2 Threads	Ndl. Thd.	502	Seaming Bags, etc. Note: No purl
2 Threads	Ndl. Thd.	503	Serging Blindhemming Break-open Seaming Note: Purl on edge
3 Threads	Ndl. Thd.	504	Seaming Knit Goods, etc. Serging Note: Purl on edge
3 Threads	Ndl. Thd.	505	Serging Break-open Seaming Note: Double Purl
4 Threads	Ndl. Thds.	512	Seaming Stitch Mock Safety (simulated safety stitch) Note: Purl on edge
4 Threads	Ndl. Thds.	514	Seaming Stitch (produces strong seams on wovens or knits) Note: same as 512 but with long upper looper
4 Threads		515 (401 & 602)	Safety Stitch Seaming
5 Threads		516 (401 & 504)	Safety Stitch Seaming
6 Threads		519 (401 & 602)	Safety Stitch Seaming
3 Threads	Ndl. Thds.	521	Hosiery Stitch Note: Break-open stitch

Figure 5-9 *500-class stitches. (Courtesy of Union Special Corporation.)*

of their interloopings catches on a sharp object. Once broken, the effort required to unravel an overedge stitch depends on the stitch; some forms of the stitch unravel easily while others are resistant. Overedge stitches tend to unravel more easily than lockstitches but not as readily as 100- or 400-class chainstitches.

VARIATIONS. The *504* is the most popular stitch type in the 500 class. It features a needle thread and two looper threads. It simultaneously sews the seam and neatens the edge by trimming and finishing it, making it a very useful stitch (Figure 5-10). Its extensibility makes it ideal for sewing knitwear, in which narrow seams are acceptable. The 504 has a **purled edge,** a series of raised loops formed by the interloopings of the looper threads at the edge. The purled edge covers the raw edge of the fabric, preventing it from raveling. The tight needle thread of the 504 creates a tighter seam than most other overedge stitches. The other even-numbered stitches, *502, 512, 514,* and *516,* also have fairly tight stitch formations for seaming. But they are not particularly strong or durable choices for seaming woven fabrics.

The *501, 503, 505,* and *521* stitches, because of their loose stitch formations, hinge open flat like a notebook; thus, they are sometimes called **break open stitches.** None are well-suited for sewing structural garment seams; they are prone to seam grin. The 501, made with a single thread, does not make a strong, tight seam, but its break-open characteristics make it useful for joining pelts in fur coats. The 503 stitch, made with two threads, is commonly used to hem T-shirts and other knit garments. The resulting, hinged-open hem closely resembles a blind-stitched hem, and the purled edge helps prevent raveling of the fabric. Manufacturers also use the 503 stitch to overedge seams. The 505, made with three threads, is similar to the 503; it is sometimes called the **square edge** or **box edge stitch.** Stitch type 521 is a three-thread overedge stitch for seaming hosiery. The arrangement of the threads in the stitch makes it strong and extremely elastic.

The 503, 504, and 505 are the most frequent choices for overedging raw edges. Some manufacturers overedge individual garment pieces before the garment is assembled. This process may be automated, with the machine serging one edge of a single garment part, pivoting at the corner and serging the next edge, and so on until all the edges are overedged.

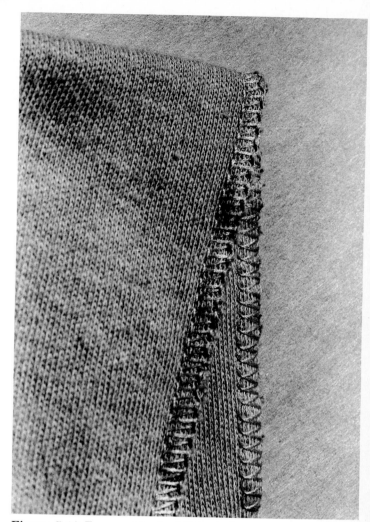

Figure 5-10 *Face and back of 504 stitch.*

SAFETY STITCHES. Perhaps the best overedge stitches for general seaming purposes are those classified as **safety stitches.** Safety stitches combine a row of overedge stitches with a row of straight lockstitches or chainstitches. The two independent rows of stitches simultaneously neaten and finish the raw edges of the seam. Safety stitches make a more durable seam than a single row of stitches. Two rows of stitches must rupture before the seam ruptures, providing a "safety" factor, thus the name. Safety stitches also create wider seam allowances than ordinary overedging, contributing to seam strength.

Identify safety stitches by the two independent rows of stitches on the face *and* back of the fabric. The row of straight stitches is parallel to the overedge stitches. A safety stitch requires more thread than stitch types consisting of a single row of stitches.

Safety stitches are used in the manufacture of shirts, blouses, jackets, pants, jeans, and skirts from both knit and woven fabrics of all weights. They are the most common stitch type used for sewing structural seams in unlined garments.

The three most common safety stitches are the *515, 516,* and *519.* They combine a row of overedge stitches with a row of 401 multithread chainstitches (Figure 5-11). These safety stitches simultaneously sew the seam twice, trimming and finishing the raw edge in just one run through the machine. Safety stitches have the same advantages and disadvantages as the stitch types used to make them.

The *517* and *518* safety stitches combine a row of stitches with a row of 301 lockstitches (Figure 5-11). These safety stitches are made by running the fabric through two different machines; a conventional sewing machine produces the lockstitch and a serger produces the overedging. The two runs require more labor and make these safety stitches more expensive to produce than those that are chainstitches. But safety stitches featuring the lockstitch have the advantages of resistance to unraveling, low bulk, minimal seam grin, and lower thread re-

quirements. The disadvantages, besides higher labor costs, are low extensibility and tendency to pucker.

MOCK SAFETY STITCH. Stitch type *512* is the **mock safety stitch** or **simulated safety stitch.** It resembles the safety stitches. Distinguish between mock safety stitches and true safety stitches by looking at the back of the stitch. On the face side they resemble a true safety stitch, with what appears as two independent rows of stitching, but on the back side the rows of stitches interloop (Figure 5-11). Mock safety stitches are strong and extensible, but once ruptured, they unravel more easily than true safety stitches. Only one row of stitches prevents a total seam rupture, as opposed to two in a true safety stitch. Mock safety stitches have a greater tendency to grin than true safety stitches. Mock safety stitches are less costly than true safety stitches because they can be produced at higher speeds. The *514* is similar in function to the 512, but does not resemble the safety stitches.

600-Class Stitches. Stitches in the **600 class** are **cover stitches,** also sometimes called *flat seam*

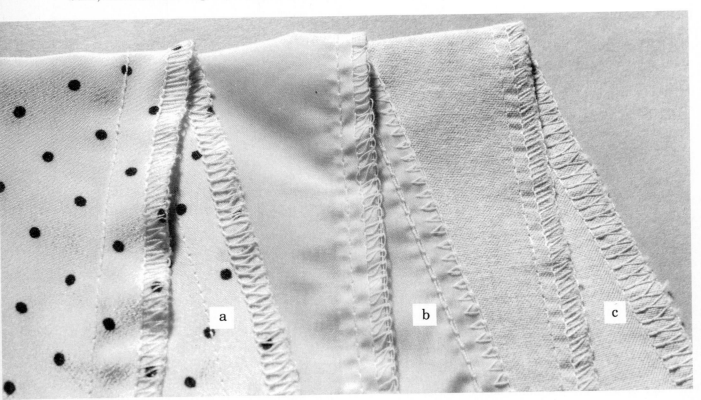

Figure 5-11 *Face and back of safety stitches made with (a) lockstitch, (b) chainstitch, and (c) mock safety stitch.*

stitches, interlock stitches, or flatlock stitches (Figure 5-12). Cover stitches sew flat seams in which the fabric plies abut or overlap slightly and are interlocked by the stitches. Occasionally, they are used to flatten the seam allowances of plain seams. Cover stitches, an advanced form of chainstitch, are characterized by their many ornamental interloopings. These interloopings appear on both the face and back side of the flat seam.

ADVANTAGES. The 600-class stitches join two fabric plies and cover the face *and* back of the seam with stitches in a single run through the machine. Thus, 600-class stitches are sometimes called **top-and-bottom-covering chain-** **stitches.** The top-and-bottom-covering capability of 600-class stitches is accomplished with the addition of *cover threads* interlooping with the needle and looper threads. The many interloopings of cover stitches yield strong and extremely extensible seams. The loops of 600-class stitches do not rupture when stretched. If torn on a sharp object, 600-class stitches do not unravel easily because of the many interloopings, although some unravel more readily than others. The 600-class stitches are not apt to pucker because most of the thread is not between fabric plies or on the seamline. The many interloopings of the stitch finish the raw edges of the fabric.

Cover stitches require little or no seam allowances, which conserves fabric. They are also

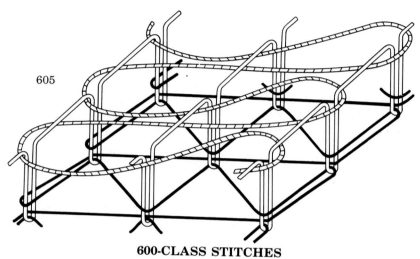

605

600-CLASS STITCHES

Appearance		Stitch Type
Top View	Bottom View	
		602 Coverstitch
		605 Coverstitch
		607 Flat Seaming Stitch

Figure 5-12 600-class stitches. (Courtesy of Union Special Corporation.)

more economical in terms of labor than the combination of a plain seam and a bottom-covering chainstitch, which requires two runs to produce a flat, comfortable seam. Machines making cover stitches run at fairly high speeds, 7,000 to 8,000 SPM.

DISADVANTAGES. Cover stitches use a lot of thread. The many interloopings of 600-class stitches, although fairly flat, can make seams uncomfortable unless a soft underthread is used. Manufacturers generally use cover stitches only on fabrics resistant to fraying and raveling; for example, knits. Cover stitches are unsuitable for sewing most woven fabrics.

VARIATIONS. The most common stitch in the 600 class is the *605* (Figure 5-13). It yields flat, strong, elastic seams for knit underwear, infant wear, swimwear, and active sportswear. The 602, similar to the 605, is also widely used. The most complex cover stitch is the *607,* which requires six threads: four needle threads, a looper thread, and a cover thread. The 607 stitch provides the best stretch, security, and smoothness of the 600-class stitches but is more costly than those requiring less thread.

STITCH LENGTH

Stitch length is an important determinant of the aesthetics and function of stitches. Manufacturers measure stitch length in terms of the number of **stitches per inch (SPI).** A standard stitch length is approximately 12–14 SPI, but stitches may be as long as 4 SPI or as short as 30 SPI. The ideal stitch length depends upon the weight, density, and type of the fabric, the purpose of the stitches, and the end use of the garment. In evaluating apparel, it is useful to be able to roughly estimate SPI at a glance (Figure 5-14). In many cases, stitch length is the best single criterion to use in quickly evaluating the overall construction quality of a garment.

Evaluating Stitch Length. Appropriate stitch length depends upon the type of fabric and its weight and density. Lightweight and loosely woven fabrics require short stitches, usually 15–20 SPI or higher. The heavyweight and densely woven fabrics call for long stitches, 5–10 SPI. Stitches too long or too short for the fabric may

Figure 5-13 *Face and back of 605 stitch.*

------------------------- 26 SPI

---------------------- 22 SPI

----------------- 16 SPI

-------------- 14 SPI

----------- 12 SPI

- - - - - - - - 10 SPI

- - - - - - - 8 SPI

— — — — — 6 SPI

— — — — 4 SPI

Figure 5-14 *Stitches per inch.*

lead to puckering (Figure 6-2). Pucker occurs when short stitches are used in densely woven or knit fabrics because the yarns of such fabrics are closely packed together. The addition of the thread from many short stitches to a densely packed yarn structure crowds the yarns of the fabric and causes the fabric to pucker. If extremely long stitches are used on lightweight or loosely woven fabrics, puckering also occurs. When the thread relaxes to its original length after being stretched during sewing, it tends to pull up or pucker the surrounding material. The puckering intensifies if there are fewer stitches and therefore less thread length to relax. The problem shows up most in lightweight and unstable fabrics because they succumb readily to the pulling.

Leather, as well as vinyl and other film fabrics, requires long stitches, 6–8 SPI. Short stitches make too many perforations in these materials and weaken the fabric. Therefore, stitches used to sew such fabrics are exceptions to the general rule that short stitches withstand more stress than long stitches.

The purpose of stitches helps determine their ideal length. For most seams, the previously discussed guidelines apply. To reinforce points of particular strain, small **reinforcement** stitches are used to help bear the stress. Reinforcement stitches, 18–20 SPI, reinforce areas that have narrow seam allowances and would otherwise rupture or ravel.

Topstitching is the use of stitches for decorative purposes (see Chapter 10). Slightly longer stitches than those used to construct the garment are appropriate for topstitching. Long stitches are more visible and therefore more attractive than short stitches for decorative topstitching. Because topstitching does not hold the structure of the garment together, long stitches do not detract from the durability of the garment.

Basting holds two or more layers of fabric in place temporarily. Because durability is not wanted, basting stitches are very long so they can be removed quickly. They hold fabric plies in position until these are permanently stitched, or hold welt pockets and skirt pleats in place until the garment is sold. Remove any visible basting before selling the garment.

Short Stitches. *Short stitches generally relate to increased stitch strength and durability.* You can point out the advantages of short stitches as buying benefits to consumers:

1. They withstand stress better than long stitches.

2. If they fail, short stitches make a smaller rupture in the row of stitches than when longer stitches break.

3. They are less apt to cause seam grin than long stitches because they make a tighter seam.

4. They deposit more thread in the seamline than long stitches, allowing the seam to be more extensible.

The general rule associating short stitches and durability is true only to a point; extremely short stitches perforate the fabric and its yarns so frequently that they may damage the fabric and actually weaken the seam.

In general, short stitches are related to high manufacturing costs. Because stitch length relates directly to the amount of labor required to sew a garment, it offers a good clue to the overall cost of manufacturing the garment. The longer the stitch, the farther a sewing machine can sew in the same amount of time. For example, if a sewing machine stitches 3,000 stitches per minute, at 10 SPI it sews 300 inches in one minute. But at 15 SPI, that same machine sews only 200 inches in one minute. Shortening the stitch length directly increases the amount of time required to sew a row of stitches and requires slightly more thread as well. Therefore, lengthening stitches is an easy way for manufacturers to cut costs. Most manufacturers producing garments in moderate-price lines use 10–12 stitches per inch, but high-quality garments are typically sewn with shorter stitches. For example, high-quality men's shirts of fine fabrics may be sewn with 25 stitches per inch or more. Stitch length has little effect on cost if the garment is manufactured in a very low-wage country. In such a case, short stitches can be put into a garment at little additional cost.

STITCH TENSION

Stitch *tension* refers to how loosely or how tautly the threads are held by the sewing machine as it sews. If the machine's tension is balanced, each stitch is formed correctly. However, if the machine holds the thread or threads too loosely or too tautly, the conformation of the stitches is altered, adversely affecting stitch appearance and lowering stitch strength. For example, tight tension stretches the thread (more than usual) as it is sewn. The thread then draws up or puckers the fabric when it eventually relaxes to its original length. Loose tension causes a loose stitch formation. To achieve consistently high-quality stitches, a trained engineer varies the tension and other sewing machine adjustments to suit the fabric.

Lockstitch Tension. Lockstitches are affected by unbalanced tension more than other stitch types. With unbalanced tension, they especially tend to pucker the fabric. Lockstitches with balanced tension contain a one-to-one ratio of needle thread to bobbin thread, which interlock in the middle of the fabric. When tension is unbalanced, the tension on either the needle thread or bobbin thread is tighter than the other, upsetting the one-to-one ratio. As a result, the threads do not interlock exactly in the middle of the fabric and are not equal in length to one another. The shorter thread, with the tighter tension, draws up the stitches and causes them to pucker the fabric.

Unbalanced tension can be visually identified. If the needle thread is tighter than the bobbin thread, the needle thread floats on the surface of the fabric and interlocks with the bobbin thread on top of the fabric instead of between the plies. Conversely, if the bobbin thread is tighter than the needle thread, the bobbin thread floats on the surface of the fabric and interlocks with the needle thread underneath the fabric instead of between the plies (Figure 5-15). Lockstitches with balanced tension appear identical on both sides of the fabric.

Balanced tension is crucial to the durability of lockstitches. Lockstitches with unbalanced tension rupture easily under stress. Evaluate lockstitch tension by pulling very firmly on each end of the row of stitches. If the tension is properly balanced, there is an equal amount of needle thread and bobbin thread in a row of stitches. Therefore, they extend to the same point and do not rupture easily. If the tension is unbalanced, there is more (or less) needle thread than bobbin thread. The longer of the two threads extends under stress, but the shorter thread breaks (Figure 5-16).

Chainstitch Tension. Perfectly balanced tension is not as important to the durability of chainstitches as it is for lockstitches. Chainstitches have more inherent extensibility in their stitch structure than do lockstitches. Therefore, the chainstitches do not rely on an equal ratio of needle thread to underthread for

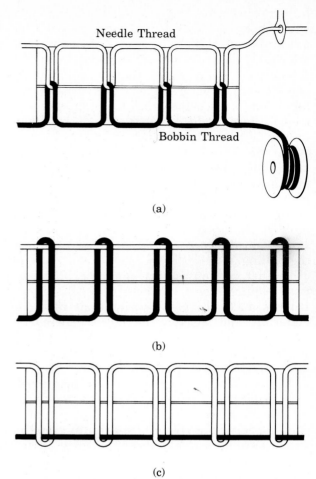

(a)

(b)

(c)

Figure 5-15 *Lockstitch tension: (a) balanced, (b) needle thread too tight/bobbin thread too loose, and (c) needle thread too loose/bobbin thread too tight. (Courtesy of Union Special Corporation.)*

the ability to "give." Balanced tension is even less important to the durability of overedge and cover stitches because of their great extensibility. However, the integrity and appearance of any stitch type is adversely affected if tension problems are severe (Figure 5-17).

SKIPPED STITCHES

Skipped stitches occur when the machine fails to sew an uninterrupted row of stitches; one or several stitches fail to interlock or interloop. The skipped stitches usually show up as a long float of thread instead of individual stitches. The result is unattractive and creates a weak spot. Skipped stitches result from the wrong needle or a defective needle; the incorrect thread for the fabric; improper sewing speed, feeding, or operator handling; misadjusted tension and

Figure 5-16 *Stitches with unbalanced tension rup-tured under stress.*

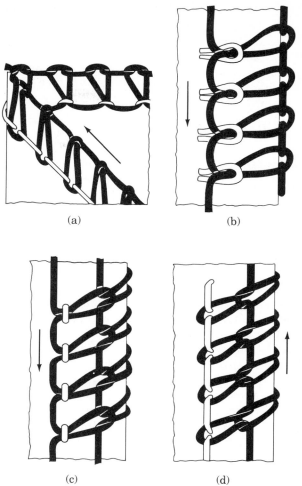

(a)   (b)

(c)   (d)

Figure 5-17 *Overedge tension: (a) balanced, (b) lower looper thread too tight/needle thread too loose, (c) lower looper thread too tight/upper looper thread too loose, and (d) upper looper thread too tight/lower looper thread too loose. (Courtesy of Union Special Corporation.)*

other machine problems. A new development on sewing machines is a skipped stitch detector so the row of stitches can be resewn as soon as the problem is detected.

STITCH WIDTH

Zigzag, overedge, and cover stitches have width as well as length. Most stitch widths or *bites* are one-eighth to three-sixteenths inch; more than one-quarter inch is unusual. Wide overedge stitches and cover stitches generally represent high quality when used to sew seams because wide stitches yield wide and thus strong seams.

Wide zigzags and overedge stitches are not suitable for lightweight fabrics. Wide bites distort lightweight fabrics because the fabric does not have the body to support wide stitches.

NEEDLES

Sewing machine needles of the correct size and type and in good condition yield high-quality

stitches. Heavy fabrics and loose weaves call for large, coarse needles. Light fabrics and tight weaves require small, fine needles. Needles that are bent, blunt, *burred* (damaged) and needles of the wrong size or type for the fabric lead to skipped stitches, needle cutting, needle heating, and needle chewing.

Needle Cutting. **Needle cutting** results when the needle cuts, or severs, the yarns of the fabric rather than slipping between the yarns. The needle damages the fabric, leaving unsightly holes, pulls, or snags. Needle cutting is a big problem in sewing knit fabrics. It is caused by a needle that is too large for the fabric, is blunt or burred, or has the wrong type of tip. Most woven fabrics are sewn with round point, *sharp tip* needles. *Ball tip* needles with slightly rounded tips should be used for sewing knits and very delicate wovens, which are prone to needle cutting. The rounded tips slide more readily between yarns of the fabric rather than severing them. Needles with flat-shaped tips are used on leathers and leatherlike fabrics to minimize needle cutting, which weakens the fabric.

Needle Heating. **Needle heating** occurs when sewing friction heats the needle, which *fuses* or melts the finishes or fibers of the thread or fabric. Needle heating results in a loss of thread strength, and therefore stitch strength. Also, buildup of the melted fibers on the needle causes it to skip stitches. Needle heating is a problem with synthetic threads and fibers that are *thermoplastic,* or heat sensitive. Large-diameter needles are prone to needle heating. Using the smallest needle possible without its breaking or cutting the thread reduces needle heating. A lubricant or special finish applied to the needle, thread, or fabric also reduces friction and needle heating. Sometimes manufacturers blow compressed air on the needle to keep it cool. However, fast sewing speeds are the main cause of needle heating, so the simplest solution to the problem is for the operator to slow down. For example, lowering the sewing speed by 2,000 SPM drops the needle temperature 160 degrees F (Glock and Kunz 1990). Lowering sewing speeds reduces productivity, so most manufacturers try alternative solutions first.

Needle Chewing. **Needle chewing** results in jagged, enlarged needle holes in the fabric. These result when the fabric does not move forward properly and the needle repeatedly enters the same area. The machine appears to "eat" the fabric as the operator and/or machine tries to force the fabric forward. Needle chews detract from the attractiveness and durability of the garment. They result from sewing machine maladjustment, poor operator technique, and choice or condition of needle.

THREAD

Thread forms the stitches that hold a garment together. Thread is often the least costly component of a garment, but its failure can cause the entire garment to fail. The strength, durability, appearance, and texture of the thread af-fect the performance of the stitches and the garment.

Strength. The strength of thread is critical to the durability of stitches. The breakage of weak thread slows down manufacturing and results in ruptured stitches. The most important aspect of thread strength is *loop strength,* or the force necessary to separate two stitches. Thread should be compatible in strength with the fabric, never stronger (see Chapter 6). Thread must withstand the same wear and care as the garment.

Threads should be fairly dimensionally stable, but must be extensible enough to withstand stress without breaking, especially in stretchy fabrics such as knits. However, if an extensible thread stretches during sewing, it puckers the surrounding fabric when it later relaxes to its original length. Cotton thread is prone to this problem.

Heavy fabrics require coarse, multi-ply threads, and lightweight fabrics demand fine threads. Large-diameter threads are strong but also are subject to abrasion and tend to cause seam distortion. Threads exposed to heavy wear, like those used to make buttonholes, should be abrasion resistant. Threads with inadequate abrasion resistance fray and wear out quickly. To minimize puckering, the finest thread possible should be used, considering the weight of the fabric and the strength and durability requirements of the seam. A strong fiber type and high amount of twist improve the strength of a thread. For example, fine, tightly twisted threads are stronger and more abrasion resistant than large, loosely twisted threads. However, too much twist causes knotting and kinking that interferes with stitch formation.

Fiber Content. Sewing thread can be made from almost any textile fiber. Most threads are polyester, nylon, cotton, or rayon. *Polyester* and *nylon* lend strength, and resistance to the chemicals used in wet processing. *Cotton* is weaker and less resistant to chemicals than the synthetics but has excellent sewability characteristics. Mercerized cotton threads are stronger than soft, unfininshed cotton threads because the finishing process strengthens the cotton fibers. *Rayon* thread is rather weak yet dyes beautifully and is lustrous; *silk* thread is rare, costly, and beautiful. Cotton, rayon, and silk threads are used when polyester or nylon threads are too strong for the fabric, and for decorative stitches.

Spun. The main categories of thread used in apparel manufacturing are spun and corespun. **Spun thread** consists of staple fibers spun into single yarns; two to six of these yarns are twisted together to make a thread. The most common thread is spun polyester. Spun threads are strong, elastic, and abrasion resistant, but subject to needle heating. They are also slick, increasing the tendency of stitches to unravel. Spun threads are generally less pleasant to the touch than corespun threads unless they are texturized for comfort. Texturizing provides soft, bulky extensible underthreads for 400-, 500-, and 600-class stitches. These stitch types expose the skin to thread buildup and are comfortable only if a soft underthread is used. Spun thread costs significantly less than corespun thread.

Corespun. Each ply of **corespun thread** consists of a spun core of polyester or nylon wrapped with cotton or other fibers. Several plies are usually twisted together to make one thread. A synthetic core makes the thread fine, strong, and elastic. Corespun threads generally have greater strength for their size than spun threads. Because of their fineness, they are less apt to cause puckering, and the imprint of the stitches is less apt to press through a thin fabric. A cotton wrapping lends the thread resistance to needle heating. Core threads, with a soft outer layer of cotton, tend to be comfortable. Overall, corespun threads have superior sewability over spun threads.

Filament. **Monofilament** is the most common filament thread. It is a clear thread made of a single filament of nylon resembling a fishing line. Clear monofilament thread is inconspicuous in a garment of any color. Therefore, manufacturers that use monofilament thread reduce the amount of time spent changing thread cones and rethreading machines when they sew different colors of garments. They also eliminate the need for a costly inventory of thread in multiple colors. Thus, monofilament thread is cost effective.

Monofilament nylon thread is very strong and abrasion resistant. However, it is *too* strong for many fabrics. When a monofilament thread ruptures, it is so slippery that the whole line of stitching readily unravels. Monofilament thread is the least comfortable type because it irritates the wearer's skin, especially if it breaks and a free end contacts the skin. For these reasons, manufacturers do not widely use monofilament thread except in low-price lines, and sometimes for hems in other price lines.

Multifilament threads consist of several filament yarns twisted together to make a very strong thread. These threads may be texturized, which reduces their high luster and gives them greater coverage, useful for cover stitches. **Texturized threads** also are more comfortable for stitches that contact the skin. They are less apt to unravel than slippery filament threads.

Color. Coordinating thread color is a mark of quality. The hue, shade, and luster of the thread should match or complement the dominant color of the fabric. Attention to a minor detail such as matching thread color not only demonstrates the overall care in constructing the garment, but also increases cost. It is costly for the manufacturer to buy enough thread to match each fabric, and to maintain a large inventory of colored thread. Many manufacturers use whatever thread they have on hand to reduce costs.

Thread should be colorfast. If a thread fades at a different rate than the rest of the garment, or if it changes color, it no longer coordinates with the garment. Although no thread is 100 percent colorfast, a thread should not bleed or crock onto the garment or accept color from the garment. White thread should not yellow.

OPERATOR ACCURACY

The accuracy of the sewing operator plays an important role in the neatness, straightness, consistency, and uniformity of stitches. Sewing machines commonly sew at 3,000 to 9,000 stitches per minute, challenging operators to do accurate work. Considering that they are usually paid by the piece, not by the hour, operators must develop great skill to achieve both accuracy and the speed required to earn a living. A skilled operator sews stitches that enhance the appearance of the garment and the durability, comfort, and fit of seams and stitchings. Crooked stitches, stitches that sew past the intended stopping point, sloppily stitched corners and curves, stitches that are an uneven distance from the edge, and misplaced reinforcement tacks are examples of substandard sewing. A close examination of stitches makes sewing inaccuracies readily apparent, even to the untrained eye.

BACK TACKING AND LATCH TACKING

Back tacking is restitching at the beginning and end of the row of stitches. Back tacking secures the stitches and prevents unraveling; it is a sign of high quality. Modern sewing machines can be programmed to automatically back tack at the beginning and end of each seam. But because it takes extra time, back tacking is often neglected. It greatly contributes to the durability of seams, especially those made with stitch types prone to unraveling. Machines that make 500- and 600-class stitch types are not capable of back tacking. To secure these stitches, **latch tacking** draws the excess thread chain at the beginning of each row of stitches into the stitches to secure them. For rows of stitches that are not latch tacked, a short chain of thread left at each end retards the unraveling of the stitches slightly (Figure 7-14).

LOOSE THREADS

Although loose threads do not affect quality if the consumer removes them after purchasing the garment, consumer perception of garment quality is negatively affected by the presence of loose and dangling threads. Dangling threads not only detract from the garment's appearance but, if pulled, may unravel the stitches. They also interfere with the functioning of zippers and other closures. However, clipping threads too short at the beginning or end of an unsecured row of stitches may lead to the unraveling of the stitches. Some sewing machines have thread trimmers that clip threads automatically at the beginning and end of each row of stitches. Or threads may be removed by an inspector at the end of the manufacturing process, often using vacuum thread clippers. Removing excess threads is time-consuming and costly, and is often neglected in low-cost garments.

Summary

Stitches are the thread arrangements in fabrics that make stitchings and seams. *U.S. Fed. Std. No. 751a: Stitches, Seams, and Stitchings* contains six classes of stitches. The classes include the 100-class simple chainstitches, 200-class handstitches and their machine simulations, 300-class lockstitches, 400-class multithread chainstitches, 500-class overedge stitches, and 600-class cover stitches. Simple chainstitches are not durable. Handstitches are usually simulated by machine except in high-price apparel. Lockstitches are the main stitches used for woven-fabric garment construction. They are abrasion resistant, reversible, nonbulky, and comfortable. Multithread chainstitches are extensible, pucker resistant, and economical. They include bottom cover stitches. Overedge stitches are made only at edges. They are the main stitches used on knitwear because they are very extensible. Safety stitches feature two rows of parallel stitches for security, consisting of a row of overedge stitches and a row of either chainstitches or lockstitches. Mock safety stitches, when viewed from the top, visually imitate true safety stitches. Cover stitches make flat seams. They cover both the top and bottom of the seam with the thread.

In general, short stitches are more durable but cost more than long stitches. However, stitch length should be appropriate to the type, weight, and density of the fabric and the purpose of the stitches. Stitch length is measured in stitches per inch (SPI). Balanced stitch tension, especially for lockstitches, avoids ruptured and puckered stitches. Needle type, size, and condition; and thread fiber, type, size, strength, color, and colorfastness should be compatible with the fabric of the garment. Operator accuracy is important in producing stitches that are neat and attractive. Back tacking or latch tacking and removal of dangling threads are signs of quality.

Stitch Quality Checklist

If you can answer yes to each of these questions regarding the garment you are evaluating, it contains high-quality stitches.

- Is the stitch type appropriate for the fabric, the design, and the end use of the garment and its location and purpose?
- Are the stitches reversible if they will be seen from both sides?
- Do the stitches avoid puckering the fabric?
- Do the stitches resist grinning?

- Are the stitches adequately extensible?
- Do the stitches resist abrasion?
- Do the stitches resist unraveling?
- Are the stitches comfortable?
- Are the stitches flat and nonbulky?
- Is the stitch length appropriate for the fabric type, weight, and density, and for the purpose of the stitches?
- Is stitch tension balanced, especially for lockstitches?
- Was the appropriate size of needle used to sew the garment, to avoid needle chews, needle heating, and needle cutting?
- Is the thread comfortable?
- Is the thread as strong as the fabric but no stronger?
- Does the thread color match or complement the garment?
- Are the stitches neat, accurately placed, continuous lines?
- Are rows of stitches back tacked or latch tacked?
- Are excess threads trimmed and removed?

New Terms

If you can define each of these terms and differentiate between related terms, you have gained a good working vocabulary for discussing the topics in this chapter. The terms are listed in the order in which they appear in the chapter.

stitch
lockstitch
chainstitch
U.S. Fed. Std. No. 751a: Stitches, Seams, and Stitchings
100-class single-thread chainstitches
basting
blindstitch
200-class hand stitches/machine-made versions
backstitch
pickstitch/prickstitch
decorative chainstitch
catchstitch
running stitch
saddle stitch

slipstitch
300-class lockstitches
stitches per minute (SPM)
plain/straight stitch
zigzag stitch
multiple-stitch zigzag stitch
lockstitch blindstitch
400-class multithread/double-locked chainstitches
two-thread chainstitch
cording stitch
bobbinless zigzag stitch
bottom cover/bottom-covering stitch
500-class overedge stitches
overlock/serge/overseam/overcast/merrow
purled edge
break open stitch
square edge/box edge stitch
safety stitch
mock/simulated safety stitch
600-class cover stitches/top-and-bottom-covering chainstitches
stitches per inch (SPI)
reinforcement stitches
balanced tension
needle cutting
needle heating
needle chewing
spun thread
corespun thread
monofilament thread
multifilament thread
texturized thread
back tacking
latch tacking

Review Questions

1. What are the main differences between lockstitches and chainstitches?

2. How is the U.S. Fed. Std. No. 751a: Stitches, Seams, and Stitchings useful to apparel manufacturers?

3. List the six main stitch classes in U.S. Fed. Std. No. 751a and summarize the performance advantages and disadvantages of each.

4. What stitch type is the most frequently used in the apparel industry? What stitch class is the most frequently used to produce knitwear?

5. How is a safety stitch different from a mock safety stitch?

6. What is the blindstitch and where is it commonly used?

7. What are the quality advantages of short stitch lengths? When are long stitches appropriate?

8. For which stitch type is balanced tension most critical? Why?

9. What are the problems that arise from using damaged needles or needles that are too large for the fabric?

10. What are the advantages and disadvantages of clear monofilament thread?

Activities

1. Find garments containing an example of each of the major stitch classes.

2. Compare the stitch length of low-price and high-price garments in the following classifications:
  a. jeans
  b. men's dress shirts
  c. women's blouses
What differences, if any, did you find and why?

3. Unravel the stitches in a seam or hem sewn with lockstitches and another sewn with chainstitches. Which one unravelled more easily and why?

4. Visit an apparel manufacturer. Find out:
  a. what types of machines they have
  b. how they decide what stitch type to use for each operation

5. Stretch a seam sewn with a lockstitch/balanced tension and another sewn with a lockstitch/unbalanced tension. Which one is stronger?

6. Sew a row of long stitches and a row (the same length) of short stitches. Which stitch length is most time efficient for sewing the same distance?

7. Examine ready-to-wear in various price lines. How are lines of stitches secured at their beginnings and ends?

8. Study the Union Special *Garment Construction Guide*. Tell how many stitch types are used in constructing each of the following:
  a. T-shirt
  b. child's overalls
  c. man's overcoat

9. Examine garments in various price lines. Is price related to neatness of the stitches? Why or why not?

10. Choose a garment from your wardrobe and write stitch specifications to duplicate it.

6

Seams: Assembling the Garment

CHAPTER OBJECTIVES

1. Differentiate between seam types.

2. Evaluate the advantages and disadvantages of various seam types.

3. Discuss the effect of seam allowance width, stays, and other features on seam performance.

Seams are used to assemble fabric panels, to create the structure and details of a garment. An examination of the seams is important in evaluating the quality of ready-to-wear because the performance of the seams is critical to the aesthetic and functional performance of the garment. Appropriate seam type and seam allowance width are especially important.

Seams are the joints resulting when two or more fabric pieces are sewn together. The **seam line** is the stitched line of a seam; it is parallel to and a specified distance from the raw edge of the fabric. The **seam allowance** or **seam margin** is the (narrow) width between the seam line and the **raw edge** or cut edge of the fabric (Figure 6-1).

Seam Performance

The aesthetic and functional performance of a seam includes its attractiveness, durability, comfort, and ease of alteration. Seam perfor-

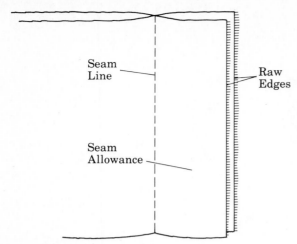

Figure 6-1 *Parts of a seam.*

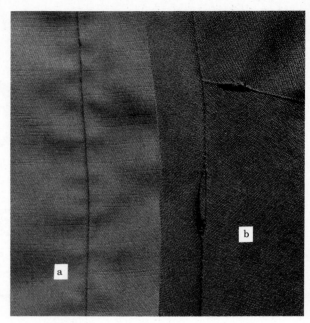

Figure 6-2 *Seam defects: (a) seam pucker, and (b) seam crack.*

mance results from the interaction between the fabric, the stitches, and the seam. Seam performance affects consumer satisfaction with the garment both at the point of sale and in use. Performance considerations for seams include smoothness, strength, and resistance to failure, balanced with cost limitations.

SEAM PUCKER

The appearance of the seams affects overall attractiveness of a garment. Straight, neat, smooth, even seams that are not twisted or rippled contribute to aesthetics. Perhaps the main factor detracting from seam appearance is puckering. **Seam pucker** is the lack of seam smoothness, or buckling of the fabric along a row of stitches (Figures 6-2 and 6-4). Seam puckering occurs in all price lines and seriously mars the otherwise pleasing appearance of a garment. In severe cases, puckered seams and stitchings also reduce durability.

Most seam puckering is categorized as either shrinkage pucker, feed pucker, structural jamming pucker, or tension pucker. Many of the causes of puckering are related to characteristics of the fabric and the stitches (see Chapter 4 and Chapter 5). For example, densely woven fabrics and lockstitches are prone to puckering.

Differential shrinkage or different rates of shrinkage between the fabric and another component, such as the thread, results in puckering (Figure 3-2). *Differential feeding* or feeding the layers of fabric through the sewing machine unevenly results in puckering. Differential feeding and the resulting material distortion may be due to uneven feeding by the sewing machine

or mishandling by the sewing operator. Sewing machines should be adjusted to evenly feed all layers of the fabric. And operators must feed the fabric evenly at the machine's pace, not pushing or pulling it through, which they sometimes do to increase their speed and earnings. Uneven feeding of the fabric layers by the sewing machine, or when the sewing operator attempts to match up unevenly cut pieces, also causes puckering. Unbalanced thread tension or a stitch length that is inappropriate for the fabric weight also leads to puckering. It may be caused as well by the sewing together of fabric plies cut on different grains, sewing speeds that are too fast, and sewing machine pressure maladjustment. *Structural jamming* occurs when needles and/or threads that are too large crowd the yarns of the fabric and cause puckering.

Joining multiple plies of fabric compounds puckering problems. For this reason, some seam types are more prone to pucker than others. In general, the least pucker occurs on the bias (unless the fabric is stretched too much as it is sewn). The most pucker occurs where stitches are made parallel to the lengthwise grain. This is apparent in the topstitching of fly front zippers on slacks. The upper part of the stitching often puckers where it is parallel to the lengthwise grain. Where the stitches curve near the bottom of the zipper placket and follow the bias, there is usually no puckering.

Although pucker cannot be completely eliminated in some cases (because of the displacement of the fabric yarns by the sewing threads), it can be reduced to an acceptable level. To produce smooth seams, manufacturers must control many factors; pucker-free seams are a mark of quality.

BULK

Bulky seams detract from a garment's smooth appearance. Although some bulk is unavoidable, construction steps that eliminate excess bulk indicate quality. Bulky seams are lumpy, unsightly, and uncomfortable. Multiple layers of fabric—especially a heavy or thick fabric—stacked up in the same area create bulk. For example, a seam type containing several fabric plies produces a strong but bulky seam. Many seam finishes that prevent raveling also add bulk.

Bulk reduces seam flexibility. Flexible seams contribute to the wearer's comfort because they allow freedom of movement. Bulky, rigid seams make the wearer uncomfortable and prevent the fabric from draping naturally, interfering with the garment's appearance. In knit garments, for example, rigid seams tend to ripple. Also, because of their inflexibility, rigid seams are subject to abrasion. Notice that the bulkiest seams in a pair of jeans, although often the strongest, also exhibit the most frosting and abrasive wear.

SEAM STRENGTH

If the seams split apart, the garment falls apart, so obviously the strength and durability of its seams affect overall garment durability. Seam strength and durability should be commensurate with the intended use of the garment and the wear and care it will receive. Good-quality seams are as strong as the fabric of the garment—they withstand the same amount of stress as the garment. Seams in some locations, such as the crotch and underarm, must withstand the extra stress that the wearer's movements cause in those areas. However, seams stronger than the fabric are unnecessary; in fact, under stress, they cause the fabric to tear near the seam.

Seam strength and durability are a result of the type and width of the seam, the strength and tendency to ravel of the fabric, and the characteristics of the stitches. The integrity of a seam may fail in one of three ways: (1) seam crack, (2) seam slippage, and (3) seam grin. All lead to unaesthetic and/or nonfunctional seams.

Seam Crack. **Seam crack** occurs when the stitches break and the seam splits apart or **bursts** (Figure 6-2). Most consumers refer to this as a ripped or split seam. Cracked seams are unattractive and may make the garment unwearable, depending on the size and location of the crack. Many consumers discard a garment when its seams rupture unless the value of the garment justifies the cost of repair.

Seams crack due to the wrong stitch type, unbalanced stitch tension, long stitch length, or incorrect needle and thread. Weak and raveling fabrics, weak seam types, and narrow seam allowances also lead to seam crack.

Seam Slippage. **Seam slippage** is a major problem in garments of woven fabrics. It occurs when the fabric pulls away from the stitches at the seamline (Figure 6-3). Seam slippage is unsightly and eventually weakens the seam to the point of cracking; however, a garment with seam slippage is usually declared unwearable for aesthetic reasons before seam crack occurs.

Slippage occurs when the thread, stitch, or seam type is stronger or more stable than the fabric. The stitches hold together, but the fabric pulls away. For example, nylon thread used to sew a silk garment leads to seam slippage. Fab-

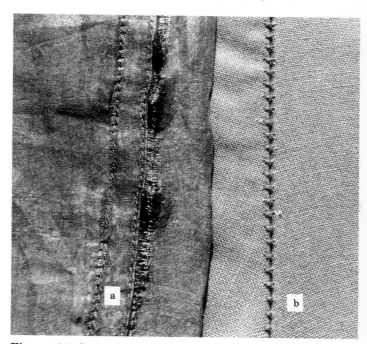

Figure 6-3 *Seam defects: (a) seam slippage, and (b) seam grin.*

rics subject to yarn slippage, with slick fibers and yarns and loose weaves, encourage seam slippage. The slippage is most evident in seams exposed to high stress and in areas that fit close to the body. Seams on the straight-of-grain slip more than seams on the bias because the same yarn is stressed along the entire row of stitches.

Seam Grin. **Seam grin** occurs when the seam-line spreads open, exposing the stitches so that they appear similar to the teeth of a grin (Figure 6-3). Grinning seams are unattractive and in extreme cases affect fit and durability. Seam grin is especially a problem in garments of knit fabrics. Garments with a snug fit have a greater tendency to grin than loose-fitting garments. Some stitch types are more prone to grinning than others (see Chapter 5). Long stitches and unbalanced tension also increase the tendency for a seam to grin. Some seam types, such as plain seams, are more apt to grin than others.

Physical Features of Seams

The performance of seams is determined by the physical features of the seam—the type and width of the seam and how it is stitched, pressed, and finished. Manufacturers choose the physical features of seams by balancing desired performance and cost.

SEAM TYPE

The types of seams used to assemble a garment influence its appearance, durability, comfort, and ease of alteration. A single garment may contain several different seam types (Figure 5-1). The choice of seam type is based on current fashion trends, the location of the seam within the garment, and the design, fit, fabric, end use, and care of the garment, all balanced with cost limitations. The cost of a seam depends on the amount of fabric, thread, and labor it requires. Additional cost is incurred if special sewing machines or attachments are needed.

Complex seams, with multiple rows of stitches, are generally strong. Multiple rows of stitching absorb more stress without rupturing than a single row of stitches; seams subjected to high stress should be stitched twice for additional strength. Topstitching also contributes strength to seams and serves as decoration. However, seam complexity increases costs. Some seam types involve multiple plies of fabric, which add strength but create unwanted bulk.

Some seam types have raw edges; these seam allowances usually require edge finishes. Finishing the raw edges of seam allowances improves their strength and appearance. It prevents raveling of woven fabrics and curling of knit fabrics. However, seam finishes generally add bulk and increase costs. Edge finishes used to finish seams are discussed in Chapter 7.

Seam types, like stitches, are defined, diagrammed, and categorized in *U.S. Fed. Std. No. 751a: Stitches, Seams, and Stitchings*. The four seam classes established by the Federal Standard are as follows:

1. *superimposed seams (SS)*
2. *bound seams (BS)*
3. *lapped seams (LS)*
4. *flat seams (FS)*

Manufacturers use variations of these basic seam types to construct ready-to-wear. The Federal Standard categorizes seams according to the fabric ply arrangement, although not always consistently. A close examination of the arrangement of the fabric plies within a seam and a comparison to the Federal Standard is required to identify the seam classification, because different seam types are quite similar. This chapter contains generalities about the seam classes and discusses the most widely used seam types within each class. For a complete listing, see Appendix B, which contains schematic illustrations of the fabric ply arrangement of each seam type.

The Federal Standard identifies each seam class by two uppercase letters, which abbreviate the name of the class (Figure 6-4). Seam types within the class are further identified with a lowercase letter or letters. Lowercase letters early in the alphabet usually represent simple variations. The letters are followed by a numeral designating the total number of rows of stitches used to make the seam. For example, SSa-1 is a superimposed seam of the simplest type, made with one row of stitches; some stitch types require more. If additional rows of stitching are added for decorative or reinforcement purposes, the number at the end of the seam

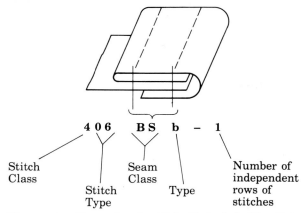

Figure 6-4 Example of a U.S. Fed. Std. No. 751a stitch and seam designation. (Courtesy of Union Special Corporation.)

type designation is higher. Combined with the stitch number, the Federal Standard seam designation accurately communicates the method of construction for any apparel production operation.

A seam type remains the same regardless of the stitch type used to sew it. For example, Figure 6-5 shows eight variations of an SS seam made with different stitch types and various edge finishes and the labor costs associated with each. Note that the least costly seam (B) and the most costly seam (H) produce garments with the same outer appearance but at a cost difference of $4.26 for just six seams. However, seam types generally lend themselves better to some stitch types than to others. Appendix C contains the *Guide for the Use of Stitches, Seams, and Stitchings* from the Federal Standard, which suggests the stitch types suited to each seam type. It also lists the typical operation performed using each seam type.

Superimposed Seams. The majority of **seams** are **superimposed (SS)** (Figure 6-6). Most superimposed seams are created by superimposing fabric plies, or stacking them on top of one another, with edges even, and sewing them together near the edge. Most major structural seams and many minor detail seams are superimposed. There are 54 variations of the SS in the Federal Standard (see Appendix B).

Plain Seams. The plain seam is by far the most common seam for joining major garment pieces. A **plain seam** (SSa), is a simple, superimposed seam. For major structural seams such as side, waist, and sleeve seams, the manufacturer sews

the fabric plies, face sides together, near the edge and then opens them out (Figure 6-7). For other plain seams, such as those joining elastic to the garment at the waist (SSt) and those closing pocket bags, the plies are not opened out after sewing but are left superimposed.

A plain seam appears as a line with no visible stitches on the outside of the garment, but the seam allowances are visible inside the garment. Plain seams may be topstitched on one or both sides of the seamline for decorative effect or to imitate other seam types, or they may be flattened with a bottom cover stitch (SSh).

Plain seams are not especially strong. They have a greater tendency to grin than other seam types. However, they are inconspicuous, nonbulky, easy to alter, and inexpensive to produce.

Ideally, each seam is pressed before another seam or stitching crosses it. The seam allowances of plain seams may be pressed to one side, or they may be pressed open, which is called **butterflied** or **busted.** Butterflying reduces bulk by distributing the seam allowances to each side of the seam line. The reduction of bulk contributes to attractiveness and comfort. Butterflied seams are found in high-quality garments, especially tailored ones. However, they increase costs because they require an extra pressing operation (Figure 6-7). When a seam crosses a previously made seam, bulk resulting from the several plies of fabric is uncomfortable and unsightly. To reduce bulk, the first seam may be butterflied before the second seam crosses it. Bulk is further reduced if the seam allowances of the second seam are also pressed open. Such underpressing improves the comfort, appearance, and sometimes the fit of the finished garment. For instance, in high-quality pants, the inseams are pressed open before the seat seam is sewn, to reduce bulk where the seams intersect at the crotch; the seat seam and outseams are pressed open before the waistband is attached, for the same reason.

The seams in low-quality garments may be pressed only at the end of construction or not at all. Often the only pressing a seam receives during production is finger pressing by the operator, who flattens the seam by hand before sewing the next seam. Of course, seams that are overedged cannot be pressed open because the seam allowances are held together by stitch interloopings.

A few plain seams, such as armhole seams and seat seams in the crotch area, are never pressed open. The seam allowances are left

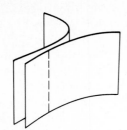

Type "A"
Plain Lockstitch Seam
This type of seam uses two threads, utilizing a lock-type stitch. Taking about 30 seconds to sew approximately 12″ = $.035 seam.

Type "B"
Sew Pink Seam
This type of seam uses two threads, utilizing a chain lock stitch costing about $.0175 per seam.

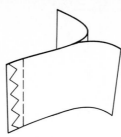

Type "C"
Overlock Seam
This type of seam uses three threads, utilizing a stretch stitch costing $.0175 per seam.

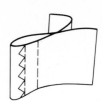

Type "D"
Safety Overlock
This type of seam uses five threads, giving the clean finish of an overlock, plus the strength and safety of a lock stitch, costing about ¢.0232 per seam, plus extra thread.

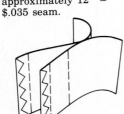

Type "E"
Double Overlock/ Lock Stitch Seam
This type of seam uses eight threads; giving a clean finish on each ply and seamed with a lock stitch costing $.07 per seam, plus extra thread.

Type 'F'
Plain Seam Pressed Open
The cost of seaming is $.035 plus the cost of pressing $.028=$.063 per seam.

Type "G"
Pinked Seam Pressed Open
The cost of seaming $.0175 plus the cost of pressing $.035 = $.0525 for seam.

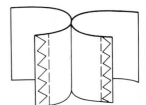

Type "H"
Double Overlock Pressed Open
The cost of seaming $.07 plus pressing $.028 = $.098 per seam.

Type "B" Seam Construction

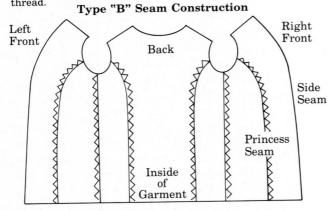

Left Front

Back

Right Front

Side Seam

Princess Seam

Inside of Garment

Type "B" & "H"

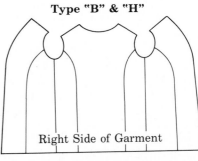

Right Side of Garment

Type "H" Seam Construction

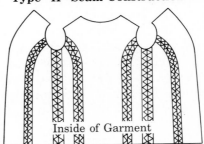

Inside of Garment

CONSTRUCTION	"B"	"H"	Note:
A. Cost to Contractor	$.0175	$.07+.028 (Press) = .098	A = Cost of type of seam
B. Cost to Manufacturer	$.0525	$.21+.02 = .23	B = 3A or 3 times Needle Time
C. Cost to Buyer	$.105	$.46	C = B+100%
D. Cost to Consumer	$.21	$.92	D = C+100%

Figure 6-5 *The labor costs of sewing 12″ seams of the same seam type but using various stitch types. The associated labor costs are calculated on a base pay of $4.20 per hour. Also shown, cost comparison and the inside and outside of garments sewn using the least costly and most costly methods. (Reprinted with permission from Bobbin Blenheim Media Corp. Copyright 1985 by Bobbin International Inc.)*

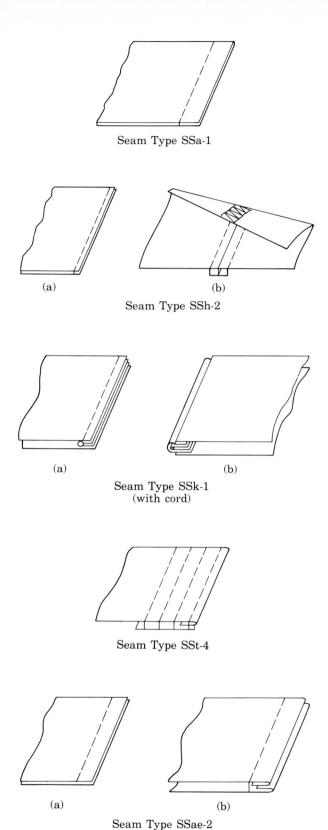

Seam Type SSa-1

(a)   (b)

Seam Type SSh-2

(a)   (b)

Seam Type SSk-1
(with cord)

Seam Type SSt-4

(a)   (b)

Seam Type SSae-2

Figure 6-6 *Superimposed seams: (SSa) plain seam, (SSh) plain seam flattened with bottom cover stitch, (SSk) enclosed seam with piping, and (SSae) French seam.*

Figure 6-7 *Plain seams: (a) butterflied, with wide seam allowances, and (b) finished together, with narrow seam allowances. Also note (a) wide, blindstitched hem (finished with hem tape), and (b) narrow, top-stitched hem.*

standing together to provide for comfort and durability and to avoid distortion of the seam.

Enclosed Seams. To make an **enclosed seam,** the manufacturer sews the fabric plies face sides together near the edge, opens out the plies, and turns them back sides together to encase the seam allowances (Figure 6-6). Enclosed seams occur only at edges, where they appear as a line with no visible stitches along the edge. The stitches and seam allowances are not readily visible inside the garment, either, because they are sandwiched between the fabric plies. The seams at most garment and detail edges are enclosed seams; for example, at the outer edges of necklines, collars, and cuffs (Figure 6-8). Enclosed seams are the second most common seam type after plain seams.

Bulk is a problem in enclosed seams because multiple layers of the garment and its seam allowances lie in the same direction, on top of one another, in the finished seam. If the manufacturer does not narrowly trim the seam allowances of an enclosed seam, the seam may be bulky and may not turn smoothly, especially at sharp curves and corners. Manufacturers often trim the seam allowances of enclosed seams extra narrow at corners to eliminate bulk; for example, in collar points. However, if seam allowances are too narrow, they fray and the seam ruptures. High-quality enclosed seams are durable, nonbulky and have sharp, flat points and smooth, flat curves. A trick couture designers use to help enclosed seams lie smooth is to clip the seam allowances on concave curves and notch the seam allowances on convex curves. They also **grade, blend, layer,** or **bevel** the seam allowances of enclosed seams, trimming each one to a slightly different length. Blending the seam allowances prevents them from making a visible imprint on the outside of the finished garment when pressed. Blending is done by hand in couture garments, and the same effect is achieved in ready-to-wear by a machine blade that trims the seam allowances at an angle.

Enclosed seams require more careful pressing than other seam types to produce the full size and intended shape of the garment piece. The lower ply of an enclosed seam has a tendency to slip out and show on the outside of the garment.

Manufacturers press the seamline of an enclosed seam about ¹⁄₁₆″ toward the underneath side to help prevent this. A *channel* is an undesirable groove that appears in an enclosed seam when the seamline is not fully pressed out toward the edge (Figure 6-9). In high-price garments, collars, cuffs, and other details may be *slipped* or *bubbled* to keep the lower ply of enclosed seams from showing at the outer edge (see Chapter 9).

A quality feature on enclosed seams is **control stitching** or **understitching** (Figure 6-8). It attaches the seam allowances to the lower ply. Control stitching keeps an enclosed seam flat and prevents its lower ply from slipping out and showing. Most collars, cuffs, and faced necklines, waistlines, and armholes require control stitching for quality results, but it is found mainly in high-price lines. Control stitching is unnecessary if topstitching is used to keep the seam flat.

French Seams. The **French seam** (SSae-2) is a "seam within a seam" (Figure 6-10). Manufacturers make French seams by sewing a narrow plain seam with the back sides of the fabric plies together. Then a slightly wider second plain seam is sewn, with the face sides of the fabric plies together, to encase the seam allowances of the first seam.

On the outside of the garment, the French

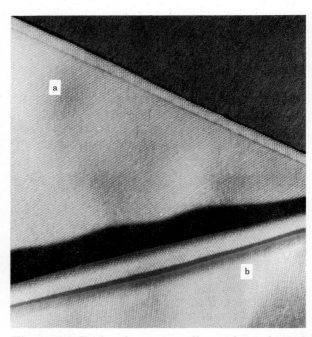

Figure 6-9 *Enclosed seam on collar with (a) channel from poor pressing and (b) facing that slips out and shows at edge (it needs control stitching).*

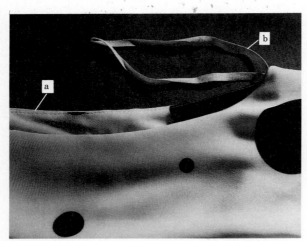

Figure 6-8 *Enclosed seam at neckline with (a) control stitching. Also note (b) hanger strap.*

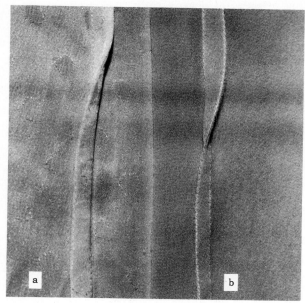

Figure 6-10 Both sides of (a) French seam and (b) mock French seam. They appear as plain seams on the outside of the garment.

seam looks like a plain seam. The main appeal of French seams is the attractive, finished appearance inside the garment; a single row of stitches is visible, but all raw seam allowance edges are hidden in the first, enclosed seam. To sum up its advantages and disadvantages, the French seam

1. Adds elegance, especially for sheer, thin fabrics with a tendency to ravel.

2. Is suitable for short, fairly straight seams, but not well-suited for long seams or extremely curved seams.

3. Is no stronger than a plain seam but, in slick fabrics, does prevent seam slippage better than a plain seam.

4. Prevents raveling by enclosing the raw seam allowances of the first seam within the second seam.

5. Is difficult to alter; it cannot be let out much to make the garment larger.

6. Is costly to make, being found mainly in high-price womenswear and lingerie.

Mock French Seams. The **mock French seam** or **false French seam** is used to imitate and is considered less elegant than the true French seam.

The mock French seam is an adaptation of the plain seam. In one version, manufacturers fold under the raw edges of the seam allowances of a plain seam and stitch them together. In the version pictured in Figure 6-10, the plain seam is merely stitched twice and trimmed close to the second stitching to resemble a true French seam. Mock French seams, like French seams, look like plain seams on the outside of the garment. However, you can distinguish the mock French seam from the true French seam because the mock French features two rows of stitching visible inside the garment rather than one.

Mock French seams are simpler and less costly to construct and can be altered more easily than true French seams, and they are strong and ravel-resistant. They can be used on long seams or curved seams, for which true French seams are unsuitable.

Lapped Seams. **Lapped seams (LS)** are made by overlapping the seam allowances of two or more fabric plies and sewing them together, with the fabric plies extending in opposite directions (Figure 6-11). Lapped seams are usually more casual looking than superimposed seams because they always have some form of topstitching. The Federal Standard contains 102 versions of the LS, making it the largest seam class (see Appendix B).

Many special-purpose seams are lapped seams. Raingear, for example, often features lapped seams because they are more waterproof than other seam types. Lapped seams attach elastic at the waistline of underwear and sportswear because they are less bulky than superimposed seams.

Manufacturers lap front panels over back panels when making lapped side seams for the smoothest, most slimming look. If a lapped seam contains gathering, easing, pleating, or tucking, it laps the less-full panel over the fuller panel.

Manufacturers produce the simplest type of lapped seam (LSa) by lapping the seam allowances without folding them under. The raw edges of the seam allowances are visible inside and outside the garment, but if a nonraveling fabric is used, the exposed raw edges are acceptable. Because lapped seams are less bulky than other seam types, they are useful for constructing garments of nonraveling materials like leather and vinyl. They may also be used to sew lace fabrics together for an uninterrupted flow of the lace motifs at seamlines (see Chapter 10).

Most lapped seam types involve folding under the seam allowances of the upper fabric ply be-

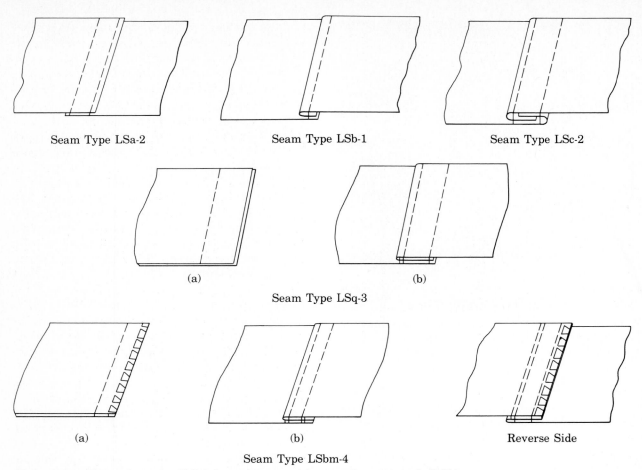

Seam Type LSa-2   Seam Type LSb-1   Seam Type LSc-2

(a)   (b)

Seam Type LSq-3

(a)   (b)   Reverse Side

Seam Type LSbm-4

Figure 6-11 *Lapped seams: (LSa) lapped seam with raw edges exposed, (LSb) lapped seam with raw edge of top ply turned under, (LSc) flat-felled seam, (LSq) welt seam is a modification of this (encased seam allowance is trimmed to pad the seam), and (LSbm) mock flat-felled seam.*

fore lapping and stitching it over the lower ply (LSb). Lapped seams of this type appear almost identical to topstitched, superimposed seams from both the face and the back of the seam. Examine the seams closely; the topstitching holds a lapped seam together, whereas the top-stitching on a superimposed seam is merely dec-orative. Lapped seams of this type are used, for example, to attach the waistband curtain to pants and to sew on patch pockets.

Lapped seams with the upper ply folded under are useful for joining unusually shaped fabric panels. For example, manufacturers producing Western-style shirts with curved or pointed yokes would find it difficult and costly to accu-rately join the yoke pieces to the shirt using superimposed seams. To solve this problem, they may press under the seam allowances of the shaped yoke, lap it over the shirt body, and top-stitch it to make the joining easier and less

costly; it also is more likely to yield smooth, durable results.

Both seam allowances of a lapped seam may be turned under. This results in a strong but somewhat bulky seam. The most common seam of this type is the flat-felled seam.

Flat-Felled Seams. **Flat-felled seams** (LSc) are the most common type of lapped seam (Figure 6-12). Manufacturers make flat-felled seams by folding under or *felling* the raw edges of both seam allowances as the seam is stitched. A skilled operator is required to feed the fabric plies accurately to the folding attachment on the sewing machine. A new development is a fell seamer that automatically forms the seam and allows even an unskilled operator to achieve excellent results using it. In either case, at least one but usually two or more rows of stitches are used to sew the seam, keeping both seam allow-

Figure 6-12 *Top and bottom of: (a) flat-felled seam, and (b) mock flat-felled seam.*

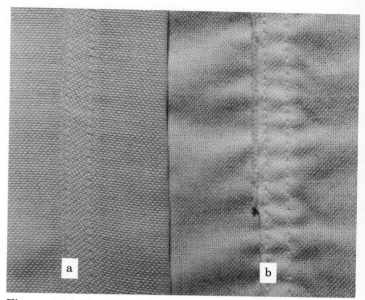

Figure 6-13 *Flat-felled seams on shirts: (a) smooth, well-made seam, and (b) puckered seam with too-narrow seam allowances, which were inadequately caught in the seam.*

ances turned under. Thus, the seam exposes no raw edges inside or outside the garment, and the seam appears identical inside and outside the garment.

As a summary of their characteristics, flat-felled seams

1. Are strong and durable; they are used in jeans, shirts, work clothing, and pajamas.
2. Prevent raveling because all the raw edges are enclosed. However, if the seam allowances are fed in so that either is too narrow, they will ravel from the stress of wear and care (Figure 6-13).
3. Are bulky and rigid in heavy fabrics.
4. Are difficult to alter.
5. Can be used only on straight or fairly straight edges.

Mock Flat-Felled Seams. The **mock flat-felled seam** (LSbm) imitates the flat-felled seam. Manufacturers produce mock flat-felled seams by sewing a plain seam using a safety stitch; then the seam allowances are pressed to one side and topstitched. Using this method, the resulting seam looks like a flat-felled seam on the outside of the garment. Inside, however, you can see the seam allowances, unlike a flat-felled seam (Figure 6-12).

Mock flat-felled seams cost less to produce than true flat-felled seams; they require less-skilled labor. They generally represent lower quality because they are not as strong or as durable as true flat-felled seams. However, if a garment does not receive heavy wear, true flat-felled seams are unnecessary and mock flat-felled seams provide the same look at a lower cost.

Tuck and Slot Seams. Most lapped seams are stitched close to the edge of the upper ply. If stitched farther back to create a small flap, the lapped seam is called a **tuck seam** because the seam resembles a tuck. **Slot seams** are a decorative variation of the lapped seam. The edges of two fabric plies are turned under and nearly abutted. They are lapped over and stitched to a narrow fabric underlay, usually of a contrasting color. The contrasting color shows through the narrow slot where the fabric panels almost touch (Figure 6-14). Slot seams are costly in both fabric and labor; they are extra costly if the seam is curved, requiring an identically shaped fabric underlay.

Welt Seams. **Welt seams** (modified LSq) are made by superimposing two plies with the raw edges uneven and sewing a plain seam; both

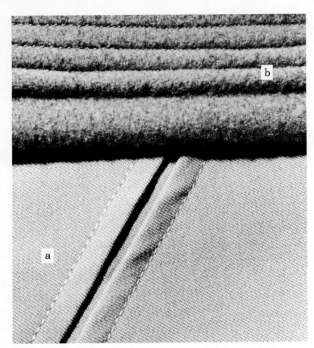

Figure 6-14 *Decorative seams: (a) tuck/slot seam, and (b) welt seam with multiple rows of topstitching.*

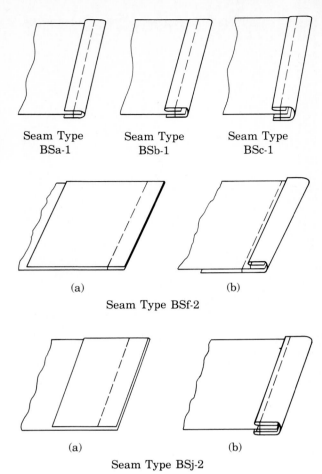

Seam Type BSa-1 Seam Type BSb-1 Seam Type BSc-1

(a) (b)

Seam Type BSf-2

(a) (b)

Seam Type BSj-2

Figure 6-15 *Bound seams: (BSa) bound seam with raw edges of binding exposed, (BSb) bound seam with one raw edge of binding turned under, (BSc) bound seam with both raw edges of binding turned under, (BSf) binding seamed on and then stitched in the ditch, and (BSj) binding seamed on and then topstitched.*

seam allowances are pressed in one direction and topstitched to catch the wider seam allowance. Dimension is provided by the narrower seam allowance which pads the area; the finished seam appears somewhat puffy, creating a decorative welt (Figure 6-14). Welt seams emphasize style lines in garments of heavy fabrics. A welt seam cannot be let out much to make the garment larger.

Bound Seams. **Bound seams (BS)** are made by using fabric binding strips to encase raw edges; bound seams are found only at edges (Figure 6-15). An attachment on the sewing machine folds the binding and holds it in position as it is stitched. Bound seams are not used to create structural seams of the garment, but to cover and finish raw edges; for example, necklines, armholes, waistlines, hems, and hem and seam allowances. Chapter 7 discusses bound seams as an edge finish, but the Federal Standard classifies bindings as seams because they fulfill the definition of joining two or more fabric plies. Eighteen variations of the BS are included in the Federal Standard (see Appendix B).

Bindings eliminate the need for additional edge finishes. Bindings produce a neat finish for edges exposed to view, prevent raveling of edges exposed to wear, and cover the raw edge to make the wearer comfortable (unless the binding adds

too much bulk). Many bindings are visible from both inside and outside the garment. Therefore, they may be decorative as well as functional.

Manufacturers use any narrow, nonbulky, flexible fabric for binding strips. Knits make a good binding because of their flexibility and lightweight. Foldover braids make good bindings because of their flexibility and varied, decorative style; however, some are bulky (Figure 10-4). Woven fabrics used as bindings are usually cut on the bias to lend flexibility, especially for use on curved edges. *Bias tape* is a woven fabric strip cut on the bias with both raw edges folded under; it is commonly used to bind garment edges (Figure 10-6).

Most bindings are attached by folding the binding over the raw edge of the garment, usually with the aid of a folding attachment on the sewing machine, and by topstitching the binding to the garment (Figure 6-16). The simplest form of binding (BSa) involves folding a strip of fabric around the raw edge and topstitching it to the garment (Figure 6-15). This method of binding is the least bulky. However, on bound garment edges it exposes the raw edges of the binding both inside and outside the garment. Therefore, this method is more often used to bind the edges of seam allowances than to bind garment edges. It requires the use of a nonraveling binding strip such as a knit or a woven tape, or the raw edges of the binding strip must be finished to prevent raveling.

A common method of binding garment edges is to fold under the upper edge of the binding strip (BSb) (Figure 6-15). This gives a finished appearance from the top side, making it useful for binding garment edges and seam allowances. It adds less bulk than folding under both edges of the binding. The lower edge of the binding must be finished to prevent raveling unless the binding is a nonraveling material.

Some seams are bound with both edges of the binding turned under before folding it around the edge (BSc) (Figure 6-15). However, turning under both edges of the binding creates bulk. Therefore, this method should not be used if the binding or garment is made of a heavy fabric. A binding with both edges turned under looks equally neat and attractive from either side, so it is useful when the binding is viewed on both sides; for example, on a reversible garment and at opening edges. Seam allowances bound this way tend to press through to the outside of the garment because of the excess bulk.

Occasionally, one edge of the binding is sewn with a plain seam to the garment; the binding is then folded around the edge and caught by topstitching (BSj). The topstitching may be **stitched in the ditch** or **crack stitched** with straight stitches placed in the crevice between the garment and the binding (BSf). Seams bound this way require considerable time and skill, but if done well the topstitches are inconspicuous.

High-quality bindings bite the fabric edge as deeply as possible. If a binding barely hangs on the edge, it is not secure. Sewing on a binding with straight stitches requires a skilled operator; the stitches must be accurately placed to catch both edges of the binding. If only one edge of the binding is caught in the stitches, the binding is not secure. Zigzag stitches, bottom cov-

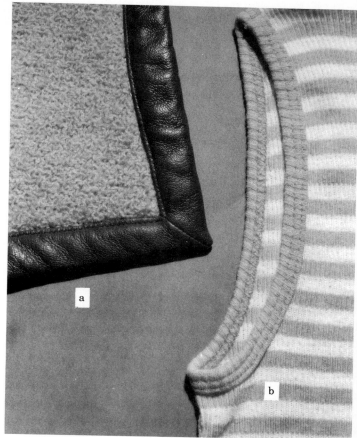

Figure 6-16 *Binding: (a) with mitered corner, and (b) on curved armhole.*

ering chainstitches, or top and bottom covering chainstitches increase the likelihood of catching both edges of the binding. They also serve as a finish for raw edges on the binding, if any.

Corners are difficult to bind; ideally, bindings should be mitered around corners (Figure 6-16). **Mitering** involves seaming or folding the binding diagonally to conform to corners. Mitered corners are less bulky and more attractive than unmitered corners. Mitering requires a skilled operator and is mainly found in high-price garments.

At most necklines, armholes, and garment and sleeve hems, the binding is attached to the flat edge and then the garment is seamed into a circle. A more costly method is to sew the garment into a circle, sew the binding into a circle, and then join the two together "in the round." This requires considerable skill and great accuracy to ensure that the two circles are the same circumference so they can be sewn together smoothly. The end of the seam joining the garment into a circle is concealed within the binding, making this method more attractive and more comfortable than bindings attached flat. High-quality garments feature bindings applied "in the round."

Flat Seams. **Flat seams (FS)** join fabric plies whose raw (or sometimes folded) edges are abutted (or sometimes slightly lapped) and sewn together (Figure 6-17). Flat seams are sometimes called **butt seams** or **exposed seams.** The joining stitches are typically 600-class cover stitches, although zigzag or bottom cover stitches may be used. Flat seams appear similar on both sides; the stitches cover the raw edges and are visible on the face and back of the seam. The Federal Standard contains only six variations of the FS (see Appendix B).

Because flat seams have little or usually no seam allowances, they are economical in fabric usage and are the least bulky of all seams. However, because they have no excess seam allowances, most flat seams cannot be let out to enlarge the garment. No excess seam allowances leave little room for error; flat seams that are not completely abutted or that are joined with too-narrow cover stitches are likely to separate and develop holes.

Flat seams are used in knit garments where thick seams are intolerable; for example, underwear, foundation garments, sweatshirts, sweatpants, and some childrenswear. Flat seams are inappropriate in garments of woven fabric because the fabric ravels and the garment splits apart at the seams.

SEAM ALLOWANCE WIDTH

The width of the seam allowances affects the strength, durability, appearance, comfort, and ease of alteration of a seam. Wide seam allowances are a construction feature worth pointing out to the consumer because they have many advantages. In general, for seams subject to stress, such as the main structural seams of a garment, wide seam allowances are a mark of quality (Figure 6-7). Their main advantages are that seams with wide seam allowances generally

1. Are stronger and more durable; they help absorb stress so the stitches are not strained, and they are less prone to seam slippage.

2. Help to slow raveling of the fabric to the seamline.

3. Help the garment hang smoothly because of their weight.

4. Provide for easy alteration, allowing the garment to be let out.

In high-quality garments, which justify the expense of extensive alterations, seam allowances as wide as one inch or more may be used in areas subject to frequent alteration. For example, the seat seam of men's pants is a common area for alteration (Figure 9-4). Side seams in skirts and inseams in pants are other seams whose seam allowances are cut wide in high-quality garments to accommodate alterations.

However, wide seam allowances require extra fabric and therefore are costly; seam allowances account for over 5 percent of total apparel fabric (Hudson 1988). High-quality ready-to-wear generally features seam allowances on major structural seams of one-half inch or wider. Low-quality garments often have very narrow seam allowances to conserve fabric, resulting in weak seams. However, to some extent, short stitches, and stitch and seam types that are strong and prevent raveling, may substitute for wide seam allowances.

Narrow seam allowances are preferable on seams where bulk is unacceptable. For example,

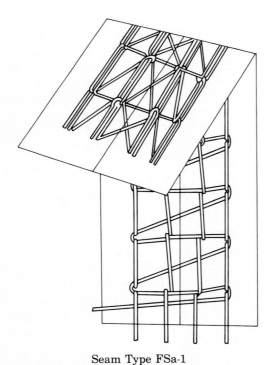

Seam Type FSa-1

Figure 6-17 *Flat seam: (FSa) ordinary flat seam.*

enclosed seams such as those in collars and cuffs are usually little more than one-eighth inch wide to reduce bulk and yield a smooth, flat edge. Wide seam allowances in these areas actually detract from quality. However, if the seam allowances are too narrow, the fabric ravels out past the stitches, creating a hole. It is difficult for operators to evenly catch all the fabric plies when sewing seams with narrow seam allowances. Therefore, the seam is usually stitched and the seam allowances simultaneously trimmed to a uniform, narrow width in detail areas where reducing bulk is important. Enclosed seams subjected to stress, such as in waistbands, call for medium-width seam allowances. A medium width is a compromise between the durability of wide seam allowances and the low bulk of narrow ones.

Wide seam allowances are unsuitable for seams in the crotch and underarm areas; they interfere with comfort and fit in these areas because they cause pulling and chafing. And wide seam allowances are unsuitable for sharp curves because they interfere with the flatness and smoothness of the curve.

Most stitch types can sew seams with seam allowances of unlimited width. An exception is seams made using overedge stitches and cover stitches; they are confined to a maximum width of about three-eighths inch. Most seam types can be made in varying widths but some, such as flat seams, are always narrow.

SEAMS SEWN FLAT VERSUS "IN THE ROUND"

It is less costly to sew seams with the fabric plies flat rather than "in the round." Manufacturers often seek to construct garments so that as many seams as possible are sewn with the fabric plies flat. The order in which a manufacturer sews the seams of a garment determines whether the seams are sewn flat or in the round. As a general rule, manufacturers sew garments together with all seams flat because it costs less; unfortunately, the finished product does not fit as smoothly and comfortably as garments in which some seams are sewn in the round. Also, seams sewn in the round are generally more attractive than seams sewn flat.

Jeans are usually constructed completely with seams sewn flat by sewing (1) the *seat seam* (center back seam), (2) the *outseams* (outer leg seams), and (3) the *inseams* (inner leg seams) in

one continuous seam. In contrast, dress pants usually have the seat seam sewn in the round, though the outseams and inseams are sewn flat. This method makes the crotch a free, upstanding seam that is more comfortable to wear, conforms better to the body's natural shape and movements, and is less apt to wrinkle or "smile" at the seat than jeans. The concept of seams sewn flat versus "in the round" are discussed repeatedly throughout the text.

SINGLE-NEEDLE TAILORING

Single-needle tailoring indicates that the manufacturer used single-needle sewing machines, even though the seams have multiple rows of stitches; each row of stitches is made in a separate run through the machine. The alternative is to use machines with two or more parallel needles to make multiple rows of stitches simultaneously. Multiple needles in the same machine sew at slightly uneven rates, producing puckered seams. Making a seam one row of stitches at a time is costly but results in a smooth seam. Single-needle seams are not significantly stronger than multiple-needle seams, but they are more attractive, and they represent higher labor costs. Many manufacturers set in shirt sleeves on men's dress shirts using single-needle tailoring, as indicated by a single row of stitching visible around the armhole on the outside of the garment, but two rows inside the garment (Figure 6-18). Armhole seams constructed this way are stronger than plain, safety stitched seams. Men's shirts are commonly labeled *single-needle tailoring*, although at lower price lines many feature limited single-needle tailoring; sometimes only the armhole is a single-needle seam.

OPERATOR ACCURACY

The skill of the sewing operator impacts seam and stitching quality. Seams that are sewn evenly, with adequate seam allowances and no raw edges exposed, are attractive, comfortable, and durable. They allow the garment to fit properly. Inaccurately sewn seams with stitches that miss the intended seamline reduce the durability, comfort, and fit of the garment. Crookedly sewn seams are unattractive and do not withstand stress well. Seams should not have accidental tucks, pleats, or gathers. Seams with

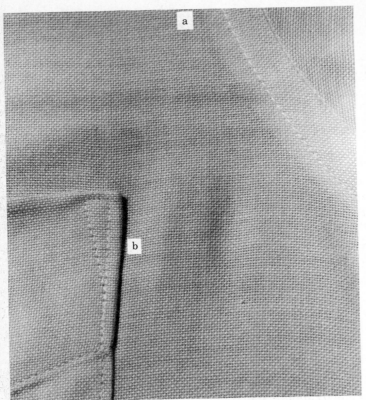

Figure 6-18 *(a) Single needle tailoring on armhole of man's dress shirt, and (b) triangular reinforcement on patch pocket.*

or stretching them. Stretching a bias-cut or knit seam as it is sewn also leads to puckering.

Seams and stitchings sewn on the bias of the fabric have a tendency to ripple and pucker. The ripple and pucker worsens if the fabric is stretched when sewn. Therefore, it is important that seams on the bias have **directional stitching** in the direction of the grain to minimize stretching. Directional stitches call for sewing from the wide end to the narrow end of the fabric plies on vertical seams, and from high side to low side of the fabric plies on horizontal seams. The vertical side seams of a flared skirt should be stitched from wide to narrow; in other words, hem to waist. The horizontal shoulder seams of a shirt should be stitched high to low, from neckline to armhole. Operators must be trained to sew each seam and stitching in the appropriate direction.

Directional stitching makes a difference in the appearance of some finished garments. For example, pockets on the fronts of jeans often ripple and pucker along the upper edge if they are stitched in the wrong direction. Long seams, such as skirt side seams, and seams close to true bias, like very flared skirt side seams, ripple and pucker from nondirectional stitching.

STAYS

The term **stay** is a very general one. It refers to any stable, narrow, nonbulky tape, ribbon, fabric strip, or other device used to stabilize a seam. A stay makes the seam "stay" the same size or shape without stretching or distorting. Stays strengthen and stabilize seams, and preserve and enhance the shape of the garment. A seam with a stay is more costly than one without, but maintains its shape and size better. Stayed seams are unlikely to rupture because the stay absorbs some of the stress of use. However, stays add some bulk to the seam. Stays that shrink at a different rate than the garment can cause puckering.

Seams subject to stress may stretch or distort if they are not stayed. Manufacturers often stay shoulder, neckline, waistline, underarm, and crotch seams, and pocket edges. In high-quality tailored garments, the armholes, lapels, collars, and other areas may be stayed. Crotch seams and inseams of better pants are often stayed with a narrow triangle of lining fabric. Any area cut on the bias is especially subject to stretching, and if it receives stress, it requires a stay to maintain its shape. Stays can be eased to the

these defects do not lie smoothly. Seams that cross other seams should be aligned on both sides of the intersecting seam, especially if the intersection is in a highly visible location.

Sometimes pieces of two different lengths must be sewn together, and the operator is supposed to ease one to the other; if the operator feeds the layers evenly, the garment does not fit as intended. A skilled operator is required to ease pieces together. The opposite type of problem occurs when an inaccuracy in pattern making results in pieces of two different lengths that are to be sewn together without easing. This being impossible, a skilled operator may feed the layers unevenly in an attempt to align them by easing them together. This unintended easing causes pucker that could be avoided by more accurate pattern making.

Sewing plies together which are cut on different grains can cause puckering. Bias to straight and lengthwise to crosswise panel joins should be avoided if possible. If panels cut on different grains must be joined, care should be taken to evenly feed the layers and avoid easing

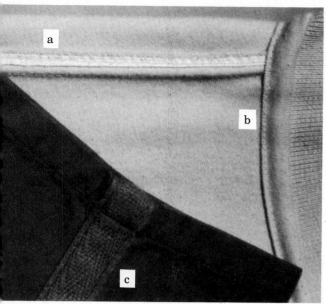

Figure 6-19 Stayed seams: (a) taped, (b) stripped, and (c) strapped.

garment to pull up the fabric and make them hug the body. This technique, although costly in labor, is useful in preventing lapels, low necklines, and large armholes and pockets from gaping. Although stays add to both materials and labor costs, they help the garment look better and last longer.

Manufacturers create **taped seams** (SSab) by staying them with narrow strips of twill tape or fabric (Figure 6-19). Superimposing the tape on the fabric plies and sewing it in as part of the seam is a common method of taping shoulder seams in better knit shirts and sweaters and waistline seams of fitted garments. Or a strip of fabric is sewn over the completed seam inside the garment, creating what are sometimes called **stripped seams** (SSf). Some T-shirt neckline and shoulder seams are taped in this manner. Such taping increases the wearer's comfort by preventing the seam allowances from chafing the skin and increases the attractiveness of neckline seams visible at the point of sale or when being worn. Continuous tape across the neck and shoulders gives the most support. Seams that feature a strip of fabric sewn over the seam on the outside of the garment are sometimes called **strapped seams** (SSag). The strapping decorates as well as reinforces; for example, the satin stripes on the side seams of tuxedo pants. Strapped seams are also found on men's and boys' briefs.

Summary

Seams are the joints between fabric pieces. The most common seam defects are puckering (lack of smoothness), excess bulk, cracking (rupturing), slippage, and grinning. *U.S. Fed. Std. No. 751a: Stitches, Seams, and Stitchings* contains four classes of seams: SS superimposed seams, LS lapped seams, BS bound seams, and FS flat seams. Superimposed seams, the most common type, are layers of fabric plies stacked on top of one another and sewn together. They include plain seams, used for most major garment seams. Butterflied plain seams, with seam allowances pressed open, cost more but are less bulky than seams which are not butterflied. Enclosed seams, superimposed seams used at garment edges, should be pressed and possibly control stitched so the lower ply does not slip out and show. The French seam, a seam within a seam, and the mock French seam, which looks similar, are other superimposed seams. Lapped seams are made by lapping the fabric ply edges; there are more different types of lapped seams than of any other seam class. Besides simple lapped seams, they include flat-felled seams, which enclose all the raw edges, and mock flat-felled seams, which look similar. Other lapped seams include tuck seams, slot seams, and welt seams. Bound seams are made by binding the edge of a fabric with a fabric strip; they are used only at raw edges. Flat seams are usually made by abutting the edges of the fabric ply and joining them with cover stitches. They are appropriate for use only on nonraveling fabrics.

In general, complex seams are durable but create unwanted bulk and increase costs. Seams with raw edges may have edge finishes to prevent raveling and improve appearance; edge finishes often add strength to the seam but increase costs and add unwanted bulk. Wide seam allowances also make seams durable and provide ease of alteration, but increase costs; narrow seam allowances are appropriate in enclosed seams. For seams joining the garment into a tube, seams sewn "in the round" are generally preferable to those sewn flat. Single-needle tailoring is also a mark of quality. Seams should be directionally stitched, with the grain, to avoid stretching them as they are sewn. Some seams have stays, nonstretch fabric strips, that reinforce the seam and prevent stretch and distortion.

Seam Quality Checklist

If you can answer yes to each of these questions regarding the garment you are evaluating, it contains high-quality seams.

- Are the seams appropriate to the fabric, end use, and price line of the garment?
- Is the seam type resistant to cracking, slippage, and grinning?
- Are the seams free of puckers?
- Are the seams nonbulky?
- Are points sharp and curves smooth?
- Are stitches accurately placed on the seamline?
- Are the seams and stitchings directionally stitched?
- Are plain seams pressed flat and enclosed seams pressed to their full dimension to avoid channels?
- As an extra quality feature, are the seam allowances of plain seams pressed open (butterflied)?
- Are the facings of enclosed seams concealed by pressing and topstitching or control stitching?
- Are bindings mitered at corners?
- Are bindings stretched around concave curves and eased around convex curves?
- Are seam allowances wide enough to withstand the wear and care of the garment without adding excessive bulk?
- Are seam allowances wide enough to perform alterations?
- Do the seam allowances have edge finishes, if needed? Do edge finishes prevent raveling of woven fabrics and curling of knit fabrics without adding excessive bulk?
- Are seams that are subjected to high stress or stretch reinforced with a stay?

New Terms

If you can define each of these terms and differentiate between related terms, you have gained a good working vocabulary for discussing the topics in this chapter. The terms are listed in the order in which they appeared in the chapter.

seam
seam line
seam allowance/margin
raw edge
seam pucker
seam crack/burst
seam slippage
seam grin
superimposed seam (SS)
plain seam
butterflied/busted
enclosed seam
grade/blend/layer/bevel
control stitching/understitching
French seam
mock French/false French seam
lapped seam (LS)
flat-felled seam
mock flat-felled seam
tuck seam
slot seam
welt seam
bound seam (BS)
stitched in the ditch/crack stitched
mitering
flat seam (FS)/butt seam/exposed seam
single-needle tailoring
directional stitching
stay
taped seam
stripped seam
strapped seam

Review Questions

1. What are the main causes of seam pucker?

2. List the four main seam classes in U.S. Fed. Std. No. 751a and summarize the performance advantages and disadvantages of each.

3. What is the advantage of single-needle tailoring?

4. What steps ensure high-quality enclosed seams?

5. What are the advantages of butterflied seams? Why are butterflied seams more costly than those that are not pressed open?

6. Is the following statement true or false regarding seams? "The stronger the stitches or thread, the better." Justify your answer.

7. When are French seams desirable?

8. Discuss the effect of seam allowance width on seam performance.

9. What are the three main types of seam failure?

10. How do even feeding and directional stitches affect quality?

11. List three seam locations that are frequently stayed.

Activities

1. Find an example of a garment with cracked seams. What would you recommend to avoid this problem?

2. Find an example of a garment with seam grin. What would you recommend to avoid this problem?

3. Find an example of a garment with seam slippage. What would you recommend to avoid this problem?

4. Find an example of a garment with seam pucker. What would you recommend to avoid this problem?

5. Find garments containing examples of each major seam class and the main types within each class. Explain how the configuration of each type is different.

6. Visit an apparel manufacturer. Find out:
   a. What types of seams do they use?
   b. How do they decide which seam types to use?
   c. What machines are required to make each seam type?
   d. Are any seams butterflied? Why or why not?

7. Examine the seam types in low-price and high-price garments in the following classifications:
   a. women's suits
   b. men's sport coats
   c. men's pants
   d. T-shirts
   e. jeans
   f. formal dresses
   g. children's play clothes
   h. lingerie
What differences, if any, did you find? Is seam type determined by price? By classification of merchandise? By location within the garment? By fabric type?

8. Compare a flat-felled seam with a mock flat-felled seam. Which is more durable?

9. Miter the corner of a piece of paper. Turn under both edges of another corner. Compare the appropriateness and bulkiness of the two methods.

10. Study the Union Special *Garment Construction Guide*. How many different seam types are used in constructing:
   a. T-shirts
   b. children's overalls
   c. men's overcoats

11. Choose a garment from your wardrobe and write seam specifications to duplicate it.

7

Edge Treatments: Finishing Raw Edges

CHAPTER OBJECTIVES

1. Discuss the methods of hemming a garment.

2. Differentiate between facings of various types, bindings, bands, plackets of various types, and other edge finishes.

3. Recognize the advantages and disadvantages of various edge treatments.

Garment edges require some form of treatment to make them attractive and durable. Edge treatments affect garment quality, whether they be on the outside of the garment (for example, necklines, waistlines, and sleeveless armholes) or on seam and hem allowance edges inside the garment. The evaluation of the treatment of a particular edge depends on the location and purpose of the edge, the fabric from which the garment is made, and the style and end use of the garment.

Edge treatments or **edge finishes** finish the raw or cut edges of a garment. Generally, consumers think of garments with neatly finished edges as being of higher quality than garments with untreated edges. Indeed, sometimes edges are poorly finished or not finished at all due to cost limitations. However, in certain situations, edges left untreated do not sacrifice quality; for example, garments made of leather or leather-like fabrics often have untreated, raw edges in order to avoid bulk. And producers of lined garments avoid finishing seam allowance edges because the lining hides the raw edges and helps prevent raveling. Manufacturers of garments made from knit fabrics with no tendency to roll or woven fabrics with no tendency to ravel also may leave seam allowances, and sometimes other raw edges, untreated without detracting from the garment's performance (Figure 7-9).

Performance of Edge Treatments

Covering raw edges makes them more attractive, which is especially important for edges visible on the outside of the garment. Edge treatments should complement the garment's fabric and style. A high-quality edge treatment is even throughout its length. It does not ripple or distort the shape or size of the edge. Curves are smooth and corners are mitered or otherwise handled to create a sharp angle. Edge finishes inside the garment do not show through to the outside. Most edge finishes add bulk to the edge, but bulk should be kept to a minimum because bulky edges detract from the appearance and comfort of the garment.

A major function of most edge finishes is to prevent raveling of woven fabrics. They also prevent the edges of light- and medium-weight knit fabrics from rolling or curling. Edge finishes contribute to the strength, abrasion resistance, and stability of edges. And finished edges usually improve the wearer's comfort, especially in locations such as armholes. Edge finish performance requirements are based on several factors, including the location and purpose of the edge, the shape of the edge, the style of the garment, and the weight and type of the fabric. Edge finishes should withstand the same wear and care as the garment. For example, edge finishes on seam allowances in the crotch and underarm areas require abrasion resistance; edges prone to distortion need stable edge finishes; heavy fabrics require nonbulky finishes; and fabrics that ravel readily demand edge finishes that prevent raveling.

Many edge finishes add unwanted bulk, some types more than others. The bulk of an edge treatment depends on the type of edge finish, the bulk of the fabric, the number of plies of fabric, and the amount of thread and other materials at the edge. Bulk can be reduced in edge

finishes by pressing open seam allowances that intersect the edge, and trimming wide seam and hem allowances that intersect the edge. However, because of the cost, these techniques are used only in high-price lines.

Some seam types have raw edges inside the garment that require finishing. Manufacturers of most low- and moderate-price garments finish the raw edges of a seam's allowances together. However, manufacturers of high-quality garments may finish the seam allowances of major structural seams separately. For example, butterflying the seam allowances of plain seams and finishing each one separately results in a smooth, nonbulky seam. However, this method costs at least twice as much as finishing the seam allowances together (Figure 6-7).

Physical Features of Edge Treatments

The physical features of edge treatments include the type of edge treatment and how well the edge treatment is executed. These factors determine the aesthetic and functional performance of the edge treatment. The following are the main types of edge treatments:

1. Hems and other edge finish stitchings.
2. Unstitched finishes.
3. Facings.
4. Bindings.
5. Bands.
6. Plackets.

EDGE FINISH STITCHINGS

Stitchings are stitches applied to finish an edge or for ornamental purposes; they do not join fabric pieces together as do seams. Stitchings are classified in *U.S. Fed. Std. No. 751a: Stitches, Seams, and Stitchings* as either *edge finish stitchings (EF)* or *ornamental stitchings (OS)* (see Chapter 10).

Edge finish stitchings (EF) are a series of stitches that finish an edge (Figure 7-1). They include hems, most seam finishes, and other sewn finishes for raw edges, such as those used to finish the raw edges of belt loops and shoulder

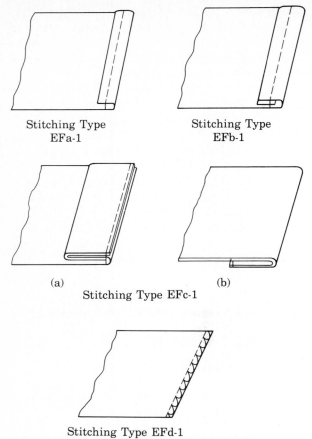

Stitching Type
EFa-1

Stitching Type
EFb-1

(a)

Stitching Type EFc-1

(b)

Stitching Type EFd-1

Figure 7-1 *Edge finish (EF) stitchings: (EFa) single-fold hem, (EFb) double-fold hem, (EFc) blindstitched hem, and (EFd) overedged.*

straps. Any stitching that finishes a raw edge without attaching a separate piece of fabric qualifies as an edge finish stitching. The Federal Standard contains 32 variations of EF stitchings. Only the most common edge finish stitchings are discussed in this chapter, but Appendix B diagrams all the EF stitchings. EF stitchings can be made using any suitable stitch type. For example, a blindstitched hem (EFc) can be made using any blindstitch, from class 100, 300, 400, or 500. Appendix C lists the apparel production operation performed by each EF stitching and the suitable stitch types.

Hems. *In general, a hem refers to any finish at the lower edge of the garment.* For example, terms such as *banded hem, bound hem,* or *faced hem* refer to lower edges finished by bands, bindings, or facings. The edge treatment used to finish the lower edge of the garment affects the overall quality impression the garment makes. (Note: Various lengths of garments are illustrated in Figure 9-2.)

As an edge finish stitching, a hem refers to turning under a raw edge and securing it to the garment. Any raw edge, not just the lower edge of the garment, may be finished with a hem, which leaves a folded edge in place of the raw one. Hems are the most common EF stitchings.

When a hem is combined with an opening, producers of high-quality garments hem the garment first and then finish the opening edge (Figure 7-2). If the garment is hemmed after the opening edge is finished, the hem tends to show at the opening edge. However, because it speeds construction, garments are often hemmed last.

Sometimes, a *hem tape* or *seam tape* is lapped over and sewn onto a raw hem allowance to cover and finish the edge (Figure 6-7). Taped edges attractively finish the hems in moderate- and high-quality dresses, skirts, and pants.

Folded Hems. The **folded hem** is a simple hem finish in which the raw edge is turned under and stitched to the garment. The edge may be folded under once (EFa), as shown in Figures 7-1, 7-2, and 7-3, or there may be a double fold (EFb), shown in Figures 7-1 and 7-4. Folded hems are the most frequently used method of finishing the lower edge of garments, as well as being a popular finish for the raw edges of details such as pockets and ruffles, and the lower edges of sleeves without cuffs.

Manufacturers of better tailored garments interface the folded hems at the lower edge of the garment and sleeves for body and durability. They cut strips of woven interfacing on the bias to use in these hems because it lends support without rigidity. The interfacing ends at the fold of the hem for a flat, crisp look, or extends slightly beyond the fold for a soft, rolled look.

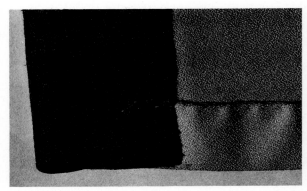

Figure 7-2 *Garment should be hemmed before facing is turned in, as shown here.*

Hem Attachment. Ideally, manufacturers hem garments "in the round," *after* all seams entering the hemline are sewn. This costs more than hemming the garment flat but represents quality construction. Low-price garments are usually hemmed flat and then seamed. An example of these two techniques is budget versus better T-shirt sleeve hems. An exception to this rule is some pleated skirts; the skirt sections are first hemmed and pleated, and then sewn together at the side seams because it would be difficult to accurately hem the skirt after it is pleated.

Secure hem attachment is important; consumers commonly complain about low-quality garments, "The hem came out the first time I wore it." But manufacturers of high-quality garments sew hems with stitch types that do not unravel at the pull of a thread. The stitches should be small and close so that the heel of the wearer's shoe or a piece of jewelry cannot catch in the hem stitches and cause them to rupture.

Manufacturers often topstitch hems, especially in casual garments and shirts that are worn tucked in (Figures 6-7 and 7-4). Topstitched hems are secure. Being more noticeable than blindstitched hems, they may serve as a decorative feature of the garment.

Most hem allowances in tailored and dress garments are attached to the garment with blindstitches (EFc). For durability, each blindstitch should fully catch a few yarns of the fabric but not take such a large bite that the stitches are highly visible on the outside of the garment (Figure 7-3). Some blindhemmers simultaneously finish the raw edge of the hem allowance with overedging (EFl).

Glued hems are common in expensive garments made of leather or leatherlike fabrics that could be weakened by the needle holes made when hems are stitched. Glued or fused hems also appear in some low-price garments, where they usually represent low quality because of poor durability and aesthetics.

Hem Width. In general, **hem allowances** (the amount turned under) in high-quality garments are wider than those in low-quality garments (Figure 6-7). Wide hem allowances require more fabric than narrow hem allowances, so they cost more, and manufacturers often sacrifice hem width in low-price garments to cut costs. Hems usually look best if they are rather wide or very narrow, not somewhere in between.

Wide hem allowances are desirable for sev-

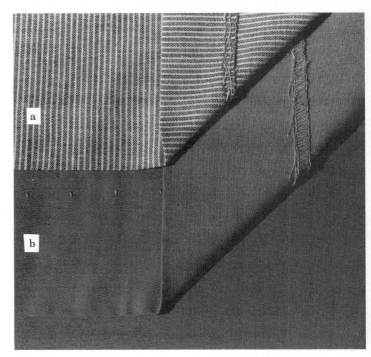

Figure 7-3 *Blindstitched hems: (a) is less visible than (b).*

eral reasons that should be pointed out as benefits to consumers:

1. The garment tends to hang smoothly when weighted by a wide hem allowance.

2. A wide hem allowance can be let down to lengthen the garment to suit different people's personal preferences regarding garment length.

3. Wide hem allowances can be let down to conform to changing fashions.

4. Wide hem allowances in dresses obscure the lower edge of the lining or the wearer's slip.

Although wide hem allowances are generally desirable, manufacturers ultimately determine hem width based on three main factors: (1) the flare of the garment, (2) the weight of the fabric, and (3) the end use of the garment, balanced with cost limitations.

GARMENT FLARE. Fairly straight garments lend themselves to hem allowances of maximum width. Narrow hems in straight garments usually appear skimpy and are often a mark of low quality. Consider a two-inch hem as a quality standard in fairly straight skirts, dresses, pants, coats, and jackets. High-price or couture garments may feature hems slightly wider than two inches, denoting generous use of fabric. However, hems wider than three inches are not usually recommended because they attract too much attention.

Garments that flare require narrow hems; the more flare, the narrower the hem. Circular skirts may have hems as narrow as one-eighth inch or, instead of a hem, have decorative stitches finishing the edge.

Wide hem allowances on flared garments require special handling. The raw edge of the hem has a greater circumference than the garment at the level to which the hem is attached; thus, the excess circumference of the hem allowance must be eased or otherwise shaped to the garment. To ease the edge, it is easestitched, and the easestitching is pulled up (see Chapter 8). The grainlines of the hem and the garment must be aligned so that the hem edge lies smoothly, without pleats or tucks, against the garment. Eased hems are costly; they are used only in high-price garments. If its edge is only slightly too full to fit the garment smoothly, a **hem** may be **wedged.** Tiny wedges of fabric are cut out and the hem edges lapped at the wedge to remove the fullness. This is common in men's pants when flared bottoms are popular. It contributes to quality if done neatly and if the cut edges do not ravel. As another alternative to easing, the hem may be flanged. Hem allowance **flanges** or projections below the hemline are cut as a mirror image of the garment above the hemline. They enable the hem allowance edge to lie flat and smooth against the garment when folded up. Flanges also help create smooth hems in tapered areas, such as close-fitting sleeves or pant legs, when the hem allowance is too small to fit the garment without flanges.

WEIGHT OF FABRIC. Garments of heavy fabrics do not require hem allowances as wide as those using lightweight fabrics. Heavyweight fabrics hang nicely with minimal hem widths, whereas thinner and less dense materials require the weight of wide hem allowances to hang gracefully. If the fabric is sheer and lightweight, and the garment is fairly straight, a hem width of up to six or eight inches may be required on a full-length skirt, for example, to give the proper hang and to balance visually with the length of the garment.

END USE. Wide hems at the lower edge of garments usually represent high quality. Sometimes, however, narrow hems are preferable. For example, a wide hem on a shirttail that is tucked in is bulky and unnecessary. Hems on accessories like ruffles, scarves, or handkerchiefs also need not be wide; narrow hems are adequate to finish the edge without adding unwanted bulk. Although they reduce costs, narrow hems are a negative feature only if they sacrifice quality.

Shirttail Hems. A **shirttail hem** (EFb) is a narrow hem that is folded under twice and topstitched in place. Most shirttail hems on shirts are about one-quarter inch wide and feature a single row of stitches. Shirttail hems on dresses may be slightly wider than on shirts and, for decoration, sometimes feature two or more rows of stitching. Manufacturers use shirttail hems on garments that have a lot of flare or an unusual shape, on garments worn tucked in such as shirts, and to give a casual look to clothing. A shirttail hem is durable and lower in cost than a wide hem because it requires little fabric. High-quality shirttail hems completely enclose the raw edge and are smooth and flat (Figure 7-4). However, bias edges on shaped shirttails often feed unevenly and stretch as they are sewn, distorting the finished shirttail hem. This detracts from the hem's appearance but is not critical if the garment is always worn tucked in.

Rolled Hems. A **rolled hem** is a very narrow hem that is rolled up to enclose the raw edge of the hem (EFw), shown in Figure 7-5. The roll of fabric, only about one-eighth inch wide, is secured to the garment with topstitching, blindstitching, or overedging. Manufacturers use

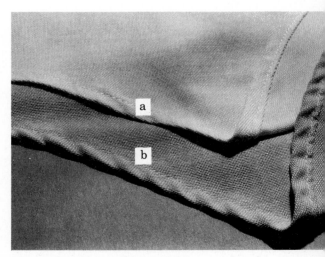

Figure 7-4 Shirttail hems: (a) is smoother than (b).

Figure 7-5 Rolled hems on scarves and a handkerchief.

rolled hems to finish the edges of garments; ruffles and other garment details; and scarves, handkerchiefs, and other accessories made of sheer or lightweight fabrics. Hand-rolled hems, secured with hand slipstitches, may be found in couture clothing.

Clean Finish. The **clean finish** is used occasionally in moderate- and high-quality garments to neatly and attractively finish edges inside the garment (Figure 7-6). To create this finish, also called **turned and stitched,** the raw edge of the seam or hem allowance is folded under once and stitched (EFa). Essentially, a clean finish is a narrow hem on the edge. Clean

finishes add bulk, so they are limited to light- and medium-weight fabrics. Nevertheless, when the garment is pressed, a ridge from the clean finish may make an impression on the outside of the garment. The clean finish does not prevent raveling but impedes its progress. Clean finishing is costly in labor because it requires four runs—(1) sewing the seam, (2) butterflying the seam allowances, and (3) and (4) stitching through the folded edge of each of the two seam allowances.

Booked Seams. **Booked seams** or **tailored seams** (SSba) are plain seams, butterflied, with the raw edges of the seam allowances folded under and blindstitched. Essentially, the seam allowances are narrowly hemmed (Figure 7-6). Booked seams are common in unlined men's jackets. They are durable but costly in terms of labor because each seam requires four operations—(1) sewing the seam, (2) butterflying the seam, and (3) and (4) blindstitching the edges of each of the two seam allowances. Booked seams are somewhat bulky.

Other EF Stitchings. *Overedging* (EFd) is the simplest and most common edge finish stitching for seam allowances, hem allowances, and other raw edges inside the garment; for example, pocket bags and facing edges. Overedging is used occasionally to finish and decorate edges visible on the outside of garments (Figure 7-7),

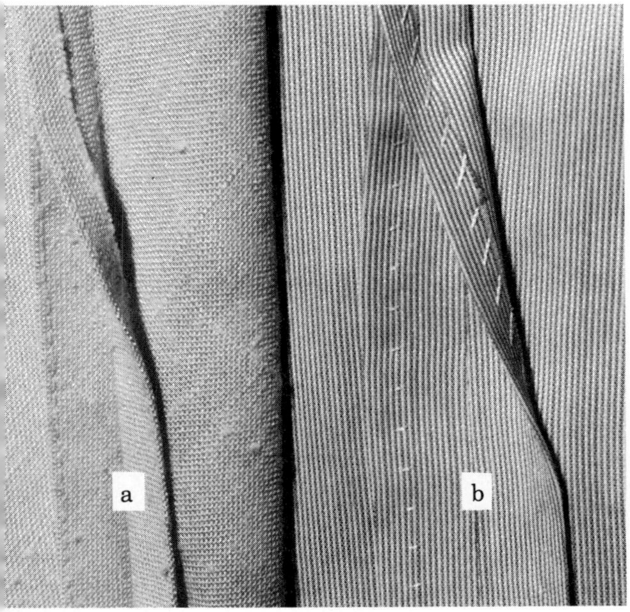

Figure 7-6 Seam allowance finishes: (a) clean finish, and (b) booked seam.

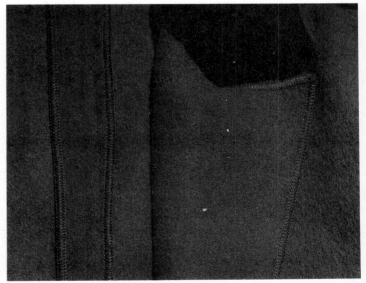

Figure 7-7 Overedging used to finish raw edges of lapels and raw edges of seam allowances in designer-label jacket. Also note black velvet/Chesterfield-style collar.

but it is not generally considered as attractive as other edge treatments in such locations. Overedging, using 500-class stitches, trims the raw edge while simultaneously overcasting it with thread. It is an effective finish because it prevents raveling by covering the raw edge with thread interloopings but does not add much bulk. For example, the lower edges of infant undershirts are sometimes overedged because they are softer and less bulky for babies to wear next to their skin than a bulky folded hem. Overedging is flexible and extensible. The hand-made version of machine overedging, found in some couture garments, is **hand overcasting;** a series of spaced, diagonal stitches cover the seam or hem allowance edges to retard raveling.

Decorative stitchings may substitute for overedging if an ornamental finish for the raw edge is desired. Figure 7-8 illustrates a few popular decorative stitchings used to finish garment edges. A series of stitches shaped, for example, as hearts, ducks, waves, or scallops can finish the edge. The **shell hem** features a scalloped effect created by a decorative shell stitch that attaches the narrow, folded hem allowance to the garment. It is used on lingerie and feminine clothing. A **lettuce edge hem** is created by the operator, who stretches the edge as it is stitched so that it ripples attractively; the edge must be stretched consistently for even ripples. The lettuce edge is used on ruffles and hems of feminine-looking apparel. This type of edge styling happens also to demonstrate clearly *why,* under ordinary circumstances, fabrics should *not* be stretched as they are sewn, to avoid unwanted rippling.

Occasionally, a manufacturer uses *zigzag stitches* at raw edges; if used on lightweight fabrics, zigzagging tends to pucker the edge. A row of *straight stitches* may be sufficient for preventing the seam allowances of knit garments from curling. However, it impedes raveling to a very limited extent.

OTHER EDGE TREATMENTS

U.S. Fed. Std. 751a: Stitches, Seams, and Stitchings limits its discussion of edge finishes to stitchings (EF stitchings). This chapter goes beyond that narrow definition to encompass other edge treatments; for example, bindings, bands, facings, and plackets that are seamed to the garment to finish an edge.

Unstitched Finishes. A simple method for finishing edges inside garments is to **pink** them; the edge is cut with a serrated blade in the factory, or with scissors by tailors in alterations departments (Figure 7-9). Manufacturers pink only opaque fabrics because the serrations show through sheer or translucent fabrics, which is unattractive. Pinking retards raveling but does not prevent it. It is an inexpensive, nonbulky edge finish, but is rarely used now to finish seam allowances because overedging prevents raveling better. A common place to see pinking is at the lower edge of pants that are unhemmed at the point of sale.

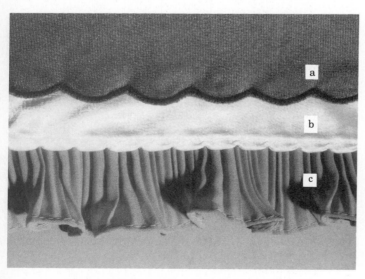

Figure 7-8 Decorative hem finishes: (a) scalloped, (b) shell hem, and (c) lettuce edge hem.

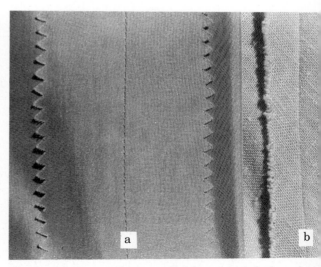

Figure 7-9 Seam allowance finishes: (a) pinked, and (b) no finish, because bias-cut edges do not ravel readily.

Manufacturers *glue* seam and hem allowances flat in garments made of leather and leatherlike fabrics. In these cases, gluing is not considered a low-quality finish, as it would be on conventional fabrics. Because leather and leatherlike fabrics are bulky and cannot be pressed, gluing down and pounding the seam allowances flattens them in a desirable manner.

An edge finish used to a very limited extent involves coating the raw edges with a heat sensitive material that is *fused* to the edges with heat. This method is effective for preventing raveling but causes discomfort when the edges contact the wearer's skin. A *liquid plastic* applied to raw edges, which dries to prevent raveling, yields similar results.

Facings. A **facing** is any piece of fabric used to finish raw edges of the garment; for example, at the neckline, armhole, and front and back openings. The facing is turned to the inside of the garment so that it backs or *faces* the garment at the edge. Facings are folded, or sewn to the garment using an enclosed seam. The three main types of facings are (1) extended facings, (2) shaped facings, and (3) bias facings.

Facings are the least conspicuous edge finish, because they are typically visible only inside the garment (except at folded-back edges, such as lapels). Occasionally a manufacturer constructs a facing to show on the outside of the garment for a novelty effect, but facings are usually designed to "face" the wearer alone. For example, a man's shirt with a **French front** is faced at center front. The smooth French front draws less attention than a **button band** (also called a placket), the band of fabric at the center front of many men's shirts (Figure 11-9).

Most facings are two to three inches wide. In low-price lines, facings may be cut narrower than two inches to conserve fabric. A common example are neckline facings in blouses cut so narrow that they slip out and show when the garment is worn (Figure 7-10). In high-price lines, some facings may be cut considerably wider than two inches. For example, a facing at the center back neckline is sometimes cut several inches wide. The main advantage of a wide, back neckline facing is that it looks attractive at the point of sale because it covers the inner construction otherwise visible when the garment is on a hanger. A wide facing also protects the fashion fabric of the garment from perspiration and body oils during wear. However, a wide facing requires extra fabric and does not

Figure 7-10 *Too-narrow facing slips out and shows on outside of blouse.*

necessarily provide greater quality; it may add unwanted bulk and create a visible line within the body of the garment. It can be difficult to keep in place if it shifts during wear and may slip out and show on the outside of the garment.

Facings in high-quality garments are tacked in place at seam allowances. Otherwise, the facing shifts position during wear and slips out to show on the outside of the garment. If not top-stitched, facings with enclosed seams require understitching or control stitching (Figure 6-8). Either keeps the facing from slipping out and showing on the outside of the garment. However, control stitching is generally confined to high-price garments. On some better garments, facings with enclosed seams also may be *slipped* or *bubbled* (see Chapter 9).

Facings add to the cost of the garment because they require additional fabric and labor. However, the cost of facings varies depending on the type used.

Extended Facings. The simplest type of facing is the **extended facing.** The fabric at the edge to be faced is extended and folded under (Figure 7-11). You can identify an extended facing by

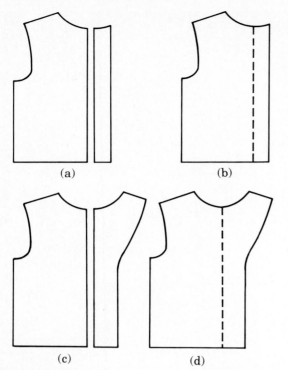

Figure 7-11 *Center front facings: (a) shaped, and (b) extended. Combination center front and neckline facing: (c) shaped, and (d) extended.*

another smoothly. The garment and facing are joined using an enclosed seam. Ideally, manufacturers attach shaped facings in the round rather than flat. You can distinguish shaped facings from extended facings by the enclosed seam (instead of a fold) at the finished outer edge of shaped facings (Figure 7-12).

Shaped facings are usually cut from the same fabric as the garment unless the garment is made from a very heavy or bulky fabric. In such cases, the facing is cut from a fabric lighter in weight than the garment, but of a matching color. Shaped facings in high-quality garments are usually interfaced for body and support. The important characteristics are that shaped facings

1. Are ideal for finishing unusually shaped necklines or hems and sleeveless armholes because they conform to any shape, including sharp corners and curves.

2. Require less fabric than extended facings because the separate pieces are laid out to better advantage.

3. Allow collar or trim to be sewn to the edge

the fold at the edge. The important characteristics are that extended facings

1. Require the least labor and add the least bulk of the facing types.

2. Are used less than shaped facings because they require more fabric. As an extension of the garment piece, the addition of an extended facing often creates a large and awkwardly shaped piece that lowers material utilization. Manufacturers of low-price garments sometimes use extended facings but often cut them narrow in an effort to compact the layout and improve material utilization.

3. Can only be used to face straight edges—to finish front and back openings, and collars, cuffs, waistbands, and other details with straight edges. The folded edge cannot conform to other shapes without pulling or buckling the garment.

Shaped Facings. **Shaped facings** are fabric pieces shaped identically to the garment edges they face (Figure 7-11). Shaped facings should be cut on the same grain as the garment piece they face so garment and facing conform to one

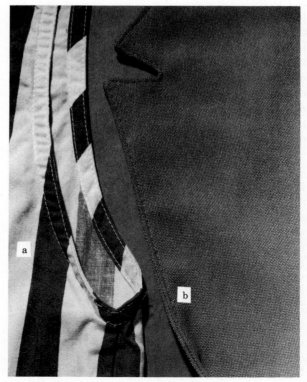

Figure 7-12 *Facings: (a) bias facing at armhole, and (b) shaped facing (note enclosed seam at edge).*

before it is faced because shaped facings are sewn on, not folded back.

4. Require more fabric for curved than for straight pieces. For example, shaped facings at the waistline cost more than straight waistbands but about the same as contour waistbands.

5. Do not absorb stress well when curved because they are cut on the bias rather than on the straight-of-grain. The stretch introduced by the bias areas of the facing should be reinforced to prevent loss of shape in those areas. For example, manufacturers stay bias-faced waistbands with a strong, nonstretch tape to prevent it from stretching out of shape during wear.

6. Allow the hem to be let down the full amount of the hem allowance when they are added to alter a hem edge.

Sometimes manufacturers combine a shaped facing with an extended facing to create a **combination facing.** For example, they combine the extended facing at the center front of a blouse with the shaped facing that fits the neckline (Figure 7-11). Combination facings reduce bulk and lower labor costs but require more fabric than shaped facings.

Bias Facings. **Bias facings** are narrow, bias strips of fabric used to face raw edges (Figure 7-12). The narrow bias strips are sewn to the raw edges to be faced and turned to the inside of the garment. The lower edge of the bias strip is turned under (usually) and then topstitched, blindstitched, or tacked to the garment to form a neat, inconspicuous facing, usually no more than about half an inch wide. The important characteristics are that bias facings

1. Require little fabric; manufacturers cut bias facings economically from the fashion fabric or purchase them as a precut notion.

2. Require no pattern making and no interfacing, thus costing less than other facing types.

3. Are useful for sheer fabrics; if they show through, they do not interfere much with the appearance of the garment because they are so narrow.

4. Are low in bulk and thus suitable for garments made of heavy or bulky fabrics.

5. Are not well-suited for use on intricately shaped edges with sharp corners or curves because of the difficulty and cost in applying them

to such edges; manufacturers face these with shaped facings.

Bindings. A **binding** covers the raw edge of the garment with a strip of fabric that is visible from both inside and outside the garment (Figures 6-15 and 6-16). The Federal Standard categorizes bindings as seams (BS) because they join together two or more pieces of fabric. However, bindings are often used as an edge finish, so they are also discussed briefly in this chapter. Edges may be *bound* by any of the methods discussed in Chapter 6. The best bindings are nonraveling, nonbulky, and comfortable, and match or coordinate with color of the fabric. Bindings may be decorative as well as functional, especially if they contrast with the color of the garment. You can distinguish bindings from bands because *bindings cover but do not extend garment edges.*

Manufacturers use bindings to decoratively finish outer garment edges such as necklines, armholes, front and back opening edges, and the lower edges of the garment and sleeves. Because bindings look the same from both sides, they are a common choice for finishing the outer edges of reversible garments. Bound seams cannot be let out much if the garment requires altering. Taking in a bound seam is labor intensive because the binding must first be removed and later sewn back on after the alteration.

Bound seam allowances (SSbh) and hem allowances look attractive inside a garment, add strength to the edges, and prevent raveling and abrasion. However, seams and hems with bound allowances are often quite stiff and bulky, and their impression sometimes presses through to the outside of the garment. Bound seam and hem allowances are costly in terms of both materials and labor; they are only found in expensive garments. An unlined garment with bound seam allowances costs more and represents higher quality than a fully lined garment in which narrow seam allowances and poor construction are covered by the lining.

A **Hong Kong binding** is a very narrow, often color-contrasting, often shiny, bias strip used to decoratively bind seam and hem allowances and other edges inside high-price tailored and couture garments (Figure 7-13). The binding strip is seamed to the edge, folded around and stitched in the ditch (BSf). Hong Kong binding is an elegant, costly finish that is valued for its ornamental appearance.

Edges are occasionally *self-bound.* One seam

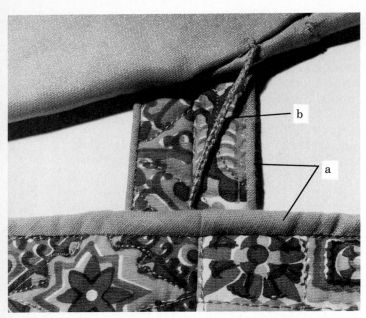

Figure 7-13 (a) Hong Kong bindings on seam and hem allowances, and (b) swing tack between garment and free-hanging lining.

allowance is extended, wrapped around the shorter seam allowance, and stitched in place.

Bands. **Bands** are pieces of fabric seamed usually to the straight raw edges of garments to extend and finish the edge. Bands are used mostly on outer garment edges. You can differentiate bands from bindings because

1. *Bands extend beyond the edge they finish.*

2. Bands are generally (although not always) wider than bindings.

A band consists of a single piece of fabric folded lengthwise or of two pieces, the band and its facing. Collars, cuffs, and waistbands are all examples of bands (see Chapter 9). Other examples are the rib knit bands at sweatshirt hems, necklines, and wrists. For these bands, a strip of rib knit fabric is folded in half and sewn to the garment. The crosswise direction of the knit fabric, the most stretchy direction, runs around the body, neck, or wrist so it can stretch when the garment is put on and taken off, but return to original size and smoothness when the garment is worn. In some garments, single-layer knit bands are used instead of folded bands; the bands are knitted with a finished outer edge.

A useful application for bands is to seam the garment, seam the band, and then join the two together in the round. However, in lower-price garments the band is usually joined to the garment while the two are in flat form and then both are joined into a circle (Figure 7-14). This finish is inexpensive, but the final seam shows at the edge, detracting from the garment's appearance; the seam is also subject to unraveling. Circular bands may be cut from tubular fabrics or knit into the correct circumference to fit the garment. This eliminates the need for seaming the band to fit, but different-size bands must be knit for each size garment produced. Such bands at the necklines of T-shirts, sweatshirts, and sweaters are sometimes called *collarettes*.

A band should be uniform in width throughout and of the correct length for the edge to which it is attached. Skilled sewing operators stretch bands applied to concave curves to prevent ripples at the outer edge; for example, T-shirt necklines gape if they are not stretched slightly as they are sewn. Operators ease bands applied to convex curves to prevent pulling at the outer edge. The wider the band and the sharper the curve of the garment edge, the more need for stretching or easing the band to fit. If the band is made from a firm material that does not lend itself to stretching or easing, a shaped band with facing is required for curved applications. Bands applied to corners or points require mitering or seaming to remove excess fullness at the angles and to shape the band to the corner or point (Figure 7-15).

Sometimes manufacturers imitate the look of a band by topstitching the garment at approxi-

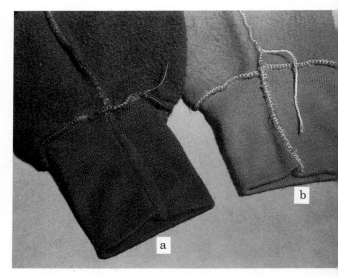

Figure 7-14 Order of band construction: (a) band joined to garment "in the round," and (b) band joined to garment flat.

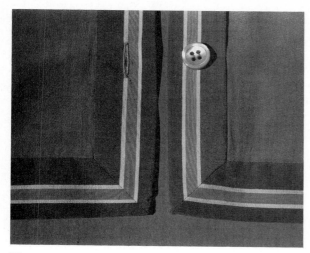

Figure 7-15 *Mitered band.*

mately the width of a band (Figure 7-16) or by turning a facing to the outside of the garment rather than the inside, and topstitching it in place.

Plackets. A **placket** is a finished garment opening that allows a body part to pass through for dressing and undressing. Plackets are required when the garment opening is closely fitted and does not stretch for dressing and undressing. They open necklines, waistlines, and sleeves, for example, so that garments can be put on and taken off easily. A fitted cuff with an opening to fit over the hand requires a coordinating placket opening in the sleeve. A shirt with a fitted collar requires a placket at the neckline to pull the garment over the head. A pair of fitted pants requires a placket opening at the waistline to pull the garment on and off over the hips. The fly front zipper placket common to jeans and men's pants is discussed in Chapter 11.

Placket edges may be hemmed, faced, bound, or banded. The resulting opening edges are closed by lapping, abutting or superimposing the finished edges and fastening them with a closure.

Slashed Plackets. Manufacturers sometimes cut a slash in a garment and turn under the raw edges of the slash to form a placket. This method is suitable only when the fabric does not ravel readily. It is not durable because the point of the placket is unreinforced.

Horizontal Plackets. A **horizontal placket** is so named because it is parallel to the sleeve open-

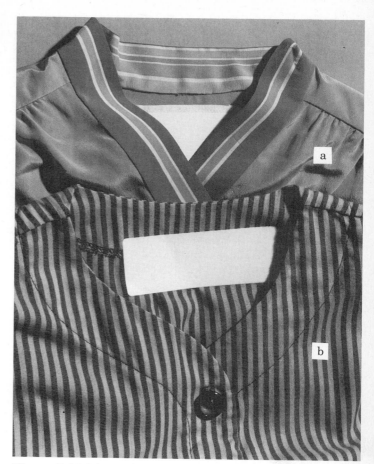

Figure 7-16 *(a) true band, and (b) topstitching imitates band.*

ing; horizontal plackets are used almost exclusively on sleeves, where they represent a simple and low-cost opening. The manufacturer cuts two clips, one or two inches apart, in the lower edge of the sleeve and then narrowly hems the area to create a finished opening (Figure 7-17). If the area has reinforcement stitching, and if the raw edge is overcast and blindstitched in place, the horizontal placket is quite inconspicuous and secure. If the raw edge is merely topstitched in place, the horizontal placket is conspicuous and insecure.

Horizontal plackets are suitable for sheer fabrics and in formal wear where a narrow, discreet placket is desired. They are not desirable if the wearer wants to roll or push the sleeves up on the arms, because the horizontal placket provides less roominess than longer, vertical plackets. Also, the horizontal placket tends to slip out and show on the outside of the garment unless a small pleat is stitched in to prevent it, a detail found in high-quality garments (Figure 7-17).

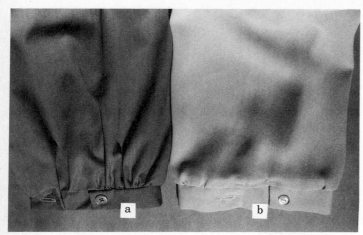

Figure 7-17 *Horizontal plackets: (a) better if invisibly stitched and with pleat, than (b) topstitched and without pleat.*

Horizontal plackets are found in garments at all price lines, in budget apparel because of the low cost and in other apparel when a nearly invisible placket is required.

Faced Plackets. Manufacturers produce **faced plackets** by cutting a straight or shaped slash in the fabric perpendicular to the edge of the garment; the slash is faced with a rectangle of fabric sewn on with an enclosed seam (Figure 7-18). If the slash is pointed, the point should be reinforced to prevent a hole from forming. Excess seam allowances at the point prevent the placket from turning smoothly and cause puckering at the point. A faced placket is fairly simple to produce, but the facing creates unwanted bulk in heavy fabrics and shows through sheer fabrics. The facing tends to slip out and show on

the outside of the garment; topstitching, control stitching, or tacking prevents this.

Faced plackets are most often found at necklines that close with a single button at the top of the placket. They are occasionally used on sleeves.

Continuous Bound Plackets. The **continuous bound placket** is one of the most widely used sleeve plackets (Figure 7-19); it is rarely used in other locations. The manufacturer binds a vertical slash in the lower edge of the sleeve with a narrow strip of fabric. To avoid puckers or a hole at the point of the placket, two common defects, the point of the slash should be reinforced with stitching, and the binding must be stitched on accurately. A well-made continuous bound placket is attractive and durable. This type of placket is somewhat bulky and should not be used in heavy fabrics.

The continuous bound placket has a tendency to slip out and show on the outside of the garment. A diagonal row of stitches or a bar tack through the upper end of the finished placket prevents this. These stitches should be placed through all layers of the binding to keep it inside (Figure 7-19). The absence of a row of diagonal stitches or a bar tack inside a continuous bound placket detracts from quality.

The side of the placket connected to the overlap side of the cuff should be turned under. The side of the placket connected to the underlap

Figure 7-19 *Continuous bound plackets: (a) with diagonal row of stitches at upper end, and (b) without a row of diagonal stitches at upper end, allowing placket to slip out and show on outside of garment.*

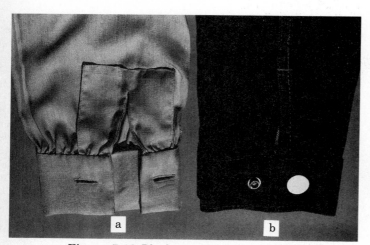

Figure 7-18 *Plackets: (a) faced, and (b) in-seam.*

side of the cuff should lie flat. A placket that does not follow these rules is the result of a production mistake.

In-Seam Plackets. The **in-seam placket** is the simplest and least expensive placket to construct (Figure 7-18). It is mainly used on sleeves and occasionally at necklines and on pant legs. A seam entering the opening at the desired position for a placket is left unsewn for the last three inches or so. The manufacturer finishes the seam allowance edges by clean finishing or overedging, and then blindstitches or topstitches them in place. The placket should be bar tacked or otherwise reinforced at the seamed end for durability.

The chief disadvantage of in-seam plackets for most sleeves is that the cuff buttons are underneath the wrist, rather than on the outside of the wrist as required. This is inconvenient to button, unattractive and uncomfortable when the arm is rested on a hard surface. However, when the in-seam placket is used in garments with two-piece sleeves, the placket is positioned correctly. Although they represent low quality when used on garments with one-piece sleeves, in-seam plackets are often used in high-quality leather and denim jackets with two-piece sleeves. In fact, the **sleeve vents** at the wrist of high-quality tailored suit and sport jacket sleeves are a form of hemmed, in-seam placket.

Tailored Plackets. The **tailored placket** consists of a bound slash (Figure 7-20). The overlap portion of the slash is bound with a topstitched strip of fabric. The overlap hides the underlap, which is bound with a narrower strip of fabric. The placket is usually interfaced and the end is topstitched for reinforcement. Manufacturers use the tailored placket on men's dress shirts (it is sometimes called the **shirt sleeve placket**) and on some casual women's blouse and dress sleeves. Variations of the tailored placket are used at the necklines of polo-style knit shirts.

The tailored placket is the most complex and costly placket to manufacture. It requires more fabric pieces and more labor than other placket types. In most cases, the production of tailored plackets on shirt sleeves is automated; automation reduces costs and produces more consistent results than manually made plackets. Poorly made plackets have holes, tucks, or puckers.

Tailored plackets draw more attention than other placket types and are an important style detail of a garment. They provide the longest opening of all placket types, allowing sleeves to be rolled up on the arm easily.

An extra button and buttonhole, the **gauntlet button,** placed on the tailored placket prevents it from gaping (Figure 7-20). Gauntlet buttons also aid in keeping sleeves in place if they are rolled up. The gauntlet button adds a touch of quality as well as extra cost to a placket.

Figure 7-20 *Tailored plackets: (a) with gauntlet button, and (b) without gauntlet button. Note that cuff on (a) has a single button, and (b) has two buttons so cuff can be loosened or tightened to alter sleeve length slightly.*

Summary

The main purpose of edge treatments is to finish raw edges both inside and outside the garment. Edge treatments should complement the appearance of the garment and prevent raveling without adding unnecessary bulk.

Hems, the most common edge treatment, are categorized as an edge finish stitching by the

U.S. Fed. Std. No. 751a. The edge is turned under and stitched to the garment. Wide hem allowances generally indicate high quality. Hem width, however, depends on the flare of the garment, the weight of the fabric, and the end use of the garment. Other edge finish stitchings include overedging and other stitches, sometimes decorative.

Facings are visible only inside the garment. They are either extended, shaped, or bias. Extended facings are a folded-under extension of the garment edge. Shaped facings are the same shape as the garment edge being faced. Bias facings are narrow, inconspicuous, and low cost. Bindings enclose raw edges with a strip of fabric; they are classified as seams by *U.S. Fed. Std. 751a.* Bands are strips of fabric that cover and extend garment edges. Bands are generally wider than bindings.

Plackets are finished garment opening edges; for example, in sleeves, necklines, and waistlines. Plackets may be hemmed, faced, bound, or banded. Horizontal plackets are inconspicuous. The facing of faced plackets tends to slip out and show. Continuous bound plackets should be diagonally stitched at the upper end to keep the placket inside the garment. Inseam plackets are appropriate on necklines and two-piece sleeves where a seam occurs at the desired position for the placket. Tailored plackets are the most complex and costly placket to construct. A gauntlet button on a tailored placket prevents it from gaping.

Edge Treatment Quality Checklist

If you can answer yes to each of these questions regarding the garment you are evaluating, it contains high-quality edge treatments.

- If the fabric has a tendency to ravel or roll, are all raw edges finished?
- Are all edge finishes even, flat, and nonbulky? Are curves smooth and points sharp?
- Is the hem wide (except when the garment is flared, made of heavy fabric, or of a style that requires a narrow hem)?
- If the garment is tapered or flared and the hem is wide, is the hem allowance eased, flanged, or wedged to help it lie smoothly?
- Is the hem attached with close, secure, inconspicuous stitches?
- If the garment is tailored, are hems interfaced?
- Are shaped and extended facings about two inches in width?
- Are facing edges invisible from the outside of the garment?
- Are facings tacked in position at seams and other anchor points?
- Do bindings completely cover raw edges?
- Are bindings securely attached?
- Are bands and bindings stretched slightly around concave curves and eased around convex curves?
- Is the garment hemmed before the opening edge is finished?
- Preferably, are facings, bindings, and bands applied "in the round" instead of flat?
- Are seam and hem allowances in unlined garments finished?
- Is control stitching used on facings with a tendency to slip out and show on the outside of the garment?
- In high-price garments, are facings slipped or bubbled?
- Are horizontal plackets and continuous bound plackets tacked to prevent them from slipping out and showing on the outside of the garment?
- Do tailored plackets have a gauntlet button?

New Terms

If you can define each of these terms and differentiate between related terms, you have gained a good working vocabulary for discussing the topics in this chapter. The terms are listed in the order in which they appear in the chapter.

edge treatment/finish
stitching
edge finish stitching (EF)
folded hem
hem allowance

wedged hem
flange
shirttail hem
rolled hem
clean finish/turned and stitched
booked/tailored seam
hand overcasting
shell hem
lettuce edge hem
pink
facing
French front
button band
extended facing
shaped facing
combination facing
bias facing
binding
Hong Kong binding
band
placket
horizontal placket
faced placket
continuous bound placket
in-seam placket
sleeve vent
tailored placket/shirt sleeve placket
gauntlet button

Review Questions

1. Why are wide hems generally desirable? In what circumstances are narrow hems appropriate?

2. Tell whether the following statement is true or false: "The opening edge should be finished first; then the garment should be hemmed." Justify your answer.

3. What extra features would you expect in the hems of high-quality tailored garments?

4. When should hems be eased?

5. How is a shirttail hem different from a rolled hem? In what types of garments is each type of hem appropriate?

6. Generally, how wide is a high-quality shaped facing? Why?

7. How does a facing, binding, or band sewn on flat versus "in the round" affect quality?

8. What might be responsible for a band rippling or pulling at its outer edge?

9. Why do some hems on knit garments ripple undesirably?

10. Why should shaped facings be cut on the same grain as the garment?

11. How does a gauntlet button add to the quality of tailored sleeve plackets?

12. How does a row of diagonal stitches or a bar tack at the end of a continuous-bound placket contribute to quality?

Activities

1. Examine the blindstitched hems in low-end and high-end garments. In your opinion, are the stitches satisfactorily inconspicuous? Did you find any differences between price lines?

2. Examine the hems in low-end and high-end garments in the following classifications:
   a. dresses
   b. men's dress shirts
   c. wool coats
   d. T-shirts
   e. men's pants
   f. women's pants

What differences, if any, did you find in hem depth? Is hem depth determined by price line? By garment classification?

3. Compare shirttail hems in low-end and high-end garments. What differences in quality did you find, if any?

4. Find an example of each of the following edge treatments:
   a. clean finished
   b. booked seam
   c. overedged
   d. pinked
   e. Hong Kong bound
   f. taped
Evaluate the quality of each. In what types of garments are these finishes used?

5. Find a garment with an example of a binding and another with an example of a band. How are the two edge treatments the same? How are they different?

6. Find garments with examples of an extended facing, a shaped facing, and a bias facing.

What are the advantages and disadvantages of each?

7. Find a garment with a too-narrow facing. Why should the facing be wider?

8. Find examples of the following placket types:
- **a.** horizontal
- **b.** continuous bound
- **c.** in-seam
- **d.** tailored placket on sleeve
- **e.** tailored placket at neckline

Which type required the most fabric and labor? The least? What is the most appropriate application for each? Evaluate the quality of each.

9. Examine the edge finishes on leather garments. How and why do they differ from those on garments of woven or knit fabrics?

10. Find a shirt with a French front and another with a button band. What are the advantages and disadvantages of each?

8

Shape and Support: Creating a Three-Dimensional Garment

CHAPTER OBJECTIVES

1. Recognize the cost and quality of shaping and supporting techniques.

2. Understand various ways of shaping garments to the human body.

3. Discuss underlying fabrics and other supporting devices used in garments.

Shaping a garment enables it to fit the wearer and achieve the desired style or look. Supporting devices help the garment retain its shape. Shaping and supporting features often distinguish a high-quality garment from one of lesser quality. Attention to shape and support is important in all garments, but especially in tailored clothing.

Tailored garments are carefully structured and detailed; they are usually closely fitted and made of woven fabrics, for example, the classic business suit. Shaping devices, underlying fabrics, and other supporting devices are critical to the aesthetic appearance of the garment, and affect the garment's functional performance as well, including fit, comfort, appearance retention, and durability.

Shaping Devices

All garments contain **shaping devices** that control the way the garment fits the contours of the body. The methods used to shape the garment, and the location and amount of added shaping affect its fit and style. In low-quality garments, pattern engineers may change or eliminate shaping devices to produce pattern pieces that are smaller or have straight edges.

This results in better material utilization and lowers sewing costs. However, the omission of shaping devices detracts from the fit and design of the garment.

A basic fitted garment is derived from a **basic block.** Manufacturers have a basic block for each classification of apparel that they produce; for example, pants or jackets. Figure 8-1 shows the basic blocks for a woman's dress and a man's suit. The designer uses shaping devices to make changes in the basic block to produce style variations. Chapter 9 illustrates a number of styles, all originating from a basic block, with varying amounts of fullness added and controlled in different locations through various shaping devices. For more information about how shaping devices are used to create different clothing styles, see Related Resources: Design and Style.

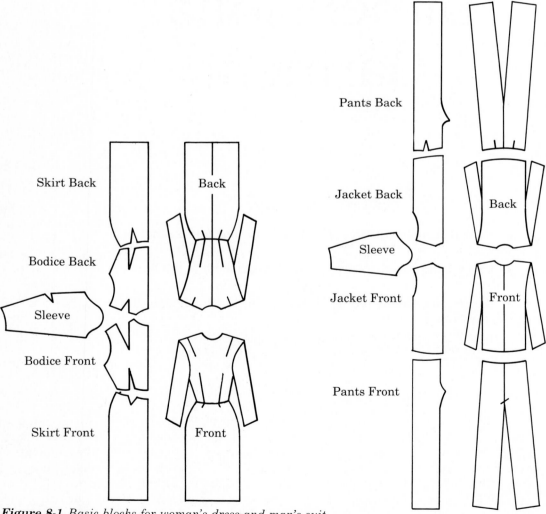

Figure 8-1 Basic blocks for woman's dress and man's suit.

DARTS

A **dart** is a triangular fold stitched to shape the flat fabric to the curves and bulges of the body. Notice the triangular *darts* in the basic blocks in Figure 8-1. Darts introduce shape into the garment, enabling a two-dimensional fabric to become a three-dimensional garment that fits a three-dimensional body.

Darts are the basic shaping device. They enable the garment to fit the body smoothly. However, a garment with darts does not usually fit as wide a range of sizes as do garments containing other shaping devices. Darts have relatively high labor costs but low fabric costs compared to other shaping devices.

Darts are almost always stitched inside the garment so that the triangular fold of the dart appears inside the garment. Occasionally, *decorative darts* are stitched so that the folded triangle appears on the outside of the garment.

Single-Pointed. Most darts are *single-pointed* (Figure 8-2). Manufacturers use single-pointed darts vertically at the back neck or back shoulders of jackets, at the waistline of bodices, skirts, pants, and dresses, and horizontally at elbows and at the bustline of women's clothing. However, a dart can originate from any seam and occur at any angle so long as it points toward the fullest part of its assigned body bulge. For example, *French darts* are diagonal bust darts that originate low in the side seams to fit the bust (Figure 8-3).

Double-Pointed. *Double-pointed darts* or *contour darts* look like two single-pointed darts joined at the wide ends to form one continuous dart (Figure 8-2). Manufacturers use double-pointed darts vertically at the waistline of jackets and dresses. Double-pointed darts nip the garment in at the waist while releasing fullness above and below it to fit the bust/chest and hip areas.

Size. Narrow darts fit small body bulges and wide darts fit large body bulges. Each dart adds to labor costs, so in low-price garments one dart is often used per body bulge where two or more narrow darts might yield smoother-fitting results. However, a single dart has the offsetting advantage of being less visually distracting than multiple darts.

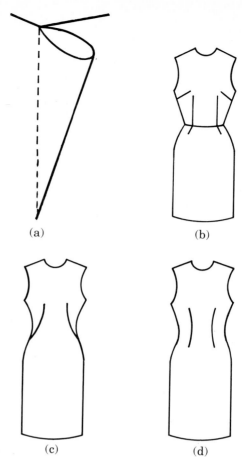

(a) (b)

(c) (d)

Figure 8-2 *Darts: (a) stitched, tapering at the point, inside the garment, (b) single-pointed, (c) French, and (d) double pointed.*

Stitching. Operators must sew darts accurately for smooth-fitting results. The stitches should be straight until they approach the tip, and then taper gradually off the folded edge (Figure 8-2). If the stitches at the dart tip are not tapered gradually, the dart bubbles or *dimples* at the tip rather than fitting the body bulge smoothly. The tip of a dart may be marked with a tiny *drill hole* or other marking to guide the operator in constructing the dart. If drill holes are used, the stitching at the dart tip must go slightly beyond the drill hole so the hole does not show on the outside of the garment. If drill holes are used in fabrics that fray, they lower the durability of the dart at the tip.

Darts with raveling stitches at the tips detract from garment appearance and are evidence of low quality standards. The stitches at the dart tip should be secured to prevent them from raveling. The usual method is to leave a short length of twisted threads at the tip of the dart.

When these threads eventually untwist, the stitches at the dart tip begin to ravel; this often happens before the garment leaves the retail store. The longer and more twisted the threads, the more durable the dart tip. The tip of a dart may be secured by backstitching. However, because backstitching causes bulk at the tip of the dart, it is not a desirable dart tip finish. The ideal finish for dart tips is a knot. This prevents the stitches from raveling, but is too costly for garments in most price lines and thus is rarely found in ready-to-wear.

Pressing. Darts should lie flat; in high-quality garments they are pressed after construction. Ideally, vertical darts are pressed toward the center front or center back of the garment; horizontal darts are pressed down. An imprint of the dart should not press through to the outside of the garment. Best results are achieved if darts are pressed over a slightly rounded surface, enhancing the shape built into the garment by the dart and preventing channels or creases at the dart tip. Darts made in thick or heavy fabrics may need to be trimmed and pressed open to reduce bulk. Double-pointed darts may require clipping at the widest point in order to lie flat.

DART EQUIVALENTS

The shaping accomplished by darts can also be created by **dart equivalents** or **dart substitutes.** Dart equivalents substitute for darts by incorporating shape into the garment in a variety of ways. Dart substitutes include the following:

seams	released darts
gussets	ease
godets	tucks and pleats
gathers	gores
drawstrings	extra fullness
full-fashioned knits	elastic
yokes	stretch fabrics

All garments contain shaping devices—either darts or dart equivalents. Darts or dart equivalents are required wherever the fabric of the garment fits a body bulge. The bust, abdomen, buttocks, shoulder blades, and elbows are bulges requiring shaping devices. Because the female figure is naturally more curvy than the male figure, women's clothing features more shaping devices than men's clothing. In some cases, de-

signers include shaping devices not for fit, but for aesthetic reasons.

The design of the garment helps determine which shaping devices are used. For example, loose styles are suited to the use of gathers or extra fullness; close-fitting styles often feature darts or stretch fabrics. The fabric and price line of the garment also influence the choice of shaping devices.

SEAMS

Not all seams are dart substitutes; many join flat fabric panels without imparting any shape. But *seams* are a common dart equivalent, especially in close-fitting garments. Dart-substitute seams perform the same function as darts by shaping the fabric panels where they are joined together. Figure 8-3 illustrates the dart shapes incorporated in some seams; fitted side seams, shoulder seams, fitted waistline

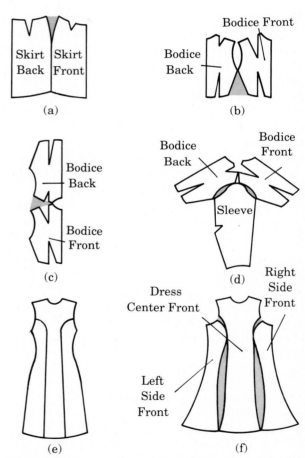

Figure 8-3 *Shaded areas show dart-substitute effect of seams: (a) skirt side seam, (b) bodice side seam, (c) shoulder seam, (d) armhole seam, (e) princess line dress, and (f) princess seams.*

seams, and set-in-sleeve armhole seams are examples of dart-substitute seams. **Princess seams,** which incorporate the bust and waist darts in womenswear, are also dart-substitute seams. They add shape to the garment and enhance fit, but cost more to cut and sew than other types of seams. Another example is better women's panties, which sometimes feature a center back seam to fit the buttocks better than ordinary panties.

YOKES

Yokes are horizontal divisions within a garment; they are usually small, flat panels of fabric at the shoulder, waist, or midriff. When seamed to the garment, some yokes help the garment fit the area above or below a body bulge (Figure 8-4). The yoke seam serves as a dart equivalent by incorporating the dart shape into the seam. Yokes called *risers* often substitute for darts at pants and skirt waistlines. *Midriff yokes* fit the garment close to the body below the bust. Yokes are frequently used in the backs of shirts and blouses to fit the garment through the shoulder blade area. They are also sometimes used in the fronts of shirts and blouses, as in Western-style yokes; these yokes are often merely decorative features that do no shaping.

Split yokes feature a seam at the center back of the yoke. Split yokes in the backs of women's jeans can improve fit considerably. In custom-made shirts, a split yoke represents better fit because the center back seam is shaped to fit the individual. In ready-to-wear shirts, a split

yoke serves no practical purpose, but manufacturers sometimes use them to give consumers the impression of quality.

GORES

Gores are vertical divisions within a garment, usually tapered panels seamed together to add shape to a garment. They serve as dart equivalents by incorporating the dart shape in the seams. Skirts are frequently gored (Figure 8-5). Two-gore skirts contain two panels, four-gore skirts contain four panels, and so on. The more gores, the higher the labor costs; however, the use of several small gores stitched together often achieves higher material utilization than a few large gores.

Gores are not always dart substitutes. Sometimes manufacturers add gores to narrow fabrics in order to widen them for cutting out garments with large pieces; for example, circular skirts.

GUSSETS

Gussets are pieces of fabric set into a seam or seam intersection to add shape and fullness to a garment (Figure 8-6). Most gussets are triangular or diamond-shaped, although some dancers' costumes feature circular gussets to provide mobility. Gussets are used in the underarm seams of garments with kimono sleeves (see

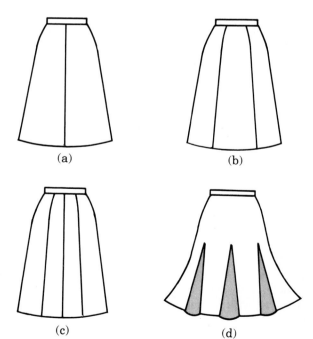

(a) (b)

(c) (d)

Figure 8-5 (a) four-gore skirt, (b) six-gore skirt, (c) eight-gore skirt, and (d) skirt with godets.

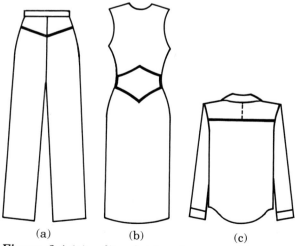

(a) (b) (c)

Figure 8-4 (a) split yoke/riser in pants, (b) midriff yoke, and (c) back shoulder yoke in shirt (dotted line indicates seam placement for split yoke).

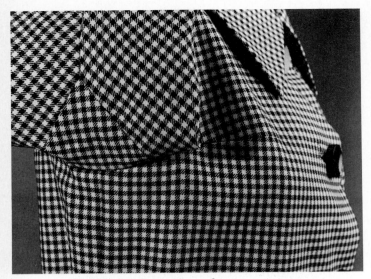

Figure 8-6 Gusset in underarm area.

Chapter 9) and in the crotch seams of sweat-pants and in toddlers' clothes to make room for diapers. Karate pants and shirts feature huge gussets that provide freedom of movement for kicking and punching. High-quality gloves have gussets between the fingers for improved finger mobility. Gussets reduce strain and wrinkling, making the garment comfortable to wear and prolonging its life.

A good-quality gusset has sharp, even points; a poorly set gusset puckers or develops holes at the points. Setting in a gusset requires an experienced operator. Gussets add to cost because of the extra fabric and skilled labor required.

GODETS

Godets are triangular fabric pieces set into a seam or slash, usually at the hem of the garment (Figure 8-5). Godets produce decorative fullness; they are mainly used in skirts but sometimes are used to cause pant or jacket hems to flare. A well-made godet has a sharp point and does not develop holes at the point.

TUCKS AND PLEATS

Tucks are stitched folds of fabric that are usually purely ornamental but occasionally serve as dart substitutes. *Pleats* are decorative, unstitched folds of fabric that often serve as dart substitutes, creating shape and releasing fullness. Trouser pleats are a good example of pleats that are dart substitutes. Not all pleats incorporate shape into a garment; many are merely

decorative. For more information about tucks and pleats, see Chapter 10.

RELEASED DARTS

Released darts result in a straight silhouette rather than a fitted garment. A released dart is a dart left unstitched. It allows the fabric to cover the intended body bulge without fitting the fabric closely to the bulge.

It is a common practice to release darts in today's ready-to-wear because of the popularity of loose-fitting clothing; darts are usually released in combination with the addition of extra fullness to the area. Releasing darts reduces cost. However, it lowers quality to release the darts in close-fitting, tailored clothing unless a dart substitute takes the place of the dart.

EXTRA FULLNESS

Extra fullness can be added to a garment; the additional fabric covers the body bulges (Figure 8-7). When loose clothing styles are popular, extra fullness is the most common dart substitute. Extra fullness allows the garment to fit a wider range of sizes than many other shaping devices. Fabric panels are cut larger to introduce additional fullness to the garment, adding significantly to the fabric costs of the garment. The extra fabric is gathered, eased, elasticized, pulled up with a drawstring, pleated, tucked, or left uncontrolled. Although it affects fit, extra fullness usually is added for style reasons (see Chapter 9).

GATHERS

Gathering is the drawing together of a series of small folds of fabric called **gathers.** The gathers

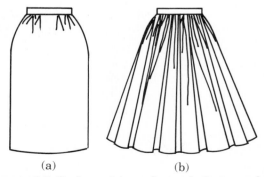

(a)   (b)

Figure 8-7 Gathers: (a) as dart substitute, and (b) with extra fullness.

are controlled and held in place by stitches. Gathers provide visible fullness. Manufacturers join two fabric edges of different lengths by gathering the longer edge to fit the shorter edge. Gathers serve as a dart substitute or to control added fullness (Figure 8-7). The more extra fullness added, the fuller the gathers (Figure 8-8). If very little extra fullness is added, the gathers may look skimpy. Full gathers require two-and-one-half to three times as much fabric as a flat, ungathered panel. Full gathers are usually confined to high-price lines because of the added fabric costs. Less full gathers require only one-and-one-half to two times as much fabric as a flat panel. They may result in tense gathers where the fabric releases minimal fullness over a large body bulge. Lightweight fabrics must be much more fully gathered than heavier fabrics for a generous appearance, requiring more fabric. Gathers in bloused areas, such as puffed sleeves, require additional fabric length as well as width to avoid a pulled and taut appearance.

Gathers take the place of darts in fitting the garment to the body. For example, gathers at the front neckline of women's dresses provide extra fullness over the bust. Gathers in women's swimsuits at the side seams near the hips and/or along the leg openings provide fit and coverage for the buttocks.

Gathers provide a soft, feminine look. They are more attractive in lightweight fabrics than in heavy fabrics. Gathers do not distort geometrically patterned fabrics, such as plaids, the way darts do.

High-quality gathers are perfectly even and fall in parallel folds. Accomplishing this requires either very skilled operators or programmable sewing machines adjusted to evenly gather the fabric. In either case, even gathers cost more to produce than uneven gathers. Gathering may also be accomplished through the use of elastic or a drawstring. Decorative forms of gathers, such as shirring and smocking, also can serve as dart substitutes (see Chapter 10).

EASE

Ease is imperceptible fullness that is drawn up and stitched in place (Figure 8-8). Manufacturers use easing to join two fabric edges of slightly different lengths, easing the longer edge to fit the shorter edge. Easing aids in setting in fitted sleeves, sewing garments to waistbands, and in sewing together seams, such as princess seams, where the edges to be joined are not identical. Easing releases about the same amount of fullness as a dart for an area where the body bulge is slight. For example, easing is used as a dart substitute at the elbow of fitted sleeves. Ease often substitutes for the back shoulder dart in tailored jackets. In low-quality garments, neither a dart nor ease is used at the shoulder, causing the garment to fit poorly through the shoulder blade area.

Easing requires a skilled operator to evenly sew a longer piece of fabric to a shorter piece. But easing requires the same amount of fabric and less labor than sewing a dart. High-quality easing looks smooth and has no tucks, pleats, or gathers.

ELASTIC

Elastic serves as a dart substitute by drawing up the longer fabric of the garment to the shorter length of the elastic. Thus, elastic applications often resemble gathering. The biggest

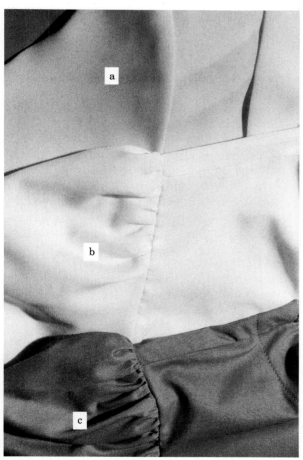

Figure 8-8 *Set-in sleeves: (a) eased into armhole, (b) slightly gathered, and (c) fully gathered.*

advantage of elastic in ready-to-wear is its stretch. However, even though elastic stretches to fit a wider range of sizes than other shaping devices, that range has a limit; too-loose elastic does not hold the garment in place properly and too-tight elastic is uncomfortable for the wearer. Elastic serves as a closure because it allows the garment to stretch for dressing and undressing but draws up to fit closely when the garment is worn. A disadvantage of elastic is that it may lose its ability to recover from stretch over time and need replacing for the garment to remain wearable.

Elastic is used at the waistline of garments, at necklines, at the lower edges of sleeves and pant legs and anywhere a gathered look and close fit is desired. When elastic is attached at a measured distance from a garment edge, the fabric that extends beyond the elastic forms a ruffle when the elastic pulls up. This ruffle is called a *header* (Figure 8-12).

Types. Numerous elastic types are available to meet various design and end use requirements (Figure 8-9). For example:

1. *Swimwear elastic* must withstand water, chlorine, sunshine, perspiration, and suntan lotions.

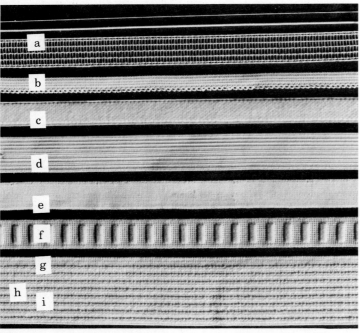

Figure 8-9 *Elastic: (a) webbing with grooves for stitching, (b) woven non-roll, (c) knitted, (d) braided, (e) plush-back, (f) knitted lingerie, (g) mesh, (h) cord, and (i) thread.*

2. *Plush-back elastic* has a soft surface for applications worn next to the skin.

3. *Lingerie elastic* is a plush-back elastic with a decorative edge or edges used on bras and feminine underwear.

4. *Stretch lace,* an elastic lace, is another popular choice for lingerie.

5. *Pajama elastic* is a wide, soft elastic used inside the waistlines of boxer shorts and pajama bottoms.

6. *Nonroll elastic* is a ribbed elastic used at the waist and in other locations where rolling elastic is uncomfortable and unsightly. However, nonroll elastic is more costly and it is bulkier and stiffer than other types.

The amount of stretch required in an elastic also depends on the end use of the garment. For example, elastic at the waist of men's underwear stretches 100–110%, at the waist of women's underwear 130–140%, and in shoulder straps only 70–80% (Glock and Kunz 1990).

Fiber Content. Elastic is made of extensible fibers, rubber, or spandex. The rubber or spandex is covered with polyester, cotton, or some other fiber to add comfort. The amount of rubber or spandex used and the structure of the elastic determines extensibility. Both rubber and spandex have excellent stretch and recovery. Spandex elastic is stronger and generally lasts longer than rubber elastic because it is more resistant to deterioration from aging, sunlight, perspiration, salt water, suntan and body oils, heat, chlorine bleach, and dry-cleaning solvents. However, some synthetic rubbers also have good resistance to degradation from the elements listed, and rubber generally costs less than spandex.

Elastic Structure. High-quality elastic may be woven, knitted, or braided. *Braided* elastic has excellent stretch. However, it becomes narrower when stretched, so it should not be stitched on (which prevents its recovery); it should be attached within a casing. *Woven* elastic is heavier and more stable than other elastics. Manufacturers use woven elastics where they need firm control, although it is generally the most costly type of elastic. *Knitted* elastic is usually soft and lightweight; it generally costs less than other types of elastic. Both woven and knitted elastics may be stitched directly to the garment or attached within a casing. Some knitted elastics have grooves knit into them so that the elastic can be stitched to the garment (in the grooves) without piercing the elastomeric fibers. However, the spacing of the sewing machine needles must match the spacing of the channels.

Width. Elastic should be of a width that is comfortable and gives the desired look. Wide elastics generally cost more than narrow elastics. The narrowest elastic is *elastic thread.* Manufacturers use elastic thread to create single or multiple rows of elasticized gathering that shape the garment and stretch with the wearer's movements. For example, elastic thread is found in tube tops, in the waist and bodice areas of shirred sundresses, and at the lower edge of ruffled blouse and dress sleeves. Round, narrow elastic is called *elastic cording.* Other elastics are an eighth of an inch or wider. Narrow elastics cause discomfort if they cut or dig into the wearer's skin. Wide elastics also cause discomfort if they twist or roll; multiple rows of stitches may be necessary to prevent this. Another solution to this problem is nonroll elastic. Very wide elastics are sometimes called *webbing.*

Seams in Elastic. Lapped seams in elastic are preferable to superimposed seams because they are less bulky. Ideally, a rectangle of stitches joins seams in elastic and is less apt than a bar tack to weaken the elastic (the needle perforations of many stitches weaken the elastic). In better garments, elastic seams may be covered with a label or a small square of fabric, or at the very least bar tacked flat. These techniques prevent fraying and make the joint flat and comfortable (Figure 8-10).

Attachment. Sometimes elastic is used in a limited area; for example, across the back of a pair of pants or a jacket. This allows the front of the garment to fit smoothly but shapes the back and allows it to stretch to accommodate a variety of sizes. In such cases, the elastic is sewn flat to the back panel of the garment before assembling the garment into a circle.

More commonly, elastic encircles an entire body part, such as the waist, wrist, neck, or leg. Most manufacturers sew all the seams of the garment that intersect the elasticized area except for one. Then the elastic is attached to the garment while both are flat. Finally, the garment and the elastic are joined into a circle using a superimposed seam. This method is inexpensive but rather bulky. In the alternative

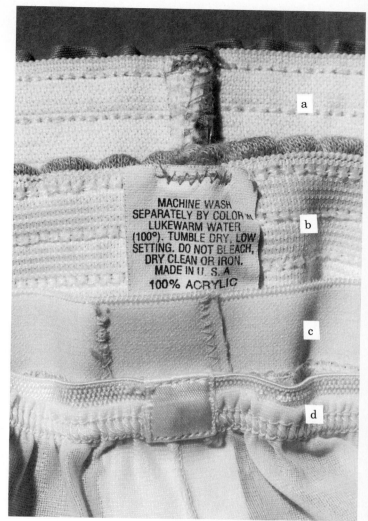

Figure 8-10 *Seams in applied elastic: (a) superimposed seam tacked flat, (b) superimposed seam covered with label, (c) lapped seam, and (d) lapped seam covered with square of satin.*

method, found only in high-quality garments, both the garment and the elastic are sewn into a circle before the elastic is attached to the garment. Attaching elastic to the garment "in the round" results in a smooth, flat, and comfortable elastic application, especially if the elastic was seamed with a lapped seam (Figure 8-10). However, attaching elastic "in the round" increases labor costs.

Manufacturers attach elastic either at the edge of the garment or within the body of the garment. For most elastic attachments, stitches show on the outside of the garment.

Applied Elastic. **Applied elastic** is stitched directly onto the garment to add shape where desired. Manufacturers commonly apply elastic at the waist level in dresses and at the waistline edges of shorts, pants, and skirts, especially in low-price lines and in childrenswear (Figures 8-10 and 8-11). As it is applied, the elastic is stretched to fit the garment. If the operator (or the programmable sewing machine) does not stretch the elastic evenly, fullness is distributed in the wrong places, detracting from the fit and appearance of the garment. The stitches used to apply elastic should be extensible (i.e., 400-, 500-, or 600-class stitches or 300-class zigzag stitches) so that they can stretch with the elastic without rupturing. If overedge stitches are used, care must be taken to avoid rendering the elastic useless by cutting it with the serger knife. To replace or alter applied elastic, all the stitches must be removed.

Applied elastic is usually found inside the garment. At garment edges, the raw edge of the garment is turned under and caught between the fabric and the applied elastic. Elastic is sometimes applied on the outside of the garment, mainly in sportswear or underwear. When elastic is applied on the outside of the garment, it is usually colorful or otherwise decorative; for example, lingerie featuring stretch lace.

Casings. **Casings** are tunnels of fabric through which elastic or a drawstring is threaded to shape the garment to the body (Figure 8-12). Although bulkier, casings are generally more comfortable to wear than applied elastic because

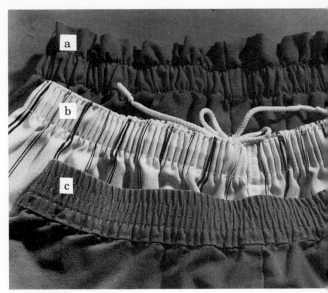

Figure 8-12 *Elastic casings at waistline: (a) with header, (b) folded casing with drawstring, and (c) formed with separate band of fabric.*

fabric rather than elastic contacts the skin. Casings generally cost more than applied elastic because of the additional fabric required.

The casing must be large enough to accommodate the elastic without straining, but not so large as to allow the elastic to twist within it. Additional rows of stitching stabilize the casing and prevent the elastic from twisting.

Most manufacturers stitch the elastic to the casing, and the casing to the garment simultaneously. However, in some high-quality garments, the elastic is not stitched to the casing but floats freely within it. *Free-floating* elastic casings are less bulky and more comfortable to wear than other casings. Another advantage of free-floating casings is that the elastic is easily altered to fit the wearer, or replaced when its elasticity is lost; merely remove a few stitches to pull the elastic out of the casing. However, because the elastic floats freely within the casing, it has a tendency to twist and roll; nonroll elastic is recommended, especially if the casing is wide. Free-floating elastic casings cost more to produce than other casings. If you can freely move the elastic about within the casing and redistribute the fabric over the length of the elastic, the casing contains free-floating elastic.

EDGE CASINGS. To make a folded casing at an edge, the raw edge is usually overedged to the elastic; simultaneously, the edge is turned under

Figure 8-11 *Elastic in body of garment: (a) applied, and (b) in casing made from seam allowances stitched to garment.*

(to enclose the elastic) and stitched to the garment. This is a fast and economical method. Another advantage of this method is that the elastic does not twist and has a reduced tendency to roll. However, this method is somewhat bulky and necessitates a stiff, bulky seam through all layers to close the garment into a circle. To alter or replace the elastic, all the stitches must be removed.

Another method for making a casing involves attaching a separate band of fabric to the garment edge (Figure 8-12). In a single step, the manufacturer folds a band of fabric lengthwise to enclose the elastic, and seams the folded band to the garment edge. This somewhat bulky method is sometimes required on unusually shaped edges, but mainly is found in low-price garments; for example, pull-on knit pants. The use of a separate band to form the casing results in smaller pattern pieces and better material utilization.

CASINGS WITHIN THE BODY OF THE GARMENT. To create a casing within the body of a garment, often the manufacturer stitches two seam allowances together, or stitches the seam allowances to the garment to encase the elastic (Figure 8-11). No stitches show on the outside of the garment if the seam allowances are stitched together. Another method for applying a casing within the body of the garment involves stitching a strip of fabric to the garment, enclosing the elastic. The fabric strip should be nonbulky and nonraveling.

DRAWSTRINGS

Drawstrings are narrow tubes, cords, or strips of fabric inserted into casings in place of or in addition to elastic (Figure 8-12). They are pulled up and tied to shape the garment to the body. The drawstring controls the fullness of the garment, pulling it up to fit or letting it out for dressing and undressing. Drawstrings are commonly used at the waist of sweatpants, windbreaker jackets, and men's swim trunks; they are also used to fit hood openings around the face.

Drawstrings require one or two openings in the casing, for each end of the drawstring to be brought to the surface and tied. One opening withstands stress better than two openings, but two openings allow for a flatter knot to be tied in the drawstring. The ends of the drawstring should be capped or knotted so they do not get lost in the casing or pulled out of the casing, requiring rethreading. The drawstring may be stitched in place halfway through the casing to keep it in position. However, this may be undesirable if the stitching interferes with the appearance of the garment, as it might on a hood, for example.

Lacing operates on a principle similar to drawstrings; it is a string or cord threaded and crossed back and forth through eyelets, grommets, or buttonholes in the garment. The lacing is pulled to shape and fit the garment, and tied to fasten the opening (see Chapter 11).

STRETCH FABRICS

Stretch fabrics help the garment fit body bulges by stretching over them. Fabrics that stretch only slightly may require the use of additional shaping devices; highly extensible fabrics need no additional shaping devices beyond the ability to stretch to adapt to the shape of the body. Therefore, no extra fabric or labor costs are required. Stretch fabrics allow the garment to fit a wider range of people than most other shaping devices. For example, most swimwear and dancewear fits mainly through its ability to stretch to the size and shape of the wearer.

FULL-FASHIONED KNITS

Full-fashioned knits are a sign of quality shaping. **Full-fashioned marks** represent increases or decreases in the number of stitches in a knitted garment section, a result of shaping the piece. Each part of a full-fashioned knit garment is knit to the desired size and shape, not cut from a large piece of fabric. The shaped pieces are sewn together for an accurately sized and shaped garment that maintains its shape and does not twist. But full-fashioned knitwear is slower and more costly to produce than are garments cut from knit fabrics. And it requires a longer lead time because the style of the garment must be determined before the knitting process begins. Sometimes manufacturers of garments cut from knit fabrics use stitches or fusing to create **mock full-fashioned marks,** which look similar but contain none of the real advantages of genuine full-fashioned marks. You can identify full-fashioned garments by noticing the increase or decrease in the number of stitches in genuine full-fashioned marks at shaped seams; for example, at the armhole seam of sweaters (Figure 8-13).

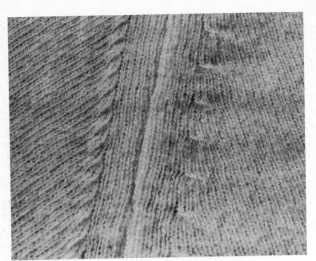

Figure 8-13 *Full-fashioned marks at sweater arm-hole.*

Underlying Fabrics

The shape of a garment is enhanced and preserved by underlying fabrics. Most garments contain one or more underlying fabrics. Although not visible from the outside of the garment, these materials help maintain the garment's shape and/or lend it other qualities such as durability and warmth. Eliminating underlying fabrics to reduce costs results in limp garments that do not maintain their original shape; the garment tends to wrinkle and stretch out of shape.

The main, outer fabric from which a garment is made is called the **fashion fabric** or **shell fabric. Underlying fabrics** or **supporting fabrics** are inside the garment; they lend support to the garment and help maintain its shape. The four types of underlying fabrics include: (1) interfacing, (2) lining, (3) interlining, and (4) underlining. These terms are used consistently, as defined in this chapter, throughout this text. However, they are used loosely, sometimes interchangeably, in the apparel industry. For example, the terms *interlining* and *lining* are commonly used to refer to what is (technically) interfacing. And underlining (technically) is commonly called lining.

The presence of supporting fabrics in a garment is usually a sign of quality. Few consumers make a purchase decision based on the underlying fabrics of a garment, but ultimate satisfaction with the aesthetic and functional performance of any garment is affected by its supporting fabrics. The choice of underlying fabrics depends on the design, fabric, and end use of the garment. Waistbands that roll, collars and lapels that bubble, and knees, elbows, seats and pockets that bag can be avoided if the manufacturer carefully selects and correctly applies supporting fabrics. However, the addition of underlying fabrics to a garment increases production costs in terms of both materials and labor.

INTERFACING

Interfacing is a supporting fabric used in almost all garments. Interfacing lends body, shape, and reinforcement to limited areas. Collars, collar bands, cuffs, buttons and buttonholes, waistbands, and other small details are usually interfaced. In tailored coats and jackets, the shoulders and lapels are interfaced; in better coats and jackets, the manufacturer also interfaces the armholes, patch pockets, sleeve hems, garment hem, and sometimes the entire garment front (Figure 8-14).

Interfacing is usually hidden between the garment and its facing, which explains the name "interfacing" (Figure 8-15). You may have to carefully rub the garment between your fingers to determine if there is interfacing enclosed between two layers.

Weight. Interfacing fabrics range from extremely lightweight fabrics (0.4 ounces per square yard), which lend soft or light support, to very heavy fabrics (4 ounces per square yard), which give crisp or heavy support (Glock and Kunz 1990). Interfacing should be the same or lighter in weight than the fabric of the garment, never heavier. A too-heavy interfacing overpowers the fashion fabric and makes the shaping look and feel artificial. Interfacings that feel papery are unappealing and reflect low quality standards. The appropriate hand of the interfacing is determined by the amount of shaping desired; the interfacing should not be too limp or too stiff to achieve the desired appearance (Figure 8-20). For example, men's dress shirt collars require a crisp interfacing; a softer interfacing is usually used in women's blouse collars; waistband interfacings require enough body to prevent the waistband from rolling.

Interfacings should withstand the same wear and care as the garment; interfacings that tear, roll, or shrink detract from quality. For this reason, some manufacturers use self-fabric inter-

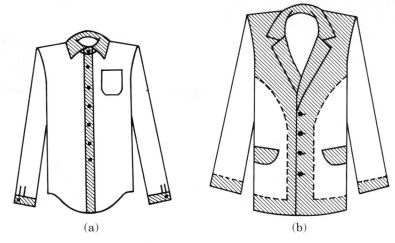

Figure 8-14 *Shaded areas should be interfaced in (a) shirt and (b) jacket.*

(a)   (b)

facings, made from the shell fabric, because they are perfectly compatible with the garment in durability, care, color, weight, and hand. However, self-fabric interfacings usually cost more than other types of interfacing.

Interfacing Structure. Interfacings are woven, knitted, or nonwoven. Each fabrication has advantages and disadvantages.

Woven Interfacing. The important features of *woven* interfacings are that they

1. Are strong.

2. Add shape without looking boardy (if not too heavy for shell fabric); this makes them effective

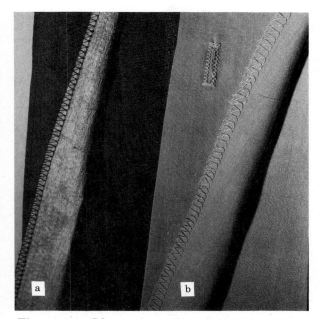

Figure 8-15 *Blouses (a) with and (b) without interfacing at center front.*

for use in tailored garments. For example, *hair canvas* and *wigan* (lighter than hair canvas) are resilient, woven interfacings made of hair fibers or blends; they are used in the traditional tailoring of better garments.

3. Do not stretch, thus adding stability to the area. Woven interfacings are used in knit garments only if the manufacturer wants to inhibit the natural stretch of the knit; for example, in button and buttonhole areas.

4. Must be cut on grain for stability or be cut on the bias in areas that must roll, fold, or drape smoothly, such as under collars, hems, and men's neckties, because fewer yarn interlacings on the bias allow the fabric more flexibility.

5. Tend to ravel.

6. Are more costly than other types of interfacing.

Knit Interfacing. *Knit* interfacings have become popular in recent years. Their important characteristics are that they

1. Stretch, making them well-suited for knit garments. At the same time, knit interfacings lend some stability because adding any fabric layer to an area makes it harder to stretch.

2. Add softer shape and drape than woven interfacings.

3. Do not ravel, but the edges may curl.

4. Must be cut "on grain." Remember, knits do not have a technical grain as do woven fabrics (see Chapter 4) but must be cut as if they did have one.

5. Cost less than woven interfacings.

6. Feature an extra filling yarn inserted through the knit structure in *weft-insertion* knit interfacings. These knit interfacings have become very popular in tailoring because they add shape and stability without sacrificing drape and flexibility.

Fiberweb Interfacing. *Fiberweb* or *nonwoven* interfacings are the most common type. They are neither woven nor knitted, but made of fibers (usually polyester or nylon) that have been entangled, glued, or fused together into a sheet of fabric. The main characteristics of fiberweb interfacings are that they

1. Generally lend good stability.

2. Are not very drapable and may interfere with the fold, roll, or drape of some face fabrics. Heavyweight fiberwebs are especially stiff.

3. Have no grain if the fibers are randomly oriented. They may be cut with the pattern pieces in any direction, fitting in the tightest possible arrangement and using the least amount of fabric. A few fiberwebs have directionally oriented fibers; they must be cut on-grain, lowering material utilization but providing greater stability than random orientations.

4. Do not ravel, but the edges of lightweight fiberwebs may curl.

5. Are often less durable than knit or woven interfacings if exposed to heavy wear and care. They have a propensity to pill.

6. Are usually the least costly type of interfacing.

Application. Manufacturers sew or fuse interfacing to the back of the garment shell fabric. Fusing is the more common method of application, but interfacing fabrications for both methods are available in woven, knitted, and fiberweb varieties.

Fusible Interfacing. *Fusible interfacings* have a heat-sensitive adhesive on the back; a hot press is used to melt the adhesive and laminate the interfacing to the back of the fashion fabric. When fusible interfacings were developed in the 1960s, quality problems associated with them were common. Fusible interfacings tended to shrink and delaminate, distorting the fashion fabric of the garment. Improved adhesives have been developed and, if properly applied, most modern fusible interfacings perform well. In fact, fusible interfacings have revolutionized tailoring. Smooth, well-shaped jackets are pro-

duced using fusibles at great savings in labor; lower labor costs make fusibles less costly to attach than sew-in interfacings. Because the fusing process is so well adapted to mass production, most tailoring is done with fusible interfacings (except in high-price lines, where sew-in interfacings are sometimes used). The important characteristics of fusibles are that they

1. Are slightly stiffer (after the melted adhesive cools and solidifies) than sew-in interfacings; fusible interfacing should barely extend into the seam allowance to avoid unwanted bulk.

2. Make the face fabric very stable. This is usually desirable except in knit garments, where the stability of fusibles restricts the stretch of the knit.

3. Provide a slightly flatter shaping than sew-in interfacings. However, high-quality fusibles are fairly pliable and supple.

4. Bond to the fibers of the shell fabric and prevent them from migrating to the surface; fusibles retard pilling, very important in shirt collars and cuffs.

5. Do not tear or roll as easily as sew-in interfacings because of being laminated to the fabric. Therefore, some fusible interfacings are more durable than sew-ins.

6. Can blister, bubble, or delaminate if applied to the garment with the incorrect time, temperature, or pressure to fully fuse the two; if the adhesive on the interfacing is uneven; or if the garment receives improper care (Figure 8-16). The interfacing may separate in a few places or throughout the area.

7. Can cause **strike-through** if adhesive leaks through the fashion fabric. It shows up either as spots or as a discoloration of the fashion fabric and may make the garment unwearable (Figure 8-16). Strike-through results from excess adhesive or improper care of the garment.

8. Can cause a puckering effect if the interfacing shrinks differently from the fashion fabric.

9. Can be fused to the facing rather than to the garment, to reduce the visibility of interfacing problems (bubbling, blistering, and strike-through). However, this method does not allow the interfacing to hide the seam allowances as does interfacing applied to the garment.

Sew-In Interfacing. *Sew-in interfacings* are held in place by the seams of the garment. The

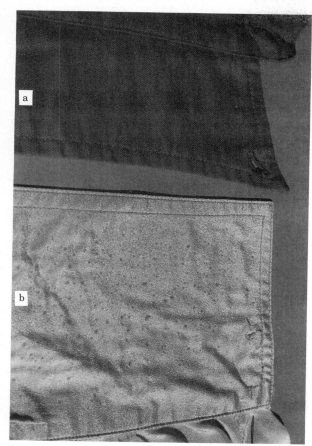

Figure 8-16 Interfacing problems: (a) bubbling, and (b) strike-through, which occurred after one dry cleaning.

interfacing should extend just beyond the garment's seamlines; beyond that adds unwanted bulk. The main features of sew-in interfacings are that they

1. Provide body without the stiffness of fusible interfacings.

2. Can hide seam allowances that might otherwise show through, if sewn to the garment rather than the facing. This is desirable in translucent or sheer fabrics.

3. Can cause slight puckering if they shrink differently from the fashion fabric; however, bubbling, blistering, delamination and strike-through are not problems with sew-in interfacings.

4. Are often preferred in knit garments; they maintain the fabric's extensibility by leaving the loops of the knit free rather than fusing them in place.

5. Sometimes are not secured at all edges; for example, at the fold of extended facings. If one or more edges is left loose, the interfacing rumples, tears, or distorts during wear and care. Manufacturers prevent these problems by securing the loose edge of the interfacing with a row of stitches. For example, interfacing in shirt cuffs is often sewn to the cuff at the upper edge to prevent the interfacing from rolling.

6. Are used extensively in finely tailored and couture apparel because of soft shaping capabilities. The skillful selection and application of interfacing is especially important in tailored garments. High-quality tailored garments possess a permanent, molded shape that has been imparted through the use of the proper interfacing, pad stitching, and careful pressing.

Pad Stitching. **Pad stitching** is one of the trademarks of fine, traditional tailoring. Hand pad stitches are many tiny hand stitches made through the sew-in interfacing and barely catching the fashion fabric. The collar and lapel are rolled slightly as the stitches are made to impart the desired rolled shape to the finished garment. Hand pad stitching is the softest and subtlest of shaping methods. However, hand pad stitching is an art found only in apparel of the highest price and quality because of the time and skill it requires. For example, men's suit brands such as Oxxford and Hickey-Freeman feature hand pad stitching in the collar and lapel areas of jackets.

Fusible interfacings had made pad stitching almost obsolete except in high-price lines, but recent innovations in automated machine pad stitching are again making pad stitching an important feature of some moderately priced tailored apparel (Figure 8-17). Machine pad stitching offers many of the subtle shaping characteristics of hand pad stitching at a much lower cost.

LINING

Lining is a replica of the garment, constructed of lightweight fabric and sewn inside the garment. The advantages of lining are that a lined garment

1. Has hidden seam allowances, making the inside attractive when the garment is taken off.

2. Helps prevent raveling of seam allowances, making a seam finish unnecessary, and prevents any raveling from showing.

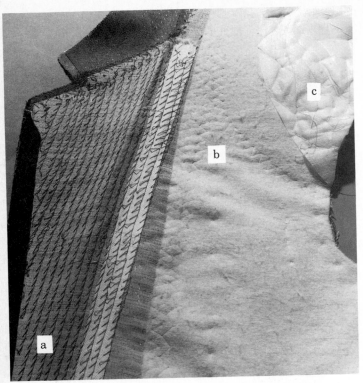

Figure 8-17 Inside of tailored man's jacket features (a) pad stitching on hair canvas interfacing, (b) floating chest piece, and (c) shoulder pad. Also note black stay tape at outer edge of lapel and white stay tape at roll line. (Jacket courtesy of Jack Henry.)

creases costs significantly. Manufacturers use *partial linings* in some garments; a partial lining extends only through the areas that require shaping and reinforcement rather than throughout the entire garment. Partial linings are common from the shoulder to the chest (called a ⅜ *lining*) in the back of tailored jackets; from the waist to below the hips in skirts; and from the waist to below the knees in slacks (Figure 8-18). Although partial linings cost less than full linings, they do not lower quality if they extend through the necessary areas. In fact, a partial lining may be more desirable than a full lining in clothing such as summer suits and sports jackets, because partial linings are cooler to wear and lighter in weight than full ones. High-quality men's jackets with a ⅜ lining usually have booked seams and otherwise impeccable inner construction. Occasionally, partially lined garments are of higher quality than similar, fully lined garments, if the manufacturer used the lining in the fully lined garment to compensate for a low-quality fashion fabric and poorly finished inner construction.

Single garment pieces such as pockets, yokes, or bibs may be lined for added strength or support. Or a small piece of lining may be used in areas subject to abrasion, such as the inner thigh area of pants. This not only protects the fashion fabric from abrasion but improves the wearer's comfort, especially if the garment is made of a scratchy fabric.

3. Is comfortable to wear because the shell fabric, the seam allowances, and other inner construction details of the garment do not chafe the skin. Comfort is especially important when the garment is made of a rough or scratchy fabric.

4. Aids the wearer in slipping the garment on and off.

5. Absorbs some of the stress, strain, and abrasion of wear, extending the life of the garment.

6. Has extra body, shape, and support, making the garment look smoother and less apt to wrinkle. The lining helps to prevent the garment from stretching out of shape, especially in stress areas such as elbows or knees.

7. Has opacity, an advantage for garments with sheer main fabrics.

8. Has extra warmth, which may or may not be an advantage, depending on the weather.

In general, garments with *full linings* are of higher quality than those without. A fully lined garment requires nearly twice as much fabric and labor as an unlined garment, which in-

Figure 8-18 Partial lining in summer-weight jacket. Note ease pleat at center back of lining and booked seams.

Lining Fabrics. A high-quality lining fabric

1. Is smooth, to help the garment slip on and off easily.

2. Is lightweight and nonbulky.

3. Is resistant to staining from perspiration and body oils.

4. Is able to withstand the same wear as the garment. A lining fabric that rips, fades or wears out before the face fabric makes the garment unwearable.

5. Has the same care requirements as the garment. For example, a dry-clean-only lining sewn into a washable garment increases maintenance costs unnecessarily.

6. Adds warmth to cool-weather garments and adds as little warmth as possible to warm-weather garments.

7. Is absorbent, for comfort.

8. Is static-free so the lining does not cling to the garment or to anything worn under it.

9. Is opaque to keep the seam allowances and other construction details from showing through inside the garment.

10. Is of a color and pattern that complements the fashion fabric of the garment.

The choice of lining fabric depends upon the fashion fabric and the end use and price line of the garment. Various fibers offer different advantages and disadvantages in lining fabrics, as summarized in Table 8-1. Most lining fabrics are woven rather than knit, for greater stability. Satin weaves are common because they help the garment slip on and off easily.

TABLE 8-1
Fibers used in lining fabrics

> *Acetate linings* Often used because they are smooth and pretty, but they require dry cleaning and are not as durable as polyester, nylon, or silk; acetate linings often wear out before the fashion fabric.
>
> *Polyester and nylon linings* Extremely durable. They are smooth but not as absorbent and comfortable as acetate and silk.
>
> *Silk linings* Luxurious and comfortable but very costly and not as durable as synthetics.
>
> *Cotton linings* Comfortable, but do not help the garment slide on and off easily.
>
> *Rayon linings* Comfortable but not very durable.
>
> *Wool linings* Rare, but provide great warmth.

Cut. In a *lined-to-the-edge* garment, the lining is an exact duplicate of the garment; the lining extends to the outer edges of the garment. The raw edges are bound, or they are finished by the enclosed seam joining the garment and the lining. Unless the outer edges are bound, the lining tends to show from outside the garment at the edges. Control stitching or topstitching helps the lining remain hidden. Self-fabric linings are least noticeable at edges but are too bulky unless the fashion fabric is lightweight. Sleeveless garments, such as vests, are often lined-to-the-edge, as are garments made of bulky fabrics, which do not lend themselves to being faced. When individual garment parts are lined, they are usually lined-to-the-edge.

Most linings do *not* duplicate the garment exactly. The lining is cut narrower and shorter than the garment, sewn to the garment facings, and hemmed shorter than the garment. A lining should be large enough so that it does not distort the hang or movement of the garment; skimpily cut linings are usually a sign of low-quality standards. Manufacturers may intentionally cut the lining smaller than the garment so that the lining absorbs the strain of wear; for example, in fitted skirts. In full or pleated garments, they often use linings smaller than the garment to reduce bulk.

Ease pleats should be added to the linings of jackets and coats. Vertical ease pleats in linings, at the center back of garments such as jackets and coats, provide adequate room for movement across the back shoulders (Figures 8-18 and 9-9). Some garments feature additional vertical ease pleats in the lining at the shoulder seams. Horizontal ease pleats in the lining at sleeve and garment hems are also required for a smooth, easy fit. Ease pleats make the lining roomier and help absorb the stress of movement, preventing distortion of the garment. Deep ease pleats indicate concern for quality. The absence of ease pleats reduces ease, decreasing the wearer's comfort and the durability of the garment. Strips of stretchy knit fabric set in the lining sometimes substitute for ease pleats in active sportswear.

Bagging. Most manufacturers apply linings by *bagging*. This method is the most common and least expensive method of inserting any lining that is attached around the outer edges of the garment. Bagging is used to line garments in all price lines. Manufacturers construct the lining and the garment separately and then sew them, with right sides together, around the outer edges. They leave an opening or gap in the stitching, forming a "bag." The entire garment is turned through this opening, and the opening is sewn shut. Although it may be inconspicuous, you can find where the opening was sewn shut in one of the sleeves or at the side seam of the garment.

Attached at the Armholes. The linings in some moderate- and most high-price jackets and coats are attached not only around the outer edges but also around the armholes. The manufacturer constructs the lining for the body and the lining for the sleeves separately. During assembly, the lining for the body is sewn to the garment around the outer edges and armholes, and then the sleeve linings are attached at the armholes; this prevents the lining from separating from the garment at the armholes as it does ordinarily. Linings attached at the armholes stay in position when the wearer moves, making them more comfortable to wear and less subject to abrasion. In the highest price lines and in couture apparel, hand stitches are used to attach the lining to the garment at the armholes. Hand stitches yield soft, comfortable results and allow the producer to distribute ease smoothly through the sleeve cap. When manufacturers apply linings by bagging them, they sometimes place tacks between the garment and the lining around the armholes. These tacks are better than nothing, but inferior to stitches attaching the lining around the entire armhole.

Free-Hanging Linings. Jacket linings are always attached to the hem of the jacket. However, **free-hanging linings** or **slip linings** are often used in skirts, pants, and coats. Because free-hanging linings are not attached to the garment hem, they do not inhibit the movement or drape of the garment. A free-hanging lining allows the consumer to examine the inner construction details of a garment. For this reason, consumers may consider free-hanging a sign of quality (compared with a lining sewn to the hem, which may hide poor-quality inner construction). For example, makers of fur coats often install free-hanging linings to show the fine workmanship inside the coat.

A mark of quality in a garment with a free-hanging lining is the use of **French tacks** or **swing tacks** (Figure 7-13). Swing tacks are about an inch and a half long, and are made of thread chains, strips of fabric similar to belt loops, or pieces of ribbon. They connect the lining hem and the garment hem at each seam allowance. Swing tacks allow the lining to move freely while preventing it from riding up.

Detachable linings are installed so they can be zipped or buttoned in and out of garments; for example, all-weather coats and jackets. They make garments versatile for wear in different kinds of weather but add significantly to cost.

UNDERLINING

Underlining involves lining each major piece of the garment individually. The pieces of underlining fabric are exact duplicates of the major pieces of fashion fabric required to make the garment. The manufacturer attaches each piece of underlining to the back of its coordinating piece of fashion fabric before assembling the garment. The two plies are then handled as one, as if the underlining were not there, as the garment is constructed.

Underlining a garment is less costly than lining it because underlining requires extra fabric but little additional labor (except in cutting). The same types of fabrics used for lining are used for underlining. However, fabrics that are crisper or more fluid (including knits) than traditional lining fabrics are appropriate for producing the desired shape in the finished garment. Each underlining piece must be cut on the same grain as its coordinating fashion fabric piece and should not pull, pucker, or distort the hang of the fashion fabric.

You can distinguish underlining from lining because all the seam allowances and other construction details can be seen on the inside of an underlined garment but are hidden by a lining (Figure 8-19). Underlining is attached to the garment at every seam, whereas lining is attached only around the outer edges of the garment. The only place the underlining and fashion fabric layers are not treated as one is if details, such as darts, are constructed separately in the underlining and in the fashion fabric, to reduce bulk.

Underlining performs many, but not all, of the functions of lining. Like lining, an underlining provides body, strength, and support to the garment, making it look smooth and preventing it from sagging or stretching. Underlining prevents sheer or translucent fabrics from being seen through. Limp, unstable fabrics often re-

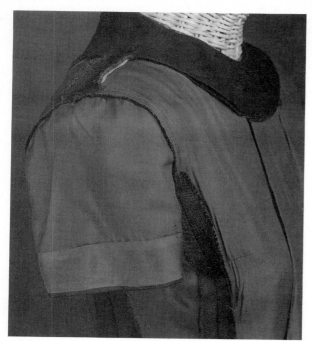

Figure 8-19 *Inside of an underlined dress.*

Manufacturers include interlinings in cold-weather clothing such as coats and jackets. Any material inserted for warmth between the fashion fabric and the lining constitutes an interlining. Interlining materials trap air, providing insulation from the cold. You cannot see a garment's interlining unless you can lift the lining.

Interlining fabrics should be lightweight and nonbulky, and should withstand the same care as the garment. Down and lambswool are traditional interlinings in coats and other cold-weather outerwear. Interlining is one place where used wool is sometimes found in apparel because used wool may not look or feel as good as new wool, but remains a good insulator. Recently developed fabrics such as the Thinsulate brand are ideal interlinings because they are designed to be extremely warm but thin, lightweight, and easy care. They are used in ski pants, jackets, and gloves. Polyester fleece is a popular, low-cost interlining in many quilted fabrics. Interlinings increase both material and labor costs.

quire underlining, especially in stress areas or for construction details that demand more body.

In some instances, underlining is preferable to lining. Underlining, unlike lining, prevents the seam allowances and other construction details from showing through to the *outside* of garments made of sheer or translucent fabrics such as lace. Therefore, underlinings, rather than linings, are often used in wedding and other formal gowns made of these fabrics. Underlinings are also used in areas prone to stretching, such as seats, knees, and elbows, where they are superior to linings in preventing stretch.

Compared to lining, some disadvantages of underlining include that it

1. Does not protect the skin from irritation by the seam allowances of the fashion fabric.

2. Does not make the garment more attractive on the inside.

3. Does not make the garment easy to slip on and off.

4. Does not prevent seam allowances from raveling.

INTERLINING

An insulative **interlining** is applied strictly for additional warmth; interlinings may incidentally add support and shape by their presence.

Supporting Devices

A number of devices are incorporated in garments to achieve or maintain the desired shape. Examples of **supporting devices** include chest pieces, shoulder pads, sleeve heads, bridles, bra cups, hoops, bustles, boning, and collar stays. All add to material and labor costs.

CHEST PIECES

Chest pieces are an important shaping device in tailored jackets and coats, mainly in menswear (Figure 8-17). The chest piece is a pad consisting of several layers of supporting fabrics. Chest pieces fill out and smooth the hollow area below the shoulder near the armhole. A high-quality chest piece creates a smooth front on the garment without hollows, ridges, or lumps.

Low-price jackets usually feature *fully fused fronts,* which means that the chest piece is fused to the jacket along with the front interfacing. Some high-price jackets feature *floating chest pieces.* Floating chest pieces are attached with loose stitches around the sides and edges. They are preferable because they float, allowing the jacket to conform naturally to the wearer's movements rather than remaining in a fixed, fused position.

SHOULDER PADS

Shoulder pads are another important shaping device in tailored jackets and coats (Figure 8-17). They are also used in shirts, blouses, and dresses as fashion demands. Shoulder pads vary from a quarter of an inch to an inch or more in thickness, depending on the desired look. They vary in style, with some creating a square shoulder look and others creating a soft look. Shoulder pads should be compatible with the recommended care of the garment and should be as durable as the garment.

Shoulder pads are made of a single layer of molded foam or layers of foam or batting, which consists of fibers fused, stitched, or tangled together. The pad should withstand the same wear and care as the garment, without lumping, rolling, or shrinking. The edges of the pad are graduated so they do not create a ridge on the outside of the garment. Shoulder pads should be covered with the garment fabric or a fabric that does not show through the garment.

Shoulder pads should be carefully positioned to follow the lines of the body for a smooth look. For lined garments, manufacturers attach shoulder pads between the fashion fabric and the lining, or fuse them in as part of a fully fused front. In unlined garments, manufacturers tack the shoulder pads to the shoulder and armhole seams; the more tacks, generally the more secure the attachment. Tacking stitches should be inconspicuous from the outside of the garment. If the tacking stitches are too tight, they prevent the shoulder pad from conforming freely to the wearer's movements and distort the garment. However, if the tacking stitches are too loose, the attachment is insecure. Consumers commonly complain that shoulder pads in blouses and dresses shift during wear, twist in the laundry, or fall out of the garment due to poor attachment. To avoid these problems, some manufacturers attach the shoulder pads to the garment with hook and loop tape; the shoulder pads are easily removed when the garment is laundered, and then replaced for wearing. However, hook and loop tape is bulky for use on lightweight fabrics. Another solution is shoulder pads not attached to the garment but made of curved foam, shaped to cling to the wearer's shoulders. Removable shoulder pads are a good selling point because they help avoid the stacked effect of pads in a blouse, jacket, or coat.

SLEEVE HEADS

Sleeve heads or **sleeve headers** are used in some tailored jackets and coats and occasionally in other types of garments. Sleeve heads consist of two or three narrow layers of shaping fabric sewn into the upper portion of the armhole and extending out into the sleeve. The purpose of sleeve heads in tailored garments is to create a soft, smooth roll in the cap of the sleeve without creating a hollow, ridge, or lump across the top of the sleeve. Without a sleeve head, the sleeve cap may be wrinkled and slightly hollow where it drops at a sharp angle from the shoulder seam. Sometimes manufacturers use crisp sleeve heads in garments with full, gathered sleeves to support the puff of the sleeve cap.

BRIDLES

Lapels in better-quality jackets and coats contain a **bridle,** a stay tape sewn at the *roll line* (the fold) of the lapel (Figure 8-17). The operator eases the lapel to the bridle, which is slightly shorter than the lapel, shaping the roll line to the body. The stable bridle holds the lapels in shape, helping them hug the body for a smooth fit. Additional fabric can be eased to the bridle in garments for women with large busts or men with highly developed chests to prevent the lapels from gaping.

BRA CUPS

Bra cups provide support, shape, and smoothness to the bustline of swimsuits, strapless evening gowns, and other garments. They often contain fiberfill or foam to enhance the bust size and shape. Such padding should withstand care procedures without lumping or disintegrating.

HOOPS AND BUSTLES

Plastic or metal circles or *hoops* may be sewn into the lower portion of a slip or underskirt to support a full skirt. Rows of stiff netting or *crinoline,* a stiff fabric, create a similar but less rigid effect. A *bustle* is a basketlike device used to expand and support the fullness and draping of the material in the back of a skirt. The popularity of hoops and bustles depends upon fashion. In this century, their use has mainly been confined to wedding and formal gowns.

HORSEHAIR BRAID

Horsehair braid is used to face and stiffen hems in wedding and formal gowns with full skirts. It is a stiff, narrow braid once made of horsehair but today made of sheer nylon. Operators sew the braid to the hem using a narrow seam allowance and stretching the braid slightly as it is applied. Because the horsehair braid was stretched slightly, it naturally pulls to the inside of the garment, keeping the hem edge turned under and in place. It is tacked to the seam allowances, so no stitches show on the outside of the garment. The horsehair braid stiffens the hem edge, making the hem stand out gracefully from the body.

BONING

Boning gives support to a garment through the use of stiff plastic (at one time whalebone) strips. Boning comes and goes in popularity as fashion demands. It was very important in womenswear in the late 1800s but today is mainly confined to formal, fitted dresses and some supportive bras, girdles, and women's swimsuits. Strapless bodices usually require boning in the side seams (and other seams in the midriff area) to shape the garment to the body and help it stay up. Heavily boned garments do not move with the wearer but mold the wearer to the shape of the garment, so boning can be quite uncomfortable. The boning is encased in fabric and sewn, on the inside of the garment, over the vertical seam allowances (Figure 8-20). Careful positioning and suitable lengths of boning for the size and design of the garment are important for appearance and wearing comfort.

COLLAR STAYS

Collar stays are thin plastic strips inserted in collars to make them "stay" flat and prevent the collar points from curling. Collar stays are used in men's dress shirts and some sport shirts. Most shirts either do not have collar stays, or the collar stays are sewn permanently inside the collar. Some high-price shirts have *removable stays*. Removable stays can be taken out when the shirt is laundered. This prevents the stays from bending or breaking, and avoids pressing the imprint of the stays through to the outside

Figure 8-20 Boning in a bra.

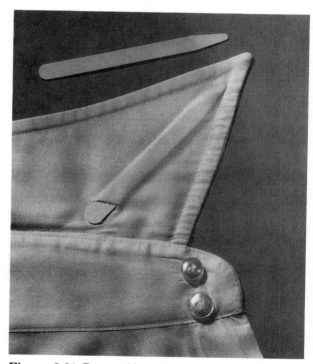

Figure 8-21 Removable collar stays.

of the collar. Extra labor costs are involved in making a collar with removable stays (Figure 8-21). Shirts with button-down collars do not require collar stays.

Summary

Garments are made from flat fabrics shaped to fit the human body. All garments contain darts or dart equivalents that introduce shape into the garment. Darts are triangular folds stitched into the fabric that shape it to fit the body. The size, length, and angle of the dart should accommodate the body bulge it is intended to fit. Seams may incorporate dart shapes to help the garment fit the figure. Princess seams, gore seams in skirts, and yoke seams are examples. Gussets, godets, released darts, and additional fabric all add extra fullness. This extra fullness may be fitted to the body with gathers (perceptible controlled fullness) or ease (imperceptible controlled fullness). Gathers and ease should be even. Elastic shapes the garment but stretches to fit a variety of sizes. Elastic is attached by applying it directly to the garment or in a casing. The highest quality garments allow the elastic to float freely in its casing. Elastic applied in the round is a sign of quality. Lapped seams are superior to superimposed seams in elastic. Too many stitches in elastic weaken it. Drawstrings may be inserted in casings instead of elastic. Tucks (stitched folds in the fabric) and pleats (unstitched folds in the fabric) may also be used to shape garments. Stretch fabrics help garments fit the body because of the ability to stretch.

Underlying fabrics provide additional shape, support, and smoothness to garments. They should be as durable as the garment and complement its color and style. Interfacing is used in detail areas. Interfacing should add the desired amount of body or crispness to the garment without overpowering it. Interfacings are woven, knitted, or fiberweb. They are usually fused into the garment; some are sewn in. Interfacing in high-quality tailored garments is pad stitched by hand or machine. Lining covers the inner construction of the garment. Fully lined garments are generally more costly but are more durable, more comfortable, and more attractive than unlined garments. Linings should have adequate ease pleats and be made of a smooth, absorbent, opaque fabric. Jacket linings attached at the armholes and free-hanging linings with French tacks in skirts reflect high quality. Underlining is constructed as one with the garment. It has many of the same advantages as lining, except it does not cover inner construction details. However, it does make them invisible from the outside of the garment. Interlinings are strictly for warmth. Other supporting devices are used to maintain shape as the design demands. Chest pieces fill out hollow areas in jackets; floating chest pieces move with the wearer. Shoulder pads enhance and even out the shoulders. They should be inconspicuous and securely attached. Sleeve heads support the cap portion of sleeves. Bridles help lapels hug the body. Hoops and bustles expand and support large skirts; horsehair braid gives hems a graceful swirl. Boning provides smoothness in bodices. Collar stays help collar points remain flat. Underlying fabrics and other supporting devices contribute to garment quality and cost.

Shape and Support Quality Checklist

If you can answer yes to each of these questions regarding the garment you are evaluating, it contains high-quality shape and support.

- Is an appropriate dart or dart equivalent used wherever there is a body bulge?
- Are darts flat with no dimple or bubble at the tip?
- Are dart tips secured?
- Are gathers even and full?
- Is ease smooth, and free of tucks, pleats, or gathers?
- Do gussets have sharp, even, secure points?
- Is elastic a comfortable width?
- Does elastic remain flat, without rolling or twisting?
- Is elastic seamed with a lapped seam?
- As a quality extra in high-price lines, is elastic attached "in the round"?

- As a quality extra in high-price lines, is the casing made first and then the elastic inserted?
- If a superimposed seam in elastic is exposed, is it tacked down or covered with a label or small square of fabric?
- Is the care of supporting fabrics compatible with that of the garment?
- Is the durability, weight, hand, and color of supporting fabrics compatible with the garment?
- Is the application of interfacings, especially fusibles, smooth and nonbulky?
- Are sew-in interfacings in tailored garments pad stitched? As a quality extra in high-price lines, are they pad stitched by hand?
- Is the garment fully lined?
- Does the lining feature generous ease pleats?
- Is the lining attached at the armholes?
- If free-hanging, does the lining have swing tacks?
- Does underlining provide desired body and/or opacity?
- Does interlining provide warmth without weight?
- Are chest pieces, shoulder pads, and sleeve heads positioned to follow the lines of the body with no visible ridges? As a quality extra, are the chest pieces floating?
- Are the shoulder pads securely attached?
- Is boning positioned attractively and for comfort?
- Does a shirt collar have collar stays? As a quality extra, are collar stays removable?

princess seam
yoke
gore
gusset
godet
released dart
extra fullness
gathers
ease
elastic
applied elastic
casing
drawstring
lacing
full-fashioned mark
mock full-fashioned mark
fashion/shell fabric
underlying/supporting fabric
interfacing
strike-through
pad stitching
lining
ease pleat
free-hanging/slip lining
French/swing tack
underlining
interlining
supporting device
chest piece
shoulder pad
sleeve head/header
bridle
horsehair braid
boning
collar stay

New Terms

If you can define each of these terms and differentiate between related terms, you have gained a good working vocabulary for discussing the topics in this chapter. The terms are listed in the order in which they appear in the chapter.

shaping device
basic block
dart
dart equivalent/substitute

Review Questions

1. Why are shaping devices like darts and dart equivalents needed in all garments?

2. List the dart equivalents.

3. Which shaping devices fit a wide range of figures? Which fit a narrow range of figures?

4. What are the characteristics of a well-made dart?

5. Name the locations where darts may be found within a garment.

6. How do seams substitute for darts?

7. Compare and contrast:
  a. gussets and gores
  b. gathers and ease
  c. yokes and split yokes

8. Why are full, even gathers considered a sign of high cost?

9. Explain how the order in which a garment and elastic are joined can affect cost and quality.

10. What are the advantages and disadvantges of
  a. lining a garment?
  b. underlining a garment?
  c. interfacing a garment?
  d. interlining a garment?

11. What are the advantages and disadvantages of fusible interfacings versus sew-ins? Wovens versus knits versus fiberwebs?

12. What are the characteristics of a good lining fabric?

13. Why should a coat or jacket lining be attached at the armholes?

14. Why is a floating chest piece superior to a fully fused front?

Activities

1. Fold a dart in a piece of paper. How does this affect the shape of the paper? Try to closely conform a piece of fabric to a dress form or human body. What is required?

2. Examine a garment with darts. Evaluate the construction of the darts for aesthetics and durability. What body bulge is each dart intended to fit?

3. Choose ten different garments at random from a store, catalog or magazine, from a historic costume collection, and from your wardrobe. What shaping devices are used in each? Does the classification of the garment influence the type of shaping device used? Does fashion influence the popularity of certain shaping devices? Do you have a personal preference for some shaping devices over others? Explain your answers.

4. Visit an apparel manufacturer. Ask
  a. To see their basic blocks.
  b. How they build shape into their garments.
  c. What cost-cutting measures they take to eliminate costly shaping devices but ensure that garments still fit the customer.
  d. What types of supporting fabrics they use and why.
  e. What other supporting devices they use.

5. Visit a high-price and a low-price bridal department or store. Examine the gowns for quality and quantity of shaping and supporting features. For example, look for horsehair braid, hoops and bustles, boning, sleeve heads, bra cups, underlining/lining/interfacing, shoulder pads.

6. Go to a thrift shop and purchase two men's suit jackets of different qualities. Remove half the lining in each. Purchase two men's dress shirts of different qualities.
  a. Examine the suit jackets for quality and quantity of shaping and supporting features. For example, look for fusible interfacing versus sew-in interfacing, fully fused fronts versus floating chest pieces, machine pad stitching versus hand pad stitching, full linings versus partial linings, sleeve heads, bridles, ease at back shoulder seams, lining attached at armholes versus not attached.
  b. Examine the dress shirts. Look for evidence of quality shape and support; for example, removable collar stays, crisp, smooth interfacing, and split yokes.

7. Visit a high-price and a low-price athletic apparel department or store. Examine the sweatpants for quality and quantity of shaping and supporting features. For example, look for elastic, gussets, and drawstrings. Why are supporting fabrics and other supporting devices *not* used?

8. Survey five male and five female friends about shoulder pads in their clothing. What do they like and dislike about shoulder pads from the standpoint of attractiveness? Comfort? Durability? From your results, what do you predict as the future of the shoulder pad in menswear and womenswear?

9

Style Variations: Focus on Design Features

CHAPTER OBJECTIVES

1. Present a vocabulary of style names, including garment silhouettes.

2. Discuss methods of producing style variations through design features, including waistlines, collars, sleeves, cuffs, and pockets.

3. Examine the impact of design features on the performance and cost of the garment.

The style of a garment is an important aspect of quality because of its strong relationship to aesthetic performance. Whether or not a style exhibits the design principles of balance, proportion, rhythm, emphasis, and unity affects its acceptance. Current fashion trends, personal preferences, and end use also affect the evaluation of aesthetics. Though the aesthetic evaluation of garment style is beyond the scope of this text (see Related Resources: Design and Style), you are given an introduction to the design features that are used to create styles. A good vocabulary of styles is necessary in all phases of apparel analysis because it enables you to communicate accurately with people in the industry. And the ability to use the correct terminology is also important in designing, writing specifications for, promoting, or selling apparel products.

The **style** of a garment or garment part results from its identifying characteristics. "A particular style of garment usually refers to the cut of its structural lines in a manner that has become recognized, accepted and named" (Davis 1980). Details added to the garment also help differentiate styles. In general, however, the color, fabric, and other details may change, but the style remains the same so long as its identifying elements do not change. The key to identifying a style is knowing what characteristics give it its style.

Along with changes in fashions, style names tend to evolve over time; as a style loses favor, its name is dropped from common usage. When the style returns to popularity, whether it happens years, decades, or even centuries later, it often receives a new name. The popularity of names for the same style changes as fashions change, with newer terms taking preference over more standard terms. Therefore, *always be alert to multiple names for the same style, and to changes in and additions to your style vocabulary.* A few styles are illustrated in this chapter to provide an introduction to style names. However, to develop a comprehensive style vocabulary, refer to Related Resources: Design and Style at the end of the text.

Garment Silhouettes

Basic, fitted garments are illustrated in Figure 8-1. Varying the silhouette of a garment yields different styles. The **silhouette,** the outline or shape of the garment, is determined by the amount and location of fullness in the garment and the methods for controlling the fullness (see Chapter 8). The silhouette of a garment can take on many forms. Figure 9-1 illustrates a few silhouettes for pants, skirts, tops, jackets, and dresses, and the associated style names.

Garment Lengths

Historically, *garment lengths* have been a vital indicator of the current fashion and the popular silhouette. The terms for garments of various lengths are illustrated in Figure 9-2. Beyond the longest length, skirts extend into *trains* that drag on the floor when the wearer walks. Wedding dresses may feature *chapel length* or the longer *cathedral length* trains.

Waistlines

Where the **waistline** of a garment occurs in relation to the wearer's waist has a significant effect on the silhouette and style of the garment. Most waistlines fall at or near the wearer's *natural waistline* (Figure 9-3). Menswear waistlines typically fall at or near the natural waistline. Womenswear waistlines are much more variable and tend to rise and fall with fashion changes. *Dropped waistlines* fall between the waist and hips. In *hip huggers,* the waistline falls at hip level (the term *hip huggers* applies to lower torso garments only). *High rise waistlines* occur slightly above the natural waistline. **Empire waistlines** occur under the bustline (the term empire applies to female clothing only). Current fashions help determine the level of the waistline.

Figure 9-3 illustrates a few common waistline styles. Waistlines within the body of the garment, as in a dress, can be fitted to the body by darts or dart substitutes such as pleats, seams, or elastic. Waistlines at garment edges may also be banded, faced, or finished by other edge treatment methods.

Waistbands

A **waistband** is a band of fabric applied to the garment at the waistline edge. It finishes the raw edge and helps the garment fit the wearer's waist when fastened with a button, hook and eye, or other closure. It may contain elastic to help the garment fit different consumers, with waistlines varying in size by several inches. Most waistbands are found at the natural waistline, but waistbands are used at other levels as fashion demands.

Manufacturers interface waistbands for body and smoothness. The interfacing should be of adequate weight and stiffness to maintain the shape of the waistband, but not so stiff that it is uncomfortable. Other waistbands are elasticized before they are sewn to the garment. Elasticized waistbands are common in low-price womenswear and in childrenswear. The operator folds the waistband over the elastic and sews the folded band to the waistline edge of the garment. Elasticized waistbands are a form of elastic casing.

Manufacturers finish the ends of the waistband in various ways. The overlapping end of the waistband is almost always finished with an enclosed seam. This is the neatest-looking and generally the most durable finish; it is also the most costly method and is somewhat bulky. Hemming the raw edge of the overlap is bulky and not a satisfactory finish in terms of appearance. If the overlap is decoratively shaped, the cost of finishing it is increased. The underlapping end of waistbands in high-quality garments is usually finished with an enclosed seam. However, because its appearance is usually less critical than that of the overlap, the underlap may be treated in various ways to reduce costs without necessarily compromising quality. One inexpensive method is to overedge the raw edge of the underlap; this is nonbulky and fairly durable but does not look as finished as an enclosed seam. A slightly more durable and better-looking finish is hemming the raw edge of the underlap after overedging it, but this adds bulk.

STRAIGHT WAISTBANDS

Most waistbands are made as straight bands (Figure 9-3). *Straight waistbands* do not conform to the natural curves of the body; they are confined to locations at or near the natural waistline and limited to a width of not more than two inches; most are about one and one-half inches wide. Straight waistbands wider than two inches either stand away where the body narrows, detracting from fit and appearance, or roll up where the body widens, causing the wearer discomfort. The waistband is cut with the lengthwise grain of the fabric going around the body because the lengthwise grain withstands more stress without stretching than the crosswise grain.

A straight waistband is constructed of either one or two pieces of fabric. You can identify a one-piece waistband, made of a single, folded piece of fabric, by the fold at the outer edge. Although not as fabric efficient as the two-piece waistband, the one-piece waistband requires less labor. Because a one-piece waistband is less bulky, it is the more comfortable alternative

when the garment fabric is bulky. Nonfusible interfacing inside one-piece waistbands may wrinkle and roll up unless secured at the outer edge with a row of stitches.

Two-piece waistbands are made of two pieces of fabric, the waistband and its facing, seamed together. You can identify a two-piece waistband by the enclosed seam at the outer edge. The raw edge of the waistband facing must be turned under, bound, overedged, or otherwise treated to prevent raveling (unless the manufacturer cuts the edge on the selvage). Edges that are overedged or cut on the selvage create the least bulk. The finished edge is secured to the garment by topstitching or stitching in the ditch.

The facing of two-piece waistbands is usually self-fabric. However, in most men's dress pants, manufacturers face the waistband with a curtain (Figure 9-4). Some better women's slacks also feature curtains. The **waistband curtain** is a prefabricated waistband facing that consists of a strip of firmly woven fabric attached to a bias-cut piece of interfacing. The lower edge of the curtain is a bias-cut fold of fabric. High-quality waistband curtains contain a stay of monofilament nylon or other material to add strength and stability without adding bulk; high-quality curtains retain their shape over time. The bias cut of the curtain allows it to hug and fit the body contours. The curtain is joined to the waistband with an enclosed seam and then tacked to pockets and seams to anchor it in place. A tack at center back is helpful because it flattens the bulk in that area. Between the tacks, you can lift a waistband curtain to examine the inner construction.

A curtained waistband is the most costly waistline finish. Curtains may contain additional stays, decorative piping or other trim, or strips of rubber or elastic to help the pants stay up and to aid in gripping the shirttail to keep it tucked in. The more elaborate the curtain, the more costly.

The operator applies the waistband curtain separately to the left and right halves of the garment; then the pants are seamed at center back. This makes the waistband easy to alter, because the waistline can be taken in or let out at the center back seam without removing the curtained waistband.

CONTOUR WAISTBANDS

Contour waistbands are shaped to fit the contours of the body (Figure 9-3). They are gener-

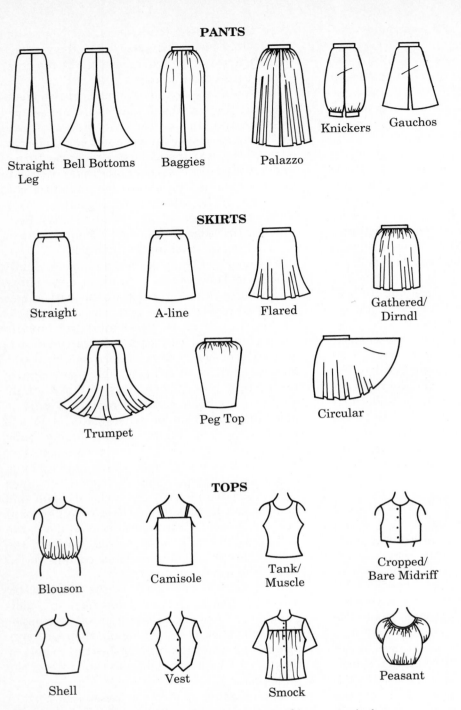

Figure 9-1 *Examples of garment styles: pants, skirts, tops, jackets, and dresses.*

JACKETS

Bolero Chanel Cardigan Blazer/ Single Breasted

Double Breasted Safari Spencer Battle

DRESSES

Shift/ Chemise/ Sack Sheath Tent/ Trapeze Shirtwaist

Figure 9-1 (Continued)

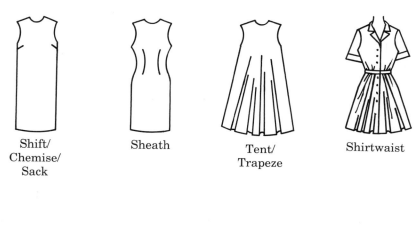

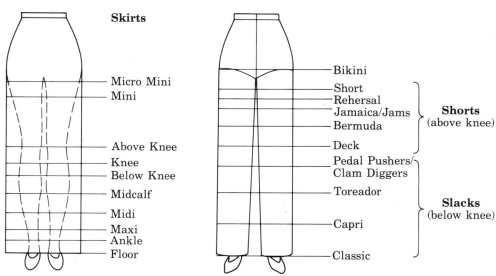

Skirts

Micro Mini
Mini

Above Knee
Knee
Below Knee
Midcalf
Midi
Maxi
Ankle
Floor

Bikini
Short
Rehersal
Jamaica/Jams
Bermuda

Deck

Pedal Pushers/
Clam Diggers

Toreador

Capri

Classic

Shorts (above knee)

Slacks (below knee)

Figure 9-2 Skirt and pant lengths.

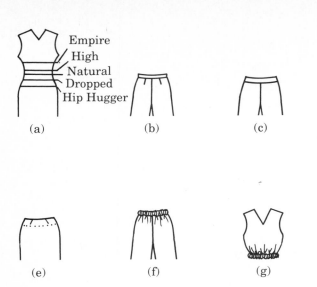

Figure 9-3 *(a) waistline levels, (b) straight waistband, (c) contour waistband, (d) waistline seam, (e) faced waistline (dotted line represents facing inside the garment), (f) and (g) elasticized casings at garment edges, and (h) elasticized casing within body of garment.*

ally required when the waistband is lower than the natural waistline. For example, women's hip hugger pants require a contoured waistband to fit the curve of the hip; a straight waistband would stick out without hugging the body. Because of their unusual shape, contour waistbands are less fabric efficient than straight waistbands and require more labor to construct. Contour waistbands have some bias-cut areas, so they are not as stable as straight waistbands. Interfacing alone is not enough to prevent a contour waistband from stretching out of shape; a stay in the waistline seam is also needed.

Figure 9-4 *(a) curtained waistband. Also note (b) wide center back seam allowances, and (c) French fly.*

Necklines

Ready-to-wear apparel features a variety of **neckline** shapes and finishes. The neckline edge is cut into the desired shape and the raw edge of the neckline finished by any edge treatment such as facing, binding, or banding. Figure 9-5 illustrates a few common neckline styles.

Collars

A **collar,** or any band applied to the neckline of a garment, is mainly decorative, although it is sometimes functional in keeping the neck warm or dry or protecting it from the sun. Some collar types finish all or part of the neckline edge; other collar types require an additional neckline finish; for example, a facing. A collar increases the cost of a garment because it requires additional fabric and labor.

COLLAR TYPES

A collar is one of three basic types: (1) flat, (2) standing, or (3) rolled (either full-roll or partial-roll). The shape of the collar's *inner edge* or neckline edge determines the collar type. The shape of a collar's *outer edge* determines its *style.*

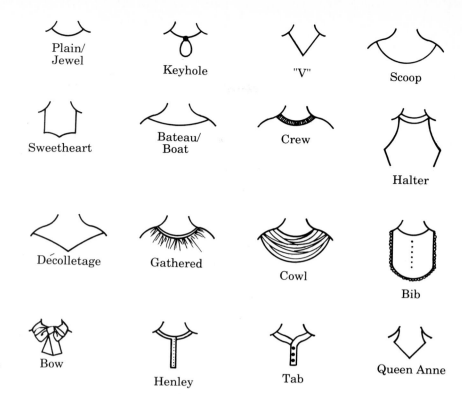

Figure 9-5 *Examples of neck-line styles.*

Plain/Jewel · Keyhole · "V" · Scoop · Sweetheart · Bateau/Boat · Crew · Halter · Décolletage · Gathered · Cowl · Bib · Bow · Henley · Tab · Queen Anne

Figure 9-6 illustrates a few common collar styles.

Flat Collars. A **flat collar** lies flat or nearly flat against the garment all around the wearer's neck. If the inner edge of the collar is shaped in a concave curve, matching the neckline edge, the result is a flat collar, for example, a sailor collar. The inner edge of the collar is attached to the neckline edge of the garment. Then the neckline is finished with a binding, facing, stitching, or other edge finish. Flat collars are used mainly on womenswear and childrenswear, rarely on menswear.

Standing Collars. A **standing collar** is a band extending straight up from the neckline edge and standing up around the neck. If the inner edge of the collar is fairly straight, the result is a standing collar, for instance, a mandarin collar. Manufacturers often apply standing collars to the neckline with the raw edge of the garment neckline sandwiched in between the collar layers as the collar is sewn on. However, if the neckline edge is not sandwiched between the collar layers, a neckline facing is required in addition to the collar to finish the neckline edge. But this method creates a bulky neckline.

A *cowl* is actually a standing collar cut high above the neckline so that it falls into folds. Manufacturers make cowls of soft, bias-cut, or knit fabrics and without interfacing so they are flexible and drapable. They face the neckline edge after sewing on the cowl, or finish the neckline seam with an overedge stitch, or flatten it with a bottom-covering chainstitch.

Rolled Collars. A **rolled collar** is a band of fabric that rolls fully or partially around the neck. A *full-roll* collar rolls all the way around the neck; a *partial-roll* collar rolls at the back of the neck and lies flat or nearly flat at the front of the neck. Full-roll collars, such as turtlenecks, have a fairly straight inner edge. They are like a standing collar, except that a full-roll collar is cut wider and folded down. The part of the collar that stands up next to the neck forms the collar **stand,** and the portion that is folded over forms the collar **fall** (Figure 9-7). If the inner edge of the collar is a concave curve somewhere between a straight line and the shape of the neckline, the result is a partial-roll collar; for instance, a convertible collar. The more concave the inner curve, the less the collar rolls. In a partial-roll collar, the fold at the back of the collar gradually tapers toward center front, where the collar lies flat or nearly flat.

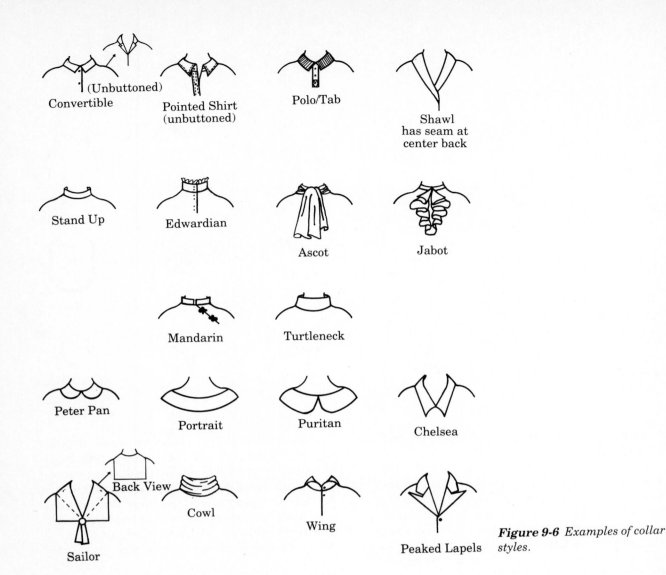

Convertible (Unbuttoned)

Pointed Shirt (unbuttoned)

Polo/Tab

Shawl has seam at center back

Stand Up

Edwardian

Ascot

Jabot

Mandarin

Turtleneck

Peter Pan

Portrait

Puritan

Chelsea

Sailor (Back View)

Cowl

Wing

Peaked Lapels

Figure 9-6 *Examples of collar styles.*

Every rolled collar features a **roll line,** where the collar naturally tends to roll. Manufacturers of better tailored jackets and coats reinforce the roll line with a stay tape so that it rolls more readily. Where the collar begins to roll depends on the level of the garment opening.

The standard *shirt collar* on a man's dress shirt is a mixture of two types; it consists of a standing collar (the *neckband*) with a full-roll collar inserted and sewn into the upper edge of the neckband to create the collar fall. Shirt collars are costly because of the extra labor and materials required; they are essentially the construction of two collars in one. However, the production of shirt collars often is completely automated so they can be accurately manufactured at a moderate cost.

COLLAR CONSTRUCTION

The fall of a rolled collar should extend far enough to cover the neckline seam of the garment (Figure 9-8). A skimpy, poorly designed collar often exposes the neckline seam where the collar is sewn to the garment. This is a mark of low quality.

The outer edges of a high-quality collar are smooth, even, and flat; points should be sharp and identical. Any trim such as lace or piping is even in width all around the collar and is applied without unwanted pleats or puckers. To achieve the best results, operators miter trim at corners, stretch it slightly around concave curves, and ease it around convex curves.

The more pieces involved, the more labor

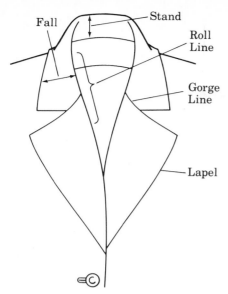

Figure 9-7 Parts of a classic, notched collar and lapels.

required and generally the higher the cost of the collar. Complex collars usually give better-looking and more durable results on tailored garments. However, simple collars are appropriate for some garments, for example, casual sportswear styles.

The application of a collar to a jacket or coat with lapels requires extra labor and attention to detail. **Lapels** or **revers** are the parts of the garment that roll or fold back above the front closure (Figure 9-7). The seam where the collar

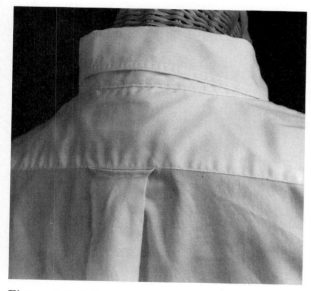

Figure 9-8 Collar exposes neckline seam. Also note locker loop and box pleat at center back below yoke.

and lapel meet is the **gorge line.** The joining of the collar and lapels is critical to the appearance of the garment and is a good indicator of the care with which it was constructed. A skilled operator must accurately match up the collar and lapels and stitch them together, exactly to the gorge line but not beyond. Otherwise, a hole or puckering may form at the end of the gorge line. All excess bulk must be removed from the area for the collar and lapels to lie smoothly. But if too much of the seam allowances is removed, a loosely woven fabric may ravel, forming a hole.

The interfacing of collars and lapels on better tailored jackets and coats features pad stitching to help the collar and lapels roll smoothly. Pad stitching builds shape and support into the collar and lapels.

Single-Layer Collars. Sometimes a single layer of fabric is used as a collar. For example, lace collars are usually a single layer. Single-layer knit collars with finished edges are used on most polo-style shirts. Although the labor cost involved in producing such a collar is low, the overall cost of the collar depends on the quality and cost of the fabric used. The fabric in a single-layer collar must have adequate body to lie smoothly.

One-Piece Collar Construction. Most collars consist of two layers of shell fabric, with interfacing between the plies; these collars may be formed from one, two, or three pieces of fabric. One-piece collar construction is simple and inexpensive. The operator folds a single piece of fabric in half lengthwise and sews the ends together, producing a two-ply collar. A one-piece collar is low in bulk because it has a fold rather than an enclosed seam at the outer edge. If nonfusible interfacing is used inside the collar, it should be secured with a line of stitches to prevent it from rolling inside the collar.

One-piece collars are uncommon because the outer edge is a fold, which cannot be shaped; thus, only full-roll collars can be made from this method because their outer edge is always fairly straight. However, the outer edges of rolled collars made from one piece tend to curl upward because the slight shaping that could prevent curling is not possible at the folded edge. Another disadvantage is that trims like lace or piping cannot be inserted in the folded edge of one-piece collars but must be topstitched on the outside. One-piece collars are mainly found on sportswear and sleepwear in low-price lines, and on inexpensive uniforms and smocks.

Two-Piece Collar Construction. Most collars are two-piece collars. Manufacturers create two-piece collars by sewing two plies of fabric, an **upper collar** and an **under collar** (a facing for the collar) together using an enclosed seam. Interfacing is placed between the layers for shape and support. Two-piece collars require more labor but are often more fabric efficient than one-piece collars because they require two small pieces of fabric rather than one large piece. On tailored garments, the under collar may be cut on the bias for a more graceful roll (Figure 9-10).

Collars on most men's suit jackets and sport jackets are **bluff-edge collars;** the under collar is made of *felt,* a nonwoven material that has no grain (Figure 9-9). Because there is no grain difference in the two halves, both sides of the under collar roll identically, and the roll is sharp and graceful because it is not controlled by fabric grain. Bluff edge collars are so called because the felt has no seam allowances at the collar edges where it is stitched to the face the upper collar; the raw edges of the felt are even with the turned under edges of the upper collar. Felt, which does not ravel, makes the bluff edge collar

less bulky than other types because only the seam allowances of the upper collar are included in the seam at the collar edges. In high-quality jackets, the felt is stitched on by hand to create a less rigid, more flexible collar.

Three-Piece Collar Construction. The three-piece collar is composed of three pieces of fabric—an upper collar, and an under collar made of two halves with a seam in the center. You can identify a three-piece collar by the vertical seam in the middle of the under collar (Figure 9-10). The under collar pieces are cut on the bias. The interfacing, if woven, is also cut in two pieces and on the bias. The bias cut aids the graceful roll of the collar, and both halves of the finished collar roll identically because of the identical grain of the two halves. This is superior to an under collar cut on the bias but all in one piece. Three-piece collars require more fabric and labor than other collar types, increasing costs.

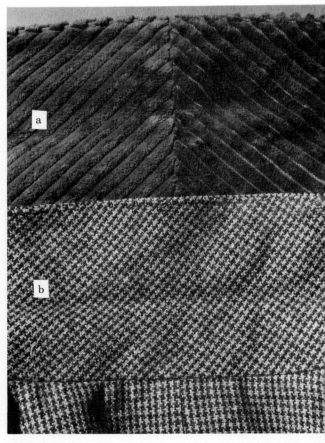

Figure 9-9 Bluff-edge collar with under collar made of felt. Also note ease pleat at center back of garment lining and decorative buttonhole on lapel.

Figure 9-10 Under collars of two jackets: (a) three-piece collar with two-piece under collar cut on the bias and seamed at center back, and (b) two-piece collar with one-piece under collar cut on the bias.

They are mainly used on high-quality tailored garments.

On two-piece and three-piece collars, the under collar and the enclosed seam at the outer edge of the collar should not be visible. The manufacturer may control stitch the enclosed seam to prevent the under collar from rolling out and showing; this is a mark of better quality found in moderate- and high-price lines. Pressing the collar so that the enclosed seam lies slightly under the edge and topstitching it in this position accomplishes the same result.

The under collars in better tailored garments may be cut slightly smaller than the upper collar, and the operator then eases them to fit as they are sewn. This procedure, known as **slipping** or **bubbling,** prevents the under collar and the enclosed seam at the outer edge of the collar from slipping out and showing; slipping pulls the seamline and the upper collar slightly under at the edge. Collars are rarely slipped in ready-to-wear because of the skilled labor required to smoothly join the two differently sized collar pieces. Slipping can be used to improve the appearance of cuffs and other garment parts that are faced and have an enclosed seam at the edge. Without slipping, an enclosed seam in a heavy fabric may appear bulky and unattractive because the seamline and facing are noticeable at the edge.

Sleeves

A **sleeve** is a covering for the arm that is attached at or near the armhole or **armscye** area of the garment. Sleeves are functional in providing modesty, warmth, or protection but are equally important for their contribution to the style of the garment; they are an important feature of the garment silhouette. They should be designed and constructed to flatter the garment and the wearer.

A sleeveless garment has no sleeves to finish its armhole edges. Consequently, the armholes of a sleeveless garment must be faced, bound, banded, edge finish stitched, or otherwise treated to finish the raw edges.

All sleeve styles fall into one of three main types: (1) set-in sleeves, (2) raglan sleeves and (3) kimono sleeves. Figure 9-11 illustrates some

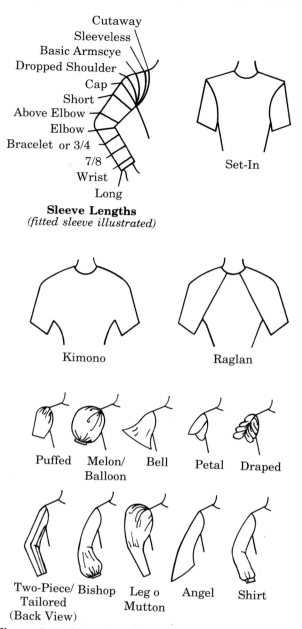

Figure 9-11 *Sleeve lengths and styles.*

sleeve styles. Variations in sleeve length are also illustrated.

SET-IN SLEEVES

Set-in sleeves are the most common type. A set-in sleeve resembles a tube hanging from the armhole. Set-in sleeves fit the body fairly closely but allow room for movement. This is accomplished through a rather complex cut and construction of both the bodice and sleeve. The sleeve has a shaped *cap* (the part above the bicep), cut larger than the armhole, that is eased to the armhole. This fits the cap to the rounded, upper part of the arm. In addition, set-in sleeves may contain extra fullness in the cap, controlled by gathers or pleats.

Set-in sleeves provide a closer, smoother armhole than any other sleeve type, while still allowing room for comfortable movement. The closer the fit of the armhole and sleeve, the higher and more extreme the curve of the sleeve cap and the more difficult it is to ease the sleeve cap into the armhole; the looser the fit of the armhole and sleeve, the flatter and more gradual the curve of the sleeve cap and the easier it is to set the sleeve cap into the armhole. Because the armhole seam is subjected to stress, especially in the lower half of the armhole, it should be stitched twice for maximum durability.

Sleeves can be set into armholes in one of two ways: (1) "in the round," with underarm seam of sleeve and side seam of garment closed, or (2) flat, with underarm seam of sleeve and side seam of garment open.

Set in "In the Round." Sleeves are traditionally **set in "in the round."** The underarm seam of the sleeve is sewn to create a tube of the sleeve, and the side seam and shoulder seam of the garment are sewn to create a round armhole. Then the tubular sleeve section is sewn to the round armhole of the garment (Figure 9-12). You can recognize sleeves set in "in the round" by examining the underarm seam intersection. If the sleeve was set in "in the round," the armhole seam is a continuous, unbroken circular seam. Setting a sleeve in "in the round" provides for the closest, smoothest fit possible while still allowing movement. The sleeve must be designed with a high, extremely curved, narrow cap that fits the rounded, upper portion of the arm. A skilled operator eases the fullness of the sleeve cap to the armhole; the finished sleeve and armhole should appear smooth and closely fitted to the body. Tiny, unwanted pleats or puckers in the armhole seam, resulting from inaccurate easing or too much fullness in the sleeve cap, detract from the quality of a set-in sleeve. Sleeves set in "in the round" are comfortable to wear because the seam allowances follow the hollow of the underarm area from front to back. A sleeve set in flat has seam allowances that protrude into the underarm from side to side and do not follow the contours of the body as comfortably. But because the application requires more time and expertise, setting a

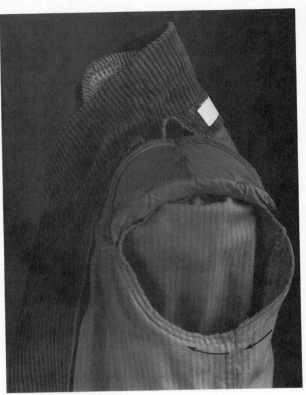

Figure 9-12 *Sleeve set in "in the round."*

sleeve in "in the round" costs considerably more in labor than setting it in flat. Sewing machines with programmable ease make the task considerably simpler, but this operation remains more dependent on operator skill than almost any other in garment construction.

Sleeves set in "in the round" look attractive in tailored and dressy clothes that require close, smooth-fitting armholes. Because sleeves are costly to set in round, this method is usually reserved for apparel in high-price lines.

Tailored coats and jackets often feature two-piece sleeves, which are always set in "in the round." The **two-piece sleeve** consists of two portions: the main sleeve piece and a second, narrow, shaped sleeve piece under the arm. The seams that attach this second piece are dart substitutes that shape the elbow area so that the sleeve follows the natural curve of the arm smoothly as it hangs in a relaxed position. Two-piece sleeves usually cost more than one-piece sleeves because of the additional labor required but they represent better quality because they improve fit.

Set in Flat. The least costly and most common way to set in a sleeve is to stitch the sleeve to the garment while both are still open and flat. The tubular shape of the sleeve and garment body are then formed by sewing the side seam of the garment and the underarm seam of the sleeve in one step. You can recognize a sleeve **set in flat** by examining the intersection of the seams in the underarm area. If the sleeve was set in flat, the side seam and sleeve seam are a single, continuous seam (Figure 9-13).

Sleeves set in flat do not fit as smoothly as sleeves set in "in the round." They tend to be cut looser than sleeves set in "in the round" to compensate for lower and less-shapely sleeve caps. Working with flat panels and little need to ease the cap to the garment makes sleeves quick and easy to set in flat and therefore less costly than sleeves set in "in the round." Because of the loose cut, sleeves set in flat are comfortable to wear but often have wrinkles of excess fabric evident in the sleeve and in the garment near the sleeve.

Men's shirts of all types and at all prices feature sleeves set in flat; in fact, sleeves set in flat are sometimes referred to simply as shirt-style sleeves. A jacket is usually worn over dress shirts, making a smooth fit less important. Sleeves in sportswear for women and children, where comfort and low cost are more important than a close fit, are also commonly set in flat. Sleeves set in flat are also the most common type at low-price lines of dressy clothes for women and children; in dressy clothes, sleeves set in flat often represent low cost and quality.

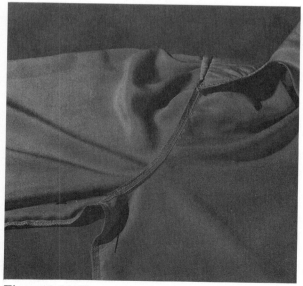

Figure 9-13 Sleeve set in flat.

KIMONO SLEEVES

Kimono sleeves are the simplest sleeves to construct because they are cut as one with the body of the garment. Because the sleeves are not sewn to the garment, labor costs are minimized. However, kimono sleeved garments may cost more than those with other types of sleeves because of poor material utilization. Material utilization is particularly low for long kimono sleeves because the pattern piece is large and unusually shaped. Garments with kimono sleeves often have seams at center front and/or center back to reduce the size of the garment/sleeve pattern piece and reduce material costs. The kimono sleeve itself may be pieced or seamed to the body of the garment to improve material utilization; the sleeve qualifies as a kimono sleeve so long as the underarm curve is cut as part of the body of the garment.

Some kimono sleeves fit close to the underarm, with obvious wrinkles at the underarm; others fit loosely, with soft folds of extra fabric at the underarm. Both types are subject to strain in the underarm area when the wearer moves, but the more fitted kimono sleeves, which feature a higher underarm curve and/or a downward-angled shoulder seam, are especially prone to strain. The underarm seam of kimono sleeves must be adequately reinforced to withstand stress; two rows of stitching in the underarm area are a must. In high-quality garments, manufacturers reinforce the underarm seam with stay tape to strengthen it.

Sometimes manufacturers add a triangular or diamond-shaped *gusset* of bias-cut fabric to the underarm of kimono sleeves (Figure 8-6). A gusset increases the roominess and comfort of the sleeve, and allows the wearer to reach farther without straining the underarm seam. Gussets require extra material and skilled labor to set the gusset into the underarm area. All the seams must match up with the points of the gusset, and the points should be sharp and free of unwanted pleats, puckers, or holes. Gussets may be added to any sleeve type to provide additional roominess but most commonly are used in kimono sleeves. They are a mark of quality.

RAGLAN SLEEVES

A **raglan sleeve** is recognizable by its characteristic diagonal seam, which runs from the underarm to the neckline of the garment. The diagonal seam attaches the tapered sleeve panel to the body of the garment (Figure 4-1).

A raglan sleeve may be attached to the garment in one of two ways, flat or "in the round." The most common and least expensive method involves attaching the flat sleeve panels to the flat garment and then sewing the side seam of the garment and the underarm seam of the sleeve in one continuous seam. If you examine the intersection of the seams in the underarm area, the side seam and underarm seam appear as one long, uninterrupted seam when constructed by this method. The alternative requires sewing the side seam of the garment, and sewing the sleeves into tubes before joining them to the garment. Then the sleeve and garment are joined "in the round." You can recognize "in the round" construction by examining the seams in the underarm area; the armhole seam is continuous and interrupts the side seam and sleeve underarm seam. This method makes the sleeve more comfortable but is more costly than the flat method, so manufacturers rarely use it in low price lines. However, "in the round" application is used in garments, at all price lines, made of tubular knits and without side seams; for example, sweatshirts and T-shirts; the manufacturer has no alternative way to join a raglan sleeve to these garments.

Raglan sleeves provide greater comfort and more reaching room than other sleeve types. They are a good choice for active sportswear and in clothing for people in wheelchairs or on crutches who require great range and freedom of arm movement. Because they do not restrain movement, raglan sleeves are also suitable in clothing for elderly people or others with limited mobility.

Manufacturers use darts or dart substitutes to release fullness in the shoulder area of raglan sleeves, to help the sleeve cover the rounded portion of the upper arm. *Split raglan sleeves* are made of two sleeve panels sewn together with a seam down the length of the arm that shapes the sleeve to the shoulder and neckline. The seam is bias, and the operator must take care not to stretch it during production, or the seam may ripple and pucker. Darted and seamed raglan sleeves typically provide a tailored look but do not fit a wide range of people. Raglan sleeves gathered to the neckline are a good choice for fitting a wide range of sizes. However, gathers provide a feminine look and are mainly used in women's and children's clothes, not in menswear. In sweatshirts and other knit gar-

ments, the stretch of the fabric serves as the dart substitute.

Cuffs

Cuffs are the banded or turned-back finishes at the lower edges of sleeve and pant legs. Crisp, well-made cuffs contribute to the overall appearance of a garment's quality.

EXTENDED CUFFS

An **extended cuff** is a band of fabric applied to the lower edge of a sleeve. An extended cuff is an extension of the sleeve; it lengthens the sleeve as it finishes the lower edge of the sleeve. Extended cuffs are the most common type of cuff used on sleeves because they control the fullness of the sleeve to fit the wrist, or arm in the case of short sleeves. Cuffs should be interfaced for smoothness and support unless they are ribbed knit bands, intended to stretch over the hand for dressing and undressing. If sew-in interfacing is used, it should be caught in a seam or secured with a line of stitches at each edge to prevent the interfacing from rolling up during wear.

Extended cuffs may be decorative, and of various widths and shapes. Wide cuffs and complex cuff shapes add to costs. On basic garments, the repetitive cuffing operation may be automated. This enables the manufacturer to achieve uniform results at a moderate cost.

Manufacturers construct extended cuff bands from a single ply of fabric folded in half or from two plies of fabric seamed together. One-piece cuff construction, identified by a fold at the lower edge, is less bulky and requires less labor but more fabric than two-piece cuffs. Two-piece cuffs are slightly more bulky than one-piece cuffs but are more fabric-efficient because they use smaller fabric pieces. Two-piece cuffs cost less in materials but more in labor because they must be seamed together. You can identify two-piece cuffs by the enclosed seam at the outer edge.

Cuffs should have smooth, even curves and flat, sharp corners. Manufacturers press and topstitch cuffs to prevent the cuff facing from slipping out and showing. In high-price garments, cuffs may be control stitched to accomplish this.

Open-Band Cuffs. **Open-band cuffs** have an opening so the wearer can fit the cuff band over the hand and then fasten it to fit snugly. Cuffs that have an opening require a placket in the sleeve that is usually buttoned closed; a zipper, tie, or other fastener may be used. The cuff should lap, front over back, and fasten on the outer edge of the wrist or arm. If the operator accidentally sets the sleeves into the wrong armholes, or puts buttonholes in the underlaps, the cuffs do not button correctly. Open-band cuffs include the following types:

1. *Barrel cuff* or *shirt cuff*—the most common type; it is a straight, open-band cuff style. Long-sleeved shirts and blouses usually feature barrel cuffs. The barrel cuff laps and buttons at the wrist (Figures 7-17, 7-18, 7-19, and 7-20).

2. *Convertible cuff*—an open band that fastens with the layers superimposed to resemble a French cuff.

3. *French cuff* or *double-cuff*—the most formal style of open-band cuff (Figure 9-14). Manufacturers construct the French cuff like the barrel cuff but twice as wide. Then they fold the cuff back on itself so that the cuff is doubled. The opening edges are superimposed, rather than lapped, and fastened with cuff links or studs through the buttonhole in each layer. French cuffs require considerably more fabric and more labor than barrel cuffs. Because of their high cost, French cuffs are mainly found in high-quality apparel and are most suitable to somewhat formal styles. For example, they are not used on button-down, oxford cloth shirts but on

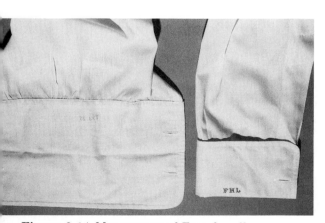

Figure 9-14 Monogrammed French cuff.

dressier shirts of fine broadcloth and on women's dresses.

Extended cuffs are constructed and then attached to the sleeve. Cuffs attached with two rows of stitches, one row to attach the cuff and a second row to secure the cuff facing, usually look smoother and more attractive than when a single row of stitches attaches the cuff to the garment.

Low-quality garments typically have one button per buttonhole on the cuff and few if any sleeve length variations available. Moderate-quality garments often have two buttons per buttonhole on the cuff (Figure 7-20). This allows wearers to make the cuff smaller or larger so that the sleeve can be pushed up or pulled down to fit varying arm lengths. High-quality garments feature a single button per buttonhole on the cuff; the manufacturer produces a variety of sleeve lengths to fit various arm lengths precisely. This increases costs because it requires more sizes to be produced by the manufacturer and carried in inventory by the retailer.

Closed-Band Cuffs. A **closed-band cuff** is an unbroken ring of fabric large enough to fit over the arm. Closed-band cuffs are inexpensive because they do not require plackets or closures. Made of ribbed knit fabric, closed-band cuffs are common in knit T-shirts and sweatshirts because they stretch over the hand and then contract to fit the wrist or arm. Manufacturers design closed-band cuffs of woven fabrics so that the cuff is large enough to pull over the hand without fitting the arm too loosely.

Closed-band cuffs of high quality are sewn on "in the round" after the sleeve underarm seam has been sewn, joining the sleeve into a tube. You can identify this method by the unbroken circular seam attaching the cuff. However, a low-cost method involves attaching the cuff to the sleeve while both are flat. Then the cuff and sleeve are joined into a tube with a single seam. You can identify this method by the sleeve underarm seam visible at the lower edge of the cuff.

TURNED-BACK CUFFS

Turned-back cuffs on sleeves and cuffed pants are formed by turning back or rolling up the lower portion of the sleeve or pant leg. Manufacturers make turned-back cuffs in one of two ways. In the first method, they hem the lower edge of the garment deeply, and turn back the finished lower edge to form a cuff. This method, because of the deep hem, requires over four extra inches of fabric length for a two-inch cuff. The second method, used on sleeves or casual pants, is to hem the lower edge of the garment narrowly and roll it up repeatedly to hide the hem. This is attractive only if the fabric and seams are reversible.

Sometimes manufacturers apply a separate extension of fabric, which is hemmed or faced and then turned back to form the cuff. If the seam attaching the extension is made on the outside of the garment, the fold of the turned-back cuff conceals the seam. Producing a turned-back cuff of contrasting fabric requires a separate extension made of the contrasting fabric. Shaping turned-back cuffs to tapered or flared sleeves or pant legs also requires a separate extension, unless the garment is flanged to fit the taper or flare. Applying a separate extension costs more in labor but less in fabric than cuffs that are extensions of the garment, so manufacturers of low-price garments often use the technique.

Pockets

A **pocket** is a small pouch or bag sewn onto or into a garment and used to carry small items. Concealed pockets are strictly functional. Nonfunctional, "fake" pockets used to complement a garment's design are strictly decorative. However, most pockets are both functional and decorative. Functional pockets include special-purpose pockets, such as watch pockets in jeans, ruler pockets in carpenter's pants, game pockets in hunting clothes, ticket pockets in men's suit jackets, key pockets in jogging shorts, and hidden money pockets in travel clothing. These pockets are shaped, sized, and reinforced according to their special purpose.

For a pocket to be functional, it must be positioned at a convenient level and angle (for example, pockets in work uniforms). And the pocket should be wide and deep enough to accommodate the hand and/or the items it is intended to hold. Pockets designed and placed to complement the garment design and to flatter the wearer contribute to aesthetics. If a garment features pockets on each side, the pockets should

be identical and level with one another. If the garment is made of a fabric with a pattern (e.g., plaid or stripe), a matched pocket reflects attention to quality but adds cost (see Chapter 10).

Pockets usually contribute to consumer satisfaction. Pockets are very important in work clothing and active sportswear, and children are especially fond of pockets in their clothing. Pockets may not seem vital at the time of the purchase, but later the wearer may wish for a pocket when he or she needs a place to put hands, wallet, or keys. Pockets are sometimes left out of garments if they show through the garment or cause a ridge on the outside of the garment. However, the main reason for leaving pockets out of a garment is to lower production costs.

The cost of a pocket depends on its complexity, size, and the fabric used. Pockets often feature decorative trims, stitchings, or other details. These decorative touches add to the cost of the pocket. The addition of pockets must be balanced with cost. Because they require additional materials and labor, pockets add to the cost of a garment. Manufacturers can justify the cost of pockets if they are important to consumer satisfaction.

TYPES OF POCKETS

There are three main types of pockets: (1) patch, (2) in-seam, and (3) slashed. Patch pockets are attached to the outside of the garment. In-seam pockets are set into a garment seam. Slashed pockets are bound or faced slits in the garment.

Patch Pockets. **Patch pockets** or **applied pockets** are pieces of fabric attached, like a patch, to the outside of the garment (Figure 5-16). Patch pockets tend to look more casual than other pocket types. Manufacturers routinely use them on the back of jeans and the fronts of shirts and jackets, but patch pockets can be placed on sleeves and pant legs or anywhere else. Patch pockets come in many shapes and sizes. Choosing and positioning them is very important because they have a great effect on the visual illusion of the garment on the wearer. For example, large patch pockets at hip level draw attention to the wearer's hip size.

Construction. Operators turn under the outer edges of patch pockets so that no raw edges are exposed when the pocket is stitched to the garment. On high-quality pockets, the sides are turned under before the upper edge of the pocket is hemmed, so that no raw edges are exposed at the top of the pocket. If the upper edge of the pocket is hemmed before the sides are turned under, the exposed raw edges near the top of the pocket should be turned or clipped at an angle so they do not show.

Pockets on basic garments, such as shirts and jeans, are made on automatic pocket setting machines that turn under the raw edges, position the pocket, and sew it to the garment. The machine forms the pockets around a *template,* a pocket-shaped piece of metal around which the pocket edges are pressed to ensure the desired shape and size. Automatic pocket setters achieve consistency from garment to garment. Therefore, the manual construction of pockets on fashion garments may be less consistent than the automated construction of pockets on basic garments.

A patch pocket with square corners is the easiest to make; it should have sharp, even corners. Although it is more costly, mitering the corners when turning them under contributes to sharp points, eliminates bulk, and prevents raw edges from showing along the pocket edges. Rounded pockets are slightly harder to make than pockets with square corners. The raw edges of a rounded patch pocket must be turned under evenly to form a smooth curve. Manufacturers may line or face unusually shaped pockets to turn under the raw edges evenly.

Applied pockets that are very large and those on tailored garments or in limp fabrics are usually lined and/or interfaced. Interfacing provides shape maintenance. A lining reduces the raveling of raw edges inside the pocket and prevents raveling edges from showing, making the inside of the pocket smooth. The lining should not show at the pocket edges.

Applied pockets may be fully lined to the top, but more commonly are lined up to the pocket hem so the lining does not show when the pocket is used. A small opening at the hem or a short slit in the lining is used to turn the pocket through after sewing the lining and pocket together. In high-quality garments, the slits and openings in pocket linings are closed, but in low-quality garments they are often left open.

Application. Manufacturers usually topstitch patch pockets to the garment; the topstitching should be placed near the edges of the pocket to keep the edges flat. Some patch pockets are fused to the garment to keep the edges flat and then topstitched for durability. On high-price garments, occasionally manufacturers stitch patch pockets to the garment invisibly from inside the pocket; they use a successive series of sewing operations on alternating sides of the pocket, rather than using one continuous line of stitches. This method is labor intensive and therefore costly, but secure and unobtrusive.

Manufacturers reinforce the opening edges of pockets so the pocket can withstand the stress of use. Rivets, bar tacks, backstitching, or stitches in the shape of a triangle or rectangle commonly secure the corner edges of patch pockets. Heavily used pockets in mid- and heavy-weight fabrics should be bar tacked or riveted for maximum reinforcement.

In-Seam Pockets. **In-seam pockets** are set into a seam of the garment, usually the side seams of skirts, pants, coats and dresses. The pocket opening of in-seam pockets occurs where the operator leaves the seam partially unsewn. The ends of the pocket opening should be reinforced with bar tacks or rivets so the pocket can withstand the stress of use. Sometimes, manufacturers incorporate the garment opening with the in-seam pocket in the side seam of skirts or pants; the upper edge of the pocket is left free at the waist, where it is lapped over the garment and fastened to close the garment.

The opening edge of in-seam pockets should be directionally stitched with the grain to avoid stretching and rippling. A stay eased to the opening edge of the pocket makes the pocket hug the body and prevents it from stretching and standing away from the body during use. This is especially important on wool and other fabrics that have the tendency to stretch.

The *pocket bag,* the pouch of fabric that forms the functional part of the pocket, hangs inside the garment. On some zip front, pleated pants and skirts, the bags of the side pockets are extended to the center front. This helps control the abdomen and keep the pleats flat, providing a smooth front. A *belly band* of lining or pocketing attached between the pockets and center front serves the same purpose.

If the garment fabric is lightweight, the manufacturer may use it to make the pocket bag. However, if the garment fabric is printed or white, a solid or flesh-colored fabric should be used for the pocket bag to prevent it from showing through; in-seam pockets are unsuitable in garments made of sheer or translucent fabrics because the pocket bag shows through to the outside of the garment. If the fabric is mid- or heavyweight, a lightweight pocket bag fabric eliminates bulk. For garments that receive heavy wear, manufacturers usually use special pocketing fabrics that are strong but lightweight and nonbulky. To reduce fabric requirements and eliminate bulk, some manufacturers use a single layer of pocketing fabric, with the garment serving as the other half of the pocket bag; the outer edges of the single ply of the pocket bag are stitched to the garment. You can recognize pockets made by this method by the pocket-bag-shaped topstitching visible on the front of the garment. This method puts stress on the fabric of the garment, especially if it is close-fitting. Single-layer pockets are typical of low-price garments, but may be used in other price lines for decorative effect.

The pocket bag should be large enough for its intended use. Work clothing and sportswear generally require larger pockets than formal clothing. Generous pocket bags indicate high quality. However, if pocket bags are too long, they cause excess bulk and, on shorts, may show at the hem.

The manufacturer must double stitch and edge finish the pocket bag for security, to prevent raveling and holes from forming later. The seam around the pocket bag should be strong but nonbulky so a ridge does not show on the outside of the garment.

Concealed. In-seam pockets are least conspicuous when the opening edges of the pocket are abutted; the seam containing the opening appears to be sewn closed, concealing the pocket (Figure 9-15). The pocket bag of a *concealed* in-

seam pocket is stitched to the seam allowances of the garment. In high-quality apparel, the manufacturer extends the seam allowances slightly and sews the pocket bag to these extensions. This requires extra fabric but prevents the pocket bag from showing at the opening, which is especially important if it is not made of the fashion fabric. Occasionally, the entire pocket bag is an extension of the seam allowance. If the shell fabric is lightweight enough to form a nonbulky pocket bag, this method yields good results because it saves the labor and eliminates the bulk of a seam. However, it requires so much extra fabric that it is rarely done except to make very small pockets.

Exposed. *Exposed* in-seam pockets are usually set into the side seam and waistline seam of the garment; they have a diagonal or curved opening edge offset from the side seam (Figure 9-16). An underlay of fashion fabric forms the exposed portion of the pocket. The underlay forms part of the pocket bag. Manufacturers use exposed in-seam pockets on the front hip of jeans (Figure 10-9) and men's pants (Figure 9-4), where they are often referred to as *quarter pockets*. Some women's skirts and pants also feature exposed front-hip pockets.

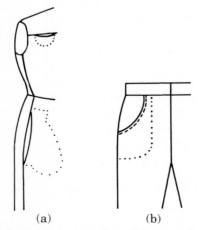

Figure 9-15 In-seam pockets: (a) concealed, and (b) exposed.

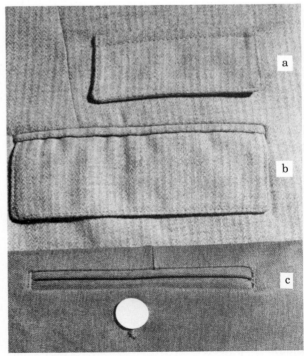

Figure 9-16 Pockets: (a) flap with no pocket, (b) flap on single welt, (c) double welt.

If the fashion fabric is lightweight, the manufacturer may use it to construct the pocket. However, if the fashion fabric is bulky or scratchy, the bag portion of the pocket should be made of pocketing fabric. In this case, the fashion fabric underlay should extend an inch or more below the opening edge, and the opening edge of the pocket should be faced with fashion fabric, so that the pocket bag does not show when the pocket gapes open (gaping is especially likely when the wearer sits). In most jeans, and in other garments at low-price lines, these recommendations are often ignored and the pocketing fabric is visible when the garment is worn. However, each extra piece used to construct a pocket adds to fabric and labor costs, which must be balanced with the comfort and appearance of the pocket.

Slashed Pockets. **Slashed pockets** are bound or faced slits within the body of the garment, for example, on tailored jackets and on the back of men's dress pants. The pocket bag is sewn behind the slit, inside the garment. Slashed pockets are the most difficult pocket to construct. If made manually, precision is often low. In most cases today, manufacturers produce slashed pockets entirely by automation. Since automation, the overall consistency and quality of slashed pockets has vastly improved and the cost has become lower. But because of the complexity, slashed pockets remain more costly to construct than most other pocket types. The more pieces used to construct the pocket, the higher the fabric and labor costs. Nonfunctional, fake slashed pockets, with no opening, are found in low-price garments.

Criteria. Marks of high-quality slashed pockets include the following:

1. They are a perfect rectangle.
2. They have even lips.
3. They are cut on-grain (unless intentionally angled for design purposes).
4. The lip of a single welt pocket meets the upper edge of the slashed opening.
5. The lips of a double-welt pocket meet, but do not overlap.
6. The lips do not sag or gape.
7. The pocket area is interfaced, and sometimes underlined, for reinforcement.

8. The pocket bag is made of a lining or pocketing fabric light enough in weight that it does not press through to the outside of the garment.
9. They are faced with fashion fabric so that the pocket bag does not show when the pocket gapes.
10. The ends of the slashed pocket are reinforced with topstitching or bar tacks. If the fabric is fraying or if there are tiny holes at the ends of the pocket, the pocket is low quality.
11. They may be basted shut so pocket stays flat and closed until the garment is sold; this basting should be removed before the garment is worn.
12. Inside men's suits, slashed pockets that extend beyond the lining into the facing of fashion fabric cost more to produce but are more accessible than those confined to the lining.

Types. Manufacturers make the simplest and least expensive type of slashed pocket by slitting the fabric and turning under the raw edges of the slash. This type of pocket sometimes is used in outerwear and active sportswear with a zipper set in the slash. It is suitable only for strong fabrics with little tendency to ravel. Quality is improved by sewing around the opening before slashing the fabric; these stitches reinforce the opening.

Most slashed pockets are bound slashes, called **welt pockets** (Figures 9-16 and 9-17). If the rectangular slash in the fabric is bound with a single *lip* or piece of the fabric, the pocket is a *single-welt pocket;* the single lip of the pocket is usually no more than about half an inch wide. If two lips are used, the pocket is a *double-welt* or *double-besom pocket;* the two lips are usually no more than about one-quarter inch wide each. A button or button tab may be used on welt pockets to secure the opening and prevent gaping. Manufacturers bar tack the ends of welt pockets to help them withstand hard use. For example, the back hip pocket on men's pants must endure a wallet being put in and taken out several times a day.

FLAP POCKETS

Flap pockets have a flap of fabric above the pocket. The flap extends down over the pocket opening. For patch pockets, the flap is sewn on above the pocket (Figures 7-10 and 10-20). For applied pockets, the flap is sewn at the opening edge. For welt pockets, the pocket flap is placed

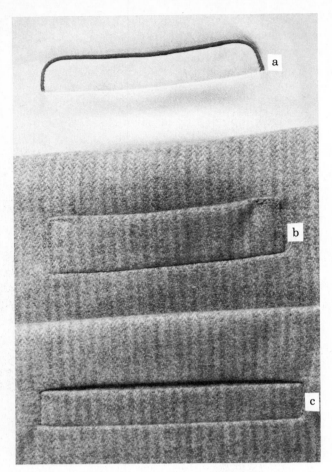

Figure 9-17 *Pockets: (a) upturned flap with piping, (b) upturned flap, and (c) single welt.*

above the single lips or between the double lips of the pocket.

The breast pocket of many tailored jackets provide an example of an **upturned-flap pocket.** Although, at first glance, they look like single welt pockets, the upturned flap is *not* a binding for a slash, but a flap that is attached to the bottom of a finished slash, extending up (not down like a regular flap). Because the flap extends up, it must be topstitched or slipstitched at the edges to keep it upturned (Figure 9-17). Another clue for telling the two pockets apart is that the flap on an upturned flap pocket is *generally* wider than a single welt.

Summary

The identifying characteristics of a garment determine its style. Variations result in different styles for its silhouette, length, and waistline; and for its neckline, collar, sleeves, cuffs, and pockets. Style is evaluated based on fashion trends, personal preferences, appropriateness, function, and principles of aesthetic design.

Waistbands are a popular band finish for waistline edges. They should be interfaced for smoothness. Straight waistbands may be faced with a curtain, the most costly waistband treatment. Contour waistbands should be stayed to prevent stretching.

A collar is one of three types: flat, standing, or rolled (either partial-roll or full-roll). The collar is constructed as either a single ply or of one, two, or three pieces that form a double ply plus interfacing. Two-piece collars are most common, but three-piece collars, with seamed, bias-cut under collars, represent the highest cost and quality. High-quality collars cover the neckline seam. They are smooth and nonbulky and the under collar does not show on the outside of the garment.

Sleeves are one of three types: kimono, which is cut in one with the garment; raglan, which is attached to the garment with a diagonal seam; and set-in, which is attached to the armhole of the garment. The underarm area of kimono sleeves should be reinforced and/or gusseted to reduce strain. Raglan sleeves provide the most room for movement. Set-in sleeves are used in most fitted and tailored garments. They fit more closely without wrinkling if they are set in "in the round" rather than set in flat. Sleeves set in "in the round" cost more in labor than sleeves set in flat. Set-in sleeves should be eased smoothly into the armhole without puckering, and the armhole stitched twice for durability.

Extended cuffs are the most common finish for the lower edges of sleeves. The cuff bands may be open or closed. Open band cuffs fasten, front over back, on the outer edge of the arm. Two buttons per buttonhole in moderate-quality garments enable the sleeve to fit a wider range of arm lengths than one button per buttonhole, which represents either lower or higher quality, depending on the number of exact sleeve lengths available. French cuffs, fastened with cuff links, are costly because of the extra fabric and labor required. Turned-back cuffs on sleeve and pant legs also require extra fabric.

Pockets usually contribute to consumer satisfaction. The main pocket types are patch, inseam, and slashed. Patch pockets are easy to construct and attach; they are usually topstitched to the garment. In-seam pockets are concealed or exposed; the ends of the opening edge should be reinforced and the pocket bag should be double stitched for durability. Slashed pockets are costly to construct because of the fabric and labor requirements. Automation has reduced the cost and increased the consistency of slashed pockets. Slashed pockets include single- and double-welt pockets and upturned-flap pockets. Flaps may be added to any pocket type.

Style Variations Quality Checklist

If you can answer yes to the following questions regarding the garment you are evaluating, it contains high-quality style variations.

- Does the style meet fashion, personal, aesthetic, and end-use functional and appropriateness expectations?
- Are waistlines stayed to prevent stretching?
- Is the waistband interfaced for body and smoothness, avoiding wrinkling and uncomfortable stiffness?
- Is the waistband a comfortable width?
- Are the ends of the waistband nonbulky and finished neatly?
- Are the center back seams of the garment and waistband sewn last for ease of alteration?
- Is the collar flat and nonbulky with smooth curves and sharp points?
- Is the collar interfaced with a suitable weight and type of interfacing?
- Is the under collar concealed?
- Does the roll of collar and lapels occur naturally without being pressed in?
- Does a rolled collar cover the neckline seam?
- Is the gorge line free of bulk, wrinkles, or holes?
- Are sleeves eased or gathered evenly through the cap?
- Is the armhole seam stitched twice?
- On tailored garments, is the undercollar made of two pieces, each cut on the bias?
- Are closely fitted sleeves set in "in the round" rather than set in flat?
- Are kimono sleeves reinforced or do they have gussets in the underarm area?
- Are sleeve seams sewn before the cuffs are attached?
- Do the cuffs lap, front over back, on the outer edge of the arm?
- Are the cuffs neatly finished?
- Are pockets positioned conveniently and attractively?
- Are pocket edges reinforced?
- Are applied pockets evenly shaped with no raw edges exposed?
- Are large applied pockets interfaced and/or lined for smoothness and durability?
- Are in-seam pockets nonbulky with the pocket bag concealed when the pocket gapes?
- Are slashed pockets even, on-grain rectangles that do not sag or spread?

New Terms

If you can define each of the following terms and differentiate between related terms, you have gained a good working vocabulary for discussing the topics in this chapter. The terms are listed in the order in which they appear in the chapter.

style
silhouette
waistline
waistband
waistband curtain
neckline
collar
flat collar
standing collar
rolled collar
stand
fall
roll line
lapels/revers
gorge line
upper collar
under collar
bluff-edge collar
slipping/bubbling
sleeve
armscye

set-in sleeve
set in "in the round"
two-piece sleeve
set in flat
kimono sleeve
raglan sleeve
cuff
extended cuff
open-band cuff
closed-band cuff
turned-back cuff
pocket
patch/applied pocket
in-seam pocket
slashed pocket
welt pocket
flap pocket
upturned-flap pocket

Review Questions

1. List the various garment lengths.

2. What are the three main collar types? What determines a type of collar? Its style?

3. How does the construction of a collar (one-piece, two-piece or three-piece) affect its cost and quality?

4. List the criteria for a well-constructed collar.

5. How does the construction of a waistband (one-piece or two-piece) affect its quality?

6. What are the three main sleeve types? How are they differentiated?

7. List the various sleeve lengths.

8. Discuss the advantages and disadvantages of sleeves set in "in the round" versus sleeves set in flat.

9. Why are pockets on basic garments often better executed than those on fashion garments?

10. Describe the various ways applied pockets are attached. What are the advantages and disadvantages of each?

11. Are pockets functional or decorative features of the garment? Support your answer.

12. What does the number of buttons per buttonhole on the cuff of a shirt tell you about its quality?

Activities

1. Find examples of the following waistline and waistband styles:
   a. straight waistband
   b. curtained waistband
   c. contour waistband
   d. seamed waistline
   e. faced waistline
   f. elasticized waistline at garment edge
   g. elasticized waistline within body of garment

2. Find examples of the following neckline styles:

a. plain/jewel	i. décolletage
b. keyhole	j. gathered
c. "U"	k. cowl
d. scoop	l. bib
e. sweetheart	m. bow
f. bateau/boat	n. henley
g. crew	o. tab
h. halter	p. Queen Anne

3. Find examples of the following collar styles:

a. convertible	j. turtleneck
b. pointed shirt	k. peter pan
c. polo/tab	l. portrait
d. shawl	m. puritan
e. stand up	n. chelsea
f. Edwardian	o. sailor
g. ascot	p. cowl
h. jabot	q. wing
i. mandarin	r. peaked lapels

4. Find examples of the following cuff styles:
   a. extended
   b. open-band
   c. barrel
   d. convertible
   e. French
   f. closed-band
   g. turned-back

5. On a tailored jacket, label the parts of the collar and lapels.

6. Find examples of the following sleeve styles:

a. set-in	h. draped
b. kimono	i. two-piece tailored
c. raglan	j. bishop
d. puffed	k. leg o' mutton
e. melon/balloon	l. angel
f. bell	m. shirt
g. petal	

7. Try on a garment with sleeves set in "in the

round" and another with sleeves set in flat. How do they differ in appearance, comfort, and fit?

8. Evaluate the construction of the following pocket types in low-price and high-price garments:
    a. applied
    b. concealed in-seam
    c. exposed in-seam
    d. single-welt
    e. double-welt
    f. upturned flap
What differences, if any, do you find?

9. Cut collars from paper with the following neckline shapes:
    a. straight
    b. slightly curved
    c. round
Try on the collars. What collar type does each produce?

10. Examine cuffs in low-price and high-price garments. Do you see any differences in the quality of construction? Why or why not?

10

Details: Aesthetic and Functional Extras

CHAPTER OBJECTIVES

1. Describe details that enhance garment function.
2. Examine the characteristics and application of trims and other decorative details.
3. Relate garment details to cost and quality.
4. Discuss the matching of patterned fabrics at seams.

Details can enhance the aesthetic and functional performance of a garment. Although details add to manufacturing costs, they also contribute to salability and to the consumer's ultimate satisfaction with the garment. The right details, properly executed, greatly enhance the attractiveness and usefulness of the garment. However, details do not necessarily indicate high quality. A poorly chosen, sloppily executed, or unnecessary detail may destroy an otherwise attractive appearance or interfere with durability or comfort. Details should be in character with the style and end use of the garment and with the weight and type of fabric. They should be neatly and securely attached and be able to withstand the wear and care to which the garment is subjected.

Some **details** improve the functional performance of the garment; others are decorative, improving its aesthetic performance. Drawing a distinction between the aesthetic and functional details is sometimes difficult. A detail originally used for a functional purpose may become valued for aesthetics. Or a decorative detail may also enhance garment function. For example, a fancy belt loop serves as both an aesthetic and a functional detail.

Functional Details

Some garment details perform a specific, practical function. These details contribute to the durability, comfort, safety, convenience, or appearance-retention of the garment. They also increase material and labor costs.

REINFORCEMENTS

Reinforcements lend strength to areas that experience hard wear or excessive strain. For example, *rivets* reinforce pocket corners (Figure 10-9). The rivet (made of copper, brass, or another nonrust metal) is forced through the fabric into a decorative metal *burr,* where the rivet expands, securing it to the burr. Rivets are an example of a functional detail that has become an important decorative feature on jeans, leather jackets, and other casual clothes.

Tacks consist of several overlapping zigzag stitches; they are used to sew on labels, and secure facings and shoulder pads. *Bar tacks* consist of a short series of zigzag stitches that overlap one another. Manufacturers use bar tacks to reinforce areas of high stress; for instance, at pocket corners, the base of zippers, and in the attachment of belt loops (Figure 10-9). When stitched in contrasting thread, bar tacks also affect aesthetics. *Arrowhead tacks* are made of stitches in the shape of an arrowhead and are used as a decorative reinforcement at pocket corners on western-style clothing.

Manufacturers sometimes place *knee patches* (patches of strong, abrasion resistant fabric) inside or outside a pair of pants at the knee. Knee patches extend the life of the pants in the knee area, which is subject to hard wear. They are most common in boys' pants. Similarly, *elbow patches* extend the life of the garment by protecting the elbow area. Most elbow patches are made of a contrasting fabric and serve a decorative purpose, as on the elbows of men's sport jackets.

A **heal guard** or **kick tape** is a layer of abrasion resistant tape sewn in to reinforce the area at the back of the hem in high-quality pants. Heel guards help the pants wear longer by protecting them from the abrasion of walking.

LOOPS

Loops are sometimes sewn inside garments and used to hang the garment up when it is not being worn. For example, a chain loop inside the necklines of high-quality coats and jackets allows the wearer to hang the garment over a hook. A fabric *locker loop,* sewn into the yoke seam on the back of shirts, was originally intended for hanging the garment but has become a decorative feature (Figure 9-8). On women's garments, manufacturers often include *hanger loops,* loops that help absorb the weight of the garment when it is hung on a hanger (Figure 6-8). Hanger loops take the strain off the seams, avoiding distortion of the garment. Hanger loops are found in moderate- and high-price lines, especially in slick garments with wide necklines, in heavy blouses and dresses with delicate shoulders (for example, sequined dresses), and in skirts.

BELT LOOPS

Manufacturers add **belt loops,** narrow fabric strips or thread chains, at the waistline to keep belts in position. The space allowed for the belt should be wide enough to accommodate the currently popular belt width. Manufacturers make most belt loops by seaming tubes of fabric, or folding narrow strips of fabric and hemming them with straight topstitching, blindstitches, or bottom-covering chainstitches. Belt loops with narrow seams or narrow folds soon ravel. *Keystone belt loops* are intricately shaped loops used in western-style clothing. *Thread belt loops* made of chains of thread are often used on womenswear; thread loops hold the belt in place until the garment is sold, after which the consumer may remove them.

On waistbands, the least bulky belt loops are sewn into the seams of the waistband. The operator must fully catch the end of the belt loop in the seam, or the belt loop may pull out of the seam under stress (especially likely at the upper edge). Some manufacturers bar tack belt loops to the waistband, which is durable. The ends of the belt loop should be turned under evenly for a neat appearance. In better garments, belt loops are often sewn in the waistline seam, and bar tacked at the upper edge of the waistband.

Manufacturers usually use five or seven belt loops on high-quality pants and skirts. A belt loop should always be located at center back to prevent the belt from riding up above the waistline. In high-quality men's pants before purchase, the center back belt loop may be sewn off-center on the waistband or placed in a pocket. After the center back seam is altered to fit the wearer, the belt loop is sewn into its correct position on the waistband. In low-price lines, manufacturers often eliminate the center back belt loop to reduce costs.

WEIGHTS

Manufacturers may place **weights** in high-quality garments to perfect drape; small, thin lead weights are encased in fabric and tacked into position (Figure 10-1). Weights increase costs but add to quality. The following are some uses of weights:

1. Most frequently, to help hems hang evenly; for example, at center front edges of heavy-weight coats to help corners hang flat. Sometimes lightweight chains serve as weights; for example, a chain at the hem is one of the signatures of a true Chanel jacket.
2. To achieve desired drape in cowl necklines of evening gowns.
3. To prevent lightweight skirts from catching a breeze and blowing up over the wearer's head.

Weights should be carefully positioned to achieve the desired effect. They should be made of a nonrust material, and care should be taken when pressing so an imprint of the weight does not show through to the outside of the garment; weights may need to be removed when the garment is cleaned and pressed.

OCCUPATIONAL CLOTHING

Occupational clothing for workers doing a particular job contains many practical features that protect the wearer, provide convenience and comfort, or improve the serviceability of the garment. For example, hammer loops on carpenter's pants provide a place for hanging tools. Employees in a fabric store may wear aprons with reinforced pockets for scissors. Industrial workers require protective clothing. Police re-

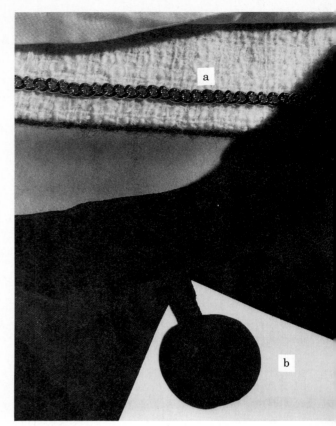

Figure 10-1 *(a) chain weight in hem of Chanel jacket, and (b) weight in neckline of evening gown.*

quire bulletproof vests. Many companies embroider workers' names on their uniforms to help customers identify them. Other functional details of occupational clothing relate to fabric characteristics. For example, soldiers require camouflage prints; fire fighters need fireproof clothing; surgeons wear gowns that have antibacterial, static-free, and low-linting characteristics. An in-depth coverage of occupational clothing is outside the realm of our discussion of ready-to-wear; to learn more, refer to Watkins, S.M. (1984). *Clothing: The portable environment.* Ames, IA: Iowa State University Press.

FORMAL CLOTHING

A number of practical details are incorporated into formal clothing to serve the wearer. For example, *lingerie strap keepers* are used inside moderate- and high-price evening gowns and other women's garments to hold bra and slip straps in place (Figure 10-2). They also keep the garment properly positioned at the neckline and

Figure 10-2 *Lingerie strap keeper at shoulder of dress.*

shoulders in garments with wide or low necklines. Strap keepers should be nonbulky so an impression does not show on the outside of the garment.

Wrist loops are attached to the trains of bridal gowns. After the ceremony, when the wearer places the loop over her wrist, the train is lifted to allow freedom of movement for walking and dancing. Other techniques may be used to shorten the train and fasten it into a bustle during the reception.

Underarm shields or *dress shields* absorb perspiration and avoid the formation of perspiration stains on the outside of the garment. Underarm shields should be carefully positioned inside the garment in the underarm area for maximum absorbency. They may be tacked in place for easy removal for laundering. Underarm shields extend the life of the garment by preventing perspiration damage. They are a mark of quality found in high-price bridal and evening gowns and in suits for men and women.

The *keeper* is the loop on the back of men's neckties. The short end of the tie is kept hidden behind the front of the tie when it is tucked into the keeper (Figure 1-2).

LINGERIE

High-quality slips are sometimes constructed with shadow panels. A *shadow panel* is an extra layer of fabric at the center of the slip for modesty; it prevents the silhouette of the legs from showing through translucent fabrics. Shadow panels increase costs.

Panties made of synthetic fibers usually feature a *cotton crotch*. This is a quality feature because of the absorbency of cotton, making the garment comfortable to wear.

Some manufacturers make bra and slip straps from elastomeric materials, which stretch with the wearer's movements for comfort. However, *stretch straps* may lose their elasticity over time, making the garment unwearable. A stretch strap that is also adjustable may be tightened if it loses its elasticity. *Adjustable straps* contain a mechanism for loosening and tightening, enabling them to fit a variety of figures.

ACTIVE SPORTSWEAR

Active sportswear often features functional details. The following are just a few of the many functional details that increase the usefulness of active sportswear:

1. *Reflective tape or designs* on jogging or biking clothing worn at night make the wearer visible to oncoming vehicles.

2. *Slits or laps* at the side seams of jogging shorts allow freedom of movement for running.

3. *Mesh-fabric vents* in the underarm area of football jerseys allow perspiration to evaporate.

4. *Grommets* (reinforced holes) in the pockets of swim trunks help water drain away and prevent pockets from ballooning out.

5. *Rubber buttons* on rugby shirts prevent contact bruises that result from hard, plastic buttons.

6. *Pads* in biking shorts cushion the buttocks from the bicycle seat.

7. *Zippers at the hems* of ski pants help the wearer put them on and take them off over ski boots.

CHILDRENSWEAR

A functional detail in infants' and toddlers' clothing is the *snap crotch* and *inseams;* the snaps make diapering more convenient. The *safety* of details on clothing for these age groups is another functional consideration. Buttons and snaps on infant and toddler clothing should be securely attached; if closures come off, the baby may swallow them. On infantwear, avoid the use of drawstrings and elastic around the neck or anywhere that a danger of strangling the baby exists. For comfort, fabric should be soft, lightweight, absorbent, flexible, extensible, and easy to launder. Also, materials used to make clothing for children size 2 and under must be nontoxic.

Design features that accommodate a child's growth are appreciated by parents. Examples include deep hems, raglan or kimono sleeves, generous armholes for set-in sleeves, dresses with undefined waistlines, separates rather than one-piece outfits, long tails on shirts and blouses, stretch fabrics, sleeve cuffs that roll down (pant leg cuffs that roll down can trip the child), elasticized waistlines or waistlines with adjustable closures, and adjustable shoulder straps/suspenders (Wingate, Gillespie, and Barry 1984). Horizontal *growth tucks* at the hem or waist of children's garments can be let out when the child grows. The main cost of growth tucks is the extra fabric required. Growth tucks are used to a limited extent in high-price line childrenswear. Because the garment has often faded more than the tucked area by the time the growth tucks are released, their value is sometimes questionable.

Self-help features that assist the child in dressing independently include conveniently placed, easy-to-manipulate closures, and large, stretch, "pull-on" openings for neck, arms, and legs. The front of the garment should be easy to distinguish from the back; for example, marked with an appliqué. Extras such as belts, sashes, and bows should be pretied and attached to the garment. Buttons should be flat, smooth, and not excessively large or small but about one-half inch in diameter. Buttonholes should be large enough to accommodate the button easily. Large zipper pulls make it easy for a child to operate a zipper.

Children's coats and snowsuits sometimes features *mitten ties* that attach the mittens to the garment with a cord; they prevent the loss of the mittens. Knee and elbow patches add durability to play clothing that receives hard wear. Straps should be secured with loops at the shoulders so they do not fall off the shoulders. Pockets, cuffs, trims, and other details should be sewn on flat, not left dangling to catch on things or trip the child. Colors that stand out make children easier to see when they are playing, increasing safety. Nonslip soles on footed pajamas are another safety feature.

MATERNITY WEAR

Maternity clothing features details that make garments expandable for the expectant mother.

Adjustable openings accommodate the enlarging abdomen. Stretch panels may be inserted in the abdominal area of maternity-wear bottoms; *stretch panels* expand as the abdomen enlarges, providing comfort and support. Stretch panels should be long enough and wide enough to avoid uncomfortable binding. They are usually concealed by long maternity tops.

Nursing garments have openings over the breasts for convenient breast-feeding. The openings are concealed by fabric overlays when not in use.

CLOTHING FOR THE ELDERLY

Clothing for the elderly should be comfortable and safe, and help them maintain their independence in dressing. For comfort, freedom of movement, and ease of dressing, choose:

1. Fabrics that stretch and give.
2. Roomy armholes.
3. Kimono and raglan sleeves.
4. Short or elbow-length sleeves.
5. Back fullness.
6. Unfitted or elasticized waistlines.
7. Large neck openings.
8. V-necklines.
9. Long, front openings.
10. Closures that are easy to grasp, or elasticized openings that eliminate the need for hard-to-manipulate closures, especially for those with limited mobility brought on by strokes or arthritis.

Avoid long, loose sleeves that can catch fire on burners or heaters, short openings, back openings, small armholes, and very close-fitting garments.

CLOTHING FOR PEOPLE WITH SPECIAL NEEDS

Clothing for people with special needs is characterized by functional details. Functional details for people with special needs should be as inconspicuous as possible and not draw attention to the disability (Figure 12-10). Disabilities and the associated clothing needs vary widely. The following are just a few examples of functional details for people with various special needs:

1. *Mastectomy bras* contain special pockets to hold the *prostheses* or breast replacements in position for women who have had breast removal surgery.

2. *Action-back pleats* are pleats in the back shoulder area of garments; for example, shirts, blouses, or jackets. They provide reaching room in otherwise fitted garments. Most action-back pleats are fairly inconspicuous. They are comfortable for crutch users and people in wheelchairs, and for anyone involved in active sports, because they increase freedom of movement and reaching in the shoulder area.

3. Underarm padding and reinforcement in clothing for crutch users provide comfort for the wearer and extend the life of the garment.

4. For wheelchair users, low pockets (on lower pant legs, for instance) provide better access than traditional pocket locations.

5. For those with limited finger mobility, hook and loop tape sewn on behind buttons makes closure easy to manipulate.

6. Loops inside garments help with pulling them on.

7. Openings that stretch (for example, cuff buttons sewn on with elastic) simplify dressing and undressing.

8. Zippered pant inseams and/or outseams allow easy access to catheters.

9. For severely handicapped people who cannot dress without assistance, clothing should be designed for easy removal and replacement.

Decorative Details

In the ideal circumstances, decorative details enhance the appearance of the garment and flatter the wearer. The choice of decorative details is strongly influenced by fashion trends, balanced with cost limitations. The right decorative detail, chosen to enhance the garment and securely attached, can greatly improve the salability of the garment. Decoration is added to collars, cuffs, sleeves, hems, pockets, garment fronts, and elsewhere on the garment. Decorative details include trims, both fabric and nonfabric, details constructed as part of the garment, and ornamental stitchings.

NARROW FABRIC TRIMS

Trims are decorative materials that adorn the garment. The term *trim* usually refers to ribbons, braids, laces, and other narrow fabric trims. Manufacturers widely use such trims to adorn childrenswear, lingerie, and bridal wear. The amount of trim used on womenswear depends upon current fashion trends; trims have very limited use in menswear.

Although trims generally enhance garment appearance, a trim that ravels, falls off, shrinks, fades, bleeds, or discolors leaves the consumer more dissatisfied than no trim at all. All trims should be compatible with the wear and care requirements of the garment. Manufacturers who test trims to verify wear properties and care requirements avoid trim problems in the finished garments.

You should develop the ability to recognize fine trims. For example, complex trims generally cost more than simple ones, and wide trims cost more than narrow ones. The fiber from which a trim is made also affects its cost. For example, cotton trims generally cost more and are softer but have a greater tendency to shrink than polyester trims; a silk trim is usually lustrous, elegant, and costly. The amount of trim and the method used to attach it affect cost. Glued-on trims generally cost less than sewn-on trims. The most costly but secure tacking attachments involve double tacking and/or adding glue to the tack. Trims are occasionally sewn on by hand because of the soft, invisible results *or* because the cost of automation cannot be justified, but hand sewing is costly and not especially durable.

Trims may be (1) applied directly to the body of the garment, (2) applied directly to a garment edge, (3) included in a seam, or (4) inset between two fabric panels. Trims should be stretched slightly around concave curves and eased slightly around convex curves to avoid distortion. The wider the trim and the more extreme the curve, the greater the amount of stretching and easing required. Trims generally add strength and stability, but also bulk.

Ribbons, flat laces, and other flat, nonflexible trims are confined to use on straight edges because they are not flexible enough to fit smoothly around curved edges. Braids and gathered laces are generally flexible and can be applied on straight edges or curves. Trim is used most effectively around corners if it is *mitered* (Figure 6-16). Mitering adds to labor cost, but trim that is not mitered at corners may appear sloppy and bulky.

Ribbon. Ribbon is a narrow, woven fabric used as a trim and to make ties and bows (Figure 10-3). Ribbon is available in a variety of widths ranging from 1/16 inch to several inches wide. Ribbons that feel papery are inexpensive and low quality. They generally do not hold up well to wear and care. Types of ribbon include the following:

1. *Grosgrain ribbon* has a dull, ribbed appearance. Manufacturers use it for decoration, but it sometimes serves a functional purpose; for example, when it faces the button placket of a cardigan sweater.

2. *Satin ribbon* is shiny and smooth; it is made with the satin weave.

3. *Velvet ribbon* has a soft, three-dimensional pile.

4. *Novelty ribbons* feature unusual weaves and/or unusual designs.

5. *Picot-edge ribbons* or *feather-edge ribbons* have tiny, decorative loops on each edge.

6. *Ruching* is a ribbon or other trim that has been gathered or pleated. Ruching requires ex-

tra material, especially if it is generously full, increasing costs.

Ribbon ends ravel readily, especially if exposed. A ravel-proof finish on the raw ends of ribbon bows is a sign of quality that most manufacturers neglect. The raveling problem usually surfaces after the purchase when the garment is worn and laundered, but garments that have been on the rack for some time may show evidence of raveling ribbons even before the garment is sold.

Braid. Braids are formed by intertwining a set of yarns according to a definite pattern to form a narrow fabric (Figure 10-4). Braids appear in many styles, most of which are referred to simply as braid. However, the following are some types of braid:

1. *Soutache braid,* a narrow braid used for decoratively trimming bolero-style jackets.

2. *Middy braid,* slightly wider than soutache braid; it is often used to trim sailor collars.

3. *Loop braid,* which consists of many loops.

4. *Scrolling,* a wavy braid.

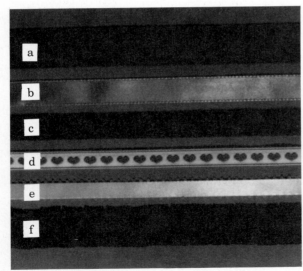

Figure 10-3 *Ribbons: (a) grosgrain, (b) satin, (c) velvet, (d) novelty, (e) picot-edge satin, (f) grosgrain ruching.*

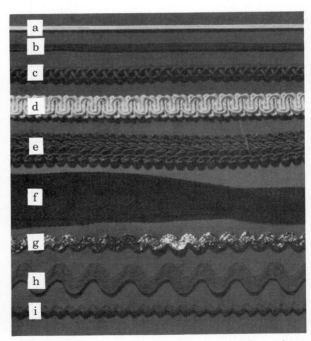

Figure 10-4 *Braids: (a) soutache, (b) middy, (c) loop, (d) scrolling, (e) gimp, (f) foldover, (g) metallic rickrack, (h) jumbo rickrack, and (i) baby rickrack.*

5. *Gimp,* a complex, highly decorative braid, sometimes used to trim high-price women's jackets.

6. *Rickrack,* zigzag-shaped trim used on children's clothing and when fashion demands it on womenswear. *Jumbo rickrack* is wide and *baby rickrack* is narrow.

7. *Foldover braid,* a general term for any braid used to bind edges. Foldover braid is available in many widths and qualities. As an edge finish binding, it is both decorative and functional.

Lace. **Lace trim** is a narrow, lace fabric (versus **allover lace,** the lace fabric from which entire garments are constructed). Lace trim can vary greatly in cost, depending on its fiber content, intricacy and complexity, width, and, if gathered, fullness. Full, gathered lace trim costs double or triple what a skimpily gathered or flat lace trim costs.

Lace making originated as a handcraft, but the vast majority of laces today are made by machine. There are many, many different types of lace, fabricated in various ways, mainly on Leavers machines, Raschel knitting machines, and Schiffli embroidery machines; knitted laces typically cost the least. Figure 10-5 shows a few popular lace trims. They include the following:

1. *Insertion,* any flat lace trim with two straight edges. It is often inset between two pieces of fabric to expose the area underneath.

2. *Galloon,* any flat lace trim with two scalloped edges.

3. *Edging,* any lace trim with one scalloped edge and one straight edge. Edging may be flat or gathered.

4. *Beading,* lace trim through which ribbon is threaded.

5. *Medallion,* an individual lace motif applied, for example, as an appliqué, collar, or cuff.

Other Narrow Fabric Trims. A number of other narrow fabric trims are used on clothing (Figure 10-6). A few miscellaneous types of trim are listed here, but many miscellaneous trim styles have no particular name and are referred to simply as trim.

1. *Piping,* a narrow, folded strip of fabric included in a seam that contrasts with the color of the garment. Piping lends itself best to fairly straight seams. It is difficult to apply around

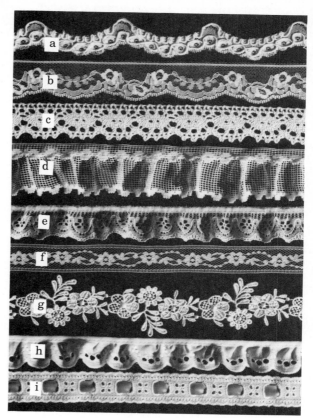

Figure 10-5 *Laces: (a) Alençon galloon, (b) Chantilly edging, (c) Cluny edging, (d) filet gathered edging, (e) Raschel knit gathered edging, (f) Raschel knit insertion (g) Venice galloon, (h) eyelet gathered edging, and (i) eyelet beading.* Note: *Technically, eyelet is not a lace, but often is referred to as one.*

sharp curves or corners; a skilled operator is required to avoid bulky or puckered results. Manufacturers use piping to decorate the inside of some lined jackets and coats as well as the outsides of garments. Seams containing piping are referred to as *piped seams.*

2. *Corded piping,* piping with a cord in it to create a round tube. Corded piping should be flexible enough that it does not distort the seam. Stiff piping is subject to abrasion, but does help reinforce the seam.

3. *Bias tape,* bias-cut strips of fabric, which may be used as a decorative binding.

4. *Seam tape* or *hem tape,* a smooth ribbonlike fabric used to trim interior seam and hem edges (Figure 6-7).

5. *Twill tape,* a twill-weave fabric used to trim casual garments; also reinforces and prevents stretch.

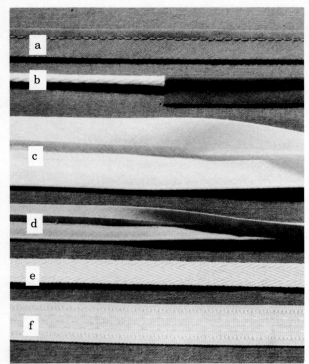

Figure 10-6 *Miscellaneous trims: (a) piping, (b) corded piping, (c) and (d) bias tape, (e) twill tape, and (f) seam/hem tape.*

6. *Fringe,* trim with even dangling yarns.
   Shimmy fringe, shiny fringe that moves when the wearer moves.
   Brush fringe, thick, even fringe that resembles a brush.
   Tassel fringe, groups of fringe tied together into tassles at intervals.
   Ball fringe, fringe with round balls hanging from the trim at intervals.

DECORATIVE DETAILS INTEGRAL TO THE GARMENT

Some decorative details are constructed as part of the garment. For example, fabric may be raveled out at the edge to form a fringe called *self-fringe.* In high-quality garments, a row of stitches just above the fringe prevents further raveling. Leather or vinyl may be slashed at frequent intervals to form self-fringe. A *tab* is a fabric strip that, when combined with a button, buckle, or d-rings serves as a functional closure as well as a decorative detail (see Chapter 11). *Epaulets* are tabs at the shoulders, often used on military uniforms, safari outfits, and trench coats. Although epaulets usually serve no func-

tion, they may be used to keep shoulder bag or camera straps from slipping off the shoulder (e.g., safari shirts).

Many details constructed as part of the garment are functional as well as decorative. For example, tucks, pleats, gathers, yokes, extra fullness, seams, and darts decorate the garment as they help shape it (see Chapter 8).

Tucks. A **tuck** is a fold of fabric, sewn together (Figure 10-7). The fold lies flat against the garment, but you can lift the fold. Tucks can be made vertically, horizontally, and diagonally on a garment. Most tucks are stitched on the outside of the garment so the folds of fabric show on the outside.

Tucks require extra fabric and labor. If a manufacturer uses numerous tucks in a gar-

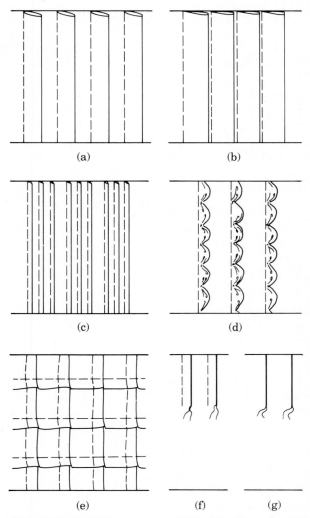

Figure 10-7 *Tucks: (a) spaced, (b) blind, (c) pin, (d) shell, (e) crossed, (f) released, and (g) inverted.*

ment, considerable extra fabric and labor are required. For example, a garment with tucks all the way across the front may require three times as much fabric as a garment with a plain front. The tucks also require skilled labor to carefully space and stitch them.

Besides the plain tuck, there are a number of variations, including these:

1. *Inverted tucks,* stitched on the inside of the garment so the folds of fabric are not visible on the outside of the garment.

2. *Released tucks,* which are partially stitched, releasing fullness and introducing ease into the garment.

3. *Dart-tucks* or *open-ended darts,* similar to released tucks. They are tapered like darts and the tips are left unstitched. Dart-tucks shape the garment, serving as a dart substitute.

4. *Pin tucks,* narrow and closely spaced tucks, such as those in tuxedo shirts.

5. *Spaced tucks,* a series of tucks that occur at regular intervals.

6. *Blind tucks,* a series of tucks that meet, each one covering the stitches of the one preceding it.

7. *Scalloped tucks* or *shell tucks,* which feature decorative stitching at the edges that draw the tuck into a shell shape (similar to the shell hem in Figure 7-8).

8. *Crossed tucks,* two sets of tucks made perpendicular to one another.

9. *Corded tucks,* which have a cord inserted in the fold of the tuck to give a three-dimensional effect.

Pleats. A **pleat** is a fold of fabric at the edge of a garment, folded back upon itself so that the pleat is comprised of three layers (Figure 10-8). The top fold of the pleat hides the back fold; you can spread open the pleat to see the back fold. Pleats are not stitched to the garment throughout their length as are tucks, although occasionally pleats are partially stitched down at the upper edge to flatten them and hold them in place. Pleats can be pressed or unpressed throughout their length for different effects. Soft, rolled pleats are appropriate in soft fabrics. Sharp, pressed pleats must be made in a crisp fabric for the proper effect. Fabrics that can be heat set have the ability to maintain the creases of pleats. Pleats in other fabrics may be edgestitched along the folds for a crisp, well-defined look. Pleats are made vertically on the garment and secured at the upper edge; they cannot be made horizontally or diagonally. Pleat types include these:

1. *Knife pleat,* the basic folded pleat; all pleats are variations of this pleat (Figure 10-9).

2. *Box pleats,* two knife pleats folded away from one another (Figure 9-8).

3. *Inverted pleats,* two knife pleats folded toward one another. Note the relationship between box and inverted pleats; when either occurs in a series, between every box pleat an inverted pleat is created and vice versa.

Knife pleats, box pleats, and inverted pleats may be used singly, in small groups *(cluster pleats),* or all the way around a garment. They are also used as a basis for the following:

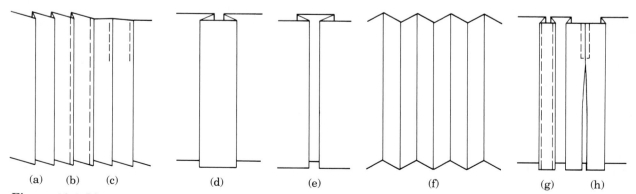

Figure 10-8 *Pleats: (a) knife, (b) edgestitched knife, (c) partially stitched knife, (d) box, (e) inverted, (f) accordion, (g) edgestitched box, and (h) partially stitched box.*

Figure 10-9 *Pleats: (a) deep versus (b) shallow.*

1. *Kick pleat,* a pleat at the hem of a skirt to give room to walk and sit; it may be a decorative feature as well.

2. *Vent,* an opening at the back hem of jackets, which allows the garment to expand for walking and sitting comfort.

3. *Gibson pleat* or *flange,* a pleat at the intersection of the shoulder and the armhole that releases fullness in the front and/or back of the garment.

4. *Accordion pleats,* repeated, evenly spaced, open knife pleats.

5. *Sunburst pleats,* smaller at the waist and larger as they near the hem. Accordion and sunburst pleats are used in skirts.

6. *Crystal pleats,* extremely narrow accordion pleats used in formal gowns and some ruffle trims.

7. *Cartridge pleats* also called *gauging,* accordion pleats drawn closed with rows of running stitches so that they resemble bold, even gath-

ers. They are used in academic and clerical robes and in high-price garments.

Considerable labor is required to accurately space and press pleats. When an entire fabric or garment requires pleating, the manufacturer usually sends the job to a contractor that specializes in pleating. The cost difference between pleats depends upon the depth. Shallow pleats require little fabric and are used in low-quality garments (Figure 10-9). Deep pleats require as much as three times the fabric needed for an unpleated garment. Full-depth pleats, with the back fold as wide as the front fold, look the same as shallow pleats when the wearer stands still, but provide more attractive fullness when the wearer moves. They also provide plenty of sitting and moving ease. However, deep pleats are confined to high-price garments because of the cost.

Creases. **Creases** pressed in pant legs are a decorative feature that add a crisp look to the garment and slim the appearance of the wearer. Front creases start at the hem and end somewhere between the crotch level and the waist. Back creases extend from the hem to the crotch level. Fabrics that can be heat set maintain a sharp crease. In fabrics that cannot be heat set, stitching along the crease helps maintain a sharp crease line; this is done mainly in children's garments. Today, some pants have a thin line of plastic dribbled under the crease line to make the crease more durable.

Ruffles. **Ruffles** or **flounces** are decorative, gathered, or pleated strips of fabric. Full ruffles are usually two-and-one-half times or more the length of the area to which they are gathered. They require more fabric than skimpy ruffles, which may be as little as one-and-one-half times the length of the area to which they are gathered. Full ruffles are found in high-quality garments. Soft, sheer, and lightweight fabrics need to be fuller than other fabrics to avoid a skimpy appearance. Ruffles should be even in width.

High-quality ruffles are gathered evenly, with no pleats or tucks. Manufacturers achieve perfectly even gathering at a reasonable cost by using machines with programmable gathering adjustments. If gathering is done by human operators, perfectly even gathering is costly and difficult to achieve. Bias-cut ruffles drape more gracefully than ruffles cut on the straight-of-grain. However, bias-cut ruffles are costly because of the amount of fabric required, and because seaming the bias pieces together is time-consuming.

Manufacturers make ruffles by hemming the long edge of a single ply of fabric to make a single-layer ruffle, or by folding a piece of fabric in half lengthwise to make a double-layer ruffle (Figure 10-10). Double-layer ruffles require twice as much fabric as single-layer ruffles; however, double-layer ruffles require less labor because they do not require hemming. Most ruffles in low- and moderate-price lines are single-layer ruffles. Single-layer ruffles have less body than double-layer ruffles, and are less attractive if the fabric has a right and wrong side and if the hem shows. However, although double-layers are considered a mark of quality in many cases, they cause more bulk than single-layer ruffles and are not suitable for all applications.

Shaped ruffles are cut in a circle and straightened for sewing to the garment. This causes an attractive ripple at the outer, unsewn edge but they remain smooth where they are seamed to the garment. A shaped or gathered ruffle at the waistline is a *peplum*; peplums are a decorative style feature used in womenswear. Wide, successive rows of ruffles are called *tiers* (Figure 10-11).

Bows. A **bow** is a ribbon or fabric strip tied into a decorative knot with loops and streamers. Long, full bows require extra material, making them costly. Fabric bows that are cut on the bias tie and drape gracefully, but bias-cut bows are also costly because they require extra material. Bows are either (1) an extension of the garment structure or (2) constructed separately and then

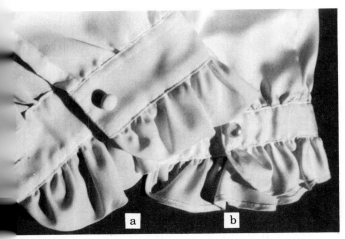

Figure 10-10 (a) double-layer ruffle, and (b) single-layer, hemmed ruffle.

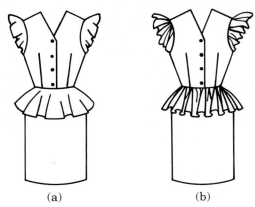

Figure 10-11 (a) shaped shoulder ruffles and shaped ruffle peplum at waist, and (b) gathered shoulder ruffles and gathered ruffle peplum at waist.

tacked, glued, or pinned in place. Ribbon bows tend to ravel and become bedraggled when laundered; in such cases, the bows should be removable for laundering.

Belts. **Belts** help hold the garment in position and shape it to the body at the waist, but they are also decorative. Belts buckle, tie, or otherwise fasten around the body. They may be made of fabric, vinyl, metal, leather, or other materials by the manufacturer or by a contractor. Stiff fabric belts are made by stitching or gluing the fabric around *belting,* a stiff interfacing; stitched belts cost more and are more durable than glued belts.

A belt often increases the *hanger appeal* of the garment, or its ability to attract the consumer when hanging on the sales rack. The addition of even a low-quality belt can significantly increase its salability. Therefore, many manufacturers purchase belts to add to the garments they produce. Belts sold on garments are generally of lower quality than the average belt sold separately. High-quality belts on garments are found only in high-price lines.

Appliqués. **Appliqués** are decorative fabric patches applied to the garment (Figure 10-12). Examples of appliqués include the Greek letters sewn onto college sweatshirts and the whimsical fabric shapes stitched onto childrenswear. **Emblems** are preembroidered appliqués, also known as patches, badges, or insignia, such as those used on scouting and military uniforms.

Stitched-on appliqués are generally more durable than glued-on or heat-sealed appliqués. A smooth, dense zigzag stitch is the most costly

Figure 10-12 *Appliqué secured with zigzag stitches.*

and durable method of attachment for most appliqués; however, the stitches should not be so close that they damage the fabric of the garment or build up at the corners of the appliqué. Emblems are best applied using a straight lockstitch. Changing thread colors to sew on multicolored appliqués is a sign of quality. Fine, clear details also add to the quality of an appliqué. High-quality appliqués have interfacing behind the stitches for reinforcement. Interfacing gives the area the body it needs to yield smooth, pucker-free stitches around the appliqué. Coating the back of the appliqué itself with plastic or fusible interfacing gives it body. Sometimes manufacturers pad the appliqué for a three-dimensional effect.

NONFABRIC TRIMS

Nonfabric trims include beads (e.g., cylindrical *bugle beads* and round *seed beads*), sequins (including large sequins called *paillettes* or *spangles*), rhinestones, flat metal nailheads, raised metal studs, rivets and burrs (as on jeans), feathers, jewels, and pearls. Real pearls and jewels are found on only the rarest and most costly couture garments; most jewels and pearls are plastic simulations. Other nonfabric decorative details include dyed and printed designs (see Chapter 4).

Most nonfabric trims are applied individually. Some may be applied in strings, which reduces cost. Gluing is the least costly method of application but is not always durable, especially when the garment is laundered. Many metal trims are cleated into the fabric; they should be adequately interfaced for durability. Stitching or cleating the trim onto the fabric costs more but is more durable than gluing. Most trim is stitched on by machine, but hand stitching may be used when the numbers being produced do not justify mechanizing the process; for example, if feathers are applied to a small production run of dresses. The manufacturer should ensure that the trim (and its method of application) withstand the care procedures recommended for the garment. Sequins, feathers, and rhinestones, for instance, may be ruined by laundering or dry cleaning.

Closures such as buttons and buttonholes, hooks and eyes, snaps, zippers, frogs, buckles, and other functional fasteners may double as decorative details (see Chapter 11). However, they may serve as decorative details only. For example, sometimes manufacturers sew nonfunctional buttons to garments strictly for decorative purposes; for example, at the wrists of tailored jackets. The buttonhole on the lapels of some tailored jackets, reminiscent of the days when men wore flowers in their lapels, is another detail more decorative than functional (Figure 9-9).

STITCHING TRIMS

Stitching trims include the **ornamental stitching (OS)** defined in U.S. Fed. Std. No. 751a (Figure 10-13). Ornamental stitchings are applied for decorative purposes. They include all forms of topstitching and other decorative stitchings that are aesthetic and have little or no functional purpose. All the ornamental stitchings included in the Federal Standard are diagrammed in Appendix B. Appendix C lists the

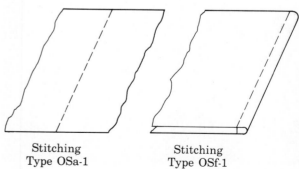

Stitching
Type OSa-1

Stitching
Type OSf-1

Figure 10-13 *Ornamental stitchings (OS): (OSa) in body of garment, and (OSf) at edge.*

apparel production operations performed by each OS stitching and the suitable stitch types.

Topstitching.

Topstitching or **accent stitching** is visible, decorative stitching done on the outside of the garment (for example, see Figures 5-16 and 7-10). Topstitching may be placed anywhere within the body of the garment (OSa) or near edges (OSf). If placed very close to an edge (within one-eighth inch), topstitching may be called **edgestitching.** Besides being ornamental, topstitching near edges (OSf) provides body, flattens and reinforces the edge, and keeps facings from slipping out and showing on the outside of the garment. Reversible edges (e.g., the front of a jacket with rolled lapels) should be stitched with lock stitches, which appear identical from both sides.

Topstitching more than any other stitching affects the appearance of the garment. It should be straight, uniform, and accurately placed on the intended line. It should not cause puckering. The thread color should match or complement the fabric. Because it is visible to the consumer, consumers use topstitching more than other stitchings to gauge quality. Manufacturers usually use straight stitches for topstitching, but decorative stitches may be used.

High-quality topstitching contributes to the garment design. Too much topstitching is a poor substitute for quality fabric and design. Remember the design credo, "Less is more," when evaluating topstitching.

Embroidery.

Embroidery is decorative stitching used to form designs or patterns. *Satin stitch* embroidery features long stitches sewn densely to create an embroidered design with a satiny look. Designs containing extensive detail and made with closely spaced stitches cost more than simple designs made with sparse stitches. Embroidery requires thread that is strong, fine, smooth and, usually, lustrous; rayon, polyester, and cotton are common choices. Embroidery found on ready-to-wear is almost always machine embroidery; machines can embroider up to 20 garments simultaneously. Hand embroidery is found only in couture and other high-price apparel, and occasionally in imports.

Cutwork consists of holes in the fabric surrounded by embroidery. Cutwork was originally a handcraft, but today it is done by machine. Cutwork decorates collars and other details on feminine garments, and it is the process used to make eyelet, a lace substitute (Figure 10-17).

Embroidery that forms the initials of the wearer's name is a **monogram** (Figure 9-14). Besides denoting ownership, monograms give an impression that the garment is custom-made, although they can be purchased ready-made and even acquired by mail order. The monogram on a man's shirt is usually placed on the pocket, cuff, on the body of the garment three to five inches above the waist, or occasionally on the collar. Tasteful shirt monograms are discreet, often white on white, and no more than one-quarter inch high. Manufacturers usually place monograms on sweaters on the chest, centered or to one side. Handmade monograms are raised and denote more prestige than the more common machine-made monograms, which are flat.

Appliqués are sometimes embroidered (e.g., emblems) so that the appliqué resembles machine embroidery. To differentiate between machine embroidery and appliqué, look for the stitches of the entire design, which are visible inside a machine-embroidered garment. If appliquéd, you see only the outline stitches of the design inside the garment. The Izod alligator is an appliqué, whereas Ralph Lauren's Polo player is machine embroidered (Figure 10-14).

Embroidery should be backed with a light interfacing to support the area. The interfacing strengthens the fabric to prevent tearing. Interfacing also prevents puckering and makes the stitches smooth and attractive. If tear-away interfacing is used, the excess interfacing should be removed after the area is embroidered. Pucker caused by embroidery, especially a problem on knits, can be reduced by using a woven backing, slowing down sewing speeds, and reducing the density of stitches (but continuing to provide complete coverage). High-quality embroidery has a high stitch count so that the embroidery covers the fabric with thread. A matching thread color also helps.

Figure 10-14 *Ralph Lauren's Polo trademark (a) is machine embroidered, and Izod's alligator trademark (b) is an embroidered appliqué.*

Trapunto is a form of embroidery that resembles quilting. In better garments, trapunto involves padding the stitched areas of the garment so they stand out in relief, producing a three-dimensional effect. Twin needles and cording provide this raised, decorative effect in most ready-to-wear (Figure 10-15).

Smocking and Shirring. Smocking and shirring are decorative stitchings that may serve as dart substitutes (see Chapter 8). **Smocking** uses decorative stitches to hold the fabric in even, accordionlike pleats. Smocking is popular in the chest area of infants' and girls' clothing; it gives slightly and enables the garment to "grow" with the child. Smocking is used occasionally in womenswear. Most smocking is done by machine. Smocking done by hand, found in high-price imported infantwear and childrenswear, is time-consuming and costly.

Shirring is permanent, parallel rows of gathers made in the body of the garment. In fact, some manufacturers use the term shirring as a synonym for gathering. Shirring made with elastic thread stretches and helps shape the garment to the body (Figure 10-16). Shirring may be done throughout the garment, as in a woman's tube top, or in a limited area, as at the bustline of a woman's swimsuit.

Hemstitching and Fagoting. Hemstitching and fagoting are ornamental stitchings that come and go in popularity, depending on fashion trends. The art of hand **hemstitching** involves pulling out a group of parallel yarns from a fabric and tying the perpendicular yarns re-

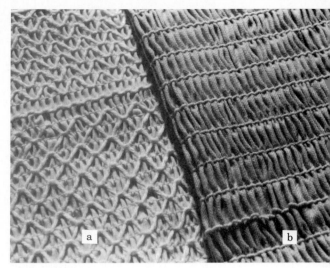

Figure 10-16 (a) smocking and (b) shirring.

maining together with decorative stitches (Figure 10-17). Machine hemstitching pierces the fabric and stitches the edges with a vibrating needle to achieve the same look. By cutting machine hemstitching, a picot edge finish is produced. Hemstitching is used to secure hems and as a decorative effect. **Fagoting** is a decorative stitching that holds together two closely spaced folded edges of fabric with ornamental stitches. Hemstitching and fagoting appear similar at a glance, like a piece of lace inset between two pieces of fabric. Both expose the area beneath the decorative stitches. However, hemstitching is an integral part of the fabric while fagoting joins two separate plies of fabric, with their

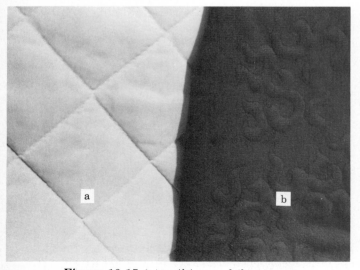

Figure 10-15 (a) quilting and (b) trapunto.

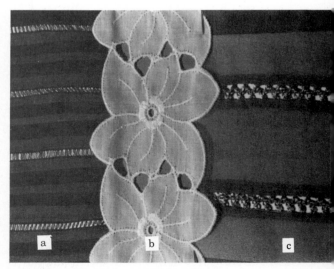

Figure 10-17 (a) hemstitching, (b) cutwork, and (c) fagoting.

seam allowances visible inside the garment. Besides being decorative, fagoting is sometimes used on "clip to fit" slips; the customer clips through one of several rows of fagoting at different levels to shorten the slip to the desired length.

Quilting. **Quilting** (SSv) joins the fashion fabric with a backing fabric and an interlining such as batting (filler), foam, or down. The quilting stitches form a slightly puffy, raised design, often in a geometric or other decorative pattern. Some quilting in low-price garments is fused ultrasonically instead of joined with stitches, if the fabric is made of thermoplastic fibers. Ultrasonic quilting is just as durable as or more durable than stitched quilting, but its appearance generally has lower consumer acceptance than stitches. Stitches cost more than fusing. Quilting is popular in coats, jackets, and vests. The fabric is usually quilted before the garments are cut and sewn.

Matching Patterned Fabrics

Some fabrics have linear patterns, such as plaids, checks, and stripes, that require **pattern matching** or lining up at seams. Matching these fabrics is necessary to achieve an attractive finished garment. Any regular, linear fabric design that is one-quarter inch or larger should be matched in the finished garment. Patterned fabrics that match at seamlines represent quality.

Matching a patterned fabric during construction is possible only if it is matched when cut. Matching increases fabric and labor costs. It requires extra time and attention during construction to plan, spread, cut, and construct a garment with matched patterns at each seam. Some manufacturers use computers to simplify the matching process during marker making and spreading. Because garment pieces must be placed on the fabric where they will match, and not where they fit closest together, fabric is wasted in layout of patterned fabrics. Because of increased fabric and labor costs, garments with matched patterns cost more than garments with unmatched patterns.

The larger the pattern, the more fabric required to match it. Typically, one extra repeat of the pattern is required for each major garment piece. Depending on the size of the pattern, matching can add significantly to fabric costs.

EVEN AND UNEVEN PLAIDS

Matching plaids requires additional fabric if the pattern is uneven. **Even plaids** contain a balanced arrangement of stripes on each side of the dominant horizontal and vertical bars. These types of patterns are easy to match. **Uneven plaids** vary in the arrangement of stripes on each side of the dominant horizontal and/or vertical bar. Uneven plaids require additional fabric for matching and sometimes limit the extent to which matching is possible. For example, uneven plaids printed on a fabric with a right and wrong side cannot radiate from center front but must move continuously around the body. This causes the two vertical halves of a garment to appear dissimilar; they are not mirror images. Stripes and other patterns may also occur as even or uneven.

CRITERIA FOR MATCHING

One important criterion for matching patterned fabric is that the dominant bars of the pattern be placed attractively on the garment. When you squint your eyes, the dominant bars appear to stand out. Manufacturers usually place the dominant vertical bar down the center front and center back of the garment and down the center of the sleeve. The dominant horizontal bar should be placed in a flattering position, at the hemline if it is straight or only slightly curved, and perhaps avoiding the hipline, the fullest part of the abdomen, and the bustline. Different designers, given the same patterned fabric, may use it in different ways to create equally interesting and beautiful but unique garments.

WHERE MATCHING IS POSSIBLE

Another important criterion for matching a patterned fabric is that it be matched at all possible seams. Seams and locations where matching is expected include the following:

1. center front and center back

2. side seams

3. collar at center back (for collars that open in front); collar at center front (for collars that open in back)

4. armhole at bust/chest level

5. shaped facings

6. sleeve plackets

7. pockets and pocket flaps

8. two-piece outfits where they overlap, so that the pattern appears continuous from top to bottom.

Places where matching *cannot* be expected because of the varying angles include the following:

1. seams with darts (seams with horizontal darts can be matched below the darts)

2. any area which contains ease or gathers (for example, shoulder seams)

3. yokes (if the yoke is a dart substitute yoke)

4. armhole backs

5. armhole fronts above bust/chest level

6. raglan sleeves

7. cuffs

8. waistline seams and waistbands.

Partial matching may be achieved in many of these areas, which is more attractive than no attempt at matching. However, complete matching throughout a fitted garment is impossible if the garment parts are properly shaped and constructed.

The "V" formed when diagonal stripes are matched at seams, especially in skirts, is called a *chevron* (Figure 10-18). Chevrons can be cre-

ated on bias-cut skirts or straight-of-grain skirts if they are flared. Even patterns are easier to chevron than uneven patterns.

Some fabrics do not lend themselves to matching. For instance, prominently woven twills angled at other than 45 degrees cannot be symmetrically matched. The garment in Figure 10-19 is an example. Examine the pattern of the fabric closely, and you will see that the poor choice of the fabric makes an otherwise well-designed and constructed jacket rather unattractive. The two halves of the garment (front, collar, lapels, and sleeves) are not symmetrical; the twills run at varying angles.

WAYS MANUFACTURERS MINIMIZE MATCHING

Simple garments with few pattern pieces, seams, and details, require little additional fabric to match and are relatively easy to match compared to more complex garments. In many

Figure 10-18 *Plaids: (a) matched to form a chevron, and (b) unmatched.*

Figure 10-19 *Poor use of patterned fabric.*

cases, simple garment designs made of patterned fabrics are more attractive than complex garment designs made from the same fabric. A simple garment design lets the pattern do the talking without fighting with it for attention. The larger or more uneven the fabric pattern, the more this general rule holds true.

Manufacturers, especially those producing low- and moderate-price lines, sometimes make garments with unmatched patterns, a sign of low quality. A compromise is matching patterns in only the most noticeable places; for example, at the center front of a button-front shirt. Other manufacturers take advantage of techniques to reduce the amount of labor and fabric required for matching patterns, but still treat patterned-fabric garments attractively. They cut the garment or parts of the garment on the bias or from a coordinating solid-color fabric. Pockets, pocket flaps, collars, cuffs, yokes, button bands, and other small pieces are frequently handled this way. Bias-cut or solid-color details provide a suitably attractive alternative to matching patterns and reduce fabric and labor costs (Figure 10-20). They are superior to unmatched seams, but do not reflect the same level of cost and quality as when the manufacturer painstakingly matches each piece of the garment when cutting and sewing.

FABRICS WITH LARGE MOTIFS

Garments cut from fabrics with large motifs, such as prominent florals or paisleys, require thoughtful planning. Simple garments with limited numbers of seams tend to complement such fabrics. If highly visible seams are involved, matching of the motifs may be advisable to prevent a broken-up appearance. For example, lace fabrics with large motifs look better if matched at seams, important in bridal and formal gowns. Squinting at the fabric may help in checking the balance of the motifs on the overall garment. Prominent motifs should not be placed over the bust or buttocks without recognizing the unflattering effect. Motifs may be centered on the chest, sleeves, or other garment parts. Of course, positioning the motifs in this way lowers material utilization, increasing costs.

Figure 10-20 Pockets, pocket flaps and yokes cut on the bias to minimize plaid matching costs.

Summary

Functional and decorative details on a garment enhance functional and aesthetic performance. Details add to cost and, generally, to quality.

Functional details include features that increase the usefulness, durability, or some other aspect of garment function. Reinforcing details reinforce stress points. Belt loops should be securely attached; a belt loop is needed at the center back of the garment. Weights contribute to the drape of the garment. Specialized, functional details improve the function of occupational clothing; dressy clothing; lingerie; active sportswear; childrenswear; clothing for mothers-to-be, new mothers; and clothing for people with handicaps and other special needs.

Decorative details make the garment attractive. Trims should be compatible with the wear and care of the garment. The fiber content, complexity, width, fullness, and method of application affect the cost of adding narrow fabric trims to a garment. Ribbon is a narrow, woven trim; braid, a narrow, braided trim; lace, a narrow lace fabric; piping, a narrow, folded fabric in a seam; and corded piping has a cord in it.

Some decorative details are constructed as part of the garment. Tucks are stitched folds in the garment. Pleats are unstitched folds in the garment. All pleats are variations of the basic knife pleat. Tucks and pleats increase fabric costs significantly. Full and double ruffles are more costly but more attractive than skimpy and single ruffles. Bows on garments should be finished so they do not ravel in use. A belt attached to a garment generally increases its hanger appeal and salability. Appliqués are fabric patches applied to garments, usually with stitches.

Nonfabric trims include beads, sequins, rhinestones, metal studs, feathers, jewels, and pearls, as well as dyed and printed designs. Stitching trims are ornamental stitchings. Top-stitching is straight stitches that accent the garment. Embroidery stitches form a decorative design. Smocking pleats the fabric with decorative stitches. Shirring is rows of permanent gathers. Hemstitching and fagoting appear similar, but hemstitching involves only one piece of fabric whereas fagoting holds together two pieces of fabric. Both expose the area beneath the decorative stitches. Quilting produces a raised design on multiple plies of fabric.

Patterns such as plaids, stripes, and checks should be matched at most seams of the garment. Matching the pattern adds to fabric and labor costs. The dominant bars of the pattern should be thoughtfully placed on the garment. Manufacturers may cut some garment pieces on the bias or from solid-color fabrics to minimize the need for matching. Matched patterns indicate quality. Patterned fabrics are most suitable for simple garments with few seams.

Details Quality Checklist

If you can answer yes to each of the following questions regarding the garment you are evaluating, it contains high-quality details.

- Will the details withstand the same wear and care as the garment?
- Are the details properly positioned and neatly executed?
- Are practical details included whenever they would enhance the function of the garment?

- Are decorative details included whenever they would enhance garment appearance?
- Are decorative trims and ruffles even in width, fully and evenly gathered, and securely applied?
- Are trims mittered at corners to avoid bulk and eased or stretched around curves to avoid distortion?
- Are trims sewn on, not glued on?
- Are the ends of ribbons and other trims finished to prevent raveling?
- Is embroidery dense, smooth, and backed with interfacing?
- Is topstitching even and straight?
- Are pleats and tucks even and on-grain?
- Are pleats full-depth?
- Are bows full and preferably cut on the bias?
- Are belts stitched, not glued?
- Are belt loops securely attached?
- Are there enough belt loops to support the belt, including one at the center back of pants and skirts?
- Are linear patterns over one-quarter inch matched at all major seams where matching is possible?
- Are patterns, including large motifs and the dominant bars of plaids, positioned attractively on the garment?

New Terms

If you can define these terms and differentiate between related terms, you have gained a good working vocabulary for discussing the topics in this chapter. The terms are listed in the order in which they appear in the chapter.

detail
reinforcement
tack
heel guard/kick tape
loop
belt loop
weights
self-help features
stretch panel
trim

ribbon
braid
lace trim
allover lace
tuck
pleat
crease
ruffle/flounce
bow
belt
appliqué
emblem
nonfabric trim
ornamental stitching (OS)
topstitching/accent stitching
edgestitching
embroidery
cutwork
monogram
trapunto
smocking
shirring
hemstitching
fagoting
quilting
pattern matching
even plaid
uneven plaid

Review Questions

1. How are rivets different from tacks and bar tacks?

2. Why should there be a belt loop in the center back of the garment?

3. What is the purpose of hanger loops?

4. What are the advantages and disadvantages of growth tucks?

5. List the criteria that garment trims should meet.

6. Differentiate between insertion lace, galloon lace, lace edging, beading, and medallion lace.

7. How is piping different from corded piping?

8. List the ways manufacturers cut the cost of matching patterned fabrics (e.g., plaids)?

9. What are the considerations when cutting garments from a fabric with a large motif?

10. How are appliqués different from monograms?

11. How is hemstitching different from fagoting?

12. List ten examples of functional details.

Activities

1. Examine low-price and high-price plaid garments. Are the plaids matched? Why or why not?

2. Examine low-price and high-price pairs of jeans. Where are reinforcements used? Are there other locations where you would recommend that reinforcements be placed?

3. Using paper, fold an example of each tuck and pleat type discussed in this chapter.

4. Examine low-price and high-price men's suit pants. Can you find any with heel guards? At what price line? How many belt loops do the pants have? Do they have a belt loop at center back?

5. Examine low-price and high-price bridal gowns. Can you find any with dress shields? Wrist loops or other functional techniques to deal with a long train? Lingerie strap keepers? What other practical details can you find? Are there any differences between price lines in the amount or quality of functional details? Decorative details?

6. Study low-price and high-price maternity garments. What functional details are used? Are there differences between price lines? In general, are these garments constructed as well as comparable nonmaternity garments in the same store? Why or why not?

7. Find garments containing the following trims, and evaluate the quality of the trim and its application:
  a. grosgrain ribbon
  b. satin ribbon
  c. velvet ribbon
  d. novelty ribbon
  e. picot-edge ribbon
  f. soutache braid
  g. middy braid
  h. loop braid
  i. scrolling
  j. gimp

k. foldover braid
l. rickrack
m. piping
n. corded piping

8. Examine low-price and high-price garments with bows made of ribbon. Are the ends of the ribbons treated to prevent raveling?

9. Find examples of the following decorative details that are constructed as part of the garment, and evaluate the quality of the detail and its application:
a. different types of tucks
b. different types of pleats
c. creases

d. ruffles
e. bows
f. belts

10. Find examples of the following stitching trims and evaluate them:
a. topstitching
b. edgestitching
c. cutwork
d. smocking
e. shirring

11. Evaluate the appliqués on low-price and high-price childrenswear. What differences, if any, did you find?

11

Closures: Securing Garment Openings

CHAPTER OBJECTIVES

1. Identify types of closures.
2. Discuss choice of closure and method of application suitable for end use.
3. Evaluate cost and quality of various closures.

Closures are critical to garment quality. Although consumers rarely purchase garments based on the closures, they often discard garments upon the failure of the closures. Although a seemingly minor component of garments, when closures malfunction, garments become unwearable. Therefore, the dependable functioning of closures is vital to ultimate consumer satisfaction.

Closures refer to the fasteners that secure garment openings. Closures unfasten to enlarge the garment for dressing and undressing, and then fasten to make the garment fit the body. Manufacturers use a wide variety of closures in ready-to-wear apparel. Closures include buttons and buttonholes or loops, zippers, hooks and eyes, snaps, and other fasteners.

The aesthetic and functional performance standards for closures are based on the end use, care, design, and fabric of the garment. To some extent, tradition indicates whether to use buttons, a zipper, or some other type of closure in a garment. For example, dress shirts are usually buttoned and pants are usually zipped. Fashion also influences the choice of closure.

Cost limitations are a factor when choosing closures; high-price garments are more likely to contain costly closures than low-price garments. Cost does not directly predict the quality of a closure, but the two are often related. All closures add to the cost of the garment, but the cost varies depending upon the particular closure and the amount of labor required to apply it to the garment. Manufacturers usually choose the closure and method of application that functions adequately at the lowest cost.

Custom decrees a sex distinction in the way the front closures of shirts, blouses, jackets, and coats are lapped; the right half of the garment laps over the left for garments intended for females, and the left half laps over the right for garments intended for males. There is no reason for this practice other than tradition. Knowledge of the way garments lap helps differentiate between garments intended for females and males.

Most women have worn clothing intended for males during their lifetime and thus accept garments that lap either way. However, most men are socialized to fasten all their garments with the left half lapped over the right. They find it extremely awkward to do otherwise. The occasional garment intended for males that mistakenly laps right over left may be rejected by the male consumer.

For slacks and skirts, because most people are right-handed, most center front openings lap left over right. Some bottoms intended for females lap right over left, but this is increasingly rare. At center back, the lapping of the garment varies. Side closures of garments fasten with the front portion of the garment lapping over the back of the garment for a smooth and attractive appearance. Side closures generally fasten on the left side for convenience because the majority of consumers are right-handed. *Surplice* or asymmetrically lapped closures cost more than symmetrical ones.

Aesthetic Performance of Closures

The closure should aesthetically harmonize with the garment; the color, size, shape, texture, and application of the closure should complement the design and fabric of the garment. An attractive, fashionable closure helps sell the garment. A savvy merchandiser knows when to invest in a better closure; for example, adding expensive buttons to improve the appearance of an otherwise ordinary garment so that it commands a higher selling price.

The application of the closure should be neat, smooth, and attractive. For example, if both sides of an opening are not exactly the same length, the fabric above and below the closure bubbles or gapes. This problem also arises when buttons and buttonholes or loops, the two halves of snaps, or hooks and eyes are improperly aligned, or when the operator attaches a zipper slider unevenly.

Functional Performance of Closures

Functional performance considerations also help determine the best closure. For example, tiny buttons at the center back of the garment are unacceptable in clothing for young children or people with limited arm mobility if they are to dress independently. All closures and applications should be comfortable, not bulky or irritating to the skin. And closures should be positioned so that the garment fits as intended.

Closures must be compatible with the garment in terms of wear and care. Quality-conscious manufacturers test closures for color-fastness, strength and durability, and resistance to heat, water, bleach, and other elements. Closures that rust, corrode, harden, break, crack, peel, melt, fade, or discolor during wear or when laundered or dry-cleaned detract from garment appearance, fit, and function. These problems with closures are especially prevalent in garment-washed apparel (see Chapter 4).

Sometimes the application of the closure is more likely to fail than the closure itself; for example, the common occurrence of buttons falling off because of insecure attachment. Consumers can sew on new buttons, but the replacement of some closures—zippers, for instance—involves too much time and skill for the average consumer to justify. In such cases, the garment is discarded as unwearable.

Physical Features of Closures

The attractiveness, utility, and durability of a closure is determined by the physical features of the closure. Physical features include the type, size, and material of the closure, and its placement, attachment, and reinforcement.

BUTTONS

Buttons have been widely used as garment closures since the Middle Ages. Most buttons are both a decorative feature of the garment as well as a functional closure. However, some buttons are strictly functional; for example, concealed button closures and buttons inside double-breasted garments to help them hang smoothly. And other buttons are strictly decorative, for example, the nonfunctional buttons at the wrist of most suit and sport jacket sleeves. These buttons imitate the functional *and* decorative buttons on the sleeves of high-price jackets, which increases costs because they require functional buttonholes. A compromise that achieves the same look is nonfunctional buttons sewn on closed, nonfunctional buttonholes.

Composition of Buttons. The least costly buttons are molded of plastic, or stamped out of a sheet of plastic. Elaborate plastic buttons cost extra. Plastic buttons can be dyed any color. They often imitate buttons made of natural materials. Plastic buttons are more uniform than natural-material buttons, but often are considered less beautiful (Figure 11-1).

Natural-material buttons comprise only about 10 percent of all buttons (Frings 1987). Buttons made of natural materials, such as wood, animal horn, leather, pearl, or metal, cost more than plastic buttons. Natural-material buttons are confined to high-price lines.

Metal buttons are made by stamping out a metal face and attaching it to a metal base. They are more durable and more expensive than metalized buttons, which consist of a metal coating over a plastic base. Metalized buttons have a tendency to chip and peel.

Covered buttons are covered with fabric. Covered buttons that match the garment utilize fabric scraps, but nevertheless require extra labor. They are an excellent choice when the desired color of button is difficult to find or when the button needs to blend in with the garment.

Typically, buttons made from leather or wood and some other buttons, such as those with rhinestones or iridescent coatings, are not washable. Buttons may be damaged by dry cleaning solvents. If the buttons will not withstand the same care as the garment, they may be tempo-

Figure 11-1 Buttons: (a) wood, (b) leather, (c) mother of pearl, (d) horn, (e) bone, (f) metal, (g) self-covered, (h) cleated on, (i) rhinestone, (j) toggle for removable buttons, (k) plastic eyed, and (l) plastic shank.

rarily attached with small clips so the consumer can remove the buttons each time the garment is cleaned. Removable buttons increase costs. *Studs* or *cuff links* are another alternative to permanent buttons; they are clasped through buttonholes in the layers being joined.

Button Size. The size of buttons is measured in **lignes** (pronounced lines), with 40 lignes equal to a diameter of 1 inch. For example, a 30 ligne button is three-quarters of an inch in diameter. Large buttons cost more than small buttons. Button size should be proportional to the size of the garment. Buttons about one-half inch in diameter are easy for preschoolers to manipulate; people with arthritis may require larger buttons.

The optimum number of buttons on a garment depends upon the size of the button and the fit of the garment. In general, large buttons are placed farther apart than small buttons. Garments designed to fit the body loosely require fewer buttons than garments that conform to the body, which require closely spaced buttons to prevent gaping. An example of this concept is that there are as many buttons on the 6-inch fly of a pair of close-fitting jeans as on the 18-inch front of a loose-fitting blouse.

Button Placement. *A button should be positioned approximately even with each horizontal stress point—bust/chest, waist, and hip levels.* Sometimes manufacturers fail to locate buttons at these stress points to reduce the total number of buttons. This is evident when a blouse with too few buttons gapes at the bust* (Figure 11-2). Manufacturers sometimes eliminate the button at hip level on shirts because this lower button does not show when the shirttail is tucked; this saves the producer money. However, the lower button preserves a straight, undistorted center front line and helps the shirttail stay tucked. For these reasons, shirts with seven-button fronts are of higher quality than shirts with six-button fronts.

Manufacturers do not place a button at waist level if it interferes with the wearing of a waistband or belt. A button should not be positioned on the hem of a garment; the lowest button usually falls at least four to six inches from the hem. The buttons on jacket sleeves are an exception; these buttons are set close together, with the lower button no more than three-quarters of an inch from the bottom of the sleeve. High-quality men's suit jacket sleeves traditionally have four buttons and women's suit jacket sleeves three buttons; men's sport coats often have only two buttons per sleeve.

Extra Buttons. Manufacturers sometimes provide an *extra button(s)* with a garment in case a button is lost. These buttons may be sewn inside the garment or attached with the hang tag. Extra buttons are highly visible and consumers often associate them with quality, although manufacturers of low-price garments sometimes attach extra buttons as an inexpensive way to imitate high-price lines.

Button Attachment. Buttons are usually sewn to the garment with a machine stitch similar to a bar tack. In highly mechanized operations, the buttons automatically feed from a hopper and are held in place by a special attachment for sewing. In other operations, operators hand-feed the buttons one at a time into the sewing machine.

A common misconception is that the more tightly a button is sewn on, the better. In fact, a button sewn on too tightly is more likely to pop off, because when the wearer moves, the button cannot give. Eyed buttons sewn tightly to a garment tend to distort the buttonhole and dent the surrounding fabric, particularly if the fabric is heavy or bulky, giving a pulled or drawn look.

In general, the greater the number of stitches used to sew on a button, the more secure its attachment. For example, Huntington Clothiers and Shirtmakers advertises that the buttons on the shirts it makes are "cross-stitched sixteen times." As important as the number of stitches used is whether the stitches are secured with *tacking stitches.* Tacking stitches are those made straight up and down after the button is sewn on, to secure the stitches. Consumers frequently complain that buttons fall off shortly after a garment is purchased; tacking prevents this. Unfortunately, many manufacturers eliminate the tacking step in the interest of saving a fraction of thread and operator time. Extra strong thread also contributes to the secure attachment of buttons, especially those receiving heavy use.

Some buttons are not sewn on, but cleated into the fabric mechanically. The security of cleated-on buttons is even more critical than that of sewn-on buttons. If a cleated-on button falls off, the consumer has no means of replacing it. Cleating on buttons tends to be a more secure attachment than sewing.

* NOTE: Gaping also may result when a wearer has a higher or lower bustline than that for which the garment is designed.

Figure 11-2 *Blouse gapes because it needs a button at bust level.*

Buttons should be *in registration* or properly oriented when they are attached. For example, an elephant-shaped button should be attached so the elephant appears to stand on its feet, not on its head.

Button Types. Buttons are either of the eyed or shank variety. Eyed buttons are slightly more casual looking than shank buttons. Shank buttons cost more to buy. Shank buttons also require more labor to attach because the fabric must be folded in exactly the right place by the operator before the buttons are sewn on. However, you can find both eyed and shank buttons on clothing of all types and at all price lines.

Eyed Buttons. **Eyed buttons,** also called *holed* or *sew-through* buttons, usually have two or four holes. When an eyed button is sewn on, the stitches should be parallel with the buttonhole. This allows the button to float in the buttonhole without distorting it.

Four-eyed buttons are more securely attached than two-eyed buttons because they are essentially sewn on twice. Manufacturers usually sew on four-eyed buttons with the holes stitched as independent pairs. Thread dragging from one pair of holes to the other is aesthetically undesirable and represents a lack of attention to detail (Figure 11-5). For a decorative look, four-eyed buttons may be sewn on with stitches forming a square or an arrow pattern. Most manufacturers promote cross-stitching as the strongest method for sewing on a four-eyed button.

To prevent distortion of the surrounding fabric, eyed buttons on garments made of heavy or bulky fabrics can be sewn on with a thread shank. A wrapped **thread shank** is created when a button is sewn on loosely and extra thread is wrapped around the stitches between the button and the garment, suspending the button away from the fabric (Figure 11-3). A thread shank allows the button to rise above the buttonhole, and the button tends to stay on longer because it has freedom of movement. So a thread shank is a mark of quality. A special machine sews on the button and constructs a wrapped thread shank, but this method remains more costly than sewing a button on flat.

The shank should not be so long that the button droops when buttoned. A button never to be buttoned should not have a shank, or the button will droop. For example, on double-breasted jackets with one row of functional but-

Figure 11-3 *(a) eyed button with thread shank, and (b) shank button.*

tons and one row of nonfunctional buttons, the functional buttons should have thread shanks and the nonfunctional buttons should not.

Shank Buttons. **Shank buttons** have a stem of plastic, metal, or cloth built into the button (Figure 11-3). The button is sewn to the garment through the shank. The shank should be sewn on parallel to the buttonhole.

A shank button has the same advantages of an eyed button with a thread shank. The button rises above the buttonhole and does not distort it. The button gives with the wearer's movements rather than popping off, so shank buttons stay on longer. Yet shank buttons found on extremely heavy or bulky fabrics may need a thread shank *in addition to* the built-in shank, a mark of cost and quality.

Some shanks, especially metal ones, sever the thread attaching the button to the garment; extra strong thread may be required. For durability, a shank button may be attached with a metal toggle rather than sewn onto the garment, but this feature is found only in high-price lines. Nylon shanks are stronger, lighter, and cheaper than metal shanks and less likely to cut the thread. Some shank buttons, such as those on denim jeans and work clothing, are cleated into the fabric.

Shank buttons tend to be bulkier than eyed buttons. A flat, eyed button is best for the lower button of shirts and blouses to be tucked in, to avoid a lump showing on the outside of the outer garment. Concealed button closures call for flat, eyed buttons so the buttons do not make the fabric over the buttons appear lumpy. On garments that button in back, flat, eyed buttons offer greater comfort when sitting or leaning back than do shank buttons. Cloth shanks offer greater comfort in such cases than do plastic or metal shanks.

Button Area Reinforcement. Interfacing should be used in button areas to reinforce the buttons (Figure 8-15). For example, button-down collars on high-quality shirts feature a small circle of interfacing beneath the collar button for reinforcement (Figure 11-4). The stress on a button sewn to only the fabric of the garment causes the fabric to tear. Two plies of fabric, if available, plus a ply of interfacing provide the ideal base for a button.

On most garments, manufacturers sew through all available fabric plies and the interfacing when applying buttons, for maximum strength. In high-quality coats and suits, buttons may be sewn through every ply except the facing. This technique trades off some durability for aesthetics because it prevents stitches from showing on the inside of the garment when it is worn unbuttoned. Sewing on buttons in this way is costly because it requires skilled labor.

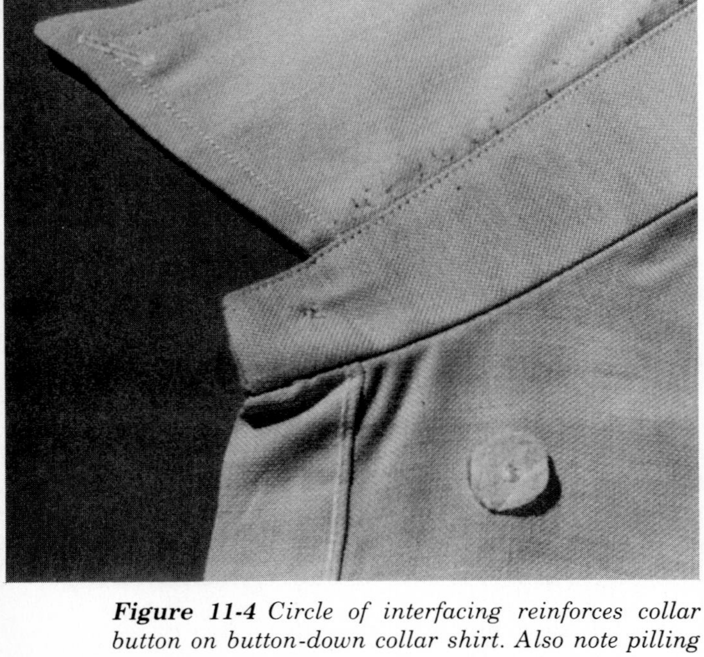

Backing Buttons. When buttons are under heavy strain or are sewn to soft fabrics, the stress may be too great for fabric and interfacing alone to support. A flat, eyed **backing button** or *reinforcement button* may be sewn on with the button, under the fabric behind the button (Figure 11-5). The backing button absorbs the stress instead of the fabric and increases the durability of the closure. Backing buttons, a sign of quality, are found mainly on coats. A square of fabric or ribbon may be substituted for a backing button in other types of garments for softer reinforcing and less bulk.

Buttonhole Length. The length of a buttonhole should be long enough so the button can slip through easily without strain or excessive wear on the buttonhole. However, a buttonhole that is too long detracts from fit and appearance, and the button does not stay buttoned. The rule for establishing buttonhole length is that it should equal the diameter plus the thickness of the button (Figure 11-6). A *ball button,* a totally round button, requires a buttonhole with a length equal to the circumference of the button. If a button is rough or unusually shaped, the buttonhole requires additional length so the button slips through easily. A button that is too rough or unusually shaped to slide easily through a buttonhole requires a snap as the functional closure; the button is then sewn over the snap for decorative effect.

Figure 11-4 Circle of interfacing reinforces collar button on button-down collar shirt. Also note pilling on collar.

Figure 11-5 Button with backing button.

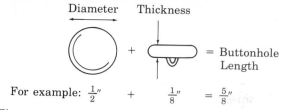

Diameter Thickness

$$\frac{1}{2}'' \quad + \quad \frac{1}{8}'' \quad = \quad \frac{5}{8}''$$

For example: $\frac{1}{2}''$ + $\frac{1}{8}''$ = $\frac{5}{8}''$

Figure 11-6 *Formula for buttonhole length.*

Buttonhole Direction. Horizontal buttonholes tend to stay buttoned. The button moves to the end of the buttonhole, which absorbs the stress when the wearer moves. If the buttonhole is vertical, the button tends to slip out of the buttonhole when horizontal stress is applied. Large, vertical buttonholes are especially vulnerable to this problem. Thus, tight-fitting clothing or areas under stress require horizontal buttonholes to keep the garment buttoned; coats, jackets, neckbands, cuffs, pants plackets, and waistbands use horizontal buttonholes. Horizontal buttonholes require more fabric than vertical ones because of the wider facing required.

Vertical buttonholes are appropriate when aesthetics is important, and when the area is loosely fitted and undergoes little stress. For example, most center front closures, especially button bands, look more attractive with vertical than with horizontal buttonholes. For garments made of knit fabrics, buttonholes parallel to the crosswise direction of the knit tend to stretch and ripple, so most buttonholes in knit-fabric garments are vertical.

Underlaps and Overlaps. Garments lap where buttons and buttonholes are used. The portion of the lap that extends beyond the button is the *underlap;* the part that extends beyond the buttonhole is the *overlap.* When the underlap and overlap are lapped, the garment fits properly. The width of these extensions depends on the size of the buttons. The underlap and overlap extensions should equal the radius of the button plus one-quarter to one-half inch. In the case of large buttons, the underlap may need to be slightly wider. Narrow extensions conserve fabric but do not provide for adequate coverage of the opening, do not support the button well, and look unattractive if the button extends beyond the extension.

Buttonhole Placement. Buttonholes should be spaced exactly as far apart as the corresponding buttons to avoid straining or bubbling be-

tween buttonholes (Figure 11-7). Manufacturers place buttonholes on the straight-of-grain of the fabric for maximum durability and shape retention. A horizontal buttonhole should begin one-eighth inch beyond the center front, center back, or lap line and extend into the body of the garment. The corresponding button is located directly across from the buttonhole, on the center front line, center back line, or other lap line. A vertical buttonhole should be located exactly on the lap line. The corresponding button is located on the lap line and one-eighth inch below the top edge of the buttonhole. If these rules are followed, the lap lines of the buttoned garment align and the garment fits as intended (Figure 11-8). These guidelines are helpful when moving a button during alteration. If they are ignored, as when buttons are placed in the middle of buttonholes, gravity and the stress of use cause the buttons to go to the ends of the buttonholes, and the garment will fit improperly.

Thread Buttonholes. Most buttonholes are made of thread. Special machines, used to make thread buttonholes, are programmed to cut open and stitch the buttonholes automatically. The machine makes six buttonholes in about 20 seconds. A sharp knife blade cuts the buttonholes open. If the knife blade dulls, the surrounding fabric may be damaged—knit fabrics run and woven fabrics exhibit pulls.

In general, the denser the stitches of a buttonhole, the more durable the buttonhole. Dense stitches withstand heavy use and prevent the fabric from fraying. The density of the buttonhole stitches is a quick clue to the overall level of garment quality (Figure 11-9). Manufacturers

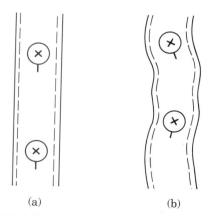

(a)   (b)

Figure 11-7 *Buttonholes should be spaced the same as the corresponding buttons to avoid the fabric bubbling between buttonholes as it does here.*

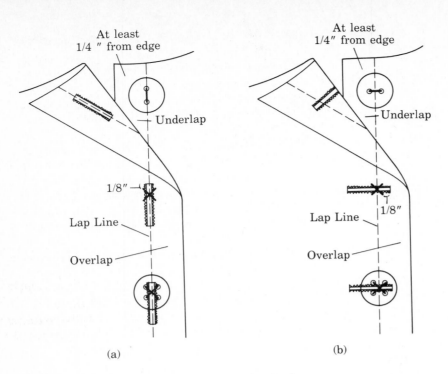

Figure 11-8 *Placement of buttons and buttonholes.*

find it much faster and therefore less costly to put fewer stitches in a buttonhole, for the same reasons that fewer stitches per inch reduce costs. A few quality-oriented manufacturers and retailers have advertised the number of stitches in their buttonholes to recommend the durability of their products. For example, Huntington Clothiers and Shirtmakers advertises that the buttonholes on the shirts it makes have "144 stitches for nonravel wearing," and Lands' End advertises a dress shirt with "130 locked stitches on each buttonhole." Lockstitched buttonholes are more durable than chainstitched buttonholes, which are easily unraveled.

Some fabrics are damaged by too-dense buttonhole stitches. For example, knits are prone to needle cutting due to dense stitches. Button-

holes must be completely surrounded with stitches. If not, fraying or tearing of the fabric is likely during use.

Buttonhole Shape. Most thread buttonholes are rectangular, especially on shirts, blouses, and dresses (Figure 11-9). A rectangular buttonhole is formed by two rows of zigzag stitches, with bar tacks at each end to withstand the stress of use.

Oval (or *fan*) and **keyhole buttonholes** are named for their characteristic shapes (Figure 11-10). The rounded ends allow the button to ride in the buttonhole without distorting the garment. Manufacturers use oval and keyhole buttonholes on tailored jackets and coats and on waistbands and pocket flaps of jeans and slacks. Oval and keyhole buttonholes are created with machine zigzag stitches or with machine stitches simulating the stitches in hand-worked buttonholes. When stitched with a machine zigzag stitch, an oval or keyhole buttonhole is not particularly durable. It does not have the bar tack to withstand stress that a rectangular buttonhole has. Stitching the buttonhole with a purled edge to imitate a hand-worked buttonhole increases the attractiveness and durability of oval and keyhole buttonholes.

Hand-Worked Buttonholes. Hand-worked (or hand-purled) **buttonholes** are increasingly rare, confined mainly to high-price menswear,

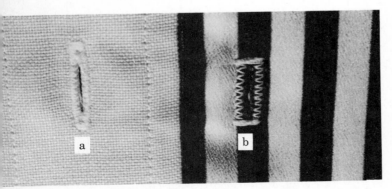

Figure 11-9 *Buttonholes: (a) densely stitched, on band, and (b) sparsely stitched, on French front.*

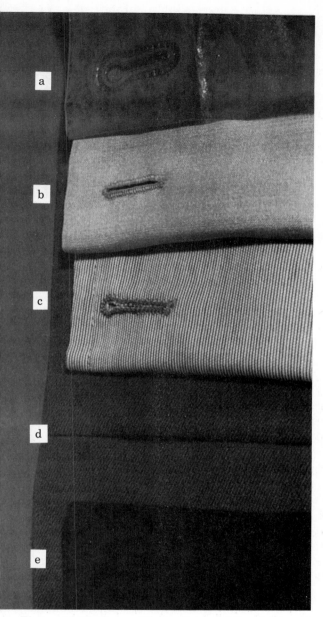

Figure 11-10 Types of buttonholes: (a) fused, (b) oval, (c) keyhole, (d) in-seam, and (e) bound.

fine imported baby clothes, and couture clothing. The purled edge consists of a series of individually knotted stitches. The stitches of hand-worked buttonholes are more irregular than machine-stitched imitations, but the two are difficult to tell apart. Because they are not as durable as machine imitations, there is no clear advantage to hand-worked buttonholes. However, they are very labor intensive and costly and therefore may influence the consumer's perception of quality if you call attention to them.

Buttonhole twist thread may be used to stitch a buttonhole, especially if the buttonhole has a purled edge. *Buttonhole twist* is a heavy, lustrous thread. It reinforces the buttonhole and provides a decorative appearance.

Bound Buttonholes. Bound buttonholes, made of fabric, are much less common than thread buttonholes. They are confined to high-price lines because of their labor intensity.

A **bound buttonhole** is a rectangular hole in the garment fabric, which is bound or faced, and backed with narrow strips of fabric that meet like lips to cover the opening (Figure 11-10). The fabric lips abut, allowing a slit for the button to pass through. A bound buttonhole resembles a miniature, double-welt pocket. It requires many steps to complete. Even when automated, a bound buttonhole is much more costly to produce than a thread buttonhole.

A well-made bound buttonhole is a perfect rectangle with even lips that meet but do not overlap. The buttonhole should not fray or expose any raw edges. A bound buttonhole is not more durable than a thread buttonhole; its primary advantage is its neat, threadless appearance. Especially in heavy fabrics, a bound buttonhole results in a smoother appearance than a regular buttonhole because it does not compress the fabric.

Bound buttonholes are prestigious because of the costly production. Bound buttonholes were once a common mark of quality in better lines of clothing. However, they are increasingly rare. They are found on some high-price and couture jackets and coats for women; they are not used much in menswear.

Slit Buttonholes. Leather and leatherlike garments usually require special buttonholes. Conventional buttonholes with dense stitches pierce the leather too many times and weaken it. Because leather does not ravel, **slit buttonholes** with raw edges are perfectly acceptable. A rectangle of machine stitching with a slit centered in the rectangle serves as a low-bulk buttonhole for leather garments. A rectangle cut in the leather with narrow strips of leather glued to the back to form lips resembles a bound buttonhole. Bound buttonholes are also appropriate for use in leather and leatherlike garments.

Faced Slit Buttonholes. A narrow, **faced slit** is the buttonhole sometimes found in high-price European clothing. Faced slits require more steps and are therefore more costly to produce than thread buttonholes, but are easier and less costly to make than bound buttonholes.

In-Seam Buttonholes. Another form of buttonhole is the **in-seam buttonhole** or *slot* buttonhole. In-seam buttonholes are rare because they are limited to designs with a seam in exactly the right location, directly over the buttons. The operator leaves the seam partially unstitched, at intervals, to create the buttonholes (Figure 11-10). In-seam buttonholes are smooth, inconspicuous, and less costly to produce than other types of buttonholes. A disadvantage is that they cannot withstand as much stress as thread buttonholes.

Fused Buttonholes. Thermoplastic (heat sensitive) fabrics may contain **fused buttonholes.** A fused buttonhole is formed by embossing the fabric with a hot die which is patterned to resemble a stitched or bound buttonhole (Figure 11-10). A slit in the fabric allows the button to slip through. In vinyls and other film fabrics, fused buttonholes are more durable than buttonholes with stitches, which would pierce and weaken the fabric. Fused buttonholes are mainly confined to low-price lines, especially raingear or other garments made entirely of thermoplastic fabrics. They do not have good consumer acceptance at high-price lines or in other types of garments, perhaps because of the stiffness and the association with low-price lines.

Buttonhole Area Reinforcement. Buttonholes should be reinforced with interfacing. Buttonholes without interfacing are not durable; they become distorted and tear away from the garment. If a strip of interfacing under a row of buttons interferes with the drape or hang of a garment made of a knit or other soft fabric, the manufacturer may place individual pieces of interfacing under each buttonhole. Most manufacturers recognize the need for interfacing in button and buttonhole areas and they seldom omit it, although they may use an interfacing with inadequate support. Figure 11-11 illustrates how a fabric with inadequate interfacing stretches and ripples in the buttonhole area.

Corded buttonholes are sometimes found in tailored garments. In a corded buttonhole, a narrow diameter cording is laid in as the buttonhole is stitched. The stitches of the buttonhole cover the cording. This creates a decorative, raised

Figure 11-11 *Inadequately interfaced buttonhole.*

effect, giving the buttonhole dimension. The cording absorbs some of the stress of use, reinforcing the buttonhole and preventing stretch.

Loops. **Button loops** are used in some garment designs, instead of buttonholes, to fasten buttons. When the two edges to be joined meet but do not lap, a buttonhole cannot be used, but a loop may be used. Loops are made of narrow tubes of bias fabric; strips of cording, braid, or elastic; or thread chains. They must have adequate size or elasticity to slip over the button. In a series, loops should be evenly spaced and identical in size; to ensure this, some manufacturers use presized, prespaced looping; for example, on the backs of wedding gowns with closely spaced loops. Loop closures are decorative as well as functional. However, they are suited only to areas that receive limited stress because they are unable to hold edges in place as precisely as do buttonholes. For this reason, loops are inappropriate as closures in areas where modesty is important. Short, wide loops hold the edges together better than do long, narrow loops (Figure 11-12). Careful placement of the corresponding button is important for attractive and functional loop closures.

When the operator sews loops into a seam, both ends of the loop should be caught securely. If not, when the loops are stressed by movement or a tight fit, they pull out of the seam.

A **frog** is a highly decorative button-and-loop closure. Frogs are made of elaborately coiled cord or braid (Figure 11-13). They are commonly used in combination with a *Chinese ball button,* which is cord or braid knotted into a ball.

A **toggle** is a decorative button-and-loop closure sewn to the face of coats, jackets, and other garments, especially those of heavy fabrics (Figure 11-13). Toggles consist of two loops; one has

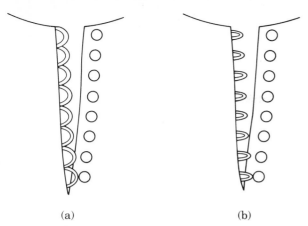

(a)   (b)

Figure 11-12 (a) Loops that are short and wide offer a more secure closure than do (b) loops that are long and narrow.

a rod-shaped button attached to it. When closed, a toggle looks like two symmetrical loops over the same button.

ZIPPERS

Zippers are a fast, easy means of getting in and out of garments. They have been widely used in ready-to-wear apparel since the 1930s; they have continued to grow lighter, more supple, and less obvious since their invention around 1900.

Because of their somewhat stiff nature, zippers are more appropriate than buttons for fairly flat areas within garments. Zippers are not well-suited to bloused areas because the stiffness interferes with the intended drape of the fabric and results in zipper hump. **Zipper hump** is the term for a wavy zipper chain (Figure 4-3). It detracts from the appearance of the garment and stresses the zipper. Although zipper hump may be due to installation in a bias seam, stretching the garment during installation, zipper tape shrinkage, or garment shrinkage, it also results from using a zipper in a fabric that is too soft to support a zipper, for example, a lightweight knit. In such situations, buttons or other closures are preferable to zippers.

Manufacturers usually choose zippers over buttons for close-fitting garments. Zippers are the better choice because, unless buttons are very closely spaced on such garments, the opening tends to gape. For example, the fitted bodices of some wedding gowns are buttoned all the way down the back with closely spaced buttons. Others combine a zipper for smooth, nongaping closure with nonfunctional buttons sewn on for

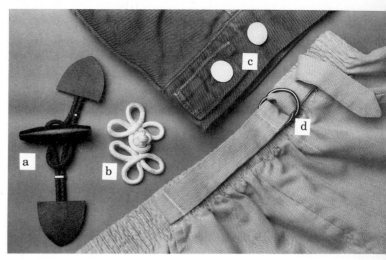

Figure 11-13 Closures: (a) toggle, (b) frog, (c) tab with button, and (d) d-ring.

a traditional, decorative look. The choice of closure depends on whether the opening is in the front or back of the garment. Zippers are usually more smooth and comfortable to lean against than buttons, so they are often best for back closures. Buttons are decorative and thus are often the choice for front closures. Very plain buttons may cost less than a zipper, but elaborate buttons usually cost more than a zipper. Also, extra fabric and labor are required to produce button closures. Therefore, zipper closures are usually less costly than button closures.

Zipper Parts. The main parts of a zipper include the tape, chain, slider, pull, and top and bottom stops (Figure 11-14). The zipper chain is composed of either continuous elements or separate elements.

Zipper Tape. The **zipper tape** is the fabric portion, which is sewn to the garment. Garment facings or linings should be sewn to the zipper tape inside the garment as a final step in zipper application. The strength of the tape affects the strength of the zipper. Woven tapes, usually of a strong, twill weave, are heavy and stiff; they are used for metal zippers in applications requiring strength and durability. Woven zipper tapes are usually made of cotton fibers or a blend of cotton and synthetic fibers. Unless preshrunk by the manufacturer before installation, these zipper tapes may shrink when the garment is laundered, causing unsightly puckering. Knitted tapes are light and flexible; they are used for plastic zippers in applications subject to low

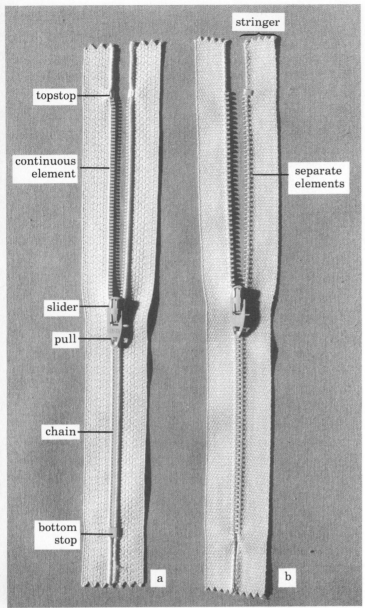

Figure 11-14 *Parts of a zipper: (a) continuous element zipper, and (b) separate element zipper.*

stress. Knitted tapes are made of synthetic fibers, usually polyester. Because synthetics can be heat set and stabilized, knitted tapes do not shrink. However, they are prone to yarn slippage, especially if low gauge and made of filament yarns. Thus, tapes with a sleazy hand should be avoided because if the yarns slip, the zipper element may become detached.

Zipper Chain. The **zipper chain** is the part of the zipper that interlocks when the zipper is closed. The zipper opening should be as long as the zipper chain. If the opening is too short, the

lower portion of the zipper is unduly stressed when the wearer dresses and undresses.

A common cause of zipper failure is *ratcheting* the zipper, or unzipping it by pulling the two sides apart rather than using the pull provided. Ratcheting damages the zipper chain and weakens the zipper. Few zippers are designed to withstand ratcheting. Ratcheting can occur in several ways. If the consumer does not fully zip and lock the zipper before laundering, ratcheting may occur. In addition, an unzipped zipper may snag the fabric of other garments in the load. When an operator in the factory pulls the zipper open incorrectly in the interest of speed, ratcheting occurs. A zipper also is ratcheted when the wearer gets dressed without fully unzipping the zipper first, or wears the garment without fastening the closure at the opening end to help absorb stress.

SEPARATE ELEMENTS. *Separate element* zippers are made up of separate **scoops,** the industry term for the *teeth* of a zipper. Separate element zippers are made by attaching the metal or plastic teeth to the zipper tape. The zipper elements are interlocked by the slider, which meshes them together to create the zipper chain. If a zipper element breaks off or pulls away from the tape, or if the elements somehow become unmeshed below the slider, the zipper no longer functions.

CONTINUOUS ELEMENT. *Continuous element* zippers or **coil zippers** are made by twisting a continuous strand of monofilament nylon into a spiral. A continuous element is attached to the zipper tape and enmeshed by the slider to create the zipper chain. Continuous element zippers do not have sharp edges, so they do not snag fabric or scratch the skin as single element zippers sometimes do. Continuous element zippers are lighter and more flexible than separate element zippers, so they are ideal for light- and medium-weight fabrics. Although continuous element zippers are strong, they cannot withstand as much stress as separate element zippers. Continuous element zippers tend to split apart when too much steady, transverse stress is applied. They are not suitable in heavy duty applications. However, because of their flexibility, they sometimes absorb sudden stress that would damage a separate element zipper. They also have the unique property of *self-healing,* by which they can be enmeshed again after splitting, unlike a separate element zipper, which is useless after it loses an element. However, this healing may be only temporary.

Zipper Slider. The **slider** is the portion of the zipper that glides up and down the chain, engaging and disengaging the two halves of the chain. The slider of the zipper has a **pull** or **tab** for easy grasping. This pull is usually unobtrusive, but occasionally is large and decorative. The pull of the zipper should fall approximately one-quarter inch below the seam above it. The slider should glide easily up and down the zipper chain. Sliders that have been crushed or spread in the manufacturing process may not glide easily. Loose, dangling threads also interfere with the slider action. The slider movement must adequately clear the fabric of the garment, of special concern if the zipper crosses a heavy or bulky seam.

Most zippers contain some sort of a locking mechanism within the slider, which prevents the zipper from unzipping by itself. The locking mechanism may be automatic, or the wearer may need to manually engage it by pressing the pull tab flat. Locking zippers withstand stress and stay zipped better than zippers without locking mechanisms. If the locking mechanism fails in a critical location, the zipper tends to ratchet open during wear, embarrassing the wearer and damaging the zipper chain.

Top and Bottom Stops. **Stops** prevent the slider from leaving the chain at either end of the zipper. Most zippers have both a top and bottom stop. A bottom stop applied directly over and enmeshing the lower teeth or coils is more durable than one with the stop placed below the zipper chain. A strong bottom stop, appropriately placed, may be the most important prevention of zipper failure. For applications that are open at the top, for example waistline or neckline applications, a bottom stop holds the two tracks together at the base, and a top stop prevents the slider of the zipper from going beyond the track at the upper edge. If no top stop is present, then the zipper elements should be caught in the seam (e.g., at the waistband) to form a stop so the slider cannot come off. When including zippers in a seam, most nylon chains can be sewn across. For metal and plastic chains, however, a few of the elements at the seam must be removed. This must be done accurately, because if a gap is left between the separate elements and the seam, the zipper slider may come off.

Zipper Size. The size of a zipper is denoted by the width of its zipper chain in millimeters. For example, a size seven zipper has a chain seven millimeters wide. The larger the size of the zipper chain, the larger the number of the zipper.

Large zippers are stronger than small ones of the same type and material. The larger the zipper, the higher its cost. A zipper must be chosen with a large enough chain to withstand the stress of the intended use, but large zipper chains may detract from the appearance of the garment. Manufacturers balance size with desired aesthetics and cost limitations.

Zipper Length. A zipper chain is more expensive than a plain seam of comparable length, so most manufacturers use the shortest zipper practical for the situation. Zippers must be long enough so that the opening created is large enough for dressing and undressing. If the opening is too small, the stress from dressing and undressing damages the seam at the base of the zipper and the lower portion of the zipper itself. Using a too-short zipper for a garment opening is a common design error leading to zipper and seam failure. However, the length of the zipper should relate to the garment design and not be so long that it is out of proportion with the garment. The most common zipper lengths used in adult clothing are 7-inch in women's skirts and slacks, 9-inch in men's slacks, and 22-inch in dresses.

Zipper Chain Composition. The material of which the zipper chain is made affects the strength of the zipper. *Metal* scoops generally yield the strongest zipper, making them suitable for applications that receive heavy use and strain, such as jeans. *Brass* is commonly used to make high-quality zipper chains because it is durable and does not tarnish or corrode readily; brass zippers are traditionally used in better pants and jeans. *Nickel* zippers are moderate in cost and durability. *Zinc* zippers have high strength and are often used in heavy-duty work clothing. The disadvantages of zinc zippers are that they corrode readily, are prone to slider difficulties, and sometimes fail in extremely cold weather. *Aluminum* zippers are the least costly and the least durable choice. Aluminum zippers discolor quickly and wear down and corrode readily so that the slider becomes difficult to move. They are sometimes found in low-price lines. They are suitable only for low-stress applications. *Alloys,* or combinations of metals, are often used to obtain the desired balance between strength, durability, and cost.

Because of their natural color, metal zippers are often less attractive than plastic zippers in positions where the zipper chain shows on the outside of the garment. Metal can be painted, but the enamel tends to wear off during use. Sometimes, a less costly metal is painted to resemble a more desirable metal; for example, brass.

Plastic zipper elements cost more than most metal scoops. Plastic elements are stronger than aluminum but not as strong as other metal elements. The advantage of plastic elements is that they can mesh closer and block out wind and water better than metal elements. Plastic elements are not as cold to the skin as metal elements when worn in cold weather. They do not corrode and they slide easily in all types of weather. Therefore, plastic elements are superior in some applications, such as ski wear and other outerwear. Also, they come in a variety of colors.

Continuous elements are usually made of *nylon*. They are more costly than nickel zippers but less costly than brass. Continuous element zippers are strong, but not as strong as most separate element zippers. However, they are adequate for most light- and medium-weight uses. One advantage of continuous element zippers is that they can be dyed to match the color of the zipper tape and the fabric of the garment. Also, they are lightweight and flexible. For this reason, they are the best choice for most garments of knit fabrics. However, in very lightweight knits, they still may be too stiff and cause zipper hump. Continuous elements melt if they contact a hot iron.

Zipper Types. The three main types of zippers are (1) conventional or regulation, (2) separating, and (3) invisible. The cost of these zippers varies depending upon the materials and construction of the zippers and the amount of labor required to install them.

Conventional Zippers. A **conventional zipper** is by far the most common in ready-to-wear apparel (Figure 11-15). A conventional zipper has a visible chain; one end, or sometimes both ends, of the zipper remain together when it is unzipped. It is the zipper type generally used in neckline, waistline, side seam, and pocket applications.

Separating Zippers. A **separating zipper** is constructed so that the two sides of the zipper separate into two different halves when unzipped (Figure 11-15). Only separate element zippers can separate. Separating zippers are found on coats and jackets with center front openings, on detachable hoods, zip-out linings,

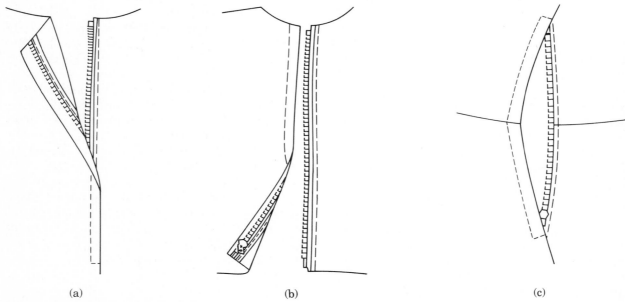

(a)   (b)   (c)

Figure 11-15 *Zipper applications: (a) one end open, conventional zipper, (b) both ends open, separating zipper, and (c) both ends closed, dress zipper.*

and garments with adjustable, zip-off lengths. To avoid malfunctioning, separating zippers should not be zipped until the parts are fully aligned and seated at the base.

Invisible Zippers. An **invisible zipper** is constructed so that the chain of the zipper is concealed beneath the tape when the zipper is closed (Figure 11-17). The only portion of the zipper that is visible on the outside of the garment is the zipper tab. Invisible zippers are mainly used when a conventional zipper would interfere with the appearance of the garment. Although containing continuous elements, invisible zippers add considerable bulk and are therefore inappropriate for garments made of very lightweight fabrics. Because invisible zippers are more costly to purchase and to apply than conventional zippers, they are rarely used except in garments such as evening wear or garments in high-price lines, in which the cost is justified.

Other Zipper Types. The following are some other types of zippers:

1. *Novelty zippers,* zippers of any of the previously mentioned types, with unusual decorative tapes, large or contrasting-color teeth and/or decorative pulls. Although in most cases zippers are concealed, occasionally the zipper is the focus of the garment; novelty zippers are used in these situations. The use of novelty zippers is greatly affected by fashion trends. However, novelty pulls serve an important function on clothing for children and the handicapped, and on active wear, such as ski wear, because they are easy to grasp.

2. *Trouser zippers,* conventional zippers with wide tapes to support double stitching. They have a durable tape, strong teeth, and a reinforced slider to withstand heavy use and frequent laundering.

3. *Dress zippers,* zippers that feature metal bars spanning the chain at both ends of the zipper to absorb stress. Dress zippers are used in side seam applications (Figure 11-15).

4. *Reversible zippers,* zippers with tabs on both sides of the slider, used in reversible garments.

5. *Two-way zippers,* which have a slider attached to each end so that the zipper can be zipped or unzipped from either end. These zippers are used in ski wear, sportswear, and clothing for the handicapped.

Zippers Assembled Before or After Application. Manufacturers apply continuous element zippers fully assembled, with the slider, pull, and stops attached to the chain and tape. However, separate element zippers are often assembled after application. The manufacturer purchases a roll of *stringer,* one side of the zipper tape with elements attached, from which lengths are cut for each zipper. The operator sews two stringers to the garment and then attaches the slider, pull, and stops. Using stringers is cost effective because it eliminates an inventory of zippers of various lengths, and there are no odd-size zippers left over. Zippers are also easy to install this way because small portions of the garment are handled as opposed to the entire garment. However, this method requires the operator to set on the slider evenly and place the stops accurately, important for smooth functioning of the zipper.

Zipper Application. The vast majority of zippers are applied entirely by machine using a straight lockstitch or chainstitch. Topstitching should be smooth, straight, and parallel to the zipper opening. Crooked stitching causes uneven stress on the zipper chain, tape, and slider. The topstitching should end approximately one-eighth to one-quarter inch below the bottom stop. Stitches placed too close to the zipper chain prevent the slider from gliding smoothly. A frequent problem spot in lapped zipper applications occurs when the operator topstitches near the zipper slider. The bulk of the slider prevents the operator from stitching close to it, causing the topstitching to curve out around it. This problem is avoided when the slider is attached after topstitching.

Occasionally, hand pickstitches are used in place of machine topstitching. A zipper applied this way is referred to as **hand picked.** If done well, the pickstitches are straight, even, and very tiny so that they are barely visible on the face of the garment. Manufacturers of better and couture garments use hand stitches when machine stitches would detract from the appearance of the garment. The advantage of a hand-picked zipper is aesthetic, but it is not as durable as a machine-stitched zipper. Because of the labor expense, hand-picked zippers are found only in very high-price lines.

Zippers are usually applied with only one end open and the other end caught in a seam; for example, at the waistline of a pair of pants. They can also be applied with both ends caught in a seam; for instance, at pocket openings or in the side seam of a dress. Separating zippers are applied so that both ends are open. This allows the zipper to completely disconnect into halves, as at the center front of a jacket (Figure 11-15).

Seam allowances in zipper applications must be wide enough so that they are caught when the zipper is stitched to the garment. Wide seam allowances help stabilize the zipper.

Slot Zippers. A **slot zipper** or centered application is characterized by two visible rows of topstitching on the outside of the garment, one on either side of the zipper chain. The lines of stitching are about one-quarter inch from and parallel to the seam line (Figure 11-16). The folded seam edges of the garment abut to cover the zipper chain. The slot application is used in center front and center back openings and for some side openings. Both conventional and separating zippers in all price lines are applied by the centered method. The slot zipper exposes the zipper chain more than do other applications.

Occasionally, manufacturers install slot zippers so that the zipper chain intentionally shows. This is known as an *exposed* zipper application, a type of slot application (Figure 11-17). Exposed applications are decorative, especially for novelty zippers. Exposed applications are required when a zipper must be inserted in a slash in the fabric, rather than in a seam or

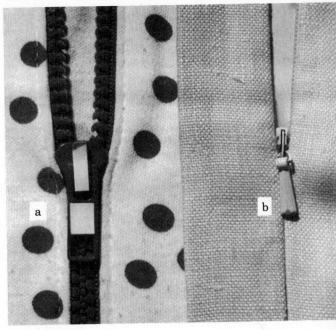

Figure 11-17 Zipper applications: (a) exposed (note plastic separate elements), and (b) invisible, using invisible zipper.

placket as most zippers are; the slashed edges of the fabric are turned under and sewn to the zipper tape, exposing the zipper chain.

Zippers in jackets or coats, especially ski wear, may feature *wind flaps* over and/or under the zipper chain. These extra fabric pieces help prevent skin irritation from a cold or scratchy zipper, and help keep wind and water away from the zipper and the wearer's skin. Such extra features add to cost as well as comfort.

Lingerie guards are ribbon or fabric strips attached behind the zipper chain so that it cannot irritate the wearer's skin or undergarments. Because it requires extra materials and labor, this feature is a mark of quality in high-price lines.

Lapped Zippers. **Lapped zippers** are characterized by only one line of visible stitching on the outside of the garment. The topstitching is on one side of the opening and is about one-half inch away from the folded seam line (Figure 11-16). It causes one folded seam edge to form a tuck that conceals the zipper closure. Lapped zipper applications are used at center front and center back garment openings and for most side openings.

The average lapped zipper application probably does a better job of concealing the zipper

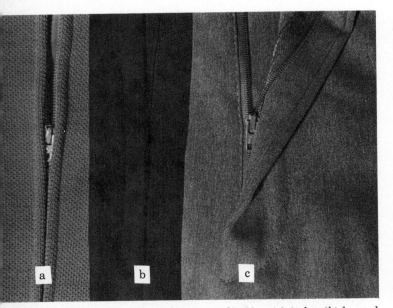

Figure 11-16 Zipper applications: (a) slot, (b) lapped, and (c) fly front.

teeth than the average slot application. But the lapped zipper insertion involves several steps and is therefore costly to construct; it is usually confined to moderate- and high-price lines.

Fly Front Zippers. The **fly front** is a form of the lapped zipper application. The fly front zipper is characterized by topstitching on one side of the opening, about an inch and a half from the folded seam line (Figure 11-16). A fly front zipper differs from a regular lapped zipper; one side of the zipper is stitched to a facing and the facing is topstitched to the garment. This allows for the wide topstitching characteristic of the fly front application. The width of the facing lends support and helps the fly front zipper withstand greater stress than a regular lapped application. If done properly, the fly front application conceals the zipper chain better than other applications. However, if the zipper is not stitched to all the fabric plies in the fly front application or if the stitches are crooked, the zipper chain may show.

Fly front applications are used in jeans, most men's and boy's pants, many women's and girl's pants, and some casual skirts. They are also used in jackets and other sportswear where an exposed zipper would interfere with the design. Because they involve more fabric and more labor, fly fronts cost more than regular lapped zipper applications.

Most fly fronts look fairly similar on the outside of the garment, but they are constructed in a variety of ways. The overlap portion conceals the zipper. The simplest overlap, often used on women's and children's garments, has an extended facing to which the zipper is stitched. This is nonbulky, comfortable, and low cost. Or the overlap may be faced with a shaped facing; this method is slightly bulky. Because men's flies are longer, extending into the curved crotch area, they usually require a separate, shaped facing.

An underlap or *fly shield* beneath the zipper protects the skin and undergarments from irritation by the zipper chain. No underlap leaves the skin directly exposed to the zipper chain. A more acceptable technique is to form an underlap by extending the fashion fabric. Some fly fronts have no underlap. This reflects low-quality standards.

In high-price garments, the underlap may consist of a separately constructed fly shield. The fly shield is faced or lined and attached behind the zipper. Although bulkier than ordinary underlaps, these fly shields are generally more comfortable and durable.

A **French fly** is found on high-quality pants. A French fly has a tab or extension on the underlap, which buttons to the inside of the pants near the waist (Figure 9-4). This provides additional support to keep the front of the pants smooth and neat.

The fly front of high-quality men's pants usually features an overlap with a shaped facing and a lined, French fly shield. Sometimes, the lower portion of the fly shield is extended for a few inches into the crotch seam to further reinforce the area. Complex fly fronts involve more pieces of both fashion fabric and lining and more labor to construct than simple fly fronts. Complex fly fronts are usually comfortable and durable but may add bulk.

The overlap and underlap of fly front zipper applications must be the same length. Both must be caught evenly in the waistband. Otherwise, the fly will buckle (Figure 11-18).

A bar tack(s) is needed near the base of all fly front zipper applications to help absorb the stress of use. Bar tacks protect the bottom zipper stop from excessive strain and to protect the fabric and seam at the base of the zipper from stress. For example, when pants are slipped on and off over the hips, the base of the zipper is stressed and the seam below it may rip out unless a bar tack or other reinforcement, such as a rivet, is present. Bar tacks placed too low do not absorb adequate stress and can lead to zipper failure, seam failure, or fabric failure at the base of the zipper.

A closure at the top of the zipper is vital to absorb the stress on the chain and slider when the zipper is closed. If the closure is too small, too weak, or if poorly attached or mislocated,

Figure 11-18 *Underlap and overlap of different lengths cause zipper to bubble.*

stress may ratchet the zipper and damage it. Garments that are too small for the wearer and worn with the waist closure left open give the same result.

Invisible Zippers. Invisible zipper applications require specially designed "invisible" zippers. No lines of stitching are visible on the outside of the garment (Figure 11-17). When properly inserted, the finished zipper installation looks like a plain seam; the only part of the zipper visible on the outside of the garment is the tab. Invisible zippers are applied with a specially designed machine attachment.

SNAPS

Snaps consist of two parts, a *ball* and *socket,* that interlock when pressed together. The ball portion of a snap is attached to the garment overlap because its thinner base does not distort the smooth surface of the overlap (Figure 11-19). The socket portion, which is indented to grip the ball portion, is attached to the underlap. Both parts of the snap should be evenly aligned. Snaps may be concealed or visible and decorative.

Most snap closures cannot withstand as much stress as buttons, zippers, or hooks and eyes. In general, most snap closures are in areas where there is little strain. Snaps in conjunction with button or zipper closures prevent garment openings from gaping. Snaps are used to hold temporary garment pieces, such as detachable collars and cuffs or dress shields, in place. Snaps may be the functional closure under nonfunctional, decorative buttons. Carefully placed snaps are a mark of quality.

Small snaps have considerably less gripping power than large snaps. The appropriate-size snap depends upon the weight of the fabric and the position and intended job of the snap. Small snaps are best at holding garment parts in desired position, while large snaps serve as actual closures. For example, a large snap used at the neckline of a lightweight dress is unnecessary, uncomfortable, and unsightly. However, the same snap used as the closure at the cuff of a medium-weight shirt is appropriate. Snap sizes range from size 4/0 (small) to size 4 (large). Snaps of the same size but different types and materials vary in durability according to the number of times they withstand repeated snapping and unsnapping.

Snap Composition. Most ordinary snaps are either steel, brass, or nickel that may be coated with nickel, zinc, or black enamel (Figure 11-20). A steel base is strongest but must be properly finished to prevent rusting. *Covered snaps* add an elegant touch to dressy clothing when a metal snap might detract from the appearance of the garment. The snap is covered with a closely woven fabric to coordinate with the garment. Covered snaps are costly to produce and are found in high-price lines. The fabric on a covered snap tends to wear out rapidly with the friction of use, so they are not practical for frequently worn garments.

Plastic snaps are an alternative to *metal* snaps. Clear plastic snaps are inexpensive, unobtrusive, and blend with any fabric. The main drawback is that they are not nearly as durable as metal snaps. Plastic snaps melt in contact with a hot iron.

Snap Placement. The appropriate placement and spacing for decorative snaps is judged in the same way as the placement and spacing for buttons. Concealed snaps are similarly spaced but

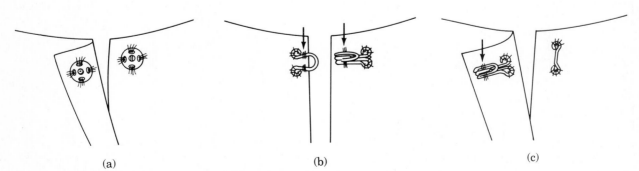

(a)   (b)   (c)

Figure 11-19 *Placement of (a) snap on an edge that laps, (b) hook and round eye on an edge that meets, and (c) hook and straight eye on an edge that laps. Arrows denote extra stitching that improves the application.*

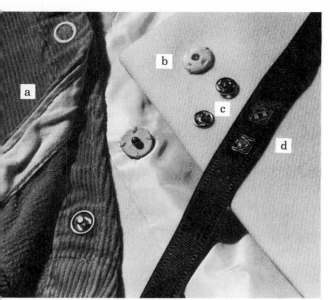

Figure 11-20 *Snaps: (a) snap tape on inseam of child's overalls, (b) covered on designer jacket, (c) metal, and (d) plastic.*

placed near the garment opening (one-eighth to one-quarter inch from the edge). A concealed snap is not visible from the outside of the garment if accurately placed and attached.

Sew-On Snaps. Most snaps are sewn on by machine. The number of stitches and whether or not tacking stitches are used affects the serviceability of machine-sewn snaps through wear and care. All four holes of a snap ball or socket should be sewn securely. Thread dragging from hole to hole detracts from appearance. Because of increased labor costs, hand-sewn snaps are used only when the expense of setting up a machine-sewn snap operation is not justified.

Garment edges that overlap require snaps sewn on flat. For abutting edges, hooks and eyes are usually substituted for snaps. In high-price lines, edges that abut may be joined by extending a snap socket from the edge or by hanging it from a thread chain.

Cleated Snaps. Decorative, cleated-on snaps are used on casual sportswear and western wear (Figure 11-20). Cleated-on snaps tend to be larger and stronger than sewn-on snaps. The portion of the cleated-on snap visible on the outside of the garment is a plain or enameled metal ring, or a plastic, colored glass, decorative metal, or mother of pearl top; cost varies widely. The cost of the snap tends to influence production cost more than the labor of attaching it,

because the process is highly mechanized. The snaps are cleated into the fabric. The fabric to which cleated snaps are attached should be adequately interfaced or reinforced, for example, with twill tape, to withstand repeated snapping and unsnapping. Unreinforced snaps tear away from the fabric in use and are a sign of low quality. Cleated-on snaps are best suited for medium- to heavyweight, firmly woven fabrics.

Snap Tape. Manufacturers often use snap tape to apply a series of snaps. *Snap tape* is a strip of fabric, often twill tape, into which the snaps are cleated (Figure 11-20), or a thermoplastic tape into which plastic snaps are fused. The snap tape is then sewn to the garment. The operator must carefully align both sides of the snap tape for the finished garment to fit properly. A major advantage of snap tape, besides the fact that it is more economical than attaching many snaps individually, is that the tape provides excellent reinforcement so that the snapping and unsnapping action does not tear the fabric. Snap tape is commonly used in the crotch of infant wear to allow for convenient diapering. Snap crotches are costly to manufacture but appreciated by parents; they are preferable to zippers in infant sleepers and other garments because urine tends to make zippers stick. Snap tape is also used in casual garments such as housecoats. However, it adds considerable bulk so is not suited to many garments. The lines of machine stitching used to attach snap tape are visible on the outside of the garment.

A major problem with snap tape and with tape used to reinforce snaps is that it may shrink during laundering. It frequently shrinks a great deal more than the fabric to which it is attached, distorting the fabric and causing "snap hump." This is another example of the need for manufacturers to test the compatibility of garment components before combining them. Testing indicates if the tape needs preshrinking before sewing it into the garment, eliminating problems for the consumer.

HOOKS AND EYES

Hook and eye closures consist of two interlocking parts, a hook and an eye, a receptacle for the hook. A hook and eye closure is comparatively stronger than a snap closure of similar size. Hooks and eyes should be used instead of snaps in areas where there is heavy strain. The majority of hooks and eyes are concealed closures, but visible hooks and eyes are used in undergarments and some sportswear.

Hook and Eye Size. Hooks and eyes vary in size; small ones are unable to withstand great stress and large ones are quite strong. Most general-purpose hooks and eyes range from small sizes for light- to medium-weight fabrics, to large sizes for heavy fabrics. Hooks and eyes are numbered from size 0 to size 3, with small sizes representing small hooks and eyes. Large, special-purpose hooks and eyes for jackets and coats are available. Heavy-duty waistband hook and eye closures fasten pants and skirt waistbands; they are a set of metal plates consisting of a raised bar for the eye and a strong, flat hook that does not slide off the eye easily (Figure 11-21).

A hook and eye should be compatible with the fabric weight and the position and intended job of the hook and eye. For instance, a small hook and eye is appropriate for neckline closures while a large, special-purpose hook and eye is necessary for securing a waistband. The hook and eye should withstand the wear and care of the garment without bending.

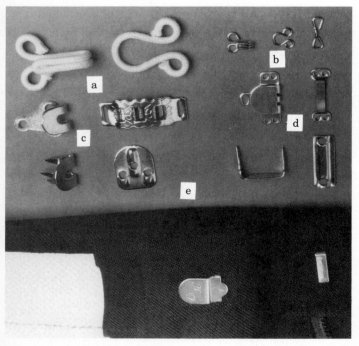

Figure 11-21 _Hooks and eyes: (a) gimp covered, (b) metal, (c) adjustable, (d) large sew-on, and (e) cleated-on (also on waistband)._

Hook and Eye Composition. Hooks and eyes are usually made of the same metals as snaps. _Bra hooks_ for bra backs have two or more sets of eyes for each hook so the wearer can adjust the bra to different circumferences. _Gimp-covered hooks and eyes_, covered with gimp to be inconspicuous, are considerably more costly than plain hooks and eyes (Figure 11-21). They are found in high-price suits and coats and in fur coats. Hooks and eyes in couture clothing may be _thread covered_ to match the garment; this is a costly technique.

Eye Types. The type of eye used with a hook varies. A _round_ (curved) metal eye is intended for edges that abut; a _straight_ or bar eye is intended for edges that overlap. Adjustable metal eyes offer more than one position for the hook (Figure 11-21). Adjustable eyes are bulky but provide for slight fluctuations in size, especially helpful at the waistline. A fabric loop, a group of threads, or a thread chain may serve as an eye for the hook. These are useful when a soft, color-matching eye is desired and when durability is not especially important.

Most hooks and eyes are applied at the stress point of the garment opening, such as at the waistline or neckline. However, hooks and eyes can be used to close an entire garment opening. When a number of hooks and eyes are sewn on, they may be prespaced and attached to a fabric strip, often twill tape. The tape is then sewn to the garment like snap tape.

Hook and Eye Placement. A hook should be one-sixteenth to one-eighth inch from the edge of the opening, with the hook end toward the opening edge. If the closure laps, the hook should be attached to the overlap and the eye attached to the underlap for ease of fastening. If the eye is curved, it is placed with the curve toward the opening edge of the garment (Figure 11-19). A well-placed, concealed hook and eye closure is not visible from the outside of the garment.

Sew-On Hooks and Eyes. Concealed hooks and eyes must be sewn on carefully so that the stitches do not penetrate the outside of the garment. They should be sewn on with several stitches for durability. The hook end of the hook ideally should be sewn to the fabric to keep the hook flat against the garment when the closure is fastened. However, this step is usually seen only in high-price lines. Hook and eye closures subject to stress should be adequately reinforced with interfacing.

Cleated Hooks and Eyes. Large hooks and eyes may be cleated on (Figure 11-21). Manufacturers most often used cleated-on hooks and eyes at waistbands. The hook and eye are cleated through the unfinished waistband. Then the prongs of the hook and eye are bent over metal reinforcing plates to hold them in place, and the waistband is completed so that the bent prongs are hidden. This closure looks neat in the finished garment. However, the hook and eye are attached to only one layer of the waistband. Separation of the waistband layers may occur unless the area around the hook and eye is secured with stitching through all layers. Hooks and eyes that are cleated on are not easily moved; the waistband must be opened up to move the hook and eye. This is not necessarily a disadvantage when used in menswear, because other areas for easily altering the waist exist. However, in womenswear it prevents simple alteration.

MISCELLANEOUS CLOSURES

Although used in fewer garments than buttons, zippers, snaps, and hooks and eyes, there are other types of closures that serve special functions or are useful for decorative purposes as well as for fastening. Hook and loop tape, d-rings, buckles, tabs, eyelets, grommets, and ties are examples of these closures.

Hook and Loop Tape. A closure that has gained popularity in recent years is pressure sensitive **hook and loop tape.** One well-known brand is Velcro. Hook and loop tape operates on the same principle as a cockle burr that clings to your clothing after a walk in the woods. The tape consists of two separate tapes that interlock to create closure when pressed together. To open, the two parts are pulled apart. The hook portion, which feels scratchy, consists of many tiny, flexible hooks embedded in a nylon fabric strip. The loop portion, which feels soft, consists of many tiny loops embedded in a nylon fabric strip. Hook and loop tape is available in various widths and gripping strengths for various uses. Generally, the coarser the hooks and loops, the greater the gripping strength and holding power of the tape. Other factors that affect the strength of hook and loop tape include the number of

hooks per inch and the amount of pressure applied to join the two portions.

Hook and loop tape is a convenient closure. It is ideal as a button, snap, or hook and eye substitute on garments for small children or people with arthritis, who have difficulty with closures requiring finger dexterity, and useful for attaching detachable items, such as shoulder pads, to garments. A disadvantage of hook and loop tape is that it adds considerable stiffness and bulk to the garment; it is incompatible with soft fabrics because its stiffness interferes with the drape of the garment. Hook and loop tape is costly but requires little labor to attach.

The larger the piece of hook and loop tape used, the greater the holding power. Long strips of hook and loop tape are effective in maintaining closure and yet are easily unlocked if pulled apart. Small circles and squares of hook and loop tape substituted for a long strip are much less effective in gripping, but are effective substitutes for buttons and buttonholes for arthritics.

Hook and loop tape is a concealed closure and can be used only in areas that lap. For comfort, manufacturers usually attach the hook portion of the tape to the underlap and the loop portion to the overlap. Machine stitches surrounding the tape and penetrating all plies of the garment are required for durable application, but the stitches show on the outside of the garment. Hook and loop tape is occasionally applied with adhesives, by heat or ultrasonically.

The two sides of hook and loop tape should be locked together during laundering. If not, the hook portion of the tape damages other fabrics in the load and collects thread and lint. Hook and loop tape melts in contact with a hot iron.

D-Rings. **D-rings** are an effective, adjustable closure named for the characteristic *D* shape (Figure 11-13). Two d-rings of the same size are required to complete the closure. The two metal or plastic rings work together to adjust the length of a fabric strip; for example, a belt or a coat sleeve tab. D-rings come in a variety of sizes to accommodate fabric strips of varying widths.

Buckles. Buckles of various types, materials, shapes, and sizes are used as functional fasteners and as decorative details. Although typically a closure for belts, buckles may also be used on straps and tabs at the ankle, wrist, shoulder, and on pockets. A buckle with a center bar usually has a prong that engages with eyelets to adjust the belt to various circumferences.

Buckles typically are made of plastic, wood, metal, or shell. Solid buckles are more durable than hollow ones, which break easily. Buckles may be fabric covered to complement the fabric of the garment. The cost and quality of buckles vary widely.

Tabs. A **tab** is a decorative fabric strip that sometimes serves as a functional closure. Tabs are used in conjunction with a button, buckle, d-rings, or other closure to secure an opening (Figure 11-13). They are frequently seen at the wrist of the sleeves of all-weather coats. They are also used on pockets, necklines, back vents, and elsewhere as the design demands.

Eyelets and Grommets. **Eyelets** and **grommets** are metal-edged holes in a garment. Eyelets and grommets are used to accept laces for lacing, to accept the prongs of belt buckles, and to accommodate cuff links. Eyelets are usually approximately one-quarter inch in diameter, while grommets are larger. Typically, grommets and eyelets are reinforced with metal tubes that are mechanically flattened in the fabric to form a metal-rimmed opening. Be aware of metals that have been painted; these finishes tend to be temporary. Grommets and eyelets should be reinforced with interfacing and multiple plies of fabric to help avoid tearing away from the garment in use. Occasionally, eyelets are made with thread, like a stitched buttonhole, instead of metal. The more densely the edge is covered with thread, the more durable. Thread eyelets are soft and not particularly durable, but are the best choice for delicate fabrics because a metal eyelet would tear away from the garment in use.

Ties. A garment opening may be closed by tying it shut. **Ties** are probably the oldest form of closure. Common locations for ties are at the waist, neck, ankles, and bottoms of sleeves. A pair of ties may be an extension of the garment; for example, the neckline of a halter top. Or ties may be attached to the garment. If included in a seam, ties must be securely attached so they do not pull out of the seam when stressed. Ties may be threaded through eyelets in the garment as in the lacing of a shoe. Or they may be a drawstring that is run through a casing; for example, at the waist of a pair of sweatpants.

Large knots or caps at the ends of drawstrings retard raveling and prevent the drawstring from getting lost in the casing.

Summary

Closures are vital to the functional performance of a garment. When a closure malfunctions, the garment is unwearable. Buttons, zippers, and other closures should be chosen for compatibility with the garment. They should complement the appearance of the garment and be able to withstand the same use and care as the garment. Placement and secure attachment are important considerations for closures. Garments for females traditionally lap right over left and garments for males left over right.

Buttons of natural materials are usually more costly than the more common plastic buttons. A button should be located even with each horizontal stress point. Manufacturers sometimes provide an extra button(s) in case one is lost. Most buttons are sewn on; they should be attached using a number of stitches and tacking stitches. Cleated-on buttons are very durable. Eyed buttons with four holes are most durable when cross-stitched. Thread should not drag between the pairs of holes. Buttons should not be sewn on too tightly to avoid distorting the fabric around them. A thread shank avoids this problem. Shank buttons have built-in shanks and are especially useful on heavy fabrics, but may still require a thread shank on very heavy fabrics. Shank buttons are bulkier than eyed buttons and cost more to attach. Reinforcement buttons should be used on the backs of buttons on coats and jackets that will receive heavy use. The length of the buttonhole is determined by the size of the button. Horizontal buttonholes tend to stay buttoned better than do vertical buttonholes. The overlap and underlap should be wide enough to support the buttons and buttonholes. The buttonhole should be carefully placed to align with its corresponding button. Most buttonholes are made of thread. Densely lockstitched buttonholes are most durable. Most buttonholes are rectangular, but some are oval or keyhole shaped to accommodate the shanks of buttons. In high-price lines, buttonholes may be hand-worked or bound. Faced slits, in-seam buttonholes, fused buttonholes, and special buttonholes in leather are variations of basic buttonholes.

Zippers are suitable for closely fitted garments because they prevent gaping. Zippers may be damaged by ratcheting. The zipper tape should be stable. The zipper chain may be composed of scoops, which are stronger, or coils, which can withstand sudden stress better. The slider of the zipper is moved up and down the zipper by holding onto the zipper tab. The zipper needs a top and bottom stop to prevent the slider from leaving the track. Zipper strength is related to the size and material of the zipper. Most metal zippers are stronger than plastic zippers, but plastic zippers are more appropriate in lightweight fabrics. Zippers may be of the conventional, separating, or invisible type. Novelty zippers, trouser zippers, dress zippers, reversible zippers, and two-way zippers are useful for special purposes. Zippers are often assembled after the tracks are applied to the garment. Zippers are applied by the slot, lapped, or invisible methods, identified by the number of rows of topstitching used to attach the zipper. Fly front zippers are a form of lapped zipper used in pants. They can be constructed in a variety of ways. A fly shield and French fly are signs of quality. Hand-pickstitched zippers are found in some high-price garments.

Snaps and hooks and eyes should be carefully positioned. They may be sewn or cleated onto the garment, with cleated-on closures generally more durable. Large snaps and hooks and eyes are stronger than small ones. Snap tape should be preshrunk, if necessary, before sewing it to the garment to avoid distorting the garment. Hook and loop tape is easy for the wearer to manipulate but adds bulk to the garment. D-rings, buckles, tabs, eyelets and grommets, and ties are other ways garment openings are fastened.

Closure Quality Checklist

If you can answer yes to each of these questions regarding the garment you are evaluating, it contains high-quality closures.

- Is the size and type of closure compatible with the garment in appearance, durability, and ease of care?

- Does the color of the closure complement the garment and retain its color?
- Is the closure application neat and secure?
- Do the garment pieces line up evenly when closed?
- Are closures positioned at all stress points?
- Are buttons sewn on with multiple stitches?
- Are tacking stitches used to secure buttons?
- Are buttonholes the correct length for buttons?
- Are buttonholes stitched with lockstitches rather than chainstitches?
- Are buttonholes on straight-of-grain?
- Does interfacing reinforce all button and buttonhole areas?
- Does thread on four-hole buttonholes not drag from one pair of holes to the other?
- Are buttons not sewn on so tightly that they distort the fabric?
- Is the underlap and overlap on button closures wide enough?
- Are loops securely attached?
- Are large, metal, separate element zippers used for heavy-duty applications?
- Are small, nylon, continuous element zippers used for lightweight applications?
- Does the zipper have a locking slider and secure top and bottom stops?
- Is the chain and tape of the zipper concealed?
- Is there a bar tack at the base of fly zippers?
- Is zipper topstitching straight and even?
- Is there a closure located at the top of the zipper?
- Are extra buttons provided?
- Are there thread shanks on buttons on heavy-weight fabric garments?
- Do buttons that will receive heavy use have reinforcement buttons?
- Are buttonholes densely and completely stitched?
- In leather and leatherlike garments, are buttonholes bound or otherwise appropriate?
- Are snaps and hooks and eyes securely and inconspicuously attached?
- Is the hook portion of hook and eye sewn flat to garment?
- As a quality extra, is the zipper hand picked?

- Do fly zippers have a comfortable, durable, nonbulky underlap and overlap?
- Do men's pants contain a French fly with a lined fly shield?
- As a quality extra, is there a lingerie guard on the zipper?
- As a quality extra, are covered snaps and thread-covered hooks and eyes used?

New Terms

If you can define each of these terms and differentiate between related terms, you have gained a good working vocabulary for discussing the topics in this chapter. The terms are listed in the order in which they appear in the chapter.

closure
lignes
eyed button
thread shank
shank button
backing button
oval buttonhole
keyhole buttonhole
hand-worked buttonhole
bound buttonhole
slit buttonhole
faced slit
in-seam buttonhole
fused buttonhole
corded buttonhole
button loop
frog
toggle
zipper hump
zipper tape
zipper chain
scoop
coil zipper
slider
pull/tab
stops
conventional zipper
separating zipper
invisible zipper
hand picked
slot zipper
lapped zipper
fly front
French fly

hook and loop tape
d-ring
tab
eyelet
grommet
tie

Review Questions

1. Where should buttons be positioned on the garment?

2. How does a thread shank add to quality?

3. What is a reinforcement button?

4. What is the purpose of a keyhole buttonhole?

5. What are the advantages of buttons versus zippers?

6. List and describe the parts of a zipper.

7. What are the advantages and disadvantages of continuous element zippers versus separate element zippers?

8. What is the advantage of a hand-picked zipper?

9. Which withstands greater amounts of stress, snaps or hooks and eyes?

10. What are the advantages and disadvantages of covered snaps? Plastic snaps?

11. What are the advantages and disadvantages of hook and loop tape?

12. Which closures lend themselves to easier manipulation by children and adults with limited finger dexterity?

Activities

1. Examine low-price and high-price women's blouses.
  a. Do the buttons appear to differ in cost?
  b. Evaluate the number of buttons and the button positioning.
  c. Is an extra button(s) included?
  d. Evaluate how securely the buttons are sewn on.
  e. Evaluate the durability of the buttonholes.

2. Repeat item 1 for men's shirts.

3. Find an example of bound buttonholes in a

woman's garment. In what price line was the garment? How do the buttonholes affect the appearance of the garment?

4. Find examples of the following types of zippers:

    a. conventional zipper

    b. separating zipper

    c. invisible zipper

In what types of garments is each type of zipper used?

5. Visit an apparel manufacturer. Find out:

    a. What types of closures do they use and why?

    b. How do they apply closures and why?

    c. What do they view as the biggest problems with closures?

6. Find garments with these zipper applications:

    a. lapped

    b. invisible

    c. exposed

    d. fly front

    e. fly front with French fly

Which application appears most comfortable? durable? costly? Which application appears least comfortable? durable? costly?

7. Examine low-price and high-price infant-wear. Examine the quality of the inseam and crotch area closures. Can any differences found be related to price line?

8. Choose ten men's garments and ten women's garments with center front closures at random from a magazine or catalog. Are they lapped correctly according to tradition? How are unisex garments lapped?

9. Survey five friends. What are their pet peeves about the quality of buttons and buttonholes? zippers? snaps? hooks and eyes? hook and loop tape? other closures? Based on their answers, what changes would you suggest manufacturers make?

10. Examine low-price and high-price jeans. How are stress points reinforced? Are there any differences according to price line?

12

Fit and Alteration: Point of Sale Concerns

CHAPTER OBJECTIVES

1. Examine the elements of good fit.
2. Present general rules for alterations.
3. Discuss the evaluation of fit.

An awareness of fit and alteration is useful to anyone in the apparel industry. If manufacturers understand fit and the need for alterations, they may thoughtfully plan garments that fit the target customer as nearly as possible and that are simple to alter. However, much of the information in this chapter is equally pertinent to sales associates and managers who provide customer assistance with fit. Fitting the customer properly and offering a competent alterations program complements a retailer's merchandise assortment by delivering the service that many consumers desire, building good will, and increasing customer loyalty to the store.

Fit refers to how well the garment conforms to the three-dimensional human body. Good fit is crucial to consumer satisfaction. However, it is often easier for customers to find colors, prices, and styles they like than to achieve a good fit. The effects of a stunning design, gorgeous fabric, and exquisite workmanship are destroyed if the finished garment does not fit the intended wearer. Garments that fit well are not only more attractive than ill-fitting garments;

they are also more comfortable. Garments that do not fit well are left hanging in the consumer's closet, seldom worn, or on the retailer's markdown rack. An estimated 70 percent of garments on markdown racks are there due to problems with workmanship and/or fit (McVey 1984).

Fit problems may be caused by careless design or construction. However, many fit problems are the result of individual characteristics of the wearer. No two bodies are alike, and even the right and left halves of the same body are not mirror images of each other. New technology promises to overcome these problems eventually. Computer systems can optically measure an individual's body in three dimensions and transmit the information to the factory. There, the data are converted to a computerized, individualized pattern. A suit designed by this method can be cut out and ready to sew within seven minutes of receipt of the measurement data (Friese 1985). The resulting garments fit accurately because the computerized scanner detects subtle nuances in the shape of the body that mere measurements cannot detect. Garments manufactured in this way cost much less than traditional custom apparel (Kuhlman 1989). However, such systems are largely experimental and not yet in widespread use.

There are varying opinions on what constitutes good fit. For example, some people like the way tight pants look and feel, whereas others prefer looser pants. A long skirt may seem more attractive or more practical to one person, and another may prefer a shorter skirt. Personal preferences regarding fit are shaped by current fashion trends and cultural influences, age, sex, figure type, and life-style. The intended end use of a garment also affects the desired fit. For example, consumers expect active sportswear to fit more loosely than spectator sportswear to allow greater freedom of movement.

Closely related to fit is the concept of the appropriateness of a garment for a particular person's figure. In other words, does the garment not only fit but flatter the wearer? You will do customers a valuable service by steering them toward garments that are most suitable for their figure. Garment design can camouflage figure flaws or use optical illusion to make figure irregularities unnoticeable. For example, although both may fit equally well, a gently flared skirt probably will be more flattering to a person with large hips than will a straight skirt. For more information, see Related Resources on Design and Style at the end of the text.

How the Apparel Industry Pursues Good Fit

Most manufacturers aim to produce apparel that consistently fits their target market because apparel that fits increases sales and customer satisfaction. Consistent fit within a brand builds customer loyalty because the customer can rely on finding a good fit where he or she has found it before. If fit is inconsistent within a brand, searching for a garment that fits becomes a frustrating and dissatisfying experience for the consumer. Consistent fit must be pursued at every step from design and pattern making to cutting, sewing, and final inspection. To achieve this, everyone involved must understand the implications of their decisions for the manufacturing process. Pattern makers who do not understand the impact of the changes they make in patterns on the fit of the finished garment are unable to achieve patterns that provide both smooth fit, and fabric and operator efficiency. For example, eased and curved seams at the elbow of a two-piece sleeve fit the arm better than do straight seams. Contoured edges on collars and yokes fit better than those with perfectly straight edges.

Retailers try to offer garments that consistently fit their target market for the same reasons. Retailers must deal with the inconsistency of fit of the same labeled size in different brands (see Chapter 3). Another challenge for manufacturers is to provide garments that continue to fit after wear and care (see Chapter 4).

DESIGNING FOR FIT AND ALTERATION

Garments may be designed to fit a wider range of people by incorporating features that enable the garment to extend or become smaller as needed. Some of these features are confined to moderate- and high-price lines. For example, high-quality childrenswear may feature straps that allow length adjustments as the child grows. Other features make the garment easy to alter so that the garment can be changed as fashion or the figure changes. For example, wide hems and seam allowances, although they increase cost, allow for garments to be let down and let out. Some high-quality childrenswear has horizontal growth tucks that can be released as the child grows taller, to accommodate his or her increased height. Very wide hems in childrenswear are also recommended because children grow faster in height than they do in width. These are all marks of quality that extend the amount of time a growing child can wear a garment. In general, men's clothing is constructed for simpler alteration than most womenswear. For example, the waistband on most men's pants is seamed at center back to allow for taking it in or letting it out easily. High-price womenswear is gradually adopting this center back waistband seam for easier alterations in pants and skirts.

In low-price lines, where a custom fit through alterations is usually not practical, design features that provide a wide range of fit are common. For example, elastic or drawstring waistlines fit a range of sizes; elastic used at the back of the waistline not only enables the garment to accommodate a variety of sizes but also fits smoothly in the front. Knit bands at the wrists and necklines stretch to fit. Loosely fitted styles, styles without darts, and garments made of stretch-knit fabrics fit a wider variety of people. Roll-up sleeves and cuffs require less exacting fit than those that are manufactured in exact lengths. Two buttons per buttonhole on shirt cuffs can be adjusted more tightly or more loosely to create slightly different sleeve lengths.

CONTROLLING FIT

Quality departments are generally concerned with ensuring that, after being manufactured, the finished garments fit as originally intended. Some manufacturers and retailers have developed extensive and detailed fit specifications that finished garments must meet. Conformance to the standards is usually checked by quality monitors who take length and width measurements of the garments at certain points. Figure 12-1 shows an example of fit specifications for the production of a sweatshirt. To pass inspection, the measurements of the garment must fall within the tolerance limits of the specifications for that particular size. The drawback of taking measurements is that they do not indicate the location of fullness and thus do not give the full picture of how well the garment will fit the body. However, taking measurements helps eliminate garments with gross departures from specifications and detects garments that have been accidentally mislabeled for size. Mail-order retailers, such as L.L. Bean, Lands' End, Sears, and

J.C. Penney, are noted for their use of measurements to check fit. Consistent fit is especially important to mail-order retailers to avoid excessive returns of garments because of poor fit.

The fit of a particular style may be checked by testing the sample garment on a model. If all samples are fitted on the same model, all designs within the company's line should fit consistently. Testing a garment on a three-dimensional form is a more precise check of the fit of a garment than measuring. **Form fitting** is done on a stationary dress form. An even better test of fit is testing the garment on a live model, often referred to as a **fit model,** an individual who represents the figure type of the target customer. A live model is preferable to a dress form because the comfort of the garment can be assessed, and its fit on a moving body can be judged. However, live models may gain or lose weight, change proportions, or become unavailable, making it difficult for a company to maintain consistent fit if they rely on live models exclusively.

Five Elements of Fit

An evaluation of fit is based on five elements: (1) grain, (2) set, (3) line, (4) balance, and (5) ease (Erwin, Kinchen, and Peters 1979). The five elements of fit are highly interrelated; they serve to describe different but related aspects of fit. For example, a garment with inadequate ease will, when worn, have poor set and distorted grain. If a garment is off-grain, it is also out of line and out of balance (Figure 12-2).

GRAIN

For good fit, the garment must be cut on **grain.** The lengthwise grain or yarns of the fabric should run parallel to the length of the body at center front and center back, down the center of the arm from shoulder to elbow, and down the center front of each pants leg. The crosswise grain or yarns of the fabric should run perpendicular to the length of the body at bust-chest, hip, and upper arm at bust/chest level. The exception to these grain rules is a garment cut on the bias, with the bias of the fabric placed parallel to the length of the body to create special effects.

Style #S111

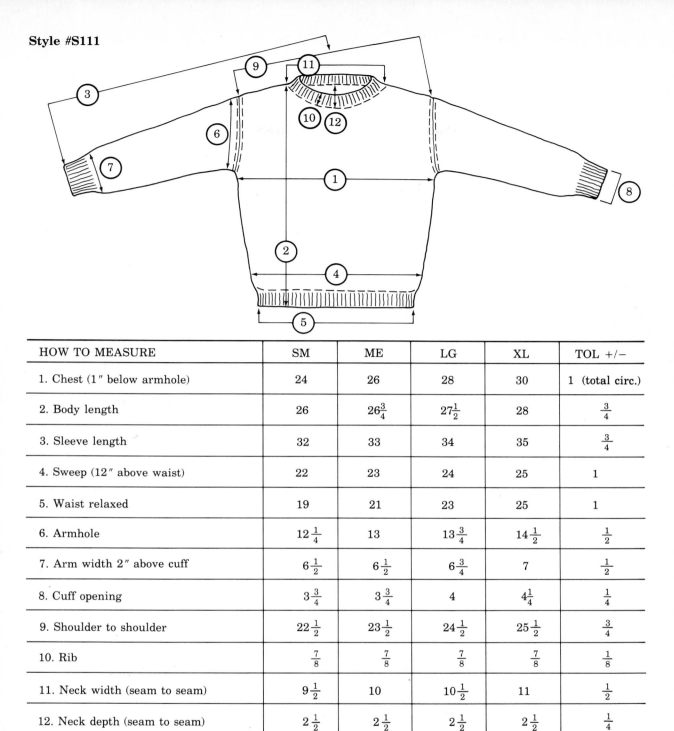

HOW TO MEASURE	SM	ME	LG	XL	TOL +/−
1. Chest (1″ below armhole)	24	26	28	30	1 (total circ.)
2. Body length	26	$26\frac{3}{4}$	$27\frac{1}{2}$	28	$\frac{3}{4}$
3. Sleeve length	32	33	34	35	$\frac{3}{4}$
4. Sweep (12″ above waist)	22	23	24	25	1
5. Waist relaxed	19	21	23	25	1
6. Armhole	$12\frac{1}{4}$	13	$13\frac{3}{4}$	$14\frac{1}{2}$	$\frac{1}{2}$
7. Arm width 2″ above cuff	$6\frac{1}{2}$	$6\frac{1}{2}$	$6\frac{3}{4}$	7	$\frac{1}{2}$
8. Cuff opening	$3\frac{3}{4}$	$3\frac{3}{4}$	4	$4\frac{1}{4}$	$\frac{1}{4}$
9. Shoulder to shoulder	$22\frac{1}{2}$	$23\frac{1}{2}$	$24\frac{1}{2}$	$25\frac{1}{2}$	$\frac{3}{4}$
10. Rib	$\frac{7}{8}$	$\frac{7}{8}$	$\frac{7}{8}$	$\frac{7}{8}$	$\frac{1}{8}$
11. Neck width (seam to seam)	$9\frac{1}{2}$	10	$10\frac{1}{2}$	11	$\frac{1}{2}$
12. Neck depth (seam to seam)	$2\frac{1}{2}$	$2\frac{1}{2}$	$2\frac{1}{2}$	$2\frac{1}{2}$	$\frac{1}{4}$

Figure 12-1 Example of fit specifications for sweatshirt.

An on-grain garment hangs evenly and appears symmetrical. If the garment is off-grain, it will not hang straight. The garment and seamlines may twist or hang crookedly because the fabric on each half of the garment behaves differently.

Deviations in grainline result when garments are not cut or sewn on grain or when the wearer's poor posture or figure irregularities interfere with the grain trueness of the garment as it hangs on the body. For further information on the role of fabric grain, see Chapter 4.

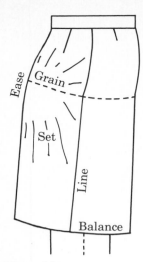

Figure 12-2 *Fit problems.*

SET

Set refers to a smooth fit without undesirable wrinkles. Wrinkles caused by poor set are not the type of wrinkles that can be eliminated by ironing the garment, but result from the way the garment fits the wearer. Set wrinkles usually occur because the garment is too large or too small, and the fabric pulls or sags where the garment does not fit. Occasionally, poor set is the result of the wearer's poor posture. Ideally, this could be corrected with improved posture, which eliminates the body bulges and hollows caused by poor posture that interfere with good set.

If a garment has poor set, the type of wrinkles and their location pinpoint the cause of the fit problem.

1. *Horizontal wrinkles under tension* indicate that the garment is narrower than the body just above or below the wrinkles. For example, skirts with horizontal wrinkles at hip level are probably too tight in that area.

2. *Loose, vertical wrinkles* indicate that the garment is too wide in that area. For example, vertical folds in the back of a jacket indicate that the garment is too wide across the back.

3. *Vertical wrinkles under tension* form when the garment is too short in an area. For example, tense, vertical wrinkles in the bodice of a dress are a sign that the bodice area is too short for the wearer.

4. *Loose, horizontal folds* indicate that the garment is longer than the body. For example,

a pair of pants on a swaybacked person will often exhibit loose, horizontal folds in the center back below the waistband because the pants are longer than the body in that area.

5. *Diagonal wrinkles* pointing to a particular body bulge indicate that the garment is too small to adequately fit that body bulge. For example, large bust/chest or buttocks, abdominal bulges, prominent shoulder blades, or a high shoulder all create diagonal wrinkles that point to the offending bulge (Figure 12-3). Adequate darts or dart equivalents to fit the body bulges solve the problem.

LINE

Line refers to the alignment of the structural lines of the garment with the natural lines of the body. Some lines of the garment **silhouette** or outline the body. For example, side seams should hang straight like a plumb line down the center of the side of the body, perpendicular to the floor. Center front and center back lines should likewise fall straight down the center front and center back of the body. Darts and seams, such as shoulder seams, should appear as straight lines that follow the body parts they are intended to fit. Other lines encompass the circumference of the body. For example, necklines, armholes, waistlines, and hemlines should be gradually curved lines that follow the circular lines of the body part they are intended to fit. Poor design or construction can result in an out-of-line garment, or figure irregularities can distort the lines of the garment.

BALANCE

Balance occurs when the garment is in equilibrium. The right and left halves of the garment appear evenly balanced, or symmetrical, when viewed from the front, back, or sides. For example, a skirt is balanced if the legs are in the middle of the skirt and not touching the front or back of the skirt. Balance relates to the elements of grain and line. Garments get out of balance if they are cut off grain, causing them to hang unevenly. Or, if the lines of a garment do not follow the lines of the body, the garment will hang out of balance. Poor posture or a lack of symmetry in the wearer's figure are likely causes of balance problems. Haphazard or uneven construction techniques may also result in an unbalanced garment.

Tense, horizontal wrinkles = too tight

Skirt too tight through hips

Jacket too tight through shoulders

Loose, vertical folds = too loose

Sleeve too loose

Shirt too loose through torso

Loose, horizontal folds = too long

Bodice too long at waist

Tense, vertical wrinkles = too short

Pants too short in crotch

Diagonal wrinkles point to body bulges

Bodice too tight across bust

Pants too tight across abdomen

Figure 12-3 Wrinkles and folds indicate fit problems.

EASE

Ease refers to the amount of roominess in a garment. Ease is the difference between the measurements of the garment and the measurements of the body of the intended wearer. There are two types of ease, fitting ease and design ease. The measurement of a garment should equal the measurement of the wearer's body plus fitting ease, plus design ease, if any.

Fitting Ease. Even a garment that appears to fit the figure closely does not have the same dimensions as the body it fits. For example, a skirt measuring 36 inches at the hip line does not fit a person with 36-inch hips. A garment must contain adequate ease beyond the actual measurements of the wearer to allow room for

ordinary movements like walking, sitting, reaching, and breathing. Ease in this context refers to basic ease or **fitting ease,** also called *movement* ease, *comfort* ease, or *garment* ease, the ease required for a comfortable fit. Minimal fitting ease is required in *all* garments, no matter what the style. Without fitting ease, a garment is uncomfortable, appears tight and wrinkled, and wears out more quickly from the strain on seams and fabric. Table 12-1 lists the approximate minimum amounts of fitting ease required in the bust/chest, waist, and hips of garments to allow for simple movement. Fitting ease is also required vertically (shoulder to waist, waist to crotch, etc.) and elsewhere in the garment (around the neck, around the arm, etc.). Some garments require additional amounts of fitting ease beyond the minimum

TABLE 12-1
Fitting ease (in inches)

	Women	Men	Children
Bust/Chest	2½	2	1
Waist	1	½	1–1½
Hip	1½–2	½	1½–1¾

Gioello and Berke (1979)

suggested, depending on the style and intended end use. For example, a baseball uniform requires more fitting ease for throwing and swinging than a business suit that is worn for sedentary activities. Clothing for toddlers generally contains fitting ease to accommodate diapers. Jackets and coats require more fitting ease than other garments because they are worn over several other layers of clothing.

Stretch fabrics substitute for fitting ease in a garment because the stretch makes up for the lack of ease. Very stretchy garments, such as rib knit shrink tops, may have negative fitting ease; for instance, a top may be cut 30 inches in circumference to stretch and fit closely to a 36-inch bust.

Design Ease. **Design ease** is extra ease in addition to fitting ease. All garments have fitting ease, but design ease is optional. Design ease gives a garment its style; it is added purely for the sake of appearance. Basic-fitting garments have only fitting ease, but other garments have design ease in addition to fitting ease. For example, design ease creates a full, pleated skirt rather than a straight one. It makes possible a gathered, puffed sleeve rather than a slim one. The amount of design ease in a garment depends on current fashion trends and the desired mood or style of the garment (Figure 9-1). Manufacturers create **oversized** garments by adding design ease.

When loose-fitting styles with design ease are popular, fit tolerances in either direction are often less strict. Leftover fitting ease goes unnoticed as extra design ease, or some of the design ease may be used as fitting ease. Although design ease makes a garment roomier, it should not be used to enable a larger person to wear the garment. If the extra roominess created by the design ease is used to accommodate a larger figure, the garment does not have the look the designer intended. For example, a fully gathered skirt with a lot of design ease might be able to go around very large hips, but it no longer appears gathered. Therefore, design ease should be excess ease that is not used to fit the body or allow for its movement. Likewise, the excess fitting ease in a too-large garment should not add to the design ease, or again, the garment does not appear as the designer intended.

Alterations

If minor fit problems exist when the garment is tried on, **alterations** may improve the fit. Some garments require alteration at the point of sale to achieve a satisfactory fit. Or alterations are needed later because of changes in fashion or a change in the weight or size of the wearer.

Most tailors believe that, "The best alteration is no alteration" (Alterations Consulting 1987). It is often true that the fewer the major alterations, the better a garment looks and lasts. However, the comfort and appearance of many clothes can be improved with simple and minor alterations that custom fit the garment to small, individual differences in wearers.

GENERAL RULES

Increasing, or *letting down* length and *letting out* width, is usually limited by the amount of excess fabric available in seams, hems, and facings. Customers may prefer the term "easing" to "letting out". New facings may be cut of another fabric to match edges that have increased in size. This is permissible if the facing does not show from the outside.

Decreasing, or *taking up* length and *taking in* width, is usually easier because it does not depend on available hem and seam allowances. Customers may prefer the term "shaping" to "taking in". Varied amounts may be taken in to the point that the alteration interferes with the style of the garment.

A common error when altering a garment is to take in or let out too much. Unless the wearer's figure is very irregular, small changes should be sufficient to correct the minor differences between the figure and the garment if the nearest correct size has been chosen. A garment usually should not be taken in more than a couple of inches on each side at the most. Small alterations in the circumference of garments sometimes can be made by moving the buttons or other fasteners slightly.

Alterations always should be made at major seams if possible; highly styled seams only should be altered as a last resort. For example, sleeves with vents cannot be altered easily.

Changes should taper very gradually from the beginning point or ending point of the alteration. If the change is made abruptly, the alteration will be obvious in the finished garment. For example, if pant legs are narrowed, the alteration should begin at the thigh and taper very gradually to the hem, or the seam will jut out at the point where the alteration begins.

CHALK MARKS

The fitter uses tailor's chalk to mark the desired alterations. This must be done carefully for accurate communication of the desired change to the alterations department or alterations contractor. Figure 12-4 illustrates the **chalk marks** for commonly performed alterations (Alterations Consulting 1987).

Remember that chalk marks are cumulative. If a skirt waist is marked to be taken in at the side seams one-quarter inch, the alteration of both sides of both seams results in a total change of one inch.

Note the marks that indicate shrinking or stretching. Sometimes complex alterations can be avoided by shrinking or stretching the fabric of the garment to mold it to the body. This can be done mainly on woven fabrics made of natural fibers, or blends containing natural fibers. Wool fibers are especially well-suited to shrinking and stretching. However, shrinking and stretching operations must combine enough heat, steam, time, and pressure for the changes to be permanent. Individual shape can be built

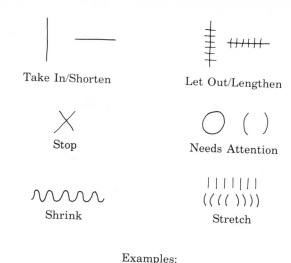

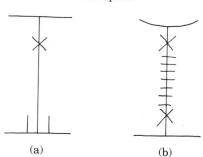

Figure 12-4 *Standard chalk marks used to indicate needed alterations: (a) take in from marks at lower edge, tapering to nothing at the "x," and (b) let out between "x" and "x."*

into suits with at least a partial wool fiber content.

AVOIDING ALTERATIONS

The effect of any alteration on the style and overall fit of the garment should be carefully considered before cutting and sewing begins because some alterations are not reversible. In any garment, but especially in unusually styled garments, one alteration affects other areas and may lead to other alterations.

Because highly altered garments rarely look as good as those that fit fairly well to begin with, it is in the best interest of the customer to start with a garment that fits relatively well. Wise retail salespeople know their merchandise and steer customers toward brands and styles that will fit with no alterations or a minimum of alterations.

Unfortunately, many customers choose a garment based on its color, style, or price, and then expect that it can be altered to fit. This is not always possible and definitely not the best way to approach the situation. Some garments may not be alterable because alterations would interfere with the style of the garment. There may be inadequate seam or hem allowances to accommodate the necessary alterations. Materials that retain needle holes or pressed-in lines cannot be let out. In other cases, as when the whole garment is too large or too small, extensive and complex alterations may destroy the appearance of the garment by causing it to look over-fitted and unnatural. When the garment is from a moderate- or low-price line, the expense of alterations may not be justified—they may end up costing more than the garment. If you are uncertain whether or not an alteration is needed, it is preferable to postpone it. The alteration can be done later if genuinely needed.

Evaluating Fit

In evaluating fit, all areas of the garment must be examined. The following sections trace the evaluation and alteration of fit from the upper body to the lower body, including the fit of the shoulders, bust/chest, neckline, collar, lapels, armholes, sleeves, waistline, hips, crotch, and length of the garment (Figure 12-5). Special sections are included on fitting suits and foundation garments, which require special attention. Fitting people with special needs is also discussed.

The customer being fitted should wear the shoes, bra, girdle, slip, shirt or blouse, belt, tie, etc. that later will be worn with the garment. Items usually carried should be put in the pockets during the fitting. These things affect the fit and help achieve accurate results. The wearer should look straight ahead, not down, during fitting. If alterations are necessary, alter the garment from the top to the bottom, taking care of the most obvious problems first. Taking care of these will often remedy other, more minor problems. *Be sure to keep the centers of the garment and the body aligned throughout the process.*

SHOULDERS

The shoulder area is the most critical when fitting upper-body garments like shirts and jack-

ets. If the garment does not fit fairly well in the shoulders, another size, style, or brand should be tried. Other areas of the garment are easier to alter than the shoulders, which should fit with little or no alteration. If these critical areas can be made to fit with a minimum of alteration, the rest of the garment usually can be altered to follow without jeopardizing the style and drape of the jacket.

In evaluating the fit of the shoulders, the shoulders should look smooth and feel comfortable. In classic garments, the armhole seam falls at the edge of the wearer's shoulder, where the bone of the arm hinges in its socket. The shoulders of the garment should be wide enough so that the sleeves hang smoothly. If the shoulders are too narrow, the sleeves will pull across the upper arm and cause wrinkles. If fashion requires shoulders that are narrower or wider, the pattern should allow sufficient ease for movement.

The shoulder slope of the garment should match the shoulder slope of the wearer. The **shoulder slope** is the angle the shoulder seam makes as it slopes away from the neck. Individual shoulder slopes vary greatly. For example, standard shirt yokes accommodate two inches of slope from the base of the neck to the shoulder, but some manufacturers cut their shirts for squarer or more sloping shoulders. Shoulder pads in jackets make accurate fit in this area less critical because the pads fill in discrepancies in the two angles. Attempts to change the width or slope of the shoulders are expensive alterations, and a different size or brand should be suggested, if possible.

The shoulder seam should lie on top of the shoulder so that it is not visible from the front or back of the wearer when viewed at eye level. An exception to this is the *dropped shoulder* style, in which the shoulder seams are purposely brought forward to create a different look.

For good fit, a shoulder dart or dart equivalent is needed in the back of the garment to smoothly fit the shoulder blade area to the body. The absence of a shoulder dart causes wrinkles emanating from the neckline or armhole because fabric is pulled from these areas to accommodate the bulge of the shoulder blades. In better jackets, ease may be substituted in the shoulder seam for the shoulder dart, yielding a smooth fit in the shoulder area. In better shirts, a shaped seam joining the yoke to the body of the shirt serves as a shoulder dart substitute. When the shoulder darts or their substitutes are

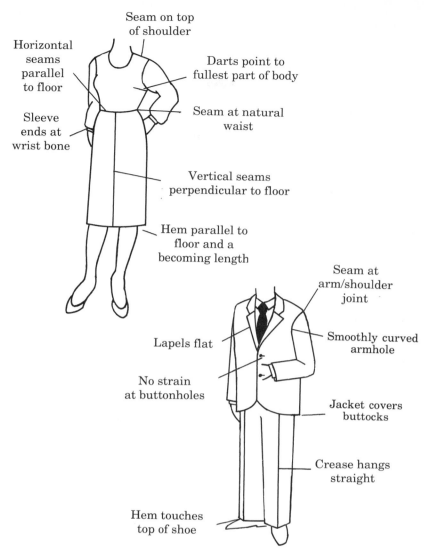

Seam on top
of shoulder

Horizontal
seams
parallel
to floor

Darts point to
fullest part of body

Sleeve
ends at
wrist bone

Seam at natural
waist

Vertical seams
perpendicular to floor

Hem parallel to
floor and a
becoming length

Seam at
arm/shoulder
joint

Lapels flat

Smoothly curved
armhole

No strain
at buttonholes

Jacket covers
buttocks

Crease hangs
straight

Hem touches
top of shoe

Figure 12-5 *Characteristics of well-fitted garments.*

omitted to speed manufacturing, the area does not fit smoothly.

If the garment seems too wide through the shoulder blades, excess fabric can usually be removed at the center back seam. Alterations of up to one inch can be made by altering the center back seam. Taking in fabric at the armholes because of excess fabric at the shoulder blades is an expensive alteration and only should be used when the excess cannot be taken up in the center back seam.

If a jacket of wool or partial wool content is too loose or too tight through the shoulder blades, the garment may be shrunk or stretched to help it fit better, also helping the collar to hug the neck better. Small amounts of one-half to three-quarters inch usually can be corrected without a sewn alteration.

Shoulder pads often are used to correct minor

fit problems. Uneven padding may help correct the appearance of uneven shoulders. Extra shoulder pads may be added for sloping shoulders, and some of the padding removed for square shoulders. However, padding should be used judiciously so that the garment does not appear stiff and become uncomfortable. Over-padding is a common fault among tailors who do not understand the correct alteration to be made.

BUST/CHEST

The bust/chest of a garment is another area that is difficult to alter; therefore, it is important to select a garment that fits smoothly through the bust/chest with little or no alteration. If the garment is too small, the seams or closures at center front and center back are likely to pull and gape open. For example, a large bust or highly developed chest often causes the button closure to gape at center front. Also, the garment may ride up because the larger body bulge takes up more length.

A well-fitted dart points toward the fullest part, or crown, of the body bulge it is intended to fit; for example, bust darts should point to the tip of the bust. The tip of the dart should end about an inch before the fullest part of the body bulge, the *crown* of the bulge. Darts that are too short or darts that extend beyond the fullest part of the body bulge result in a bubble at the dart tip. If two (or more) darts are used to fit the same body bulge, they may be placed with their points equidistant from the crown or with one pointed directly at the crown and the other, usually the shorter and smaller one, placed near the edge of the bulge. Darts occurring anywhere in the garment, as at the waist, shoulder, or elbow, should follow these same general rules. The current practice of eliminating darts to speed construction creates diagonal wrinkles on bodice fronts.

If there is a slight hollow in the chest area near the arm, it can be filled in with a chest piece, typical of men's jackets. Chest pieces can be added or removed to fill in or smooth out this hollow area.

NECKLINE

Another critical area in fitting upper body garments is the neckline. The circumference of the neckline of a garment should be large enough to fit without pulling or chafing but not so large that it gapes. The neckline should lie smoothly around the base of the neck without buckling or bubbling. The neckline shape should be chosen to flatter the wearer's face shape.

A basic neckline should cross the wearer's prominent vertebrae at center back and the base of the throat depression at center front. The front of a basic neckline should be lower than the back to accommodate the natural forward tilt of the head (Figures 4-2 and 5-8). Manufacturers that do not distinguish garment fronts and garment backs in this way compromise quality fit for faster production.

Cutting a neckline circumference bigger fits a larger neck more comfortably. But care must be taken—as little as one-quarter inch cut off the entire circumference results in as much as a three-inch change in neck circumference. This same concept affects armhole circumference.

Pullover necklines must be large enough to fit over the wearer's head. Even if banded with a stretchy rib knit, the neckline may not be large enough unless properly designed.

COLLAR

As for the neckline, the collar should be fitted carefully because it frames the wearer's face. The most important factor in the fit of the collar is neck circumference. The circumference of the collar should be about one-quarter inch larger than the neck measurement, or just large enough so that you can insert two fingers between the neck and the collar. A properly fitted collar is smooth and stays in place when the wearer moves. It should not be so tight that it pulls; a tight collar is uncomfortable and makes the neck look fat. But neither should the collar be so loose that it gapes (Figure 12-6).

The **collar slope** or vertical height also should be considered. The most flattering slope—low, medium, or high—depends on the wearer's neck length. Specifying the slope of a shirt is possible only when ordering custom- or semi-custom-made shirts. However, different manufacturers cut garments with slightly different slopes, so try various brands until the

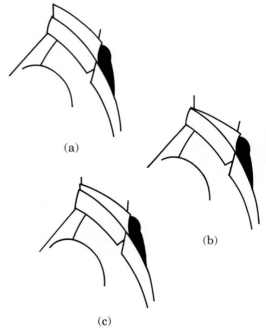

(a)

(b)

(c)

Figure 12-6 (a) collars too loose and shirt collar slope too high for jacket, (b) collars too tight and shirt collar slope too low for jacket, and (c) collars fit correctly and shirt collar slope correct for jacket (about one-half inch shows).

desired effect is achieved. If necessary, the collar can be shortened or raised. When a shirt and jacket are worn together, the back of the shirt collar should extend about one-half inch above the jacket collar.

Popular collar styles generally depend on fashion. However, the shape that is chosen should flatter the wearer's face. The length of the collar points also depends somewhat on fashion. However, narrow collar points are scaled to small people and wide collar points to large people. The **spread** of the collar, the distance from collar point to collar point, should be chosen to flatter facial shape and to accommodate the type of knot tied in the necktie, if one is worn.

The collar on a jacket of wool or partial wool content that stands away from the wearer's neck often can be shortened by merely shrinking it with steam. The collar may be shortened by shrinking it up to three-quarters inch. More than that requires an alteration.

When wrinkles or bulges occur directly below the collar, they should be eliminated. A small ripple or bubble below the collar sometimes can be corrected by steaming the center back seam of a jacket or by removing some of the shoulder padding. If the ripple or bubble is large, it may require the lowering of the collar.

LAPELS

Lapels should lie flat and smooth against the chest, without gaping or sagging. They should taper gradually from the neckline to the level of the top button. They should roll naturally; the roll line of each lapel should not be artificially pressed in but should form on its own as a result of the interfacing and other shaping techniques that were used.

Classic lapels are three to three and one-half inches wide. However, as fashions change, lapels become wider or narrower. Narrowing the lapels is a costly alteration but is possible. Making the lapels wider usually is not possible. The width of a man's necktie should be proportional to the width of the jacket lapels and shirt collar; wide ties are appropriate for wide collars and lapels, and narrow ties for narrow collars and lapels.

ARMHOLES

Armholes must fit well for the garment to be comfortable and attractive. The circumference of the armholes should be large enough so they do not pull at the front and back of the garment but not so large that they gape. In well-fit armholes, the base of the armhole is cut close to the armpit but not so close that it is actually felt—about an inch below the armpit. This provides adequate comfort, that is, room for movement without shifting the garment, and close fit without wrinkles in the armhole area. If armholes are too snug, they bind and are uncomfortable. If sleeveless armholes are too loose, they may be comfortable but expose too much of the body. When armholes with sleeves are too large or low, they are actually less roomy and comfortable because movement is restricted in much the same way that a low crotch in a pair of pants impedes walking. Blouse or shirt armholes generally are cut higher than jacket or coat armholes.

Armholes should be shaped so that the front of the armhole is more deeply curved than the back. This provides freedom of movement (because arm motions are usually in a forward direction) and smooth fit. Asymmetrical sleeve caps, reflecting the forward pitch of the shoulders, generally provide better fit than symmetrical armholes. However, manufacturers often cut armhole fronts and backs identically so that the sleeve cap is symmetrical, compromising fit for faster production and fewer errors in setting sleeves in the wrong armholes. For most children's casual garments and sleepwear, and for low- and moderate-price men's shirts and womenswear with loosely fitting armholes, symmetrical sleeve caps have become the rule. Asymmetrical sleeve caps are found only in better tailored garments.

Armholes can be enlarged by cutting the underarm curve lower. If cut around the entire circumference of the armhole, the garment will be too small in the front and back of the garment at chest level and across the shoulders.

SLEEVES

Sleeves that fit well are attractive and comfortable. The circumference of a basic sleeve should be loose enough so that it does not bind or wrinkle horizontally around the arm. Tight sleeves are a problem for people like athletes with highly developed biceps. Sleeves can be as loose as desired; the only limit occurs if a jacket is to be worn over the sleeves, in which case full sleeves will bulge under the jacket sleeve and look lumpy. The sleeve *style* affects the desired amount of design ease in a sleeve (see Chapter 9).

For set-in sleeves, the *position* of the sleeve in the armhole, often referred to as the set of the sleeve, is an important indicator of good fit. A well-set sleeve hangs at a slight angle toward the front of the body, much as the relaxed arm hangs at the side. The lengthwise grain of the sleeve is parallel to the length of the upper arm. The crosswise grain should be parallel to the floor and perpendicular to the lengthwise grain at bust/chest level. The underarm seam of a long sleeve should fall at the center of the underneath part of the wrist. Sleeves sometimes are set in too far forward or too far back. An off-grain sleeve binds, wrinkles, or twists. As little as half an inch of tilt can cause a problem. If the sleeve is set in too far back, it pulls against the front of the arm. If the sleeve is set in too far forward, it strains across the back of the arm. Correctly set sleeves are attractive and comfortable and are definitely an indicator of quality.

Sleeve caps should be larger than the armscye of the garment and eased to the garment. In many low-price garments, the design provides for little ease because it requires a skilled operator to set an eased sleeve into an armhole. An eased sleeve allows the sleeve to fit the rounded portion of the upper arm more smoothly than an uneased sleeve, which pulls and wrinkles, making the sleeve unattractive and uncomfortable. Gathered sleeves provide fitting ease plus design ease and are slightly easier to set in than eased sleeves.

WAISTLINE

Waistline fit is important for comfort. The circumference of the waistline should not be so tight that it binds or rolls. It should return to its natural position after the arms are raised and lowered and should allow plenty of room for breathing and eating. It should not be so loose that it stands away from the body, droops, or adds excess bulk when tucked into or worn under another garment. Waistline circumference is determined partly by the style of the garment. For example, men's tapered shirt styles are more fitted at the waist than traditional dress or formal shirts, which fit closer than most sport shirts.

The narrowest part of the garment should fall at the wearer's waist. If there are buttons at the waist, the garment should not strain at the closures (however, a slight indentation at the waist

is permissible in men's jackets). A jacket should be full enough so that the wearer can sit down with it buttoned. When fitting men's suits, the bottom buttons of single-breasted jackets and vests are left unbuttoned; the bottom or middle button of double-breasted jackets may be left open, depending on which is more flattering.

Pants and skirts should be supported at the waist, not the hips. If a garment rests on the hips, the waistline of the garment is too large or the hips of the garment are too small for the body. Hip-hugger styles are an exception.

The waist circumference cannot be let out more than the width of the available seam allowances. Waistbands of men's pants are often constructed to allow for ease of alteration, with the final seam sewn through the seat and the waistband at center back. Waistbands of men's pants usually can be taken in or let out at the center back seam no more than one and one-half to two inches. Taking in the waist more than that brings the rear pockets too close together and causes the legs to twist. Alterations greater than two inches must involve the side seams as well as the center back seam, if the pockets allow it. Only a few women's garments are constructed to allow for easy alterations of the waistband. Therefore, women's and children's garments usually require the removal of the waistband so that the seams of the garment can be taken in or let out. If the garment is let out very much, the waistband will not be long enough to be sewn back on. For this reason, most low- and moderate-price women's apparel, some men's apparel, and childrenswear at all price lines feature full or partial elastic at the waist to fit a wider variety of figures without precision alterations.

Waistline seams should be slightly curved, although they will appear straight when worn. Although a curved seam is more difficult to cut and sew, it fits the body better than a straight seam. Many manufacturers cut the waistlines of garments straight to speed manufacturing. For example, elastic waist shorts, pants, and skirts are easier to sew if the waistline is cut straight, but the resulting fit is less accurate than if the waistline is shaped into a slight curve. And although the waistband is usually straight, the waistline to which it is sewn should be curved and eased to the straight waistband so that the garment fits the body. The curve of the waistline should dip slightly lower in the back of women's clothing and rise slightly in men's clothing.

HIPS

The fit of the hip area is critical when fitting lower-body garments like pants and skirts. If there is adequate room in the hips, other parts of the garment usually can be altered to fit.

Garments with adequate room in the hip and thigh area fit smoothly without pulling, wrinkling (*smiling*), or riding up. Pockets, pleats, or vents that gape often indicate the garment is too tight in the hips. If the garment has excess ease in the hip or thigh area, loose, vertical folds form. This is desirable in garments such as full, gathered skirts to which the manufacturer added design ease for style purposes, but undesirable in a garment intended to fit closely.

CROTCH

Pants and other **bifurcated** (having two legs) garments require a well-fitted crotch for comfort and durability. A properly designed crotch fits a majority of customers with the hip and waist size of the garment. The customer may suggest at the time of fitting that the crotch is too tight. Unless the condition is extreme, the crotch will become more comfortable when it relaxes slightly through wear and when the customer is less conscious of it than at the time of fitting. Before altering the crotch, determine that there is no play or give in the crotch area and that it really needs altering. Garments with the inseams sewn first and the crotch seam sewn second are most comfortable. Although it reduces cost when the inseams are joined in one continuous seam, the garment is less comfortable to wear.

Crotch Length. **Crotch length** refers to the measurement of the crotch from the waistline in front to the waistline in back as measured between the legs (Figure 12-7). Allow an addi-

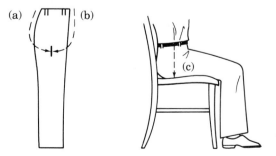

Figure 12-7 (a) back crotch length and (b) front crotch length (a and b added together equal total crotch length), and (c) crotch depth, or rise.

tional one inch or so for fitting ease. Crotch length includes both body length and body thickness; thicker bodies require longer crotch points and deeper crotch curves. The back of the crotch seam should be longer and more deeply curved than the front because the back side of the body is generally more curved than the front; the necessary shape and depth of the curve depends on the individual wearer. When manufacturers cut garment fronts and backs identically, they compromise quality fit for faster production time.

Diagonal wrinkles often result where the crotch curve is not long enough in the back to accommodate the size of the buttocks. Or, if the wearer has a large abdomen, diagonal wrinkles may indicate the need for greater front crotch length. Sometimes the curve of the crotch leaves little room for alteration, so suggest a change in style or size if crotch length is a serious problem. However, usually the inseams are let out or taken in at crotch point to lengthen or shorten the crotch. The crotch point of the front and/or the back can be extended to create additional crotch length only if wide enough seam allowances are provided at the inseams. When the crotch needs to be lengthened beyond the width of the seam allowances, a small piece of extra material called a crotch piece may be added. Crotch length can be changed at the crotch points no more than about one and one-half inches total without twisting the legs of the pants. Additional adjustment may be made at the waistline by removing the waistband and raising or lowering it. An alteration in crotch length is also referred to as changing the thigh or stride. Take care when making other alterations near the crotch area, or you may inadvertently affect crotch length—always start other alterations above or below the crotch area to avoid accidentally distorting it.

Rise. Crotch length is closely related to **rise** or **crotch depth** (Figure 12-7). The two terms are sometimes used synonymously. However, rise constitutes only part of crotch length—the measurement from crotch level to the top of the waistband (you can measure rise on a seated figure by measuring from the chair seat to the wearer's waist level plus an inch or so for fitting ease). Some better lines of pants offer a choice of rise—short, regular, or long. The desired rise depends on the length of the wearer's torso, and the waistline level and ease of fit desired. Men's suit pants generally feature a higher rise than men's sport pants and are usually worn just about even with the navel, so that the waistline seam lies just above the hip bone. Men's sports pants usually have a shorter rise than suit pants and may be worn slightly lower on the hip. English suits usually have shorter rises than American suits; thus, changing suit styles may be more effective than drastic alterations. Unless fashion dictates otherwise, women's pants usually fit at the natural waist—the narrowest part of the female body.

Wrinkles emanating upward from the crotch area indicate a too-high, tight crotch; the seam causes chafing and discomfort. Wrinkles emanating downward from the crotch indicate a low, loose crotch; it bags and sags, restricts walking, and has an increased probability of ripping from the strain of movement. If the rise must be lengthened or shortened, the entire waistband can be raised or lowered slightly, but this is a costly and difficult alteration. Rise is also lengthened or shortened by changing the crotch length, but this sometimes causes a problem where none existed.

GARMENT LENGTH

Garment length is very important to consumer satisfaction with a garment. Consumers usually have definite opinions about the sleeve length, skirt length, pant leg lengths, etc. that they prefer, and they are easily able to determine if the garment meets their criteria by looking in the mirror. Therefore, special attention should be paid to altering the garment to the length desired by the consumer. The desirable length depends on current fashion trends, the end use of the garment, and the body type and size, lifestyle, and attitude of the wearer. For example, childrenswear should be hemmed short enough so that it does not pose a stumbling hazard or get underfoot when the child stoops.

About 75 percent of alterations are changes in the length of the garment (Brinkley and Aletti 1976). Alterations to shorten the garment are limited only by the style of the garment. Alterations to lengthen the garment are limited by seam allowance or hem width. In the case of hems, the amount of fabric can be maximized by facing the edge, with the facing forming the turned-under portion of the hem.

Jackets. The appropriate length of a basic jacket is determined by the wearer standing with arms at sides. If the fingers are curled up,

the hem of the jacket should fall into that curl. The front of the jacket is usually about half an inch longer than the back. Men's jackets should cover the wearer's buttocks, and the hem should be parallel to the floor. If a vest is worn, it should cover the waistband of the pants or skirt.

Women's basic jackets follow the same rules, but the length of fashion jackets varies depending upon trends. Often, shorter jackets are in better proportion to shorter women and longer jackets to taller women. The length of the skirt also affects the desirable length of the jacket. Slightly shorter jackets may be in better proportion with skirts than with slacks. However, proportion rules are sometimes overruled by fashion trends.

Coats and jackets usually can be lengthened as much as the hem and the style will allow. Shortening the length of a coat or jacket is costly and complicated. It often affects the style of the garment and it makes re-altering the coat or jacket to its original length impossible. Most jackets can be shortened only one to two inches maximum without the hem interfering with the position of the pockets. If the garment is lined, the lining must be lengthened or shortened the same amount as the garment.

Other Upper-Body Garments. For upper body garments such as shirts and blouses that have shirttails, the back may be cut longer than the front so it does not come untucked when the wearer bends or reaches. The length of a shirttail should be at least six inches below the waist so that it will stay tucked when the wearer moves. If it is too much longer, it will add unwanted bulk and distort the pants or skirt into which it is tucked. Shirts and blouses without tails may be any length prescribed by fashion.

The fronts of women's upper-body garments worn untucked should be cut longer than the backs to accommodate the bust curve and prevent the garment from riding up in front. Upper-body garments with waistline seams must have adequate length in the upper torso to prevent tense vertical wrinkles from forming at the waist. However, too much length will result in soft horizontal folds at the waist. Sometimes, this blousing is a desirable fashion effect, and extra length is added for style purposes. If the garment is intended to blouse, the blousing should not be used up in fitting the length of the body, nor should excess fitting ease add more to the blousing.

Men's neckties should be tied with the *dimple*

(indentation) centered under the knot. Methods of knotting a tie include the four-in-hand, Windsor, and half Windsor knots. The knot chosen should complement the shirt collar spread; a smaller knot is generally dressier than a large knot. The end of the tie should reach the top of the belt buckle when tied. For tall men, this may necessitate buying a longer-than-average tie. Short men should tie a knot that takes up more of the length of the tie to achieve the proper fit. Standard ties range from 52 to 58 inches long. If a coordinating pocket square is worn, it should extend about half an inch above the breast pocket.

Sleeve Length. Sleeves can be any length but should flatter the wearer, not adding unwanted visual weight to the figure, especially at the bustline or hipline. Long sleeves should cover the wrist bone when the arm is bent slightly at the elbow. When a shirt or blouse and a jacket are worn together, the shirt or blouse sleeves should extend one-quarter to one-half inch beyond the jacket sleeves (Figure 12-8). If the shirt or blouse has French cuffs, its sleeves may extend as much as an inch beyond the jacket sleeve to display the cuff links. Cuff width should be proportional to collar width. Each sleeve length should be checked separately because the two arms on the same person usually vary slightly in length.

Most sleeves can be shortened any amount desired. Sleeves can only be lengthened if there is excess fabric in the hem. The length of a sleeve can be maximized by facing the sleeve

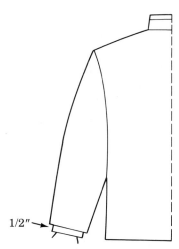

Figure 12-8 *Sleeve length covers wrist bone when arm is bent slightly at the elbow, and shirt sleeve extends about one-half inch below jacket sleeve.*

hem so that all the hem allowance can be let down.

Jacket sleeves usually can be altered at the wrist by re-hemming. However, this is not possible if there are working buttonholes or some other feature that prevents the alteration. In such cases, the sleeve may have to be removed from the armhole and lengthened or shortened at the armhole end of the sleeve. This is a complex and costly alteration, and in such cases, the amount the sleeve can be lengthened is limited by the width of the sleeve seam allowance at the armhole.

Skirt Length. Skirt lengths generally are dependent on fashion trends. Skirt length generally is referred to in inches "below the band," from the lower edge of the waistband to the lower edge of the hem. The **sweep** of a skirt hem refers not to its length, but to its circumference at the hem. A skirt length should be chosen to flatter the wearer. In general, shorter-than-average skirts provide more pleasing proportions when worn by short women, and longer-than-average skirts are better for tall women. The hem of the skirt should cover the fullest part of the leg and expose the most slender part. Basic skirts are often hemmed at or just below the knee. Floor length skirts generally are hemmed half an inch to an inch above the floor. All hems should be parallel to the floor unless they are unusually styled; for example, handkerchief hems. Large body curves, for example a protruding abdomen or buttocks, require additional length to cover the bulge and maintain a level hem.

Some skirts may be shortened at the waist. Raising the garment at the waist simultaneously shortens the hemline. This method is recommended for skirts with permanently pressed pleats or when the hem is unusual, such as a handkerchief hem, border lace, or border print hem, which are difficult or impossible to re-hem. This method also may be used for dresses if there is a waistline seam. If the skirt is flared, raising it at the waistline will make the skirt larger through the waist and hip areas, so this alteration sometimes is used to change for that reason.

When hemming dresses and skirts, the fitter should measure up from the floor a uniform distance. The yardstick or hem marker should be kept a uniform distance from the garment while the hem line is being marked, or variation will occur in the measurements. The fitter should move around the wearer rather than asking the wearer to turn. If a yardstick is used, it must be kept perpendicular to the floor for accuracy; hem markers are on a stand, which ensures hem straightness.

Pant Length. Pant leg lengths are critical to consumer satisfaction and should be marked carefully. The proper length of pants depends greatly on fashion trends. However, for basic pants, there are two choices (Figure 12-9). The pants should either just skim the top of the shoe or they should be slightly longer so that they **break.** A break refers to the slight indentation that occurs between the knee and ankle when the pants hit the top of the shoe and are slightly longer. High-quality men's suit and sport slacks and some women's pants are sold unhemmed. The consumer is expected to have them altered to a precise fit. The length of each pant leg should be checked separately because the two legs on the same person frequently vary slightly in length. If pants are cuffed, cuff width should be proportional to the width of the waistband, and the width of the jacket lapels, shirt collar, and tie, if any.

Many men's dress pants and some women's pants are **canted** (Figure 12-9). The backs of the slacks legs are cut from one-half inch to one inch longer than the fronts, causing the hem to fall at an angle from the front to the back of the pant leg. The lower back edge should fall where the heel and sole of the shoe meet. This ensures that the back of the shoe is covered better than if the pants were hemmed straight all the way around. Canting sometimes features a small snip in the hem at center front so the fabric can be spread and a tiny pleat placed in the hem at

center back. If neatly made, this adds to quality rather than detracts from it. It indicates attention to detail and an attempt to perfect the hang of the hem.

Cuffed pants are hemmed straight rather than canted so that they are parallel to the floor. If cuffs are used on the bottom of pants, they should be similar in width to the waistband. Generally, wider pant leg cuffs and waistbands are used with wider jacket lapels, shirt collars, and shirt cuffs. Narrower-than-average cuffs or no cuffs flatter short people and wider-than-average cuffs are suitable for tall people.

SUITS

A suit is usually a large investment and is worn for important occasions. Therefore, most customers expect excellent fit as one of the most important criteria in purchasing a suit. Alterations are often done to perfect the fit of a suit by a customer who might tolerate the same imperfections of fit in more casual or sporty garments. The pants of a suit are usually fitted first, followed by the vest, if any, and then the jacket.

The fit of women's jackets is largely determined by fashion trends. Fit, ranging from closely fitted to unconstructed styles, depends on currently popular styling.

The fit of men's suits depends partly on the style. There are three basic styles: (1) American cut, (2) European cut, and (3) British cut. The differences between these styles are rather blurry. For example, some American-made suits may be more of a British cut than some British-made suits. However, there are some generalizations about the typical fit features of each cut.

American-cut jackets, called **standard cut** in the United States, are usually the most conservative. They may also be the most comfortable. American-cut jackets are usually single breasted. The shoulders usually are padded only slightly; this jacket also is referred to as a *natural-shoulder* style. The jacket hangs from the shoulders and drapes loosely rather than fitting the body. The jacket tapers only slightly at the waist. The armholes are cut slightly low for comfort. The lapels are notched, medium in width, and the jacket often features a single, center back vent. A type of American cut jacket is the *Ivy league* or *sack jacket.* It has a full body and unpadded shoulders. Pants worn with American-cut jackets may be cuffed or uncuffed. Less formal suits may feature jackets of a loosely fitted style referred to as *unconstructed.*

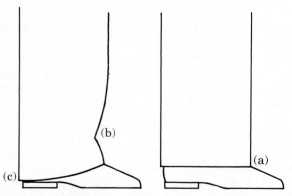

Figure 12-9 *Pant leg: (a) skims top of shoe, (b) breaks slightly above the shoe, (c) canted, about an inch longer in back than in front.*

European-cut jackets are sleeker, more angular, and more highly shaped and closely fitted than American-cut jackets. They tend to flatter a slimmer man more than a heavier one. The shoulders are built up and padded heavily and squarely, and the jacket is fitted at the waist. The armholes are cut high and tight, and the lapels often are peaked and either narrow or wide, depending on fashion. European-cut jackets are often double breasted and, if so, have two back vents or none at all. Pants worn with European-cut jackets seldom are cuffed. Vests usually are not worn with European-cut suits.

British-cut jackets fall somewhere in between American-cut and European-cut jackets. They have slightly padded shoulders like American-cut jackets and a somewhat fitted waist like European-cut jackets. British-cut jackets usually have two deep vents in the back of the jacket. They tend to fit the body more than merely hanging from the shoulders as an American-cut suit does. Pants worn with British-cut jackets often are cuffed.

The fit of a man's suit is also determined by its **drop.** The drop of a suit is the difference between the measurement of the chest of the jacket and the waist of the pants. A six-inch drop is fairly standard in men's suits in the United States. A greater-than-average drop of seven to nine inches provides a good fit for a man with a highly developed chest and trim waist (sometimes called an *athletic cut*). Recommend a smaller-than-average drop for men with larger waists than chests. Another designation is *gentlemen's cut,* with ample room to accommodate a figure with a spreading waistline.

FOUNDATION GARMENTS

Well-fitted foundation garments are essential for comfort and to provide, as their name indicates, a smooth foundation for outer clothing. Bras and girdles require special attention during fitting.

A well-fitted bra provides proper support for all the wearer's activities. Because bodies and busts come in many shapes and sizes, various styles and brands should be tried until good fit is achieved. Seamed bras provide more support than seamless stretch bras; generally, the more seams and stitchings, the firmer the support. A large bust often requires the support of an *underwire,* a plastic or wire support under the cup. *Minimizer* bras press the breasts to the sides

rather than lifting them outward, making the bustline appear smaller. A small bust may be enhanced by *maximizer* bras with an underwire, light fiberfill lining, and/or foam padding. When fitting a bra, look for the following:

1. The support of a bra should come from under the cups, not from the straps. Bra straps should rest comfortably on the shoulders without digging into the flesh. The bra should stay in position when the wearer lifts her arms.

2. The lower edge or *band* of the bra should be straight around the body and parallel to the floor. If it rides up, it does not provide proper support.

3. The band should be snug but not so tight that it is uncomfortable. There should not be a bulge above or below the band.

4. The wearer should lean forward so her bust lies naturally in the cups of the bra. If the cups are not fully filled, a smaller cup size is indicated. If there is a bulge of flesh above the cup, a larger cup size is needed. The center of the bra between the cups should lie flat against the sternum.

5. If the bra contains an underwire, it should rest against the rib cage, *not* the bust. Underwire bras should be carefully fitted, because a poorly fitted underwire is not only extremely uncomfortable but can damage delicate tissue.

Girdles should fit snugly but without pinching or restricting breathing. If the girdle features boning, it should follow the curves of the body to control without cutting. If there is a bulge above the waistline, a larger size or a high-rise style should be tried. If there is a body bulge below the girdle, a longer style should be tried. If the girdle rides up, it is probably too small in the hips. For panty-style girdles, be sure the girdle is deep enough in the crotch to prevent binding or chafing and is not restrictively tight.

Fitting Special Markets

While some general rules for fitting have been introduced in this chapter, there are many special markets that have unique characteristics. From infancy to old age, the human body changes, requiring special fitting. Various life circumstances also require special fitting for some people. Attention to the fit of their clothing flatters the wearer and provides greater comfort and convenience for people at all stages of life and in all circumstances.

CHILDREN

Infants are born with heads two-thirds their adult size. Rapid growth enables the infant to double its height and triple its weight in the first year of life, but the growth of its head continues to outpace the growth of its body. Because infants' and children's heads are disproportionately large in comparison to their bodies, their pullover necklines are frequently cut too small. More than five pounds of pressure may occur when sliding a neckline over the head, and this causes discomfort (McVey 1984). To avoid this problem but maintain a close fit at the neckline, lapped, snapped, or buttoned neckline openings may be added to facilitate comfortable dressing and undressing.

Clothing for a baby must help it maintain a constant body temperature, because the ability of the baby's body to do so is not fully developed. Clothing must provide adequate ease to accommodate a diaper and ease for activities like learning to sit, crawl, and walk.

Toddlers also grow rapidly, but more slowly than infants. They grow faster in height than in circumference, causing them to lose their "baby fat" and become more muscular. They have short necks, round chests, and prominent abdomens. Clothing must provide enough ease for the extremely active toddler without being so loose that it gets in the way.

Preschoolers continue to grow more in height than in circumference. Their abdomens decrease in size and their shoulders get broader. They require clothing that allows ease of movement for their constant activity.

Infants and children have short arms and legs in proportion to their bodies. Obviously, young children's bodies are not proportioned like those of adults. Childrenswear is frequently cut in proportions all wrong for the child it is intended to fit; the arms and legs are cut in proportions that look right to adults when compared to the size of the garment, rather than in proportion to the body of the child. These garments are purchased because they have proportions that look like clothing for miniature adults. These

grandmother clothes, so-called because grandmothers are often the ones who cannot resist buying them, are often purchased as gifts without the child trying them on first. Such garments are rarely returned; therefore, the manufacturer does not receive many complaints, and continues to produce the same ill fit in the next season's line (McVey 1984).

Elementary school children are proportioned similarly to adults. Growth slows somewhat, with the child continuing to grow faster in height than in circumference.

Growth speeds up as children approach puberty. Their legs, arms, and feet grow most rapidly. As girls mature, their hips and shoulders broaden, waistline becomes smaller, and eventually the bust develops. Boys grow taller and broader in the shoulders and chest. Girls mature earlier than boys, but their growth slows or stops after sexual maturity. Boys mature later but continue to grow in height and weight through their early twenties. The rapid growth of adolescents causes them to outgrow their clothing quickly.

PREGNANT WOMEN

Pregnant women have special fitting problems. During the first trimester, few changes are evident except for slightly larger breasts. During the second trimester, the waistline begins to rise and expand. As the waistline expands, the curvature of the lower spine increases to help balance the body. The waistline continues to rise until a few weeks before the baby is born, when it becomes lower. Hips and thighs increase in size. The hands, legs, and feet may swell. Garments for pregnant women must be larger in circumference through the bust, waist, hips, and thighs, and longer in front to accommodate the protruding abdomen and increased curvature of the spine.

OLDER ADULTS

The bodies of adults may continue to change as they age, although these changes depend somewhat on heredity and can be postponed by proper diet and exercise. Weight gain is typical of many middle-aged adults. The aging of women often is accompanied by an increase in bust, waist, hip, and thigh measurements. The bustline is lower, but this can be controlled by a well-fitted support bra. The shoulders may round slightly or greatly. These changes require more length and width in the back bodice and less in the front to fit the figure smoothly. Men's aging often is accompanied by an increase in waist and hip measurements and a larger abdomen. Men's and women's buttocks tend to flatten, requiring less length and width in the back of pants and skirts, with more in the front. Garments that are loosely fitted in these areas are most flattering.

Elderly adults may lose the weight they gained in middle age. Legs and arms may lose their shape as muscle tone decreases. Longer skirts, pants, and sleeves usually are preferred to short ones. Elderly people become as much as five inches shorter than their earlier adult height because of reduced cartilage in their spinal columns and because of osteoporosis (Farmer and Gotwals 1982). Osteoporosis may lead to a dowager's hump, with the head forward, hollow chest, and increased neck circumference. V-necklines, but not low ones, tend to be most comfortable and attractive. Women require a lower bustline in garments. Garments with soft fullness over the bust but that do not accentuate the bustline are most flattering. Raglan or kimono sleeves provide maximum freedom of movement. A garment should not fit so loosely that it catches on things or becomes a fire hazard near burners or heaters.

OBESE

Obese people, like anyone else, require clothing that fits well. Too-loose or too-tight clothing draws attention to a person's heaviness. There is not a single solution for fitting overweight people because they may be large all over or they may be top heavy or bottom heavy. However, obese men tend to be largest through the abdomen. Obese women tend to have a lower bustline. They may find raglan and kimono sleeves without distinct armscye seams easier to fit, more flattering, and more comfortable than set-in sleeves. Dresses without waistline seams eliminate the need to locate the less distinct waist and draw attention away from its circumference and the protruding abdomen. Dresses that pull on over the head or close in front are preferable to those that close in back. Men and women may find slightly loose v-necklines and open, flat collars more comfortable and more flattering than very high, closely fitted

ones. Shoulder pads may help to visually balance people who are overweight.

HANDICAPPED

Other individuals who may have special fitting needs are those who are physically handicapped. They are not easily put into one category because their needs vary greatly. For example, people using crutches or walkers require extra ease across the back shoulder area of the garment and through the upper part of the sleeves to allow them to move the crutches. Their shirts and blouses need to be cut longer to stay tucked; overblouses are perhaps a better choice. Skirts may need to be hemmed to correct the tilt caused by the changed posture. The garments of crutch users need to be cut high under the arm to prevent abrasion.

People who use wheelchairs also require extra ease across the back shoulder area of the garment and through the upper part of the sleeves. This gives them a longer reach and allows them to operate the wheelchair manually. Short jackets are more comfortable for the seated figure. Lower-body garments should be cut shorter in front and longer in back to accommodate the seated figure comfortably without bunching up in front (Figure 12-10). If a person must use a wheelchair for years, the waist and hips enlarge, the front torso shortens, the back torso lengthens, and the shoulders may become broader from operating the wheelchair. The fit of their clothing needs to accommodate these physical changes. If necessary, clothing can be fit to smoothly cover leg or foot deformities or braces. However, clothing must not be so long or loose that it gets in the way of the operation of the wheelchair.

Thousands of people have a problem with incontinence, a partial or total loss of bowel and/or bladder control. Full garments are desirable because they conceal absorbent pads, waterproof pants, or other collection devices. Zippered pant legs or otherwise easy access to catheters is important. If the wearer needs assistance in changing pads, clothing should be easy to remove and replace.

Women who have had a mastectomy, or surgical removal of the breast(s), require garments with necklines and sleeves that fit to conceal the affected areas. Garments may require padding in addition to the prosthesis or replacement body part to fill in any hollow areas. Garments

E&J AVENUES™ OFFERS MORE TO FIT YOU AND YOUR LIFESTYLE

When you order from Avenues, you receive more than just great looking styles. You receive body-engineered fashions designed for the wheel chair user. This means more comfort, easier dressing, and a more attractive fit than "stand"-ard designs. Most of the features are hidden, though, so you'll need to look for them. As you leaf through Avenues, note the special numbers after every item. They refer to the illustrations of fashionable, functional benefits that you won't want to miss.

DISCOVER THE E&J AVENUES™ ADVANTAGE!

Eliminate binding, bunching, and gaping for better comfort and fit with our SEATED SHAPE and ELASTIC WAISTBANDS

Get a grip on pants for speedier dressing with INSIDE WRIST LOOPS

Place your carry-alongs within easy reach with ACCESSIBLE POCKETS

Enjoy quick dressing ease, hidden in attractive designs with FULL SIDE SKIRT OPENINGS

Simplify dressing and changing with HIDDEN PANT ZIPPERS (In leg or crotch seams)

Opt for neat, custom-tailored appearance with SHORT CUT JACKETS

Allow freedom of arm movement (even in office attire) with ACTION BACK PLEATS

Select easy closure options with HIDDEN VELCRO-STYLE FASTENERS or FINGER RINGS FOR TROUSERS

Figure 12-10 *Clothing for wheelchair users. (Courtesy of Everest & Jennings Avenues, 3233 E. Mission Oaks Blvd., Camarillo, CA 93012. (800) 848-2837.)*

should be designed and constructed to allow moving and reaching without binding and chafing the sensitive surgical area.

Summary

Fit is influenced by fashion trends, personal preferences and the intended end use of the garment. Fit is evaluated based on five elements: grain, set, line, balance, and ease. The lengthwise grain generally should run parallel to the center front and center back of the garment and the center of the sleeve. The crosswise grain should run perpendicular to center front and center back at the bust/chest and hip levels. Set is smooth fit with no undesirable wrinkles. The lines of the garment should follow the silhouette and circumference lines of the body. Garments that are balanced appear symmetrical from side to side and front to back. Garments require adequate fitting ease to provide comfort and allow room for movement. Additional ease for style reasons is design ease.

Good fit is partly the result of the manufacturer's careful design, production, and inspection of the garment. Fit also depends on the figure of the individual wearer. Garments require alteration at the point of sale for a custom fit. However, the total effect of any alteration should be considered before it is executed, with changes based on knowledge and skill. Alterations should be minimal; if drastic alterations are required, another size or style of garment should be suggested instead.

The shoulder and chest are the most critical areas to fit in upper-body garments. The neckline, collar, and lapels should fit smoothly. Armholes should be comfortable. The hipline is the most critical area to fit in lower-body garments. The waistline should be comfortable. Crotch length and crotch depth are important in bifurcated garments. The length of the garment, especially pant leg and sleeve lengths, is important to consumer satisfaction. Pant legs hemmed longer in back than in the front are called canted.

Suits require careful fitting. The cut of women's suits is determined by fashion trends. Men's suits fall into three main categories as follows: standard or American cut, the more closely fitted and highly styled European cut, and the British cut, which falls somewhere in between.

Foundation garments, such as bras and girdles, also require careful fitting. Both should be comfortable and provide support.

Fit must be adapted to the changes people experience as they age. Children are proportioned differently from adults, and their clothing should fit accordingly. Necklines should be large enough to fit over their heads without causing discomfort. Sleeves and pant legs should be short in comparison to the body of the garment. Young children grow faster in height than in circumference. Adolescents grow rapidly.

Pregnant women require garments longer in the front than in the back and that accommodate their enlarged bust, hips, and thighs. Older adults tend to gain weight as they age. The bustline may lower, shoulders round, and buttocks flatten. The very elderly tend to lose weight and muscle tone and become shorter. Clothing should reflect these trends if it is to fit comfortably and attractively. Obese people require clothing that is neither too loose nor too tight and allows plenty of freedom of movement. Comfortable sleeves, necklines, and waistlines are important. Handicapped people, depending on their particular disability, require clothing that adapts to their patterns of movement. It is important that clothing for people with special needs appear similar to what the rest of the population wears. Helping the customer achieve good fit is a service that differentiates a retailer from the competition.

Fit and Alteration Quality Checklist

If you can answer yes to each of these questions regarding the garment you are evaluating, it fits well.

- Is the garment on grain?
- Does the garment set on the figure smoothly without wrinkling?
- Do the lines of the garment follow the lines of the body?
- Is the garment evenly balanced?
- Does the garment have adequate ease without having too much?

- Has the best fitting brand, style, and size been chosen before deciding to alter?
- Can the garment be altered without disturbing its style?
- Are the seam and hem allowances adequate for the necessary alterations?
- Is the customer dressed during the fitting as he or she will be when the garment is worn later (undergarments, shoes, etc.)?
- Were the most serious problems altered first?
- Does the shoulder slope of the garment match that of the wearer's shoulders?
- Does the armhole seam fall at the end of the wearer's shoulder?
- Does the shoulder seam lie on top of the wearer's shoulder?
- Does the garment contain dart or ease in the back of the shoulders?
- If possible, is the alteration accomplished with shoulder pads, chest pads, or shrinking or stretching with steam?
- Do darts point toward, and end about one inch from, the crown of the body bulge?
- Do the shoulders and chest of jackets and other upper-body garments fit smoothly and comfortably?
- Do the hips of skirts, pants, and lower-body garments fit smoothly and comfortably without pulling or riding up?
- Is the neckline/collar comfortably sized without gaping?
- Are pullover necklines large enough to fit over the head?
- Does the shirt collar extend one-half inch above the jacket collar?
- Are the armholes fitted without chafing?
- Does the sleeve hang naturally from the armhole?
- Does the waist fall at the natural waist or desired waist level?
- Is the crotch high enough for the wearer to walk easily and low enough to avoid chafing?
- Is the crotch curved the same as the wearer's body?
- Does the garment length flatter the wearer, and reflect current fashion and the personal preferences of the customer?
- Does the tip of the necktie reach the belt buckle?
- Do long sleeves hit at the wrist bone when the arm is bent slightly?
- Do the shirt sleeves extend about one-half inch beyond the jacket sleeves?
- Do the pant legs skim the tops of the shoes, or break slightly?

New Terms

If you can define each of these terms and differentiate between related terms, you have gained a good working vocabulary for discussing the topics in this chapter. The terms are listed in the order in which they appear in this chapter.

fit
form fitting
fit model
grain
set
line
silhouette
balance
ease
fitting ease
design ease
oversized
alterations
chalk marks
shoulder slope
collar slope
spread
bifurcated
crotch length
rise/crotch depth
sweep
break
canted
American/standard cut
European cut
British cut
drop

Review Questions

1. List features that allow a garment to fit a wider range of people.

2. How is fit evaluated using the five elements of fit?

3. How are wrinkles used to diagnose fit problems?

4. Explain the difference between fitting ease and design ease.

5. A customer has selected a garment that will require extensive alteration to fit properly. What is your advice? Justify your answer.

6. Draw and define the standard alteration chalk marks.

7. What is the most critical area to fit when fitting upper-body garments? lower-body garments?

8. List the criteria for fitting each of these body parts:
  a. shoulders
  b. bust/chest
  c. neckline
  d. collar
  e. lapels
  f. armholes
  g. sleeves
  h. waist
  i. hips
  j. crotch
  k. garment length: jackets
                               other upper body
                                  garments
                               sleeves
                               skirts
                               pants

9. Compare and contrast the three basic suit cuts for men.

10. What are the criteria for fitting a bra? a girdle?

11. Trace the physical development of an infant through old age and explain the impact of physical changes on fit.

12. What are the special challenges in fitting pregnant women? the obese? people with physical impairments?

Activities

1. Evaluate the fit of a classmate's clothing based on grain, set, line, balance, and ease.

2. Visit a nursing home or a center for the physically handicapped. Observe how the patients' clothing fits and ask them what their main problems are in trying to find clothing that fits.

3. Compare maternity clothes to regular clothes for women. What differences in fit, if any, are incorporated into the maternity clothes?

4. Compare the proportions of clothing for toddlers to that of adults. What, if any, are the differences and why?

5. Compare the length of children's trouser legs, using various brands of the same size. If differences are found, which brand is better and why?

6. Compare the neckline circumferences (when stretched) of children's T-shirts, using various brands of the same size. If differences are found, which brand is better and why?

7. Study a costume history book. How has fashion influenced the perception of good fit during the past 200 years?

8. Visit a store or a custom tailor shop where fine suits are sold. Ask to observe some fittings. Find out what chalk marks are used to communicate the desired alterations.

9. From a magazine or catalog, select five examples of garments containing only fitting ease and five examples of garments containing both design *and* fitting ease.

10. Have five people who claim to wear the same labeled size try on the same garment. What variations in fit are found between these individuals? What challenges does this pose for the apparel industry?

11. Watch people while attending a business or social function. Informally evaluate the fit of ten individuals' clothing while you are standing in line or seated in an audience. What suggestions would you make to help each person achieve better fit?

12. Try the same, basic skirt style on five different women. Determine the most flattering skirt length for each person, measured in inches below the waistband.

13. Visit a men's suit department or store. Find a suit in each of these cuts:
  a. American/standard
  b. European
  c. British
  d. unconstructed

Related Resources

GENERAL

AATCC Technical Manual. Research Triangle Park, NC: American Association of Textile Chemists and Colorists. Published annually.

ALEXANDER, P. R. (1977). *Textile products: Selection, use, and care.* Boston: Houghton Mifflin.

ALLEN, H. (1986). *Introduction to sewn products: Overview* (videotape). Raleigh: North Carolina State University.

ALLEN, H. (1986). *Introduction to sewn products: Production and quality* (videotape). Raleigh: North Carolina State University.

American Apparel Manufacturers Association. (1985). *Elements of an apparel quality control program.* Washington, DC: Author.

American Apparel Manufacturers Association. (1979). Avoiding zipper problems. *Bobbin,* (May), 76–84.

American Apparel Manufacturers Association. (1973). *Improving apparel performance.* Washington, DC: Author.

American Apparel Manufacturers Association. (1988). *Go for the apparel* (videotape). Washington, DC: Author.

American Association for Textile Technology, Inc. (1972). *A guide to garment evaluation.* New York: Author.

Annual Book of ASTM standards: Textiles. Philadelphia: American Society for Testing and Materials. Published annually.

Apparel Industry Magazine. Atlanta, GA. Published monthly.

Apparel Tech. (1990). *Apparel analysis* (slide set). Kansas City, MO: Author.

ASQC Textiles and Needle Trades Division Transactions. Milwaukee, WI: American Society for Quality Control. Published annually.

Bobbin Magazine. Columbia, SC. Published monthly.

CARR, H., & LATHAM, B. (1988). *The technology of clothing manufacture.* Oxford, England: BSP Professional Books.

COLGATE, A. I. (1988). A match for a clean cut. *Bobbin,* (March), 86.

Consumer Reports. (1988). How to buy a blazer. *Consumer Reports,* (September), 548–553.

Consumer Reports. (1986). The good gray suit. *Consumer Reports,* (August), 502–510.

DHIMAN, B. (1988). Matchmakers make match. *Bobbin,* (March), 81–84.

DOLCE, D., & DEVELLARD, J. P. (1983). *The consumer's guide to menswear.* New York: Dodd, Mead & Co.

ERWIN, M. D., KINCHEN, L. A., & PETERS, K. A. (1979). *Clothing for moderns* (6th ed.). New York: Macmillan.

FEATHER, B. (1984). *Ready-to-wear quality signals.* Columbia, MO: University of Missouri-Columbia Extension Division College of Home Economics.

FRINGS, G. S. (1991). *Fashion from concept to consumer* (3rd ed.). Englewood Cliffs, NJ: Prentice-Hall.

GANG, E. S. (1989). Trim's no kid stuff. *Bobbin, 30*(5), 106–107.

GEWEN, B. (n.d.). *Brief history of the ILGWU.* New York: International Ladies' Garment Workers' Union.

GILL, P. (1987). Quality comes first. *Bobbin, 28*(12), 58–66.

GIOELLO, D. A., & BERKE, B. (1979). *Fashion production terms.* New York: Fairchild.

GLOCK, R. E., & KUNZ, G. I. (1990). *Apparel manufacturing: Sewn products analysis.* New York: Macmillan.

GROGAN, J. (1987). Press for success. *Bobbin, 25*(11), 56–68.

HARTENSTINE, W. (1987). Still pressing for the grand slam. *Bobbin, 26*(10), 92–95.

HOFFMAN, A. M. (1979). *Clothing for the handicapped, the aged, and other people with special needs.* Springfield, IL: Bannerstone House.

HOLLEN, N. R. (1981). *Pattern making by the flat-pattern method.* Minneapolis, MN: Burgess.

HOLZAPFEL, M. (1986). The physics of pressing. *Bobbin*, 25(11), 72–74.

HORN, M. J., & GUREL, L. M. (1981). *The second skin* (3rd ed.). Boston: Houghton Mifflin.

HUDSON, P. B. (1988). *Guide to apparel manufacturing*. Greensboro, NC: MEDIApparel.

Iowa State University (1986). *Mass production procedures in apparel manufacturing: Tape 1, Overview of apparel manufacturing; Tape 2, Eiseman tradition; Tape 3, Eagleknit makes basics right; and Tape 4, JH Collectibles story* (videotapes). Ames, IA: Author.

JARNOW, J. A., GUERREIRO, M., & JUDELLE, B. (1987). *Inside the fashion business* (4th ed.). New York: Macmillan.

JEWELL, D. L., & FIEDOREK, M. B. (1984). Quality in clothes: How to recognize it. *New Woman*, (November), 102–103.

KEFGEN, M., & TOUCHIE-SPECHT, P. (1986). *Individuality in clothing selection and personal appearance: A guide for the consumer* (4th ed.). New York: Macmillan.

KIDWELL, C. B., & CHRISTMAN, M. C. (1975). *Suiting everyone: The democratization of clothing in America*. Washington, DC: Smithsonian Institution Press.

KOZLOSKY, J. (1981). Strike back. *Bobbin*, 22(9), 90–94.

LEWIS, V. S. (1976). *Comparative clothing construction techniques*. Minneapolis: Burgess.

MEDIApparel. (1988). Creation of a quality garment (slide set). Greensboro, NC: Author.

MEHTA, P. V. (1984). *An introduction to quality control for the apparel industry*. Japan: J.S.N. International.

Meridian Education Corporation. (1990). *Judging clothing workmanship* (videotape). Bloomington, IL: Author.

Reader's Digest Association, Inc. (1978). *Reader's Digest complete guide to sewing*. Pleasantville, NY: Author.

RUSS, W. V. (1984). Hints on avoiding zipper problems. *American Society for Quality Control Textiles and Needle Trades Division Transactions, 12,* 59–65.

RYAN, M. S. (1966). *Clothing: A study in human behavior*. New York: Holt, Rinehart & Winston.

SCHOER, J., & PARALIS, J. (1984). Interfacings do enhance a garment's appearance. *Apparel World*, (August), 12–16.

Sears Roebuck Company. (1985). *Women's apparel manufacturer's handbook*. Chicago: Author.

SIEBEN, W. (1987). Unpublished manuscript. St. Paul, MN: Author.

SOLINGER, J. (1988). *Apparel manufacturing handbook: Analysis, principles, and practice* (2nd ed.). New York: Van Nostrand Reinhold.

STAMPER, A. A., SHARP, S. H., & DONNELL, L. B. (1991). *Evaluating apparel quality.* (2nd ed.). New York: Fairchild.

STONE, E. (1987). *Fashion buying*. New York: McGraw-Hill.

TRAY, A. I. (1985). Information that helps sell apparel. *Bobbin,* (January), 118–120.

WATKINS, S. M. (1984). *Clothing: The portable environment*. Ames, IA: Iowa State University Press.

WEBER, C. (1985). Quality: The inside story. *Bobbin*, 27(1), 180–186.

WINGATE, I. B., GILLESPIE, K. R., & BARRY, M. E. (1984). *Know your merchandise: For retailers and consumers* (5th ed.). New York: McGraw-Hill.

DESIGN AND STYLE

CALASIBETTA, C. M. (1986). *Essential terms of fashion*. New York: Fairchild.

CALASIBETTA, C. M. (1975). *Fairchild's dictionary of fashion*. New York: Fairchild.

DAVIS, M. L. (1980). *Visual design in dress*. Englewood Cliffs, NJ: Prentice-Hall.

HILLHOUSE, M. S. (1963). *Dress selection and design*. New York: Macmillan.

HUMPHRIES, M. (1986). *Apparel anatomy*. Ontario, Canada: Author.

IRELAND, P. J. (1987). *Encyclopedia of fashion details*. London: B.T. Batsford.

MORGANOSKY, M. (1989). Consumer evaluations of apparel form, expression, and aesthetic quality. *Clothing and Textiles Research Journal, 7,* 11–15.

PICKENS, M. B. (1973). *The fashion dictionary*. New York: Funk & Wagnalls.

TATE, S. L. (1984). *Inside fashion design* (2nd ed.). New York: Harper & Row.

TRANQUILLO, M. D. (1984). *Styles of fashion: A pictorial handbook*. New York: Van Nostrand Reinhold.

VARIATIONS IN CONSUMER QUALITY PERCEPTIONS

AJZEN, I., & FISHBEIN, J. (1980). *Understanding attitudes and predicting social behavior*. Englewood Cliffs, NJ: Prentice-Hall.

CREEKMORE, A. S. (1963). *Clothing behaviors and their relation to general values and to the striving for basic needs*. Ph.D. Thesis, Pennsylvania State University.

FRANCIS, S. K., & DICKEY, L. E. (1984). Dimensions of satisfaction with purchases of women's dresses: Before and after garment care. *Journal of Consumer Studies and Home Economics, 8,* 153–168.

GALBRAITH, R. L. (1981). Consumer comments on textile and apparel quality. *American Society for Quality Control Textile and Needle Trades Division Transactions,* 94–98.

HARRINGTON, E. C. J. (1965). The desirability function. *Industrial Quality Control, 21,* 494–498.

HOWARD, J. A., & SHETH, J. N. (1969). *The theory of buyer behavior*. New York: John Wiley & Sons.

JACOBY, J., & OLSON, J. C. (1985). *Perceived quality: How consumers view stores and merchandise.* Lexington, MA: D.C. Heath.

MADDOX, R. N. (1981). Two-factor theory and consumer satisfaction: Replication and extension. *Journal of Consumer Research, 8,* 97–102.

MAYNES, E. S. (1976). *Decision-making for consumers: An introduction to consumer economics.* New York: Macmillan.

MCCULLOUGH, J. S., & MORRIS, M. A. (1980). Development of a model for quality grading of textile products. *Home Economics Research Journal, 9*(2), 116–123.

MYERS, J. H., & ALPERT, M. I. (1968). Determinant buying attitudes: Meaning and measurement. *Journal of Marketing, 32,* 13–20.

NORTON, M. J. T., NELSON, C. N., & SIEBEN, W. A. (1986). Apparel quality from consumers' perspective: Do expectations match in-use experience? *American Society for Quality Control, Textile and Needle Trades Division Transactions.*

SWAN, J. E., & COMBS, L. J. (1976). Product performance and consumer satisfaction: A new concept. *Journal of Marketing, 40,* 25–33.

PRICE AS A CUE TO QUALITY

FRENCH, N. D., WILLIAMS, J. J., & CHANCE, W. A. (1972). A shopping experiment on price-quality relationships. *Journal of Retailing, 48*(3), 3–16.

FRIEDMAN, M. (1967). Quality and price consideration in rational consumer decision making. *Journal of Consumer Affairs, 1,* 13–23.

GALE, A., & DARDIS, R. (1970). Predicting product performance by price. *Journal of the American Association of Textile Chemists and Colorists, 2*(10), 23–27.

GARDNER, D. M. (1971). Is there a generalized price-quality relationship? *Journal of Marketing Research, 8,* 241–243.

GARDNER, D. M. (1970). An experimental investigation of the price/quality relationship. *Journal of Retailing, 46*(3), 25–41.

HATCH, K. L., & ROBERTS, J. A. (1985). Use of intrinsic and extrinsic cues to assess textile product quality. *Journal of Consumer Studies and Home Economics, 9,* 341–357.

JACOBY, J., OLSON, J. C., & HADDOCK, R. A. (1971). Price, brand name, and product composition characteristics as determinants of perceived quality. *Journal of Applied Psychology, 55*(6), 570–579.

JUNG, A. F. (1983). Price-quality relationship: An empirical investigation. *Journal of Consumer Studies and Home Economics, 7,* 1–6.

SPROLES, G. B. (1977). New evidence on price and product quality. *The Journal of Consumer Affairs, 11*(1), 63–77.

SZYBILLO, G. J., & JACOBY, J. (1974). Intrinsic versus extrinsic cues as determinants of perceived product quality. *Journal of Applied Psychology, 59*(1), 74–78.

VALENZI, E. R., & ANDREWS, I. R. (1971). Effect of price information on product quality ratings. *Journal of Applied Psychology, 55*(1), 87–91.

WHEATLEY, J. J., & CHIU, J. S. Y. (1977). The effects of price, store image, and product and respondent characteristics on perceptions of quality. *Journal of Marketing Research, 14,* 181–186.

WHEATLEY, J. J., CHIU, J. S. Y., & GOLDMAN, A. (1981). Physical quality, price, and perceptions of product quality: Implications for retailers. *Journal of Retailing, 57*(2), 100–115.

INDUSTRY EFFORTS TO CONTROL QUALITY

BEST, A., & ANDREASEN, A. R. (1976). *Talking back to business: Voiced and unvoiced complaints.* Washington, DC: Center for the Study of Responsive Law.

BESTERFIELD, D. H. (1986). *Quality control* (2nd ed.). Englewood Cliffs, NJ: Prentice-Hall.

COLGATE, A. I.. (1988). Pinning down quality. *Bobbin,* (March), 85.

CROSBY, P. B. (1989). *Let's talk quality.* New York: McGraw-Hill.

CROSBY, P. B. (1984). *Quality without tears.* New York: McGraw-Hill.

CROSBY, P. B. (1979). *Quality is free.* New York: McGraw-Hill.

DUNLAP, D. (1978). Quality control in the cutting room. *Bobbin,* (February), 76–86.

FEIGENBAUM, A. V. (1983). *Total quality control* (3rd ed.). New York: McGraw-Hill.

GAVLAK, M. (1984). Product performance specifications: A retailer's perspective. *ASTM Standardization News, 13*(7), 16–18.

JACOBSEN, R., & AACKER, D. (1987). The strategic role of product quality. *Journal of Marketing, 51*(October), 31–44.

KOLBECK, W. B. (1984). Quality assurance: Is your program up to date? *Bobbin,* (August), 81–92.

LATTURE, W. E. (1981). Improving quality through the analysis of returned garments. *American Society for Quality Control Textile and Needle Trades Division Transactions,* 50–59.

LESTER, R. H., NORBERT, L. E., & MOTTLEY, H. E. JR. (1977). *Quality control for profit.* New York: Industrial Press.

LOVELESS, H. L. (1983). A quality control blueprint. *Apparel Industry Magazine, 44*(April), 32–34.

MCVEY, D. C. (1983). Getting a grip on quality. *Apparel Industry Magazine, 44*(November), 20–26.

MEHTA, P. (1982). Final inspection. *Bobbin, 23*(6), 27–31.

PETERS, T. J. (1982). *In search of excellence: Lessons from America's best-run companies.* New York: Harper & Row.

RAO, V. A. (1985). Total quality: A commitment to excellence. *Bobbin, 26*(10), 41–45.

STEINIGER, L. B., & DARDIS R. (1971). Consumers' textile complaints. *Journal of the American Association of Textile Chemists and Colorists, 3,* 161–165.

STOHLMAN, D. (1985). Developing your statistical Q.C. program. *Bobbin,* (September), 188–210.

WEINTRAUB, E. (1986). Evaluating and improving quality. *Bobbin, 27*(10), 26–28.

ZARUBA, J. F. (1982). Steps to in-process inspection. *American Society for Quality Control Textile and Needle Trades Division Transactions, 10,* 72–80.

CAD/CAM

BERNARD, H. (1987). Retailers realize CAD benefits. *Apparel Industry Magazine,* (November), 69–75.

KOSH, K. (1990). Pattern quality, MU and CAD/CAM systems. *Apparel Manufacturer, 2*(8), 11–16.

KOSH, K. (1987). Computer systems automate design function. *Bobbin,* (February), 51–64.

Microdynamics. *Futuresafe* (videotape). (1988). Dallas, TX: Author.

SANTORA, J. E. (1986). Microdynamics Incorporated. *Bobbin,* (February).

TRAY, A. I. (1987). Computer designs' third dimension. *Bobbin,* (February), 58–59.

WORKMAN, J. E., & CALDWELL, L. F. (1988). The future belongs to computer aided design and manufacturing. *What's New in Home Economics,* (January/February), 6–7.

SEWING ROOM TECHNOLOGY

HEISEY, F. (1984). The future of apparel production and construction. *Journal of Home Economics, 76*(3), 8–13.

JONES, S. (1986). Future trends and needs. *Bobbin,* (April), 108–123.

LOWER, J. (1987). Robotics advance softly. *Bobbin, 28*(9), 106–113.

ONDOVCSIK, M. (1985). The unit production system. *Bobbin,* (October), 50.

SPIEGEL, S. (1986). Technology of the '80s allows style flexibility. *Bobbin,* (November).

(TC)2 Today (videotape). (1990). Raleigh, NC: Textile/Clothing Technology Corporation.

WALSH, W. (1984). Sewing room automation. *Bobbin,* (September), 256–260.

WILCOX, J. L. (1985). The apparel industry in 1995. *American Society for Quality Control Textile and Needle Trades Division Transactions,* 52–56.

COSTING

ALLEN, H. (1986). *Introduction to sewn products: Costing* (videotape). Raleigh: North Carolina State University.

American Apparel Manufacturers Association. (1965). *The effect of style variation upon manufacturing cost.* Washington, DC: Author.

COLE AND ASSOCIATES. (1983). *Practical apparel costing.* Shelbyville, TN: Author.

GAETAN, M. (1979). Garment costing: Method or madness. *Bobbin,* (March), 32–47.

STURDIVANT, L. (1985). Costing and apparel manufacturing. *Bobbin,* (September), 226–232.

WHITE, R. (1984). Costing and apparel manufacturing. *Bobbin,* (December), 88–94.

INTERNATIONAL TRADE

American Textile Manufacturers Institute. (1987). *Textile and apparel imports: A national concern.* Washington, DC: Author.

American Apparel Manufacturers Association. (1980). *Apparel trade primer.* Washington, DC: Author.

American Textile Manufacturers Institute. (n.d.). *It's good business to buy American.* Washington, DC: Author.

American Textile Manufacturers Institute. *Textile Hi-Lights,* (published quarterly).

ARPAN, J. S., DE LA TORRE, J., & TOYNE, B. (1982). *The U.S. Apparel Industry: International Challenge, Domestic Response.* Atlanta: Georgia State University.

Boston Consulting Group. (1985). *Analysis of garment sourcing economics.* Boston: Author.

Crafted With Pride in U.S.A. Council. (n.d.). *Fact sheet.* New York: Author.

DARDIS, R., SPIVAK, S. M., & SHIR, C. (1985). Price and quality differences for imported and domestic men's dress shirts. *Home Economics Research Journal, 13,* 391–399.

DE LA TORRE, J., JEDEL, M. J., ARPAN, J. S., OGRAM, E. W., & TOYNE, B. (1978). *Corporate responses to import competition in the U.S. apparel industry.* Atlanta: Georgia State University.

DICKERSON, K. G., (1991). *Textiles and Apparel in the International Economy,* New York: Macmillan.

DICKERSON, K. G., & BARRY, M. (1980). Family clothing: The economics of international trade. *Journal of Home Economics, 72,* 35–39.

DICKERSON, K. G., & HESTER, S. B. (1984). The purchase of a shirt: International implications. *Journal of Home Economics, 76,* 20–25.

East vs. west: What Americans really think about imports. (1988). *Chain Store Age,* (January), 13–15.

KING, JR., R. (1988). Made in the U.S.A. *Forbes,* (May 16).

National Retail Merchants Association. (n.d.). *The costs of protectionism: Textile and apparel import quotas.* New York: Author.

TOMPKINS, J. A. (n.d.). *The myth of moving offshore.* Raleigh, NC: Tompkins Associates.

U.S. Customs. (1989). *HS: Harmonized commodity description and coding system.* Washington, DC: Author.

U.S. Customs Service. (1990). *Importing into the United States.* Washington, DC: Author.

VIGDOR, I. (1989). The global facts. *Apparel Industry Magazine,* (May), 58–59.

QUICK RESPONSE

BOWER, J. L., & HOUT, T. M. (1988). Fast-cycle capability for competitive power. *Harvard Business Review,* (November/December), 110–118.

COTTON, R. E. (1986). QR's bottom line. *Apparel Industry Magazine,* (July).

DOLEN, P. Z. (1989). Quick response: What's in it for you? *Apparel Industry Magazine,* (September), 86–88.

GRAVENSLUND, W. J., & DINKELSPIEL, J. D. (1990). Updating QR: New retail mindset needed. *Women's Wear Daily,* (May 3), 13.

JONES, S. H. (1988). QR depends upon quality. *Apparel Industry Magazine,* (June), 40–43.

KURT SALMON ASSOCIATES. (1986). Quick response for retailing. *The KSA Perspective,* (January).

KURT SALMON ASSOCIATES. (1986). New technology for quick response. *The KSA Perspective,* (March).

SWIFT, R. E. (1984). *Quick response: The ultimate in quality and service.* New York: Crafted With Pride in U.S.A. Council.

THOME, J. T. (1986). QR gains as industries cooperate. *Apparel Industry Magazine,* (October), 20, 22.

WEINTRAUB, E. (1986). Study probes use of QR to combat apparel imports surge. *Daily News Record,* (December 8), 11.

WHITE, R. (1985). Quick response: What is it? *Apparel Industry Magazine,* (December), 40–42.

BAR CODES

ALDRICH, J. (1989). EGI: The new wave. *Bobbin,* (April), 50–52.

BROCKETT, R. (1989). VAM: The next logical step. *Bobbin,* (April), 76–84.

CAVENDER, D. (1988). A code to link by. *Bobbin,* (March), 110–112.

Connections. (1989). *Supplement to America's Textile International, Apparel Industry Magazine and Apparel Merchandising,* (March).

DYSART, J. (1989). The fear of EDI. *Apparel Industry Magazine,* (September), 90.

KNIGHT, K. (1986). Bar code tech quickens response. *Bobbin,* (April), 86–96.

REDA, S. (1988). Decoding UPC and EDI. *Apparel Merchandising,* (August), 51–53.

ROBINS, G. (1989). New role for the buyer. *Stores,* (December), 34–37.

THALL, N. (1988). UPC catalog—What to expect. *The KSA Perspective,* (January).

FIBER CONTENT LABELING

American Apparel Manufacturers Association. (1987). *The labeling book.* Washington, DC: Author.

U.S. Federal Trade Commission. (1986). *Questions and answers relating to the Textile Fiber Products Identification Act.* Washington, DC: Author.

U.S. Federal Trade Commission. (1986). *Questions and answers relating to the Wool Product Labeling Act and Regulations.* Washington, DC: Author.

U.S. Federal Trade Commission. (1986). *Rules and regulations under the Textile Fiber Products Identification Act.* Washington, DC: Author.

U.S. Federal Trade Commission. (1986). *Rules and regulations under the Wool Products Labeling Act of 1939.* Washington, DC: Author.

U.S. Federal Trade Commission. (1980). *Rules and regulations under the Fur Products Labeling Act.* Washington, DC: Author.

U.S. Federal Trade Commission. (n.d.). *A direct marketer's guide to labeling requirements under the textile and wool acts.* Washington, DC: Author.

CARE

American Society for Testing and Materials. (1981). *D 3938-81 Guide for evaluation of textile products in relation to refurbishing described on care labels.* Philadelphia: Author.

FEE, J. M. (1985). Care labeling issues. *American Society of Quality Control Textile and Needle Trades Division Transactions, 13,* 57–71.

International Fabricare Institute. (1988). *American national standard: Fair claims guide for consumer textile products.* New York: Author.

OEHLKE, N. (1988). Who's writing your care label? *Apparel Industry Magazine,* (May), 106.

Solving the care label dilemma (videotape). Silver Spring, MD: International Fabricare Institute.

U.S. Federal Trade Commission. (1984). *Trade regulation rule: Care labeling of textile wearing apparel and certain piece goods.* Washington, DC: Author.

U.S. Federal Trade Commission. (1984). *What's new about care labels.* Washington, DC: Author.

U.S. Federal Trade Commission. (1984). *Writing a care label.* Washington, DC: Author.

SIZE

American Apparel Manufacturers Association. (1982). *How to size and label products for export sales.* Washington, DC: Author.

American Society for Testing and Materials. (1989). *D 4910-89 Standard tables of body measurements for infants, ages 0 to 18 months.* Philadelphia: Author.

DELK, A. E., & CASSILL, N. L. (1989). Jeans sizing: Problems and recommendations. *Apparel Manufacturer, 1*(2), 18–23.

GIOELLO, D. A., & BERKE, B. (1979). *Figure types and size ranges.* New York: Fairchild.

National Bureau of Standards. (1973). *Voluntary product standard PS 54-72: Body measurements for the sizing of girls' apparel* (withdrawn 1983). Washington, DC: U.S. Department of Commerce.

National Bureau of Standards. (1972). *Voluntary product standard PS 45-71: Body measurements for the sizing of apparel for young men (students)* (withdrawn 1983). Washington, DC: U.S. Department of Commerce.

National Bureau of Standards. (1971). *Voluntary product standard PS 36-70: Body measurements for the sizing of boys' apparel* (withdrawn 1983). Washington, DC: U.S. Department of Commerce.

National Bureau of Standards. (1971). *Voluntary product standard PS 42-70: Body measurements for the sizing of women's patterns and apparel* (withdrawn 1983). Washington, DC: U.S. Department of Commerce.

National Bureau of Standards. (1953). *Commercial standard CS151-50: Body measurements for the sizing of apparel for infants, babies, toddlers and children* (withdrawn 1983). Washington, DC: U.S. Department of Commerce.

BRAND NAME

Behling, D. U., & Wilch, J. (1988). Perceptions of branded clothing by male consumers. *Clothing and Textiles Research Journal, 6*(2), 43–47.

Bender, D. (1984). Finding the fakes. *Apparel Industry Magazine,* (January), 40–41.

Kurt Salmon Associates. (1988). Private label development for retailers. *The KSA Perspective,* (January).

Private label. (1984). *Stores,* (September), 30, 66.

Sloane, L. (1988). Private-label clothes find new buyers. *New York Times Consumer's World,* (February 20).

CRAFTED WITH PRIDE IN THE U.S.A.

Elrick & Lavidge, Inc. (1986). *Crafted With Pride in the U.S.A. campaign: An awareness and impact research tracking study.* Atlanta: Author.

Gallup Organization, Inc. (1985). *Consumer perceptions concerning the quality of American products and services.* Princeton, NJ: Author.

Key results of consumer preference: Research studies by four independent polling organizations. (n.d.). New York: Crafted with Pride in U.S.A. Council.

Summary of research findings. (n.d.). New York: Crafted With Pride in U.S.A. Council.

FABRIC

American Apparel Manufacturers Association. (1978). *Guidelines for purchasing by specification and vendor evaluation & rating system.* Washington, DC: Author.

American Textile Manufacturer's Institute. (1986). *Worth Street Textile Market Rules.* Washington, DC: Author.

Blackmon, A. G. (1975). *Manual of standard fabric defects in the textile industry.* Graniteville, SC: Graniteville Co.

Coats, J. P. Ltd. (1984). Fabric: How it sews. *Bobbin,* (September), 118–121.

Coats & Clark, Inc. (n.d.). *Grain in fabric.* Stamford, CT: Author.

Fortess, F. (1989). Technology tailored to fabric. *Bobbin,* (May), 86–92.

Fortess, F. (1985). Objective evaluation of apparel fabrics. *Bobbin,* (June), 130–138.

Fortess, F. (1985). Purchasing fabric by performance specifications. *Apparel World, 6*(1), 30.

Gioello, D. (1985). Hand of fabric primer. *Bobbin,* (April), 122–126.

Gioello, D. A. (1982). *Understanding fabrics: From fiber to finished cloth.* New York: Fairchild.

Gioello, D. A. (1981). *Profiling fabrics: Properties, performance, and construction techniques.* New York: Fairchild.

Hollen, N., Saddler, J., Langford, A. L., & Kadolph, S. J. (1988). *Textiles* (6th ed.). New York: Macmillan.

Joseph, M. L. (1986). *Introductory textile science* (5th ed.). New York: Holt, Rinehart, & Winston.

Kolbeck, W. B. (1984). The receipt and inspection of fabric: A primer. *Bobbin,* (April), 45–49.

Lyle, D. S. (1982). *Modern textiles* (2nd ed.). New York: John Wiley & Sons.

Lyle, D. S. (1977). *Performance of textiles.* New York: John Wiley & Sons.

Powderly, D. (1987). *Fabric inspection and grading.* Columbia, SC: Bobbin International.

Powderly, D. (1988). Mine eyes have seen the defect. *Bobbin,* (March), 100–107.

Powderly, D. (1985). Making the grade. *Bobbin,* (October), 150.

Rees, T. (1990). FAST fabrics. *Apparel Industry Magazine,* (March), 82–84.

Rudie, R. (1990). Prints heat up fashion. *Bobbin,* (May), 54–60.

Simplicity Pattern Company, Inc. (1979). *All about plaids.* New York: Author.

Tortora, P. G. (1987). *Understanding textiles* (3rd ed.). New York: Macmillan.

U.S. code of federal regulations, part 1602 to 1632, subchapter D—Flammable Fabrics Act regulations. (1988). Washington, DC: U.S. Government Printing Office.

U.S. Military Standard MIL-STD-105D. (1963). Washington, DC: U.S. Government Printing Office.

Willis, R. F. (1985). Color monitoring: The instrumental requirements for color control. *American Society for Quality Control Textile and Needle Trades Division Transactions, 13,* 40–44.

Wingate, I. B., & Mohler, J. F. (1984). *Textile fabrics and their selection.* Englewood Cliffs, NJ: Prentice-Hall.

STITCHES, SEAMS, AND STITCHINGS

Baugh, C. (1984). Needle problems and how to avoid them. *Bobbin,* (January), 180–182.

Coats, J. P. Ltd. (n.d.). *The technology of thread and seams.* Glasgow, Scotland: Author.

Crum, R. J. (1983). *Methods of joining fabrics: A technical literature survey.* Manchester, United Kingdom: Shirley Institute.

Escott, D. (1978). The mechanics guide: Stitches, seams, and stitchings (Federal Standard). *Bobbin, 20*(2), 84–108.

Ferla, R. (1987). To sew a fine seam. *The New York Times Magazine,* (June 7), 50–63.

Henderson, H. R. (1985). Down with seam pucker. *Apparel Industry Magazine,* (January), 48–50.

Italiano, L. (1985). Seam construction. *Bobbin,* (April), 73–74.

Kolbeck, W. B. (1983). A neglected tool. *Bobbin, 24*(7), 139–142.

McGinnis, J. (1984). Seam pucker: Causes and solutions. *Apparel World, 5*(8), 63–64.

Murphy, M. (1984). Needle problems and solutions. *Bobbin,* (January), 182–185.

Pfaff. (1983). Seam pucker: A solution. *Bobbin,* (March), 193–196.

Reader's Digest Association, Inc. (1979). *Reader's Digest complete guide to needlework.* Pleasantville, NY: Author.

Sandow, K. (1990). Seam puckering. *Apparel Manufacturer, 2*(9). 14–18.

Sandow, K. (1990). Skipped stitches. *Apparel Manufacturer, 2*(7), 46–49.

The Thread Institute, Inc. (n.d.). *Voluntary guide to colorfastness in thread.* Washington, DC: Author.

Union Special. (1983). *Garment construction guide.* Huntley, IL: Author.

Union Special. (1980). *Lockstitch formation type 301.* Chicago: Author.

Union Special. (1978). *Overedge stitch formation type 504.* Chicago: Author.

Union Special. (1976). *Stitch formation type 401.* Chicago: Author.

Union Special. (1974). *Thread consumption.* Chicago: Author.

Union Special. (1971). *Stitch formation type 605.* Chicago: Author.

Union Special. (1971). *Stitch type 401 formation & pucker control.* Chicago: Author.

Union Special. (n.d.). *Inside Union Special.* Chicago: Author.

Union Special. (n.d.). *The mechanization of sewing.* Huntley, IL: Author.

U.S. Fed. std. no. 751a: Stitches, seams, and stitchings. (1965). Washington, DC: U.S. General Services Administration.

FIT AND ALTERATION

Allen, A. (1987). Perfect fit. *Threads Magazine,* (August/September), 70–73.

Alteration Consulting (1987). *The simple art of fitting* (4th ed.). Chicago: Author.

Brinkley, J., & Aletti, A. (1976). *Altering ready-to-wear fashions.* Peoria, IL: Chas. A. Bennett.

Burns, M. A. (1976). *Altering ready-to-wear.* Philadelphia: J.B. Lippincott.

Carlin, D. (1962). *Alteration of men's clothing* (3rd ed.). New York: Fairchild.

Dolce, D., & Devellard, J. P. (1983). *The consumer's guide to menswear.* New York: Dodd, Mead & Co.

Farmer, B. M., & Gotwals, L. M. (1982). *Concepts of fit.* New York: Macmillan.

Friese, P. (1985). Made-to-measure marvel. *Apparel Industry Magazine,* (August), 66–72.

Johnson, M. (1964). *Mary Johnson's guide to altering and restyling ready-made clothing.* New York: E.P. Dutton.

Kuhlman, P. (1989). Making non-contact. *Bobbin,* (March), 64–68.

McVey, D. C. (1984). Fit to be sold. *Apparel Industry Magazine,* (February), 24–26.

Taylor, G. (1979). Patterns vs. people. *Bobbin, 20*(8), 170–182.

List of ASTM and AATCC Standards

ASTM Standards Relating to Textiles—Yarns, Fabrics, and General Test Methods, Fibers and Zippers

D 76–89	Specification for Tensile Testing Machines for Textiles
D 123–89c	Terminology Relating to Textiles
D 204–82(1986)	Methods of Testing Sewing Threads
D 276–87	Test Methods for Identification of Fibers in Textiles
D 434–75	Test Method for Resistance to Slippage of Yarns in Woven Fabrics Using a Standard Seam
D 461–87	Test Methods for Felt
D 519–78(1983)	Test Method for Length of Fiber in Wool Top
D 541–87	Specification for Single Jute Yarn
D 579–89	Specification for Greige Woven Glass Fabrics
D 580–89a	Specification for Greige Woven Glass Tapes and Webbing
D 584–77(1983)	Test Method for Wool Content of Raw Wool—Laboratory Scale
D 629–88	Test Methods for Quantitative Analysis of Textiles
D 737–75(1980)	Test Method for Air Permeability of Textile Fabrics
D 861–89	Practice for Use of the Tex System to Designate Linear Density of Fibers, Yarn Intermediates, and Yarns
D1059–87	Test Method for Yarn Number Based on Short-Length Specimens
D1060–85	Practice for Core Sampling of Raw Wool in Packages for Determination of Percentage of Clean Wool Fiber Present
D1113–78(1983)	Test Method for Vegetable Matter and Other Alkali-Insoluble Impurities in Scoured Wool
D1117–80	Methods of Testing Nonwoven Fabrics
D1230–85	Test Method for Flammability of Apparel Textiles
D1234–85	Method of Sampling and Testing Staple Length of Grease Wool

D1244–81(1986)	Practice for Designation of Yarn Construction
D1282–89a	Test Method for Resistance to Airflow as an Indication of Average Fiber Diameter of Wool Top, Card Sliver, and Scoured Wool
D1283–85	Test Method for Alkali-Solubility of Wool
D1284–87	Test Methods for Relaxation and Consolidation Dimensional Changes of Stabilized Knit Wool Fabrics
D1294–86	Test Method for Tensile Strength and Breaking Tenacity of Wool Fiber Bundles—1-in. (25.4-mm) Gage Length
D1334–72(1983)	Test Method for Wool Content of Raw Wool—Commercial Scale
D1336–72(1977)	Test Method for Distortion of Yarn in Woven Fabrics
D1388–64(1975)	Test Methods for Stiffness of Fabrics
D1422–85	Test Method for Twist in Single Spun Yarns by the Untwist–Retwist Method
D1423–88	Test Method for Twist in Yarns by the Direct-Counting Method
D1424–83	Test Method for Tear Resistance of Woven Fabrics by Falling Pendulum (Elmendorf) Apparatus
D1425–89	Test Method for Unevenness of Textile Strands Using Capacitance Testing Equipment
D1440–77(1982)	Test Method for Length and Length Distribution of Cotton Fibers (Array Method)
D1441–87	Practice for Sampling Cotton Fibers for Testing
D1442–80	Test Method for Maturity of Cotton Fibers (Sodium Hydroxide Swelling and Polarized Light Procedures)
D1445–75	Test Method for Breaking Strength and Elongation of Cotton Fibers (Flat Bundle Method)
D1447–89	Test Method for Length and Length Uniformity of Cotton Fibers by Fibrograph Measurement
D1448–84	Test Method for Micronaire Reading of Cotton Fibers
D1464–79(1984)	Test Method for Differential Dyeing Behavior of Cotton
D1518–85	Test Method for Thermal Transmittance of Textile Materials
D1574–87a	Test Method for Extractable Matter in Wool and Other Fibers
D1575–83	Test Method for Fiber Length of Wool in Scoured Wool and in Card Sliver
D1576–84	Test Method for Moisture in Wool by Oven-Drying
D1577–79	Test Methods for Linear Density of Textile Fibers
D1578–88	Test Method for Breaking Load of Skeins
D1682–64(1975)	Test Methods for Breaking Load and Elongation of Textile Fabrics
D1683–81	Test Method for Failure in Sewn Seams of Woven Fabrics
D1684–84	Practice for Lighting Cotton Classing Rooms for Color Grading
D1770–88	Test Method for Neps, Vegetable Matter, and Colored Fiber in Wool Top
D1774–79	Test Methods for Elastic Properties of Textile Fibers
D1775–81	Test Methods for Tension and Elongation of Wide Elastic Fabrics
D1776–85	Practice for Conditioning Textiles for Testing
D1777–64(1975)	Method for Measuring Thickness of Textile Materials
D1907–89	Test Method for Yarn Number by the Skein Method
D1908–89	Test Method for Needle-Related Damage Due to Sewing in Woven Fabric

D1909–86	Table of Commercial Moisture Regains for Textile Fibers
D2050–87	Terminology Relating to Zippers
D2051–86	Test Method for Durability of Finish of Zippers to Laundering
D2052–85	Test Method for Colorfastness of Zippers to Dry cleaning
D2053–86	Test Method for Colorfastness of Zippers to Light
D2054–86	Test Method for Colorfastness of Zipper Tapes to Crocking
D2057–85	Test Method for Colorfastness of Zippers to Laundering
D2058–87	Test Method for Durability of Finish of Zippers to Dry cleaning
D2059–87	Test Method for Resistance of Zippers to Salt Spray (Fog)
D2060–85	Methods for Measuring Zipper Dimensions
D2061–87	Test Methods for Strength Tests for Zippers
D2062–87	Test Methods for Operability of Zippers
D2101–82	Test Methods for Tensile Properties of Single Man-Made Textile Fibers Taken from Yarns and Tows
D2102–87	Test Method for Shrinkage of Textile Fibers
D2118–84	Practice for Assigning a Standard Commercial Moisture Content for Wool and Its Products
D2130–88	Test Method for Diameter of Wool and Other Animal Fibers by Microprojection
D2165–78(1983)	Test Method for pH of Aqueous Extracts of Wool and Similar Animal Fibers
D2252–85	Specification for Fineness of Types of Alpaca
D2253–88	Test Method for Color of Raw Cotton Using the Nickerson-Hunter Cotton Colorimeter
D2255–87	Test Method for Grading Cotton Yarns for Appearance
D2256–88	Test Method for Tensile Properties of Yarns by the Single-Strand Method
D2257–89	Test Method for Extractable Matter in Textiles
D2258–86	Practice for Sampling Yarn for Testing
D2259–87	Test Method for Shrinkage of Yarns in Boiling Water or Dry Heat
D2260–89	Tables of Conversion Factors and Equivalent Yarn Numbers Measured in Various Numbering Systems
D2261–83	Test Method for Tearing Strength of Woven Fabrics by the Tongue (Single-Rip) Method (Constant-Rate-of-Extension Tensile Testing Machine)
D2262–83	Test Method for Tearing Strength of Woven Fabrics by the Tongue (Single Rip) Method (Constant-Rate-of-Transverse Tensile Testing Machine)
D2402–78	Test Method for Water Retention of Fibers (Centrifuge Method)
D2462–77(1983)	Test Method for Moisture in Wool by Distillation with Toluene
D2475–88	Specification for Wool Felt
D2480–82	Test Method for Maturity Index and Linear Density of Cotton Fibers by the Causticaire Method
D2494–81	Test Method for Commercial Mass of a Shipment of Yarn or Man-Made Staple Fiber or Tow
D2495–87	Test Method for Moisture in Cotton by Oven-Drying
D2497–80(1985)	Tolerances for Man-Made Organic-Base Filament Single Yarns
D2524–85	Test Method for Breaking Tenacity of Wool Fibers, Flat Bundle Method—⅛-in. (3.2 mm) Gage Length

D2525–76(1983)	Practice for Sampling Wool for Moisture
D2594–87	Test Methods for Stretch Properties of Knitted Fabrics Having Low Power
D2612–78	Test Method for Fiber Cohesion in Sliver and Top in Static Tests
D2630–83	Test Method for Rubber Property–Adhesion to Fabrics (Strap Peel Test)
D2644–81(1986)	Tolerances for Yarns Spun on the Woolen System
D2645–85	Tolerances for Yarns Spun on the Cotton or Worsted Systems
D2646–87	Test Methods for Backing Fabrics
D2654–89a	Test Methods for Moisture in Textiles
D2678–82	Practice for Spinning Tests on the Cotton System for Measurement of Yarn Properties
D2720–77(1983)	Recommended Practice for Calculation of Commercial Weight and Yield of Scoured Wool, Top, and Noil for Various Commercial Compositions
D2724–87	Test Methods for Bonded, Fused, and Laminated Apparel Fabrics
D2811–77(1983)	Methods for Spinning Tests on the Cotton System for Measurement of Spinning Performance
D2812–88	Test Method for Non-Lint Content of Cotton
D2816–76(1985)	Test Method for Cashmere Coarse-Hair Content in Cashmere
D2817–76(1985)	Specification for Maximum Cashmere Coarse-Hair Content in Cashmere
D2904–86	Practice for Interlaboratory Testing of a Textile Test Method that Produces Normally Distributed Data
D2905–88	Practice for Statements on Number of Specimens for Textiles
D2906–88	Practice for Statements on Precision and Bias for Textiles
D2968–89	Test Method for Med and Kemp Fibers in Wool and Other Animal Fibers by Microprojection
D3025–86	Practice for Standardizing Cotton Fiber Test Results by Use of Calibration Cotton Standards
D3106–89	Test Method for Permanent Deformation of Elastomeric Yarns
D3107–75(1980)	Test Method for Stretch Properties of Fabrics Woven from Stretch Yarns
D3108–88	Test Methods for Coefficient of Friction, Yarn to Solid Material
D3135–87	Specification for Performance of Bonded, Fused, and Laminated Apparel Fabrics
D3136–88	Terminology for Permanent Care Labels for Consumer Textile and Leather Products Other Than Carpets and Upholstery
D3181–89	Practice for Conducting Wear Testing on Textile Garments
D3217–79	Test Methods for Breaking Tenacity of Man-Made Textile Fibers in Loop or Knot Configurations
D3218–87	Specification for Polyolefin Monofilaments
D3333–79	Practice for Sampling Man-Made Staple Fibers (Intent to Withdraw)
D3334–80	Method of Testing Fabrics Woven from Polyolefin Monofilaments
D3412–86	Test Method for Coefficient of Friction, Yarn to Yarn
D3511–82	Test Method for Pilling Resistance and Other Related Surface Changes of Textile Fabrics: Brush Pilling Tester Method

D3512–82	Test Method for Pilling Resistance and Other Related Surface Changes of Textile Fabrics: Random Tumble Pilling Tester Method
D3513–81	Test Method for Overlength Fiber Content of Man-Made Staple Fiber
D3514–81	Test Method for Resistance of Apparel Fabrics to Pilling (Elastomeric Pad Method)
D3657–88	Specification for Zipper Dimensions
D3659–80(1986)	Test Method for Flammability of Apparel Fabrics by Semi-Restraint Method
D3660–81	Test Method for Staple Length of Man-Made Fibers, Average and Distribution (Fiber Array Method)
D3661–79	Test Method for Staple Length of Man-Made Fibers, Average and Distribution (Single-Fiber Length Machine Method)
D3692–89	Practice for Selection of Zippers for Care-Labeled Apparel and Household Furnishings
D3693–80(1985)	Specification for Labeled Length per Holder of Sewing Thread
D3773–89	Test Methods for Length of Woven Fabric
D3774–89	Test Methods for Width of Woven Fabric
D3775–85	Test Method for Fabric Count of Woven Fabric
D3776–85	Test Methods for Mass per Unit Area (Weight) of Woven Fabric
D3777–79(1984)	Practice for Writing Specifications for Textiles
D3786–87	Test Method for Hydraulic Bursting Strength of Knitted Goods and Nonwoven Fabrics—Diaphragm Bursting Strength Tester Method
D3787–80a	Test Method for Bursting Strength of Knitted Goods—Constant-Rate-of-Traverse (CRT) Ball Burst Test
D3817–89	Test Method for Maturity Index of Cotton Fibers by Fibrograph
D3818–79(1984)	Test Method for Linear Density and Maturity Index of Cotton Fibers (IIC-Shirley Fineness/Maturity Tester)
D3822–82	Test Method for Tensile Properties of Single Textile Fibers
D3823–88	Practice for Determining Ticket Numbers for Sewing Threads
D3882–88	Test Method for Bow and Skewness in Woven and Knitted Fabrics
D3883–85	Test Method for Yarn Crimp or Yarn Takeup in Woven Fabrics
D3884–80	Test Method for Abrasion Resistance of Textile Fabrics (Rotary Platform, Double-Head Method)
D3885–80	Test Method for Abrasion Resistance of Textile Fabrics (Flexing and Abrasion Method)
D3886–80	Test Method for Abrasion Resistance of Textile Fabrics (Inflated Diaphragm Method)
D3887–80	Specification for Knitted Fabrics
D3888–80(1985)	Definitions of Terms Relating to Open-End Spinning
D3937–82	Test Method for Crimp Frequency of Man-Made Staple Fibers
D3938–81	Guide for Evaluation of Textile Products in Relation to Refurbishing Described on Care Labels
D3939–80	Test Method for Snagging Resistance of Fabrics (Mace Test Method)

D3940–83	Test Method for Bursting Strength (Load) and Elongation of Sewn Seams of Knit or Woven Stretch Textile Fabrics
D3990–89a	Terminology Relating to Fabric Defects
D3991–85	Specifications for Fineness of Wool or Mohair and Assignment of Grade
D3992–85	Specifications for Fineness of Wool Top or Mohair Top and Assignment of Grade
D4031–81(1987)	Test Method for Bulk Properties of Textured Yarns
D4032–82	Test Method for Stiffness of Fabric by the Circular Bend Procedure
D4108–87	Test Method for Thermal Protective Performance of Materials for Clothing by Open-Flame Method
D4120–82	Test Method for Fiber Cohesion in Roving, Sliver, and Top (Dynamic Tests)
D4157–82	Test Method for Abrasion Resistance of Textile Fabrics (Oscillatory Cylinder Method)
D4158–82	Test Method for Abrasion Resistance of Textile Fabrics (Uniform Abrasion Method)
D4231–83(1989)	Practice for Evaluation of Men's and Boys' Home Launderable Woven Dress Shirts and Sport Shirts
D4238–83	Test Method for Electrostatic Propensity of Textiles
D4270–86	Guide for Using Existing Practices in Developing and Writing Test Methods
D4271–88	Practice for Writing Statements on Sampling in Test Methods for Textiles
D4356–84	Practice for Establishing Consistent Test Method Tolerances
D4390–84	Practice for the Evaluation of the Performance of Terry Bathroom Products for Household Use
D4391–87	Terminology Relating to the Burning Behavior of Textiles
D4392–87	Terminology for Statistically Related Terms
D4465–85	Performance Specification for Zippers for Denim Dungarees
D4466–85	Terminology for Multicomponent Textile Fibers
D4467–85	Practice for Interlaboratory Testing of a Textile Test Method That Produces Non-Normally Distributed Data
D4522–86	Performance Specification for Feather-Filled and Down-Filled Products
D4523–85	Terminology Relating to Feather-Filled and Down-Filled Products
D4524–86	Test Method for Composition of Plumage
D4604–86	Test Methods for Measurement of Cotton Fibers by High Volume Instruments (HVI) (Motion Control Fiber Information System)
D4605–86	Test Methods for Measurement of Cotton Fibers by High Volume Instruments (HVI) (Special Instruments Laboratory System)
D4685–87	Test Method for Pile Retention of Corduroy Fabrics
D4686–87	Guide for Identification of Frequency Distributions
D4697–87	Guide for Maintaining Test Methods in the User's Laboratory
D4723–87	Index and Descriptions of Textile Heat and Flammability Test Methods and Performance Specifications
D4724–87	Test Methods for Degree of Filament Yarn Entanglement by Needle Insertion Methods
D4770–88	Test Method for Evaluation of Man-made Fiber Batting Used as Filling in Outerwear Apparel

D4772–88	Test Method for Surface Water Absorption of Terry Fabrics (Water-Flow Test Method)
D4845–89	Terminology Relating to Wool
D4846–88	Test Method for Resistance to Unsnapping of Snap Fasteners
D4848–89	Terminology Relating to Tensile Properties of Textiles
D4849–89	Terminology Relating to Yarn and Related Terms
D4850–89	Terminology Relating to Fabric and Related Terms
D4853–88	Guide for Reducing Test Variability
D4854–88	Guide for Estimating the Magnitude of Variability from Expected Sources in Sampling Plans
D4855–88	Practice for Comparing Test Methods
D4910–89	Standard Tables of Body Measurements for Infants, Ages 0 to 18 Months
D4911–89	Tolerances for Man-Made Yarns Spun on the Parallel Worsted or Modified Worsted System
D4920–89	Terminology Relating to Moisture in Textiles
D4964–89	Test Methods for Tension and Elongation of Elastic Fabrics (Constant-Rate-of-Extension Type Tensile Testing Machine)
D4965–89a	Terminology of Seams and Seam Finishes in Home Sewing
D4966–89	Test Method for Abrasion Resistance of Textile Fabrics (Martindale Abrasion Tester Method)
D4970–89	Test Method for Pilling Resistance and Other Related Surface Changes of Textile Fabrics (Martindale Pressure Tester Method)
D4974–89	Test Method for Thermal Shrinkage of Yarn and Cord Using the Testrite Thermal Shrinking Oven
E 4–83a	Practices for Load Verification of Testing Machines
E 105–58(1975)	Recommended Practice for Probability Sampling of Materials
E 337–84	Test Method for Measuring Humidity with a Psychrometer (The Measurement of Wet- and Dry-Bulb Temperatures)
G 23–89	Practice for Operating Light-Exposure Apparatus (Carbon-Arc Type) With and Without Water for Exposure of Nonmetallic Materials
G 24–87	Practice for Conducting Natural-Light Exposures Under Glass

AATCC Test Methods and Procedures

Method	Test Method
2-1988	Colorfastness to Fulling
3-1985	Colorfastness to Bleaching with Chlorine
6-1986	Colorfastness to Acids and Alkalis
7-1988	Colorfastness to Degumming
8-1988	Colorfastness to Crocking: AATCC Crockmeter Method
9-1988	Colorfastness to Stoving
11-1988	Colorfastness to Carbonizing
15-1985	Colorfastness to Perspiration
16-1987	Colorfastness to Light: General Method
16A-1988	Colorfastness to Light: Carbon-Arc Lamp, Continuous Light

Method	Test Method
16C-1988	Colorfastness to Light through Glass: Daylight
16D-1988	Colorfastness to Light: Carbon-Arc Lamp, Alternate Light and Darkness
16E-1987	Colorfastness to Light: Water-Cooled Xenon-Arc Lamp, Continuous Light
16F-1988	Colorfastness to Light: Water-Cooled Xenon-Arc Lamp, Alternate Light and Darkness
16G-1985	Colorfastness to Light: Determination of Fastness Above L-7
17-1985	Wetting Agents, Evaluation of
20-1985	Fiber Analysis: Qualitative
20A-1989	Fiber Analysis: Quantitative
21-1983	Water Repellency: Static Absorption Test
22-1985	Water Repellency: Spray Test
23-1988	Colorfastness to Burnt Gas Fumes
24-1985	Insects, Resistance of Textiles to
26-1988	Ageing of Sulfur Dyed Textiles: Accelerated
27-1985	Wetting Agents: Evaluation of Rewetting Agents
28-1985	Insect Pest Deterrents on Textiles
30-1988	Antifungal Activity, Assessment on Textile Materials: Mildew and Rot Resistance of Textile Materials
35-1985	Water Resistance: Rain Test
42-1985	Water Resistance: Impact Penetration Test
43-1985	Wetting Agents for Mercerization
61-1989	Colorfastness to Laundering, Home and Commercial: Accelerated
62-1988	Oils, Wool; Oxidation in Storage
66-1984	Wrinkle Recovery of Fabrics: Recovery Angle Method
70-1988	Water Repellency: Tumble Jar Dynamic Absorption Test
76-1987	Electrical Resistivity of Fabrics
78-1985	Ash Content of Bleached Cellulosic Textiles
79-1986	Absorbency of Bleached Textiles
81-1988	pH of the Water-Extract from Bleached Textiles
82-1989	Fluidity of Dispersions of Cellulose from Bleached Cotton Cloth
84-1987	Electrical Resistivity of Yarns
86-1985	Dry cleaning: Durability of Applied Designs and Finishes
88B-1989	Smoothness of Seams in Fabrics after Repeated Home Laundering
88C-1989	Retention of Creases in Fabrics after Repeated Home Laundering
89-1985	Mercerization in Cotton
92-1985	Chlorine, Retained, Tensile Loss: Single Sample Method
93-1989	Abrasion Resistance of Fabrics: Accelerator Method
94-1987	Finishes in Textiles: Identification
96-1988	Dimensional Changes in Commercial Laundering of Woven and Knitted Fabrics Except Wool
97-1988	Extractable Content of Greige and/or Prepared Textiles
98-1988	Alkali in Bleach Baths Containing Hydrogen Peroxide
99-1988	Dimensional Changes of Woven or Knitted Wool Textiles: Relaxation, Consolidation and Felting
100-1988	Antibacterial Finishes on Textile Materials: Assessment of
101-1989	Colorfastness to Bleaching with Peroxide
102-1987	Hydrogen Peroxide by Potassium Permanganate Titration: Determination of
103-1989	Bacterial Alpha-Amylase Enzymes Used in Desizing, Assay of
104-1988	Colorfastness to Water Spotting

106-1986	Colorfastness to Water: Sea
107-1986	Colorfastness to Water
109-1987	Colorfastness to Ozone in the Atmosphere Under Low Humidities
110-1989	Whiteness of Textiles
111-1988	Weather Resistance: General Information
111A-1988	Weather Resistance: Sunshine Arc Lamp Exposure with Wetting
111B-1988	Weather Resistance: Exposure to Natural Light and Weather
111C-1988	Weather Resistance: Sunshine Arc Lamp Exposure without Wetting
111D-1988	Weather Resistance: Exposure to Natural Light and Weather through Glass
112-1989	Formaldehyde Odor in Resin Treated Fabric, Determination of: Sealed Jar Method
114-1985	Chlorine, Retained, Tensile Loss: Multiple Sample Method
115-1986	Electrostatic Clinging of Fabrics: Fabric-to-Metal Test
116-1988	Colorfastness to Crocking: Rotary Vertical Crockmeter Method
117-1989	Colorfastness to Heat; Dry (Excluding Pressing)
118-1983	Oil Repellency: Hydrocarbon Resistance Test
119-1989	Color Change due to Flat Abrasion (Frosting): Screen Wire Method
120-1989	Color Change due to Flat Abrasion (Frosting): Emery Method
124-1989	Appearance of Fabrics after Repeated Home Laundering
125-1986	Colorfastness to Water and Light: Alternate Exposure
126-1986	Colorfastness to Water (High Humidity) and Light: Alternate Exposure
127-1985	Water Resistance: Hydrostatic Pressure Test
128-1985	Wrinkle Recovery of Fabrics: Appearance Method
129-1985	Colorfastness to Ozone in the Atmosphere Under High Humidities
130-1981	Soil Release: Oily Stain Release Method
131-1985	Colorfastness to Pleating: Steam Pleating
132-1985	Colorfastness to Dry cleaning
133-1989	Colorfastness to Heat: Hot Pressing
135-1987	Dimensional Changes in Automatic Home Laundering of Woven or Knit Fabrics
136-1985	Bond Strength of Bonded and Laminated Fabrics
139-1985	Colorfastness to Light: Detection of Photochromism
140-1985	Dyestuff Migration: Evaluation of
141-1987	Compatibility of Basic Dyes for Acrylic Fibers
142-1989	Appearance of Flocked Fabrics after Repeated Home Laundering and/or Coin-Op Dry cleaning
143-1989	Appearance of Apparel and Other Textile End Products after Repeated Home Laundering
144-1987	Alkali in Wet Processed Textiles: Total
145-1985	Color Measurement of the Blue Wool Lightfastness Standards: Instrumental
146-1989	Dispersibility of Disperse Dyes: Filter Test
147-1988	Antibacterial Activity Assessment of Textile Materials: Parallel Streak Method
149-1985	Chelating Agents: Chelation Value of Aminopolycarboxylic Acids and Their Salts; Calcium Oxalate Method
150-1987	Dimensional Changes in Automatic Home Laundering of Garments

151-1985	Soil Redeposition, Resistance to: Launder-Ometer Method
152-1985	Soil Redeposition, Resistance to: Terg-O-Tometer Method
153-1985	Color Measurement of Textiles: Instrumental
154-1986	Thermal Fixation Properties of Disperse Dyes
155-1986	Transfer of Disperse Dyes on Polyester
156-1986	Transfer of Basic Dyes on Acrylics
157-1985	Colorfastness to Solvent Spotting: Perchloroethylene
158-1985	Dimensional Changes on Dry cleaning in Perchloroethylene: Machine Method
159-1989	Transfer of Acid and Premetallized Acid Dyes on Nylon
160-1987	Dimensional Restoration of Knitted and Woven Fabrics After Laundering
161-1987	Chelating Agents: Disperse Dye Shade Change Caused by Metals; Control of
162-1986	Colorfastness to Water: Chlorinated Pool
163-1987	Colorfastness: Dye Transfer in Storage; Fabric-to-Fabric
164-1987	Colorfastness to Oxides of Nitrogen in the Atmosphere Under High Humidities
166-1988	Dispersion Stability of Disperse Dyes at High Temperature
167-1988	Foaming Propensity of Disperse Dyes
168-1989	Chelating Agents: Active Ingredient Content of Polyaminopolycarboxylic Acids and Their Salts; Copper PAN Method
169-1989	Weather Resistance of Textiles: Xenon Lamp Exposure
170-1989	Dusting Propensity of Powder Dyes: Evaluation of
172-1989	Colorfastness to Non-Chlorine Bleach in Home Laundering
173-1989	CMC: Calculation of Small Color Differences for Acceptability

Procedure	**Evaluation Procedure**

1	Gray Scale for Color Change
2	Gray Scale for Staining
3	AATCC Chromatic Transference Scale
4	Standard Depth Scales for Depth Determination

B

Seams and Stitchings

Diagrams in *U.S. Fed. Std. No. 751a:*
Stitches, Seams, and Stitchings

Schematic Index of Seams and Stitchings in Alphabetical Order by Class

Seam Class SS (Superimposed)

SSa	SSb	SSc	SSd	SSe
SSf	SSh	SSj	SSk	SSl
SSm	SSn	SSp	SSq	SSr
SSs	SSt	SSu	SSv	SSw
SSx	SSy	SSz	SSaa	SSab
SSac	SSad	SSae	SSaf	SSag
SSah	SSaj	SSak	SSal	SSam
SSan	SSac	SSap	SSaq	SSar
SSas	SSat	SSau	SSav	SSaw
SSax	SSay	SSaz	SSba	SSbb
SSbc	SSbd	SSbe	SSbf	SSbg
		SSbh		

Seam Class LS (Lapped)

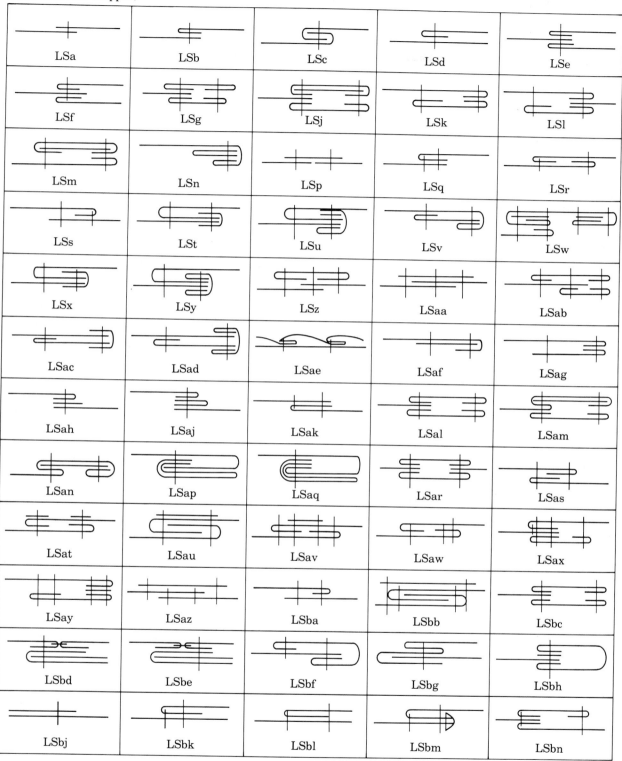

LSbo	LSbp	LSbq	LSbr	LSbs
LSbt	LSbu	LSbv	LSbw	LSbx
LSby	LSbz	LSca	LScb	LScc
LScd	LSce	LScf	LScg	LSch
LScj	LSck	LScj	LScm	LScn
LSco	LScp	LScq	LScr	LScs
LSct	LScu	LScv	LScw	LScx
LScy	SScs	LSda	LSdb	LSdc
		LSdd		

Seam Class BS (Bound)

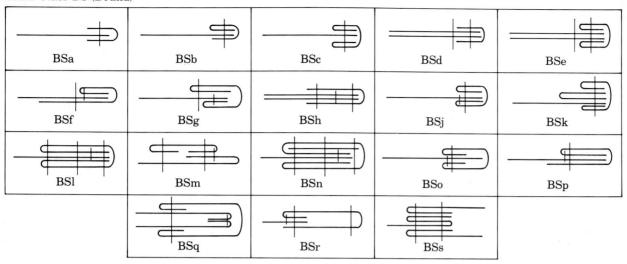

Seam Class FS (Flat)

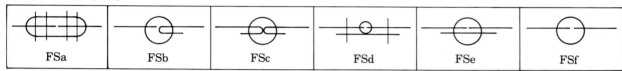

Stitching Class OS (Ornamental)

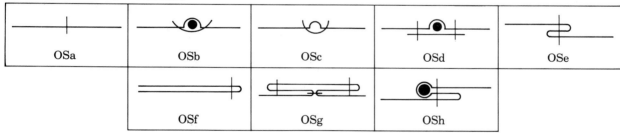

Stitching Clss EF (Edge Finishing)

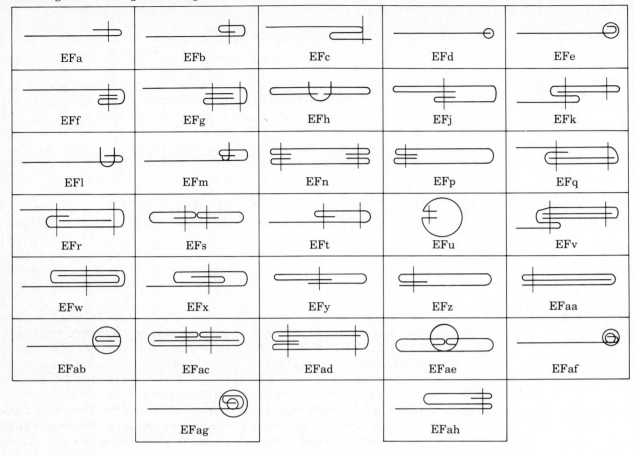

EFa	EFb	EFc	EFd	EFe
EFf	EFg	EFh	EFj	EFk
EFl	EFm	EFn	EFp	EFq
EFr	EFs	EFt	EFu	EFv
EFw	EFx	EFy	EFz	EFaa
EFab	EFac	EFad	EFae	EFaf
	EFag		EFah	

C

General Applications to Typical Operations

Applications of Stitches, Seams, and Stitchings in *U.S. Fed. Std. No. 751a: Stitches, Seams, and Stitchings*

Seam Type	Operation	Types of Standard Stitches Suitable
Superimposed seams		
SSa–1	Basting	101.
	Seaming (straight)	301, 401.
	Seaming (zigzag)	304, 404.
	Seaming (overedge)	501 to 513.
	Seaming (using waxed thread)	101, 201, 301.
SSa–2	Seaming and serging	301, 401, 501 to 507, 602, 515 to 519.
SSb–1 and SSb–2	Seaming (straight)	301, 401, 302, 402.
	Seaming (where similar stitch is essential on both surfaces)	301.
SSc–1 and SSc–2	Seaming	301, 401, 302, 402.
SSd–1	Seaming	301, 401.
SSe–2 and SSe–3	Seaming and edge finishing Making cuffs, collars, etc., and edge stitching on coats and shoes	301, 401, 302, 402.
SSf–3	Taping or staying	301, 401.
SSh–2	Cover seaming	302, 402, 406.
SSj–1	Seaming	201, 301, 401.
SSk–1	Seaming and cording	201, 301, 401.
SSl–1	Seaming	201, 301, 401.
SSm–1	Seaming or felling, where a blind stitch is required	103.
	Padding lapels, felling tapes, etc.	103.
SSn–1	Seaming	101, 301, 401.
SSp–1	Seaming	301, 401.

Seam Type	Operation	Types of Standard Stitches Suitable
Superimposed seams—Continued.		
SSq–2 and SSq–3	Seaming	301, 401, 302, 402.
SSr–1	Seaming	301, 401.
SSs–1 and SSs–2	Seaming and staying	301, 401.
SSt–2 to SSt–4	Seaming and taping	301, 401.
SSu–2 to SSu–4	Attaching elastic	301, 401.
SSu–2	Making pocket jettings	301.
SSv–1 to SSv–3	Quilting	301, 401.
SSw–2	Seaming	301, 401.
SSx–2	Seaming (crotch pieces and linings to trousers)	301, 401.
SSy–2	Seaming	301, 401.
SSz–3	Seaming	301, 401.
SSaa–1	Taping (coat fronts and armholes)	301.
SSab–1	Taping (coat fronts and armholes)	301.
SSac–3	Taping (crotch seams on trousers)	301.
SSad–3	Seaming and staying	301, 401.
SSae–2 and SSae–3	Seaming	301, 401.
SSaf–2	Seaming and staying	301, 401.
SSag–3	Seaming and staying	301, 401.
SSah–3 and SSah–4	Seaming	301, 401.
SSaj–3	Seaming	301, 401.
SSak–1	Attaching slide fasteners	301, 401.
SSal–2	Attaching slide fasteners	301, 401.
SSam–2	Seaming	301, 401.
SSan–2	Seaming	301, 401.
SSao–2	Seaming	301, 401.
SSap–3	Seaming	301, 401.
SSaq–2	Seaming	301, 401.
SSar–3	Attaching end of left fly lining to crotch seam	301, 401.
SSas–4	Attaching buttonhole strips	301, 401.
SSat–2	Attaching buttonhole strips	301, 401.
SSau–2	Staying	301, 401.
SSav–2	Seaming and welting	301, 401.
SSaw–2	Seaming and welting	301, 401, 504.
SSax–2	Seaming and welting	301, 401, 504.
SSay–2	Making waistbands	301, 401.
SSaz–1	Seaming neckties	104.
SSba–3	Book seaming	103 and 301 or 401.
SSbb–3	Seaming and staying	301, 401.
SSbc–1	Attaching interlining to cuff	103, 306.
SSbd–1	Seaming	301, 401.
SSbe–2	Seaming and edge finishing	301, 306, 401.
SSbf–3	Seaming and welting	301, 401.
SSbg–3	Seaming and welting	301, 401.
SSbh–3	Seaming	301, 401.
Lapped seams		
LSa–1	Seaming knitted materials or underwear and similar garments	602, 603, 604, 605.
LSa–1 and LSa–2	Seaming	301, 401, 402, 406, 407.
	Seaming (using waxed thread)	101, 201, 301.
LSb–1 and LSb–2	Seaming	301, 401, 402, 406.
LSc–1 to LSc–4	Seaming	301, 401.
LSd–1 to LSd–3	Attaching pieces to body of material	301, 304, 401.
LSe–1 to LSe–3	Seaming	301, 401.
LSf–1 and LSf–2	Seaming	301, 401.
LSg–2 to LSg–4	Facing (center plaits, stays, etc.)	301, 401.
LSj–2 and LSj–4	Facing (center plaits, stays, etc.)	301, 401.
LSk–2 and LSk–4	Facing (center plaits, stays, etc.)	301, 401.

Seam Type	Operation	Types of Standard Stitches Suitable
Lapped seams—Continued.		
LSl–2 and LSl–4	Facing and seaming (center plaits, stays, etc.)	301, 401.
LSm–2 and LSm–4	Facing (center plaits, stays, etc.)	101, 301, 401.
LSn–1	Facing (center plaits, stays, etc.)	301, 401.
LSp–2 and LSp–4	Joining with overlapping strip	301, 401.
LSq–2 and LSq–3	Seaming	201, 301, 401.
LSr–2	Seaming	301, 401.
LSs–2	Seaming	301, 401.
LSt–2	Seaming	301, 401.
LSu–2	Seaming	301, 401.
LSv–2	Facing and staying	301, 401.
LSw–4	Joining band (plain, elastic, etc.)	301, 401.
LSx–2 and LSx–3	Seaming	301, 401.
LSy–2 and LSy–3	Seaming	301, 401.
LSz–3 and LSz–4	Seaming	301, 401.
LSaa–3	Seaming	301, 401.
LSab–3 and LSab–4	Banding	301, 401.
LSac–2	Facing and binding	301, 401.
LSad–2	Facing and binding	301, 401.
LSae–1	Undersewing cushion	301, 401.
LSah–1	Seaming	301, 401.
LSaj–1	Seaming	301, 401.
LSak–2	Seaming	301, 401.
LSal–2 and LSal–4	Facing (center plaits, stays, etc.)	301, 401.
LSam–2 and LSam–4	Facing (center plaits, stays, etc.)	301, 401.
LSan–2 and LSan–4	Facing (center plaits, stays, etc.)	301, 401.
LSap–1	Finishing	301, 401.
LSaq–1	Finishing	301, 401.
LSar–2 to LSar–4	Facing and seaming	301, 401.
LSas–2	Seaming and gathering	301, 401.
LSat–2	Seaming and staying	301, 401.
LSau–2 to LSau–4	Seaming	301, 401.
LSav–4	Seaming and reinforcing	301, 401.
LSaw–3	Seaming	301, 401.
LSax–4	Seaming	301, 401.
LSay–4	Sewing-on band with elastic	301, 401.
LSaz–4	Seaming and staying	301, 401.
LSba–2	Seaming	301, 401.
LSbb–4	Seaming and staying	101, 301, 401.
LSbc–2 to LSbc–4	Facing	301, 401.
LSbd–2	Seaming	301, 401.
LSbe–2	Seaming	301, 401.
LSbf–2 to LSbf–4	Binding (center plait)	301, 401.
LSbg–1	Seaming	301, 401.
LSbh–1 and LSbh–2	Binding, inserting tape between binding and body material	301, 401.
LSbj–1	Attaching pieces to body material	301, 401.
LSbk–2	Attaching pieces to body material	301, 401.
LSbl–2	Attaching pocket flaps and belt loops	301, 401.
LSbm–3 and LSbm–4	Seaming	301, 401.
LSbn–2	Seaming	301, 401.
LSbo–3	Seaming	301, 401.
LSbp–2	Joining yoke to shirt	301, 401.
LSbq–2	Joining yoke to shirt in loosely woven material	301, 401.
LSbr–3	Seaming	301, 401.
LSbs–1	Attaching slide fasteners	301, 401.
LSbt–2	Attaching slide fasteners	301, 401.
LSbu–2	Attaching slide fasteners	301, 401.
LSbv–3	Attaching slide fasteners	301, 401.

Seam Type	Operation	Types of Standard Stitches Suitable
Lapped seams—Continued.		
LSbw–3	Seaming and binding	301, 401.
LSbx–2	Forming welt on set-in pockets	301, 401.
LSby–2	Forming welt on set-in pockets	301, 401.
LSbz–2	Forming pocket welts	301, 401.
LSca–2	Forming pocket welts	301, 401.
LScb–2	Top edge of hip pocket with a stay and facing	301, 401.
LScc–2	Top edge of hip pocket	301, 401.
LScd–3	Top edge of hip pocket	301, 401.
LSce–2	Forming welt on bottom edge of set-in hip pockets	301, 401.
LScf–2	Attaching cuffs, waistbands or collars	301, 401.
LScg–2	Attaching cuffs, waistbands or collars	301, 401.
LSch–2	Attaching cuffs, waistbands or collars	301, 401.
LScj–3	Attaching cuffs, waistbands or collars	301, 401.
LSck–3	Attaching cuffs, waistbands or collars	301, 401.
LScl–3	Attaching cuffs, waistbands or collars	301, 401.
LScm–3	Attaching cuffs, waistbands or collars	301, 401.
LScn–3	Attaching cuffs, waistbands or collars	301, 401.
LSco–4	Attaching cuffs, waistbands or collars	301, 401.
LScp–4	Attaching cuffs, waistbands or collars	301, 401.
LScq–4	Attaching cuffs, waistbands or collars	301, 401.
LScr–4	Attaching cuffs, waistbands or collars	301, 401.
LScs–3	Attaching left fly to trouser fronts	301, 401.
LSct–2	Attaching waistband linings	301, 401.
LScu–2	Finishing bottoms of caps	301, 401.
LScv–3	Seaming curtains on waistbands	301, 401.
LScw–3	Making sewn-on belts or bands	301, 401.
LScx–3	Making sewn-on belts or bands	301, 401.
LScy–3	Seaming and staying	301, 401.
LScz–2	Seaming	301, 401.
LSdb–2	Facing	301, 401.
LSdc–3	Trouser crotch seam	301, 401.
LSdd–2	Cut-on shirt front	301, 401.
Bound seams		
BSa–1 and BSa–2	Binding, bound seaming	301, 401, 304, 404, 406.
BSb–1 and BSb–2	Binding, bound seaming	301, 401, 304, 404.
BSc–1 and BSc–2	Binding, bound seaming	301, 401, 304, 404.
BSd–2	Seaming and binding	301, 401.
BSe–2	Seaming and binding	301, 401.
BSf–2	Seaming and binding	301, 401.
BSg–2	Seaming and binding	301, 401.
BSh–3	Seaming and binding	301, 401.
BSj–2	Binding, bound seaming	301, 304, 401, 404, 406.
BSk–1	Binding and welting	301, 401.
BSm–3	Facing pockets	301, 401.
BSn–4	Binding flag headings	301, 401.
BSo–2	Binding, bound seaming	301, 304, 401, 404, 406.

Seam Type	Operation	Types of Standard Stitches Suitable
Bound seams—Continued.		
BSp–2	Making pocket welts	301, 401.
BSq–2	Seaming and binding	301, 401.
BSr–2 and BSr–4	Seaming and binding	301, 401.
Flat seams		
FSa–1	Seaming	304, 404, 606, 607.
	Attaching collars, cuffs, borders, etc. to knitted articles	602, 603, 606.
	Attaching edging, lace, etc.	601, 602, 603.
FSb–1	Seaming	304, 602, 603, 606.
FSc–1	Seaming	304, 404.
FSd–3	Seaming and staying	304, 404.
FSe–1	Seaming and staying	304, 404.
FSf–1	Hosiery toe closing	521.
	Seaming fur pelts, or seaming with overedge stitching where a flat butted seam is desired	501 thru 505.
Ornamental stitching		
OSa–1 to OSa–3	Ornamental	101, 102, 104, 201, 203, 204, 301, 302, 303, 304, 305, 306, 307, 309, 310, 311, 312, 402, 403, 404, 405, 406.
OSb–1	Cording	102, 302, 402, 406.
OSc–1	Cording	102, 302, 402, 406.
OSd–2 and OSd–3	Cording	101, 301, 401.
OSe–1	Tucking or plaiting	101, 301, 401.
OSf–1	Tucking and mock seaming	101, 301, 401.
OSg–3	Making box or inverted plait	301, 401.
OSh–3	Welting	301, 401.
Edge finishing		
EFa–1 and EFa–2	Hemming (one fold)	101, 102, 301, 302, 401, 402, 406.
EFb–1 and EFb–2	Hemming (two folds)	101, 301, 401, 402, 406.
EFc–1	Blind hemming (woven)	301.
	Bind hemming (knit)	301, 401, 502, 503, 505.
EFd–1	Edge finishing (serging)	502, 503, 504, 505.
	Ornamental edge finishing	304, 502, 503, 504, 505, 601, 603, 604, 605, 607.
EFe–1	Ornamental edge finishing (zigzag)	304, 404.
EFf–1	Hemming with elastic tape	101, 301, 401.
EFg–2	Hemming with elastic tape	101, 301, 401.
EFh–1	Making loops or straps	406.
EFj–1 and EFj–3	Making straps	301, 401.
	Making straps (using waxed thread)	101, 301.
EFk–2 and EFk–4	Cut-on center plait (shirt fronts)	301, 401.
EFl–1	Blind hemming	103, 301, 306, 401, 502, 503.
EFm–1	Blind hemming	103, 301, 306, 401, 502, 503.
EFn–2 and EFn–4	Making straps or loops	301, 401.
EFp–1 and EFp–2	Making straps or loops	301, 401.
EFq–2	Inserting elastic in hems	301, 401.
EFr–2	Inserting elastic in hems	301, 401.
EFs–2	Making straps or loops	301, 401.
EFt–2 and EFt–4	Hemming shirt fronts	301, 401.
EFu–1	Making drawstrings or loops	301, 401.
EFv–2 and EFv–4	Cut-on center plait (shirt fronts)	301, 401.
EFw–1	Hemming (three folds)	101, 301, 401, 402, 406.

Seam Type	Operation	Types of Standard Stitches Suitable
Edge finishing—Continued.		
EFx–1	Hemming	101, 301, 401, 402, 406.
EFy–1 and EFy–3	Making straps or loops	301, 401, 406.
EFz–1 and EFz–2	Making straps or loops	301, 401, 406.
EFaa–1 and EFaa–2	Making straps or loops	301, 401, 406.
EFab–1	Hemming	502, 503, 504, 505.
EFac–2	Making straps or loops	301, 401.
EFad–2	Making straps or loops	301, 401.
EFae–2	Making straps or loops	103.
EFaf–2	Edge finishing	501, 502, 503, 504, 505.
EFag–2	Edge finishing	501, 502, 503, 504, 505.
EFah–1	Hemming	301, 401.

Glossary

Acceptable quality level The limit of defective garments in a random sample below which the entire lot is accepted and above which the entire lot is rejected.

Aesthetic performance The attractiveness of a garment; how well the garment meets aesthetic expectations.

Allover lace Lace fabric from which garments are constructed.

Amalgamated Clothing and Textile Workers Union of America (ACTWU) One of two major unions for workers in the apparel industry.

American Apparel Manufacturers Association (AAMA) A trade organization for U.S. apparel producers.

American Association of Textile Chemists and Colorists (AATCC) An organization that publishes standards for textile testing to provide industry-wide consistency.

American cut Cut of a jacket that hangs from the shoulders and drapes loosely rather than fitting the body; also known as standard cut or natural-shoulder style.

American National Standards Institute (ANSI) U.S. member organization of International Standards Organization.

American Society for Quality Control (ASQC) A professional organization for people interested in quality.

American Society for Testing and Materials (ASTM) An organization that publishes standards for textile testing to provide industry-wide consistency.

American Textile Manufacturers Institute (ATMI) A trade organization of U.S. textile manufacturers.

Apparel quality Degree of excellence; conformance to requirements; the extent to which a garment meets expectations.

Applied elastic Elastic stitched directly onto the garment to add shape where desired.

Appliqué Decorative fabric patch applied to the garment.

Armscye The armhole of a garment.

Back tacking Re-stitching at the beginning and end of a row of stitches.

Backing button Flat, eyed button sewn on under the fabric behind a button, to reinforce the button.

Backstitch Secure form of stitching where one small stitch is taken backward for every large stitch taken forward.

Balance As an element of fit, this refers to the garment being in equilibrium from side to side and from front to back.

Balanced tension Equal tension on needle, bobbin, and/or looper threads.

Band Straight (usually) pieces of fabric seamed to the raw edges of a garment to extend and finish the edge.

Bar codes Black lines and spaces read by a laser beam; used to electronically identify a product.

Basic block Basic pattern used to produce a basic fitted garment.

Basting Long, loose temporary stitches.

Bespoke High-quality, custom-made men's suits.

Better Term that refers to the highest of the mass merchandise price lines.

Bias Any direction that is not the lengthwise or crosswise grain of a woven fabric.

Bias facing Narrow, bias strips of fabric used to face raw edges.

Bifurcated Garments having two legs, for example, pants.

Binding Strip of fabric that covers the raw edge of the garment and is visible from both inside and outside the garment; does not extend the edge.

Blend More than one fiber type mixed together in a fabric.

Blindstitch Stitch that joins layers of fabric without the needle thread fully penetrating the top layer.

Bluff-edge collar Collar with under collar made of felt and with no seam allowances at the collar edges.

Boning Stiff plastic strips sewn to garment seams to add shape and support.

Booked Plain seam, butterflied, with the raw edges of the seam allowances folded under and blind-stitched; also known as *tailored seam*.

Bottom cover stitch Stitch that features two or three parallel rows of straight stitches visible on the face side and many thread interloopings on the back side to flatten the area and conceal raw edges by covering them with thread.

Bound buttonhole Rectangular hole in the fabric that is bound or faced, and backed with narrow strips of fabric that meet like lips to cover the opening.

Bound seam (BS) Seam made by using fabric binding strips to encase raw edges.

Boys' sizes Size classification for boys approximately 7 to 17 years old.

Bra size The number equal to under-bust measurement plus five or six inches, whichever results in an even number.

Braid Narrow trim formed by intertwining a set of yarns according to a definite pattern.

Break Slight indentation that occurs between the knee and ankle when the pants hit the top of the shoe and are slightly longer.

Break open stitch Stitch that, because of the loose stitch formation, hinges open flat like a notebook.

Bridge Price line covering the gap between two price lines.

Bridle Stay tape sewn at roll line of lapel to prevent gaping.

British cut Jacket cut that falls between American cut and European cut.

Budget Term that refers to the lowest of the mass merchandise price lines.

Bundle Cut pieces grouped for assembly line production.

Butterflied Seam allowances of a seam that are pressed open or *busted*.

Button band Vertical band of fabric at the center front of a shirt through which buttonholes are made; also called a placket.

Button loop Circle made of fabric strip, cording, braid, or elastic that encircles a button, substituting for a buttonhole.

Buying benefit Performance advantage that results from the garment's physical features.

Canted Pants with the backs of the legs cut slightly longer than the fronts, causing the hem to fall at an angle from the front to the back.

Care Labeling Rule Federal law requiring that all apparel sold in the United States have a permanent label that provides full instructions for the regular care of the garment.

Casing Tunnel of fabric through which elastic or a drawstring is threaded to shape the garment to the body.

Catchstitch Stitch that looks like a series of uneven X's; a flexible, extensible stitch as well as a decorative one.

Certification Seal of approval issued by a certifying agency.

Chapter 98 A provision in the Harmonized Commodity Description and Coding System allowing offshore production; policy was formerly called Item 807.

Chest piece Pad used to fill out and smooth the hollow area below the shoulder near the armhole.

Children's sizes Classification of clothing sizes for the child of approximately 3 to 6 years of age.

Childrenswear Classification of clothing for children.

Clean finish Edge treatment made by folding under the raw edge once and stitching it in place; essentially, a narrow hem on the edge; also called *turned and stitched*.

Closed-band cuff Unbroken ring of fabric large enough to fit over the arm.

Coil zipper Continuous-element zipper with interlocking, twisted, spiral strands of monofilament nylon.

Collar slope Vertical height of the collar.

Collar stay Thin, plastic strip inserted in collar to make it stay flat and to prevent the collar points from curling.

Collection Same as a line, but suggests higher prices.

Colorfastness Ability to retain original color.

Combination facing Shaped facing combined with an extended facing.

Computer aided design (CAD) Computerized system used to enhance performance of design tasks.

Computer aided manufacturing (CAM) Computerized system used to enhance performance of manufacturing tasks.

Computer integrated manufacturing (CIM) System that links all computerized facets of a business electronically for efficient management.

Continuous bound placket Bound slash in the fabric perpendicular to the edge of the garment.

Contractor Person or company hired by the manufacturer to do part or all of the work in producing a garment; also called *jobber* or *outside shop*.

Conventional zipper Zipper that has a visible chain, and one or both ends of the zipper remain together when it is unzipped.

Control stitching Understitching used on enclosed seams; stitches the seam allowances to the lower ply to keep the seam flat and to prevent the lower ply from slipping out and showing.

Cording stitch Stitch that secures creases; two rows of straight stitches appear on the top side with a looper thread underneath.

Corespun thread Thread that consists of a spun

core of polyester or nylon wrapped with cotton or other fibers.

Cost per wear Purchase price divided by the number of times the garment is worn to assist in determining value.

Costing Estimating the total cost of producing a garment.

Counterfeit Fake copies of currently popular branded apparel, accompanied by the illegal use of the rightful producer's brand name or trademark.

Country of origin Nation in which a garment was produced.

Courses Loops that run across the back of a plain knit fabric.

Couture Term used to refer to high-price, designer-named ready-to-wear; true couture is high-quality, custom-made clothing.

Crafted With Pride in the U.S.A. Certification label of the Crafted With Pride in the U.S.A. Council that promotes garments made in the United States.

Crotch length Measurement of the crotch from the waistline in front to the waistline in back, as measured between the legs.

Cup size The letter, ranging from AAA to F, that represents the difference between bra size and bust measurement at the fullest point.

Cut Number of loops per square inch of knit fabric; also called *gauge*.

Cutwork Holes in a fabric, surrounded by embroidery.

D-ring Two d-shaped rings that work together with a fabric strip to create an adjustable closure.

Dart Triangular fold stitched to shape the flat fabric to the curves and bulges of the body.

Dart equivalents *Dart substitutes* that incorporate shape into the garment in a variety of ways.

Decorative chainstitch Stitch that is identical to 101 single-thread chainstitch except chain appears on the face side of the fabric rather than the back side.

Denier System used to designate filament fiber and yarn size; the larger the number, the larger the fiber or yarn.

Design ease Extra ease in addition to fitting ease that gives a garment its style.

Designer Person who develops the style of a garment; in the highest sense, describes couture or haute couture apparel; as a price line, may include work by popular, high-price ready-to-wear designers all the way to merchandise that bears the name of a non-existent person.

Die Cutting device in the shape of piece to be cut; used to cut out small, complex pattern pieces.

Dimensional stability Ability to maintain original shape and size.

Directional stitching Sewing in the direction of the grain to minimize stretching.

Double ticketing Labeling clothing with both a junior size and a misses size, for example, 5/6 or 11/12.

Drop In a suit, the difference between the measurement of the chest of the jacket and the waist of the pants.

Dye lot Fabrics from same dye bath, producing color consistency.

Ease Imperceptible fullness drawn up and stitched in place; as an element of fit, it refers to the amount of roominess in a garment.

Ease pleat Pleat in the lining that provides adequate room for movement and a smooth, easy fit.

Edge finish stitching (EF) A series of stitches that finishes an edge.

Edge treatment A *finish* of the raw or cut edges of a garment.

Edgestitching Topstitching placed very close to an edge.

Emblem Preembroidered appliqué; also known as a *patch*, *badge*, or *insignia*.

Embroidery Decorative stitching used to form designs and patterns.

Enclosed seam A seam where the operator sews the fabric plies face sides together near the edge, opens out the plies and turns them back sides together to encase the seam allowances; occurs only at edges, where it appears as a line with no visible stitches along the edge.

End use Intended use of a garment.

European cut Sleek, angular, highly shaped, and closely fitted cut of a jacket.

Even plaid Plaid that contains a balanced arrangement of stripes on each side of the dominant horizontal and vertical bars of the plaid.

Extended cuff Band of fabric applied to the lower edge of a sleeve.

Extended facing Facing formed by extending the fabric at the edge to be faced and folding it under.

Eyed button Button that is sewn to the garment through holes in its face.

Eyelet Small, metal- or thread-edged hole in a garment.

Fabric Assessment by Simple Testing (FAST) Fabric evaluation system that measures four main fabric characteristics critical to garment appearance and performance; less costly alternative to Kawabata Evaluation System.

Faced placket Finish at an opening edge made by facing a slash in the fabric, perpendicular to the edge of the garment.

Faced slit Slit in the fabric, faced to serve as a buttonhole.

Facing Piece of fabric used to finish raw edges of the garments; the facing is turned to the inside of the garment so that it backs or faces the garment at the edge.

Fagoting Decorative stitching that holds together two closely spaced folded edges of fabric with ornamental stitches.

Fall Part of the collar that is folded over the stand.

Fashion fabric Main, outer fabric from which garment is made; also called *shell fabric*.

Fiber Fine, hairlike structure; raw material from which fabrics are made.

Filament yarn Yarn composed of long, filament fibers.

Fit model Individual who represents the figure type of the target customer and on whom fit is tested.

Fitting ease Ease required for a comfortable fit.

500-class overedge stitches Stitches formed, as the name implies, over the edge of the fabric, encasing the edge in thread interloopings; also called *overlock, serge, overseam, overcast,* or *merrow*.

Flammable Fabrics Act Law that establishes minimal flammability standards for apparel, with the strictest standards for children's sleepwear.

Flanges Projections below the hemline cut as a mirror image of the garment above the hemline, enabling the hem allowance to lie flat and smooth against the garment when folded up.

Flat collar Collar that lies flat, or nearly flat, against the garment all around the wearer's neck.

Flat seam (FS) Joint in which raw edges are abutted (or sometimes slightly overlapped) and sewn together; also called *butt seam* or *exposed seam*.

Flat-felled seam Seam with the raw edges of both seam allowances folded under as the seam is stitched; a strong and durable seam.

Fly front Type of lapped-zipper application with wide topstitching; used at the center fronts of jeans and other garments.

Folded hem Hem with raw edge turned under and stitched to the garment.

Form fitting Testing fit on a stationary dress form.

400-class multithread chainstitches *Double-locked* stitches formed by a needle thread passing through the fabric and interlooping with a looper thread.

Four Point System The most popular fabric-rating system; used to assign penalty points to a fabric based on the number and size of defects.

Free-hanging lining Lining not attached at the garment hem; also called *slip lining*.

Free trade Policy favoring unrestricted imports in the interest of the free flow of goods between nations.

French fly Tab or extension on fly-front underlap that buttons to the inside of the pants near to waist for a smoother look.

French front Shirt front that is faced at center front.

French seam A "seam within a seam"; operator sews a narrow plain seam with the back sides of the fabric plies together and then sews a slightly wider plain seam with the face sides of the fabric plies together to encase the seam allowances of the first seam.

French tack Thread chain, strip of fabric similar to a belt loop, or a piece of ribbon, about an inch and a half long, connecting the hem of a free-hanging lining and the hem of the garment at each seam allowance; also called *swing tack*.

Frog Highly decorative button-and-loop closure made of elaborately coiled cord or braid.

Full-fashioned mark Mark that represents increases or decreases in the number of stitches in a knitted garment section, a result of shaping the piece.

Fully-let-out Method for making the most expensive type of fur garment in which pelts are cut into narrow diagonal strips and sewn back together so that each pelt becomes a long, narrow panel that covers the length of the wearer's body.

Functional performance Performance features other than appearance, namely, the garment's utility and durability.

Fur Products Labeling Act (FPLA) Federal law regulating labeling of fur products.

Furnishings Men's items other than clothing or sportswear, including shirts, ties, underwear, sleepwear, and accessories.

Fused buttonhole Buttonhole formed by embossing the fabric with a hot die which is patterned to resemble a stitched or bound buttonhole; a slit in the fabric serves as the buttonhole.

Garment dyeing Dyeing the finished garment.

Garment washing Washing or *rinsing* the completed garment before it is sold to soften, preshrink, and/or fade the garment before it goes to the consumer.

Gathers A series of small folds of fabric, controlled and held in place by stitches and providing visible fullness.

Gauntlet button Button and buttonhole placed on a tailored placket to prevent it from gaping.

General Agreement on Tariffs and Trade (GATT) International agreement promoting free trade.

Girls' sizes Classification of sizes fitting girls approximately 7 to 11 years old.

Godet Triangular fabric piece set into a seam or slash, usually at the hem of a garment.

Gore Vertical division within a garment, usually tapered panels seamed together to add shape to a garment.

Gorge line Seam where collar and lapel meet.

Grade To trim the seam allowances of an enclosed seam, each to a slightly different length; also called *blend, layer* or *bevel*.

Grading Increasing and decreasing the dimensions of a pattern to reflect the various sizes to be produced.

Grain As an element of fit, refers to need for lengthwise yarns to run parallel to length of body at center front and center back, down the center of the arm from shoulder to elbow, and down the center front of each pant leg; the crosswise yarns should run perpendicular to the length of the body at bust/chest, hip, and upper arm at bust/chest level.

Greige goods Undyed, unfinished fabrics.

Grommet Large, metal-edged hole in a garment.

Gusset Pieces of fabric set into a seam or seam intersection to add shape and fullness to a garment.

Hand Broad term for the tactile sensations resulting from touching, moving, or squeezing the fabric with the human hand.

Hand-worked buttonhole Buttonhole with raw edges covered by hand-purl stitches; very labor-intensive, rare, and costly.

Hand picked Application, usually of a zipper, with hand pickstitches.

Half sizes Size classification for shorter-than-average adult women with a full, mature figure; sometimes marketed as women's petites.

Haute couture Term for the most fashionable and exclusive couture apparel.

Heat set Process in which fabric is heated and then cooled in desired shape to maintain dimensional stability.

Heel guard Layer of abrasion-resistant tape sewn in to reinforce the area at the back of the hem in high-quality pants; also called *kick tape*.

Hem allowance Amount turned under in a hem.

Hemstitching Pulling out a group of parallel yarns from a fabric and tying the remaining perpendicular yarns together with decorative stitches, or the machine imitation of this process.

Hand overcast Series of spaced, diagonal stitches covering the seam or hem-allowance edges to retard raveling.

Hong Kong binding Very narrow, often color-contrasting bias strip used to decoratively bind seam, hem allowances, and other edges inside high-price tailored and couture garments.

Horizontal placket Finish at an opening edge of a garment so named because the placket is parallel to the opening.

Horsehair braid Braid that faces and stiffens hems in wedding and formal gowns with full skirts.

Hook and loop tape Fastener that consists of two separate tapes that interlock to create closure when pressed together; a popular brand name is Velcro.

In-seam buttonhole Seam that is left partially unstitched to create a buttonhole.

In-seam placket Finish at an opening edge of a garment made by leaving a seam unsewn for the last few inches of the edge.

In-seam pocket Pocket that is set into a seam of the garment, usually the side seams of skirts, pants, dresses, and coats.

Infants'/babies' sizes Classification of clothing sizes for infants from birth to approximately the age of 18 months, or old enough to walk.

Inside shop Manufacturer-owned and -operated factories.

Interfacing Supporting fabric usually hidden between garment and its facing; lends body, shape, and reinforcement to limited areas of the garment.

Interlining Insulative layer applied strictly for additional warmth between the lining and the fashion fabric.

International Fabricare Institute (IFI) Association of professional dry cleaners and launderers.

International Ladies Garment Workers Union (ILGWU) One of two major unions for workers in apparel factories.

International Standards Organization (ISO) An international organization with representatives from many nations that concentrates on international standardization.

Inventory Goods in the factory waiting to be processed or in a warehouse waiting to be sold.

Invisible zipper Zipper constructed so that the chain is concealed beneath the tape when the zipper is closed.

Junior sizes Size classification for short, slender women with youthful figures.

Just in time (JIT) No wasted time between each step of production.

Kawabata Evaluation System (KES) Fabric evaluation system that quantifies the statement of difficult-to-measure fabric performance specifications.

Keyhole buttonhole Buttonhole with characteristic keyhole shape; rounded end allows button to ride in the buttonhole without distorting the garment.

Kimono sleeve Sleeve cut as one with the body of the garment.

Knock off The legal copying, with or without modification, of a design shown by another firm under a different brand name.

Lab dip Samples that illustrate a fabric's possible colorations from which the manufacturer can choose.

Lace trim Narrow lace fabric.

Lapped zipper Application characterized by only one line of visible stitching on the outside of the garment; the topstitching is on one side of the opening.

Lapels Parts of the garment that roll or fold back above the front closure; also called *revers*.

Lapped seam (LS) Seam made by overlapping the seam allowances of two or more fabric plies and sewing them together, with the fabric plies extending in opposite directions.

Latch tacking Technique of drawing the excess thread chain of 500- and 600-class stitches at the beginning of each row of stitches into the stitches to secure them.

Lettered sizing The use of letters of the alphabet, rather than numbers, to designate size.

Lettuce edge hem Hem created by stretching the edge as it is stitched so that it ripples attractively.

License When a manufacturer (the licensee) pays a fee to an individual or company (the licensor) for the privilege of affixing the licensor's name, trademark, or logo to the licensee's products.

Lignes Used to measure button size; 40 lignes are equal to a diameter of one inch.

Line Series of related designs; as an element of fit, it refers to the alignment of structural lines of the garment with the natural lines of the body.

Lining Replica of the garment, constructed of lightweight fabric and sewn inside the garment.

Lockstitch blindstitch The most durable type of blindstitch; used to secure hems in high-quality garments.

Loop Circle (made from cord, thread chain, or strip of fabric) used to hang the garment or to suspend articles from the garment.

Loss leader Style sold at a loss to attract buyers to a line.

Low labeling Recommending a more conservative care method than the garment requires.

Manufactured fibers Fibers formed through human effort; also called *man-made fibers.*

Manufacturer The person or company ultimately responsible for all the steps in producing a garment.

Marker Plan that indicates how all the pattern pieces of the garment should be arranged on the fabric to achieve the most efficient layout.

Market potential price The highest price that the market will bear without dampening sales too much.

Material utilization (MU) Percentage of fabric utilized by a particular marker arrangement.

Men's sizes Size classification for clothing that fits the average adult man.

Merchandiser Person who formulates the line for a manufacturer to satisfy the company's target market.

Misses sizes Size classification fitting the adult women of average proportions; also called *missy sizes.*

Mitering Seaming or folding a corner diagonally for sharper, less bulky corners.

Moderate Term that refers to a middle-ground, mass merchandise price line.

Modular manufacturing Technique that replaces the traditional assembly line; operators are grouped into teams, or modules.

Monofilament thread Clear thread resembling a fishing line and made of a single filament of nylon.

Monogram Embroidery that forms the initials of the wearer's name.

Multi-Fiber Arrangement (MFA) Under GATT, seeks an orderly growth in the openness of world trade in textiles and apparel; allows for tariffs and quotas.

Multifilament thread Several filament yarns twisted together to make a very strong thread.

Multiple-stitch zigzag stitch Stitch made in much the same way as a regular zigzag stitch except that each diagonal portion of the zigzag is made up of more than one stitch.

Nap-one-way (NOW) Fabric spread with each ply of fabric facing up.

Nap-either-way (NEW) Fabric spread face to face.

Nap-up-and-down (NUD) Napped fabric from alternate layers is sewn together so nap is consistent within each garment.

National brand Brand developed by a manufacturer and sold to many retailers; also called *name brand* or *manufacturer's brand.*

National Retail Merchants Association (NRMA) Trade organization of retailers.

Natural fibers Fibers that occur naturally in the environment.

Needle chewing Damage that occurs when a needle causes jagged, enlarged holes in the fabric.

Needle cutting Damage that occurs when the needle cuts, or severs, the yarns of the fabric rather than slipping between the yarns.

Needle heating Damage that occurs when sewing friction heats the needle, which then fuses or melts the finishes or fibers of the thread or fabric.

Notions All materials, other than fabric, required to produce a garment; also called *findings* or *sundries.*

Number A style offered as part of a manufacturer's line.

Off-grain Distorted fabric grain.

Off-pressing Final pressing after construction.

Off-shore production Contracting with foreign manufacturers to make goods.

100-class single-thread chainstitches Stitches interlooping one needle thread and having no underthread.

100 percent inspection Examination of every garment.

One-size-fits-all A garment that will stretch to fit many figure types and sizes.

Open-band cuff Cuff that has an opening so that the wearer can fit the cuff band over the hand and then fasten it to fit snugly.

Operator Person who sews garments together in a factory.

Ornamental stitching (OS) Series of stitches applied for decorative purposes.

Overhead costs Expenses of operating a business over and above the direct costs of producing garments.

Pad stitching Tiny stitches made through the interfacing and barely catching the fashion fabric; softly and subtly shapes collars and lapels.

Patch pocket Pieces of fabric attached, like a patch, to the outside of the garment; also called *applied pocket.*

Pattern design system (PDS) Computer system that enhances performance of pattern design tasks.

Pattern matching Lining up stripes, checks, plaids, and other linear patterns at seams.

Per sample buying Traditional buying in which buyers select from manufacturers' lines.

Permanent press Chemical finish that helps garments maintain their shape and pressed appearance after many washings and wearings; also called *durable press*.

Petites Size sub-classification for shorter-than-average women.

Physical inventory Actual count of the merchandise.

Pickstitch Tiny, decorative backstitch; also called *prickstitch*.

Pictograms Body measurements indicated on a sketch of the human body to communicate size internationally.

Piece dyeing Dyeing fabric in the fabric stage.

Piece goods A term for fabrics.

Piece work System in which operators are paid according to the number of garments they complete rather than by the hour.

Pink To cut an edge with a serrated blade or scissors; pinking retards raveling.

Placket Finished, structural opening in a garment that allows a body part to pass through for dressing and undressing.

Plain seam Simple, superimposed seam; appears as a line with no visible stitches on the outside of the garment, but the seam allowances are visible inside the garment; the most common seam for sewing structural garment seams.

Plain stitch A single, straight, continuous row of stitches that looks the same on both sides of the fabric; the stitch made by conventional, home-sewing machines; also called *straight stitch*.

Plain weave Weave in which filling yarns pass alternately over and under warp yarns; simplest and most common weave.

Pleat Fold of fabric, folded back upon itself so that the pleat is comprised of three layers; occurs vertically only.

Precost Preliminary estimate of what it will cost to produce a garment; also called *quick cost*.

Prêt à porter/prêt French term for ready-to-wear.

Price line Clustering of merchandise priced at approximately the same price; stores may carry low-price, moderate-price, and/or high-price lines.

Princess seam Dart-substitute seam that incorporates the bust and waist darts in womenswear.

Private label Brand developed by or for a specific retailer; also called *private brand* or *store brand*.

Production costing Detailed, accurate costing that enables the manufacturer to accurately predict the cost of producing a garment.

Production pattern Pattern designed for optimal efficiency in mass manufacturing; also called *hard pattern*.

Protectionism Policy favoring the regulation of imports to protect the domestic industry; also called *fair trade*.

Pull Portion of the zipper that is grasped to operate the slider; also called *tab*.

Purled edge Series of raised loops, as a result of the interloopings of looper threads at an edge.

Quality control (QC) Department in a company that establishes quality standards and searches for ways to consistently achieve the desired level of quality; also called *quality assurance (QA)* or *quality department*.

Quick response (QR) Strategy of U.S. manufacturers for responding more quickly to the retailer's needs than foreign manufacturers can.

Quilting Stitching that joins the fashion fabric with a backing and an interlining; the stitches form a slightly puffy, raised design, often in a geometric or other decorative pattern.

Raglan sleeve Sleeve attached to the garment with a diagonal seam that runs from the underarm to the neckline of the garment.

Random sampling Examining a representative sample of the garments rather than all of them; also called *statistical sampling*.

Ready-to-wear clothing (RTW) Apparel that is mass produced; in its broadest sense, includes any garment that is not custom-made for the wearer.

Registered number (RN) Number registered with the federal government that identifies a specific manufacturer.

Reinforcement stitches Small stitches used to help points of particular strain bear stress.

Released dart A dart left unstitched, resulting in a straight silhouette rather than a fitted garment.

Retail price The price retailers charge consumers.

Retailer One who sells apparel to consumers.

Ribbon Narrow, woven fabric used as a trim and to make ties and bows.

Rise Measurement from crotch level to the top of the waistband; also called *crotch depth*.

Roll line Area where the collar and lapel naturally tend to roll.

Rolled collar Band of fabric that rolls fully or partially around the neck.

Rolled hem Very narrow hem rolled up and stitched to the garment to enclose the raw edge of the hem.

Ruffle Decorative, gathered, or pleated strips of fabric sewn to the garment; also called *flounce*.

Running stitch Stitch made by the needle being passed up and down through the fabric, always moving forward, creating a space between each stitch.

Saddle stitch Decorative running stitch, each ¼ inch to ½ inch long.

Safety stitch Stitch that combines a row of overedge stitches with an independent row of straight lockstitches or chainstitches.

Satin weave Weave in which filling yarns pass over or under several warp yarns at one time, creating a smooth-faced fabric.

Scoop Tooth of a separate element zipper.

Seam Joint resulting when two or more fabric pieces are sewn together.

Seam allowance Narrow width between the seam line and the raw edge of the fabric; also called *seam margin*.

Seam crack Damage that occurs when stitches break and the seam splits apart; also called *seam burst*.

Seam grin Unsightly result that occurs when the seamline spreads open, exposing the stitches so that they appear similar to the teeth of a grin.

Seam pucker Lack of seam smoothness that detracts from the appearance of the garment.

Seam slippage Damage that occurs when the fabric pulls away from the stitches at the seamline.

Self-help features Details that assist the wearer in dressing independently.

Selling point Physical feature of the garment that makes it desirable.

Selvages Woven edges of the fabric.

Separating zipper A zipper that unlinks at both ends and separates into two different halves when unzipped, unlike a conventional zipper that remains linked at one or both ends when unzipped.

Set As an element of fit, refers to smooth fit without undesirable wrinkles.

Set-in sleeve A sleeve formed by sewing a tube of fabric into the armhole. If *set in flat*, the sleeve is stitched to garment while both are still open and flat; then the tubular shape of the sleeve and garment are formed by sewing the side seam of the garment and the underarm seam of the sleeve in one step. If *set in "in the round,"* the underarm seam of the sleeve is sewn to create a tube of the sleeve, and the side seam and shoulder seam of the garment area are sewn to create a round armhole; then the tubular sleeve section is sewn to the round armhole of the garment.

Shade lot Fabrics grouped together for color consistency.

Shank button Button with a stem of plastic, metal, or cloth built into the button.

Shaped facing Facing is shaped identically to the garment edges it is sewn to and which it faces.

Shell hem Hem that features a scalloped effect created by a decorative shell stitch that attaches the narrow folded hem allowance to the garment.

Shirring Permanent, parallel rows of gathers made in the body of the garment.

Shirttail hem Narrow hem folded under twice and topstitched in place.

Shoulder slope Angle that the shoulder seam makes as it slopes away from the neck.

Single-needle tailoring Using single-needle sewing machines to construct a garment; generally produces smoother, flatter, but more costly seams than using multiple-needle machines.

600-class cover stitches *Top-and-bottom-covering chainstitches* with interloopings appearing on both the face and back; used to sew flat seams in which the fabric plies abut or overlap slightly and are interlocked by the stitches.

Size classifications Groups of sizes according to age and/or body types of consumers.

Skin-on-skin Method for making a fur garment in which whole pelts are sewn together.

Sleeve head Layers of shaping fabric sewn into upper portion of armhole and extending out into sleeve; also called *header*.

Sleeve vent Type of hemmed, in-seam placket at the wrist of high-quality tailored suits and sport jacket sleeves.

Slipping Cutting the under collar slightly smaller than the upper collar and easing the two together as they are sewn; also called *bubbling*.

Slipstitch "Invisible" form of the running stitch, used to join a folded edge to another play of fabric (the stitches are hidden in the fold).

Sloper A company's basic pattern; also called a *basic block*.

Slot seam Decorative lapped seam in which the edges of the two fabric plies are folded under and nearly abutted; they are lapped over and stitched to a narrow fabric underlay, usually of a contrasting color.

Slashed pocket Bound or faced slits within the body of the garment with the pocket bag sewn inside the garment.

Slit buttonhole Buttonhole with raw edges; a slit in the fabric that serves as a buttonhole.

Slider Portion of the zipper that glides up and down the chain, engaging and disengaging the two halves of the chain.

Slot zipper Application characterized by two visible rows of topstitching on the outside of the garment, one on either side of the zipper chain.

Smocking Stitching that uses decorative stitches to hold the fabric in even, accordion-like pleats.

Solution dyeing Dyeing of manufactured fibers before the fibers are formed, while they are still in the liquid stage; also called *dope dyeing*.

Sourcing Finding a contractor.

Specification buying Buyers requesting goods made to meet their requirements and standards rather than choosing from manufacturers' lines.

Specifications (spec) Exact standards for the production of a garment.

Split Layers of a hide other than the top layer.

Sportswear Casual separates that can be mixed and matched.

Spread Distance from collar point to collar point.

Spun thread Staple fibers spun into a thread.

Spun yarn Yarn composed of short, staple fibers.

Square edge stitch Stitch with thread interloopings forming a square or box effect at the edge; also called *box edge stitch*.

Stand Part of the collar that stands up next to the neck.

Standing collar Band extending straight up from the neckline edge and standing up around the neck.

Stay Any stable, narrow, non-bulky tape, ribbon, fabric strip, or other device used to stabilize a seam.

Stitch Thread interlooping that holds a garment together.

Stitched in the ditch Straight stitches placed in the crevice between the garment and a binding or band; also called *crack stitched*.

Stitches per inch (SPI) Measurement of stitch length.

Stitches per minute (SPM) Sewing speed.

Stitching Stitches applied to finish an edge or for ornamental purposes; does not join fabric pieces together as do seams.

Stock keeping unit (SKU) Numbering system used by a company to identify a particular item.

Stops Parts of the zipper that prevent the slider from leaving the chain at either end of the zipper.

Straight-of-grain Includes both lengthwise and crosswise grains because they follow the straight yarns of the fabric.

Strapped seam Seam with stay sewn over the completed seam on the outside of the garment.

Strike-through Unsightly results when adhesive from fusible interfacing leaks through the fashion fabric.

Stripped seam Seam with stay sewn over the completed seam inside the garment.

Style The cut and other identifying characteristics of a garment.

Superimposed seam (SS) Seam created by superimposing fabric plies, or stacking them on top of one another, with edges even, and sewing them together near the edge.

Sure care symbols Symbols that indicate the recommended care method and may be used internationally to provide universally understood care labeling.

Sweatshop Factory in which the owner reaps profits from the sweat of the workers, who are under compensated.

Sweep Circumference of hem.

Tab Decorative fabric strip that sometimes serves as a functional closure.

Tack Reinforcement that consists of several overlapping zigzag stitches; used to sew on labels, secure facings and shoulder pads, and reinforce areas of high stress, for instance, at pocket corners, the base of zippers and in the attachment of belt loops.

Tailored Having trim, simple lines; usually refers to garments that are carefully structured and detailed, usually closely fitted and made of woven fabrics; for example, the classic business suit.

Tailored placket A bound slash; the overlap portion is bound with a topstitched strip of fabric and the underlap is bound with a narrower strip of fabric; also called *shirt sleeve placket*.

Taped seam Seam with stay tape superimposed on the fabric plies and sewn in as part of the seam.

Tensile strength Ability of the fabric to resist a pulling force; also called *tenacity*.

Tex System used to designate fiber or yarn size; the larger the number, the larger the fiber or yarn.

Textile and apparel pipeline Channel of distribution through which a garment passes, from the fiber producer all the way to the ultimate consumer.

Textile/Clothing Technology Corporation Coalition of industry, education, government, and labor; concentrates on research and development into cutting-edge manufacturing techniques and training to advance apparel-manufacturing technology and enhance the competitiveness of the U.S. apparel industry; usually abbreviated *(TC)2*.

Textile Fiber Products Identification Act (TFPIA) Federal law requiring that all apparel sold in the United States have a permanent label that identifies fiber content, manufacturer, and country of origin.

Texturized thread Thread processed to give it greater bulk, thus reducing luster, improving sewability and coverage, and increasing the wearer's comfort.

Thermoplastic Heat sensitive; melts when exposed to high temperatures.

Thread count Numbers of yarns per square inch of woven fabric.

Thread shank Thread wrapped around the stitches between the button and the garment, suspending the button away from the fabric.

300-class lockstitches Stitches composed of a needle thread interlocked with a bobbin thread.

Toddlers' sizes Classification of children's clothing sizes for the child from 18 months to approximately 3 years of age.

Toggle Decorative button-and-loop closure consisting of two loops; one has a rod-shaped button attached to it.

Tolerance The difference between the allowable minimum and maximum of a specification.

Top grain leather Top layer of a hide; also called *genuine leather*.

Topstitching Visible, decorative stitching done on the outside of the garment; also called *accent stitching*.

Trademark A registered brand name or symbol.

Trapunto Form of embroidery that resembles quilting.

Trim Decorative material that adorns the garment.

True bias Fabric direction that occurs at a 45-degree angle to the lengthwise and crosswise grain of woven fabrics; has the highest degree of stretch of any fabric direction.

True to size A garment that fits about the same as most other garments of the same labeled size.

Tuck Fold of fabric, sewn together; may occur at any angle.

Tuck seam Decorative lapped seam stitched away from the edge to create a small flap of fabric.

Turned-back cuff Formed by turning back or rolling up the lower portion of the sleeve or pant leg.

Twill weave Weave in which filling yarns float over or under two or more warp yarns in a staggered progression; resulting fabric has diagonal ridges.

200-class stitches Stitches created by hand or on machines that pass a single thread through one side of the material and then the other.

Two-piece sleeve Sleeve consisting of two portions, the main sleeve piece and a second, narrow, shaped sleeve piece under the arm.

Two-thread chainstitch The most common 400-class stitch; consists of a needle thread interlooping with a looper thread.

Under collar Facing of the collar.

Underlining Lining each major piece of the garment individually and then handling the two plies as one as the garment is constructed.

Underlying fabric Fabric inside the garment that lends support to the garment and helps maintain its shape.

Underpressing Pressing during construction.

Uneven plaid Plaid that varies in the arrangement of stripes on each side of the dominant horizontal and vertical bars of the plaid.

Union shop Factory in which the workers are union members.

Unit production system (UPS) System that replaces the traditional assembly line; garments are sent to each operator's station via computer-controlled, overhead transporters, thus improving flow of garments through the factory and eliminating the time spent in handling bundles.

Universal Product Code (UPC) *See* Bar code.

Upper collar Visible portion of the collar.

Upturned-flap pocket Flap attached to bottom of a finished slash, extending up and topstitched or slip-stitched in place.

U.S. Fed. Std. No. 751a: Stitches, Seams, and Stitching Federal document that diagrams and defines the conformation of stitch, seam, and stitching types.

Value Relationship between price and quality.

Vanity sized Expensive lines cut large to appeal to consumers who desire to think of themselves as wearing a small-labeled size.

Vat dye Most colorfast type of dye.

Vendor marking Price marking of the goods at the factory by the manufacturer, instead of in the store by the retailer.

Vertical integration Situation that occurs when the same firm is responsible for multiple steps in the production or marketing of a product.

Voluntary Interindustry Communications Standards (VICS) Group with representatives from all facets of the apparel industry who determine the standards for electronic data interchange for the industry.

Waistband curtain Pre-fabricated waistband facing that consists of a strip of firmly woven fabric attached to a bias-cut piece of interfacing; the lower edge of the curtain is a bias-cut fold of fabric.

Wales Loops that run up and down the face of a plain knit fabric.

Warp Yarns that run parallel to the selvages; consists of yarns held taut by the loom during weaving; also called *lengthwise grain*; a *warp knit* is made with the yarns running vertically.

Wash and wear Fabric finish that reduces wrinkling; garment may require some touch-up pressing.

Wear testing Wearing and caring for the garment under normal circumstances to determine quality.

Wedged Hem with tiny wedges of fabric cut out of a too-full hem allowance to help it fit smoothly against the garment.

Weft Yarns that run perpendicular to the selvages; in weaving, consists of yarns woven over and under the lengthwise yarns to create the fabric; also called *crosswise grain*; a weft knit is made with the yarns running horizontally across the fabric.

Weights Small, thin pieces of metal encased in fabric or chains tacked in place to perfect the drape of the garment.

Welt pocket Bound, slashed pocket.

Welt seam Decorative lapped seam with dimension created by a narrow seam allowance caught between the garment and a wider seam allowance by topstitching; the narrow seam allowance pads the area.

Wicking ability Rate at which a fabric diffuses moisture.

Wholesale price The price that manufacturers charge retailers.

Wholesale representative Agent of the manufacturer; sells finished garments to retailers for a commission; also called *sales representative*.

Women's sizes Size classification for adult women of average height with full, mature figures.

Wool Products Labeling Act (WPLA) Federal law regulating the labeling of wool products.

Yarn Continuous strand of fibers; the thread used to make fabric.

Yarn dyeing Dyeing yarn prior to weaving or knitting the fabric.

Yarn number System used to designate staple-fiber yarn size; the larger the number, the smaller the yarn.

Yarn slippage Tendency of the yarns in a fabric to shift under stress.

Yoke Horizontal division within a garment; small, flat panel of fabric usually at the shoulder, waist, or midriff.

Young men's sizes Size classification designed for young men with developing builds.

Zigzag stitch Stitch made by the needle moving from side to side to produce a symmetrical zigzag pattern; the chief advantage is elasticity.

Zipper chain Part of the zipper that interlocks when the zipper is closed.

Zipper hump Unsightly defect that results when the zipper chain does not lie flat and smoothly, but instead creates waves in the fabric where the zipper is applied.

Zipper tape Fabric portion of a zipper.

Index

Returns, 18-19
Revers, 199
Ribbing, 91
Ribbon, 220
Rickrack. *See* Braid
Rise. *See* Crotch depth
Rivets, 215
Robotics, 31
Roll line, 182, 198-199
Rolled hem, 154-155
Ruching, 220
Ruffles, 224-225
Running stitches, 112-113

Saddle stitches, 112-113
Safety, 80, 217-218
Safety stitches, 118-120
Sales reps. *See* Wholesale representatives
Sample garments, 27
Sample patterns, 26
Sanforized, 100
Satin stitches, 227
Satin weave, 89-90
Scalloped hems, 156
Screen printing, 98-99
Scrolling. *See* Braid
Seam allowances, 144-145
Seam bulk, 133
Seam burst, 132-133
Seam crack, 132-133
Seam grin, 133-134
Seam pucker, 132-133
Seam slippage, 133-134
Seam tape, 221-222. *See also* Hem tape
Seams
   as dart equivalents, 170-171
   classes, 135-144
      bound seams (BS), 142-144, 159-160
      flat seams (FS), 143-145
      lapped seams (LS), 139-142
      superimposed seams (SS), 135-139
   general applications to typical operations, 307-311
   labor costs of, 136
   performance, 131-132
   related resources, 290
   schematic diagrams of, 301-302
   sewn flat, 143-145, 160, 202-203, 205
   sewn "in the round", 143-145, 160, 202, 205
   types, 135-144
Self-help features, 218-219
Selling points, 3
Selvages, 93
Serge. *See* Overedge stitches
Serviceability, 2-3
Set, 264-265
Set-in sleeves, 201-202
Sewing room technology, 287
Shade lots, 75

Shadow panel, 217
Shank buttons, 239-240
Shaping devices, 168-177
Shell fabrics, 178
Shell hems, 156
Shirring, 228
Shirt sleeve plackets, 163
Shirttail hems, 154
Shoulder pads, 182, 186
Shrinkage, 77, 132
Signature labels, 64. *See also* Brand names
Silhouettes, 192, 194-195, 264
Single-needle tailoring, 145-146
Sizes
   childrenswear, 56-58
   classifications, 54
   expressed as body measurements, 55-56
   international, 63
   lettered, 56
   menswear, 61-63
   one-size-fits-all, 56
   pictograms, 63
   related resources, 289
   voluntary standards, 55
   womenswear, 59-61
Sizing, 101
Skewed fabric, 95-96
Skin-on-skin furs, 87
Skipped stitches, 124-125
Skirt lengths, 192-195
Skirt styles, 194
Sleeves
   heads, 186
   lengths, 201
   styles, 201-204
Slipping, 201
Slipstitches, 112-113
Sloper. *See* Basic block
Slot seams, 141-142
Smocking, 228
Snagging, 79
Snap crotch/inseams, 217, 253
Snap tape, 253
Snaps, 252-253
Soil release, 101
Sourcing, 38
Soutache braid. *See* Braid
Special needs clothing, 218-219, 277-281
Specifications, 14-17, 36, 72-74, 107, 263
Sportswear, men's, 61
Spun thread, 127
Spun yarns, 87-88
Standard care terms, 49-51
Static, 80, 101
Stayed seams, 146-147, 182
Stitch tension, 123-124
Stitches, 105-109
   chainstitches, 109-113
   classes, 107-122
      100 single-thread chainstitches, 109-111